The Fate of the Russian Revolution, volume 2

The two Trotskyisms confront Stalinism

Debates, essays and confrontations

Edited and with an introduction by Sean Matgamna

D1512712

Second edition

The Fate of the Russian Revolution volume 2

The two Trotskyisms confront Stalinism

Debates, essays and confrontations

Edited and with an introduction by Sean Matgamna

Second edition

Printed by Imprint Digital, Exeter EX5 5HY

ISBN: 978-1-909639-31-7

This second edition published 2015 by Workers' Liberty
20E Tower Workshops
Riley Road
London SE1 3DG
020 7394 8923
awl@workersliberty.org
www.workersliberty.org

A shape with lion body and the head of a man,
A gaze blank and pitiless as the sun,
Is moving its slow thighs, while all about it
Reel shadows of the indignant desert birds...
What rough beast, its hour come round at last,
Slouches towards Bethlehem to be born?

W B Yeats

The socialists consider it their principal, perhaps even their only,
duty to promote the growth of this consciousness among the
proletariat, which for short they call its class consciousness.
The whole success of the socialist movement is measured for
them in terms of the growth in the class consciousness of the
proletariat. Everything that helps this growth they see as useful
to their cause: everything that slows it down as harmful.

G V Plekhanov

Underground Trotskyist publications in Europe during World War 2: the French Trotskyist paper *La Vérité* remained illegal for some time after the collapse of Nazi rule in France. *Arbeiter und Soldat* was a publication of French Trotskyists and German soldiers, aimed at German soldiers in France. The Nazis killed over 20 French and German Trotskyists when they suppressed it.

CONTENTS

CONTENTS

CONTENTS

Titles given here to some of the excerpts are ours rather than those in the original. Each of chapters 1 to 12 contains one main debate, series of exchanges, or confrontation of opinion, and then background articles (titles in italics).

Illustrations

Introduction: The Two Trotskys

Part 1: Trotsky Of The Enigmas

DURING MOST OF THE 20TH CENTURY, and the 21st century so far, revolutionary-socialist politics has been some form of Trotskyism. It is rooted in the anti-Stalinist tradition that began with Lenin's 1922 attack, from his deathbed, on Stalin's Russian-chauvinist policy in Georgia, and continued with his attempt to remove Stalin as General Secretary of the ruling party. The Left Opposition of Trotsky, in October 1923, picked up the thread and augmented it.

The Left Opposition, and then the United Opposition (of Zinoviev-Trotsky), took into themselves some of the criticisms made by earlier Bolshevik oppositions to Lenin and Trotsky – the well-known Workers' Opposition, the less-well-known Democratic Centralists, and others. The Democratic Centralists joined the United Opposition. The leaders of the Workers' Opposition, Kollontai and Shlyapnikov, went over to Stalin.

For the Trotskyists – in Trotsky's lifetime they preferred to call themselves Bolshevik-Leninists – it has been a very long march through the 20th century and beyond, and over sometimes strange, unexpected, uncharted, often bewildering terrain. Central to it has been the fight against Stalinism, the attempt to understand and categorise it, the battle to wipe the labour movement clean of it.

The Trotskyist tradition is nourished by the memory of immense working-class victories – the October 1917 workers' revolution in Russia, the Bolshevik victory in the civil war, the foundation of the Communist International in 1919. It is shaped, and also mis-shaped, by the catastrophic defeats of the working class by Stalinism, fascism, and pluto-democracy. The Trotskyist tradition encompasses the historical experiences of the working-class movement in which it participated, and which it analysed, discussed, disputed about. There is no other authentic Marxist-communist tradition.

George Santayana's aphorism is not less true for having become a cliché: "Those who cannot remember their past are condemned to repeat it". Those who do not know their own history cannot learn from it. A revived revolutionary socialist movement will have to learn from the Trotskyist tradition. As Rosa Luxemburg explained:

"What does the entire history of socialism and of all modern revolutions show us? The first spark of class struggle in Europe, the revolt of the silk weavers in Lyon in 1831, ended with a heavy defeat; the Chartist movement in Britain ended in defeat; the uprising of the Parisian proletariat in the June days of 1848 ended with a crushing defeat; and the Paris Commune ended with a terrible defeat. The whole road of socialism – so far as revolutionary struggles are concerned – is paved with nothing but thunderous defeats. Yet, at the same time, history marches inexorably, step by step, toward final victory! Where would we be today without those 'defeats', from which we draw historical experience, understanding, power and idealism? We stand on the foundation of those very defeats, because each one contributes to our strength and understanding".

A reviewer of *The Fate of the Russian Revolution*, volume 1, dismissed it as "sectariana". Aim at the sky and you are sure to hit the mark! Certainly the texts in that volume, and its introduction, like this one, dealt with the politics, problems, conundrums, debates, and disruptions of small and very small organisations. But those were the organisations that attempted to continue and develop the political ideas and practical projects of the early Communist International after that organisation had been transformed into a corrupt and vicious political instrument of the ruling oligarchy in the USSR. The concerns and disputes of those small groups dealt with all the political questions that comprise the history of the 20th century. These were the concerns that exercised the minds of thinking people for most of that century. George Orwell is widely respected today for his integrity, truth-telling, and dogged honesty. Yet Orwell's viewpoint was a variant of that of the Trotskyist movement, and, certainly, he was strongly influenced by it.

Trotsky's Evolving Analysis

THE MURDEROUSLY ANTI-WORKING-CLASS totalitarian state which claimed to base itself on the 1917 workers' revolution in Russia was less than two decades old when Trotsky was struck down. In historical time it was a new phenomenon. For Marxists it was as unexpected and strange as the great continent of America which loomed up before him had been for Christopher Columbus when he thought he was en route to India and the East.

From the very beginning of his exile from the USSR in 1929, Trotsky and his comrades had many disputes among themselves about the exact nature, the class content, and the historical implications and perspectives, of Stalinism, and of the territory over which Stalin ruled. Similar discussions and disputes occupied the Bolsheviks jailed and exiled inside the USSR, until Stalin killed them all. The USSR itself went through great convulsive changes: the final destruction of the labour movement and the Bolshevik party; the reduction of the working class itself to what Trotsky would name as semi-slavery; the breakneck industrialisation and forced collectivisation. Trotsky constantly re-thought, reconceptualised, readjusted his thinking, on the USSR as on other issues. He worked by extrapolation, deduction, prognostication on events. He concretised, adjusted, changed, or abandoned his projections in the light of experience. Often events would lead him to apply a new description to the USSR, and also to say that the new description had already been valid for some time. In 1936, for example, when for the first time he called Stalin's regime "totalitarian", he wrote: "The regime had become 'totalitarian' in character several years before this word arrived from [Hitler's] Germany". (Sources for this, and other Trotsky quotes: p.116).

By the end of Trotsky's life, events, and in the first place the development and unfolding of Stalinism in the USSR and (in 1939-40) beyond its borders, had driven him into a politics of bewildering complexity, Jesuit subtlety, and seemingly extravagant self-contradictions. Trotsky bequeathed to his surviving comrades a large quiver of half-evolved and half-eroded "positions", ambivalences, and contradictions. The ideological history of the post-Trotsky Trotskyists is the story of their attempts to work through those half-developed and half-eroded ideas in relation to yet-new and again-unexpected world events.

In 1930, Trotsky broke with the biggest group in the Left Opposition outside Russia – the German Leninbund – on their attitude to Russia's conflict with China over the Chinese Eastern Railroad. Trotsky was vehemently on the Russian government's side. Until 1933 Trotsky thought that the Stalinist aspects of the Russian state could be "reformed" out of existence. Even then he postulated a special type of reform. He expected the bungling and irrationally-run Stalinist system to encounter disaster. The bureaucracy would begin to break up. The party which Stalin had stifled and paralysed would regroup and reconstitute itself as a Bolshevik party. In that way the working class would regain direct power. In 1933 he shifted to the belief that a "political" revolution would be needed to break the Stalinist dictatorship. At that stage he still wrote of a resurgent Bolshevik party carrying out "police measures" against the bureaucracy. In 1936 he deepened and sharpened what he meant by "political revolution", defining it in fact, if not in name, as a full-scale working-class revolution against the USSR's "sole commanding stratum" and its state machine.

The direction of Trotsky's politics on the USSR all through the 1930s was unmistakable. He inched closer and closer to abandoning the idea that the USSR was a degenerated (and degenerating) workers' state. At the beginning of the 1930s he was in public a critical defender of the Russian state. By the end he was publicly denouncing the Russian bureaucracy's rule as "worse" than that of any ruling class in history, and publicly calling for a new revolution against it. He compared Stalin's rule unfavourably with pre-war Hitler's.

The separation in the ranks of the Trotskyists in 1940 was the definitive branching-off of two Trotskyisms, for two reasons. It was at the end of Trotsky's life, and his last word on the subject of Stalinism. And it marked a decisive turn for Stalinism – the beginning of the Russian expansion that would by 1945 see Russia in control of half of Europe.

Trotsky Of The Paradoxes

AT THE END Trotsky was the theorist of a Russian "degenerated workers' state" in which, on his own account, the workers were slaves or "semi-slaves".

From the writing of *The Revolution Betrayed* (1936) onwards, Trotsky consistently referred to Stalin's Russia as an oligarchic "totalitarianism". In the programme Trotsky wrote for the September 1938 conference of the Fourth International, he said, and the movement that adopted the programme repeated after him, that Stalin's regime was uniquely reactionary and repressive, different from (pre-war) Nazi Germany "only in more unbridled savagery". "The Soviet bureaucracy has all the vices of a possessing class without having any of its 'virtues' (organic stability, certain moral norms, etc.)". The bureaucracy was "the sole privileged and commanding stratum". It "devour[ed] a lion's share of the modest national income", worse than in the USA: "The higher layer of the bureaucracy lives approximately the same kind of life as the well-to-do bourgeois of the United States and other capitalist countries". "In the USSR there are twelve to fifteen million privileged individuals who concentrate in their hands about one half of the national income, and who call this regime 'socialism'. On the other hand there are approximately 160 million people oppressed by the bureaucracy and caught in the grip of dire poverty". "Historically, no class in society has ever concentrated in its hands in such a short time such wealth and power as the bureaucracy has concentrated during the two five year plans".

And yet, Trotsky still thought, this bureaucracy was not a ruling class.

The rule of the slave-driving elite, wrote Trotsky, "from the standpoint of the interests and position of the popular masses... is infinitely worse than any 'organic' exploitation. The bureaucracy is not a possessing class, in the scientific sense of the term. But it contains within itself to a tenfold degree all the vices of a possessing class". From the point of view of the workers, the economy functioned worse than capitalism did. The workers suffered "the classic methods of exploitation... in such naked and crude forms as would not be permitted even by reformist trade unions in bourgeois countries". "The relations between people... in many respects are still lagging behind a cultured capitalism". "The Soviet economy today is neither a monetary nor a planned one. It is an almost purely bureaucratic economy... Industry, freed from the material control of the producer, took on a super-social, that is, bureaucratic, character. As a result it lost the ability to satisfy human wants even to the degree to which it had been accomplished by the less-developed capitalist industry".

And yet, Trotsky vehemently insisted, this bureaucracy was not yet a ruling class. In an important sense the "semi-slave" working class was still the ruling class.

Trotsky himself pointed out that: "The means of production belong to the state. But the state, so to speak, 'belongs' to the bureaucracy". And yet he argued that the state-owned economy rooted in the October Revolution continued to give the system its "degenerated" but still workers'-state character. The revolution in Stalinist Russia which Trotsky advocated would smash the bureaucratic state, replace it with the organs of a democratic workers' state (soviets), destroy the bureaucrats' plans for the economy, and replace them with working-class planning, democratically decided, vetted, supervised, and adjustable. And yet he insisted that this revolution which he advocated with mounting urgency was something less than the revolution he advocated against capitalism. Why? Because in both Stalinism and in a post-Stalinist working-class system of social organisation there would be state ownership. It would be ownership by a different state, and a different kind of state, "owned" by a radically different social group, the working class, in place of the Stalinist autocracy; but the common factor of state ownership made this for Trotsky a "political", not-quite-fully-social, revolution.

He was the keeper of the terrible chronicles of the rise and consolidation of Stalinism on the graves of millions of workers and peasants, of the revolutionary working-class movement, and of Bolshevism. Yet he greeted Stalin's statification of property in eastern Poland in 1939-40 as "the strangled and desecrated October Revolution serv[ing] notice that it was still alive".

Trotsky was a bitter critic of the foreign policy that in 1939-41 flowed from the Hitler-Stalin pact of August 1939. It was more than a non-aggression pact, he said. It was a partnership. He denounced

"Hitler's quartermaster" and "jackal" Stalin. And yet he was for the "unconditional defence" of the USSR in its international dealings, that is defence irrespective of the Russian government's policies and actions, and even when it acted, as in Poland, in partnership with the Nazis. He condemned the USSR's invasions of Poland (17 September 1939) and Finland (30 November 1939). And yet, when the Finns resisted, he was for the victory of Stalin's army over the Finnish people.

He insisted that "we are and remain against seizures of new territories by the Kremlin", and that conquest in Poland by the Stalinist state was turning the people into "semi-slaves". And yet he could not side with those "semi-slaves", actual or future, for fear of the effect on the fate of that same state and of what was unique to it because of the working-class October Revolution: nationalised property and some form of economic plan, with all the evils he had angrily described, stigmatised, and urged the workers to resist and destroy.

Trotsky was a proponent of the theory that the totalitarian bureaucracy was historically, for a short time, a locum for the working class and for the October Revolution because it retained statified property; and yet he was a mortal opponent of that bureaucracy from its early days. Advocate of a thoroughgoing revolution to extirpate the bureaucracy, he nonetheless felt obliged to defend its state in international affairs, "unconditionally", whatever it did and even when he condemned it, so long as it remained the custodian and defender of the statified property. In practice, in face of a stabilisation and expansion of Stalinism which Trotsky had not expected, this attitude raised Russian nationalised property above all other concerns. In Finland, it raised it above the freedom of the working class to organise itself, to think, and to formulate and express its own politics.

Trotsky interpreted "defence of the USSR against imperialism" to mean wanting it to be victorious even when it was engaged in an attempt to reduce the Finns (and thus the free Finnish labour movement) to what he had described as "semi-slavery" (in relation to Poland, three months earlier). He was an inveterate defender of the rights of the oppressed nationalities in the USSR. And yet he defended the USSR in its war to subjugate the Finns because he thought the Russo-Finnish war would quickly merge into the Second World War. He denounced Stalin's policy in Finland sharply. He wrote: "During the war with Finland, not only the majority of the Finnish peasants but also the majority of the Finnish workers proved to be on the side of their bourgeoisie. This is hardly surprising since they know of the unprecedented oppression to which the Stalinist bureaucracy subjects the workers of nearby Leningrad and the whole of the USSR". And yet he felt obliged to side with Stalin in Finland.

Shortly after Stalin's invasion of Poland – in partnership with Hitler's Germany and as agreed by the Hitler-Stalin pact – Trotsky wrote: "In every case the Fourth International will know how to distinguish where and when the Red Army is acting solely as an instrument of the Bonapartist reaction and where it defends the social basis of the USSR". He bitterly condemned Stalin's policy in Poland and Finland. Yet when in 1939-40 some of Trotsky's comrades tried to separate off what should be "defended", "unconditionally", from what should be condemned as an expression of the oligarchy and its drives, appetites, and interests; and when they argued that "defence of the USSR" could not be "unconditional", he denounced and condemned them. Trotsky described the invasions of Poland and Finland as above all an "extension of the territory dominated by bureaucratic autocracy and parasitism". And yet he still felt obliged to "defend" the Stalinist system's forcible extension by Stalin beyond the USSR's borders because the alternative, once the USSR was engaged, was or might be defeat for the progressive potential of the USSR's nationalised economy. Against "conjunctural defeatism" (.siding with the USSR in wars only "conjuncturally", i.e. in some circumstances), he recalled the legend of "Columbus and the egg". Christopher Columbus challenged his companions to make an egg stand on its end. When they couldn't, he smashed one end of the egg on the table, flattening it. Thus he could make the egg, the no-longer-quite-itself egg, stand on that end. After Columbus's example, anyone could do the same thing. Thus too with defeatism: do it once, on the periphery of the World War, where inevitably there would be cross-currents and complications, and you would find it much easier to do in other situations. Trotsky feared that the "conjunctural defeatism" which he himself had seemed to advocate ("the Fourth International will know how to distinguish...") might slide into a comprehensive defeatism. He feared to disorient his comrades when (soon, in the World War), the Stalinist system would collapse, the bureaucracy would shatter, and the fate of what appeared to be the remaining legacy of the 1917 revolution would become the living axis of politics.

In fact, the collapse didn't happen. The bureaucracy didn't shatter. And most of those who were "Russian defeatists" in the Finnish war would soon reject "defence of the USSR" entirely.

For fear of the spread of a general Trotskyist defeatism, Trotsky took a position which flew in the face of his denunciations of what Stalin was doing and would do in Finland. His stance meant taking a position on Finland motivated not by what was happening and would happen with a Russian victory there, but by concern for something else, general defence of USSR against the big imperialist powers. By way of the "Columbus and the egg" parable, he said plainly that that was what he was doing. When Max Shachtman tried to insist on answers, on their merits, to the "concrete questions", Trotsky angrily dismissed him as a mere coiner of journalistic jargon.

Trotsky was an international socialist who, feeling the need for auxiliary theses beyond those of the "degenerated workers' state" and the "progressive economy" to buttress defence of the USSR, reached for arguments indistinguishable from those of the Russian Marxist social-patriot George Plekhanov for defending the Tsar's Russia in World War One: Russia would be reduced to a colony if it were defeated. When a comrade, Simone Weil, who was to become well known as a mystical philosopher, pointed this out, he responded gnomically that she had a "right to understand nothing".

I discussed these issues in greater detail in the introduction to *The Fate of the Russian Revolution* volume 1. Some of these paradoxes are plain flat contradictions. Most can be understood in terms of Trotsky's increasingly feverish attempts to grasp and define the new Stalinist system and to hold on to the perspective on contemporary history as an "era of wars and revolutions", on the certainty of which the Bolsheviks had made the October Revolution. Yet, as we will see, the later political evolution of his co-thinkers in the 1939-40 dispute would mock his fear that it would set an open-ended precedent if the Trotskyists came out for "conjunctural defeatism" against the USSR in the Russo-Finnish war. The precedents set by Trotsky's "Russian defencism" on Finland, and by his speculations about social upheavals triggered by the "Red Army" in eastern Poland and, maybe, Trotsky thought, in Finland too – those would be the "precedents" that would begin to reshape and warp "Orthodox" Trotskyism within a year of Trotsky's death.

The Significance For Trotsky Of Statified Industry

TROTSKY READ OFF the class character of the USSR from the origins in the 1917 working-class revolution of the statified property that characterised it. At the same time he remembered and said that the statified property in Stalin's USSR was radically different in kind from the statified property in the early workers' state, as well as far more pervasive. It was not less radically different from the statified property of a future regenerated USSR, after a new workers' revolution, under working-class control and planning. He argued that the fully statified property was inexplicable apart from the working-class revolution which had overthrown the old ruling class. "The first concentration of the means of production in the hands of the state to occur in history was achieved by the proletariat with the method of social revolution, and not by capitalists with the method of state trustification". The Russian system was unique.

This was central to Trotsky's reasoning. What he saw as the post-bourgeois nationalised economy in Russia was unique in the world. It could not have come into existence without the prior destruction by the working class of the Russian bourgeoisie. When the revolution came to be isolated, and declined, the bureaucracy expropriated the working class and made itself, in Trotsky's words, "the sole master of the surplus product". The Stalinist bureaucracy did not create the nationalised economy; its rule was a negation but also a continuation of the revolution, by way of the survival of nationalised property. It performed no essential function in the economy that the working class could not have done better. The bureaucracy was a parasitic formation on the workers' state, an epiphenomenon, not an independent force in history. Without the working-class revolution there could have been no statified economy in the USSR.

Because, as he believed, the bureaucracy was so unstable and historically unviable, the nationalised property still gave the state a predominant, albeit a residual, working-class character. Or, more exactly, a "post-working-class-revolution and not-yet-definitively-anything-else" character.

As yet the USSR remained a degenerated and degenerating workers' state. Or, more precisely, so Trotsky thought and said, it was better to go on seeing it like that for a while longer, until all the contradictory variables were tested, as they would be, in the World War. "Might we not place ourselves in a ludicrous position if we affixed to the Bonapartist oligarchy the nomenclature of a new ruling class just a few years or even a few months prior to its inglorious downfall?" Trotsky had admitted in September 1939 that the USSR as it was might have to be reinterpreted as a "bureaucratic collectivist" society. The lynchpin of his entire position by 1939-40 was: wait a while.

Trotsky saw the nationalised economy as the empirical evidence that the revolution had not been entirely destroyed, and thus for his "degenerated workers' state" theory. But the criterion was not just the nationalised economy "in itself". It was the nationalised economy as seen in the perspective of its origin, the workers' revolution, and then of the revolution's "political" defeat by the bureaucracy. Trotsky saw the nationalised economy as necessarily, as well as in terms of historical fact, linked to the October Revolution. There was no other way it could have come to exist. The criterion was a question of four elements.

One: the agency, the working class and its revolution.

Two: the empirical evidence of what remained of October, the statified property.

Three: the fact that the level of statification in the USSR was, then, unique in the world.

And four: the fact that the statified economy of Russia bore some resemblance, even in its grossly deformed Stalinist reality, and in a backward country, to the social administration of the economy that the working-class revolution, as the heir to advanced capitalism, would create.

The origin of the statified property in the 1917 revolution reinforced this fourth consideration. But, for Trotsky, it could not have been nationalised property "alone".

From 1937, he began to dismantle and remodel his own edifice of theory, when, "for the sake of argument", he separated his idea that Russia was still, in a very deformed sense, a workers' state, from the idea that the system of statified and bureaucratised planning was historically progressive. It was progressive, he argued, because it developed the forces of production in an epoch of great and all-pervasive capitalist decline. Against a French comrade, Yvan Craipeau, who argued that Stalin's USSR was an exploitative class state, Trotsky wrote: "When we are faced with the struggle between two states which are — let us admit it — both class states, but one of which represents imperialist stagnation and the other tremendous economic progress, do we not have to support the progressive state against the reactionary state?... Whatever its modes of exploitation may be, this new society is by its very character superior to capitalist society. There you have the real point of departure for Marxist analysis!"

And there, too, in Trotsky's idea, you have the starting point for the post-Trotsky Orthodox Trotskyist theory of the "deformed" (deformed, not degenerated) workers' states. These would be states approximating Russia in their structure, and consequently would be considered progressive and labelled "workers' states" to signal that progressiveness; but states which the working class, as a class, had played no part in creating, as in Yugoslavia, China, Vietnam, Cuba.

In that 1937 polemic with Yvan Craipeau, Trotsky presented Russia's nationalised economy as progressive per se. Two years later, in *The USSR in War* (September 1939), he wrote that it would be progressive only if and when the bureaucracy ceased to rule over it. "In order that nationalised property in the occupied areas [of eastern Poland], as well as in the USSR, become a basis for genuinely progressive, that is to say socialist, development, it is necessary to overthrow the Moscow bureaucracy". He declared in his open letter to the Russian workers of May 1940 that "the surviving conquests of the October Revolution", "the nationalized industry and the collectivized Soviet economy", would "serve the people only if they prove themselves capable of dealing with the Stalinist bureaucracy, as in their day they dealt with the czarist bureaucracy and the bourgeoisie". In plain words, by then Trotsky saw the statified economy of the USSR as progressive only on condition that the working class took power there. (This volume, p.637).

On one level, this was as big an innovation as his shift in September 1939 to the view that it might become necessary to re-conceptualise the USSR, exactly as it was, without further "degeneration", as a form of exploitative class society. And it raised the question: what was now left of Trotsky's post-1937 reasons for "defending the USSR"?

Trotsky: Feverish Flux

TO RECAPITULATE: TROTSKY BELIEVED that in the Stalinist system, the state-owned economy was a result of the destruction of the old ruling classes by the working-class revolution and, ultimately, a product of the new economic foundation laid by that revolution. The workers had been politically expropriated by a bureaucratic counter-revolution. And socially, too: in his attempt to distinguish between grades of counter-revolution Trotsky did not in any degree deny that. What he proposed that the working class should fight for against the bureaucracy – destruction of the totalitarian state apparatus, soviet democracy, a working-class-controlled economic plan, etc. – spelled it out clearly.

The new autocracy drove the people like the worst slave-masters in history; it had a concentrated power over society unparalleled in history. Yet it maintained, and indeed after 1929-30 had vastly extended, statified property. It was the autocracy's form of property, rooted in their political counter-revolution, their political expropriation of the working class, and in their way of administering the socio-economic system – but also, more fundamentally, it was rooted in the great transformation accomplished by the October Revolution. The ruling oligarchy maintained that which in broad socio-economic and historical terms distinguished the USSR from the capitalist world.

In Trotsky's view, this was a "transitional" phenomenon of necessarily short duration, an unexpected phase in the protracted decline and degeneration of the October Revolution, albeit one which, because the fetters of capitalism had been thrown off, still allowed a tremendous development of the forces of production. Trotsky knew and said that much of the economic success of the 1930s depended on the savage slave-driving of the workers and the rural population by the autocracy; and he believed that they could not possibly go beyond a very partial and patchy catch-up towards the level of advanced capitalism. He put forward a programme of working-class self-defence and political reassertion against the autocracy. He analysed and described the system, which he considered unviable, as a flux of history, degenerating at an accelerating rate, rather than having degenerated finitely into a durable socio-economic formation. For decades after World War Two, almost all observers, friendly or hostile, would see the USSR as an established, and, so-to-speak, settled and stabilised, socio-economic formation. Trotsky saw it not at all like that. For him it was a temporary conjunction of contradictions which had to give way, and soon, either to bourgeois counter-revolution or to a working-class "political" revolution against the autocracy. Before September 1939, when he declared that a new way of conceptualising the USSR (as it was) might in due course be necessary, he saw the system as a freak of history arising from the political destruction of working-class power in the USSR, combined with the anachronistic maintenance of economic forms rooted in the October Revolution, whose survival in such conditions had been possible only because of the prolonged crisis of world capitalism after 1929.

Repeatedly Trotsky saw the downfall of this system as imminent – in the crisis of collectivisation before 1933 (when there was a temporary consolidation), and with the beginning of the purges in 1935-6, which he initially saw as the death convulsions of the system. Trotsky thought it certain that Russia would be drawn into the World War, and that in the war its current regime would collapse one way or another, under capitalist conquest or under workers' revolution.

In other words, Trotsky's analyses of Stalinism at the end of his life were in a feverish flux, and seen by Trotsky himself as provisional and ongoing.

A New Organic Socio-Economic Formation "In One Country"?

TO UNDERSTAND why Trotsky refused to "affix to the Bonapartist oligarchy the nomenclature of a new ruling class", we need to stand back from the immediate situation of 1940. In refusing at the start of World War Two to classify the USSR as a class-exploitative society, Trotsky stood on the self-same ground as when in 1924 and after he rejected the Stalin-Bukharin theory of socialism in one country. The immediate focus of the disputes in the mid 20s around the doctrine of socialism in one country, the ideological banner under which the bureaucracy consolidated its power, was, properly, its short-term political implications. Socialism, that is, a developed socialist society on a higher level than the most advanced capitalism, and in one country? So there would be no other working-class revolution in the whole epoch in which socialism was being constructed in the USSR? The Communist Parties throughout the world would no longer work to make revolutions in their own countries? They would function mainly as frontier guards to "defend" and serve the interests of the state in which socialism was being built?

Plainly, in this schema, there would be no other working-class revolutions, and the non-Russian CPs would become international guardians and diplomatic and political pawns for the government of the socialist state a-building. And in fact they did, and very quickly. There was also a more profound theoretical reason for rejecting socialism in one country.

The programme of working-class communist revolution is grounded on the level of production attained by capitalism *on a world scale* and on the basis of the worldwide division of labour. Only that level of production, and what could be developed out of it by the working class, would provide the necessary minimum social and economic basis for a socialist society and for abolishing classes. A "socialism" in a backward country, confined to its own resources and inevitably severing at least some of its connections with the world market, could only be a sham. As Marx had reasoned: "A development of the productive forces is the absolutely necessary practical premise [of communism], because without it want is generalised, and with want the struggle for necessities begins again, and that means that all the old crap must revive". In the mid 20s Trotsky put forward an ambitious programme of economic development, which the Stalinists and Bukharinites rejected. But the idea that the USSR, in isolation, in parallel to capitalism, could build itself all the way to socialism was a new version, on a gigantic scale, of the projects of 19th-century utopian socialists, who would set out to create new societies in the wildernesses of the USA or some such "virgin" place.

Marxists argued that socialism would have to develop from capitalism, and be won by the proletariat, that is, by one of the classes within capitalism and created by capitalist society. It could never come from outside advanced capitalism, rise in competition with it, and go on to surpass it. For Trotsky in 1939-40, the idea of the USSR being a new form of class society implied that it was not a freak of history, an "accidental" combination of circumstances, but a relatively stable, "historically established" and viable system. The objections to the idea of a new stabilised "bureaucratic collectivist" system emerging in isolation on the edges of capitalism and then surpassing it were identical to the objections to "socialism in one country".

Trotsky in the late 1930s took it as a fact that capitalism had ceased to develop on a world scale and was in historical regression. Short of socialist revolution, a series of world wars and with them "the eclipse of civilisation" were certain. It was only in such a world of catastrophically declining capitalism that Stalinism could survive and prosper and, so he wrote, if generalised internationally, stabilise as a new form of exploitative class society.

Trotsky admitted, in effect, the theoretical possibility that the USSR was already established as a new exploitative class society, a semi-slave society. But a definite conclusion that it was so would mean a big step away from his general conceptions of necessary historical evolution. So he held back. That Russia was still a "degenerated workers' state" was not something Trotsky put forward as a long-term perspective. He said plainly that it was a very short-term perspective. He did not envisage long-term Stalinism in one country, or in many backward countries. When he described the USSR as a "transitional" formation, as he sometimes did, he did not mean what that expression came to mean for his Orthodox followers: a stable society in transition to socialism.

Trotsky thought of Stalin's autocracy as too unstable for it to venture on international expansion more than marginally. "The idea of Stalin's sovietizing Germany is as absurd as Chamberlain's hope for the restoration of a peaceful conservative monarchy there", he wrote (December 1939). James P Cannon, the man who would shape post-Trotsky Orthodox Trotskyism, was even more clear-cut than Trotsky on this. "Stalin could take the path of Napoleonic conquest not merely against small border states, but against the greatest imperialist powers, only on one condition: that the Soviet bureaucracy in reality represents a new triumphant class which is in harmony with its economic system and secure in its position at home, etc.... If such is really the case, we certainly must revise everything we have said on the subject of the bureaucracy up to now..." (Letter to Trotsky, 8 November 1939). The time-frame in Trotsky's argument that the USSR could not develop as an alternative economic model in parallel to capitalism was vastly mistaken – out by half a century. But his fundamental reasoning about the impossibility of a new social order developing on the edges of advanced capitalism and in competition with it rather than from its inner contradictions and historical achievements – on that he was not mistaken. The USSR, after competing with a revived and thriving capitalism for decades, and being drawn into arms competition with the USA which it could not sustain, went down to defeat and destruction.

Trotsky In The 1939-40 Dispute And In The Split

BY THE EVE OF LEON TROTSKY'S DEATH in August 1940, the American Trotskyist organisation, which was by far the most important of the Trotskyist groups, had split over "defence of the USSR" in Poland and Finland and over how the Trotskyists should organise and conduct their party affairs. (There would have been no split on "defencism" had it not been for the organisational disputes and the "Cannon regime" in the party). Two currents of Trotskyism had begun the process of complete separation, but as yet only begun. It would take most of a decade before the evolution of two distinct species was, more or less, complete. To change the image: in 1940 the two Trotskyisms were two dialects of one political current. By 1950 the dialects had evolved into two political languages, whose speakers often no longer understood each other.

There is no question where Trotsky stood in the split and the events that led up to it – solidly with Cannon and the "defenders of the USSR". Indeed, he was the main political writer on that side of the divide. On the underlying political and theoretical issues the picture is nothing like as clear-cut.

In the long essay *The USSR in War*, which Trotsky finished in mid-September 1939, he broke radically new ground. For the first time he accepted that the USSR, as it was, without further degeneration, might have to be reclassified as a new and hitherto unknown type of class-exploitative society. If the world war produced not the overthrow, one way or another, of Stalinism, but the spread of Stalinist-type regimes across the world, then "it would be necessary in retrospect to establish that in its fundamental traits the present USSR was the precursor of a new exploiting régime on an international scale". When some of his American comrades (some of them in mockery) branded such an idea as "revisionism", he replied in October 1939 with *Again and Once More on The Question of the USSR*, in which he dismissed such condemnation as know-nothing dogmatising.

"Some comrades evidently were surprised that I spoke in my article of the system of 'bureaucratic collectivism' as a theoretical possibility. They discovered in this even a complete revision of Marxism. This is an apparent misunderstanding. The Marxist comprehension of historical necessity has nothing in common with fatalism.... [If the working class fails to take power], fascism on one hand, degeneration of the Soviet state on the other, outline the social and political forms of a neo-barbarism..."

He suggested that the "further decay of monopoly capitalism, its further fusion with the state and the replacement of democracy wherever it still remained by a totalitarian regime" might produce a similar structure.

If Stalin's system on a world scale would be an exploitative slave society, what was the Stalinist one-sixth of the world, in the USSR? Logically, there was only one answer to the questions posed by Trotsky's reasoning: Russia was already an exploitative slave society. Trotsky had said explicitly that, looking back from the future, the socialists might have to accept that the USSR was already in 1939 the "precursor of a new exploiting régime on an international scale".

Was there some additional quality which the Russian Stalinist system would get from participation in a worldwide network of similar states? Yes, there was: stability, and the elimination of pressure and rivalry from an inimical advanced capitalism. But in terms of the social structure, and the roles of social groups in it, especially of the working class, in this putative slave-society world, Stalinist Russia would remain itself.

Trotsky believed that the USSR would give way either to a workers' revolution or to capitalist restoration, and soon. The great test would be the world war which was already being fought, and which would reach Russia ten months after Trotsky's death. The war would decide the fate of the USSR.

"Defence of the USSR" had been seen as defending a Russia under attack from imperialist states, and on the defensive. In eastern Poland the USSR was expanding its territory as Hitler's partner in imperialist rapine and plunder. Was Russia, then, to be seen as imperialist? The disputes that erupted around that question were heated, but more about terminology and historical perspective than about the substance of what Russia was, and what it was doing.

The majority of the peoples of the USSR were not Great Russians, but members of distinct nations. The Bolsheviks, in 1917 and after, had had to tear down the walls of what had been called the Tsarist "prison-house of nations". At the very start of the Left Opposition against the rising oligarchy, Lenin, from his deathbed, had indicted the Georgian Stalin for his "Great-Russian chauvinist" treatment of Georgia. As Stalinism developed, its rigid bureaucratic centralising Russian state power subordinated all segments of the apparatus to firm Moscow control. It thereby made the formal autonomy of the smaller nations in the USSR more or less meaningless. In this way, Stalin re-erected, and higher than before, the walls of the old Great Russian prison-house of nations.

The Trotskyist proposals to smash the bureaucracy and revive Bolshevism in the USSR meant also freeing the channels of self-determination for the smaller peoples in the USSR. In 1939, when Trotsky had called for the independence of a soviet Ukraine, he had to defend the idea against both dogmatic semi-Trotskyists (the Oehlerites, a mid-30s breakaway from the American party) and such reflex Russian patriots and chauvinists as Alexander Kerensky, the one-time Russian prime minister whom Lenin and Trotsky had chased out of Petrograd in October 1917. The implications of the call for Ukrainian independence ran right through Stalin's internal USSR "empire". In 1939 Trotsky published bitter criticism of Stalin's "shameful and criminal" invasion of Poland. He refused to use the term "imperialism" for the USSR, but in fact the terms of his refusal to do so conceded that Stalinist expansion amounted to imperialism "in the widest sense of the word". "History has known the 'imperialism' of the Roman state based on slave labour, the imperialism of feudal land-ownership, the imperialism of commercial and industrial capital, the imperialism of the Tsarist monarchy, etc. The driving force behind the Moscow bureaucracy is indubitably the tendency to expand its power, its prestige, its revenues. This is the element of 'imperialism' in the widest sense of the word which was a property in the past of all monarchies, oligarchies, ruling castes, medieval estates and classes. However, in contemporary literature, at least Marxist literature, imperialism is understood to mean the expansionist policy of finance capital..."

Stalin invaded Finland on 30 November 1939, after Russia's demand for military bases in Finland was rejected. Trotsky denounced that invasion too. "The invasion of Finland", he wrote, "indubitably provokes a silent condemnation by the majority of the population in the USSR". But, seeing the conflict as inseparable from the world war, he favoured the victory of the USSR. He feared that the Finnish conflict would lead to British and French intervention. Over Finland, far more than in relation to Poland, he insisted that the necessary condemnation of Stalin's invasion was secondary to a more basic question: "defence of the USSR". "Behind the Finnish question, as behind the question of the errors and crimes of the Kremlin, stands the problem of the existence of the USSR. Its defeat in the world war would signify the crushing not only of the totalitarian bureaucracy but also of the planned state economy; it would convert the country into a colonial booty for the imperialist states".

The Trotskyist Schism: The Orthodox And The Heterodox

STALIN'S INVASION OF POLAND TRIGGERED a dispute in the American Trotskyist movement between a majority led by James P Cannon and a minority led by Max Shachtman. It would end with a split down the middle of the party on 16 April 1940. The Heterodox Trotskyists launched themselves as the Workers Party ten days later, on 26 April 1940. They produced a single-sheet issue of *Labor Action* in time for May Day 1940, and by then they had already produced the April number of the *New International* magazine as their publication (as editors, Burnham and Shachtman had been the registered owners). The first weekly *Labor Action* appeared on 20 May 1940.

As always in such splits, a lot of people simply quit. The Workers Party consolidated as members fewer than the number of SWP and YPSL (youth group) people that they had had in the faction fight. The dispute was nothing like as clear-cut as it is almost universally summed up as having been. Contrary to most retellings, the dispute was not about whether the USSR remained a "degenerated workers' state" or must be reckoned as a new exploitative class state. And it was not about whether or not to "defend the USSR" against big-power invasion. With not many exceptions, the minority, the future "Heterodox Trotskyists", including Max Shachtman, agreed with Trotsky that Russia was a "degenerated workers' state". Shachtman had "doubts"; but Trotsky too had "doubts", and expressed them in September 1939 by sketching out alternative futures for the USSR. The minority also agreed that against a big imperialist onslaught the Trotskyists should and would "defend the USSR". The faction fight in the American Trotskyist movement was focused politically on whether "defence of the USSR" could guide them in the war which Russia waged against Finland between 30 November 1939 and March 1940; and, organisationally, on the "Cannon regime" in the SWP, which the opposition defined as "Zinovievite". That meant: akin to the Communist International around 1924-6, in its early stages of political corruption and debasement by demagogy, and of party-machine rule.

At the start, when Poland was invaded, Albert Goldman moved a motion to "approve of Stalin's invasion of Poland". Goldman would shift radically in the mid 1940s and join the Shachtman Workers Party, but in 1939-40 he was a leading writer and speaker for the Cannon group. Cannon as well as Shachtman opposed Goldman's motion to "approve" the invasion. Cannon's attitude, as Shachtman recounted it, was that it was "purely a military question and we were in no position to express ourselves affirmatively or negatively on it".

Trotsky, in his first comment for the public press, wrote that the invasion was "not a question of emancipating an oppressed people, but rather one of extending the territory where bureaucratic oppression and parasitism will be practised". "The Red Army received the order to defeat in Poland those who had been defeated by Hitler. This is the shameful and criminal task that the Red Army was assigned by the jackals of the Kremlin".

Cannon and his group then condemned the invasion, and they would also condemn Russia's invasion of Finland. So they now agreed with the minority? No. The majority insisted that the real, basic, and primary question was "defence of the USSR", in effect that they should also "defend" what they denounced – Russia's invasion of Finland. Cannon and his comrades saw the minority's views as sliding towards a general renunciation of "defence of the USSR", and on that they were right. Shachtman and his comrades saw the majority's views as sliding towards alignment with Stalinist imperialism and "bureaucratic revolution", and they were right too. But that all lay in the future.

The dispute became fierce after the USSR's invasion of Finland on 30 November. In Finland, unlike in eastern Poland, there was an ongoing war, which produced a lurch by the Cannonites to what they called "Soviet patriotism" (*The Militant*, 9 December 1939: though that was accompanied by Trotsky's anti-Stalinist polemics.)

The dispute was immediately about whether in their underlying "theoretical" approach (as distinct, for example, from Trotsky's journalistic comments), the Trotskyists should want Russia to win in Finland. Should they, when and if possible, help Russia to win? Should they tell the Finnish labour movement (which would be extirpated if Stalin occupied Finland) to wish for Russian victory over the Finnish people, and act where possible to facilitate that victory? Faced with such questions, Trotsky's whole system of politics began to disintegrate because of its inner contradictions.

The split process took on a momentum of its own. On one side, Cannon and his comrades had initially declared that the organisation could not "afford the luxury of a new discussion". Trotsky had insisted that there should be discussion. But when Cannon and his comrades started denouncing the minority as the "petty-bourgeois opposition", guilty not of mistaken views within a Marxist common framework but of capitulation to US public opinion, Trotsky joined in. The minority responded by raising the demand that they be allowed to put out a public bulletin of their own, with their distinctive views on the USSR, while still contributing to, supporting, and circulating the SWP press.

The split came on 16 April 1940. The USSR's war in Finland had finished on 13 March 1940. The USSR was 14 months away from war, the USA 20. For some time after April 1940, in nearly every respect the new organisation set up by the minority, the Workers Party, would be a smaller twin of the SWP. The precipitating factor for the split was not the heat of a current political dispute, but the majority's refusal to let the minority publish a public bulletin. In fact the majority rushed to a split without even waiting to see whether the minority would break party discipline and publish a bulletin.

Armed with a resolution from the 5-8 April conference, the Cannon group confronted the Shachtman group at the SWP Political Committee on 16 April 1940 (see *The Fate of the Russian Revolution* volume 1, p.270). Cannon produced a two-part proposal. The first part said: "That the committee accepts the convention decisions and obligates itself to carry them out in a disciplined manner". The leaders of the convention minority abstained on that. The second said that those members of the SWP National Committee (a broader body) who abstained were suspended from the SWP. And that was that. According to Shachtman, "When Cannon had us 'finished off', he turned from his watch to his colleagues with the triumphant remark, 'Only four and one-half minutes!'" For Cannon it was the dawn of a new era, of a "tightened-up", "Cannonite" SWP.

Nobody saw the demand for a special minority bulletin, or its prohibition, as matters of principle. Two things ruled out conciliation: the baiting and demonisation of the "petty-bourgeois opposition", and the minority's experience of being refused even a hearing in some Cannon controlled SWP branches (including Minneapolis, the most important branch outside New York: see p.509). Why sensible people – if they did not want a split – would think two competing parties better than a public minority bulletin is not self-evident. The argument, essentially, was that this opposition, especially degenerate, "petty bourgeois", bending under the pressure of public opinion, could not have a bulletin, or even much space in the SWP press. The production of a minority bulletin with a line on the USSR different from that of the majority might, under the impact of events, have led to a split at a later stage; but in the meantime the duplication of effort from having two competing Trotskyist groups with very similar politics would have been avoided; and the politics would have been clearer. The best outcome would, of course, have been that the two groups, in a common party discussion, positively interacted with and modified each other. Had the SWP of April 1940 not split, it is inconceivable that the wild quasi-Stalinist zig-zags of *The Militant* in the first few months of the Russo-German war (see below) could have happened. The strange ideas which the Orthodox deployed – "Trotsky's Red Army", the description of the USSR as "the workers' state" without qualification, etc. – could not have been imposed on the organisation by the simple say-so of Cannon and his co-thinkers in the editorial office.

But the Shachtman minority intended to produce their own bulletin, in violation of the 5-8 April congress decisions, and thus there was approximate justice in the SWP Political Committee's decision to split the organisation? Everything suggests that the minority had indeed intended to do that. But then why not wait for them to act and proceed against them when they acted and for what they did?

A majority anxious to avoid a split would have been conciliatory within the decisions they had won at the convention. It would have been eager to make it plain that the minority would not be discriminated against in party activity, positions, etc. It would have followed Trotsky's recommendations from October 1939: to avoid linking the political argument to "the perspective of personal degradation, i.e. demotions, loss of prestige, disqualifications" and to establish "all the organisational guarantees for the minority". The timing and content of Cannon's motions were designed to produce the opposite effect. The majority wanted a split. Cannon's *Struggle for a Proletarian Party*, written and published just before the split, makes that plain.

Old Antagonisms And The Test Of Events

SUBSEQUENT EVENTS GAVE an unanswerable verdict on the charge of "petty-bourgeois renegacy" that was the banner of the Cannonites in their drive for a split. The "petty bourgeois opposition" did not bend under bourgeois public opinion when the US entered the war in December 1941. If anything it was the "proletarian majority" who aligned themselves with bourgeois and petty-bourgeois "pressure", in their pro-USSR stance after 22 June 1941, and in an initial fudging on opposition to the war (see below).

The Orthodox would continue for a decade and more to describe James Burnham as the inspirer of the minority. But four weeks after the founding of the Workers Party, Burnham wrote a letter of resignation, announcing that he no longer had anything in common with Marxism or a Marxist party. Trotsky, he wrote, had been right about him. (See *The Fate of the Russian Revolution* volume 1, p.383). That Burnham had been a central SWP leader, writer of resolutions and articles, co-editor of the magazine, was true. The idea that he was the central leader of the minority – making them, after his departure, "Burnham's orphans" – never made much sense. It was a factional gambit.

Sharp conflicts of the previous decade of the US Trotskyist movement welled up in the SWP of 1939-40 and broke it in two. When he sent Trotsky his polemic *The Struggle for a Proletarian Party*, just before the April 1940 SWP conference, Cannon wrote, in a covering note: "The dam of ten years patience has been broken down" (*Dog Days: James P. Cannon vs. Max Shachtman in the Communist League of America, 1931-1933*, p.6). In 1933, the Trotskyists had come very close to splitting along roughly the same organisational lines as those on which they would split in 1940. Cannon had the majority of the National Committee against Shachtman and Martin Abern and was determined to hold on to it, one way or another. On all the big political questions, there were no differences between the groups. The origin of the group-clique conflict lay in the period immediately after the formation of the separate Trotskyist organisation when Cannon had a personal — and perhaps political — crisis, and had to get an outside job for a period of two and a half years. He largely withdrew from work at the office and got into conflicts with the de facto leadership of the organisation, Shachtman and Abern. Cannon resisted and opposed them on such things as publishing a biweekly and then weekly paper. A monthly was the best they could do, he argued.

There was no political basis for the intense factional conflict then. So Trotsky thought. He diagnosed the difference between the two groups as, on one side, comrades with a long political experience, even before the formation of the American Communist Party, and on the other, younger comrades. In "the local organisations... the workers, particularly those with trade union experience, go more with the majority, whereas the intellectuals, etc., who, come over to the organisation more or less on ideological grounds, go more with the minority. This categorisation is not quite exact, but it is by and large correct." Trotsky linked it to the fact that in the whole previous period the group had been concerned above all with propaganda. "The mere fact that both factions have a different social composition and the different traditions is not enough to necessitate a split, since every party arises from various groups, elements, etc, is not socially homogeneous, and is a melting pot... The current situation coincides with the beginning of more energetic external work. Whether the League will become a melting pot through this work — that is the question that counts" (*Dog Days*, pp.462-3).

Cannon and his friends used various mechanical ploys, such as depriving Martin Abern of a vote on the leading committee while one of theirs was away, trying to co-opt a Cannon supporter onto the committee, and so on. They excluded Abern from the organising and administrative work which, by all accounts, he was most suited to, and Cannon least suited to. A secretariat consisting of Cannon and Abern was being proposed by the minority. Trotsky commented: "The question of the secretariat is also not quite clear to me. Of course, it is quite natural that Cannon was proposed as secretary, but if I were in Cannon's place I might say, 'I would in fact like a representative of the minority to work as a second secretary'. That would be an attempt to settle the disputed issues collectively, and through day-to-day collaboration frictions might indeed be eased. The personal-organisational disputes are out of proportion to the maturation of the principled differences. It seems to me, in fact, that on the part of the majority an element of organisational 'ultimatism' has played a role..." (*Dog Days*, p.465).

What in Cannon's account of 1939-40 was called "Abernism", the substitution of personal for political ties, is often a real issue in politics, whether it is called "Abernism" – or "Cannonism". In 1939 Shachtman cited as part of the evidence that a "Cannon clique" ran the organisation the moves by Cannon to cinch up a "Cannonite" majority on the Political Committee before the differences had been clearly established.

Early on in the 1939-40 dispute, according to Shachtman, Cannon offered him an amicable split in which they would share the resources of the organisation. Cannon did not deny it, but it was, he said, a joke.

Trotsky, in joining in the demonisation of the minority as "petty bourgeois", did the very opposite of what he had recommended in October 1939. If he had lived, he would have seen in the political activity of the alleged "petty-bourgeois capitulators" – in their stand against the USA in the war – the clearest possible evidence that he had been mistaken. Trotsky would have worked to eliminate the consequences of his mistake. Cannon was unwilling and perhaps unable to register the "mistake" that had allowed him to gain a control of the organisation such as he never had in its first eleven and a half years. Reunification was incompatible with the Cannonite-Zinovievite party into which the SWP was reshaped after 1940.

The Workers Party had been born politically premature and only half-formed. They had to sort themselves out politically on the Russian question. The discussion in the WP in 1940 produced three positions, other than those who remained degenerated-workers'-staters as (most likely) the bulk of the minority had been in April 1940.

C L R James and Raya Dunayevskaya argued that Russia was state capitalist, and in fact a "fascist" state. Two groups of "bureaucratic collectivists" emerged. A group around Joseph Carter and including Hal Draper developed towards the view that Russia exemplified a new reactionary form of class society which theoretically could (so it was implied, though their earlier statements did not say this) spread to be dominant in the world. They were impervious to Trotsky's considerations about the shape of history and the impossibility of a new form of society arising in "one country" (or a cluster of countries) on the margins of capitalism and then competing successfully with it. Max Shachtman was not so impervious. At first he developed an analysis almost identical with Trotsky's, only calling "bureaucratic collectivist" what Trotsky called "degenerated workers' state". As did Trotsky, Shachtman saw the USSR as a freak of history, a one-off, and with at least some potentially progressive content. He remained within Trotsky's strictures and theoretical structures.

Max Shachtman published an article in *New International* of December 1940, *Is Russia a Workers' State?*, expounding the majority view of the Workers Party (*The Fate of the Russian Revolution*, vol.1, pp.272ff). In 1946, in response to the consolidation and expansion of the Stalinist empire, the majority, Shachtman included, adopted a variant of the view of Joseph Carter. In this they paralleled (as we shall see) the establishment by the Orthodox in the mid-1950s of a quasi "socialism-in-one-country" perspective on the USSR as a "degenerated workers' state" stably in transition to socialism, and likely soon to overtake and surpass the capitalist world.

Trotsky's Ambivalent Legacy

THE TROTSKYISTS SPLIT. Four months later Trotsky was struck down by a Stalinist assassin, on 20 August 1940, and died the next day. By then most of the Trotskyist groups in Europe had been scattered and driven underground by Nazi conquest of their countries.

Trotsky bequeathed to his surviving comrades a great political heritage, but also a number of seriously mistaken ideas. As well as on Stalinism, Trotsky bequeathed mistaken views on the historical prospects of capitalism; and on the prospects of bourgeois democracy.

In *The USSR in War* (September 1939) he wrote: "The disintegration of capitalism has reached extreme limits, likewise the disintegration of the old ruling class. The further existence of this system is impossible". This huge and too absolute underestimation of the resilience of capitalism would warp and derail his comrades' thinking for many years after his death.

As for bourgeois democracy: Trotsky and the Trotskyist movement believed that there were important differences between fascist regimes and bourgeois democracy. In pre-Hitler Germany, Trotsky appealed for a workers' united front to defend the "elements of proletarian democracy" embedded in the framework of bourgeois democracy. For France, the "program of action" which Trotsky drafted in 1934 declared that "as long as the majority of the working class continues on the basis of bourgeois democracy, we are ready to defend it with all our forces against violent attacks from the Bonapartist and fascist bourgeoisie", but with the Trotskyists' own class-struggle methods. In the Transitional Program of 1938, Trotsky wrote: "The Fourth International does not discard the program of the old 'minimal' demands... Indefatigably, it defends the democratic rights and social conquests of the workers".

In World War Two, both fascist and bourgeois-democratic powers formed imperialist blocs. That fact ruled out seeing the war as simply "democracy versus fascism". But Trotsky went further, arguing that in the war bourgeois democracy would disappear. All regimes would become fascist or authoritarian. There would be no difference. This was not a real answer to the question of what weight defending bourgeois democracy should have in the war. It was an evasion. It was to substitute a judgement of how things would evolve for things as they actually were; or, to judge some things as they were and others by what one thought they would become. It was too mechanical and fatalistic.

In March 1939 Trotsky responded to Palestinian Trotskyists who argued "it is necessary to renounce defeatism in countries which are even of doubtful democratic virtue, but which are at war with the leading fascist countries" by saying that iron "socio-historical laws" ruled out any bourgeois-democratic outcome. He wrote this remarkable passage: "Fascism is the inevitable product of decaying capitalism, insofar as the proletariat does not replace bourgeois democracy in time. Just how is a military victory of decaying democracies over Germany and Italy capable of liquidating fascism, even if only for a limited period? If there were any grounds for believing that a new victory of the familiar and slightly senile Entente (minus Italy) can work such miraculous results, i.e., those counter to socio-historical laws, then it is necessary not only to 'desire' this victory but to do everything in our power to bring it about. Then the Anglo-French social patriots would be correct".

Even if bourgeois democracy were likely to collapse soon, that generalisation faded out such questions as the life or death of working-class organisations in the next months or years. Was that all that was to be said? Was the truth that both blocs were imperialist so overwhelming that it wiped out all concern with defending bourgeois democracy in the war, that is, with defending the existence of labour movements in Nazi-unconquered Europe (and in the USA)? Or: in 1939-40, Russian conquest of Finland would have meant the destruction of the Finnish labour movement. Why was that only a detail? The Trotskyists' predictions proved to be seriously mistaken. In Britain, for example, war-time regulations were introduced against strikes, but not rigorously enforced. After the fall of France, the Labour Party joined a coalition government with the Tories and Liberals, under a Tory prime minister. The Home Secretary was Herbert Morrison, who had been a conscientious objector in World War One. After the formation of the coalition government with Churchill, the organised working class moved to massive acceptance that fascist invasion should be resisted, but it did so in its own way, not under state compulsion. The shop stewards' movement expanded during the war. The Home Guard – "arming the people" – was feared as a potential threat to the ruling class, organised by men of the left such as Tom Wintringham, who had fought the fascists in Spain.

Despite the (patchily-enforced) wartime regulations against strikes, it could be argued that in Britain there was an expansion of bourgeois democracy during the war. Even the conscript army was not quite the old army. Lectures and talks became forums for real discussions in which leftists could and did speak freely. The Eighth Army had fought in North Africa and in Italy. In 1944 their "soldiers' parliament" responded to howls in the bourgeois press against striking engineering apprentices in Tyneside by coming out for the right to strike and declaring that this right was one of the things they were fighting for. This was a Britain in political ferment, working its way towards the Labour landslide election victory of 1945, the creation of the modern welfare state, and the more or less peacefully-won independence of India, Pakistan, Burma, and Sri Lanka which followed. The Labour election victory was not our socialist revolution, but progress it undoubtedly was.

The main British Trotskyist group, the Workers' International

League, following the SWP-USA, took up the so-named "proletarian military policy". It meant that the Trotskyists accepted the need for a war against fascism and the threat it posed to the labour movement, but distrusted the way the government conducted and was likely to conduct that war. The policy of the British (and US) Trotskyists in the war was at least a close relative of "revolutionary defencism". It had a real meaning in Britain, under threat of Nazi invasion, which it did not have in the USA.

Shachtman's Heterodox group, the Workers Party, believed that bourgeois democracy would go down before authoritarianism in the war no less than Cannon's Orthodox SWP and the now-shadowy Fourth International which the SWP ran from New York did. *Labor Action* reported on 3 June 1940 that all civil liberties had been ended in Britain. "The Churchill government [has] rushed bills through... which give the Cabinet totalitarian powers equal to those of Hitler. The new powers wipe out all the guarantees of civil liberties and individual rights won in long and hard struggles... for over a thousand years". That was to substitute expectation for analysis and accurate reporting. The difference between the Workers Party and the SWP was that though the WP could be misled by such ideas, they did not regard them as fetishes. They did not believe, as Cannon did, that the prestige of the leadership rested on never being wrong, that is, in practice, on covering up when inevitably they did get something wrong. As Shachtman recorded: "Before the war, we had all declared in our analyses that once the war got under way, the political differences between the totalitarian and the democratic countries would dwindle rapidly... Refusing to be guided by disproved assertions of yesterday, we established the facts early in the war and proceeded to orient our activities accordingly" (*Five Years of the Workers Party*, April 1945).

In the USA, despite wartime regulations, repression of socialists was a great deal less than it had been in World War One and its aftermath. "Pluto-democracy", democracy dominated by the rich but still allowing leeway to the working class, thrived. And then, from 1943-5, in the Europe liberated from fascist rule and Nazi occupation, the development of bourgeois-democratic regimes confronted the Trotskyists with yet another unexpected development.

The Workers Party adjusted early and fully. The SWP and its co-thinkers in Europe did not. They insisted that bourgeois-democratic regimes – "new Weimar Republics" – were impossible in post-war Europe. There would at best be Bonapartist regimes, semi-dictatorial regimes under which the state machine, led by some self-said

Napoleonic hero like De Gaulle in France, would rise above parliament and society. As late as 1949 (in an article by Ernest Mandel [Germain] in *Fourth International* of April 1949) the Orthodox were arguing that "the characteristic form of the state in our time [is] the totalitarian state within whose framework the police dictatorship (open, as under fascism, or thinly veiled, as [in] the regimes now being established in several Western European countries) corresponds to the extreme concentration of economic and state power and to the permanent crisis of the regime". Obscurantisms cross-bred and multiplied.

The Fallibility Of Trotsky

IT IS IMPOSSIBLE not to attach to Trotsky much of the blame for what happened in 1939-40 and for the malign consequences that warped the post-Trotsky Trotskyist movement. How much his personal condition and the circumstances he lived in contributed to that can only be surmised. Was the raging at the "petty-bourgeois opposition" (and his tolerance of Cannon's raging factionalism) displaced feeling about the world he saw taking shape? In the diary he kept for a while in 1935 while living in France, he compared himself to a wise old physician compelled to watch helplessly as fools, charlatans, assassins, and traitors destroyed someone very dear to him. Five years later he had to discuss the question: what if the working class and labour movements fail? What sort of world will it be then? At the worst reckoning, he said it would be a world in which the Marxists would have to work out a "minimum programme" to defend "the slaves of the new bureaucratic collectivist society". In his "testament", written in February 1940, he asserted his right to decide when to die, if his health continued to deteriorate; that is, to commit suicide.

W B Yeats in old age defined himself, mind, spirit, and awareness, as a sentient creature "tied to a dying animal". Trotsky embodied Bolshevism and the legacy of the workers' revolution in Russia, but it was Bolshevism tied to a dying animal – to an old, tired, dying animal, confronting an increasingly hellish world in which the hopes and beliefs that had sustained him politically for over four decades were put in question by events and by the "syphilitic" and "leprous" (his words) condition to which Stalinism had reduced so much of the working class movement. There is no mystery in Trotsky's exasperation with Shachtman and his comrades or in his alliance with Cannon. There is no mystery in his fallibility. We need to record it, try to learn from it, pick up the pieces, and move on.

The Fourth International And The USA's War

THE TWO TROTSKYIST GROUPS, Cannon's SWP and Shachtman's Workers Party, moved apart politically after April 1940 also in their responses to the USA in World War Two. Neither supported the Allies in the war, though the Orthodox continued to support China in its war against Japan. (The Heterodox saw China as having become an American tool in the war). The Workers Party responded to US embroilment in the World War after 7 December 1941 in what might be called the traditional early-Comintern way. Immediately on the US entering the war the WP issued a ringing manifesto that denounced the war. It appeared on the front page of *Labor Action* of 15 December under the headline "World in Flames" (this volume, p.569).

The war was an imperialist war on both sides, said the WP. They were opposed to the USA going to war, and they did not want the US government to win. The working class should not abate its class struggle during the war, but accelerate it.

Against the government, the WP backed pacifists opposing the war and refusing to fight in it. The young men of the Workers Party and the YPSL, however, believed that they should go with their generation, and let themselves be conscripted into the armed forces. A high proportion of the Heterodox Trotskyists, who were generally younger than the Orthodox, were taken into the military machine, seriously sapping the strength of the small party. The remaining activists of the "petty-bourgeois opposition" took the wartime opportunities for jobs in industry. Hal Draper and Anne Draper, for example, became shipyard workers.

The predictions and "warnings" to the minority that their refusal to back the USSR in Finland was the first "social-patriotic sinfall" of the Trotskyists in the war, and the deduction that this political tendency would not swim against the patriotic tide of mainstream America once the USA entered the war – those were shown by what the Heterodox did in the war to be the opposite of the truth. The Workers Party behaved in the full spirit of Liebknecht, Luxemburg, Eugene Debs, Lenin and Trotsky. For them it was all politically and personally straightforward.

And the Orthodox Trotskyists? The SWP's response to the US entering the war was downright strange. The front-page lead headline of the issue of *The Militant* just after the US entered the war told the reader: "War reinstates 1917 Espionage Act". And John G Wright wrote of an imminent Russo-Japanese war. Nothing at all on the USA's war itself.

The Militant did not comment directly on the USA's entry into war, or declare that the SWP was opposed to this war by the USA, until the issue of 24 January 1942, 47 days or nearly seven weeks later. When it finally did comment on the war, it did so not in the name of the SWP as an organisation, but in a personal statement by James P Cannon, its National Secretary.

On 3 January 1942, an editorial in the left-hand column of the front page of *The Militant* carried the headline, pushing the paper's masthead aside to the right of the page: "How labor can strike Hitler a mortal blow" (see this volume, p.573). How? Workers' and farmers' governments in Britain and the USA would evoke an anti-Hitler revolution in Germany. The article was linked to the war, but in political substance it could have been written at any time since Hitler came to power in 1933. In January 1942, it signalled that the SWP was in the fight against Hitler: "We Trotskyists want the destruction of Hitlerism and a 'lasting peace'." That seems to have been the point of publishing the article then. Thus, the Orthodox started printing advice (albeit addressed to the working class) on how to down Hitler before they had said plainly whether they supported or opposed the USA in the war. The signal given was that they supported it.

From the point of view of the USSR and its defence, the USA's entry into war against Hitler, and thus into alliance with the USSR, was very good news. That had to be one of Cannon's concerns in the six weeks or so in which he mulled over his response. The gap between the USA's entry into war and the SWP's response suggests that for them the response was not at all straightforward. In the epoch of the "Proletarian Military Policy" (see below) so much had changed – on conscription, on their attitude to militarism, and on the general necessity of an "anti-fascist" war – and the Orthodox had, as we shall see, become such whole-hog "patriots" for the USA's Russian ally — that everything connected with the war had become a more or less new question.

The Cannonites would eventually proclaim as one of the chief crimes or mistakes of Stalin, reliance on his bourgeois allies, the USA and Britain. Cannon had evidently to work hard to arrive at that position.

The Militant of 24 January 1942 announced that the "Trotskyist leader" Cannon had issued a statement, which it summarised. Dated 22 December 1941, the full statement was printed in *Fourth International* for January 1942, which, the paper reported, had come out just then (i.e. not at the start of the month). The "22 December" statement had either been kept hidden for a month, or backdated by a month. *The Militant* did not print it in full until 7 February, two calendar

Socialist Appeal, 5 September 1939. The tone of the Orthodox Trotskyists on the war changed dramatically in 1941.

months after Pearl Harbour and the USA's entry into the war.

Later, Cannon would be angered by any reference to the SWP's tardiness. At the SWP Convention ten months later, he denounced those who said he had hesitated as "liars". Remember, he said, that the SWP leaders did not repudiate their anti-war politics in the court room. That "deed" (or non-deed), he asserted, spoke louder than any written statement could. "No misunderstanding has been possible... Those who pretend otherwise are liars and provocateurs, not misunderstanding people and not honest opponents" (*The Militant*, October 2, 1942). Not doing the opposite, not declaring positive support for the war, was stronger than an explicit statement against the war could be... Cannon, in his evidence at the Minneapolis Trial (27 October to 8 December 1941) in which, eventually, he and 17 other SWP members were sentenced to go to jail for "advocating the overthrow of the US government", had expounded the SWP's general attitude to imperialism and imperialist war, and that section of the evidence was published in *The Militant* dated 6 December 1941, the day before the Japanese attack on Pearl Harbour.

Probably the SWP leaders feared that their organisation would be outlawed. They expected the severe repression that opponents of World War 1 had faced from the "liberal" government of Woodrow Wilson. But whatever the SWP's calculations, to issue – as the WP did – a ringing and far-reaching denunciation of an American war which they opposed was, surely, their first political duty.

The Proletarian Military Policy

ON 27-29 SEPTEMBER 1940 the Orthodox Trotskyists called a conference and made a new departure which according to Cannon "telescoped", so that they would be "carried out simultaneously", the tasks of defeating Hitler's fascism and those of overthrowing the

US bourgeoisie (*Socialist Appeal*, 26 October 1940). This, the Orthodox said, was "proletarian militarism", for an age of all-pervasive militarism. They based themselves on some remarks of Trotsky's ("Discussions with Trotsky", 12-15 June 1940: Writings 1939-40 pp.251ff).

The Trotskyist organisation would now have to be "a party of a new type"; it would have to "adapt itself to universal militarism... be highly centralised, with iron discipline in its ranks". It would no longer oppose conscription, as it had done up to then (in a front-page lead article on 29 June 1940, for example). Rather, it would support military training but demand that it be done under the control of the trade unions, and that union-run, government-financed schools for officers be set up. This was, the Orthodox said, the extension into military affairs of the daily struggle of the unions in the factories with the bosses. In fact it was a proposal that the trade unions contend with the government for control of the army. So they would back the USA in the war against fascism? No, they explained. It was an inter-imperialist, not an anti-fascist, war. The ruling class could not properly wage an anti-fascist war or be trusted with doing so.

As far as I know, the Orthodox made no effort (and neither did the Heterodox) to organise their comrades drafted into the armed forces for political work there.

For a while, much was made of this "new" approach in the press of the Orthodox. Then it subsided to a reference in the regular eight or nine point platform which appeared in *The Militant* each week, together with an occasional call in the press for trade-union officers' training schools. That may mean that criticisms of it had hit home. But the approach was not abandoned. For example, *The Militant* contributed "constructively" to the public debate opened up by a dispute in 1943 between the US commanders demanding a larger army, and dissenting Democrat and Republican politicians (*The Militant*, 20 February 1943). In practice the shift meant that the Orthodox dropped their once-vociferous opposition to conscription and softened their opposition to the war into one of de-facto political acquiescence, but with the caveat of a "demand" for trade-union controls that could not possibly be realised without an advanced state of dual power [1: *notes on pp.114-6*] in the country and in the armed forces. In the SWP's daily reality, what was left was acquiescence in the war, with big caveats, and glorying in the victories of the USA's ally Russia.

The proposal to take control of the armed forces out of the hands of the government – outside of a situation of dual power or revolution – was seen by the Orthodox as a demand that would be transitional to that dual power. In reality the idea that the army was separable from the state, while that state was stable, was political fantasy-mongering, abracadabra politics. The political acquiescence was real and immediate, as was the propaganda that militarism could not be resisted and that the proletariat therefore needed its own version of the all-pervasive militarism, its "proletarian military policy". At first this stance included nasty and envenomed condemnation of pacifists resisting induction into the army (see, for example, "Paralysing poison from the ivory tower of pacifism", by Joseph Hansen, *Socialist Appeal* 9 November 1940). Later they took a warmer attitude to pacifist conscientious objectors. (Cannon wrote in 1944 urging *The Militant* to defend the Jehovah's Witnesses jailed for conscientious objection, such as he met in the same prison as himself).

The Workers Party polemicised against the new "proletarian military policy". Max Shachtman wrote that "the Cannonites have given an important finger to the devil of national defencism" (*Labor Action*, 4 November 1940).

In the trade unions the Orthodox pursued a deliberately cautious policy. This was explained as "preserving the cadre". On party guidance, SWP trade unionists tried to keep their heads down. By contrast, the Workers Party members were open and visible as revolutionaries and militants. They openly sold *Labor Action*. The SWP dismissed the Workers Party approach as that of people merely "visiting" in the unions. Whatever our judgement might be of the tactical advisability of caution in this or that case, the overall policy meant that the SWP avoided sharp clashes with the trade union bureaucracy. James P Cannon reckoned that the government and FBI offensive against the SWP which resulted in the Minneapolis jailings had been triggered by Daniel Tobin, leader of the Teamsters Union, and his friends in the Roosevelt administration. Felix Morrow, one of those jailed, later said that the Minneapolis case had been a "shot across the bows" of the SWP from the government – and that Cannon had heeded it.

Appendix: What Did Happen In "Eastern Poland" In 1939-40?

TROTSKY'S TENTATIVE INTERPRETATIONS of what happened in eastern Poland when Russia took over were seminal for later "Orthodox" Trotskyism. What really happened there has been pieced together by the historian Jan Gross, in his book *Revolution from Abroad*, from testimonies written by inhabitants who were deported to the USSR. The history tells us where exile Mensheviks got their stories from when they wrote accounts of a sort of social revolution accompanying the Russian invasion. Those accounts had an influence on

Trotsky – he said so – and in the Trotskyists' debates. It also shows that those stories misrepresented what was happening, taking superficials as fundamentals and ignoring fundamentals.

Germany had already invaded from the west on 1 September, sixteen days before the Russian troops entered the east. In the east the big majority of the population were Ukrainian, Belarusian, or Jewish, and Poles were mostly colonists or administrators. The Polish government machine had substantially collapsed by the time the Russian troops arrived. "Killings, beatings, and destruction of property went on throughout eastern Poland for days before the Red Army actually occupied any given area and continued for several days afterwards. Ethnic hatred ran deep in the Ukrainian and Belarusian countryside, and it filled the power vacuum created by the collapse of the Polish administration with blood". There was an addled social dimension to the violence, since Poles and Jews (the main victims) dominated the better-off classes.

"Through the western Ukraine and western Belarus, in hamlets, villages, and towns, the Red Army was welcomed by... visible, friendly crowds... largely of... Belarusians, Jews, and Ukrainians". Hatred of Polish rule ran deep. It led many to think that Stalinist rule must be better. Jews especially welcomed the Russian army, calculating that the alternative was the rabidly anti-semitic German army or pogroms by local Ukrainian anti-semites. In a couple of villages allotted to Russia by agreement with Hitler, but occupied by the Wehrmacht before 17 September, the German army organised demonstrations to welcome the Russians!

The Moscow government instructed its military commanders in Poland to let the spontaneous reprisals and chaos continue their course for a while. The chaos continued and intensified. Stalin was nervous and uneasy about the invasion. Despite protests from its German allies, Moscow publicly explained its invasion as action "in order to aid Ukrainians and Belarusians threatened by Germany". It supplied Russian Army commanders with political slogans. "For twenty years you lived under the yoke of the masters who drank your blood, and now we have liberated you and we give you freedom to do with them as you please". Moscow supplied its troops with cash to buy supplies in the occupied territories, to stop them looting and antagonising the local people. The looting came later.

After a short while the Russian occupying army set up bodies of local government. To staff them, they often selected those who had led the ethnic violence, or mere criminals released when the Russian troops opened the Polish jails. Officials, police, school principals, etc.

from the old regime were arrested. The Russian army encouraged land seizures and redistributions, though as a very short prelude to "collectivisation" – appropriation of the land by the Russian state.

Waves of arrests and deportations to the USSR (some to labour camps, some just to remote regions) followed. Hundreds of thousands of people were deported. The prisons were filled again – so full that in some of them prisoners had to try to sleep standing up. When in 1941 Germany invaded, those prisoners were either shot en masse or force-marched to the USSR, in a smaller-scale rendition of the death marches from some concentration camps which the Nazis organised in 1944-5 when facing defeat and exposure by the Allies.

Theodore Dan and the pro-Stalin Mensheviks, and after them Trotsky, were very badly mistaken about eastern Poland in 1939.

Part 2: The Orthodox And Russia In The War

A New Russian Empire?

DURING THE WAR the divisions between the two Trotskyist tendencies widened and deepened. The two dialects of one political language in 1940 were becoming different languages. What follows is a detailed examination of the responses of the Orthodox Trotskyists to the Russo-German war after June 1941, when Hitler launched his blitzkrieg against the USSR – of what the slogans and the polemics of the Orthodox in the 1939-40 faction fight led to in political practice during the war. The extensive quotations are used so that there is no room for serious dis-

James P Cannon in 1922

pute on the subject.

Rejection of the idea that Russia was or could be an oppressive empire had been a political foundation stone of the Orthodox in 1939-40. At least, it was taken as a foundation-stone by the Orthodox after June 1941. Although he tacitly agreed that the USSR was what in other powers was called imperialist – "the tendency to expand its power, its prestige, its revenues" – Trotsky refused to call the USSR an empire or its activities imperialist. He refused to use the same term for Russia's domineering, annexationist, and plundering activities as for the capitalist empires doing the same thing [2]. To use the same term for the USSR as for finance-capital imperialism, he said, could only cause confusion.

Events would show that refusal to call what Stalin's Russia did by its proper name, imperialism, and the combining of that refusal with indiscriminate "defencism", would generate dire confusion in the Cannonite groups.

Trotsky had not baulked at calling the USSR a "counter-revolutionary" degenerated and degenerating workers' state. Logically he need not have baulked at calling it an "imperialist" degenerated workers' state. He did baulk. And his Orthodox comrades of 1939-40 would go on baulking as Russia took over half of Europe. All through the war, and after it was over, at every turn, in every seizure of territory or demand for territory, they saw only the USSR "defending" itself. They would explain the USSR's vast post-war empire in Europe as a mere buffer or glacis for Russia's defence. They would apologetically define, or even champion, Russian expansion as "defensive" actions, at root politically legitimate.

The Workers Party had already caught on to the trend of Russian development in relation to Poland (1939), Finland (1939), the Baltics (invaded by Stalin in June 1940), and eastern Romania (invaded by Stalin in June-July 1940). While the SWP was wrestling with its own self-stifling dogmas and political fantasies, the Workers Party was straightforward in registering events and commenting on them from a working-class internationalist viewpoint. The Workers Party's commentaries were work by people who read the serious bourgeois press and thought about what was new and unexpected; those of the post-Trotsky Orthodox, the work of people who extrapolated from old resolutions about different realities; who, instead of analysing events fully, properly, and honestly, looked in them for elements that would confirm themselves, and Trotsky, as "correct" and "prophetic". They would construe things way beyond common sense, or dialectical sense, or any sense, to make them fit old schemas. We will find ample evidence of that as we sift through their commentaries during the war.

Neither the Workers Party, the Heterodox, nor the SWP, the Orthodox, expected the USSR to survive the world war. Neither expected the USSR to expand as it did. Cannon least of all. Recall that he had written: "Stalin could take the path of Napoleonic conquest... only on one condition: that the Soviet bureaucracy in reality represents a new triumphant class which is in harmony with its economic system and secure in its position at home..." When the USSR did expand, the Heterodox registered the facts, thought about their implications, and understood what Stalin was doing. They understood that what they had described as Stalinist imperialism in eastern Poland and Finland was integral to the USSR's role in the war. The Orthodox responded by holding to the formulae which Trotsky had used, while – and this is central to the whole story – radically changing their political and class content. They moved away from Trotsky's ideas, but by way of unacknowledged reinterpretation of formulae rather than explicit rethinking. From 1943 onwards, "defence of the USSR" became defence of the Stalinist empire being built.

The Heterodox On The USSR In World War 2

IN JUNE 1941 HITLER INVADED the USSR. The Orthodox proclaimed that they were for the defence of the Soviet Union "under any circumstances and in all conditions". They made no conditions on their support: as long as nationalised property existed in Russia, they would be for Russia no matter what it did.

In June 1941 the Workers Party was not in principle opposed to "defending the USSR". The majority then considered it to be a comparatively "progressive" though class-exploitative society. The Workers Party took its stand on the politics of Lenin and Trotsky during the First World War, and now applied those politics to the Second World War and to all the participants in the war, including the USSR.

In both world wars there were, of course, many subsidiary conflicts and wars – wars, in which, had they occurred separately, the socialists would have taken sides. For instance, with the Serbs in the Austro-Serb conflict, which had triggered the general war in 1914. Or even with Belgium: though Belgium itself possessed a large colonial empire, it had been occupied by Germany in 1914. But, so Lenin had argued, to support, say, the Serbs, meant siding against peoples similarly oppressed in the UK-French, bloc. In the Second World War, Russia was first part of Hitler's imperialist bloc (1939-1941) and then, after the Nazi invasion of the USSR on 22 June 1941, of the British-

American bloc, in both phases gaining new territory. From 1943-4 it was a major imperialist power in its own right. In both periods of Russia's alliances, the Workers Party refused to support either bloc by way of supporting the USSR. Their attitude to the USSR was a function of their attitude to the whole war.

To choose one of the blocs was, so to speak, a political "Sophie's Choice". "Sophie's Choice" was first a novel and then a movie. In it, a woman is confronted with the terrible sudden demand that she choose which one of her two children will live and which will die. If she refuses to choose the Nazis will kill both of them immediately. She must choose, instantly. In her panic she shouts "Take the little girl!"; and of course it destroys her psychologically. Choosing the better of the imperialist blocs was for the Workers Party a political variant of "Sophie's choice" [3]. In its own terms, the Workers Party followed, perhaps too mechanically, what since the First World War had been Leninist politics on inter-imperialist war. With them, there was no big innovation, because they recognised no difference in principle between the world wars. The self-called Orthodox were the political innovators.

The Orthodox In The Russo-German War: The First Phase

"DEFENCE OF THE USSR" in all circumstances and by any method was the core policy of the Communist Parties, their guiding principle to which anything might be sacrificed and everything Marxist and communist was. Once the Russo-German war was on, the post-April-1940-split Cannonites too made "defence of the USSR" their highest and most urgent priority.

They did not sacrifice "everything" to it. They did not, like the Stalinists, counterpose "defence" of Russia to the working-class struggle in their own countries. But a very great deal was reshaped and subordinated to the defence – in particular, their attitude to the class struggle in the USSR. Throughout the war they failed to tell the American workers the truth about the USSR, the US ruling class's ally and accomplice in the war. Interpreting "defence" as propagandist defence, they told lies by deed and by omission. They would never tell the full truth about the Russian empire, or about the events and issues that polarised the world after 1945. Their comments on the conflicts after 1945 between the US-led bloc and Russia were usually limited to blaming the US-led bloc alone and attributing "aggression" to it alone. Commitment to the USSR, which was now becoming Stalin's imperial USSR, coloured, reshaped, distorted, and limited their whole body of politics.

During the six months faction fight in the SWP and in the period after the April 1940 split and before the German invasion of Russia, roughly a year, "defence of the USSR" figured relatively little in the press of the SWP, the Orthodox, or "official", Trotskyists. Publicly, Trotsky's writings represented the face of the Orthodox to the world at large, and he wholeheartedly denounced Stalin's policy and activity in both Poland and Finland. "Defence of the Soviet Union" was then very much an internal party matter, an "orientation issue", though one seen as of fundamental importance.

In *Socialist Appeal* of 3 November 1939, for example, Felix Morrow wrote: "The AFL convention adopted a resolution for a boycott against all Soviet goods.... No revolutionist can support either the Anglo-French-American camp or the Hitler-Stalin camp in the American labor movement. The task of the revolutionist is to build and recruit into the third camp: the camp of revolutionary struggle against war. On all questions connected with the war, the third camp stands on a different program than that of the two war-camps. This is equally true of our attitude to the Soviet Union. We neither join the democratic war-mongers in their war against the Soviet Union, nor do we join the Hitler-Stalin camp in their justification of Hitler and Stalin."

In 1940 *The Militant* welcomed the Russian annexations of the

New International, April 1940

three Baltic states and of eastern Romania, without the condemnations Trotsky had hurled on the invaders of Poland and Finland. "Sovietisation of the Baltic step forward" was the headline on Albert Goldman's article in *The Militant* (27 July 1940: see *The Fate of the Russian Revolution* vol.1 p.357, and this volume p.250). Trotsky was silent, though this was an explicit expression of what in the faction-fight had been denounced as a matter of Trotsky and the orthodox giving credence to Stalinist "bureaucratic-proletarian revolution". Whether he would have remained silent had he remained alive longer is not to be known.

The paper of the Orthodox (*Socialist Appeal*; from February 1941 *The Militant*) carried other reports and commentary on the USSR that were in the same root-and-branch anti-Stalinist vein as all the coverage in *Socialist Appeal* had been before September 1939 and to a great extent continued to be during the faction fight inside the Socialist Workers Party. In *Socialist Appeal* of 14 September 1940, for example, John G Wright reported on "Stalin's new labour laws... chaining the workers to the factories like industrial serfs".

When Nazi Germany invaded Russia on 22 June 1941, the Orthodox were electrified. They immediately elaborated politics on the war that were... a political and ideological half-capitulation to Stalinism! The first post-invasion issue of *The Militant* shouted in its front page headline: "Defend the Soviet Union!" This appeared above a Manifesto from the SWP which called, as basic Trotskyist politics did, for the overthrow of the Stalinist bureaucracy, but now in a sharply qualified way. "For the sake of the Soviet Union and of the world socialist revolution, the workers' struggle against the Stalinist bureaucracy must be subordinated to the struggle against the main enemy – the armies of Hitler Germany. Everything we say or do must have as its primary object the victory of the Red Army". Everything? Everything we *say*?

The ordering of priorities had also been Trotsky's: first, defence, and, second to that, "political revolution". But with Trotsky it referred to what the Trotskyists in the USSR would do: they would not act so as to hinder military defence against the invader. Right from the start, the Orthodox conflated and confused two distinct things: military defence, in the USSR itself, and "defence of the USSR" in the outside world, in the USA, for example, by way of selective and sometimes lying accounts of Stalinist society. Where Trotsky had been among the sharpest critics of Russian Stalinist society, the Orthodox now took to asserting that the USSR gave the workers great benefits which, in the war, they were eagerly defending. That was not true, and it was not implied in the idea that nationalised property should be defended. The Trotskyists had previously identified and stigmatised lies about beneficent Stalinism as typical of the pro-Stalinist "Friends of the USSR" who were defenestrated by Trotsky in *The Revolution Betrayed* in the persons of the aged Fabian socialists Sidney and Beatrice Webb (Lord and Lady Passfield). [4]

On the masthead of *The Militant* of 28 June 1941 the new Orthodox printed a quotation from Trotsky, undated. "To defend the USSR, as the main fortress of the world proletariat, against all the assaults of world imperialism and of internal counter-revolution is the most important duty of every class-conscious worker". Those words were culled from an article Trotsky wrote in 1931: from before the Trotskyists decided, in 1933, that a "political" revolution to overthrow the bureaucracy had become necessary. The choice of this quotation, which they would frequently use as a motto during the war, was the first public signalling of what they were going to do: – jump back eight years and, episodically, lop off much of the politics on Stalinism which the Trotskyists had developed over the last decade of Trotsky's life.

The manifesto in *The Militant* of 28 June 1941 advocated what appeared to be the old politics on the USSR — what Trotsky and Cannon had advocated in 1940: defend the USSR; make a political revolution against the totalitarian Stalinist oligarchy. The Orthodox did it in the quasi-sacerdotal style that would come to be one of their trade-marks: "Workers and peasants of the Soviet Union! We appeal to you in the name of our martyred leader, Comrade Trotsky. His voice would now be urging you on to revolutionary war against Hitler. This was the hour of danger which Trotsky was destined to turn into the hour of proletarian triumph – but his noble and heroic mind was crushed by Stalin's pick-axe. Since he has been denied the happiness of participating in your decisive battles and final victory, let Trotsky henceforth participate invisibly in your struggle. Let his voice, stilled by Stalin but living on in the movement which bears his name, advise you in your struggle for a better world. Avenge his death by destroying Hitler, overthrowing the Cain in the Kremlin, and reviving the Soviet democracy which in the heroic years of the October revolution made possible the victory over imperialist intervention".

The old Trotskyist politics were weakened and reshaped by a new mode of reporting. Over the next months *The Militant* ran front-page photographs issued by the Moscow regime (workers receiving arms, workers forming guerrilla detachments, collective farmers bringing in the harvest, etc.). It proclaimed that the Russian were fighting Hitler with uniquely high morale. The Russians fought so wonderfully well (said *The Militant*) and their morale was as high as it magnificently was, because they had "something to fight for" – the nationalised property. The Russian workers knew they were defending the October Revolution. Contrast France, they said. There, the bourgeois ruling class had surrendered to Hitler [5]. There was no such class in the USSR. And what of the bureaucracy, what Trotsky, without contradiction from Cannon, had called "the sole privileged and commanding stratum", which "contains within itself to a tenfold degree all the vices of a possessing class"?

Even if the reports of especially high morale were true, and they were not, this radical mis-reporting of – that is, lying about – the society and politics erected by the counter-revolutionary autocracy on nationalised property was no necessary part of "defence of the USSR", as the Trotskyists had it before 22 June 1941. Worse: The accounts of USSR morale repeated by the Orthodox, after Stalin and the Stalinist-friendly bourgeois press, posed urgent questions to Trotskyists. Were there then no consequences for Russian morale of Stalinist misrule? The picture which the Orthodox gave of the war implied that the answer to this very important question was: "no"; or "not much". They said, and kept on saying throughout the war, that USSR morale was uniquely high, and it was so because the people believed they owned the state property. In that belief, *The Militant* repeatedly said, they were right: they did.

In Trotsky's time, the Trotskyists had said the opposite. They had characterised the idea that the people in the USSR owned what the state owned as "the fundamental sophism" on which vast Stalinist edifices of lies had been erected. Trotsky had written: "State property is converted into socialist property in proportion as it ceases to be state property. And the contrary is true: the higher the Soviet state rises above the people, and the more fiercely it opposes itself as the guardian of property to the people as its squanderer, the more obviously does it testify against the socialist character of this state property". Or again: "The means of production belong to the state. But the state, so to speak, 'belongs' to the bureaucracy". Now the Orthodox reported the USSR very differently.

The 28 June 1941 manifesto explained the Soviet Union as follows: "The Soviet Union can be best understood as a great trade union fallen into the hands of corrupt and degenerate leaders. Our struggle against Stalinism is a struggle within the labor movement. Against the bosses we preserve the unity of the class front, we stand shoulder to shoulder with all workers. The Soviet Union is a Workers' State, although degenerated because of Stalinist rule. Just as we support strikes against the bosses even though the union conducting the strike is under the control of Stalinists, so do we support the Soviet Union against imperialism".

Trotsky too had used that analogy. It is difficult to imagine one stranger or more maladroit. Stalin's USSR held millions in slave labour camps, held all workers in a totalitarian vice, routinely and frequently used mass murder as a political tool against the working people. It was a state power "more savage and unbridled" than that of pre-war Nazi Germany, as the Fourth International had said in the program of its 1938 congress. Even the worst gangster-ridden union in the USA came nowhere near the horrors inflicted on the workers in the USSR. This analogy worked only to suggest that the Stalinist totalitarian state was less terrible than in fact it was. Indeed, the Orthodox would assert in plain words that the USSR – the whole USSR, bureaucracy as well as the workers – was part of the labour movement (this volume, p.601).

James P Cannon, as National Secretary of the SWP, sent a telegram to Stalin: "Trotskyists all over the world, now as always, are solidly for the defense of the Soviet Union. In this hour of grave danger to the achievements of the October revolution, we demand that you release all Trotskyist and other pro-Soviet political prisoners who are now in jails and in concentration camps, to enable them to take their proper place in the front ranks of the defenders of the Soviet Union. Your crushing of workers' democracy has increased the terrible danger to the Soviet Union. We demand the revival of Soviet democracy as the first step in strengthening the struggle against German Nazi imperialism and the capitalist world" (*The Militant*, 5 July 1941).

Cannon also said this to Stalin: "The Trotskyists in this country, in the Soviet Union and everywhere in the world say to the Soviet government: place us in the most dangerous posts, we are ready and shall unhesitatingly accept". In this parody of self-abasing "loyalty", Cannon pledged the Trotskyists to active service for a state that habitually murdered people of their political species as soon as it identified, or thought it had identified, them. Cannon knew that the American Trotskyists would of course never be asked to act on this pledge. There was a broad streak of exhibitionist political masochism in post-Trotsky Orthodox Trotskyism [6].

Throughout the war many USSR soldiers fought bravely. The regime developed an effective nationalist, chauvinist, and Orthodox-Church-religious appeal. On the whole, though, USSR morale was worse, not better, than that of the other major powers in the war. Around one million USSR soldiers ended up fighting with the Germans. There were whole units in Hitler's armies made up of USSR deserters: two Ukrainian divisions, many units from the Baltic states, and over 250,000 in "Cossack units" (sometimes including non-Cossack, but called "Cossack" because Hitler had decided that Cossacks were not Slavs and, unlike the "sub-human" Slavs, "racially acceptable"). The German Sixth Army, fighting at Stalingrad, included at least 50,000, maybe 70,000 "Hiwis", so-called "volunteer helpers" recruited from the peoples of the USSR. Many "volunteered" because their only alternatives were forced labour or death in prisoner-of-war camps, where the Nazis treated the Slavic USSR prisoners as the sub-human "Untermenschen" that their racist zoology proclaimed them to be. Some were really prisoners of war conscripted into ancillary labour – digging trenches and latrines, running field kitchens, looking after horses, etc. But many were front-line fighters. A considerable number of Hiwis stuck with the Germans even after they were routed at Stalingrad. It is a measure of the political seriousness of the Orthodox by that point that in *The Militant* and in *Fourth International* there was not one word about Stalin's August 1941 decree that the family of every soldier who surrendered should be "deprived of all state allowance and assistance". In July 1942 Stalin added that every army should organise "barrier units" to be stationed behind the front line and shoot waverers and those who tried to retreat [7].

July 1941: A "Minimum Program" For Russia At War?

THE SUBORDINATION OF THE OVERTHROW of the Stalinist autocracy to "defence of the USSR" now began to reshape and redefine the Cannonites' operational politics on Stalinism. Inside a month of the German invasion of Russia the Orthodox issued a new manifesto which marked an enormous shift in their politics on the USSR. Under a streamer above the masthead, "For unconditional defence of the Soviet Union", they printed "A Program Of Victory For The Soviet Union". It was aimed at supporters of the Communist Party USA [8].

"We stand for the unconditional defense of the Soviet Union. The Stalinist leaders try to fool their rank and file into believing that the Trotskyists do not defend the Soviet Union. The word 'unconditional' is plain enough. It means that we set no conditions whatsoever before we defend the Soviet Union. We do not demand that Stalin make any concessions to us before we defend the Soviet Union. We defend the Soviet Union because the foundation of socialism established by the

October revolution of 1917, the nationalized property, still remains and this foundation it is necessary to defend at all costs" (*The Militant*, 19 July 1941: p.290 of this volume).

The foundation of socialism? Even under the totalitarian bureaucracy? Nationalised property alone, regardless of who "owned" the state? We have seen that Trotsky, in his last letter to the workers of the Soviet Union (May 1940: this volume, p.637), posed things very differently: for the existing nationalised property to be the foundation of socialism the working class would first have to take it out of the hands of the bureaucracy. It would only prove to be progressive if it could be taken out of the hands of the ruling autocracy.

"It is to assure victory in the struggle against Hitler that our party presents a minimum program of imperative tasks for the Soviet Union". For whom in the Soviet Union? "Whether the Stalinist bureaucracy accepts or rejects this program, we shall defend the Soviet Union. But we insist that this minimum program is vital in order to strengthen immeasurably the fighting power of the Soviet Union.

"1. Release all pro-Soviet political prisoners. Restore them to their rightful place in industry and the Red Army.... The release of this great army of pro-Soviet political prisoners, kept in jail solely because Stalin feared their opposition to his false policies, is imperative for the salvation of the Soviet Union.

"2. Revive the democratically-elected Soviets. Workers' democracy in the trade unions....

"3. Legalization of all pro-Soviet political parties. Their right to present their programs to the masses. Every political party that is for the defense of the Soviet Union must be given the right to exist as an open political organization, to present its program, and to agitate among the masses for that program. Without these rights, there can be no true democracy. [9].

"4. For revolutionary unity with the German working class. For the Socialist United States of Europe.... The Soviet government must call upon the workers of Germany to join hands with the Soviet Union to create the Socialist United States of Europe..."

The Orthodox asked Stalin's Soviet Union to "undermine Hitler by pledging to the German workers that the defeat of Hitler will not mean a second and worse Versailles [Treaty] but will begin the creation of the Socialist United States of Europe... The imperialist states cannot possibly make this pledge to the German workers. Only the Soviet Union, the Workers' State, can thus cement revolutionary unity with the German proletariat. The Soviet Union must clearly state its peace terms – the Socialist United States of Europe, the right of all nations to self-determination".

The Workers' State could, and in 1917 had done so. The degenerated workers' state? To call Russia simply "the Workers' State", to elide the enormous and basic caveat that it was a monstrously "degenerated" workers' state, to combine that with the suggestion that because Stalin's Russia was "the Workers' State" it could generate and embody a Bolshevik program – all that had nothing in common with the Trotskyist analysis and program as the new Orthodox had had it before 22 June 1941. As a comment on reality, the suggestion that Stalin's Russia was uniquely well-placed to make a democratic and socialist proposal was absurd: a lie-bearing Stalinist absurdity.

The list of desiderata was not a "minimum" but a comprehensive program, *almost* the whole Trotskyist program against Stalinism. Missing only was the idea of a workers' anti-Stalinist "political" revolution. In its place was an appeal to Stalin to do what for Trotsky, and for Cannon up to that point, could only be done by that new working-class "political" revolution.

The real imperial Stalinist Russia could not conceivably offer such peace terms. It ran and would continue to run a brutally chauvinistic and spectacularly inhumane war. At the end of the war it would try to grab as much of Germany as it could. It would capture as many German slave labourers for deportation to the USSR as it could. It would deprive many nations, including the German nation, of self-determination. All those horrors were already part of what the Stalinist bureaucracy did where it ruled.

This aberration of the Orthodox was rooted both in their dogma that Russia could never be an imperialist power, whatever it did, and in their translation of "defence of the nationalised property" into the idea that Stalinist society was "better" for its workers than anything else in the world. There was nothing in the pre-1941 Trotskyist policy of defending the USSR that demanded or licensed any of this fantastic quasi-Stalinist rigmarole. It would have been less absurd to demand such a program from Winston Churchill or Franklin D Roosevelt than to express it as "demands" to Stalin.

Program And Agency

WHAT THE MILITANT DEMANDED could only be achieved as part of a revolution against the totalitarian autocracy. However achieved, it would amount to a revolution. Cannon and his comrades could not but know that as well as Stalin would. The propaganda gambit here – directed at their American audience – was made absurd by being couched as socialist demands addressed to Stalin. It was implicitly to lie about the USSR and Stalinism, to suggest that Stalin could conceivably do the things demanded. Or that (because of nationalised property!) Stalin was more likely to do these things than Roosevelt or Churchill. In terms of real-world politics, it was an appeal to the Stalinist autocracy for self-reform and self-abolition. It was a wilful denial of what Trotsky and they themselves had known and said about the Stalinist regime for a decade. When they said it was a "minimum program", they meant that it was the Trotskyist program without "political revolution", the Trotskyist program reduced to free-floating advice and suggestions, the program but without telling the full truth about Stalinist Russia, the program but without invoking the Russian working class as the agency that could achieve it.

The manifesto spoke of "tasks... for the Soviet Union". The key terms in any political statement, "who" and "whom", were missing. The tremendous divisions within the USSR, between the workers and working farmers on one side and the privileged bureaucratic ruling elite on the other, were glossed over or denied by talking of tasks for "the Soviet Union" as an undifferentiated whole. As late as December 1943 an official SWP policy document written by Bert Cochran would rhapsodise about "the amazing unity of the Soviet peoples" (p.314 of this volume).

By calling the manifesto a minimum program, the SWP meant to underline that, as people who put "defence of the USSR" first, for now they did not call on the Russian workers to make a new revolution — a "political revolution" — against the autocracy. They were splitting off the "tasks" from the question of the agency which would carry them out and from the revolutionary method it would have to use. By presenting the program as a series of "demands" on Stalin for self-reform, Cannon aimed to "take the harm out of them" for a Stalinist audience: the SWP were no longer "counter-revolutionary Trotskyites", you see, but utopian socialists! This separation of task from agency and class would for many decades be central to the politics of the new Orthodox Trotskyists.

Thus, in their day-to-day propaganda and agitational work, in deference to "defencism" and the hoped-for Communist Party audience, they suspended or neutralised their own full politics, and came to purvey reform-Stalinist politics for the USSR. And they were getting into the habit of believing what they wanted to believe, what was emotionally satisfying or likely to be organisationally fruitful for them. They were beginning to work themselves loose from the trammels of doctrine, of program, and of the centrality of the working class in revolutionary Marxist politics. To an enormous extent, they were beginning to cut themselves off from reality too.

Lenin defined the self-destroying "opportunism" that led to the collapse of the Second International in 1914 as a way of working that took the line of least resistance and greatest temporary advantage, losing sight of whether those activities were or were not consonant with the stated overall goal and purpose of the movement. Shachtman and his comrades alleged that Cannon's tendencies in the labour movement were opportunist in that sense: the sacrifice of the long view to short-term considerations; the concoction of "lines" and gambits that did not fit with or advance the overall educational work and purpose of the organisation. The artificially and inorganically constructed Orthodox "lines" of the World War Two period were a giant example of that pattern. Cannon steered by instinct and political appetite, not by theory, program, history, or, too often, fact. Awkward facts could be simply ignored.

In the next issue of *The Militant*, on an inside page, a picture of captured German soldiers accompanied the headline: "Red Army Forces Still Intact. Soviet Masses Are Fighting To Defend October's Gains". Stalin and his "lackeys" were criticised for depriving the soldiers of "weapons the October Revolution put in their hands" — a socialist appeal to the German workers in uniform (26 July 1941). The 19 July 1941 program would in time dwindle to this "proposal": that a working-class appeal be made to the German armies by the Russian autocracy. [10].

In fact, this was charlatan stuff. The Kremlin did "appeal" to the workers, though not, of course, in the internationalist and Marxist terms the Orthodox Trotskyists called for [11]; it had set the Communist Parties in Nazi-occupied Europe to organising armed resistance in many countries.

In a speech printed in *The Militant* on 30 August 1941 Cannon obliquely explained a likely origin of the comments of the Orthodox on Russian morale. "What [those who expected the collapse of the USSR] overlooked was the one most important and most fundamental element in war.... [It] was elucidated by Comrade Trotsky in our last talk with him in Mexico, fourteen months ago, the element of morale. The great battle of France was raging – we asked him to give us his opinion of the military prospects of that fight. And again and again he repeated. 'It depends on the morale of the French army. If the French army really has the morale to fight, Hitler cannot win, not even if he comes as far as Paris'... The Russian workers and peasants... know better than all the renegades... who have turned their backs on the Soviet Union in the hour of danger... Trotsky said more than once, that the beginning of a war of imperialism against the Soviet Union would arouse [an] outburst of genuine revolutionary patriotism and fighting spirit in the Russian masses... By their tremendous demonstration of fighting heroism, the Russian masses have said once again that the revolution in Russia is still alive..." (p.297, this volume).

In August 1941 *The Militant* revived its excited agitation about high Russian morale. "Red Army Blasts Myth of Hitler Strength", an article by "George Stern" with a picture of captured German soldiers, claimed: "The Red Army stand against Hitler's legions has come as a revelation to the rest of the world. Churchill and Roosevelt have greeted it as 'magnificent' and the press gives surprised recognition to the fact that the Red Army has exploded the myth of Nazi invincibility" (*The Militant*, 9 August 1941). Another headline in that issue, over an article by George Breitman (see p.299, this volume), shouted: "Red Army Morale Astonishes Its Enemies". A subordinate headline asserted: "Soviet Soldiers Fight Bravely Because They Have Something Worth Defending".

Under a crosshead, "Trotsky's predictions now come true", Breitman triumphantly told the reader that in 1934 Trotsky had written: "Within the USSR, war against imperialist intervention will undoubtedly provoke a veritable outburst of genuine fighting enthusiasm. All the contradictions and antagonisms will seem overcome or at any rate relegated to the background. The young generations of workers and peasants that emerged from the revolution will reveal on the field of battle a colossal dynamic power..." Trotsky (so wrote Breitman) "was able to foresee this stubborn resistance chiefly because he understood the class character of the first workers' state and, as a result, the determination of the workers and peasants, even under the parasitic Stalinist bureaucracy, to hold on to what they have". And what of events after 1934, such as the great slaughter of 1934-8?

This article had some of the quality of hysteria, of a flood-tide of emotion breaking its banks. Breitman was responding to explanations given by the Nazis and others for their failure to have in Russia the quick and easy victory they had expected. "Unlike the European armies, the [Russian] soldiers have something to fight for, and they know it!" The European and American soldiers "know that it is not the people who will benefit from the results of the war, but their masters, the imperialists, and that the lives of the worker-soldiers are being thrown away in a cause that is not theirs." The broad mass of workers in Europe and the USA understood all that? Nationalism and chauvinism, or simple "defend-my-home-and-family" ideas, had vanished from among them?

Breitman felt obliged to admit: "The Nazis have maintained a certain high discipline in their armies". But that was only skin deep. The German army too was made up of "men who know they are not fighting for their own interests. The Red soldiers, on the other hand, not only have something to fight against... but they also have something to fight for." German morale would collapse, therefore it need not be evaluated as something existing now.

A subtitle prepared the reader to be told "What the Red Army Defends". "The October revolution destroyed the political power and the economic power of the capitalist class... In spite of all the crimes and blunders of the Stalinist bureaucracy since then, the economic foundation established by the Russian Revolution still exists. It is this for which the Soviet troops are willing to give their lives rather than capitulate".

The Red Army soldier knew that "he is not fighting for the benefit of a gang of bosses who will continue to exploit him after the war just as viciously as before. He knows that he is fighting for himself and his children, to preserve what he has left of the greatest revolution of all time, the nationalized economy which must exist and be extended before society can go ahead to socialism, peace and plenty." Experience had "shown the Russian masses the superiority of living in a workers' state, even though isolated and degenerated under Stalinism". Here, "defend the nationalised economy" was translated into direct "Friends of the Soviet Union" style fantasies – and lies – about Stalinist society.

This article was crude Stalinist propaganda, utterly at odds with the realities of the USSR and with what the Trotskyists had truthfully been saying about Stalinism for most of a decade. But it was in accord with the US government, the US press, Hollywood. In politicians' speeches, in newspapers, and in a number of mainstream films, a fantastically false picture of the USA's Russian ally was being presented. The "capitulation" of the Orthodox to the Stalinist nonsense about the glories of "the Workers' State" was simultaneously a "capitulation" to bourgeois and petty-bourgeois opinion and pressure.

The young George Breitman was merely following "the line". The "minimum program" printed in *The Militant* had plainly said that the Stalinist system already had "the foundation of socialism".

The people of the USSR resisted the Nazi invaders who openly called the Slavs subhuman ("Untermenschen"), and treated them accordingly, murdering, starving, and enslaving the people in areas they conquered. The Orthodox took all that the Stalinists said about high morale as hard fact; ignored the evidence of widespread low morale; ignored examples of high morale during the war in other countries. They refused to see the obvious reason — apart from being driven by a murderously coercive state — for mass Russian self-defence. For it they substituted their own notion — the people of the USSR were "defending nationalised property". The Orthodox spun a story, instead of giving honest reports, accounting, and analysis. Their political "lines" were being cut loose from the basic politics of the Trotskyist account of the USSR.

Breitman's article was the most extreme and explicit case as yet of the substantial collapse, in the camp of the Orthodox Trotskyists, of the working class content of Trotsky's politics on Stalinism. It was still only a beginning!

"Trotsky's Red Army" In World War 2

TO KEEP THIS IN PERSPECTIVE and in context, it needs to be underlined that the SWP continued to make vigorous propaganda against the American Stalinist party. It argued that the American workers should prosecute their own class struggle in war time. It held consistently to the view that for US workers the "best way to help the USSR" was to fight and win the class struggle at home. It opposed the often spectacular strikebreaking, scab-herding, and shameless class collaboration which was the American-Stalinists' contribution to "defending the Soviet Union". The Orthodox denounced Stalinism in general and carried historical articles about the conflict between Trotskyism and Stalinism. When in 1943 it became known that two leaders of the Polish Bund, Wiktor Alter and Henryk Ehrlich, had been killed by the Russians, the SWP would join in the outcry against Stalin.

But soon they took a further large step into a world of political make-believe, in an article by John G Wright, "How Leon Trotsky Organized The Red Army" (*The Militant*, 16 August 1941). It was nothing less than an attempt to claim, on behalf of Trotsky and, therefore, for themselves, the credit that was now, for many Americans, beginning to attach to the Russian Army. They discovered that the Army that existed in 1941 was not after all Stalin's Army, but still "Trotsky's Red Army"! They spun off into political delirium [12].

A defining idea, for the Cannonites as for Trotsky, was that the state-owned means of production could rationally be separated out from the totalitarian state and those who controlled it. That idea was now extended to the claim that the army of that state also had a political and class character unchanged and uncorrupted by those who controlled it (and who in purges four years earlier had massacred over 15,000 of its officers). Like the statified means of production, this "Red Army" was a continuation of the October Revolution, nestling inside the Stalinist putrefaction, like the honey bees in the bible story inside the carcass of the dead lion. The Red Army of 1941, so John G Wright wrote in plain words, was a "conquest of October", and, like nationalised property, it retained the fundamental character it had had a quarter-century earlier. As late as October 1944 James P Cannon would write from his prison cell rebuking the editors of *The Militant* for allowing someone to use the expression "Stalin's Red Army". It wasn't Stalin's Red Army, but Trotsky's, Cannon insisted (letter of 22 October 1944).

John G Wright said it explicitly: "The name of Leon Trotsky is inseparably bound up with the formation, life and victories of the Red Army... No one will succeed in obscuring the connection between his role in organizing and building the Red Army and its successes, including the present heroic resistance of the Red soldiers against the Nazi onslaught." The Army too was a great "conquest of the revolution". "Long after Stalin concentrated political power in his own hands, he had to leave the command of the Army in the hands of those who commanded it under Trotsky". Stalin, said Wright, had little control over the major armed body of the totalitarian state! "It is the Army of the October Revolution and the Civil War – Trotsky's Red Army – that is now fighting so heroically".

As a critic of this thesis said: to believe that you have to believe in ghosts (see p.354, this volume). In the SWP press John G Wright, Felix Morrow, and others would develop this idea all the way to imagining that the "Red" Army in the war was something other than the instrument of Stalin; that it was an instrument of working-class politics and working-class socialist revolution.

Wright separated off the core of the USSR state machine, the army, from the Stalinist counter-revolution: then, had there in fact been a counter-revolution at all? One consequence of this sort of thinking would be that the Orthodox sometimes seemed to be uncertain about whether or not the bureaucratic autocracy really ruled. In late August and early September 1941, as we will see, they would write things which could only make sense if the bureaucracy were very weak or had faded away and lost control of the USSR.

Wright's idea was a radical departure from Trotsky's analysis of Stalinist Russia and from the positions held by the Fourth International at Trotsky's death. Trotsky had seen the Army as one of the prime sources of the bureaucratisation that engulfed the revolution. The habit of command, of hierarchy, had spread from the Army to the party and society. Discussing the idea that he should have organised a military coup against the bureaucracy, Trotsky replied that that would only have been another, and maybe a quicker, route to bureaucratism. In *The Revolution Betrayed*, written in 1936, he had written: "The restoration of officers' castes 18 years after their revolutionary abolition testifies to the gulf which separates the rulers from the ruled, to the loss by the Soviet army of the chief qualities which gave it the name of 'Red'".

The Second Phase: The Leningrad Delirium

UNCHECKED POLTICAL DELIRIUM breeds more delirium. In *The Militant* of 30 August and 6 September 1941 – it needs to be said bluntly – the Orthodox went very close to outright political dementia. Their critical judgement, their memory and their sense of reality, were temporarily paralysed. They came close to suggesting that the Stalinist regime in Russia had ceased, or was ceasing, to exist.

The German siege of Leningrad, which would continue for 882 days, was beginning. Workers' battalions were organised from Leningrad factories, those that had not been evacuated – on the initiative of the Stalinist autocrats and police and under their control. The people of the city were willing to resist: the Nazis declared in leaflets dropped into the city that: "We will level Leningrad to the earth and destroy Kronstadt to the waterline" (Harrison Salisbury, *The 900 Days*, pp.209-10, 208). On 30 August 1941 the front page headline of *The Militant* announced: "Workers Arm To Save Leningrad". Subheads: "Masses Inspired By Memories Of October 1917. Kremlin Finally Compelled To Make Appeal To Traditions Of The October Revolution As Workers Rally For Defense To The Death".

"In the hour of gravest danger to Leningrad, birth-place of the October Revolution, its proletarian inhabitants are mobilizing arms in hand to defend their city to the death against the German army. A tremendous revolutionary resurgence is sweeping the masses. Leningrad today is witness to scenes having their only parallel in the heroic days of the civil war, when, in October 1919, Yudenich's army was crushed by the aroused might of the armed Leningrad proletariat....

"In tremendous mass meetings the workers are shouting forth their defiance of the imperialist enemy. From every factory and shop, picked units of workers are joining the regular troops to help hold the battle lines and are filtering through to the enemy's rear to aid the guerilla detachments."

In fact the "units of workers" were "picked", organised and controlled by the Stalinist state apparatus. *The Militant* drew and coloured the picture as if the workers were no longer under the physical or political or ideological control of the bureaucracy's murdering political police, the GPU. The Kremlin, said *The Militant*, had been "compelled" to play a positive role in rousing the working class: "Up to the last moment, the Kremlin had held back the mobilization of the workers. Up to the last moment, Stalin suppressed the traditions of the October Revolution, appealing instead to the traditions of the Napoleonic era.... Today, however, a Voroshilov is compelled to proclaim to the workers of Leningrad... 'Leningrad was and is and shall forever remain the city of the great October Revolution'." Everything was changed!

The Militant writers operated by seizing on reports in the bourgeois press, reports filtered through the Stalinist censorship, that would fit their "theses", their hopes, and their desires, and then, like a space rocket escaping its scaffolding as it rises, wildly extrapolated from that. From a mere 4,000 miles away, they knew themselves to be able with certainty and precision to judge the ideas in the heads of Russian workers – who would have been shot for speaking critically about Russia and its rulers.

"The masses of Leningrad are demonstrating that that is the appeal for which they have been waiting" (!). "Once again, as in the days of Lenin and Trotsky, they are surging forward, ready to die in defense of the conquests of the October Revolution".

All this was false, arbitrary, political self-projection – self-indulgent foolishness. *The Militant* did everything that could be done by excited words, the flashing of romantic revolutionary images and reminiscences, and the arbitrary assignment of motives – the people defended nationalised property – to paint a picture of revolutionary workers acting outside the political control of the Stalinist bureaucracy. They substituted their own concerns and fantasies for the likely concerns of Leningrad workers facing Nazi enslavement. They wrapped up Russian-Stalinist realities in ideological red ribbons, appealing political mirages, fantasies mistaken for hard fact, and blissful self-induced political amnesia.

That 30 August 1941 issue of *The Militant* editorialised in the same vein: "Leningrad is in danger. The imperialist wolf-pack is closing in upon the city. Workers, understand what this means. Leningrad is the hearth of the October Revolution. The most glorious traditions of revolutionary struggle cluster around this proletarian center. Despite the degeneration of the workers' state under the Stalinist regime, these glorious traditions inspire the working class of Leningrad. Once again, as in 1905 and 1917, the Leningrad workers are rising and arming themselves to cope with their class enemy. Barricades are going up. The factory workers who constituted the Red Guard of Lenin's day are practising armed drill..." The same factory workers? The leading Bolshevik workers of the revolution had survived the civil war and Stalin's butcherings?

"This mass rising" – who have they risen against? what resistance did they meet with? what was the political result of their rising? – "is the supreme manifestation to date of the resurgence of the revolutionary spirit of 1905 and 1917. The proletarian power that created the USSR now springs forth to save it from destruction". Power? For Marxists the term usually denotes state power, and they had already, through John G Wright (sponsored and backed, certainly, by Cannon), claimed that Stalin did not "really" control the army, the military core of the state machine. But *The Militant,* in its fantasy-addled language, may here have just meant energy or strength.

Lack of political self-appraisal and self-criticism, a fondness for easy demagogy, too-loose and loosening ties to the theoretical and programmatic moorings of their starting-point politics, and the absence of an independent-minded opposition in the post-1940-split party, here reduced them to political raving [13]. Where the Trotskyists in Trotsky's time had seen the nationalised industry as the sole, albeit large, survival from the October Revolution, submerged in the totalitarian filth, and Stalinist society as an exceptionally vicious parody of a class-exploitative system, Trotsky's self-named "disciples" now saw a survival of the workers' revolution itself in the whole society.

"The proletarian revolution within the Soviet Union exhibits irrepressible vitality. Despite the injuries laid by Stalin's regime upon the revolutionary proletariat, its living forces well up in a mighty stream. Stalin, who disarmed the workers years ago, is now compelled to rearm them. The Stalinist bureaucracy takes this step with misgivings, at the most critical hour of its existence, in order to save its own skin. But that does not lessen the objective significance of the act. The arming of the people gives testimony that the workers' state endures... Leningrad is not, like Paris and Brussels, ruled by a powerful capitalist clique which could oppose the arming of the people and their fight to the death against the fascists." And the Stalinist autocracy? The Nazis too, in 1944-5, "armed the people" in the Volksturm, and hundreds of thousands of them died resisting the Allies in the last months of the war. There was no capitalist clique in Berlin either? Or in Britain? In Britain, and not under a totalitarian state but as part of a functioning bourgeois-democratic political system, the government armed the people, creating the "Home Guard".

When Trotsky (and Cannon after him) said the bureaucratic autocracy had all the vices of all the ruling classes and seized a proportionately greater share of the social product in Russia than the rich in the advanced capitalist countries, that it deprived the workers even of the basic necessities of life, they were wrong? It wasn't true? It had ceased to be true? The Russian workers hadn't noticed? Politically serious people would feel obliged to say how all that fitted into the picture they were now drawing of Russian Stalinist society. In this vein, the Orthodox were not being serious political people; they were being irresponsible demagogues and fantasists. Above all: demagogues.

"The workers have no selfish private property interests to protect at the expense of others". The workers decide? They rule? "The readiness of the Leningrad workers to offer up their lives to save their city demonstrates that they know they are defending, not the privileges of Stalinist bureaucrats, but the nationalized property and other remaining conquests of the revolution". If they withstood the siege, the nationalised property would be in the hands of the workers and not of the autocracy and its state?

"The Stalinist regime fears the people in arms as the forerunner of new revolutionary struggles. But even more do they fear the loss of Leningrad and further victories for the fascists, which would endanger their rule from within and from without. Under these compelling circumstances they have been obliged to approve the arming of the masses. But they did not permit the people to take arms until the danger was poised at their heart. Now suddenly they sound the alarm and call upon the workers to save them from the consequences of their own ruinous policies." The Stalinist bureaucracy was projecting a roughly revolutionary orientation...?

The Militant continued: "The Stalinist propaganda machine strives to conceal the real character of this mass uprising... The masses of the USSR lack the necessary class organs through which to exercise their creative energies and mobilize their maximum forces. The Soviets, the trade-unions, Lenin's Bolshevik Party, the Young Communist League – all these indispensable class agencies have been destroyed by the Stalinist regime... These institutions must be reborn and resume their commanding place in Soviet life. The arming of the people [by the Stalinist regime] is the first step in this direction. The class in arms possesses power to demand and to win the restoration of its political rights and its democratic institutions. The Soviet proletariat is in a position to move forward and regain all that has been taken from it by the Stalinist reaction". The workers, or "the masses", now shared "dual power", or something not far from it? [1]

And even in its ecstatic delirium, *The Militant* did not forget denunciations, damnings, and fatwas against the Heterodox Trotskyists: "The Russian workers exhibit no signs of defeatism. Such renegacy belongs to the petty-bourgeois radicals in the capitalist countries. The independent revolutionary proletariat is moving to the forefront in the Soviet Union on the wave of a resurgent revolutionary tide. This class movement imparts a new dynamic force to the defense of the workers' state. This can be the beginning of the renewal of the Russian Revolution".

They recalled their "minimum program", and now addressed it to "the masses". "The program for victory presented by our party can be realized in life through the action of the Soviet masses themselves". Here at least the proposals were aimed in the right direction – at the workers and the other "masses". "We urge the unconditional defense of the Soviet Union against imperialist attack as the elementary duty of the working class. The stubborn resistance of the Red Army and the mass rising of the urban proletariat demonstrate how both recognize the necessity for defending to the last ditch the remaining achievements of their revolution." Not only the urban proletariat, but also the "Red Army", is a political force independent, or becoming independent, of the bureaucracy?

"Down with Stalin's ruinous policies!" – defined as "faith in imperialist alliances", instead of appealing to the German workers – and "drive out the Stalinist bureaucracy". Those phrases were surely better than silence on the bureaucracy, but still too far from a plain reiteration of the necessity for working-class revolution against Stalin and the autocracy.

The front page headlines of *The Militant* of 6 September 1941, the second number issued under the imprimatur of political bedlam, told its readers: "Masses Defend Soviet Cities. Hold Nazi Army At Odessa, Kiev And Leningrad. Traditions Of October 1917 Inspire Masses To Fight To Death Against Imperialists". This outdid the previous issue in at least one respect. It carried a straightforwardly Stalinist cartoon on the front page, headed "A Tale of Two Cities". It had two panels, labelled "Paris" and "Leningrad". In "Paris" we see a bourgeois on his knees, representing the French bosses, offering a giant key to a big thug stamped with a swastika, Hitler. In "Leningrad" we see the Hitler figure crouching, almost on his knees, and looming above him, much larger, is a muscular worker grimly

The Militant, 6 September 1941

rolling up his sleeves. The Stalinist autocracy is no part of the picture.

They were still working on their translation of the idea that Russia remained a degenerated workers' state because of the nationalised economy rooted in the 1917 revolution into the idea that the class character given to the "workers' state" by nationalised economy pervaded everything and made it a state equipped with "the foundation of socialism", one where "the masses" – the slave-driven masses – knew by experience "the superiority of living in a workers' state".

"Surrounded by vast, heavily mechanized Nazi force, the armed workers of Odessa, side by side with the Red Army, are holding the invaders at bay". The misreporting here, as if the workers were the independent protagonist on the Russian side, could only be deliberate. And they were, and would be throughout the war, above all experts on Russian morale: "As in Leningrad and Kiev, the proletarian masses of Odessa are rallying to the defense of the Soviet Union, spurred on by the memories and traditions of the October Revolution. Eye-witness reports from the beleaguered Ukrainian city relate the tremendous effect produced on the workers' morale last week when a unit of Black Sea Marines paraded through the city's streets singing the Kablochka, famous fighting song of the Civil War of 1918-1921. Stirred by this revolutionary song, the populace danced in the streets and morale soared to a high pitch". It would have been well to remind the readers and themselves that all reports coming out of Russia had passed through the Stalinist censorship. In fact Odessa fell to Romanian troops a few weeks later. Russia's Black Sea fleet evacuated the Russian troops in Odessa, but not the Jewish population, some 75,000 to 80,000 of whom were murdered by the invaders after the city fell.

"In Leningrad... workers at the end of their factory shifts engage in vast defense drills... In mortal fear for its own existence, the Stalinist bureaucracy is finally forced to rally the workers by appeals to the real tradition of the Soviet Union – the October Revolution... All evidence points to the one inspiring fact: the October Revolution still lives and fights on". Their gratitude for a few words – Voroshilov's reference to Leningrad as "the city of the Great October Revolution" – and their satisfaction with them, was not only pitiable but also evidence of their deep political demoralisation and disorientation.

Someone reading all this without knowing what happened next would have thought that the SWP was going over to a species of critical Stalinism, on the basis of out-of-control fantasy and self-delusion. In fact that's what, politically speaking, they did. Then they backtracked, recalled to something like sense by Natalia Sedova Trotsky and by their own better political selves. Episodes of similar delirium would be a recurrent feature of the Orthodox over the decades to come.

This, I think, was the first appearance in the history of the Trotskyist movement of this sort of wilful, knowing or half-knowing, misrepresentation and downright falsification of reality in order to spin consoling fantasy. Of course mistakes had been made before then – recently, about Russia's Stalinist armies in Poland and Finland. But there is no just comparison of Trotsky's mistaken view of Poland and Finland and the Stalinist invasion with this wilful cutting loose from reality and the Marxist – notionally their own – program.

There is no such thing, it has been observed, as a "sincerometer" in politics. That Cannon sincerely lost his sense of reality at different points in World War 2, is, I think, a matter of recorded fact. That he calculated and postured and assumed positions for organisational advantage is, I think, a certainty. Where calculation started and sincere delusion, whipped up among themselves by a small group of like-minded people, ended, is impossible to know.

As we will see, in late 1941, in the SWP's retreat from the Leningrad delirium, and again in 1944, Cannon would back down from positions in which he seemingly had a great emotional investment, in face of rebukes from Natalia Sedova Trotsky.

The Third Phase: Natalia Sedova's First "Intervention"

THE WIDE-EYED CREDULITY AND FANTASY was abruptly abandoned in the next issue of *The Militant*, 13 September 1941. Someone had poured a bucket of political ice water over the too-heated Orthodox – Natalia Sedova Trotsky. So too, perhaps, had the unfolding events in Russia. The Nazis had completely surrounded Leningrad on 8 September, starting a siege which would last for two and a half years. Kiev would surrender on 19 September. Now there was a dramatic shift in *The Militant*'s coverage of the war and the USSR. No explanation for the shift was offered. No explanation would ever be offered for the two weeks of delirious triumphalism in August-September 1941.

"Catastrophe faces USSR as result of Stalin's rule. Stalin's purges beheaded Red Army", *The Militant* told its readers in its 4 October 1941 front-page headline, over an article by Natalia Sedova Trotsky. "The German army keeps advancing deeper and deeper into the Soviet Union. The fascists have seized Kiev, they are marching on Kharkov, Rostov, the Donets Basin. They are in a position to occupy Crimea. They can occupy Leningrad. The heroic Red Army is not attaining its goal despite its high morale, despite its frightful sacrifices, despite the millions of fighters who perish... It is necessary to undertake a resolute campaign against the criminals responsible for the defeats. Irrefutable facts are now confirming with invincible force the diagnosis made by Leon Trotsky on the basis of an all-sided analysis of the general political and economic conditions in the USSR. It is necessary by means of the merciless blows of fact to lay bare unceasingly, with all our energy, the causes for the defeats of the Red Army. The time has come to remind all workers daily, hourly, of the crimes of the Kremlin regime and its chieftain. The questions I raise are questions of the greatest importance. Everything must be concentrated on them, everything else must be subordinated to them. For the fate of the Soviet Union is now being decided."

Sedova angrily dismissed the idea exulted in and rhapsodised upon by *The Militant* that the use of guerrillas by the regime constituted independent working-class intervention in Russian political life and military affairs. She related it to old intra-Bolshevik disputes of the Civil War period. "What is the truth about guerrilla warfare? Stalin has come back to it, he has returned to the guerrillaism against which Lenin and Trotsky fought so relentlessly during the civil war in the revolutionary Soviet Union. Stalin needs guerrillaism as a facade, as something to show, something to fool the people with. By guerrillaism he tries to cover up the absence of strategists, the absence of a genuine revolutionary and planned leadership of the war; he distracts public opinion by means of the heroes of guerrilla warfare. But in a correctly conducted war there is no need at all of guerrillas; they can only be a hindrance and incur disproportionate sacrifices. Who benefits by this?"

Natalia Sedova's article, dated 25 September 1941, was a tacit reprimand to the Orthodox. They accepted it meekly. It is probable that there had been an exchange of letters before Sedova's article appeared.

A front-page editorial, "Trotsky showed Road for the Victory of the Soviet Union", once again proclaimed the immediate "minimum program", as demands on "the Soviet government": "release pro-Soviet political prisoners; revive the democratically-elected Soviets; legalise all pro-Soviet political parties; seek revolutionary unity with the German working class. For the Socialist United States of Europe".

After 4 October 1941, for about a year, during which the war went badly for the USSR, *The Militant* repeated the themes of Natalia's angry article. Why such defeats? Stalin had beheaded the "Red" Army by purging most of its top commanders shortly before the war. The idea of the overthrow of the bureaucracy reappeared occasionally, though in an addled form in which the "Red" Army, as it was, as a whole, or more or less as a whole, was to rank equal to the working class as the agency for this "political revolution".

"The Soviet masses and the Red Army must rid the country of the bureaucratic regime which constitutes the chief internal obstacle to the victorious defence of the workers' state" (*The Militant*, 25 October 1941). Correlated with reality, this would be a call for a military coup!

"Resurgence Of The Soviet Masses"

IN THE MAGAZINE *FOURTH INTERNATIONAL*, January 1942, John G Wright published a "think-piece" on "The USSR in War". A cross-head sums up the article: "Resurgence of the Soviet masses". Wright wrote of the "enthusiastic response" to the decree of "universal military training" from October 1941. In many cities workers were "arming and drilling" even before the official decree. "There is considerable evidence that the initiative for this measure did not originate at the top". Evidence from where? Wright did not tell his readers.

The "worker detachments", wrote Wright, were "not... guerrillas fighting behind enemy lines". They "coordinate their activities with those of the regular army". Moscow, wrote Wright, "kept silent about the role of these proletarian militias". So how did Wright come to know better? "The bureaucracy is not enthused by the prospect of an armed and trained population". (In fact, three battalions of Leningrad civilians were formed and sent into battle with little training. The third such battalion had only one day's training). All through the piece, Wright implied, without saying it, that the "worker detachments" were politically independent working-class groups, or becoming independent. He wrote of "the trade unions", as if the Stalinist labour-front organisations for controlling the workers were real trade unions. A "section of the trade union activists and trade union organisers" had gone into the army. Activists? Organisers?

"The contradiction between the political needs of the regime and the military tasks of the country is being brought to the breaking point". The Communist Party of the Soviet Union "holds no meetings, conducts no political agitation, accepts no new members... The party has been a hollow shell for many years. The war has cracked the shell". There is "growing pressure from below... Under the hammer blows of events the ranks of the bureaucracy are being shattered". Workers' control, not stifling bureaucratism, was necessary in the factories to maximise production. There was "rising confidence and self-action among the Soviet masses".

Wright's basic idea was that the contradiction between the needs of war and bureaucratic rule was an absolute one – the bureaucrats could conduct no adequate war effort – and the contradiction was shattering the Stalin regime. It was impossible for the bureaucracy to adjust and survive. The Stalinist structures in Russian society were crumbling. In the early 30s Trotsky had believed that the mechanisms of Stalinist rule were falling apart under the stresses of forced-march collectivisation and industrialisation. Something like that was in Wright's mind now, and of course the Orthodox "knew" that the bureaucracy was in no degree a ruling class, but only a flimsy encrustation on Russian society: it could be easily sloughed off.

Even in the period when defence of the USSR was downplayed, the idea theorised by Wright that the "Red" Army was a proletarian force autonomous or semi-autonomous from the bureaucracy would be kept alive and developed. A front-page cartoon in *The Militant* of 15 August 1942 claimed it was "Trotsky's Red Army" (p.175, this volume).

1941-2: Taking Stock

FOR ABOUT A YEAR, up to the turn of the tide in Russia's favour at Stalingrad after 19 November 1942, the Orthodox expected Russia to be overwhelmed. Coverage of Russia lessened. The fluctuating moods of the Orthodox were registered in *The Militant*'s use of the

1931 quotation from Trotsky — "To defend the USSR... is the most important duty of every class-conscious worker" — as a heading for its editorial page. It was there, then it wasn't, then it was again. It ran from 9 August 1941 to 13 December 1941, then it was dropped for a year, reappearing only from 19 December 1942 until 31 March 1945.

On 25 October 1941 *The Militant* spoke out against the Stalinist regime in renewedly sharp terms. "Stalin Orders GPU Rule For Moscow. Turns To Open GPU Terror To Bolster Regime. Edict Aimed at Silencing All Those Who Criticize Or Oppose Kremlin's War Policy", it reported on page one – as if "GPU rule" in the USSR were startling news. *The Militant* did not report the background of a new order by Stalin, which was that the Germans had taken the important city of Rostov almost without a fight. The USSR troops had panicked and fled. That defeat, and the bureaucracy's visible measures to move government operations from Moscow to Kuibyshev (further east), created panic and flight from Moscow. Stalin responded by moving up the GPU from its usual second-line role to front-line policing in Moscow, with powers to shoot there and then anyone whose talk they overheard and did not like.

John G Wright wrote on Stalin's decree that it was "only the latest link" in a series of decrees (all of European Russia under martial law, 22 June; GPU-controlled political commissars in the army, 16 July, and in the navy, 21 July) instituting "the investment of the GPU with open and sweeping powers not only over the population, but over the Red Army itself".

Wright thought the overthrow of Stalin was now very close. "Stalin's monstrous bureaucratic apparatus of repression began crumbling on the eve of the second World War. The war has violently speeded up this process of disintegration. We are now witnessing the final stages of the death agony of Stalinism... Every day, every hour of the struggle brings additional overwhelming proof that the Soviet Union can be successfully defended only by the reconstitution of the Soviets and the return to the policies of Bolshevism" (*The Militant*, 8 November 1941). The Soviet Union could only be defended after a "political" revolution? A revolution whose achievement was ruled out in deference to the priority of defence? Therefore, in reality, it couldn't be defended at all? Essentially, that's what they still thought.

On 1 November *The Militant* issued advice to "the masses" living under the GPU terror. "The Soviet masses, while they continue the military struggle against the fascists, must take steps to provide a leadership for the fronts that is qualified, trained and capable of leading them to victory... While the struggle against Stalinism, the chief internal obstacle to the successful defense of the USSR and the organizer of its defeats, must be subordinated to the defense of the military front against the imperialists, the Soviet masses must take the first favorable opportunity, without weakening the front against the imperialists, to remove the bureaucratic regime..."

This new formulation had the merit of pointing once again toward the need for a working-class revolution against Stalin and the autocracy. But the idea that the "Soviet masses" could change the army leadership while Stalin still held power (or did he? remember that his power was "crumbling") was another bizarrity to add to the growing collection. The Proletarian Military Policy for the USA may have infected their thinking here – the idea that the trade unions, without taking power or at least achieving "dual power", could take over the training of the US armed forces.

The Socialist Workers Party held a Plenum-Conference on 11 October 1941, in Chicago (this volume, p.304). "Only our analysis of the anti-revolutionary character of Stalinism explains to the workers why the Kremlin has refused to arouse the masses of Europe and undermine Hitler in Germany". The Heterodox Trotskyists were never far from Cannon's concerns. "Our program for the revolutionary defense of the Soviet Union has been confirmed not only against the Stalinists, but also against all the petty-bourgeois renegades who denied the Soviet Union its character as a workers' state and who refused to defend it." Cannon had a new "proof" that the USSR was a workers' state: "The unparalleled morale with which the Red Army and the Soviet Union masses rallied to the defense of the workers' state can only be explained by our analysis of the class character of the Soviet Union. The Soviet masses, despite the oppression which they are under from the Kremlin bureaucracy, proved to be wiser politically than the 'cultured' petty-bourgeois snobs who abandoned the Soviet Union; the masses were able to distinguish between the Soviet Union and Stalinism" (*The Militant*, 18 October 1941). In fact, of course, Stalin and his GPU were absolutely inseparable from the reality of the USSR.

Cannon told the conference: "From all indications, Stalin and his gang are carrying their work to its predestined end. Stalin and Hitler together are dealing the Soviet Union what appears now to be its most catastrophic blow. The bitter truth can no longer be concealed by any blustering. The reality is too glaringly obvious now". He was plain about his organisational calculations: "We should intensify our work among the Stalinists; try to reach them at all costs; fix the responsibility for the catastrophe of the Soviet Union where it really belongs – on the shoulders of Stalin and his gang; and try to win over every possible Stalinist worker to the movement of the Fourth International". And again he did not forget to curse, damn, and anathematise the Shachtmanites. "In such an hour as this, we see again how absolutely right were Trotsky and the majority of our party and the International in defending the Soviet Union to the very end; in establishing such a clear record that if we have now come to the catastrophe... nobody can justly say that one iota of responsibility clings to the Fourth International. We remain loyal to the Soviet Union in spite of everything, and that gives us the political and moral right to approach the disillusioned Stalinist workers. It is not so with the petty-bourgeois elements who deserted our ranks on account of the Russian question. What position are they in to approach a sincere Stalinist worker who in his heart believed, and believed with justice, that the Soviet Union was a great fortress of the proletariat?..." (*The Militant*, 15 November 1941).

Self-righteous bragging was never absent for long. Typically, Cannon here judged, and urged his comrades to judge, the rightness or otherwise of an analysis or a programmatic position by how it would "play" to an audience, not by whether it was true to reality or not.

The SWP summed up again a year later, in an October 1942 convention resolution."We are proud of our record on the Russian question... Not one stain of dishonour will fall upon the banner of the Fourth International... The Fourth International [never] failed in its duty of defending the Russian revolution to the very end. That is one of the proudest assets of our movement". The October 1942 convention still believed that "unless the revolution rises and conquers in the capitalist world and the Soviet workers throw the Stalinist usurpers off their back, the Soviet Union will inevitably be crushed". No one else but themselves understood the USSR and therefore no one else but themselves understood world politics."The events affecting the Soviet Union... are incomprehensible except to those who are guided by the Trotskyist analysis of the character of the Soviet Union. We alone have accurately explained the course of the USSR, we alone do not have to conceal what we said yesterday... Petty-bourgeois deserters turned their back on the USSR which they suddenly termed 'imperialist', but we... explained that by the seizures of the Finnish, Polish and Baltic territories, the Kremlin bureaucracy was not pursuing imperialist aims but was in its own bureaucratic and reactionary way seeking to safeguard the defences of the Soviet Union" (*The Militant*, 17 October 1942; p.305 of this volume). Trotsky, of course, had said a great deal more about the Kremlin in Poland and Finland. Here was another leitmotif for the decades ahead:

Everything imperialistic-seeming the USSR did or would do, was done only for purposes of the legitimate defence of the workers' state.

Cannon and his comrades let their "Soviet patriotism", as SWP resolutions called it, lead them into very strange territory. Lauding nationalised property, they slipped into lauding Stalinist totalitarianism. The resolution said: "The Red Army and war production were free from the fetters which private property imposes upon 'national defense' even in wartime; no profiteers existed to limit war orders to monopoly corporations. The 'scorched earth' policy could be applied by a land without private property with a determination and planfulness which are impossible to capitalist countries. The moving of industrial plants from endangered areas to places deep in the interior, the building of a second railroad across Siberia – such gigantic economic actions in wartime were made possible only by the system of nationalised property".

This rodomontade about the superior efficiency of nationalised economy in the war was entirely Stalinist. The nationalised economy did not run itself. People made the decisions, decisions about other people. The Stalinist bureaucracy made the decisions. The "second railroad across Siberia", presumably the Baikal-Amur mainline, was constructed by the captive slave labour of 100,000 German prisoners-of-war. Only 10% would survive to be repatriated. All that was faded out in order to present a picture of the pure glories of nationalised property.

What they hailed here was the totalitarian power, ruthlessness, and inhumanity of the bureaucracy. Not nationalised property permitted that ruthlessness, but the totalitarian concentration of power in the hands of people who had the strength, imperviousness, and ruthlessness casually to kill off millions of "their own" people. Even the picture they painted of the capitalist states for contrast with the USSR was false and in substance a senseless glorification of Stalinist totalitarianism: the governments in both Britain and the USA had taken direct political control of industry, and they ran, as in World War One, effective capitalist war economies. The bluster here contrasted Stalin's system of totalitarian slave-driving favourably with the capitalist state-directed war economy in states that essentially preserved most of the bourgeois-democratic rights and liberties.

The program for democratisation was there too in the resolution, but how it all fitted together was still far from clear. In truth, it did not fit together. The October 1942 resolution did not explain the sudden collapse after two weeks of their wild fit of enthusiasm in August-September 1941. It "processed" it into a smooth "story-line".

"After five months of terrible defeats, workers from the factories joined the heroic Red Army warriors at the gates of Leningrad and Moscow and helped recover Rostov... in an outburst of proletarian revolutionary endeavour". Why was it revolutionary? In relation to what was it revolutionary? Because they "defended nationalised property", and doing so was ipso facto "revolutionary"? That is not how they had presented things in August-September 1941.

All this specious pseudo-explanation and demagogy stood on forceful assertion, misrepresentation, political dishonesty, bluster — and on a party system which made it very difficult for anybody to challenge the incumbent leaders. Such self-righteous demagogy could not but smother political discussion and dissent in the SWP, and any attempt at honest accounting. Thus the first fruit of the "tightening-up" of 1940, James P Cannon's "Bolshevisation" of Trotskyism, was to make possible this flood of irresponsible, capricious, and self-indulgent "apparatus politics" and "apparatus story-lining".

The Fourth Phase: After Stalingrad

A FOURTH PHASE in the responses of the Orthodox came with Russia's successes in the war, as the third phase had come with its defeats. In November 1942 the Russian army encircled the German army at Stalingrad. It was the turning point in the war. Russian strength, success, and territory began steadily to increase. The new cycle of enthusiasm and delusional politics on Russia was signalled with a front page headline on 5 December 1942: "Red Army's Offensive Staggers Germans At Stalingrad And Rzhev". And they knew what to do next, and what "tasks" they should set for Stalin's Russia: "The Task Now Is To Arouse German Revolt". And the "tasks" in the USSR?

"The military victories of the Red Army can be extended and turned into decisive victories. The ferment in Germany" – in response to a hypothetical Russian appeal to the German workers – "can completely disrupt Hitler's rear and facilitate Soviet victory. But for this a correct revolutionary policy is necessary. The Soviet masses, while fighting with all their energy against Hitler's attack, must convince their German brothers that they are allies who will fight with them against the imposition of a new Versailles [Treaty] and for the creation of a workers' government in Germany". Unless "Soviet masses" included the Stalinist regime, that was rampant nonsense, with no grip on any reality.

"As in 1918-19, today [a revolutionary appeal] can not only save the Soviet Union but can lead to the emancipation of all the workers of Europe". This line made even less sense now that the "Red" Army was beginning to advance. They saw no contradiction between the emancipation of the workers – of Europe or of Russia – and Russian military victory. Such talk as there had been about the overthrow of the bureaucracy subsided again.

On 5 December 1942 the SWP added "Defence of the USSR" as a ninth point to the previously eight-point policy platform in *The Militant*, and on 19 December 1942 they restored to the editorial page the 1931 quotation from Trotsky — "To defend the USSR... is the most important duty of every class-conscious worker". It would remain there until 31 March 1945. In mid-December 1942, they brought out, under the title *In Defence of Marxism*, a very one-sided selection of Trotsky's articles on Poland and Finland from 1939-40 (omitting the articles he had written for the public press to condemn Stalin's invasions, those he wrote after April 1940, and the May 1940 manifesto of the Fourth International). By that time much of the content of the book, Trotsky's polemics against the "petty-bourgeois" who would capitulate to US public opinion in the war, had been disproved by events, and its reproduction without comment on that disproof was therefore wilful libel on the Workers Party. A proper collection of what Trotsky wrote on Russia between, say, the USSR's turn to Germany in March 1939, or from the Hitler-Stalin pact in August 1939 to his death in August 1940, including his articles and drafts for the public press, would have been very valuable politically. Instead, the SWP produced a "cut out" Trotsky, limited to his internal polemics, to back up their own current politics. *In Defence of Marxism* was the first big example of "Apparatus Marxism" in the Trotskyist movement.

The introduction to the first edition of *In Defence of Marxism* (this volume, p.467), written by Joseph Hansen and William F Warde (George Novack), acting as Cannon's amanuenses, was an important document in the history of the Fourth International. It enshrined the Orthodox myth that the origin of the two Trotskyisms lay in the "renegacy" of "petty-bourgeois traitors". The introduction asserted, as allegedly bedrock Trotskyist principle, ideas flatly contradicted by the two major articles by Trotsky in the book, *The USSR in War* and *Again And Once More*. Hansen and Novack held forth on "dialectics"; but, in asserting that the "workers' state'" characterisation of the USSR and commitment in all circumstances to its defence were fixed parts of the "program of the Fourth International", they were utterly undialectical. Trotsky's point was the changeability of the USSR and therefore of Marxist assessments of it. What in Trotsky was a matter of ongoing investigation and successive approximations, in Hansen and Novack became a matter of barebones dogma. The Orthodox experts on materialist dialectics were creaking crass old-fashioned metaphysicians in their own attitudes to the USSR. In August 1943 the SWP followed up *In Defence of Marxism* with a book of Cannon's writings during the 1939-40 dispute, entitled *The Struggle for a Proletarian Party*. For decades, those two books would be international pillars of the Orthodox version of Trotskyism. As the question of "defending the USSR" receded in military terms with the successes of the Russian army, it became more prominent in the weekly and monthly publications of the Orthodox. According to what they had said in 1939-40, in the first place Trotsky and in the second place Cannon, it was now time to reassess the "degenerated workers' state" characterisation of Russia in the light of the survival of and imperialist expansion by Stalin's regime in the war. Instead, they veered off on a binge of vicarious proto-Stalinist triumphalism.

The emotions proper for revolutionary socialists in relation to the October Revolution and working-class movements in general were unleashed full-blast in support of Stalin's Russia. Russian military successes were successes of "Trotsky's Red Army"; of the October Revolution; of nationalised and planned industry; of the absence (thanks to the workers' revolution) of capitalists to hinder success, act as a fifth-column, or be a sell-out leadership such as the bourgeoisie in France had been when facing Hitler.

A regular contributor to *The Militant* in those years, Louis Jacobs, would comment in a document distributed at the 16-19 November 1944 SWP convention that calls for the overthrow of Stalin were there when things were going badly for Stalin's army, and absent when it was doing well. That was just.

The "Class Significance" Of Russia's Victories

THE STRANGE IDEA of claiming the "Red" Army for Trotskyism had started in Wright's article in 1941 and was epitomised in the front-page cartoon published in *The Militant* of 15 August 1942, before the turn of the tide in the war. Their use of the term "Trotsky's Red Army" for the Russian military helped the Orthodox ride the floodwaters of mass popular enthusiasm in the USA for the "Red Army" and "Uncle Joe" Stalin's Russia. The idea of "Trotsky's Red Army" had an ideological function in addition to its usefulness in a labour movement in which the "Red" Army was extremely popular. The USSR's army had survived Hitler's onslaught and was now scoring military successes against the Germans. It was doing deeds that the Orthodox had not believed it capable of. They explained the suc-

71

cesses by conjuring up the idea that this pillar of Stalin's state was not "really" Stalinist. Splitting off the "Red" Army (in their heads) from the Stalin regime had an extra daftness of its own; but the method and pattern was the same as with the splitting-off of the nationalised economy as a thing-in-itself separable from the people who ran and served it and from the social relations they set up within it. This method would play a very great role with the post-Trotsky Orthodox Trotskyists as, between the end of World War 2 and, say, the outbreak of the Korean war five years later, they struggled to comprehend a world they had never expected and the role in it of Stalin and Stalinism.

In 1939-40 Trotsky had written that the Russian Army in Poland and Finland could evoke revolutionary mass activity: Stalin would use it and then strangle it. The facts proved to be different, and in the Fourth International Manifesto of May 1940, Trotsky acknowledged that "Stalin did not find any support whatever in Finland... the invasion of the Red Army assumed the character of direct and open military violence". In 1943-4 the Orthodox took Trotsky's previous ideas about the Russian army evoking revolutionary activity, and applied them to the "Red" Army advancing on Europe. There would be an "impetus inevitably imparted by the Red Army advances to the revolutionary moods and movements of the masses and to an overturn in political and property relations", so they said as the Army entered Poland (*The Militant*, 8 January 1944); and the victorious Red Army, Trotsky's Red Army, would not let itself be used for Stalinist repression, or not all of it would.

Felix Morrow in *The Militant* of 20 February 1943: "Even before the Nazis are beaten, the fundamental class attitude of the capitalists toward the Soviet Union is revealing itself. They know that behind the Soviet victories and making them possible is the nationalized property system created by the October revolution. They are not too sure – and with good reason! – that the bureaucratic regime of Stalin will last long after a definitive Soviet victory over the Nazis. They fear that in place of Stalin... there will arise again the democratic Soviets in the spirit of Lenin and Trotsky – the spirit of the world socialist revolution. That's what capitalist reaction fears will be the outcome of Soviet victory. For exactly the same reason all workers truly loyal to their class are fervent supporters of the Soviet Union, knowing that its victory is also the victory of workers everywhere". The front-page headline the next week, 27 February 1943, warned: "New anti-Soviet manoeuvres reported. USSR Menaced By Finnish 'Peace' Move, Polish Plan, Vatican Plots". *The Militant* would worry much about things like that from now on. The Orthodox would back Russia's claims to the borders Stalin desired.

Two questions were confused and entangled here: the likely behaviour of Russia as a burgeoning military-imperialist power, and the "class character" of the USSR and of the areas it seemed now to be able to take under its control. The reasonable expectation that Russia would take what it could was mixed up with the notion that Russia, as a workers' state, would impart a "workers'" or "workers' state" character to a large part of Europe. The idea was sometimes that the "Red" Army would inspire working-class revolution and maybe help it along, and sometimes of the Army (which, remember, for the Orthodox, was not Stalin's "Red Army" but "Trotsky's") not letting itself be used against the workers.

Albert Goldman, in his column in *The Militant*, would explain "Why The Reactionaries Are Worried About Soviet Gains" (27 February 1943). "The magnificent victories achieved by the Red Army in recent months have inspired all the defenders of the Soviet Union with new hope... What worries some of the big capitalists is the possibility that the Red Army will reach Berlin before the British and American armies [and] of the Soviet Union extending its influence to Germany and to all of Central Europe... It is almost impossible to conceive of the Red Army's marching into Germany without a social revolution following". Whose social revolution? "They are worried that regardless of Stalin a social revolution will come as a result of a defeat of Hitler by the Soviet armies..." The ghosts of Ttrotsky's misunderstandings of Finland and Poland, in 1939-40, could be seen dancing wildly inside this and the many similar assessments.

What did all this mean in the SWP branches? The same issue of *The Militant* carried a report that inadvertently answered that question: "Speaking on 'The Class Meaning of the Soviet Victories' to an intensely interested New York audience of well over a hundred, Felix Morrow, editor of *Fourth International,* stated that the first victories of the Red Army have already revealed the fundamental hostility between the capitalist states and the workers' state. Listing a series of anti-Soviet moves by the capitalist 'friends' of the USSR, he quoted [British cabinet member] Lord Beaverbrook's admission that the Red Army had captured in two months more equipment from the Nazis than they had received from England and the US since the start of the war. The victories of the Red Army have caused panic not only amongst the Nazis but among the reactionaries in the United Nations who fear that the new confidence and high morale of the Red Army bodes ill for their plans to make a deal with Stalin guaranteeing them against a Socialist Europe".

The delusions and fantasies that ran riot in *The Militant* for two or three weeks in August-September 1941 had revived in a lower key. "The stranglehold of the Stalin bureaucracy has progressively weakened with every new Red Army victory and its consequent rise of morale among the Soviet masses. The Red Army is fighting for a Socialist Europe as well as a Socialist Russia, Morrow declared, and they will never submit to any underhanded deal to preserve capitalism in Europe for the benefit of the very same imperialist powers that attempted to overthrow the October 1917 Revolution".

Max Shachtman's response in *Labor Action* (15 March 1943) will serve as an interim summing up. "Felix Morrow... says: 'The stranglehold of the Stalin bureaucracy has progressively weakened with every Red Army victory'. Where, when, how? Nowhere, thus far, not even in the pages of *The Militant*, have we read of a single important (or for that matter, unimportant) fact to support this absurd contention. A weakening of the stranglehold of the bureaucracy would manifest itself in any number of concrete ways... a moderation of the terror regime, increased independent class activity of the workers, etc. Will such things, especially the last-named, take place? They will... As yet, there is no sign, no evidence, for Morrow's assertion. A totalitarian regime is weakened in wartime when it suffers military setbacks. To speak now, especially now, of a weakening of the bureaucracy's stranglehold on the country and its people is, at the very best, wishful thinking. Rise of morale among the Soviet masses? If by 'morale' Morrow is referring in general to the readiness of the masses to fight, to make sacrifices, then substantially the same thing could be said about the 'morale' of the Germans and the Japanese. Didn't their morale hold up, and rise, with the big victories of their armies? And isn't it still pretty high, according to most reports? What does this fact, by itself, prove about Russia that it does not prove about Germany or Japan?

"There is no evidence – again we emphasise, as yet – of any rise in the class morale of the Russian workers. Such a rise would show itself in the development of organised opposition, however primitive, to the counter-revolutionary regime; in the development of an independent class movement, of a socialist consciousness, of internationalist spirit. That will come. But where is there a single sign of it now?

"According to Morrow, not only is the 'Red' Army fighting for a socialist Russia (which does not exist except in the lying propaganda of the Kremlin) but also for a socialist Europe. With all deference to the delicate eardrums of our readers, we say again: Nonsense! But this time, especially dangerous nonsense. There is no such thing today as a Red Army. It once existed. It was organised by Trotsky and the Bolsheviks. It was the army of the workers, of the people, of the socialist revolution. But Stalinism destroyed that army! Hasn't Morrow heard? He can find the whole story told and analysed in Trotsky's writings. What is 'Red' (that is, socialist, internationalist, democratic) in the Russian army today?... The Stalinist army is the army of the Bonapartist counter-revolution. Does Morrow get this? – the army of Bonapartist counter-revolution, not the army of socialism!... What Morrow says is, at the best, apologetics for Stalinism. If it is 'fighting for a socialist Europe as well as a socialist Russia', that is welcome news. It would be a miracle – and we don't believe in miracles. The Russian masses will really be fighting for a socialist Russia and Europe when they have first destroyed the rule of bureaucratic totalitarianism, rid themselves of the poison of Stalinist chauvinism, and taken control. Not before! To disseminate the idea that the Stalinist army is fighting for a 'socialist Europe as well as a socialist Russia' is to disseminate the most vicious pro-Stalinist propaganda, and thereby help destroy the prospects of a truly socialist Russia and Europe. Morrow evidently does not know that the rule of Stalinism is the rule of slavery. Morrow evidently does not read Trotsky, who wrote that the victory of the 'Red' Army in Poland (which it divided with the Hitlerite pirates in 1939) meant the subjugation of the 'liberated' masses to Stalinist slavery.

"Because of the dangerous illusions created among some workers here and in Europe by the 'victories of the Red Army', the revolutionary socialist should and will emphasise: The extension of Stalinist rule means the extension of a new slavery. Call it bureaucratic collectivism, as we do, or 'degenerated, counter-revolutionary workers' state', as Trotsky did, it is nevertheless a totalitarian slavery that Stalinist rule represents, a slave-master oppression which crushes everything that is noble, progressive, democratic, socialist and internationalist in the working class that comes under its heel. Be irreconcilable toward imperialism, be it in the form of fascism or 'democracy'. But be no less irreconcilable to Stalinism. Whoever teaches differently is either an outright enemy of socialism, or a well-meaning obstacle in its path". (The whole article is in *The Fate of the Russian Revolution* volume 1, p.414-6).

The Orthodox Defend The Victorious USSR

AT THE START OF JANUARY 1944 18 SWP leaders and Trotskyist leaders of the trade unions in Minneapolis went to jail, some for a year, some for 16 months. The FBI had raided the party headquarters in Minneapolis just as Hitler's invasion of the USSR started, and the defendants, convicted of "advocating the overthrow of the government" were sentenced the day after the Japanese attack on Pearl Harbour on 7 December 1941. Now, after two years of appeals, they went to jail. The court decisions included an instruction from a judge that the books and other such material seized in the FBI raid of 1941 should be burned. Among those jailed were James P Cannon, Felix Morrow, and Albert Goldman. A serious political dispute had already developed between them.

Goldman was the SWP's attorney. His summing-up speech in the Minneapolis courtroom had been issued by the SWP as a pamphlet, a companion to the pamphlet *Socialism on Trial* which comprised the courtroom question-and-answer sessions between Goldman, as attorney, and Cannon, as defendant, about the politics of the SWP. Felix Morrow was the editor of the SWP's monthly magazine, *Fourth International*. The 1940 split had taken out of the SWP those who had been the party's leading intellectuals and most qualified theorists. Shachtman, in an analogy with factory workers and perhaps seriously, described James Burnham as a "skilled" intellectual and himself as "semi-skilled". After the split, Goldman and Morrow replaced them as the leading party intellectuals. Goldman had been the main speaker for the Cannon faction at the conference in April 1940.

Goldman and Morrow had been in favour of allowing the minority to put out a public bulletin that would express their views on Russia. (Cannon's refusal to agree to that was the immediate cause of the 1940 split). They had also been among the most sure and vehement of the Orthodox. Goldman had at first proposed that the SWP "approve" the Russian invasion of eastern Poland. He had written in *The Militant* approving the annexation of the Baltic states in June 1940. In many of the journalistic skirmishes between the SWP and the Workers' Party after the split, it was either Goldman or Morrow who defended the SWP viewpoint.

Morrow had been editor of *The Militant* during the August-September 1941 Leningrad delirium. He had written some of the worst and most disorienting nonsense about the "class meaning" of Russian successes in the war. But he was an honest man. He learned from his mistakes. By 1946 he would have abandoned the "degenerated workers' state" account of Russia in favour of a very rudimentary state-capitalist account, as would Goldman.

Goldman was a downright and candid man. For instance, early in 1943 the Nazis had revealed their discovery of the bodies of 10,000

Polish officers, massacred in April-May 1940 and buried in the Katyn forest, in Russia near the Polish border. It is reckoned that in total the Stalinists killed about 22,000 captured Polish officers at that time. Stalin claimed that the story was a Nazi fabrication, and that the Nazis themselves had killed the Polish officers. Though the SWP was still in full "Soviet patriot" mode, and Goldman too, he weighed the evidence in *The Militant* (8 May 1943), including the record of Stalin in such matters, and concluded that it was at least a serious possibility that the Katyn massacre was the work of the Russians.

On current politics, Goldman and Morrow had begun to differ from Cannon and others in the latter half of 1943, over how the prospects of socialist revolution in Europe had to be seen after the experience of the "Italian revolution" of July 1943. The Fascist Grand Council had voted out Mussolini and installed a new government, which switched to the Allied side in the war. *The Militant* (and Goldman and Morrow) had hailed this as "the revolution", a working-class revolt. After a while Goldman and Morrow felt obliged to record that it had been a palace coup, not a revolution, though great crowds had come out to welcome it.

From the experience of Italy they began to argue that a series of democratic slogans – against the monarchy, for the republic, for restoration of parliamentary democracy, etc. – would play an important part in preparing the European labour movements to take power. The SWP leaders responded, and would continue for years to respond: "Roosevelt and Churchill are absolutely right when they calculate that the choice is either a Franco-type dictatorship [i.e. like the fascist regime in Spain, with which the USA and the UK had friendly relations] or the socialist revolution. There is no alternative. There exists no middle-of-the-road program" (*The Militant*, 4 December 1943). There was no space at all for democratic demands. In this epoch of working-class revolution such democratic demands were no longer a proper and necessary part of their program as they had been for the 1938 Fourth International. At the SWP National Committee plenum (effectively, a small national conference) in October 1943 Goldman and Morrow moved amendments to the resolution on Europe. It seems to have been the bureaucratic chicanery with which the central administration of the SWP met the amendments that, at that point, brought them into sharp conflict with the party regime.

In jail, from January 1944, two groups formed among the Trotskyists, one around Goldman and Morrow, the other around Cannon. Out of jail, in early 1945, a Goldman-Morrow minority took shape, arguing against what they saw as the ultra-left and sectarian politics for Europe of the SWP and the European Trotskyists who, effectively, followed the SWP. They were heavily influenced by the Workers Party on those political questions, and in their experience-born views on the bureaucratic nature of the Cannon regime in the SWP. They were also, perhaps, influenced by Natalia Sedova's criticism of the SWP leaders and their attitude to Stalinist Russia. They would soon begin to champion reunification between the SWP and the Workers Party. [14]

The Warsaw Rising And James P Cannon

ONE OF THE THINGS that the critics inside the SWP may have learned from was the strange episode of Cannon's letters from prison on policy towards the advancing "Red" Army. The interim SWP leaders while the 18 were in jail veered a little, in response to events, from the "Trotsky's Red Army" and automatic "Soviet patriot" line, and they came into conflict with the jailed James P Cannon.

As the Russian Army approached Warsaw in August 1944, Polish nationalists and others, including a large part of the workers of Warsaw, rose in rebellion against the Nazis in anticipation of the Russian entry into the city. They wanted to assert Polish self-liberation, as also the French who rose in August 1944 as the Americans approached Paris wanted French self-liberation. In response, the Russian Army ceased to advance. For nine weeks the Warsaw insurgents fought magnificently and were slowly destroyed by the Nazis. 150,000 Poles died. The Russian Army did not budge. Eventually it occupied the corpse-strewn ruins of the city. Stalin later expressed his view of the rising: a "criminal act of an anti-Soviet policy".

The interim SWP leaders editorialised in *The Militant* and the magazine *Fourth International* that the Russians had betrayed the Warsaw fighters. When he read the editorials, Cannon came close to denouncing the SWP leaders as traitors – to the "Red" Army. (This volume, p.326).

"The editorial again fails to put explicitly and unmistakably our slogan 'Unconditional defense of the Soviet Union' against all imperialists... The Moscow charge that the London 'Polish government in exile' ordered the uprising without consulting the Red Army command is brushed aside without being clearly stated, much less analyzed in the light of the current Soviet-Polish negotiations.

"No consideration is given to the question of whether or not the Red Army was able at the moment to launch an all-out attack on Warsaw in view of its long-sustained offensive, the Nazi defensive preparations along the Vistula, the necessity to regroup forces and mass for new attacks after the not inconsiderable expenditure of men and material in reaching the outskirts of Warsaw, the fact that there was a lull along virtually the entire Eastern front concurrent with the halt before Warsaw, etc.

"Nor does the editorial take up the question of the duty of guerrilla forces – and in the circumstances that is what the Warsaw detachments are – to subordinate themselves to the high command of the main army, the Red Army, in timing such an important battle as the siege of Warsaw..."

Cannon was vibrantly aware of his responsibilities: "Great care should be taken in treating the Polish and similar questions... We must never forget that our party statements and editorials are now regarded as programmatic documents and taken with the greatest seriousness by the revolutionary workers of the entire world.... [Our] carefulness... has given all our resolutions since the death of the Old Man their thought-out character and made them stand up from year to year as supplements logically flowing from one unchanging program, and, like the program itself, needing no fundamental revision".

Natalia's Second Intervention

NATALIA SEDOVA WROTE to the SWP endorsing the editorial Cannon complained of and declaring: "You seem to be hypnotized by the slogan of the 'defense of the USSR' and in the meantime profound changes, political as well as moral-psychological, have taken place in its social structure. In his articles, especially the last ones, L.D. [Trotsky] wrote of the USSR as a degenerating workers' state and in view of this outlined two possible paths of further social evolution of the first workers' state: revolutionary and reactionary. The last four years have shown us that the reactionary landslide has assumed monstrous proportions within the USSR... The Red Army, at the basis of whose organization were lodged the principles of the October overturn, and whose (the Red Army's) goal was the struggle for the world revolution, has become transformed into a nationalist-patriotic organization, defending the fatherland, and not against its bureaucratic regime but together with its regime as it has taken shape in the last decade. Do you recall the answer of L.D. to the question put to him in the Politburo in 1927: whether the Opposition would defend the USSR in case of war? 'The socialist fatherland — yes; Stalin's regime — no'.... At the present time there is only one danger threatening the Soviet Union — that is the further development of black reaction, the further betrayal of the international proletariat. This is precisely the direction in which it is necessary to sound the alarm... It is necessary to hammer away at one point: to warn against the consequences of Russian victories; to warn, to sound the alarm on the basis of the elements that have already been disclosed with complete clarity..." (This volume, pp.335ff).

Cannon retreated. He wrote a letter from jail proposing a shift in "emphasis" to "defence of the European revolution against Stalin". That letter was published inside the SWP so as to make it seem that he was independently proposing the same sort of shift as that advocated by Sedova. As we've seen, he had in fact just written to the opposite effect.

The SWP decided at its November 1944 conference to drop the 1931 quotation from Trotsky about defending the USSR which had been in its editorial masthead most of the time since June 1941, and to substitute another quotation from Trotsky, this time from the May 1940 manifesto: "Only the world revolution can save the USSR for socialism. But the world revolution carries with it the inescapable blotting out of the Kremlin oligarchy". Despite the conference decision, the 1931 quotation continued on the masthead, most likely because Cannon wanted it, until the end of March 1945. The cutting edge of its replacement was still concern with defence of the USSR, and the new quotation was still far too far from a plain statement that the Russian bureaucracy should be overthrown by a new working-class "political" revolution; it was, nonetheless, progress of sorts.

The Fifth Phase: Free-Swirling Confusion

LEAVING ASIDE ALL OTHER QUESTIONS for the moment, it was already plain from experience that Russia would expand into as much territory as it could and hold as much as it could, for as long as it could. Britain and Russia had jointly occupied Iran in August-September 1941. After the end of the war, in 1946, when Britain had evacuated Iran, Russia stayed on for some months in its northern part of the country. Stalin withdrew from Iran only under intense US pressure. At the end of the war he laid claim to Italy's ex-colony Libya. Stalin's oligarchy had immense and growing power. After looting and pillaging the countries they occupied, they would want to assimilate property forms in those countries to Russia's. In any case, much of the means of production in the countries Russia occupied was already state property. In Czechoslovakia, the most industrially advanced of the territories being occupied by "Trotsky's Red Army", the Nazis had expropriated around 70% of industry, putting it into the hands of the German state or German companies. In August 1945, a coalition government under the bourgeois liberal Edvard Benes decreed the nationalisation of two-thirds of industry. The question was not whether or not industry would be nationalised, but whether this nationalisation constituted in any sense, no matter how limited, a workers' revolution.

The problem many of the Orthodox had in registering the plain facts and trends arose out of the idea that nationalised property akin to Russia's in and of itself might define a species of Stalin-made bureaucratic "workers'" revolutions. Certainly replicas of the Stalinist system created by the activity of the Russian Stalinist state would have the same characteristics that the "degenerated workers' state" formula cherished and defined as the essential remaining "workers'" element in the "degenerated workers' state" [15].

Either Stalin could carry through revolutions – from above – to make workers' states, or the whole "degenerated workers' state" notion for the USSR was wrong. This dilemma paralysed them politically for a long time. They would not cut themselves out of it in the only way possible: by redefining the USSR. [16]

In an SWP Political Committee discussion on 2 August 1949 about the "class character" of Eastern Europe, Cannon would say:

"I don't think that you can change the class character of a state by manipulation at the top. It can only be done by revolution which is followed by fundamental change in property relations. That is what I understand by a change of the class character of a state. That is what happened in the Soviet Union... I don't think there has been a social revolution in the buffer countries and I don't think Stalinism carried out a revolution... The role of Stalinism is not revolutionary at all. It gave an impulse to the revolution in this sense, that the victories of the Red Army stimulated the revolutionary movement. But the actual role of Stalinism was to strangle that revolution, to suppress the mass movement of the workers and to re-stabilize the capitalist state and capitalist property relations. The fundamental role they played there was counter-revolutionary...

"If you once begin to play with the idea that class character of a state can be changed by manipulations in top circles, you open the door to all kinds of revision of basic theory... Nationalization plus the [state monopoly of] foreign trade, is not the criterion of a workers' state. That is what remains of the workers' state created by the Russian Revolution. That is the remnants of the Russian Revolution. That is why the Soviet state is called 'degenerate'. There is a tremendous difference whether a state has nationalized property relations as a result of a proletarian revolution, or whether there are certain progressive moves toward nationalization, by the Stalinists in one case or by

English reformists in the other..." (SWP IB vol.11 no.5, Oct 1949).

The whole political tragedy of Orthodox Trotskyism is there, dissected and laid out. Cannon said it clearly: "Nationalised property... is not the criterion of a workers' state". A working-class revolution is necessary for the class character of a state to go from "bourgeois" to "working-class". Cannon was clear, and in terms of Trotsky's theory of the USSR as we have discussed it in this introduction, entirely correct. But the nationalised property was held to be what empirically linked Stalinist Russia back to the revolution. Stalin was creating in a number of countries as much as "remained" of the October revolution. To judge things in the satellites according to which class held political power would destroy the position that Russia remained a degenerated workers' state because of nationalised property. In Russia, nationalised property was held to identify who held power. Either the whole Russian question had to be rethought, or nationalised property in Russia's satellites defined them as some sort of workers' states. (Not degenerated workers' states: a new term would eventually emerge, "deformed workers' states").

If you made it a "programmatic" dogma that the USSR was a degenerated workers' state, and would remain so as long as nationalised property survived, then an inexorable logic pushed you to a similar position for the satellites. Cannon would have to change his 1949 position, shared with John G Wright, and go with those who called the satellites "deformed workers' states". The alternative was to conclude that he had been wrong in 1940 and in the war years that followed.

The morally, politically, and intellectually self-destroying method was there on display too: "The victories of the Red Army stimulated the revolutionary movement". The wartime dogma was recycled, processed, and slipped in as one part of a "story". It was dealt with, as the Leningrad delirium of August-September 1941 had been dealt with in its time, by inserting a smoothed version into a fabricated storyline. Cannon would not say that he, and the others on the SWP Political Committee, were wrong in their expectations in 1943-5. If there really had been Russian-army-stimulated "revolutionary movements" in the areas conquered by Stalin, then *The Militant* and *Fourth International* had been seriously remiss in not reporting them...

Thanks in part to the remonstrations of Natalia Sedova Trotsky and in part to experience, the Orthodox recoiled in late 1944 from their ideas about "Trotsky's Red Army" and Stalinism being "objectively revolutionary". Then they lurched back in 1945-6: assertions by the SWP that war against Russia was imminent (a judgement few in the world shared) licensed keeping "defence of the USSR" at high tension. In 1946 two members of the SWP-USA made a detailed analysis of *The Militant*'s response to news concerning the USSR between the end of war in Europe, May 1945, and June 1946. They published it in the Internal Bulletin of the SWP (this volume p.375). On the large-scale pillaging and removal of industrial equipment by the Russians from areas they had conquered, in 56 issues, there appeared two articles by Morrow, one by Goldman, and only four other brief items. Millions of women and men in "enemy" countries were deported to forced labour in the USSR. In 56 issues *The Militant*, except in the Morrow and Goldman articles just mentioned, carried no reference (though the deportations were very graphically depicted in a cartoon by Laura Gray: this volume, p.174). The USSR had seized large numbers of countries and territories: the mentions of that in *The Militant* were very few, and tended to explain away the expansion as being "defensive".

An SWP resolution in February 1946 advocated that workers in Eastern Europe "tolerate the presence of the Red Army" in the name of its alleged help in "the fulfilment of agrarian reform and the state-isation of the means of production" – with the proviso that they should rethink if the Russian Army "hindered in any way whatsoever the free development of the working-class movement" (p.394, this volume)! That encapsulated the de facto pro-Stalinist policy of the Orthodox. They lurched again to a more anti-Stalinist policy. A resolution calling for the withdrawal of Russian troops from the countries they occupied was adopted by the Fourth International in June 1946 and published by the SWP in August 1946. But they never made an explicit self-correction. After 1948 and the Tito-Stalin split, they lurched again. "Objectively revolutionary" Stalinism, which they would criticise and condemn but nevertheless felt compelled to support, would dominate their picture of the world for decades after that.

How The War Re-Shaped Orthodox Trotskyism

WE NEED TO SUM UP what the war period did to immediately post-Trotsky Orthodox Trotskyism, as embodied in James P Cannon and his close circle. In the responses of the Orthodox Trotskyists to the USSR at war, the Trotskyism of Trotsky was pulped and pulverised, mashed up, deconstructed and reconstructed, reduced to detached and recombinable segments. A bit like the horse in Picasso's "Guernica": you can see that in straightforward terms it is a horse, yet in naturalistic terms it is also not a horse. The limbs are all higgledy-piggledy.

They slid back years to outlived Trotskyist attitudes, before the Trotskyists declared for "political revolution" in Russia, and let much of the further development of Trotskyist thinking on the USSR in the mid and late 1930s fade to the background. They detached their agitation and propaganda from their own theory as they had it before June 1941, and sometimes designed agitation according to whatever selection from the old Trotskyist ideas would "play" best with Stalinist-inclined workers in the USA.

In most of their day-to-day journalism they dispensed with "degenerated" and called the USSR simply "the workers' state". They ascribed to Stalin's "workers' state" qualities and possibilities that both Trotsky at the end, and the Cannon of 1940, would have dismissed as either weak-minded fantasy or downright lies.

They based much of their commentary on the USSR at war on what Trotsky had called "the fundamental sophism of the bureaucracy", the idea that the people owned what the Stalinist state owned. They embraced the Stalinist idea that just by having nationalised property the USSR embodied "the foundation of socialism". They wrote that the USSR workers were defending that foundation because they knew from experience that it was the best place in the world for workers to live. (Breitman: experience had "shown the Russian masses the superiority of living in a workers' state"). They patched together unreliable reports of high morale in the USSR and erected "morale" into a criterion for determining the class character of the USSR at that point.

They related to the USSR of the bureaucrats as if major social elements of the revolution – not just, as in Trotsky, the nationalised property – had survived, or had revived. They used the "trade union analogy" to pretend to readers of *The Militant* that the USSR bureaucracy was no worse than the worst trade-union bureaucracy in a bourgeois-democratic society. They said that the USSR was part of the working-class movement, bureaucratic autocracy, slave-labour camp guards, and all. They denounced the USSR's ruling autocracy, but would also glory in the "unity" of the people of the USSR.

Most of their adverse comments on Russian Stalinism during the war were solely-political criticism, most importantly of Stalin's failure to issue a "class appeal" to German workers and to assure them that at the end of the war there would be no repetition of the terrible Versailles Treaty of 1919. By making their proposals "demands" on the bureaucracy, they cut the political criticism off from the Trotskyist social criticism. They deployed the absurd claim that the "Red" Army, a central part of the Stalinist state apparatus, was not Stalinist, had not "really" experienced the Stalinist counter-revolution. They wrote of this "Red" Army bringing socialist revolution with it, and not, as Trotsky had described it for eastern Poland, bringing "semi-slavery" on its bayonets and tanks. In this "Trotsky's Red Army" make-believe, they pioneered a technique they would later use to pretend and half-pretend that Tito's Yugoslavia and Mao's China were not really Stalinism.

At some points, notably August-September 1941, they implied that the power and control of the bureaucracy were being sloughed off, implicitly begging the question: had there really been a Stalinist counter-revolution at all? And the question: hadn't Trotsky's and their own denunciations of Stalinism been exaggerated and false to reality? What they said about the USSR's high morale implied that yes, they had.

They turned "defence" of the USSR into defence of Stalin's imperial Russia. They presented every Russian demand for territory, or for conquest and occupation by Stalin's army, as a legitimate or at any rate an arguably defensive measure by the USSR. Thus, in the war and after, they translated "defence of the USSR" into pixilated partisanship for the Stalinist bureaucratic empire that was spreading into east and central Europe and the Balkans.

The subordination of "political revolution" to "defence", for the Orthodox, sometimes came to mean couching their politics in the form of a program of reforms of the existing USSR system. Such an approach, promoting the idea that the bureaucracy could do this, might do that, could not but radically inhibit workers influenced by the Communist Party in drawing the conclusions that Trotskyists had already drawn about the USSR from the early mid-1930s onwards. (It was also a prefiguration of the later "defencism" of the Orthodox for Yugoslavia, China, North Korea, Vietnam, Cuba, etc.)

Episodically they detached Trotsky's program for "political revolution" against Stalinist totalitarianism from the working class as its agent and reduced it to a series of "demands" on Stalin (and later on Tito, Mao, Ho Chi Minh, or Fidel Castro), implying the autocrats could conceivably carry them out. From a working-class program, they transformed it into a species of utopian socialist advice to the rulers. They pretended, by "demanding" it of them, that the Stalinist autocrats might conceivably wage an internationalist working-class war.

They pushed the whole notion of "defence of the USSR" towards an interpretation (which did not emerge fully until the mid-1950s) that the Stalinist socio-economic formation was a stabilised system which could develop from the existing "foundation of socialism" to something near socialism itself. Ideologically, that was a giant step towards "socialism in one country".

These traits, which I have isolated here, the better to see and define them, were not of course the whole face of the Orthodox. *The Militant* carried routine anti-Stalinist commentary, especially against Stalinism in history. But its telling silences at crucial times and on very important issues added more or less heavy, neutralising, qualifications.

The focus and the emphasis of the Orthodox oscillated, but within a narrow circle. The totality of their Orthodox "Trotskyism" combined elements of Trotsky's Trotskyism with their own accommodation to the bureaucracy by way of "defending the USSR". They were compelled, in the general picture they gave of the USSR, to invent more virtues for it than that nationalised property remained and was historically progressive. And the qualification that Trotsky had added from late 1939, that the nationalised property was only potentially progressive, and would be really progressive only on condition that the workers overthrew the bureaucracy, disappeared from their picture. They filled the yawning gap between the reality of the totalitarian state, and the high-morale-inducing society they portrayed, by misreporting and fantasising about the USSR.

In an important sense, it all flowed from the stark contradictions in their politics on the USSR. The state which represented the progressive survival of the October Revolution was also the agency for enslaving and half-enslaving Russian workers and those whom it conquered. The complex theoretical and historical reasons for Trotskyist "defencism", as Trotsky had them in 1939-40, were impossible to explain in agitation and propaganda aimed at non-political, or superficially or newly political, people. That problem had at the time of the 1939-40 dispute been resolved by Trotsky's public denunciation of Stalin in Poland and Finland, coupled with "defencism" mostly confined to esoteric reasoning inside the Trotskyist organisation. The war and the US-Russian alliance made "defencism" now the public focus. Why? became an imperative immediate question. The US state was now for the "defence of the USSR" too. Stark condemnation of Stalinism would have pitted the Orthodox against the massive pro-Russian sentiment in the labour movement and against bourgeois public opinion. Cannon boldly solved this dilemma. He deployed as reasons for "defending" the USSR a large chunk of the lies the CP-USA and the "Friends of the Soviet Union" deployed: workers defended the USSR because they knew the advantages of living in a "workers' state". Then the Orthodox added a big element of pseudo-

Trotskyist fantasy. Theycombined trimming their political sails to the winds and moods around them with bombast about their imperviousness to the pressures of public opinion, their unchanging "finished program", their disciplined organisation, their firmness against "revisionism", and their "class loyalty" to the USSR. "And after twenty years of hard work, of study, of struggle, the Fourth International, the movement of living Bolshevism, has hammered out a finished program, has welded together a tested cadre, has created a firm organizational structure. It stands today, just as Lenin's small band of Bolshevik internationalists during the last war, unyielding, intransigent, confident of its destiny to lead the working class in the next great revolutionary offensive, confident of its future successes and its final triumph" (editorial in the magazine *Fourth International*, January 1945).

The result was what a critic inside their own ranks, Louis Jacobs, called "apparatus politics". Apparatus politics and "Apparatus Marxism" could and did combine strident Orthodoxy about verbal formulae with flat opportunism and never acknowledged or accounted-for fumbling in real political tests. It had a long future before it.

All this anticipated and cleared the way for the political transmogrification that would overcome the Orthodox Trotskyists at the end of the 1940s, and be codified by the "Third World Congress" (in fact the first congress of a new Trotskyist movement) in 1951. All that would unfold in the decades after World War 2 was there already, not always fully explored or fully developed, in the "positions", makeshifts, political and theoretical self-editing, Trotsky-selecting and Trotsky-editing, of the Orthodox during the war.

In a 1946 polemic against C L R James and others in the Workers Party who were moving towards rejoining the SWP – they would do so in July 1947 – Irving Howe neatly summed up the records of the Orthodox and the Heterodox in the war:

"When the SWP hailed the advancing Stalinist army as 'the liberating Red army', when the SWP national secretary called upon the workers of Warsaw to subordinate their struggle to the oncoming Stalinist army – was that the SWP's 'inestimable advantage' over us, their means of espousing the 'full Trotskyist tradition'? When the SWP press discovered that the workers in Russia 'owned' the factories and the land and that that was the cause of their determined resistance – was that the SWP's 'inestimable advantage?'

"When the SWP the week after the [USA's entry into] war [in December 1941] responded by printing a learned dissertation on criminal syndical laws while we of the 'Menshevik' WP responded by printing a bold declaration against the imperialist war – was that the SWP's 'inestimable advantage?' When the SWP played ostrich in the trade unions and finagled with bureaucrats while our comrades boldly and with some success pursued a class struggle line in the unions – was that their 'inestimable advantage' over us? When the SWP national secretary spoke of 'telescoping' the struggle for socialism with defense of country – was that their 'inestimable advantage'?" (Workers Party Internal Bulletin, 28 March 1946).

Part 3: The Orthodox And The Heterodox After The War

The Orthodox After The War

BY APRIL 1946 Max Shachtman could comment: "It is hard to find anyone in the Fourth International who will today offer, with any measure of conviction, an argument in favour of 'unconditional defence' of Stalinist Russia. Many of the Trotskyist militants in this country and elsewhere, who opposed us vigorously in 1940, are today abandoning this outlived and now reactionary slogan". The Second Congress of the Fourth International, in April 1948, would officially amend the slogan to the ambiguous and open-ended "defence of what remains of the conquests of October".

"Others go further in our direction", wrote Shachtman, "by abandoning the preposterous theory that Russia today represents any kind of 'workers' state'... The...'workers' state' theory, in whose demolition we are proud to have pioneered, is dying in the Fourth International and there is pretty nearly nobody around with enough belief in it to try to save it".

But there was no conscious, open, and clear-cut self-correction. The minorities in the Orthodox Trotskyist groups in the USA (Goldman-Morrow), in France, and in other countries, who did slough off the "degenerated workers' state" formula, and did openly attempt self-correction, were demagogically beaten down with charges of "revisionism" and dispersed. The Trotskyist groups had grown around the end of the World War, but then from 1947 the political climate turned very unfavourable for Trotskyists of all stripes.

The April 1948 Second Congress of the Fourth International defined the East European satellite states as capitalist police states. There, in effect, the Orthodox gave the same answer as the James-Dunayevskaya segment of the Workers Party had given in its definition of the USSR as a fascist state-capitalism. If state capitalism, rather than "degenerated workers' state" or "bureaucratic collectivism" was true for Russia's satellites, then it was true for the USSR too. Fetishisation of the "degenerated workers' state" term for Russia kept them from saying, or seeing, that.

The sorting-out would come in the wake of another startling shift. Exactly 68 days after the close of the Second Congress, a split between Stalin and the Tito Stalinists ruling Yugoslavia became public, complete with mutual vituperation. Untypically among the European Stalinist regimes, the Yugoslavs, at the head of a peasant army during the World War, had taken and held power without any important help from Stalin's army.

Just a few days after the public Tito-Stalin split, the Fourth International, which had very recently characterised Yugoslavia as a capitalist police state, that is, some sort of fascistic state, wrote an open letter to the Yugoslav Communist Party, addressing the YCP leaders as "Comrades". It offered "to assist [them] in resolving the present crisis in communism along proletarian and Leninist lines". Within the next year they would, most of them, decide that the other satellite states – Czechoslovakia, Poland, Romania, Bulgaria, Albania, East Germany, North Korea – were also "deformed workers' states" and should also be "defended". The long gestation of full-blown post-Trotsky "Orthodox Trotskyism" was nearly over. The political changes had become qualitative. This was a new political tendency, a hybrid combining strands of Trotskyism as Trotsky had it, of pre-1933 Trotskyism, and of the 1930s "Right Communist" Opposition of Heinrich Brandler, Jay Lovestone, and others, who advocated reform not revolution for Russia.

The difference between the Orthodox Trotskyists, as their doctrine solidified in 1949-51, and Trotsky, was vast. The difference between them and the Workers Party (the Independent Socialist League from 25 April 1949) was now one of two radically different world outlooks. The Orthodox Trotskyists' jump on Yugoslavia and Eastern Europe ate into everything else in their politics. On Yugoslavia and then China, then North Vietnam, then, a decade and a half later, Cuba, the Orthodox jumped back explicitly to the "reform" Trotskyism before the movement's decision in 1933 that a new, "political", revolution was necessary in Russia, and to the "reform" Trotskyism to which they had reverted implicitly and erratically during World War 2 in relation to the USSR. It would be 20 years after Mao conquered all of China before the Fourth International decided that a "political revolution" was necessary. (The SWP-USA had been for a "political revolution" from as soon as it decided that China was a "deformed workers' state", in 1955, later than the rest of the Fourth International).

The new reformism vis-a-vis some Stalinist states was not the old "reformism". The pre-1933 Trotskyist "reformism" meant orienting to the elements of the Bolshevik party, assumed to be still a force despite Stalin's destruction of party functioning, and still loyal to the ideals of the 1917 workers' revolution. In a sharp crisis of the system – which the Trotskyists expected to come, and very soon – all those elements would be shaken up. The party would recompose itself, its functioning would be restored, and the bureaucracy could be sloughed off.

There was no equivalent agency in the new "reformist Trotskyism". It was a matter of advocating reform for states identical in structure to the Russian state in its fully-Stalinised, post-counter-revolution condition. In some instances the reform proposals were addressed as advice to the rulers in the style of 19th century utopian socialists petitioning governments. Yet those who had taken and held power in those states had done so at the head of totalitarian parties and armies that were not working-class in their membership or in any Marxist sense at all. The Yugoslav CP did loosen up its totalitarian rule after 1948, and it made some reforms, but they went nowhere near allowing the existence of a workers' movement or independent communist organisations. After 1950-1 the Yugoslav CP would back the United Nations (US-led) forces in the Korean war, while the Orthodox Trotskyists backed the North Koreans and their Russian and Chinese sponsors. The Yugoslav Stalinists would eventually denounce the Orthodox Trotskyist Fourth International, which had loudly backed them against Stalin and organised international work brigades to go and help build roads in Yugoslavia, for being too soft on... Russian Stalinism!

In Czechoslovakia, the Communist Party had been a mass working-class party before the Nazis took over. The final act in creating a full replica of Stalinist Russia, in February 1948, was a grim parody of a workers' revolution, in its way something new in Stalinism: working-class demonstrations, strikes, and other activities were staged and regimented by the Stalinists who had long before acquired real state power as a gift from Moscow. *The Militant* assessed the Stalinist action as a victory for Czech capitalism: "Stalinists utilise mass pressure to make deal with Czech capitalists" (8 March 1948). In all the world only one Trotskyist organisation thought the Stalinist action in Czechoslovakia good and desirable. The Revolutionary Communist Party in Britain welcomed it in an article in its *Socialist Appeal* (March 1948), signed by its secretary Jock Haston: "Capitalists routed in Czechoslovakia". Such was the political chaos that would grip the

Fourth International that the people who published that article would also make valid criticisms of the delusions about Yugoslavia which the other Orthodox Trotskyists held from July 1948.

In June 1950 Stalinist North Korea invaded the bourgeois South. It was acting as Russia's proxy. After December 1950 large Chinese armies fought in Korea. The US and its allies, including Britain, responded to the June 1950 invasion with full-scale war, for which they got the backing of the United Nations, since Russia had temporarily quit the Security Council. The SWP at first responded with a "Third Camp" stance – "Let the Korean people decide their own fate free from US or Kremlin" (*The Militant*, 3 July 1950). Here too, as at the start of the USA's war in December 1941, James P Cannon took some weeks to decide what he thought. But then, with an Open Letter to the President and Congress (31 July), he threw the Orthodox Trotskyists behind the Stalinists. Cannon simply redefined the political picture, fading out the Stalinist dimension in Korea. It was not Stalinism but the Korean Revolution, part of the world-wide Colonial Revolution, that confronted the USA and its allies. The technique was familiar from the political performance of the Orthodox during the World War. It was a further turning point in consolidating the new Orthodoxy. In the following three years, up to Stalin's death in March 1953, the Fourth International would elaborate a world view that expanded the idea of war-revolution that had exercised the Dan Mensheviks, the SWP, and some European Trotskyists, in 1943-5.

World War Three, which many people far from Trotskyism then expected too, would be an international class war. In it, the European mass Stalinist parties would rally to the USSR and lead revolutionary mobilisations as the Russian army marched across Europe to the Atlantic. The Stalinist-led forces would establish systems and regimes similar to those of the East European satellites and the USSR itself. This would be the next, albeit "deformed", stage of the world socialist revolution. The Orthodox Trotskyists were its advocates by way of their "perspectives" and "predictions" and orientations, which in Europe included entry into the big and authoritarian Stalinist parties of Western Europe.

This new "war-revolution" perspective differed from that of the SWP in 1943-5. It had never been sufficiently clear whether the "Red" Army, or workers roused by it, would make the revolution, but the SWP had talked of the "Red" Army stimulating working-class revolutionary movements that it would not be able to control or repress, and indeed would not want to control or repress, even if ordered to. There was none of that in the 1950-53 war-revolution thesis. The result would not be socialist revolutions beyond the power of Stalin to quell, as the 1943-5 line had it, but Stalinist states set up by the "Red" Army, with more or less local support. The Fourth International's main leader, Michel Pablo, even wrote speculatively of "centuries" of Stalinist and semi-Stalinist deformed workers' states ("Where Are We Going?", SWP International Information Bulletin, March 1951).

The Revenge Of "Bureaucratic Collectivism"

IN HIS SPECULATION about Stalinist states covering much or all the world for "centuries", Pablo came close to defining the Stalinist states as "bureaucratic collectivist", that is, states of a substantial new type of ruling class. It was what Trotsky had outlined hypothetically in 1939 as a global slave-society, but now re-evaluated as a first wave of socialist revolution. Curiously, Pablo, who separated from the Fourth International in 1963, by the late 1960s had come explicitly to call the Stalinist systems bureaucratic class states. He remained a "defencist" against capitalist imperialism for those states.

In that he merely brought his own publicly-expressed half-thoughts of the early 1950s to their logical conclusion. A number of "anti-Pabloite" Orthodox Trotskyists took an essentially similar course, disguising it from themselves in the idea that "deformed workers' states" were so sharply distinct from "workers' states" that the "deformed workers' state" was a separate stage in history, not necessarily connected to working-class action (and therefore should not be accommodated to in the way that Pablo had accommodated to it around 1950). These were "bureaucratic collectivist" ideas in an ill-fitting "deformed workers' state" shell, advocated for example by the Grant tendency (Militant, the Socialist Party, Socialist Appeal) and the once-noisy Spartacists.

"Workers' state", in this version of "deformed workers' state" doctrine, signified nothing about the relation of the state to workers, and nothing at all but an encoded expression of approval. The only difference on the level of basic theory between this sort of "deformed workers' state" doctrine and the "bureaucratic collectivist" idea of the Workers Party/ ISL was a difference of political attitude and of historical evaluation: an attitude of "defending" and lauding and helping along the expansion of Stalinism (because it was historically progressive), as against the WP/ISL's horrified rejection of it (as a historically regressive totalitarian tyranny). And in that rejection, the WP/ISL, and not the Orthodox, were the Trotskyists.

A sizeable section of the Pablo-Mandel international, the Latin American Bureau, split away in 1962, led by Juan Posadas. Advocacy of the "demand" that Russia and China start the war-revolution came to be one of their central policies. The other Orthodox Trotskyists said that the Posadas group was deranged, and it surely was. When Hal Draper defined the Orthodox Trotskyist Fourth International of the early 1950s as "borderline crackpot", he erred, if he erred, on the side of restraint and mealy-mouthedness [17].

The great expansionary wave of Stalinism that ran from the 1940s until it broke in Afghanistan, in Russia's colonial war of the 1980s, was revolutionary against the bourgeoisie, but also counter-revolutionary against the working class and against all elements of bourgeois democracy and political liberty, that is, against much of the historical achievements of bourgeois civilisation over centuries, not to speak of socialism. The Stalinist revolutions were in no sense or degree working-class revolutions. Under them, the working classes were the immediate victim of repression, labour movements of extirpation, Trotskyists simply of murder. They had none of the characteristics that had led Trotsky to believe that Russia remained some kind of degenerated and degenerating workers' state.

Thus, in their own way the Orthodox Trotskyists had arrived at a theory of what Trotsky had described in its future projection as "bureaucratic collectivism", while yet rejecting that term for Russia and the other Stalinist states. They rejected the suggestions which Trotsky had given for reviewing the class character of the USSR in the light of events in World War 2, as they had "suspended" his (and their own) program of political revolution for much of the war. They developed a concept of "deformed workers' state" that was a new theory of a new form of society, connected only by thin verbal formulae to Trotsky's theory of Russia as a "degenerated workers' states". Trotsky made a well-known joke that even though James Burnham did not recognise the dialectic, the dialectic recognised him. The Orthodox Trotskyists refused to recognise any variant of the theory of bureaucratic collectivism, but the theory, in a thin disguise and with pro-Stalinist politics, recognised and took possession of them.

The Orthodox became political satellites of the Stalinist bloc in world affairs – outspokenly so from 1950 and the Korean war. They did not become uncritical supporters of either the foreign or (most of) the domestic policy of Stalinists in power. For the "autonomous" Stalinist states, those not set up by the Russian army, they did as the SWP had done in 1941 with its "minimum program" for defence of the USSR: they advocated "reforms" that would have amounted to a revolution. As in the pioneering model in 1941, these "demands" had their head and executive organs lopped off. The demands – which of course were a form of propaganda in the Orthodox Trotskyist press, aimed at their own milieu – were separated off from the necessary conclusion: a workers' revolution. On one level they were advice to the rulers to cut off their own horns, claws and tails. They were a species of utopian socialism.

James P Cannon, who was in some ways always better, or trying to be better, than the movement he had educated and miseducated, made a confused revolt in 1953 against some of the trends that the Orthodox Fourth International developed around the ideas of the August-September 1951 Third World Congress. He split the Orthodox Fourth International, accusing the Pablo-Mandel leadership of conciliation with Stalinism; of failing to support the East German workers when they rose in 1953 with demands that the Russian army, which was shooting them, should withdraw from Germany; and of liquidating the small independent Trotskyist groups into the big Stalinist parties. Cannon was in part driven by an internal SWP faction fight with people who claimed to be acting "for Pablo", and he explicitly refused to "go back to 1940", or even to the Third Congress of 1951. When one of his comrades, Sam Gordon, argued in a private letter that what Cannon denounced was rooted in the positions of the Third Congress, Cannon responded that they should recognise no major errors as having been made by the Third Congress or themselves. Prestige and calculation of factional advantage ruled then, as they had since Trotsky's death and always would. The consequence for the "anti-Pabloite" segment of the Fourth International was that they arbitrarily asserted their own picture of reality, as they had during World War 2, and didn't bother too much with logic, theories, the recent past, or the implications of positions taken or not taken. They cut loose from the theorising of the Third Congress and of Pablo, as earlier from that of Trotsky [18].

Those who sided with Cannon in 1953 – the British Healyites and French Lambertists – would evolve into the worst regime-ridden, undemocratic, and irrational organisations in the Trotskyist archipelago. In 1979 the SWP itself went the same way, transformed by its own party machine, under new control. It soon expelled almost all the older Orthodox Trotskyists and transformed the group into a semi-Stalinist sect rigidly aligned with the Castro regime in Cuba.

That was not a matter of political logic only, or of the habit of establishing a political line for short-term advantage. It happened, could happen, only because the organisations of the 1953 Cannonite "International Committee of the Fourth International" were under the control of strong bureaucratic machines.

When the SWP and the Mandel grouping reunited in 1963 (minus Pablo), the Healyites and Lambertists rejected the reunification, and went their own, increasingly bizarre, ways. In 1967, the Healyites came out for Mao's Cultural Revolution – a debauch of wild physical and intellectual wrecking and destruction by "Red Guard" youth controlled by the Maoist army.

The mainstream "Orthodox Trotskyists", with Mandel, zig-zagged wildly, playing political chameleon to many other political tendencies, Stalinist and non-Stalinist. In the 1950s and most of the 1960s they operated as factions inside social democratic parties and official Communist Parties. Then in the late 1960s and the 70s they grew into sizeable organisations, usually ultra-left, in a number of countries.

From the 1980s, they generally declined. After the collapse of Stalinism in Europe and the USSR in 1991, they officially declared that their "deformed workers' state", "post-capitalist society", or "transitional society" descriptions of Stalinism must be critically reviewed. Their well-known writer, Daniel Bensaid, explicitly repudiated all those formulas. Their summary of their adjustment after 1991 was, however, "new epoch, new program, new party", which in practice means they have become proponents of building ill-defined "broad left" parties rather than of parties of the type advocated and built by Lenin and Trotsky. In Britain their small group attached itself to George Galloway's ill-born and ill-fated "Respect party".

Why The Shachtmanites Declined And The Cannonites Survived

IN THE MID 40S THE SHACHTMANITES REVISED their version of "bureaucratic collectivism" to see Stalinism as a viable world system able to compete with advanced capitalism and likely to supplant it unless the workers first made a socialist revolution in the advanced capitalist countries. It was, they decided, very urgently a case of socialism or barbarism. Stalinism was barbarism.

They drew sharp, angular, truth-centred but often too abstract lines and definitions – in World War 2, in their characterisation of the mass Stalinist parties, in their trade-union work. In their belief that Stalinist bureaucratic collectivism was a viable alternative to advanced capitalism, they paralleled the view which the Orthodox took, though with a different evaluation, from the mid 1950s. The Heterodox never ceased to see capitalism as in retreat before Stalinism and historically vulnerable to its predatory competition. Stalinism did expand enormously, and was still expanding for many years after Shachtman's death in 1972. But in the years after World War 2, when Stalinism was expanding into backward countries, capitalism had reorganised itself in its two-thirds of the world, which included the most developed areas, and it began to flourish again. The Heterodox refused to take sides in the Cold War; but they thought and said that the bourgeois West was "better", economically, socially, politically, and in general civilisation, than the Stalinist East, and they were always under a pressure of political logic to side with "the West" as the lesser evil.

In the decades of capitalist prosperity, their commitment to the working class and its movement subjected their revolutionary politics and perspectives to great pressure. Trade-union routines drained off much of their politics. They were pushed towards going where most of the unions were politically immersed, in the Democratic Party.

Their hostility to Stalinism and to the Stalin-controlled workers' movements, and their stringent rationalism, deprived them of the sheltering and sustaining illusions and delusions that the Orthodox would repeatedly avail themselves of when they let themselves see the "world revolution" advancing by way of Tito, Mao, Ho Chi Minh, or Castro. The democratic structure of the Workers Party and ISL cut away the sectism that can sometimes scaffold even the most intellectually and politically feeble organisations and enable them to survive and grow. In the 1950s and after, the bulk of the Shachtmanites slowly biodegraded into social democracy.

In the early 1950s, a section of the younger leaders of the group (since 1949, called the Independent Socialist League) – Irving Howe, Stanley Plastrik, Emanuel Geltman, Jack Ranger, and others – hived off to found a new journal, *Dissent*, which still appears today, after they are all dead. One of them, Irving Howe, would in 1965 produce the best one-volume anthology of Trotsky's writings. The ISL produced a politically high-grade weekly paper and a quarterly journal. But many of its members dwindled, in their activity, to being mere trade unionists. They were greatly under pressure, from the realities of the American labour movement and its politics, to participate in Democratic primaries when the trade unions did, as they did. In 1958 the ISL fused with the small Socialist Party. Some former ISL people, around Max Shachtman, gained great influence in the Socialist Party. In 1961 Shachtman refused to condemn the CIA-backed invasion of Castro's Cuba, and the Shachtmanites divided again. Shachtman and some of his long-time close associates, for example Al Glotzer, evolved to backing the US against Stalinism. Shachtman wound up in the Democratic Party; he died in November 1972.

But as long as the Heterodox Trotskyists of the Workers Party and the ISL were alive as a revolutionary political tendency, they did not become in any way or degree supporters of the bourgeois-democratic capitalist system, as the Orthodox Trotskyists became critical supporters of varieties of Stalinism. It took Max Shachtman 21 years of erosion and demoralisation after the death of Trotsky to adopt the same attitude to bourgeois-democratic capitalism that the Cannonites had taken to Stalinism less than 21 months after Trotsky's death.

Hal Draper, who had disputed with Shachtman over Cuba, produced scholarly books of great value. Some of Draper's younger co-thinkers linked up with the British IS (forerunner of the SWP), and acted as revolutionary socialists where they could. Despite a dispersal in 1976-7, when pressure from the British IS for greater control broke the American group into half-a-dozen splinters, they continue to do that. But, on the whole, the Heterodox Trotskyist current had withered to very little by the time the revolutionary left revived in the late 1960s, and its legacy has had to be rediscovered in libraries rather than being passed on directly through living political organisations.

If the outlook of the Heterodox was aridly chaste and truth-centred, that of the Orthodox was full of sloppy political and historical fantasies, delusions, and adulterations, and it was polluted by promiscuous association with reactionary regimes.

The Orthodox had the weight of Trotsky's authority on their side. They presented their ideas about Stalinism as the only consistent development from Trotsky's (in fact very different) ideas. And they survived for the same reason that the Stalinists did. The Stalinist parties were Stalinist even when their politics were bourgeois-conformist. In Britain, for instance, they were against the Labour Party leaving its coalition with the Tories in May 1945. Even after Labour had won the general election in July 1945 the Communist Party advocated a new coalition that would include the Tories. Even Labour's right wing was to the left of this Stalinist party! What made the Communist Party Stalinist and prevented its sometimes bourgeois-conformist politics leading to full conciliation with the bourgeoisie was that its core commitment was to the Russian Stalinist state. That kept it in the orbit of Russia, and at odds with the local bourgeoisie, no matter how much the Stalinists became mired in the local bourgeoisie's politics. So too with the Orthodox Trotskyists: their "defencism" kept them from recoiling from Stalinism towards bourgeois democracy. The Heterodox had no such moorings.

1700 years ago Catholic Christianity fought for supremacy with Arian Christianity. The Arians were rational for their times, severely sensible, impatient with such ideas as that Jesus was god. The Catholics dealt in intellectual gibberish like the Trinity, the idea that god is both three persons and one. They absorbed pagan cults and worshipped local pagan gods as Christian saints. But the Catholics' myths and monkish fantasies catered for emotional and other needs in their congregations that the Arians could not cater for or hope to satisfy. The Heterodox were the Arians, and the Orthodox the Catholics, of post-Trotsky Trotskyism. The "Catholic" Orthodox, by virtue of their fudging of issues and their revolutionary fantasies and delusions, and their willingness to accept or adapt to alien political movements, were the better equipped to survive in an age of Stalinist expansion and of the widespread credibility of Stalinism even in the political eye of its critics and its bourgeois outright enemies.

Dogmatic Marxism And Apparatus Politics

A WEEK AFTER TROTSKY'S DEATH on 21 August 1940, a big memorial meeting for him was held in New York. Al Glotzer represented the Workers Party there, but the main speaker was James P Cannon. His speech was printed in *The Militant* (6 September 1940: p.527 of this volume).

Cannon's powerful and moving speech for Trotsky was also a clear declaration of what Marxism was to be for the Orthodox now that Trotsky, its eminent practitioner, was dead. It was the manifesto of a new Trotskyism. "The mighty ideas of Trotsky are... a clear guide to action in all the complexities of our epoch, and a constant reassurance that we are right... He worked against time to pour out through his pen the whole rich content of his mighty brain and preserve it in permanent written form for us..."

Marxism was now the texts of Trotsky – and earlier leaders, but primarily of Trotsky, who had unpacked his mind of all it contained and "laid up a literary treasure for us, a treasure that the moths and the rust cannot eat". Not said, but implied – and it would be the guiding rule for the Orthodox – was the idea that Marxism as a process of scientific investigation had more or less come to an end. Now those whom Cannon himself called Trotsky's "disciples" had to "apply" Trotsky's "teaching" (as they sometimes put it). They themselves would, of course, have to pick and choose at each time whatever of Trotsky's written "treasure" they thought relevant. Marxism was now a set of texts and old analyses, positions, and predictions, for deployment by "Trotsky's disciples". They would defend it and construe it in current politics.

Before the 1940 memorial meeting, an attempt had been made to bring Trotsky's corpse to New York for the ceremony. As well as being an undeserved insult to the Mexican people, whose government had given the live Trotsky refuge, this was bizarre – the idea of a Marxist political event organised around the specially imported carcass or ashes of the great dead man. The American government's refusal to give permission saved the Orthodox from this mummery, and they had the memorial without the corpse.

More than 40 years later in London, the Workers Revolutionary Party, the organisation (now defunct) that had once been the Cannonites' section in Britain but had long ago separated from them, somehow got hold of Trotsky's death mask and used it rather as Cannon had wanted to use Trotsky's body. They organised a mass meeting at which the centrepiece was the death-mask. It was a mix of showmanship, idolatry, kitsch religion, and all-round mumbo-jumbo.

The WRP had come close to realising Cannon's ambition half a century later. Cannon, however, did do with Trotsky's thinking what he couldn't do with Trotsky's corpse.

Cannon took on the role of St Peter, to whom Jesus Christ had supposedly said: "Thou are Peter" – his name up to then had been Simon; Peter meant "rock" – "and upon this rock I will build my church". Peter was, so the Catholic Church said, the first pope, the "vicar on Earth" of the departed Christ. For the Trotskyist movement, Cannon also took a role similar to that played for the "De Leonites" (the Socialist Labor Party) by Arnold Petersen after the death in 1914 of the SLP's central figure, Daniel De Leon – De Leon's dogmatising and sterile "vicar on Earth".

That this was Cannon's conception of Marxism would be demonstrated again and again all through the 1940s, the formative period of Orthodox Trotskyism. Much of their history in that period was a succession of more or less demented blunders rooted in a fixation on Trotsky's "predictions" and on verbal formulae taken from Trotsky.

We have seen that Trotsky had said that bourgeois democracy would soon give way in all the combattant states to fascism or authoritarianism. That proved to be not true of the USA, Britain, etc. during the war. It was proved not true in Italy after the fall of Mussolini in 1943, and in France as the Nazis retreated in 1944. But the Orthodox – or most of them: the British RCP was comparatively sensible about it – insisted, and insisted again, long after the actual establishment of new bourgeois-democratic states in Western Europe, that only authoritarian or "Bonapartist" police states could emerge there.

The Orthodox understood Trotsky to have believed that all imperialisms were equally predatory, the British and American as predatory as Hitler's. Therefore, they concluded, the triumphant USA would treat the European peoples liberated from German rule just as the Nazis had. That conclusion was by 1943-4 far from sensible. Yet long after the war was over, and the Americans were not behaving like the Nazis in Europe, the Orthodox clung to their belief.

Trotsky had predicted that during and immediately after the war there would be mass working-class anti-capitalist risings and socialist victories. That had been a plausible idea before the war, rooted in the experience at the end of World War One; but it did not happen. The war in Europe ended on 8 May 1945 (and in Japan on 2 September). Ah, but had the war *really* ended? At a public meeting on 4 November 1945, Cannon addressed himself to that question. No, the war hadn't ended, he said. Only "careless thinkers" believed it had (p.546 of this volume). The Marxists, Trotsky's disciples, knew better. There was only a pause in the ongoing and unended war. Trotsky's predictions would yet be proven true. His Marxist foresight would be vindicated.

Everyone, well-prepared and experienced speakers at public meetings too, sometimes gets carried away with an idea, or makes exaggerations. There was a sane and reasonable idea within the ridiculous claim that World War 2 was not over. Many smaller wars continued. Lines were already being drawn for a possible World War 3. But sensible people would see the exaggeration, or have it pointed out to them, and modify or retract.

Not Cannon. Not the "disciples". When Felix Morrow proposed to have the SWP repudiate the idea that World War 2 was not over, the rest of the SWP Political Committee rallied to Cannon. Morrow's motion was "factionally motivated", and therefore it was not necessary to separate the SWP from the idea, expressed by the Leader of the Orthodox in a major public speech printed in their paper, that World War 2 was still going on (p.549 of this volume). Thereafter the broad idea that the war was not over was repeated again and again in *The Militant*, in a toned-down and not-crazy form. For example, "Only Militant warned 'There is no peace!'" (16 March 1946). To re-assert the idea in some form, while silently retreating from the letter of what Cannon had said, became a point of honour with the Orthodox.

The accumulating effect of this prestige-heavy and politics-light approach to Marxism was to change the public persona of the organisation from one of reasonable Marxists in touch with reality (and, where necessary, with their own fallibility) into one that was quirky, arbitrary, capricious, a little eccentric, sometimes very eccentric. Reading the Orthodox papers and magazines of the 1940s, you get the feel of people not reasoning things through but tacking, trimming, and manoeuvring with "smart" formulations and gambits cut loose from their notional political doctrine and the Marxist framework. You get the feel of agitation-led "lines" and commentaries and not honest or free discussion of unexpected or problem-raising events – of an edifice dominated by apparatus politics and calculations about likely short-term political effect – above all of arbitrariness and caprice.

There was a famous dispute, recorded in Lenin's *What Is To Be Done?*, between Lenin and the future Menshevik (and future Stalinist) Alexander Martynov about the relationship for Marxists between agitation and propaganda. Martynov thought agitation and propaganda were separate things that, so to speak, sometimes didn't talk to each other. Agitation was measured by its results as a "call to action". Lenin, following Plekhanov, argued that agitation was bound by the theory and basic propaganda of the movement. There could be no such thing as doctrine-free agitation, no separate category of slogans which were "calls to action". Agitation on specific questions flowed from the basic doctrine and purposes of the Marxist movement, and led back to them.

In Cannon and the Orthodox after Trotsky's death, for example in their jugglings about Russia, there is a loosening or breaking of the link between agitation (which Plekhanov defined as one or a few ideas reaching a large audience) and propaganda (many ideas, reaching a few), and theory.

On the one hand, the Orthodox sometimes practised daft fidelity to the letter of Trotsky; on the other, when it suited them, they could ignore Trotsky's reasoning. Not only Trotsky, but also Cannon, had based their assessment of the Stalinist USSR in 1939-40 on the idea that it was unviable even in the short term, and certainly incapable of large expansion. Russia had survived and seized half of Europe. The Workers Party asked the Orthodox: what about that? On this the Orthodox were not at all "Trotsky-to-the-letter" people. They made a joke of it. Shachtman thinks he has a "promissory note" from Trotsky and from History! Ha! Ha! Ha! These were pick-and-choose dogmatists.

One reason for their fixation on, for example, the idea that bourgeois democracy was impossible in post-war Europe, was their own inability to elaborate revolutionary working-class politics based on the same premises, norms, and methods as Trotsky in unexpected realities. The truth about all dogmatists is that in practice they pick and choose what to do empirically, according to pressures, perceived opportunities or dangers, pet ideas, brainstorms, and then fit dogma to deed. Even when the text-fetishists get hooked in the wheels of a dogma which runs away with them – the idea about bourgeois-democratic regimes being impossible in post-war Europe, for example – on the whole they match dogma to deed, not deed to dogma. Marxism becomes not method and precept but afterthought and rationalisation: apparatus Marxism.

In Orthodox Trotskyism, the tendency over decades came to be for "the party" and what was considered to be good for "the party" to become the all-defining supreme good – to become what the USSR was to the Stalinised Comintern. There are very few things people calling themselves Trotskyists have not done for organisational advantage. Much of the time, for many of the "Orthodox" Trotskyist groups, everything – perceptions of reality, "perspectives", truth, consistency, principle – is up for "construing" and reinterpretation in the light of perceived party interest. Their "Marxism" is "Apparatus Marxism": it exists to rationalise what the party apparatus thinks it best to do. The idea of the "finished" or "unchanging" program has sometimes been presented as a barrier to opportunism, but in fact has become a licence for it: any emphasis, extrapolation, or selective reading is justified so long as it remains or can be claimed as remaining within the limits of the barebones formula.

This is "Marxism" with its eyes put out, chained to the millwheel, "Apparatus Marxism". Apparatus Marxism is a peculiarly rancid species of "Marxism" from which everything "objective", disinterested, spontaneous and creative is banished. Creativity is incompatible with the prime function of "Apparatus Marxism": rationalising for "the party" and its apparatus. Creativity and, so to speak, spontaneity, is the prerogative of the all-shaping, suck-it-and-see empirical citizens who staff the "Party" apparatus. Everything is thereby turned on its head. The history of the Orthodox Trotskyist, or Cannonite, organisations is a story shaped by this conception of the relationship of Marxism to "the revolutionary party" – as a handmaiden of the apparatus.

"Apparatus Marxism" is both blind and sterile because it is not and cannot be a guide to honest analysis and to practice consistent with theory. It exists to rationalise a practice that is in fact guided by something else – usually, the perceived advantage of the organisation. For Marxists, the unity of theory and practice means that practice is guided by theory, a theory constantly replenished and sometimes modified by experience. In "Apparatus Marxism", the proper relationship of theory to practice and of practice to theory is inverted.

Our predominant Marxist culture today is largely made up of the various "Apparatus Marxisms", protected, as behind high tariff walls, by the "party" regimes they serve. Demurrers or questioners of cloistered certainties are inimical to that culture, which, progressively over the 1940s, reshaped the Orthodox Trotskyists and their policies. James P Cannon was the Zinovievist cuckoo in Trotsky's small nest. It was not all negative Zinovievism. Cannon stood for a serious attitude to organisation, and that was necessary. But the Zinovievism eventually, as Cannon himself seems ruefully to have recognised in the 1960s, "strangled the party" (p.621, this volume). Grown fully, and without Trotsky restraining him, Cannon bit off the heads of a lot of the smaller birds in the nest or pushed them out. With Trotsky's help in 1939-40, he tried to bite off the head of some of the bigger birds: in the first place Shachtman. He "bumped off" a succession of leading SWP intellectuals in 1939-40 (Shachtman and others), 1943-6 (Morrow, Goldman, van Heijenoort), and 1952-4 (Cochran, Braverman), until he had left only the Cannon cultists, George Novack and Joseph Hansen, and, until his death in 1956, John G Wright, who was certainly a patronised member of Cannon's inner circle. Cannon, again and again, urged that the organisation become "tighter", more "centralised". Farrell Dobbs, who succeeded Cannon as secretary of the SWP and served in the post until the 1970s, summarised in 1941 how those close to Cannon had seen the April 1940 split: "the petty-bourgeois minority... tried to force the party to renounce the defense of the Soviet Union. They tried to turn the organization into the shambles of a social democratic debating society" (*The Militant*, 13 September 1941). Eventually the "tightening" and the "centralisation" squeezed the life out of the organisation.

The question of Cannon's ascribed pre-eminence in the organisation had been a contentious issue since about 1929. The notion – and it was Cannon's governing notion – of a fixed "prestige" for certain leaders, and a common leadership duty to maintain it, could not but play a deadly role. Inevitably a leader's prestige fluctuates. Everyone, even a Trotsky, sometimes makes mistakes, is slow to understand or too hasty or one-sided in response. To try to stop the natural fluctuation of prestige involves putting the judgement, and the freedom to think and express themselves, of the organisation's members in a bureaucratic straitjacket. It comes to involve falsification of the political records, covering-up, and the stifling of anyone who might politically undermine the leaders' prestige. A serious revolutionary socialist will practise a politics of truth and honest dealing, and inescapably that involves being unpopular sometimes. That, as they say, goes with the territory. Valid prestige based on honest dealing in politics can come only from having been right on a number of occasions, despite unpopularity. That is the "prestige" which Lenin had in the Bolshevik party, for example. It is very different from prestige based on pretend-omniscience and an eternal bureaucratic struggle to maintain it.

Cannon, in his "Notes on the Party Discussion", produced during his battle with Goldman and Morrow (SWP Internal Bulletin vol.7 no.2, April 1945), was surely right that "workers will not stay in a kibitzers' club. They won't talk back to the articulate smart alecks, and they won't write letters to the national office, either. They 'vote with their feet'." And, certainly, from that must flow some regulation as to time, occasion, and place for discussion, and broad guidelines for the chairing of such discussions in branches. But the gap between "kibitzers" and workers who can gain confidence in abstract debate and attend meetings only by effort against the pressures of social conditions and of long and tiring hours of work, demands not just restraint on the "kibitzers" but a "levelling-up" of the workers by education, experience, and discussion. As Gramsci put it: "Education, culture, the spreading of knowledge and experience – this is the independence of the masses from the intellectuals". Or again: "Marxism is antithetical to this Catholic position [of an iron discipline over the intellectuals so that they do not pass beyond certain limits of differentiation] ... If [Marxism] asserts the need for contact between the intellectuals and the simple people it does so, not in order to limit scientific activity and maintain unity at the low level of the masses but precisely in order to build an intellectual-moral bloc which makes politically possible the intellectual progress of the masses and not only of a few groups of intellectuals... [This] means working to produce cadres of intellectuals of a new type who arise directly from the masses though remaining in contact with them and becoming the stay of the corset."

In fact, Cannon offered as solution a levelling-down. What did the "kibitzers" of the 1945 SWP want to discuss? General politics, issues in dispute inside and outside the SWP, current events, Marxism... That such things be discussed by the membership is a necessity for a healthy party organisation. To stifle the "articulate" people who want to discuss those things in deference to new working-class (and other) members – or, with Cannon in 1945, in deference to a hoped-for big "influx of new, politically-inexperienced worker militants" which in fact never came – is to stultify the organisation, cramp the functioning of its cadres, and cut off the development of new worker activists. It is to make discussion of complex political issues into a preserve of an intellectually-privileged caste within the organisation, of just a few leaders (or one leader) and their personal political friends, sheltered from criticism. And a consequence of that is progressively to lower the intellectual and political level of the "top" layer in the organisation itself.

That deadly "dumbing down" could already be seen in the SWP-USA in the early 1940s. It did not eliminate petty-bourgeois intellectuals, and in any case they should not be eliminated; it just added another requirement for entry into complex discussions: selection by or subservience to the leading group, the apparatus, or "the leader". It led to a lowering of the level of the "intellectuals": a Wright for a Shachtman, a Novack for a Morrow, a Hansen for a Goldman, or a Dobbs for a McKinney, was not progress. If entirely party-trained intellectuals, without a "petty-bourgeois" (that is, a wide) educational background, are made the ideal, then they are likely to be narrow and one-sided. Cannon's approach tended artificially to cut the party off from contributions not only from independent-minded but also from better-trained intellectuals. In an apparatus-ruled party, no-one can know or say more than the apparatus and its leader says, or licenses them to say.

John G Wright, who conjured up the "Trotsky's Red Army" nonsense, was not a negligible man. He translated important texts and wrote some valuable articles. He, like Cannon, was one of the last of the Orthodox to accept the formula that the new Stalinist states were "deformed workers' states". Even so, in the early 1940s, he had the position he had in the SWP press by virtue of membership in a clique around Cannon. Novack and Hansen were selected over time, and survived, by dint of their intellectual and political biddability and willingness to operate within limits set by the apparatus, that is, to one degree or another, by their intellectual and political lack of independence and of personal political integrity, in a word, by their corruptibility. The levelling-down and stultifying gradually killed intellectual life in the SWP, and paved the way for the coup in 1979, when apparatus-made and now apparatus-controlling younger leaders revolutionised the organisation from above. They made it a Castroite sect and expelled the remaining veteran Trotskyists (except, notably, George Novack, who remained subservient even to the Castroite "leadership" and apparatus). The smaller would-be Trotskyist groups around the SWP reported in the mid-80s an episode that in its symbolism summed up the whole tragic story. The new SWP leaders threw out Cannon's personal collection of pamphlets and documents, placing them in a dumpster. When they found interested people with respect for Cannon rescuing the documents, they put a guard on the dumpster until it was hauled away. The paths of artificial prestige sooner or later lead only to the historical dumpster.

Their junking of the "old Cannonism" could happen the way it did – through clique control of the apparatus – only on the basis of further development of the apparatus control Cannon created after the 1940 split. One of the veterans expelled after the 1979 coup, Frank Lovell, described the regime after 1953 like this: "Disagreements that developed within the National Committee were smoothed over and remained unresolved. The leaders in the national office made decisions by consensus and discouraged any general discussion within the ranks of the party about the correctness of their decisions or the best way of implementing them. This sufficed to keep the organization together... But this method tended to have a stultifying effect. It discouraged political initiative and debate". (Introduction to *In Defence of American Trotskyism*, FIT pamphlet 1992).

Cannon And Shachtman

THE HONEST CRITIC of the Trotskyist movement — of both the Cannon and Shachtman segments of it, which are intertwined in their history and in their politics — must remind himself and the reader that those criticised must be seen in the framework of the movement as a whole. Even those who were most mistaken most of the time were more than the sum of their mistakes, and some of them a great deal more. The US Trotskyists, Shachtmanites and Cannonites alike, mobilised 50,000 people in New York in 1939 to stop fascists marching into Jewish neighbourhoods of that city. When some idea of the extent of the Holocaust became public, the Orthodox responded vigorously (and the Heterodox would have concurred): "Anger against Hitler and sympathy for the Jewish people are not enough. Every worker must do what he can to aid and protect the Jews from those who hunt them down. The Allied ruling classes, while making capital of Hitler's treatment of the Jews for their war propaganda, discuss and deliberate on this question endlessly. The workers in the Allied countries must raise the demand: Give immediate refuge to the Jews... Quotas, immigration laws, visa – these must be cast aside. Open the doors of refuge to those who otherwise face extermination" (Statement of the Fourth International, *The Militant*, 3 April 1943).

We, the Orthodox – the writer was one of them – identified with the exploited and oppressed and sided with them and with the labour movements of which we ourselves were part; with people struggling for national independence; with the black victims of zoological racism. We took sides always with the exploited and oppressed. To those we reached we brought the basic Marxist account of class society in history and of the capitalist society in which we live. We criticised, condemned, and organised against Stalinism. Even at the least adequate, the Orthodox Trotskyists generally put forward proposals that in sum meant a radical transformation of Stalinist society, a revolution against Stalinism. Always and everywhere the Orthodox Trotskyists fought chauvinism. When some got lost politically, as they sometimes did and do, it was usually because of a too blandly negative zeal for things that "in themselves" were good, such as anti-capitalism and anti-imperialism. We mobilised political and practical support for movements of colonial revolt. French Trotskyists, living in a world gone crazy with chauvinism of every kind, set out to win over and organise German soldiers occupying France. They produced a newspaper aimed at German worker-soldiers: some twenty French Trotskyists and German soldier sympathisers lost their lives when the Nazis suppressed it. The Orthodox Trotskyists even kept some elements of feminism alive in a world in which it was long eclipsed. Michel Pablo, in a French jail for helping the Algerians in their war of independence, applied himself to studying and writing about "the woman question". Large numbers of people shared the view of the Trotskyists on specific questions and worked with them or in parallel to them. The Trotskyists alone presented and argued for a whole world outlook that challenged the outlook of the capitalist and Stalinist ruling classes. We embodied the great truths of Marxism in a world where they had been bricked up alive by Stalinism. We kept fundamental texts of anti-Stalinist Marxism in circulation.

Read the accounts of the day to day mistreatment of black people in the USA in the mid 20th century — Jim Crow in the South, where blacks had been slaves, segregation in the North, all-pervasive humiliations, exclusions, beatings, mob lynchings, burnings, the systematic ill-treatment of children as of grown-up black people. Work through even a little of that terrible story and you run the risk of despairing of the human race. The Trotskyists, consistently and unswervingly challenging Jim Crow, championing and defending the victims of injustice, showed what they were. To have been less would have been despicable. That does not subtract from the merits of those who did what was right and necessary, when most people did not.

James P Cannon and Max Shachtman, the main representatives of the two currents of Trotskyism, were, in my judgement, heroes, both of them. Cannon, when almost all of his generation of Communist International leaders had gone down to Stalinism or over to the bourgeoisie, remained what he was in his youth, a fighter for working-class emancipation. I make no excuses for the traits and deeds of

Cannon which are shown in a bad light in this volume. It is necessary to make and keep an honest history of our own movement if we are to learn from it.

After Trotsky's death Cannon found himself, and fought to remain, the central leader of the Trotskyist movement, a job which, as the Heterodox said, he was badly equipped politically to do. Moving by instinct and the great tradition of which he was part, he steered a course between what he saw as the twin evils, Stalinophilia and Stalinophobia — as he might have said, between Deutscher and Shachtman. That was a long way from being politically or intellectually adequate. He did the best he could, in a world that had turned murderously hostile to the politics he worked for and the goals he fought to achieve. More than once he must have reminded himself of the old lines, "The times are out of joint. O cursed spite/ That ever I was born to set it right". James P Cannon remained faithful to the working class and to revolutionary socialism. Such a book as his *History of American Trotskyism* cannot be taken as full or authoritative history, but it has value as what Gramsci called a "living book": "not a systematic treatment, but a 'living' book, in which political ideology and political science are fused in the dramatic form of a 'myth'." Socialists today can learn much from both Shachtman and Cannon.

In his last decade (he died in 1972), Max Shachtman followed the US trade unions into conventional politics and dirty Democratic Party politicking. He took up a relationship to US capitalism paralleling that of the Cannonites to Stalinism of different sorts and at different times. Politically that was suicidal. But those who, again and again, took similar attitudes to one Stalinism or another forfeit the right to sneer and denounce. Shachtman got lost politically at the end of the 1950s; the Cannonites got lost politically, in relation to Stalinism, twenty years earlier!

When Trotsky in 1939-40, living under tremendous personal strain, reached a crossroads in his political life and fumbled and stumbled politically, Max Shachtman, who had tremendous and lasting regard for Trotsky and a strong loyalty to what he stood for, had the integrity and spirit to fight him and those who — Cannon and his comrades in the first place — were starting on a course that would warp and distort and in serious part destroy their politics in the decade ahead and long after. The Prometheus myth has been popular amongst socialists, supplying names for organisations and newspapers. As punishment for stealing fire from the gods and giving it to humankind, the Titan Prometheus is chained forever to a rock in the Caucasian mountains and vultures eternally rip at his liver. Shachtman picked up the proletarian fire Trotsky had for a moment fumbled with and carried it forward. Generations of mockery, obloquy, misrepresentation, and odium where it was not deserved, have been his punishment for having been right against Trotsky and Cannon. This book is intended as a contribution to the work of those who strive to refurbish and renew the movement that in their own way both James P Cannon and Max Shachtman tried to serve, and served.

Historiography

MOST HISTORIES of the Trotskyist movement are what might be called "apparatus historiography". They are tendentious, selective to the point of distortion or outright falsification. The histories are written for purposes other than providing accurate chronicles or analyses. It sometimes reaches the point that there is very little real history in the stories of themselves and their opponents that some Trotskyist organisations tell.

That was true of the Workers Revolutionary Party of Gerry Healy, now long defunct but once the biggest activist organisation of the revolutionary left in Britain. But not only extremely degenerated organisations fail to provide accurate history. Even honest academic-style efforts such as those of Robert Alexander fail miserably [19]. This volume tries to provide a broader political picture by presenting in their own words the different sides of every dispute it covers. Of course, even then selection can serve to distort. All I can offer the reader is assurance that I have not knowingly held back anything that would change the picture my selection paints.

The reclamation of a true picture of our own history is one of the most important tasks of revolutionary Marxists today – an essential element in reconstituting a viable revolutionary socialism. As with Lenin's work on State and Revolution, the reanimation of revolutionary Marxism requires that we dig down into our own roots.

The "Shachtmanites" have in my opinion suffered worst in the handed-down history of the revolutionary movement after the death of Trotsky. And yet in the 1940s and 50s they continued and elaborated an alternative strain of Trotskyism from that of the Cannon tendency, whose literature has for most people today and for more than three quarters of a century has defined "Trotskyism". The historical reputation of the Shachtmanites has largely been defined by the Cannonites' account of them. Peter Drucker's biography, *Max Shachtman and his Left* (1994), and the first volume of *The Fate of the Russian Revolution* (1998), have opened things up quite a bit in the last two decades, but for many people, still, the very tendentious selection of polemical texts by Trotsky put together by Cannon and his comrades in 1942 under the title *In Defence of Marxism* has frozen the image of the Shachtmanites. Generations of Trotskyists have been cut off from the ideas of "the other Trotskyists" – and thereby from many ideas of Trotsky himself, major aspects of whose thinking were jettisoned by the Cannonite "Orthodox Trotskyists". The history of that time is told usually by supporters of the Orthodox. It is told, when it deals with the Shachtmanites, as if the Heterodox were aberrant and the Orthodox were balanced, properly pro-USSR but adequately anti-Stalinist. Pretty much the opposite is true. The Orthodox went prolifically haywire after June 1941. In important respects they ceased to be Trotskyists at all, as that term had been understood before June 1941.

A valuable and honest book like Peter Drucker's account of Max Shachtman is diminished by the author's apparent belief that there was, side by side with the WP/ISL, a balanced or more balanced Trotskyism. (He is a member of the Mandelite Fourth International). There surely was not. It is not possible to understand the WP-ISL without a properly filled-in background of the politics and activities of the Orthodox. One can't be understood without consideration of the other. For the Workers Party in the 1940s and well into the 50s, it is a case of: what can they know of Shachtman, who only Shachtman know? It not possible to clear space for the real history of the two Trotskyisms without demolishing the myths and self-serving misrepresentations of the Orthodox, which occupy the space now.

The story of the Orthodox Trotskyists told in this introduction and in the documents in this book is one of political confusion, bewilderment, inadequacy, and defeat. Of a small political tendency being overwhelmed by events and, despite its revolutionary, working-class, anti-Stalinist best intentions, magnetised by the Stalinist USSR as it conquered and consolidated a great European empire. Of a small political tribe that got lost trying, half-blind, to work its way through the murderous maze of mid 20th century history.

From the standpoint of broad, long-term, impartial history, there is no mystery here, and there should not be much surprise. The Fourth International was a very small political tendency. It was heavily dependent on one person, Trotsky, who was, you could say, a visitor from another world, the lost world of Russian and international Bolshevism. He was removed by the assassin at the decisive turning-point of mid-20th century history. So, soon, were many of his most experienced comrades, victims of Stalin and fascism.

The fate of the Polish Trotskyists in the war is only an extreme example of the fate of the whole tendency. They were targeted by the German and Russian totalitarians who turned Poland into a battlefield and then a slaughterhouse. They were hunted by Nazis and Stalinists, as communists and Trotskyists, as Poles, and (a very large proportion of them) as Jews. Not a single member of the Trotskyist organisation in Poland survived the war. At the end of the war, the Stalinists in Greece slaughtered several hundred Trotskyists. The Nazis had already killed the Greek Trotskyists' outstanding leader, Pantelis Pouliopoulos. In Vietnam the members of the sizeable Trotskyist organisation were massacred in 1945-6 by the Vietnamese Stalinists, led by Ho Chi Minh. In China, the members of the Trotskyist organisations were killed by the Guomindang or the Stalinists, or put in Maoist jails for decades.

Even before that, the leaders of the Fourth International in Europe were killed as the International was being proclaimed in 1938. Rudolf Klement, a German émigré, was kidnapped and murdered on the eve of the Fourth International congress; his body, without its head, was found floating in the Seine. Leon Sedov, son of Natalia Sedova and Leon Trotsky, and an important leader of the Fourth International in his own right, was murdered in a French hospital in February 1938.

This slaughter was inflicted on a political tendency faced with the theoretical and political conundrums that exercised Trotsky at the end of his life. Many quit in despair, exhaustion, and disgust, or a combination of them. Like the First International, whose centre was moved from Europe to the USA after the Paris Commune, the Fourth had its centre relocated to New York early in World War 2. In Europe, underground Trotskyist organisations continued to exist and fight. All their expectations were proved false, their expectations of Stalinism too. Stalinism survived and prospered and kept its grip on the working-class movement. That shaped everything else.

In other words, this is the history of a movement which suffered a comprehensive defeat. One of the modes of its defeat was that it was, to a serious extent, conquered and politically overwhelmed by Stalinism. In the name of "defending the USSR", it turned itself into a group of auxiliary frontier guards, albeit highly critical ones. It went into a political and historical blind alley, a cul-de-sac.

That is the story of a historical tragedy. But it is not the whole story. That is what makes the "other Trotskyists", the Heterodox, so important for the future of revolutionary socialist politics. In parallel to and in polemic with the Orthodox, on issue after issue and in general, they elaborated a politics of consistent anti-Stalinism as well as consistent anti-capitalism. Where the Orthodox built on Trotsky's mistakes at the end of his life, the Heterodox built on the whole record of Trotskyist anti-Stalinism and anti-capitalism.

The Heterodox too were organisationally scattered and dispersed, even more radically so than the Orthodox. The surprising thing is not their setbacks, but that they were able to do the work they did for two decades and more. Their political legacy, not that of the more numerous and seemingly more successful Orthodox, is the one on which a renewal of revolutionary Marxism is possible.

In history, revolutionary movements suffer defeat and again defeat. That is in the nature of things for movements confronting the entrenched might and power of ruling classes. There are no words of explanation and consolation that can make that historical reality less bitter. But the movement continues, because the bourgeois oppression to which revolutionary socialism is the opposite and the antidote continues. The defeated bear their defeat honourably, and work to prepare the future. Brave young people pick up the fallen banners. They try to learn from the past.

To learn from the past we must know the past. To renew and build on the history of the Trotskyist movement it is necessary to know that history. It is necessary to know the whole heritage; to know that, important as the Orthodox organisations are, theirs has not been the only strand of Trotskyism, or the best. The Heterodox are pivotal in the history of Trotskyism, and in its future. Don't mourn: study, think, and organise! Or, as James Connolly used to put it: hope, and fight!

The Alliance For Workers' Liberty

THE ALLIANCE FOR WORKERS' LIBERTY, which had distant origins as "1953", that is, sharply anti-Stalinist "Cannonites", made our way to the Third Camp politics of the Heterodox Trotskyist tradition by our responses to successive political events, rather than by way of a sudden conversion. Then we revised our ideas about the history of the Trotskyist movement: we "went back to 1940", to the parting of the ways of the two main Trotskyist currents. The AWL has for practical purposes, that is, in our political response to events, been in the Heterodox Trotskyist camp since the late 1970s, though some formal explanations and changes of "position" were made later. The Russian invasion of Afghanistan in December 1979, and our decision to argue for the withdrawal of USSR troops – alone of Orthodox Trotskyist organisations – is a convenient point from which to date our allegiance to the "Third Camp" tradition. Despite its vicissitudes, and despite the fact that it does not come down to us as a neatly-codified package transmitted by a continuous chain of organisational and intellectual activity, that tradition, and the formulations of its politics form a rich heritage. As well as the political disputes, mistakes, and degenerations, there is also a magnificent record of indomitable devotion and courage in the fight for socialism against both capitalism and Stalinism.

This Volume, Volume One, And Volume 3

IN THE FATE OF THE RUSSIAN REVOLUTION, volume 1, I assembled key texts of a strand of Trotskyist thinking which had been confined to the archives for many decades, the "Heterodox Trotskyism" of Max Shachtman, Hal Draper, C L R James, Al Glotzer, and others. This volume continues that work of rediscovery. It documents the fact that the characteristic ideas of later "Orthodox Trotskyism" – "objectively revolutionary" Stalinism; socialist revolution by "bureaucratic impulse" or by Stalinists being "compelled" by circumstances; the supposed self-sufficiency of a "party" apparatus with an allegedly "finished" program; the fetishisations of some formulas of Trotsky's, such as that the USSR was a "degenerated workers' state" – had developed within a year or so of Trotsky's death in 1940, though it took another decade for them to develop into a locked-down system. It makes the case that revolutionary socialists today who want to find clean political ground on which to rebuild, in labour movements where seepage from many decades of Stalinism still poisons the ground, must go back to re-examine the old debates and the flaws and lacunae in the political legacy which Trotsky left at his death – back to 1940.

My original plan was to cover all the important disputes and debates that helped form the two basic strands of the Trotskyist movement in one sizable volume. That proved impossible. There will be a third and final volume. Important issues are being held back for the third volume, most notably perhaps on the Trotskyists and the Jewish question in the period of the Holocaust.

In producing this volume I owe much to Martin Thomas for suggestions and insights, for much discussion and argument, for the index, and for pre-print technical work, and to Gemma Short for technical work.

Sean Matgamna, October 2015

Notes

This is an edited and expanded version of the introduction printed in the first edition of this volume.

1. Dual power would mean the working class maybe expressing itself through workers' councils (soviets) so strong that they vied directly with the government for political and social control – the disintegration, enfeeblement, and paralysis of the bourgeois state and the coming into being of a rising and strengthening working-class movement with authority comparable to that of the state, as in Russia before the October revolution.

2. In fact the policy adopted on Trotsky's initiative in mid 1939 of championing the independence of a "Soviet Ukraine" against Moscow rule implied that the USSR was an empire in the sense that pre-World-War-1 Austro-Hungary was, and in the 1930s the Trotskyists defined Poland, Czechoslovakia, and Yugoslavia as imperialist states – states with national minorities held against their will. Ukraine vanished from the SWP press during the war.

3. On the lines of Lenin's and Trotsky's arguments in World War 1, the strongest argument against "defending" or siding with Britain – the Britain of the labour movement and the trade unions – against the Nazis would be Britain's alliance with the USSR, the real Stalinist USSR, not the imaginary one that still for Cannon and his comrades shone with the glow of the October Revolution.

4. It is a strange fact of history that the serious and detailed critical accounts of Stalinist society available in the West in the 1930s were mostly limited to the works of Trotsky and his comrades, and those of disillusioned ex-sympathisers of the CP. In Britain, it was a "Right Book Club", run by the publisher Hutchinson's, a weak parallel to the very strong "Left Book Club" of Victor Gollancz and the Communist Party, that published Victor Serge's book on Russia, Eugene Lyons' *Assignment in Utopia*, and *I Was A Soviet Worker* by Andrew Smith (a sympathiser who went to the USSR). In the era of the great capitalist slump, there was eager sympathy for "the Russian experiment" among liberals and reform-socialists, and even some aristocratic Tories. There was a tremendous wide credulity for the Stalinist account of USSR society. The *New Statesman* and *Tribune*, like *The Nation* and *The New Republic* in the USA, were Stalinist propaganda sheets on everything connected with Russia.

5. The post-Hitler-Stalin-pact pro-German defeatism of the strong French Communist Party had, of course, been a factor in that.

6. The open letter, too – the appeal to Stalin as if to an errant comrade-in-arms – was a precedent. Similar appeals to Stalinists in power – in Yugoslavia, the USSR, China, etc. – would punctuate the later political history of the Orthodox like interjections from a victim of political Tourette syndrome.

7. Richard Overy, *Russia's War*, chapter 5; Antony Beevor, *Stalingrad*, pp.184-5, 385, 84-5; Antony Beevor, *Berlin*, p.113.

8. During World War Two the Communist Party USA would have over 100,000 members at its peak, and great strength in the trade unions.

9. And what of communists who want to overthrow the autocracy, but might not be willing to subordinate themselves meekly to Stalin in the war or join the Orthodox in their pledges of loyalty?" If the Cannonites ruled in Russia, the "petty-bourgeois renegades" of the Workers Party would be outlawed? They

wouldn't qualify for release from Stalin's jails?

10. *The Militant*'s proposal of the Socialist United States of Europe as an immediate alternative to the war seemed to take the existing German empire as a given starting point, ignoring the conquered European peoples and their national rights and possible inclinations. That may have been rooted in Trotsky's 1915 "Peace Program", in which he argued that if Germany united Europe, then socialists should fight within that Europe for its transformation into a democratic federation. It is plain in hindsight that Trotsky underestimated the upsurge of nationalism that conquest would trigger in the forcibly "united" nations of Europe. The caricature of Trotsky's 1915 idea in the press of the Orthodox in World War 2 was an aspect of their blindness towards the national liberation movements that would develop in some of the Nazi-occupied countries.

11. And so at the outbreak of war in 1939 did the Nazis. They issued an appeal to the working class of the world – in the form of a call from Robert Ley, gauleiter of Hitler's police-state "unions". In Britain that appeal was reprinted in the press of the anti-war but often confused Independent Labour Party.

12. This sort of mental operation would be a model for many other political rationalisations in the future, as for instance to explain how Mao Zedong's peasant army could make a working-class revolution in China, as they believed it had.

13. The lack of internal party critics with enough self-confidence to call the SWP leaders to order also contributed. It was sometimes said, approvingly, of Stalin's USSR in World War 2 that it had no disloyal "fifth column" because all the "fifth columnists" had been shot. James P Cannon, too, faced no revolt or "fifth column" in his ranks because, politically speaking, he had shot them.

14. These important critics from within Orthodox Trotskyism as it took shape themselves fell down before the contradictions and difficulties of the time. Goldman and some of his co-thinkers joined the Workers Party in June 1946. Goldman remained active until 1948, when he left the Workers Party, differing with them about the Marshall Plan of US aid to Europe (Goldman was for it). He then quit political activity. Morrow did not leave the SWP with Goldman. He was expelled in November 1946, and left politics at that point. Another significant critic, Louis Jacobs, distributed his document "We arrive at a line" in late 1944 and then dropped out of the SWP, writing occasionally for the WP press. Jean van Heijenoort, wartime secretary of the New York based Fourth International, dropped out too.

15. See Trotsky's *Letter to Borodai* of late 1928, in which he defined political reformability as the criterion of a workers' state, and Shachtman's discussion of Trotsky's later shift to nationalised property as the empirical criterion. *The Fate of the Russian Revolution* volume 1, pp.300-309.

16. At least one Trotskyist tendency, Lutte Ouvrière, argued right up until the end that Stalinist Russia had one class character, and the structurally identical satellite states another.

17. In Posadas, the patterns of 1940-5 and of the war-revolution perspective of

1950-4 were upfront. After all, if War-Revolution would be a stage forward towards socialism, as the Fourth International in 1951-3 had believed, then serious socialists should indeed advocate it. Some time in the 1970s the author listened to a British Posadist exulting in the "transformations" and "regeneration" that had taken place in the USSR. He cited tremendous working-class gatherings and marches in Moscow. Hadn't we heard? No. What had happened? What working-class demonstrations? It turned out that he was talking about the annual official Stalinist May Day march and military display.

18. In 1953 Cannon indicted Pablo, Mandel, etc. for thinking that the Russian state could project "a roughly revolutionary orientation" in the imminent Third World War, which would be a War-Revolution.

19. Alexander's accounts of Trotskyist movements in the two countries I know about in some detail because I have been active in them, the UK and Ireland, are not even a reliable chronology. Even such a "standard" work as Isaac Deutscher's biography of Trotsky fails, at least in its third volume, which tells the story of Trotsky's last exile, after 1929. Deutscher radically misrepresents Trotsky's views on Stalinism at the end of his life by "splitting" Trotsky into two, assigning views that were Trotsky's to other anti-Stalinists whom he fought with, and narrowing Trotsky down to something not too far from Deutscher's own critical pro-Stalinist politics.

Quotations from Trotsky, by page number • 5, "totalitarian": RB ch 5 • 5, "police measures", W33-4 p.8 • 6, "savagery", W38-9 p.325 • 6, stratum, RB ch 9 • 6, "lion's share", "same as US bourgeois", W39-40 p.144 • 6, "twelve to fifteen million", W39-40 p.115 • 6, "no class ever", W37-8 p.444 • 6-7, "all the vices" W38-9 p.325 • 7, "classic exploitation", RB ch 4 • 7, "behind a cultured capitalism", RB ch 5 • 7, "bureaucratic economy", W32-3 p.224 • 7, "state belongs", RB ch 9 • 7, "strangled", W39-40 p.197 • 8, "quartermaster", W39-40 p.76 • 8, "jackal", W39-40 p.92 • 8, "against seizures", UW • 8, "semi-slaves", AO • 8, "during war with Finland", W39-40 p.166 • 9, "in every case", AO • 9, "extension", UW • 10, Simone Weil, W37-8 p.331 • 11, "the first concentration", RB ch 9 • 11, "ludicrous", UW • 12, "sole master", *Stalin* vol.2 p.240 • 12, "both class states", W37-8 p.27 • 13, "only if", W39-40 p.166 • 16, "as absurd", W39-40 p.124 • 19, "history has known", AO • 19-20, "silent condemnation", "behind the Finnish question", W39-40 p.144 • 21, "not a question", W39-40 p.91 • 21, "shameful and criminal", W39-40 p.92 • 27, "fascism inevitable", W38-9 p.210 • 43, "to defend", W30-1 p.229 • 44, "state property", RB ch 9 • 72, "not any support", W39-40 p.201 • W signifies the volumes of Trotsky's writings, RB Revolution Betrayed, UW The USSR in War, AO Again and Once More.

Our thanks to Marty Goodman, the Riazanov Library Project, and the Marxist Internet Archive for their work in making many of the texts used here more accessible and available. Most of the non-Trotsky quotations are from texts in this volume: they may include cuts not indicated by ellipses which can be identified from the full texts. The texts have the old usage of "man" for "human being", "he" for "she or he", etc.: that reflects their times, rather than indifference by the speakers and writers to women's liberation.

Timeline

1914-18: Breakdown of world capitalism into world war. 1914: Collapse of the Socialist International into national segments almost all of which back "their own" governments in the war.

1917, November: Russian workers' revolution. 1918-1922: Workers' state defends itself against civil war and invading armies from 14 other countries.

1918, November, and 1919: German revolution in which the Kaiser is overthrown but workers are eventually defeated. Rosa Luxemburg, Karl Liebknecht, Leo Jogiches and others are killed.

1922, December: The dying Lenin, after condemning the "Great Russian chauvinist" policy of Stalin in Georgia, tries to remove him as general secretary.

1923, October: Trotskyist Left Opposition formed, to fight bureaucratisation of the Russian regime.

1924: Lenin dies. Stalin and Bukharin proclaim as the communist goal "socialism in one country".

1927, July: Trotsky proclaims his "Clemenceau thesis": in the event of war the Opposition will criticise and seek to replace the Stalinist leadership. Stalin replies: "These cadres can be removed only by civil war". November-December: United Opposition of Trotsky and Zinoviev defeated: oppositionists expelled from Communist Party of Soviet Union and sent into exile inside USSR.

1928: The American James P Cannon and the Canadian Maurice Spector read Trotsky's *Critique of the Draft Programme of the Communist International* in Moscow. They form Trotskyist groups on their return to North America, and are expelled from the Communist Parties.

1928-9: Stalin turns to forced-march industrialisation and collectivisation. The Russian labour movement is destroyed and replaced by police-state "unions". Many of the exiled oppositionists go over to Stalin and support the new policies, keeping their misgivings private.

1929, February: Trotsky deported to Turkey

1929: Stalinists expel formerly leading groups in Communist Parties which had been allied with Bukharin in the USSR. They form "Right Communist" groups, for a while much stronger than the Trotskyist groups.

1929, October: New York Stock Exchange crash starts descent of capitalism into the Great Depression.

1930, February: Trotsky breaks with the Leninbund, the biggest organisation in the International Left Opposition: he supports Russia, and they China, in the conflict over the Chinese Eastern Railway.

1930, April: First international conference of the Left Opposition, in Paris.

The Left Opposition groups see themselves as expelled factions of the Communist Parties.

1933, January: Hitler is allowed by the mass Communist Party of Germany, which has its own armed militia, to come to power peacefully. Trotsky and the Left Opposition call for a new, Fourth, International: at first it is conceived of as a broad regroupment of communists, not only Trotskyists. They come out for a working-class "political revolution" in the USSR against the bureaucracy. They reject the idea that the USSR has become an exploitative class state.

1934, January-February: "Congress of Victors" in the USSR: Stalinists celebrate apparent economic successes. December: assassination of Leningrad Stalinist boss, Sergei Kirov, becomes signal for the start of the Great Terror in the USSR. 1108 of the 1966 delegates to the Congress of Victors and 98 of the 139 Central Committee members elected there are sent to labour camps or killed.

1936-8: Moscow Show Trials.

1936, June: International conference of the Movement for the Fourth International.

1936, October, to March 1937: Hunger strike by the Trotskyists in the Vorkhuta labour camp.

1936-7: Spanish revolution. Workers take control of industry in Catalonia, but anarchist leaders cannot consolidate the workers' power and some of them instead join bourgeois coalition governments. May 1937: Stalinists and bourgeois forces crush workers' rising in Barcelona, and kill many anarchists and members of the POUM (party formed by merger of Spanish Trotskyists with Spanish "Right Communists"). Trotsky's criticism of POUM (which also joins bourgeois coalition government in Catalonia) alienates forces which had tentatively gravitated towards the movement for Fourth International.

1937, December: Formation of the Socialist Workers Party in the USA by expelled members of the Socialist Party, which the Trotskyists had joined in 1936.

1938: Stalinists murder all the Trotskyists held in their jails and forced-labour camps such as Vorkhuta.

1938, September: A purely Trotskyist Fourth International proclaimed at a one-day conference near Paris. Max Shachtman chairs, James P Cannon is a delegate.

1939, April: Fascists triumph in Spain. August: Hitler and Stalin sign military pact. September: World War 2 starts. Invasions of Polish state by Hitler (1 September: seizing the west) and Stalin (17 September: seizing the east). Beginning of crisis in Trotskyist movement over "defence of the USSR" in Poland. November: Stalin invades Finland, meets fierce resistance. Intensified dispute among Trotskyists.

1940: April: The US Trotskyist movement splits. James P Cannon leads one faction, who keep the name SWP and will soon call themselves Orthodox Trotskyists; Max Shachtman the other, the "Heterodox Trotskyists", who form the Workers Party. Trotsky allies with Cannon.

1940, May: Emergency conference of the Fourth International in New York. Its manifesto, written by Trotsky, includes an implicit self-criticism on Finland and the prospects for Stalinist-sparked revolution there. It elects a new executive to replace the old one, the majority of which had backed the US minority on "defence of the USSR" in Poland and Finland, and confirms move of the centre of the FI to New York for the duration of the war.

1940, August 20-21: Trotsky is murdered by the Stalinist Ramon Mercader.

1940, September: SWP adopts new policy on war, "proletarian military policy", following a half-formulated suggestion of Trotsky.

1941, June 22: Hitler invades USSR. The Communist Parties across the world, which had been making propaganda in favour of the peace terms offered by Hitler, swing to supporting the Allies and oppose strikes and class struggle during the war. June 27: FBI raids SWP's Minneapolis office. SWP leaders and leading trade-unionists indicted for "advocating overthrow of government".

1941, December: USA enters war. James P Cannon and 17 other SWP members found guilty of "advocating overthrow of the government": they will be jailed in 1944, after appeals are exhausted.

1942, November: Tide of Russo-German war turns at Stalingrad. December: Foundation text of "orthodoxy", *In Defence of Marxism*, published

1944-5: Russian army advances into eastern and central Europe. May 1945: end of war in Europe. August 1945: USA atom-bombs Hiroshima and Nagasaki, and Japan surrenders. Beginning of the nuclear age and cold war between the USSR and the big capitalist powers.

1945-7: Talk of reunification between the two Trotskyist currents: final outcome is that a section from the Cannonite "Orthodox" secede to Shachtman's "Heterodox", and a section of the "Heterodox" — CLR James and others — secede to the "Orthodox".

1948, February: Prague Stalinist "coup". April: Second congress of Fourth International, in Paris, the last on its founding principles.

1949, April: Workers Party renames itself Independent Socialist League

1949, August: Russia acquires atom bomb. Drift to World War 3 gives way to long international stalemate based on "balance of terror".

1950, June, to 1953: Proxy war between Russia and China, on one side, and USA and its allies including Britain, on the other, in Korea.

1951, August-September: Third congress of Fourth International codifies a radical change in outlook and politics. It is in fact the founding conference of a consolidated new "Orthodox Trotskyism".

1953, March: Death of Stalin. Relaxation of totalitarian terror regime in USSR and its East European satellite states. Beginning of international "thaw".

1953, June: Workers' uprising against Stalinism in East Germany.

1953, July: Korean war ends.

1953, November: Cannon leads an anti-Stalinist split-off from the Fourth International.

1956: Hungarian and Polish revolutions against Stalinism.

1958, September: Independent Socialist League merges into the small Socialist Party.

Max Shachtman speaks in an SWP election campaign. To his right on the platform, James P Cannon. *Socialist Appeal*, 5 September 1939

Glossary

Abern, Martin — One of the founders of the US Trotskyist movement. Sided with the minority in the 1940 split and was in the Workers Party/ ISL ("Harry Allen" in their press) until his death in 1949.

Benson, Herman — Also known as Ben Hall. Active in the Workers Party; later and still (at age 99) in Association for Union Democracy

Braverman, Harry — Writer for SWP in the 1940s, under the name Frankel; split 1953; later prominent in the journal *Monthly Review* and author of the book *Labour and Monopoly Capital* (1974).

Breitman, George — Editor of SWP paper *The Militant* 1941-3 and 1946-54. Expelled from SWP 1984 as it turned to Castroism. Died in 1986.

Browder, Earl — General secretary of US Communist Party from 1930 to 1945. Scapegoated by Stalin when shifting the Communist Parties from their extravagant pro-Allied-government and strike-breaking line in World War 2 and expelled from CP in 1946. Remained broadly Stalinist in his politics to the end.

Bruno — Bruno Rizzi, crank who published a book in 1939 discussed by Trotsky. Rabid anti-semite, advocated fusion of fascism and Stalinism. See *The Fate* vol.1 pp.315ff.

Bukharin, Nikolai — Old Bolshevik; "left communist" in 1918; ally of Stalin 1924-8; purged by Stalin 1929, killed 1938.

Burnham, James — Leading writer and speaker for SWP in late 1930s. Went with Shachtman in 1940 split, but then almost immediately dropped out and soon became well-known as a right-wing writer.

Cannon, James P — Founder of US Trotskyist movement. Leader of SWP after 1940 split and until 1954, when he retired as national secretary and moved to California. Died in 1974.

Carter, Joseph — Founder-member of US Trotskyist movement; leading member of Workers' Party in the 1940s. Rejected the "degenerated workers' state" description of the USSR as early as 1937, though he then described it as a class state halfway regressed to capitalism, rather than as "bureaucratic collectivist". Within the Workers Party, advocated the version of "bureaucratic collectivism" that would become party policy in 1946-7.

Cassidy — see Morrow

Cochran, Bert — Also known as E R Frank. Leading writer for SWP in 1940s. Split from SWP in pro-Stalinist direction in 1953. In old age, supported the journal *New Politics*, which continued politics similar to WP and ISL.

Deutscher, Isaac — Author of the best-known biography of Trotsky. Active in Polish Trotskyist movement 1932-8; stopped writing for the British Trotskyist press at fall of France in 1940. Later a writer and mainstream-press journalist. Believed Stalinism reformable. Backed the Stalinists in the East German rising of 1953 and in the Hungarian

121

revolution of 1956.

Draper, Hal — Leading writer for Workers Party and ISL until the end. In the 1950s, edited *Labor Action* and wrote a great deal of it. Later wrote the multi-volume *Karl Marx's Theory of Revolution*.

Farrell, James T — Novelist (known for the Studs Lonigan trilogy) sympathetic to the SWP and then to the Workers' Party.

Foster, William Z — Trade union activist; founder member of Communist Party USA and chief leader of it 1929-1932 and 1945-57.

Frank, E R — see Cochran

Frankel, Harry — see Braverman

Galicia — Western Ukraine: in 1939 part of Polish state

Glotzer, Albert — Founder-member of US Trotskyist movement; a leader of Workers Party/ISL after 1940 split. Prolific writer in the WP/ISL press in 1940-50. Became a social democrat.

Goldman, Albert — Also called Morrison. Trotsky's lawyer. Leading figure in SWP until 1944; oppositionist after 1944; joined Workers Party 1946; quit politics 1948.

GPU — Stalinist secret police. Called KGB after 1941, and sometimes referred to by name of "commissariat" of which it was part, NKVD. A controlling force in the Communist Parties throughout the world through its agents in their committees.

Hall, Ben — see Benson

Hansen, Joseph — Leading writer for SWP from 1940s until his death in 1979

Heterodox — Used in this book to denote the "Third Camp" Trotskyists who argued for a working-class "camp" opposed to both capitalism and Stalinism

ISL — Name of the Heterodox Trotskyist organisation after 1949. Dissolved into the Socialist Party in 1958.

Jacobs, Louis — Also known as Jack Weber or A. Roland. A founder member of US Trotskyist movement; went with majority in 1940 split; developed criticisms of SWP in 1944; quit SWP in late 1944; wrote occasionally for the WP press thereafter.

James, C L R — Activist and writer of Trinidadian origin in the Trotskyist movement in Britain from mid-30s, in USA 1938-50. With Raya Dunayevskaya, led minority in Workers Party arguing that USSR was state-capitalist. Their grouping, the "Johnson-Forrest Tendency", left the WP in 1947 and joined the SWP, then quit the SWP in 1951. James became well-known as a writer. He also used the name Johnson.

Johnson — see James

Labor Action — Weekly paper of Workers Party, then of ISL, 1940-1958

Logan — see van Heijenoort

Lore, Ludwig — An early leader of the Communist Party USA who was expelled for alleged Trotskyism, but became a freelance journalist sympathetic to the USSR and in the 1930s a spy for the USSR

Lovestone, Jay — A leader of Communist Party USA until 1929; then leader of a "Right Communist" group until 1940; later, right-wing operator in US and international trade unions using tactics learned in the Stalintern.

Macdonald, Dwight — Radical journalist, active into the 1970s. Wrote for *Socialist Appeal* before split; was a semi-detached member of Workers Party 1940-1. Edited journal *Politics* in 1944-9.

Mandel, Ernest — Also known as Germain. A leader of the Orthodox Trotskyists in Europe from before the end of World War 2 to his death in 1995. The "Karl Kautsky" of the post-war Fourth International.

Mannerheim, Gustaf — Finnish general. Chief of the White forces in Finnish civil war, 1918, and (under a social-democratic and liberal coalition government) of Finnish forces in 1939-40 Russo-Finnish war. President of Finland 1944-6, during which time he negotiated peace with the USSR and switched Finland to the Allied side in World War 2.

Martin — see Cannon

McKinney, Ernest Rice — Trade-union activist, and previously activist in African-American movements; joined Trotskyists in 1934; joined minority in 1940 split; national secretary of WP in the 1940s; quit around 1950.

Menshevik — Faction in Russian Marxist movement after 1903 split. They opposed the October 1917 workers' revolution. In the 1930s and 40s they had a sizeable exile organisation, with relatively good contacts within the USSR

Militant, The — Paper of the SWP from February 1941 (before then: *Socialist Appeal*). No relation to the British paper Militant (1964-1997).

Morrison — see Goldman

Morrow, Felix — Leading writer and speaker for SWP after 1940 split. In SWP dissident minority 1944-6. Expelled from SWP, and dropped out, 1946.

Moscow Agreement — of October 1943, between US, UK, and USSR, to continue fighting war as allies

Novack, George — Also known as William F Warde. Leading writer for SWP in 1940s and after. Only one of the "old guard" to support the new Castroist politics of SWP after 1979.

Orthodox — A self-description for the strands of Trotskyism holding more or less to variants of the ideas which would be codified by the Third Congress of the Fourth International in 1951.

Pablo, Michel — Also known as Raptis. A leader of the Orthodox Trotskyists in Europe from before the end of World War 2. Separated from the Fourth International in 1963-5 and formed his own international current, which dispersed in the 1990s, some of its activists going back to the Mandelite Fourth International.

Poland, eastern — The eastern part of the Polish state as it was in 1939, invaded by the USSR in September 1939, is sometimes referred to in the documents in this book as "eastern Poland", "west Ukraine and west Byelorussia", "Polish Ukraine", or "Polish Galicia". It was a Polish-ruled area in which most of the people were Ukrainian or Byelorussian.

Raptis, Michel — see Pablo

Rizzi, Bruno — see Bruno

Shachtman, Max — Leading figure in US and international Trotskyist movement from 1928. Leader of Workers Party and ISL after 1940. In old age, wound up trying to be a sort of "Fabian", a behind-the-scenes puller of strings in the trade union movement.

Sedova, Natalia — Trotsky's companion from 1903 to his death; active as a socialist before she met Trotsky, and after his death until her own in 1962. Severe critic of James P Cannon's current in the 1940s; broke publicly with the Fourth International in 1951.

Socialist Appeal — Paper of the SWP. Renamed *The Militant* in February 1941.

Socialist Workers Party — see SWP

Swabeck, Arne — Also known as Ben Webster, or as Simmons. Founder-member of US Trotskyist movement and close comrade of Cannon. Secretary of the organisation for a while in the 1930s. In old age, became a Maoist and was expelled from SWP in 1967 for writing a letter to Gerry Healy of the British Socialist Labour League praising their support for the Chinese Cultural Revolution.

SWP — In this book, always refers to the Socialist Workers Party USA, the name which the US Trotskyist movement took in 1937 and which the Orthodox retained after the 1940 split. No direct relation to today's SWP in Britain.

Trotsky, Natalia — See Sedova, Natalia

van Heijenoort, Jean — Also known as Daniel Logan. Trotsky's secretary for many years; member of SWP in 1940s; in SWP dissident minority with Goldman and Morrow from 1944; expelled from SWP in 1947, then quit politics; later became famous writer on mathematical logic; in old age was murdered by his wife.

Vérité, La — Main French Trotskyist paper in 1940s

Warde, William F — see Novack, George

Weber, Jack — see Jacobs, Louis

Wolfe, Bertram — A leader of Communist Party USA until 1929; member of "Right Communist" group 1929-40; later an anti-communist liberal and author of the book *Three Who Made A Revolution*.

Workers Party — Organisation of the Heterodox Trotskyists after 1940. Renamed itself Independent Socialist League (ISL) in 1949.

Wright, John G — Also known as Usick Vanzler. Leading writer for SWP from 1940 to his death in 1956.

Zinoviev, Gregory — Old Bolshevik, close collaborator of Lenin in World War One; president of Communist International until 1927; allied with Trotsky in United Opposition 1926-7, then capitulated to Stalin. Shot after first Moscow Show Trial. See also Zinovievism.

Zinovievism — The form of politics and organisation inculcated in the Communist Parties by the Communist International under Zinoviev's leadership in 1924-5. It included a drive for "monolithic" organisation and, in politics, a demagogic hunt for "deviations" and revisionists.

Trotsky explains: August 1940

125

Daily Worker, 27 June 1925

Against the stream

A discussion in April 1939 between Trotsky and C L R James [Johnson] about how the Trotskyist groups could have been right about so many political issues in the 1920 and 30s — for example in Trotsky's prescient warnings after 1930 of the Nazi threat in Germany — and yet remain so small as organisations. They discussed how those groups could rationally aspire to decisive political action.

TROTSKY: Yes, the question is why we are not progressing in correspondence with the value of our conceptions which are not so meaningless as some friends believe. We are not progressing politically. Yes, it is a fact which is an expression of a general decay of the workers' movements in the last fifteen years. It is the more general cause. When the revolutionary movement in general is declining, when one defeat follows another, when Fascism is spreading over the world, when the official "Marxism" is the most powerful organization of deception of the workers, and so on, it is an inevitable situation that the revolutionary elements must work against the general historic current, even if our ideas, our explanations, are as exact and wise as one can demand. But the masses are not educated by prognostic theoretical conception, but by the general experiences of their lives. It is the most general explanation — the whole situation is against us. There must be a turn in the class realization, in the sentiments, in the feelings of the masses; a turn which will give us the possibility of a large political success.

I remember some discussions in 1927 in Moscow after Chiang Kai shek [Chinese bourgeois nationalist leader] stilled the Chinese workers. We predicted this ten days before and Stalin opposed us with the argument that Borodin was vigilant, that Chiang Kai shek would not have the possibility to betray us, etc. I believe that it was eight or ten days later that the tragedy occurred and our comrades expressed optimism because our analysis was so clear that everyone would see it and we would be sure to win the party. I answered that the strangulation of the Chinese revolution is a thousand times more important for the masses than our predictions. Our predictions can win some few intellectuals who take an interest in such things, but not the masses. The military victory of Chiang Kai shek will inevitably provoke a depression and this is not conducive to the growth of a revolutionary faction.

Since 1927 we have had a long series of defeats. We are similar to a group who attempt to climb a mountain and who must suffer again and again a downfall of stone, snow, etc. In Asia and Europe is created a new desperate mood of the masses. They heard something analogous to what we say ten or fifteen years ago from the Communist Party and they are pessimistic. That is the general mood of the workers. It is the most general reason. We cannot withdraw from the general historic current, from the general constellation of the forces. The current is against us, that is clear. I remember the period between 1908 and 1913 in Russia. There was also a reaction. In 1905 we had the workers with us. In 1908 and even in 1907 began the great reaction.

Everybody invented slogans and methods to win the masses and nobody won them — they were desperate. In this time the only thing we could do was to educate the cadres and they were melting away. There was a series of splits to the right or to the left or to syndicalism and so on. Lenin remained with a small group, a sect, in Paris, but with confidence that there would be new possibilities of a rise. It came in 1913. We had a new tide, but then came the war to interrupt this development. During the war there was a silence as of death among the workers. The Zimmerwald [anti-war] conference was a conference of very confused elements in its majority. In the deep recesses of the masses, in the trenches and so on, there was a new mood, but it was so deep and terrorized that we could not reach it and give it an expression. That is why the movement seemed to itself to be very poor and even this element that met in Zimmerwald, in its majority, moved to the right in the next year, in the next month. I will not liberate them from their personal responsibility, but still the general explanation is that the movement had to swim against the current. Our situation now is incomparably more difficult than that of any other organization in any other time, because we have the terrible betrayal of the Communist international which arose from the betrayal of the Second International. The degeneration of the Third International developed so quickly and so unexpectedly that the same generation which heard its formation now hears us, and they say, "But we have already heard this once!"

Then there is the defeat of the Left Opposition in Russia. The Fourth International is connected genetically to the Left Opposition; the masses call us Trotskyists. "Trotsky wishes to conquer the power, but why did he lose power?" It is an elementary question. We must begin to explain this by the dialectic of history, by the conflict of classes, that even a revolution produces a reaction.

Max Eastman wrote that Trotsky places too much value on doctrine and if he had more common sense he would not have lost power. Nothing in the world is so convincing as success and nothing so repelling as defeat for the large masses. You have also the degeneration of the Third International on the one side and the terrible defeat of the Left Opposition with the extermination of the whole group. These facts are a thousand times more convincing for the working class than our poor paper with even the tremendous circulation of 5000 like the [US Trotskyists'] *Socialist Appeal*.

We are in a small boat in a tremendous current. There are five or ten boats and one goes down and we say it was due to bad helmsmanship. But that was not the reason. It was because the current was too strong. It is the most general explanation and we should never forget this explanation in order not to become pessimistic — we, the vanguard of the vanguard. There are courageous elements who do not like to swim with the current — it is their character. Then there are intelligent elements of bad character who were never disciplined, who always looked for a more radical or more independent tendency and found our tendency, but all of them are more or less outsiders from the general current of the workers' movement. Their value inevitably has its negative side. He who swims against the current is not connected with the masses. Also, the social composition of every revolutionary movement in the beginning is not of workers. It is the intellectuals, semi-intellectuals, or workers connected with the intellectuals, who are dissatisfied with the existing organizations. You find in every country a lot of foreigners who are not so easily involved in the labor movement of the country. A Czech in America or in Mexico would more easily become a member of the Fourth than in Czechoslovakia. The same for a Frenchman in the US. The national atmosphere has a tremendous power over individuals.

The Jews in many countries represent the semi-foreigners, not totally assimilated, and they adhere to any new critical, revolutionary or semi-revolutionary tendency in politics, in art, literature and so on. A new radical tendency directed against the general current of history in this period crystallizes around the elements more or less separated from the national life of any country and for them it is more difficult to penetrate into the masses. We are all very critical toward the social composition of our organization and we must change, but we must understand that this social composition did not fall from heaven, but was determined by the objective situation and by our historic mission in this period.

It does not signify that we must be satisfied with the situation. Insofar as it concerns France it is a long tradition of the French movement connected with the social composition of the country. Especially in the past the petty bourgeois mentality — individualism on the one side, and on the other an élan, a tremendous capacity for improvising.

If you compare in the classic time of the Second International you will find that the French Socialist Party and the German Social Democratic Party had the same number of representatives in parliament. But if you compare the organizations, you will find they are incomparable. The French could only collect 25,000 francs with the greatest difficulty but in Germany to send half a million was nothing. The Germans had in the trade unions some millions of workers and the French had some millions who did not pay their dues. Engels once wrote a letter in which he characterized the French organization and finished with "And as always, the dues do not arrive."

Our organization suffers from the same illness, the traditional French sickness. This incapacity to organization and at the same time lack of conditions for improvisation. Even so far as we now had a tide in France, it was connected with the Popular Front. In this situation the defeat of the People's Front was the proof of the correctness of our conceptions just as was the extermination of the Chinese workers. But the defeat was a defeat and it is directed against revolutionary tendencies until a new tide on a higher level will appear in the new time. We must wait and prepare a new element, a new factor, in this constellation.

We have comrades who came to us, as Naville and others, 15 or 16 or more years ago when they were young boys. Now they are mature people and their whole conscious life they have had only blows, defeats and terrible defeats on an international scale and they are more or less acquainted with this situation. They appreciate very highly the correctness of their conceptions and they can analyze, but they never had the capacity to penetrate, to work with the masses, and they have not acquired it. There is a tremendous necessity to look at what the masses are doing. We have such people in France. I know much less about the British situation, but I believe that we have such people there also.

Why have we lost people? After terrible international defeats we had in France a tide on a very primitive and a very low political level under the leadership of the People's Front. The People's Front — I think this whole period is a kind of caricature of our February Revolution. It is shameful that in a country like France, which 150 years ago passed through the greatest bourgeois revolution in the world, that the workers' movement should pass through a caricature of the Russian Revolution.

JOHNSON: You would not throw the whole responsibility on the Communist Party?

TROTSKY: It is a tremendous factor in producing the mentality of the masses. The active factor was the degeneration of the Communist Party.

In 1914 the Bolsheviks were absolutely dominating the workers' movement. It was on the threshold of the war. The most exact statistics show that the Bolsheviks represented not less than three-fourths of the proletarian vanguard. But beginning with the February Revolution, the most backward people, peasants, soldiers, even the former Bolshevik workers, were attracted toward this Popular Front current and the Bolshevik Party became isolated and very weak. The general current was on a very low level, but powerful, and moved toward the October Revolution. It is a question of tempo. In France, after all the defeats, the People's Front attracted elements that sympathized with us theoretically, but were involved with the movement of the masses and we became for some time more isolated than before. You can combine all these elements. I can even affirm that many (but not all) of our leading comrades, especially in old sections, by a new turn of situation would be rejected by the revolutionary mass movement and new leaders, fresh leadership will arise in the revolutionary current.

In France the regeneration began with the entry into the Socialist Party. The policy of the Socialist Party was not clear, but it won many new members. These new members were accustomed to a large milieu. After the split they became a little discouraged. They were not so steeled. Then they lost their not-so-steeled interest and were regained by the current of the People's Front. It is regrettable, but it is explainable.

In Spain the same reasons played the same role with the supplementary factor of the deplorable conduct of the Nin group. He was in Spain as representative of the Russian Left Opposition and during the first year we did not try to mobilize, to organize our independent elements. We hoped that we would win Nin for the correct conception and so on. Publicly the Left Opposition gave him its support. In private correspondence we tried to win him and push him forward, but without success. We lost time. Was it correct? It is difficult to say. If in Spain we had an experienced comrade our situation would be incomparably more favourable, but we did not have one. We put all our hopes on Nin and his policy consisted of personal manoeuvres in order to avoid responsibility. He played with the revolution. He was sincere, but his whole mentality was that of a Menshevik. It was a tremendous handicap, and to fight against this handicap only with correct formulas falsified by our own representatives in the first period, the Nins, made it very difficult.

Do not forget that we lost the first revolution in 1905. Before our first revolution we had the tradition of high courage, self-sacrifice, etc. Then we were pushed back to a position of a miserable minority of thirty, or forty men. Then came the war.

JOHNSON: How many were there in the Bolshevik Party?

TROTSKY: In 1910 in the whole country there were a few dozen people. Some were in Siberia. But they were not organized. The people whom Lenin could reach by correspondence or by an agent numbered about 30 or 40 at most. However, the tradition and the ideas among the more advanced workers was a tremendous capital which was used later during the revolution, but practically, at this time we were absolutely isolated.

Yes, history has its own laws which are very powerful, more powerful than our theoretical conceptions of history. Now you have in Europe a catastrophe, the decline of Europe, the extermination of countries. It has a tremendous influence on the workers when they observe these movements of the diplomacy, of the armies and so on, and on the other side a small group with a small paper which makes explanations. But it is a question of his being mobilized tomorrow and of his children being killed. There is a terrible disproportion between the task and the means.

If the war begins now, and it seems that it will begin, then in the first month we will lose two-thirds of what we now have in France. They will be dispersed. They are young and will be mobilized. Subjectively many will remain true to our movement. Those who will not be arrested and who will remain, there may be three or five, I do not know how many, but they will be absolutely isolated.

Only after some months will the criticism and the disgust begin to show on a large scale and everywhere our isolated comrades, in a hospital, in a trench, a woman in a village, will find a changed atmosphere and will say a courageous word. And the same comrade who was unknown in some section of Paris will become a leader of a regiment, of a division, and will feel himself to be a powerful revolutionary leader. This change is in the character of our period.

Fourth International, May 1941

Part 1: Stalinism

Socialist Appeal, 16 July 1938. (It was a Stalinist catchphrase that the USSR would "catch up with and outstrip" the West)

Socialist Appeal, 22 October 1938

1. Stalin's Russia, a socialist community?

In 1950, at the height of Stalinism's prestige, Max Shachtman debated with Earl Browder (1891-1973), who had been the general secretary of the Communist Party of the USA from 1930 to the mid-1940s, when it was at the height of its influence, with 100,000 members. In 1946 Stalin got Browder expelled from the Communist Party, using him as a scapegoat when shifting the Communist Parties from their extravagant strike-breaking and pro-Allied-government line in World War 2 to a more obstreperous stance. Browder remained broadly Stalinist in his politics. Max Shachtman (1904-1972) was the main writer of the Trotskyist movement, after Trotsky himself, in Trotsky's lifetime. In the 1940s he was one of those who developed "Third Camp" Trotskyist politics, in contrast to the Orthodox Trotskyists who sided critically with the Stalinist "camp" against the USA and its allies. In old age he wound up abandoning independent working-class politics and siding with the US-led "camp" in Vietnam, becoming a mirror image of the Orthodox Trotskyists. In 1950, it was very rare for people aligned with the Communist Parties to debate with any Trotskyist. The idea that the USSR was socialist was commonplace well beyond the CPs.

The only really existing socialism

Earl Browder (1950)

LADIES AND GENTLEMEN, friends: is Russia a socialist community? This is the question presented by our sponsors tonight, the Eugene V. Debs Society of Brooklyn College. I assume that you are not interested in the proper usage of words so much as in estimating the significance of the new society in Russia for the world and for America in particular. I will discuss history, therefore, rather than philology. I speak for myself alone as a student of Marxism, and not on behalf of any organisation. I address myself to those who seek the truth as the prime value in life. Now to our subject.

I am aware, of course, that some people deny the right of the Union of Socialist Soviet Republics to use its own chosen name. They say it is not socialist because it does not conform to their preconception as to what socialism must be like. There are many varieties of so-

Throughout the texts, insertions in square brackets [...] are editorial notes.

cialism and there is little profit in disputes as to their right to use the name. The USSR has not asked our permission to use the name socialist. It has proclaimed itself a socialist country for about 33 years, has organised the new type of economy under that name, and has achieved certain successes, for which it has paid a very heavy price. It sustained its right to existence as a socialist country by victory in the greatest of all wars.

Words are useful to explain history, but they have no primary role in determining history. On the contrary, it is history which determines the meaning of words. The only type of socialism existing in the world of fact as distinct from ideas is that of the USSR. You may like it or not, understand it or not — but there it is. It is a fact, a very important one. It is the course of prudence and wisdom to recognise facts and try to understand them. It is a question of history as to whether the new system in Russia which calls itself socialist is an entirely new variety of socialism or whether it realises a pre-existing body of ideas identified by that name. Specifically, this is the question — whether the Russians are correct in claiming their new system as a realisation of the body of ideas known as Marxism, or scientific socialism. This is a question the answer to which is capable of proof by reference to objective facts and not merely by citation of theories.

Marxism is an interpretation of history which explains the progress of society as a product of the expansion of the forces of production of the material means of life, that is, the development of economy. The stage of the development of the productive forces determines the political and ideological superstructure of society which are crystallised into a system of social organisation. The social system grows rigid but the productive forces continue to expand, and conflict ensues between the forces of production and the social conditions of production. This conflict finally reaches a stage in which a fundamental change of the social conditions becomes necessary to bring them in harmony with the continued growth of production. This is the stage which produces revolution, a relatively brief period in history in which outmoded social forms are discarded and new ones are created which free the shackled productive forces for a new leap forward in their expansion.

Marxism traces this process in past history from the primitive tribal commune through slavery, feudalism, early capitalism in the form of simple artisan manufacturing, the rise of modern capitalism in power-driven machinery, and the final stage of capitalism marked by huge trusts and monopolies and the trend toward state capitalism, in which state power becomes the collective capitalist. Marxism conceives of the new system of socialism as the necessary outcome of all previous history made possible and necessary only by that previous history. Because capitalist society has expanded the productive forces so enormously, the social conditions under which it arose lag behind and become fetters holding back the further growth of productive forces.

Socialism is nothing more nor less than the social, political and ideological system which breaks the fetters upon economic growth created under capitalism and opens the way to a new period of economic and social expansion on a much larger scale. So long as bourgeois society, that is, capitalism, reigned supreme throughout the world and dominated the lands of free capitalist development, the dispute between various schools of thought was conducted primarily on the level of theory, that is, the struggle between ideas, as to which most correctly foreshadowed the next stage of development in history which had still not appeared in fact, in life.

But in 1917 the Russian Revolution introduced a new phase, that of testing theories in their practical application in life. Socialism was introduced as a living reality. It is now to be tested not only in theory, in the mind, in thought, but also by reference to fact, to objective reality, to the real world. The question as to whether Russia is a socialist community is thus reduced to the question of fact, as to whether this new system has introduced a higher stage of economic development into the world. Since the new system has existed for one-third of a century, since it has overcome the challenges to its very existence, it may now be judged first of all by this test.

What do the facts show? Has the new system in Russia proved itself to be socialist in this Marxist sense by demonstrating a higher stage in the growth of the forces of production? In past history, it has not always been possible to give final proof of this nature in economics of the progressive character of great political changes so soon after such a change was initiated. American independence, for example, was judged by most European intellectuals throughout the 19th century as having condemned America to the status of a backward and uncivilised nation. Such a distinguished mind as that of Charles Dickens, for example, reporting on a personal visit of inspection to America, delivered the judgement of backwardness against it, which, if his premises were granted as being the decisive ones, was annihilatingly conclusive. Even American intellectuals suffered from a crippling sense of inferiority to Europe from which they have not entirely liberated themselves in 1950.

We know today, however, that Dickens and all who followed that line of judgement on America's role in world progress were profoundly mistaken. They were misled by exclusive preoccupation with secondary and irrelevant matters. Despite the handicap of lacking self-conscious understanding of her historical role, America was in the vanguard of political progress during the 19th century. What Dickens and his school of thought considered the root of American backwardness, namely, its deep cleavage from the older civilisations of Europe, was in fact the absolutely necessary precondition to realisation of America's tremendous productive potentialities which finally made America the giant of the bourgeois world, the highest expression of productive forces under the now declining capitalist system. Liberation from Europe and its outmoded social and political system alone could and did clear the ground for the free development of America's potential productive forces. This was the foundation, the moving force of America's role in the vanguard of world progress throughout the 19th century. Everything else was secondary or irrelevant to this basic consideration.

My central thesis in tonight's debate is that the role played by America in the 19th century in leading the development of the world's productive forces under capitalist society has passed to Russia in the 20th century in the development of the world's productive forces to a stage higher than capitalism, which is the foundation of socialism. The evidence which proves this thesis is known to all, even if it is still generally overlooked by Americans for much the same reasons that Dickens overlooked the American vanguard position in the 19th century, because of preoccupation with secondary matters.

The new system called socialism came to power in Russia about one-third of a century ago. It took over a backward, shattered and defeated country, the chief laggard among the great powers. It had been defeated and shattered precisely because of its backwardness, its huge heritage of medieval reaction that had crushed the potentialities of progress of its peoples for centuries, keeping its vast area and population outside the main current of historical progress. Under its new system called socialism, the Russian people and the smaller nationalities which had formerly composed the Russian Empire speedily forged ahead from last place among the great powers of Europe and Asia to a position of unchallenged pre-eminence as the first. In the whole world, only the USA is today at all comparable in power and influence with the USSR. This radical transformation of world power relationships reflects primarily in the case of both the USA and the USSR the growth of the productive forces. Not only did the new socialist system overtake and surpass all other powers in Europe and

Asia; in its rate of growth it has already surpassed America. In broad historical outline, this fact is seen in the span of 150 years required for the rise of America to its present position as one of the two world giants compared with the span of 30 years required by the USSR to make the same transition.

Let us bring this broad historical fact into closer focus and examine some of its details. Let us compare the highest rates of economic growth measured in decades of the two great powers as exhibited in manufacturing production, the heart of modern economics.

In the five decades of the 20th century, American economy experienced only two periods of relatively rapid expansion. These were concentrated in the ten years 1914-1924 and the similar period of 1938-1948. In the first, volume of manufacture rose from an index of 100 to 266, about one and two-thirds times; and in the second, when the similar index figures were 100 and 180, something less than double. These are the decades of maximum growth of American manufacturing industrial production.

The new socialist economy system went into full operation in the USSR in 1928 with the inauguration of the Five Year Plan. In the ensuing decade of 1928-1938 the growth of production in manufacturing industry is measured by the index figures of 100 and 700, a sevenfold increase, or more than four times the high American rate of the decade of 1914-1924. During the following decade of 1938-1948, Soviet socialist economy suffered the most extreme disruption and destruction ever visited upon any country in modern times through the invasion of Hitler's army. It lost about 40 per cent of its industrial area where its oldest industries were located, and when the enemy was driven out everything had been systematically destroyed, down to the individual dwellings. Its entire economy had to be switched to war production and entirely subordinated to war economy. The country went on to a military subsistence basis. Direct war losses exceeded the total capital value of the country in 1928.

Yet the socialist economy overcame these war losses and reached the end of the decade in 1948 with a net growth over 1938 of about 60 per cent, that is in the same general scale of magnitude experienced in America during the period without direct war devastation. When allowance is made for replacement of direct war losses, it is clear that the rate of growth of socialist manufacturing industry was even greater than in the previous decades.

In the light of this evidence, if the proposition is valid that the growth of productive forces is the basis for progress, then the new system in Russia called socialism is the most progressive that history has ever produced. This is progress on a hitherto unknown level. It is revolutionary progress. The economy of the USSR has satisfied the basic test of socialism that is set up by the theory of Marx and Engels in full and in a relatively short historical span of time.

Our newspapers and magazines tell us in a thousand variations that Soviet production figures are mere Potemkin villages built by Bolshevik propaganda. It is true, of course, that statistics can be falsified. But Soviet statistics of production were confirmed in resistance to the Nazi invasion backed up by the industry of conquered Europe. Modern war is first of all a battle of production. When Hitler lost the war, those who denied the validity of Soviet production records lost their argument. Artillery, planes and tanks were the direct means whereby the war was won. Such things as modern armaments, including atom bombs, do not come from falsified statistics. They are produced only by modern industry with the highest technique, with the most highly skilled labour, and with the most advanced and socially organised science. For all these things have come into existence so recently and so rapidly, and so little was inherited from a previous stage of development, they prove the existence of a progressive society of the highest order able to readjust itself quickly to changing social problems and conditions. They presuppose a rapidly rising standard of literacy and education, stable and improving conditions of life for the masses and the other most necessary accompaniments of progress. They guarantee continued peacetime progress.

Many Americans fail to correlate the different parts of their thinking. They believe simultaneously that the USSR is powerful and that it is backward and unprogressive. But a backward, unprogressive nation cannot become powerful. A nation that has become powerful can turn blackly reactionary. That is what happened to Germany under Hitler and might happen to America to the same full extent if the American people do not stop the process.

But if Russia under her new system was really as pictured by official American propaganda today, or by my opponent, she could no more master all the elements of economic progress and develop them to a higher stage than could Chiang Kai-shek in China. Political reaction puts a halt to all progress, as American science is feeling so keenly today under the hysteria of the current Red scare. Political reaction results in a decline of power, not its rise. Reaction can only loot the treasures produced by the past but cannot create new ones.

It is true that the economic progress of the new socialist system is not fully translated at once into the abundance of the luxuries of life. Life remains hard and austere in Russia. The main bulk of the economic gains go to the support and development of three phases of Soviet life which are not included in the average American's conception of the good life. These are, first, the expansion of the means of production, that which in capitalist America we call accumulation of capital and in which the average citizen here plays no conscious part. Second, an enormous expansion and intensification of public education in science. And third, the guarantee of national security by a military establishment able to meet all possible dangers. From the point of view of the Soviet peoples, these three are the supreme necessities of life, and their satisfaction by the new socialist system is the final proof to them of its superiority. If these things had not been always their first consideration, the result would have been that Hitler would today be ruling them and the world. They are, therefore, willing to wait a while for fine clothes, rich foods, refrigerators and radios in every home, and all those lighter amenities of life which make up the popular concept of good living that has been created for America, not so much by their enjoyment directly by the people as by the influence of Hollywood movies.

The Cold War that rages between the USA and the USSR hinges primarily around the American refusal to recognise the Soviet requirements of national security, and as this Cold War has developed it has become an official American policy, a crusade to halt the spread of socialism in other countries. The world is being organised in two blocs between which there is constantly diminishing practical contact and understanding. This is the major problem for America and the world today. The Cold War is bringing more hardships to the American people, and if not halted may well bring catastrophes, if not of war itself, then of economic crisis which might be almost as damaging.

It is folly to expect to solve the Cold War by preaching the desirability of socialism to America. But it is an essential contribution to bringing this war to an end, to spread a more realistic understanding of what the new socialist system really is, and the facts about the relationship of forces between the socialist and capitalist parts of the world. It is certainly not impossible to rouse and organise an effective public opinion that will demand and secure a halt to and eventually a settlement of the Cold War. But mutual vilification of Russia and America certainly is not a serious contribution to anything, not even to a real struggle between the two. I must sadly admit that I have no complete blueprint for achieving peace between Soviet socialism and American capitalism. But I do know what are some of the essential conditions for such a peace. First of all, I know what all America is slowly beginning to recognise, that war as a method of attempting to settle the disputes involved has become entirely impractical for either side. A military decision of the rivalry between capitalism and socialism is impossible. No one can win a war of world proportions. War was scientifically defined in former times as the continuation of policy by military means. But this definition is no longer accurate. A major war today makes sense for no conceivable policy. It means only a collapse of policy. The advance of military technique has reached the point at which between major powers it can bring only mutual extermination of mass populations. Between the major camps in the world there exists a military stalemate. If there is not to be war, then peace must be organised.

The Trotskyite slogan of neither war nor peace was always stupid. But today it serves the suicidal war party to quiet the people while moving surreptitiously toward war. There is no condition of peace in the world until its main terms in state relationships have been defined and generally accepted. The terms of such a peace cannot be dictated by either side of the present Cold War, and America must understand that it is impossible to deny to the USSR those measures of security which the USSR considers essential and already has the power to take over by her own unilateral action if necessary. Among these measures are the elimination of Germany and Japan as bases for possible hostilities against the USSR. It may be difficult for Americans, who have not experienced hostile armies on our soil since the War of 1812 with England, to understand the importance of this to Russia, who suffered major attacks from her neighbours twice in one generation. For our own good, we should make an effort of the imagination as to what lengths America would go, placed in a similar situation, to guarantee that Germany and Japan would not be able to invade a third time.

A defined peace settlement between the great powers is thus a modus vivendi, a way of living together without war between antagonistic systems. It is no refutation of this idea to say that the two systems are irreconcilable. America herself was founded on two irreconcilable systems within the body of a single nation, the system of commodity production by free labour, and the system of slavery, with an unstable and explosive modus vivendi between them. The terms of such a problem were very fully explored in American history, where for several generations the central theme of wisdom and statesmanship was to maintain this modus vivendi, to reconcile the irreconcilable. Without this wisdom and statesmanship of early American leaders, the American continent would have been Balkanised for a century, and world progress would have received a major setback. It would have been historic folly and irresponsibility to demand a showdown settlement between the two systems as a condition for establishment of the United States as a single nation. It will be equally folly and irresponsibility to demand the final conflict between capitalism and socialism as the condition for the establishment of a functioning United Nations organisation under a defined peace settlement.

As matters stand now, America is losing battle after battle of the Cold War. This fact, after several years in which our statesmen and newspapers assured us of victory after victory, is now being generally recognised. So long as the USA was supposed to be winning the Cold War, we were assured that peace was not necessary. Now that the USA is admittedly losing the war, we are told that peace must wait until the US is winning again. According to these formulae from our supposedly wise men, the time to make peace will never come, until the Soviet Union runs up the white flag and agrees to accept a counsellor appointed by Washington. If King George III had adopted a similar position toward the revolting American colonies in the last years of the 19th century, he would have been much more realistic than the present American attitude toward the Soviet Union which was never our colony — and may I predict never will be? King George III knew when he was licked, and signed a peace treaty, which did not prevent Great Britain from enjoying some years of prosperity thereafter. And today the British themselves, in accepting largesse from America, congratulate us on having won the War of Independence, proving thereby that the political passions of a historical moment do not last forever.

The main problem of the world today is peace. This problem has different connotations for different countries. For much of Europe the struggle for peace has become indissolubly united in the immediate struggle for socialism. In America the struggle for peace has an immediacy that is not shared by the issue of socialism. For America the realisation of these two goals is not to be achieved at the same time, even though both are a part of the same continuous historical process. In America all adherents of socialism have the duty to fight for peace as a form of co-existence of the two systems, capitalism and socialism. It is fortunately a fact that the leaders and spokesmen of the new socialist system in the Soviet Union clearly recognise the historical necessity for a long-term peaceful co-existence of the two systems, organised in business-like and mutually beneficial relations between the states involved, as a basic component of Soviet policy. This fact is itself further evidence of the socialist, in the Marxist sense, character of the new system in Russia. Socialism developed on Marxist principles is essentially peaceful. It has no urge toward war, and finds no profit in it. It justifies and supports wars of national liberation, and wars of defence against reactionary invasion. It does not justify war as an instrument for the spread of socialism to unwilling and unprepared peoples and nations. Socialism is not a commodity for export and import. Socialism cannot be imposed on the points of bayonets. Socialism must be firmly grounded in the material conditions and the history of each major nation before it can be realised there. Socialism requires the free choice of conscious people as the main condition for its realisation. These are fundamental principles of the Marxist theory of socialism, and these principles are deeply imbedded in the new society that has arisen in Russia under the banner of Marx and his disciples. What conditions does America, continuing under capitalism, require from a peace settlement in order that it shall be mutually beneficial to both sides? What America needs above all, without the slightest doubt, is to have markets for the surplus products of her industry and fields of investment for surplus capital, both of which far exceed the capacity of the domestic market. That is indeed the aim of the Cold War, to obtain such markets by conquest and subjugation, by all means of coercion short of shooting war and by the threat of shooting war. This type of market is the traditional one of the past, but it is no longer possible to achieve. Markets on the scale America requires can only be organised by agreement, not seized by power. Such markets must be mutually beneficial to all the peoples involved, not merely to America. Such markets cannot be gained by crusading against socialism, but only by co-operating with socialism, which must be an essential and growing part of those markets. The Cold War, or any conceivable hot war, cannot produce the needed markets for America. But a durable peace with the socialist part of the world can and will do so. Peace, and only peace, will open up the markets of the world on a new and larger scale than ever before — the rise of socialism has enlarged the world market, not diminished it — once America is ready to make peace with socialism, instead of trying to wipe it out.

One of the most confusing things about our American ruling class in modern times is its habit, when it is about to embark upon some historic line of development, to firmly proclaim to the world its determination to do the exact opposite. Thus, at the opening of the 20th century, America adopted the Sherman anti-trust law, which declared trusts and monopolies in industry to be outside the law, to be destroyed. This step initiated a period of the most feverish growth of the greatest trusts and monopolies the world has ever seen. The more these monopolies dominate American life, all the more does the American bourgeoisie pledge its allegiance to the ideology of free enterprise, of which monopolies are the negation.

When the Second World War was shaping up, and during its first period of the phoney war, it was certain that America would be in it. The only uncertainty was which side America would be on. The American ruling class solemnly and emphatically proclaimed neutrality in its determination not to join the war under any conditions. The rule seems to be that the American bourgeoisie firmly and resolutely faces the past and then moves into the future by backing up. Under this rule, we may possibly assume the present war-like attitude of the American bourgeoisie really represents its preparation to move into peace, backward as usual. We may say of this method, not that it is the best one, but that it is better to make progress by moving backward than not to make progress at all. The technique of backing into the future is possible only for an established ruling class with a great apparatus of power under its control. It is not at all suitable for a democratic mass movement of the people, the leadership of which must make crystal-clear the immediate objectives for which it fights. It is a fatal weakness for a democratic mass movement to permit any ambiguity in the definition of its immediate goals.

In the fight for peace and the mobilisation of the American masses for peace, we may set the immediate goal as the establishment of peaceful coexistence of two systems, or we may declare that peace can be achieved only by establishing socialism in America. The first aim, properly, energetically and intelligently pursued has the possibility of raising a powerful peace movement in America that will influence the course of history. The second course, while it has much lower potentialities of immediate power and influence, is at least intelligible even if mistaken in its judgement.

But to try to combine both aims in one single mass movement, as seems to be taking place in America, produces nothing but chaos, confusion and disunity among the masses. It produces a combination of the weakest sides of both approaches and loses the strength of both. It produces a movement of the limited aim of the first and the limited mass influence of the second: it is a sterile hybrid. That is why in America we have the most tremendous, diffused and unorganised peace sentiments and aspirations but the most pitifully weak organised mass movement for peace. Only political idiots can believe that socialism can be smuggled into America, that this country can be backed into socialism, manoeuvred into a fundamentally new system of society without its own knowledge. There are such idiots, of course, on both the Right and Left, and their influence makes of American politics a bedlam of confused babbling. They dominate the newspaper headlines, even if not the thinking of the country. They run the party machines, they write the slogans of the day.

But when socialism comes to America, it will not be through the back door. It will come only when a Marxist party, having won the confidence of the working class through its correct leadership in the struggle for all progressive measures short of socialism, is able further to convince the majority of the country that socialism, that is, the social ownership and operation of the means of production, has become necessary also in America. Are there steps which the country takes toward socialism without knowing it? Yes, of course, there are. Everything of a progressive nature is a step toward socialism. Even the building of every new great modern factory is a step toward socialism. If Mr. Taft and Mr. Dewey want to halt all steps toward socialism, they will have to pass a law against the building of modern industry. These are the most powerful steps toward socialism that are being taken in America today.

But a socialist society is not created by steps toward socialism. Socialism is a result of conscious social building, planned and conducted by the organised workers who have won political power and supported by the majority of the population. There are no short cuts and no new routes by which America can reach socialism. Every country must find its own path and its own forms for the transitions of history, but in the finding of its own path and its own forms, it will be working out the universal laws of social development, and it will not be going in violation of those laws, which are the laws of science, not the decrees of some political authority.

Yes, the new system of social organisation in Russia, the Union of Socialist Soviet Republics, is socialist, the kind of socialism of which Marx and Engels conceived as the inevitable product of historical progress. We in America have much to learn from it as the first manifestation of socialism in life, in history. We will learn, however, through thinking, and not through imitation. Those who wish us to imitate the Soviet Union would follow the method of the old chicken farmer who, to encourage his hens to lay bigger and better eggs, hung the egg of an ostrich above their nests on which was a placard reading: "Look at this and do your best." That system does not work with chickens; it will not work with men.

Stalin murdered the socialists

Max Shachtman (1950)

MR. CHAIRMAN, COMRADES and friends: I have been waiting for an occasion like this for a long time — more than twenty years! Like so many of you, I have waited patiently for a free and public debate between a revolutionary socialist and a spokesman of the Communist Party, authorised to defend the position that the Stalinist regime in Russia represents a socialist society.

It seems that the only way you can get a Stalinist to defend this position in fair debate, like tonight, is when he has been cast out of the inner darkness into the outer light, and branded publicly as an agent of capitalism and as an enemy of the Soviet Union. So, for a debate with the genuine article, we must still wait patiently, or, rather, impatiently. Meanwhile, beggars can't be choosers: I must content myself with the second-hand article, the somewhat used (applause) — don't take away my time, please — the somewhat used, or, as I read the *Daily Worker,* the somewhat abused article.

I am not here debating this evening — that was not my understanding of the subject — war or peace. Any time Mr. Browder is ready to debate that with me, 24 hours' notice will suffice. I can state, and it will be adequate for the purpose tonight, that our organisation and I with it are uncompromisingly opposed to the Cold War, uncompromisingly opposed to American imperialism, to American capitalism, to the American capitalist regime and to the American capitalist ruling class, uncompromisingly opposed to the atom bomb or its use. We didn't endorse it in the last war; we didn't approve of it in the last war. And if Mr. Browder is prepared to debate that, I will also give him an answer on the "stupid Trotskyist slogan of neither peace nor war" that he won't forget for a year.

Our debate simply concerns one of the most vital questions of our time — indeed, the most vital question, and I start on it from these fundamental considerations: if the cold horror of Stalinist despotism, that vast prison camp of peoples and nations, represents the victory of socialism, then we are lost; then the ideal of socialist freedom, justice, equality, and brotherhood has proved to be an unattainable Utopia; then the National Association of Manufacturers is right in saying that while capitalism is not perfect and has a couple of defects here and there, socialism is a new slavery; then we must be resigned to that appalling decay of modern civilisation that is eating away the substance of human achievement. But if it can be shown that Stalinist Russia is not socialism, that it has nothing in common with socialism, that it is only another and very ominous lesson of what happens to society when the working class fails to fight, and extend its fight, for socialism, or when its fight is arrested or crushed; if it can be shown that Stalinist Russia is a new barbarism which results precisely from our failure up to now to establish a socialist society, to extend the Revolution of 1917 that took place in Russia — then, despite the agony that grips the world today, there is a hope and a future for the socialist emancipation of the race. It is from that standpoint and no other that I will seek to show that Stalinist Russia has nothing at all in common with socialism. The best way to begin is by defining socialism.

Socialism is based upon the common ownership and democratic control of the means of production and exchange, upon production for use as against production for profit, upon the abolition of all classes, all class divisions, class privilege, class rule, upon the production of such abundance that the struggle for material needs is completely eliminated, so that humanity, at last freed from economic exploitation, from oppression, from any form of coercion by a state machine, can devote itself to its fullest intellectual and cultural development. Much can perhaps be added to this definition, but anything less you can call whatever you wish, but it will not be socialism.

Now, if this definition is correct — as it has been considered by every socialist from the days of Marx to the days of Lenin — then there is not only not a trace of socialism in Russia, but it is moving in a direction which is the very opposite of socialism.

It is absolutely true that by their revolution in 1917 the Russian working class, under the leadership of the Bolsheviks, took the first great, bold, inspiring leap toward a socialist society. And that alone, regardless of what happened subsequently, justified it and made it a historic event that can never be eliminated from the consciousness of society. But it is likewise true that the working class of Russia was hurled back, it was crushed, and fettered and imprisoned, and that every achievement of the revolution, without exception, was destroyed by the victorious counter-revolution of the Stalinist bureaucracy which now rules the Russian empire with totalitarian absolutism. Let's examine a few decisive aspects of life in Stalinist Russia as it is, not in the propagandist mythology but in the incontrovertible reality.

The most heavily emphasised claims — we heard them here only tonight — of Stalinism are based upon the tremendous growth of industry. The figures are exaggerated; the figures are juggled and twisted; but I don't have the time to dwell upon that, and I have no need to do so. I will simply grant without hesitation that under Stalinist rule, under Stalinist rule, Russia has experienced a vast increase in the industrialisation of the urban and rural economy. But I will add the following comments which will throw some light on the social significance of this increase:

First: if we were to accept every single one of the exaggerated figures on industrialisation in Russia, how would that prove that there is socialism in Russia? At the end of the 19th century, over 50 years ago, Russia in six years more than doubled her production of cast iron and steel, almost doubled her production of coal, naphtha. Lenin wrote at that time — I am quoting him — "The progress in the mining industry is more rapid in Russia than in Western Europe and even in North America.... In the last few years the production of cast metal has tripled." And so on and so forth. Russian industrial output under the Czar doubled between the Russo-Japanese War and the beginning of the World War. The Czar built the Trans-Siberian, for example, the longest railway in the world. But that didn't show that Russia was a "socialist community" — it was what it was, Czarist autocracy.

Between 1932 and 1937, according to the official Stalinist statistics, the total value of the Russian heavy-industry products increased 238 per cent. That's impressive. But in the very same period, 1932-1937, heavy-industry production in Japan — a country far less endowed with population and natural resources — increased by 176 per cent. That, too, is impressive. But nobody thought of saying — nobody, I hope, will — that this proves the existence of socialism, or — to be statistically exact — three-fourths socialism in Japan.

The Communist Manifesto over a hundred years ago went out of its way to pay tribute to the bourgeoisie which, as it said, "has accomplished wonders far surpassing Egyptian pyramids, Roman aqueducts and Gothic cathedrals," but Marx and Engels didn't, therefore, call capitalist society a socialist community. We will see in a minute what wonders the Stalinist bureaucracy has accomplished and what it has surpassed. The statistics of production by themselves tell us nothing whatever about the social nature of production.

Second: Labour productivity, in industry and agriculture, to this hour is much lower in Russia than it is in the United States, the outstanding capitalist country in the world, which, from the socialist standpoint, i.e., this capitalism of ours — is exceedingly backward. According to *Planned Economy* for December, 1940, the Russian miner, in spite of the vicious speed-up system of Stakhanovism, produced less than half the tonnage of the American (370 tons as against 844).

What's more, while production in an American mine is three times as large as in a comparable Russian mine, the latter uses eleven times as many technicians, twice as many miners, three times as many office workers, and twelve times as large a supervisory staff. Twelve times as large a supervisory staff! — wherever you go, the dead hand of bureaucratism in Russia!

According to another journal, *Problems of Economy* for January, 1941, agricultural labour in America exceeds the productivity of the Russian kolkhoznik: 6.7 times in the production of wheat, 7.7 times in oats, 8.1 times in sugar beets, 3.1 times in milk and 20.1 times in wool. Now, the function of technique is what? It's to economise human labour, and nothing else. Socialism must guarantee society a higher economy of time than is guaranteed by capitalism, but by capitalism at its best! Otherwise socialism represents no advance. What kind of socialism is it where the productivity of labour is so inferior to that which prevails in an advanced capitalist state?

Third: Browder wrote a book a few years ago — *What is Communism?* I read it — a very radical book. He referred to the construction of Boulder Dam, to the fact that Roosevelt was very proud of it. What did Browder ask in commenting on that? He said, this dam, achievements similar to it — what have they contributed to the material welfare of the American workers? That's the challenge he threw in the face of the American bourgeoisie in connection with Boulder Dam. Legitimate question to ask of it. It's not less but more legitimate to ask it of those who claim that the industrialisation in Russia is socialist in character, that the big technological advances there prove that Russia is a socialist community. And is that not what we are discussing right now? Now let's look — official figures.

I want to emphasise first of all that I'll not refer to Russia during or since the devastation of the country by the war. I will refer to 1939 and the years before it. It makes no difference really. As early as 1935 the Stalinists officially announced that socialism had already been established in Russia — and irrevocably at that!

At the end of the Second Five Year Plan, in 1937, the output of steel was four times as great as in 1913, the last pre-World War I year in Russia — dairy products lower than 1913; petroleum products three times higher than 1913 — tea was available only to one-third the extent of 1913. There's a big airplane industry, non-existent in Czarist Russia, absolutely. But in 1912, Russia had 1,166,000 department stores, wholesale units and retail shops, which the consumer depends upon — while on October 1, 1937, according to *Planned Economy* of 1938, issue No.2, with a population far greater — no less than

160,000,000 — there were only 228,000 distribution stores and 98,000 warehouses. The plan for rolled steel was completed almost 100 per cent; they now have a big chemical industry; but the plan for the production of soap was not even 40 per cent completed. Browder refers so lightly, as we Americans can, to radios and refrigerators, and television, and other Hollywood products, that even we don't really enjoy and that the Russians don't care about. Tea, we're talking about, not television sets! Soap! The production of machines is twenty times as high as in 1918, at the end of the Second Five-Year Plan. But wages were lower than in pre-war Russia — real wages.

Which brings me to my fourth comment: The only valid criterion for socialist industrialisation — and we're not talking about industrialisation in general, are we? We're talking about whether Russia is a socialist community — the only valid criterion, I repeat, for that, is the improved economic welfare of the workers — that's a minimum, that's basic. What's happened to wages — what's happened to real wages — under Stalinist rule? In other words, what's the real standard of living for the masses under Stalinism — not in terms of television sets, not in terms of radios, refrigerators, and Buick automobiles. No, not many workers have them here, not as many as should. We're talking about ordinary standard of living. Have real wages kept pace with the growth of industrialisation, which has been great — with the growth of production, which has been great — with the growth of the national income, which has been great? By Stalin's official figures or any official figures? No, they have declined! The real facts are hard to find in the official Stalinist press, which does everything to conceal and twist them out of shape. The Stalinist press for years has not published one single line officially about prices of commodities. You don't find that there. But although it's hard to find, it's not impossible. I will take my figures only from the Stalinist press, in Russia.

According to *Pravda*, May 14, 1938, the average wage of workers in 1938 was 259 rubles a month. Bear that figure in mind. That's *Pravda*. What could the Russian worker buy with this wage? What could he do with it? Inadvertently *Pravda* itself tells us. On April 8, 1938, it reports that food for a patient in a Moscow hospital costs 7 rubles a day, that is, 210 rubles a month. On May 17th of the same year, it says, and I quote, "The fee for a child in a Pioneer camp should not be more than the cost of maintenance, 250 to 350 rubles a month." Now everybody knows that hospitals and children's camps do not provide the richest variety of food, the best food. Not at all. Everybody knows that hospitals purchase in large quantities; they purchase collectively, they prepare collectively. Things are cheaper. If a hospital patient requires for food 210 rubles a month, if a kid in a Pioneer camp requires from 250 to 350 rubles a month for food, what could the Russian worker buy with an average wage of 259 rubles a month? That's not after the Hitler invasion; that's in 1938, after socialism had irrevocably been established in Russia. The average is wretched, but it doesn't yet tell the whole story, because we have to find out what are the extremes. Averages are the most deceptive things in the world sometimes.

What about inequality? There is no country in the world, bar none, where inequality is as great, as deep, as extensive as it is in Stalinist Russia — nowhere. In the United States, the spread between the poorest-paid and the best-paid worker is what — three to one, four to one, and, in extreme cases, five to one? Is it much more than that — in extreme cases? — between the best paid and the poorest paid? In Russia, according to a very objective and fair economist and statistician, Dr. Abram Bergson, in his book on *The Structure of Russian Wages*, in October 1934 — I am quoting him now — "the earnings of the highest paid Soviet worker were more than 28.3 times the earnings of the lowest paid worker at that time." And it's much worse today. 1947, average annual wage: 7,100 rubles. The Stalinist press reports all the time earnings of some workers between 10 and 15 thousand rubles a month, that is, 120 to 180 thousand a year, when the average is 7,100. Typical report is in *Trud*, the labour paper, so-called, for January 1, 1949, which reports that three Donbas miners averaged 60 to 75 thousand rubles for the three years 1946-1948. Now if with the lowest paid the average is 7,100, is it an exaggeration to assume that the lowest paid do not go over 3,000? That makes a ratio of what between the lowest paid and the highest paid? — anywhere from 50 or 60 to 1! Find me a working class anywhere in the world that shows that disparity. Now if that's how it is among workers, imagine the gap between workers and the ruling class — the factory directors, the managers, the army and navy officers, the brass, the millionaire kolkhozniks, as they call them in the Stalinist press, the bureaucrats of all varieties, stripes, ranks, sizes and weights!

The Russian Revolution established the socialist principle: no official is to be paid more than the average worker — the skilled worker, if you wish; no functionary, no official. That's the principle of the Commune, said Lenin. Marx praised that principle, as the only socialist standard. That's one of the means, he repeated a thousand times, for shattering bureaucratism, for making possible rotation in office, for introducing workers' democracy as the prelude to socialist democracy. No official above that of the skilled worker in income. And then he added later on, when the problems became a little more complex than he had imagined, if we have to pay a lot more to bourgeois "spetzes," the specialists — he repeated that a hundred times later on — it is only because we are forced to. But, he said, that's not socialism; that's a concession to capitalism, that's a violation of the socialist principle, the Commune principle; that's a retreat from socialism! There are a thousand quotations from Lenin, and I refer to them not because they are quotations but because they are correct.

What did Stalinism do to this Commune principle, this principle of Bolshevism? We have already seen the division of the workers into paupers at one end and aristocrats at the other. What about the ruling classes themselves, the bureaucracy of all shades? Here is the decree of January 17, 1938. (Remember the average worker is earning an average in that year of 259 rubles a month, according to *Pravda*.) The decree provides that deputies, deputies, that is hand-raisers, Russian Gil Greens, get a thousand rubles a month, plus 150 rubles expenses for every day's session they attend; presidents of the eleven federated republics, as they are jocularly called in Russia, get 12,500 rubles a month; presidents and vice-presidents of the Union get 25,000 a month. What does that mean, that figure? One hundred times more than the average worker's wage, 100 times more! A 10,000 per cent increase as over the average wage of the worker! That's socialism? Why, John L. Lewis would almost break his back getting that kind of socialism! Show me such a spread in that miserable capitalist-exploited United States — and that's what it still is! Wouldn't the National Association of Manufacturers be delighted with such a differential in this country? The only thing they'd have to worry about is to conceal their delight. It would be too, too revealing, would it not? That's what you call socialism? You make a mockery of that ideal!

In 1939, Marshal Voroshilov — under socialism we have marshals! living ones and dead ones! — Voroshilov announced publicly that a lieutenant in what they jocularly call the Red Army is to get 625 rubles a month, a colonel 2,000 a month. Now, relatively speaking, is an American colonel better off, as compared to the average worker's wage in this country? Not at all. Between 1934 and 1939, according to official statistics, wages for workers increased, nominally, 120 per cent; for army lieutenants, 240 per cent; for generals 305 per cent. I say nothing about the exceptional privileges that the bureaucracy, including the brass, enjoys in Russia. You call that socialism? Is that what you expect to introduce into this country, openly or behind the back, or any other way? Go peddle your socialism to the Pentagon Building!

When the Russian workers yearn for greater equality, what does Stalin, the leader of the country, say? He answers to this at the 17th Congress of the Party in 1934, that it is, and I'm quoting — this is the leader of socialism, its spokesman and idealist, its best disciple — it's "a reactionary, petty bourgeois absurdity worthy of a primitive sect of ascetics but not of a socialist society organised on Marxian lines." That's what the yearning for equality is. Naturally, the applause from the assembled bureaucrats was deafening! It would be just as deafening and enthusiastic at a convention of the National Association of Manufacturers, wouldn't it, if you could get anybody to advocate it openly there. And that's where it belongs, and it also belongs in a convention of the Stalinist ruling class, the collectivist bureaucracy. It's an abomination to socialism.

There is not a working class in a single modern country — modern country — that's as brutally exploited as the working class of Russia, not one as cynically disfranchised and deprived of its elementary rights. The Russian worker has no trade unions. The Russian worker cannot determine hiring and firing — forbidden by law — wage scales, working days, working conditions. Trade unions are pure and simple speed-up organisms of the state. And what organisms! I quote, just typical, believe me, from *Izvestia* of May 16, 1937, that the central trade union committees are composed entirely of appointed officials. What's Lewis got that they haven't got? We hear from Andreyev, a Political Bureau member, in *Pravda* of December 9, 1935, and I'm quoting: "The wage scale must be left entirely in the hands of — whom, under socialism, whom? — the heads of industry. They must establish the norm." No wonder unions hold no conventions and leaders are appointed by the state. In no modern country do the workers have to endure the regime applied to the Russian workers.

Every worker must carry a labour book. Are we to have that under socialism in this country, introduced in the back door, the front door, or whatever door you want to? It was first introduced by the imitation Bonaparte, Napoleon III, in 1854. It was introduced into Germany in 1935 by whom? Hitler! And you've got it now in Russia, don't you? It lists all your fines, your dismissals from work with the reason therefor, your insubordinations.

The decree of September 24, 1930, reaffirmed on August 11, 1940, in the Russian press, not in the press of the NAM, says that workers are forbidden to leave their factory without permission of the employer, the boss, the director; violation of that is desertion, and the penalties go up to 10 years in prison.

The decree of October 11, 1930, renewed January 1941: Worker must accept work wherever he is ordered to be or to go.

Decrees of December 16, 1932, reaffirmed June 26, 1940: Absence from work without justification can be punished by dismissal, involving loss of the so-called trade union card and lodging; three latenesses totalling 20 minutes per month are equal to an absence.

The Czar, the Czar — not the socialist one, the real one — had the system of internal passports. The revolution abolished them, because, as they said — the Bolsheviks said — it's a police means for oppressing the people. Naturally, Stalinism reintroduced the internal passport on December 27, 1932. It exists to this day. It lists your parents, your grandparents, their class position and social activity; the members of your present family; the divorce record of the bearer; dismissals from work, the reasons for them; organisations you belong to; decorations, if any; dates of subscriptions to the "voluntary" loans, and how much you subscribed. Without stamped authorisation on your internal passport, you cannot take a train out of the city, you cannot move from one city to another, you cannot be absent from home for more than 24 hours at a stretch. And permission is granted only by the bureau of the GPU in the factory. You cannot leave the country without authorisation; you cannot get authorisation.

On June 6, 1934, they adopted a new decree on "flight" abroad, that is, leaving the country without permission which you can't get. It's punishable by death, and if there are extenuating circumstances — ten years in prison. That's a permanent, not a wartime, regulation. It's not applied to the military personnel but to the civilian population.

Article III provides, under the socialism of Stalin, that if adult members of the military personnel family helped him to flee abroad, or failed to denounce him to the authorities in time, five to ten years in prison for them, with loss of wealth. Other members of the traitor's family living with him or dependent on him, even if they knew nothing about the preparations for the flight — this is Article III — lose their citizenship and get five years in Siberia. It's the system of hostages, in peacetime, for the civilian population. Tell me another country in the world that has it.

The Czarist regime, the regime of Nicholas the Bloody, abolished capital punishment for all crimes except assaults on the Czar, political assassination. In Stalinist Russia, they have the death penalty for counterfeiting gold or silver money; acts of sabotage — and almost anything is interpreted as that; for strikes in enterprises, death penalty: for illegal slaughter of cattle, death penalty.

On April 7, 1935, another decree. As reported in *Izvestia*, for example: All children from 12 years upward, guilty of theft, violence, murder or attempted murder, go to criminal courts and may be punished to the full limit of the law, which includes the highest measure of social defence, which is translated, as you know, as execution. From 12 years on. Am I vilifying Stalinist Russia? I'm giving you a photograph of it. Where else will you find such barbarism?

The workers have no rights! The workers live in terror! If I'm told, by the way, I almost forgot — if I'm told: but how do you explain, didn't they whip Hitler? Doesn't that show superiority? Doesn't that show it's socialism? — I'm aghast! The most powerful army in Europe at the beginning of the 19th century was whose? Napoleon's! The man who spread bourgeois rule over feudal Europe. Napoleon! The Grand Army of the Republic! Who whipped him? Czar Alexander, with his serf army, with his Marshal Suvorov. They fought well, didn't they? Does that prove that bigoted, semi-feudal, backward, Czarist Russia of the early 19th century was socialist, or that Czar Alexander was the best disciple of Lenin, or that he was the sun who radiates light throughout the world, as you read about Stalin in the Stalinist press, or that he created the world, as you read about Stalin in the Stalinist press? No he was the Czar, the autocrat of all the Russias.

Bernard Shaw went to Russia in 1931 and he made a broadcast about his visit to the United States, and here is what he said — listen: "A considerable share of the secret of the success of Russian Communism consists in the fact that every Russian knows that if he will not make his life a paying enterprise for his country, then he will most likely lose it. An agent of the GPU will take him by the shoulder and will conduct him to the cellar of this famous department and he will simply stop living. And his relatives will be politely informed that they need have no anxiety about him because he's not coming home any more." Who am I quoting — a vilifier of Russia? A man who wants to create war, not peace? Bernard Shaw! And where do I take it from, this excerpt? *Pravda*, May 13, 1932, where it is printed without one word of comment!

We hear a lot about housing. I wish I had the time. Housing conditions have grown worse for the workers under Stalinism. The legal minimum is a miserable six square meters, about six by ten feet, per person, the minimum required for hygiene. Nizhni Novgorod, about which we have figures from the Stalinist press: five by seven, as compared with larger quarters before, in 1928. Moscow: average floor space, habitable floor space in 1937, a decline as against 1928. But on March 9, 1936, *Izvestia*, Mr Dyelukin, the Moscow construction chief, announced that in 1937 the city will build 400 buildings with apartments of two or five main rooms, with latest improvements and servants' rooms of six square meters, with master rooms of from 12 to 24 square meters. Who's that for? Who? The worker? The skilled worker? The workers live, as everybody in Russia calls them, in "coffins."

We hear a lot about rest homes. I hope it will be referred to, then I will refer to it in my rebuttal. We'll see what the rest homes are like, and who they're for, and who enjoys them, and what kind there are for the heads of industry, and for the workers who get them. The Russians like to employ a phrase: gynat e peregnyat, catch up with and outstrip! Catch up with and outstrip the capitalist world. In inequality, gynat e peregnyat, far exceeding anything that we know in any modern country. Don't insult the good name of socialism by applying it to this brutal regime of exploitation and social inequality.

Lenin wrote early that the legislation on women alone would justify the Bolshevik revolution. He was right. It was the most advanced in the world, admired not only by socialists but by every sincere reformer. What has Stalinism done to the status of Russian women? Take two things, which are not only sufficient by themselves, but which amply and accurately reflect the whole social structure, the whole social situation of women under Stalin.

First, divorce: Engels said, and so rightly, a long time ago, when love is at an end, "a separation becomes a blessing for both parties and for society." Under socialism, he said, "humanity will be spared the useless wading through the mire of a divorce court." Lenin said, and not once, it is impossible to be a socialist and a democrat without immediately demanding complete freedom of divorce.

On July 8, 1944, there is a decree, printed next day in *Izvestia*, and what does it do? It reforms the divorce laws. Now you have to go through two courts and drag your case through the mire, and there is no formal basis now for allowing divorces; it is entirely up to the judge. The proceeding is humiliating, it's drawn-out, expensive. The mere registration fee is now raised from 500 to 2,000 rubles. Do you know what the wage of the worker is? Do you know who can now enjoy divorce legally? Not only that, but they now record your divorce in your labour book. You not only have to wade through the mire but they splash some of it on you permanently.

Infinitely worse, infinitely more shameless and depraved is the Stalinist legislation on abortion. The decree of June 27, 1936 — in spite of numerous protests, so great that they had to be printed in the Stalinist press! — a penalty of two years in prison for the physician performing the abortion; public rebuke to the mother for the first offence, 300 rubles' fine for the second. Abortion is a dreadful business, and every socialist, every human being with intelligence, with feeling, must recoil from this blow at what might become a human life. But we are neither hypocrites nor religious bigots. If a law prohibiting abortion is an abomination in this country, in the United States, it's a double abomination in a country like Russia. Just think! A low standard of living; hospital service which is exceptionally poor. You can't buy shoes for kids. *Pravda* of March 30, 1938, reports — this is an absolutely typical and current picture — "To buy shoes, a coat or a change of underwear for the newly-born, the parents spend a great deal of time going from one store to another. For the entire railway district of Moscow with more than 100,000 inhabitants there was only one store for infant wear, and this store has been a long time without infant underwear or shoes for school children. Because of the lack of goods, the store sold underwear only six or seven days in the month. In the stores of the capital city (Moscow itself) mothers searched in vain for an infant bathtub or a round basin for bathing the baby and a tub for washing the clothes." Say what you want about Russia, that's the situation. Let us not blame Stalin for that. Let's say that is not his fault at all. But to prohibit abortion under those circumstances? To force the woman to have an unwanted child under those conditions? At a time when contraceptives are at a premium, when diapers are almost impossible to get, when there is little or no food, when you cannot find a baby basinette or a basin for washing its underwear, when it's even hard to find a nipple for the baby's milk bottle — the dirty, mailed fist of the bureaucracy grabs the working woman by the throat and snarls at her: "Breed!":

The law of 1936 provides that mothers of more than six children get 200 rubles' premium annually for five years for each additional child; mothers of ten children receive 5,000 rubles at birth of each additional child, and so on. The bureaucracy does not hesitate to intervene into the most sacred and intimate precincts of the personal life of the working woman. We need more labour slaves; more cannon fodder! Here is your bribe! Produce! If you're with child, whether you want it or not, whether it is a child of love or not, whether you can afford it or not, produce! Breed! That's socialism? You call that monstrosity, copied straight from Mussolini, straight from Hitler, you call that socialism? You have the nerve to speak before an audience when that happens? I say to the Stalinists everywhere: Go try to peddle it to the women who have freedom and fearlessness enough to give you their answer.

You have destroyed the Russian Revolution. You have garrotted it! Lenin wrote a hundred times: "The proletariat cannot achieve the socialist revolution unless it is prepared for this task by the struggle for democracy; (I'm quoting) victorious socialism cannot retain its victory and lead humanity to the stage when the state withers away unless it establishes complete democracy." Where is there democracy in Stalinist Russia today? What democratic rights does the worker have? The right to vote for Stalin whenever Stalin decides to allow what he calls an election? Is that the kind of elections Browder proposes for the United States? It would be interesting to hear something about that! Does the worker have the right to organise a trade union, to elect his own officials? Does he have the right to form a political party of his own — except for the Communist Party, as it is called jocularly? Do I have that right in Russia? Let me hear from an expert! Does Norman Thomas have it? Does Wallace have that right in Russia? Does Browder have that right in Russia? What would happen if he tried to exercise that right? Let me hear from some political idiots to whom Browder refers! What would happen if he tried to exercise that right in Russia? Isn't he an agent of American imperialism? Isn't he a class enemy spreading the poison of the bourgeoisie? I know that's true — that's what he is — I read that in a pamphlet by that pitiable Robert Thompson. I read it in the *Daily Worker*. Now, suppose Browder tried to exercise that democratic right in Russia?

Does the worker have the right to read any paper but the Stalinist press in Russia — any? Does he have the right to listen to any broadcast but the Stalinist broadcast? Does he have the right to organise a public meeting of his own, like here — not just this one, but any one? Does he have the right to put forth his own candidacy in the election? I want to nominate Browder! Can I do it? Can he run? Does he have the right to recall a single significant public official? Lenin considered that right absolutely indispensable for a workers' state, let alone for socialism! He underscored it a thousand times, laid the heaviest stress on it. He pointed to the Commune as a model. Not only election of all officials, but recall, recall, so that if the scoundrel doesn't turn out right you can yank him out of office. Show me a single Stalinist official of any consequence who has ever been recalled by the workers and peasants of Russia. One! The GPU recalls — that's all — and that is not only all but it's fatal, too!

Does the worker have the right to strike? Where? Does he have the right to move from one city to another without police permission?

Stalinism has destroyed every right that the Russian workers ever had! Name me one of the tiny miserable rights that the workers had under Czarism, under Czarism, in Russia. They were miserable, tiny, microscopic — name me one that he has in Stalinist Russia today. You call that tyranny socialism? I know Stalin has given him "security." We have heard that; we hear it time and again: He's given a roof over his head; he's fed two or three times a day; he's given all the work he can stand — and a lot more! And there's no unemployment like under capitalism — and that is a curse of capitalism that you can never get rid of, that's true. But we're talking about if there's socialism in Russia. Is it a socialist community? If that is socialism, Browder, among others, has already had two experiences in socialism in the United States alone: one in World War I in Leavenworth Federal Penitentiary; the other in World War II in Atlanta Federal Penitentiary. Those are nationalised penitentiaries, commonly owned. He had work there. The bourgeoisie gave it to him as it is given to all other political prisoners, and to all prisoners in general. But at least he could get out when his term was up! Can the Russian worker? No, it's flight and treason; his family is held as hostage; he is imprisoned for life.

Look at what they have done to the great emancipating principles of the Russian Revolution! They butchered the whole revolutionary generation, with one or two exceptions! Not a word from Browder about that. A trifle! Industry is progressing — gynat e peregnyat! They wiped out the whole leadership of Bolshevism, of the October uprising, of the victory in the Civil War! Are they any better than the Czar? No, worse by far! Under Czarism from 1826 to 1905, almost a century, 102 persons were executed for political reasons, 102! In the period of black reaction from 1905 to 1906, after the revolution, the blackest reaction cost the lives of 4,352 people. That's all! That's horrible! That's all! And they've murdered tens of thousands of the same kind of revolutionists that the Czar murdered by the hundreds. There were just twenty-two members of Lenin's Central Committee in October, 1917, the eve of the insurrection, the people who organised the insurrection: three of them died more or less normally — Lenin, Dzerzhinsky, Uritsky; two are still alive — Kollontai, Stalin. Five out of the 22. Where are the other 17, where are the other 17 who founded the Russian Revolution? Seventeen others shot as mad dogs, as fascists, as spies, as wreckers, as counter-revolutionists, as enemies of the people, as enemies of the working class, enemies of socialism, by Stalin. Stalin murdered five out of the seven chairmen of the Soviet executive committee; almost all the members and candidates of the

Soviet executive; the heads and the leaders of practically every Republic — Ukraine, Georgia, White Russia, Uzbekistan, Transcaucasia — all the others. The majority of the commission that wrote the Stalin Constitution, the most democratic Constitution in the world — the majority of the commission that wrote it became fascist and were shot down like dogs. Two out of five marshals of the Red Army; three army group commanders out of six, ten army commanders out of fifteen, 57 army corps commanders out of 85, 110 divisional commanders out of 193, 202 brigade commanders out of 400 shot as mad dogs, spies, agents of Japan, of England, of France, of Germany. Thousands of lesser officers! The whole life of these men was devoted to the fight for socialism. They breathed, they thought, they dreamed, they ate, they drank nothing else. What happened to drive them — if we are to take Stalin's version of these butcheries — what happened under Stalinism that drove them away from Stalinism, away from socialism, and into the arms of arch-reaction, Hitlerite fascism? That's if we take your version! Isn't that the most damning indictment that Stalin could make of his own socialism? That practically every one of the leaders in the fight for it, with trivial exceptions, hated and feared and despised his socialism so much that rather than share it, rather than tolerate it, they sold themselves to the most reactionary, the most sordid, the most rotten and corrupt imperialists in the world? You murdered the leaders of the Red Army, its great captains in the civil war, its giants, its architects, and its epic heroes. Then Stalin was free to destroy the army of socialism, of course, and establish the army of reaction which he has now.

The International — you sing it, don't you? Not in Russia; it's no longer the national anthem. They have a new national anthem of how "Great Russia established an indestructible union." Great Russia! The term "general" was hated under the Czar, restored by Stalin. "Marshals" — that rank was destroyed under the Czar — restored by Stalin. Ranks, grades, class divisions, distinctions, privileges — restored by Stalin. And who were made the inspirers and models of the army? Under the names of whom did they go out to fight for socialism? Marshal Suvorov, the man who crushed the national revolution of Stanislav Poniatovsky, and Thaddeus Koscziuszko, the man who drowned in blood the peasant uprising of Pugachev! They even made medals — and the big breasts of the generals and marshals to this day are loaded down with them, aren't they, or Suvorov and his right-hand man Kutuzov. They created an Order of Bogdan Khmelnitzky, the Ukrainian Ataman who centuries ago first introduced mass pogroms against the Jews and the Poles. It was under their banner, with their names on his lips, that Stalin sallied forth for his socialism! That's what he has; Suvorov socialism, Khmelnitzky socialism! But not socialism as we ever understood it; not socialism to which we aspire with every fibre of our passion for freedom and the comradeship of man!

What have they done to the Bolshevik revolution, with its noble sentiments, its noble ambitions, and its noble goal? They've destroyed it and made Russia a nation of slave labour. Doesn't every child know that there are millions of slave labourers in Russia? I don't have the time, I will in my rebuttal; I will read you from the kodex, the photostatic copy of the kodex for "corrective labour institutions," as they call them there — 10 millions of them at an absolute minimum. Here in "correction camps," federal penitentiaries and state penitentiaries, we have what? — from US Census Bureau — 141,000 odd in state and federal penitentiaries out of a population of 145 million, five out of every 5,000 in prison. In England, 30,000 out of a population of 50 million, three out of every 5,000. In Russia, 10 million at least out of approximately 180 million, 277 out of every 5,000! Is that a sign of socialism? Is that what your socialism leads to!

(Interruption by Chairman Mills asking Shachtman to conclude. Shachtman asks for an extension which he will take from his summary if Browder doesn't object.)

I want to conclude hastily.

I say even if Browder wants it, he'll never live to see it!

What does he have to say about Tito? One word! One word! We're discussing war or peace, Tito is an element in it. Why must Tito and his regime be liquidated? Aren't theirs the same — the same regime as in Russia, same medals, same economy, same politics, same structure? He must be liquidated because he insists on exploiting the Yugoslav people instead of letting the Russians do it! That's why he must be crushed, must he not? He must be crushed like Rajk was crushed in Hungary, like Gomulka is about to be crushed in Poland, like Kostov was crushed in Bulgaria.

Browder's loyalty to Stalinism cannot be questioned, can it? His defence of Stalinist socialism, of Stalinist Russia, can't be questioned, can it? You heard it yourself. But supposing this same Browder were in Russia, what would happen to him, what would have happened to him as far back as 1946? Suppose this same Browder, who calls Russia socialist, were in Hungary or Bulgaria, what would be his fate? Or suppose Browder's Stalino-socialists were successful in establishing their socialism in this country, with Foster, and Green, and Dennis, and Childs and Minor and Don and all the rest of that perfidious crew at the head of it — (turning to Browder) they are perfidious, aren't they? — who would be the first to go? Who would be the first to get the GPU bullet in the base of his skull? Who would be the first to be denounced in the obituary articles as a counter-revolutionary mad dog, a viper, a restorationist, a wrecker? Who would it be — Browder or Shachtman? That's a sporting proposition!

(Interruption by Chairman Mills: Time's up.)

When I saw him standing there at the podium, I said to myself: Rajk was the general secretary of the Hungarian Communist Party, and was shot, or hanged, or garrotted. Kostov was the general secretary of the Bulgarian Communist Party. And when I thought of what happened to them, I thought of the former secretary of the American Communist Party, and I said to myself: There, there but for an accident of geography, stands a corpse!

Earl Browder sums up

AS I LISTENED to the passionate indictment of that monstrous reaction that spreads from the East, the backward, barbarian East, gradually engulfing the progressive and civilised West, I had a feeling that, well, now, if this is true, I'd better enlist in the crusade that is led by those who formulate policy today, to wipe out this menace which is worse than Hitler, because it is so much more efficient, because it can even make progress in the material development of life while it is destroying everything which we hold dear, which makes life worth living.

And as I was debating and listening in this war to destroy the Soviet Union for which a recruiting sergeant made a very effective appeal this evening, I was forced to hesitate a little, because I had to ask myself: what is happening in Poland today, which had been engulfed by the monster, and what is happening in Italy today, which has been saved from the monster and saved for our higher concept? And I happen to know that in Poland being engulfed by this monster has meant for the first time in history that Poland has been able to rise and begin to organise its life, and is organising it in a way that even every simple honest capitalist who has gone there has had to speak of it with admiration. For the first time in history the land of Poland is in the hands of the masses who cultivate it. For the first time in history, landlordism has been abolished. For the first time in history, the economy of Poland is rising. And I turn and I look at Italy, or France, which America has saved from the monster. And what do I see in Italy? The saving of Italy from the monster has been at the cost of riveting again upon the Italian farmers the rule of the most bloodsucking class of landlords that has been seen outside of Eastern Europe, where it has been destroyed.

We heard a lot today about declines in living standards. It is strange that you didn't hear a word about the decline of the living standards of the Italian masses who've been saved from that monster. We saved France from the monster, and yet in this morning's newspapers you may read how the average monthly salary of the French workers has declined since the day of liberation from the Nazis. Since the Americans went in to direct French affairs, the average wage of the French worker has declined from $50 a month — a month! — to $24.50 a month. The price of saving the French workers from this monster was to slash wages in half. Slice them in half!

What is happening to wages in Russia and in those countries who have been swallowed by the monster, those countries where they are building socialism of the kind which is objected to by my opponent? It is quite well established that the standard of living of the workers and of the peasants has risen steadily in every one of these countries. You may say very cheaply and very easily it is a lie, but figures of production do not lie. My opponent this evening can make great play with the development of his sort of statistics to prove that the material standard of life of Soviet workers today is lower than in 1914. But in order to give you that lie, he has to conceal from you simple, basic facts of production in the Soviet Union. He tells you the bureaucrats enjoy all the production in the Soviet Union. Well, in 1914, the standard of production of shoes, for example, to take one little thing, was 29 million pairs per year. In 1948, the production of shoes was 380 million pair. 350 million new bureaucrats, I suppose, put on shoes. The production of textiles in the Soviet Union in 1948 was four times the production of textiles in 1914. I suppose those trillions of metres of textiles produced above that of 1914 are all worn by the bureaucrats of the Soviet Union. There must be an enormous number of them. The whole country is composed of bureaucrats, of course.

It is silly to contend, and nobody does, that life is easy in the Soviet Union and problems are solved. I made it clear in my presentation that the rise in the material standard of life in the Soviet Union in no way corresponds to the rise of total production. I explained why that is so, because for the future of socialism, especially in a country which begins as one of the most backward in the world, it is necessary to go through a prolonged period, which would be quite unnecessary in America, of the basic accumulation of capital, that is, the accumulation of the material means of modern production — to have enormous expenditures in mass education to lift a whole nation up which had been kept back for centuries, to lift it up to modern standards of literacy and science. And that it above all is necessary to provide a national defence for that country, in order that socialism should not be made into an illusion by its destruction in a world of enemies. I heard not one word from my opponent about these things. Are these things important, or is immediate consumption the only test of socialism, as he says?

I say to you that anyone who can talk like that about the problems of building a new socialist society in a country where the forces of production were not developed by capitalism, that such a person is committing a vulgar fraud when he speaks to you in the name of Marx. There is nothing of Marx in that whole approach. There is only the vulgar demagogy of such schools of socialism as, for example, that of the famous Disraeli of Great Britain. You probably know the name only as one of the great founders of the British Empire. But at the same time, Disraeli the Tory was a socialist of sorts, a violent enemy of capitalism — the kind of socialism that wants to protect the working class from the evils of industrialisation and substitute the benevolent protection of the kind-hearted men like Disraeli who founded the British Empire or developed it to a higher stage. The socialism of the Tory Disraeli is equally respectable with that socialism that has been expressed here by my opponent.

Marx said that the course which brings socialism and makes socialism inevitable is the expansion of the productive forces which reach a limit under capitalism beyond which they cannot go until they have discarded capitalism and adopted socialist forms, abolishing private ownership. My opponent this evening rejects this basic principle of Marxism. In so doing he moves to the position of the reactionary forms of socialism if it is to be dignified by that name. Utopian, clerical socialism, not Marxist socialism, certainly; a Christian socialism, perhaps.

We heard a great deal about democracy and the necessity for the thorough realisation of democracy as the precondition for the establishment of socialism. I yield to no one in my valuation of democracy, but when it is brought forward to us as the precondition for the realisation of socialism that thorough democracy must be achieved, I can only tell the gentleman that he has a touching faith in the possibilities of capitalism which I cannot share. I have learned from Marx and Engels that socialism is the precondition for the full realisation of democracy, not that the thorough realisation of democracy is the pre-condition for the realisation of socialism. If the fullest realisation of democracy is possible before you have socialism, what's socialism necessary for? Socialism is a means of reaching the full development of democracy. If you can get it before you have socialism, you won't need the means.

In the same way, the substitution of the goal as the obstacle pre-venting us from getting the means is used on this question of con-sumption: Of course, the final purpose of all production is to give the good things of life to men, women and children to enjoy. Of course, that's the final aim. But when my opponent this evening comes here to tell you that because the new socialist system in Russia has not given all those good things, therefore, it is not socialism, and that that is the only test of whether it is socialism or not, what he is actually doing is telling you that because you can't have the goal of socialism today, he is going to destroy in your minds the understanding that the means of reaching that goal is being created. And because of its being created today, he is denouncing it to you here as false.

I listened with amazement to the statement that the growth of the forces of production in Russia are simply repetition of what has been repeatedly, and everywhere where it was attempted, done under cap-italism. That message, I am quite sure, would be applauded in the United States Chamber of Commerce, in the National Association of Manufacturers. But it happens to be a flat falsehood. I cited to you the basic figures to show to you that — and these figures cannot be successfully challenged — to show to you that in the Soviet Union four times the rate of the growth of production in America is now normal in the Soviet Union; that we are comparing the normal rate in the Soviet Union with the highest rates in American history so that the average rate is much faster than that. My opponent this evening tells you that's merely capitalism normally at work, a bureaucratic capitalism but capitalism nonetheless. Exploitative society, he says, which I presume is a pseudonym for continued capitalism. When given all those good things, therefore he makes this concession to capitalism, I assure you it is quite unwarranted. Capitalism does not have such possibilities of the growth of production any longer.

He also described to us with great admiration about how the rate of productivity per worker is four to six or eight times as much in America as in Russia. That is true and proves exactly the opposite of what he was trying to tell us. It is true we have the technical achieve-ments of productivity in America far beyond anything they have in the Soviet Union. Why then do we not have the growth of the economy as a whole that should result from it? Because capitalism prevents the utilisation of these techniques. Why, with a much more backward technique in the Soviet Union are they able to make greater progress than America? Because socialism gives such higher utilisation of the forces of production that a backward — technically considered — country can outstrip the most technically advanced capitalism today.

The chairman tells me I have about two minutes left. I really have taken more time than I considered was necessary to answer the shoddy presentation of the anti-Soviet case that was placed before you tonight.

Max Shachtman sums up

MR. CHAIRMAN, COMRADES and friends: My opponent did a very imprudent thing. He mentioned a name he should have left unmentioned — the National Association of Manufacturers. I was afraid he would — I hoped he would not. I have here a pamphlet, *Communists and National Unity*, an interview of *PM* — that's a New York newspaper, or was — with Earl Browder, dated March 15, 1944; interview with Mr Harold Lavin, assistant managing editor of the New York newspaper *PM*.

"Question by Mr. Lavin of Mr. Browder: 'I had a discussion with two friends of the National Association of Manufacturers; and I must say that you would get along with them fine. In large sections they almost sound word for word like you.' Answer by Mr. Browder: 'That's fine. I'm awfully glad to hear that. I'm not sorry when you say that leading members of the NAM talk like me. My report to the Plenum of our party was distributed to every delegate at the economic conference of the NAM, and I am told most of them read it through.'"

Now. I'm a socialist. I don't distribute my literature at the NAM. I don't defend the NAM. I have no friends among them. I don't defend its social system. I've been combatting it for 30 years almost to the day — I'm about to celebrate a modest anniversary — I've never relented in it! I didn't support American imperialism in the war! I didn't support the throwing of the atom bomb! I didn't defend the system of American capitalism and point out how it can grow.

(There is a slight break here between reels; voice unclear.)

I give a whole series of absolutely unassailable facts. I refrain as carefully as possible from taking them from enemy sources. I take them from the official Stalinist sources. I don't take accidental or incidental little things that appear in any newspaper; I take the central items which describe the regime and how it operates.

Typical is the reply. Typical is the reply. "What about Italy?" "What about France?" it's become a joke, a rotten joke. You know of the timid American visitor who is being shown around in Moscow, its glories, taken into the magnificent subway with its marble panels — by guide, of course. They wait... they wait 5 minutes, 10 minutes, 15 minutes. The timid American says: "Your trains don't run very often." "Yes, what about the Negroes in the United States?"

But I'm not defending the persecution and lynching of Negroes in the United States. I'm not defending the Marshall Plan. I'm not defending the landowners in Italy. I'm not defending the landowners in Poland. I'm not defending the bourgeoisie in France. I'm opposing them. And I opposed them when Browder was on their side! Wasn't he? I was never allied with them. Browder was. The Communist Party was. Stalin was.

My comrades were murdered because they were accused of having made a pact with Hitler. Browder says, of course, there were no documents to prove it. The Opposition, he says in one pamphlet, were clever enough to burn their documents. But there's one document that was not burned. It was printed in the *Daily Worker*, wasn't it, by Mr. Browder? And he had an article on it, didn't he — when he could write in the *Daily Worker*! And the signature of Hitler or von Ribbentrop was on that document, wasn't it? What Russian signature was on it? Trotsky's? Rakovsky's? Tukhachevsky's? Whose signature was on this document of alliance with Hitler and Soviet Russia?

You talk to me, a revolutionary socialist and an internationalist, about Italy? Who cares about Italy tonight? I'll discuss Italy with you in another debate! I'll discuss American imperialism with you in another debate! I have a few words to say about it. I'll repeat the things I've been saying for thirty years.

I'm talking about: is Russia a socialist community? That's supposed to have been the subject of the debate tonight. Not one of the things I spoke about were referred to or dealt with, were they? My speech "called for a crusade of the progressive West against the reaction." Why? Why? Who said anything about "the progressive West"? Yes, Browder once spoke about that. Not I. I never did.

When Browder was an internationalist, when he opposed the imperialist war of 1917 in this country, what did the patriots say to him? On what basis was he railroaded to prison, along with hundreds and thousands of revolutionary socialists, of IWW's? What did they tell him? "By criticising the United States you're working for the Kaiser!" Browder spit in their faces, didn't he? Debs spit in their faces! Haywood spit in their faces! Kate Richards O'Hare spit in their faces! Now he tells me that I'm recruiting for a crusade against Russia!

In 1917 when he was a socialist, when he was a revolutionist, Browder said: "I'm against German imperialism. I'm against American imperialism." Among other examples, his was one I learned from. I haven't changed: I'm against Stalinist imperialism! I'm against American imperialism! I'm against their Cold War! I'm against their atom bomb! I'm against their H-bomb! I'm against the war that they're preparing for the destruction of civilisation. Doesn't Browder know that? Of course! But years of training in the Stalinist movement teach you how to "answer" criticism of Stalinist Russia.

Browder was the editor of the paper of the Trade Union Educational League when I first met him, it was a good paper, and it was well edited. And I remember how it used to expose the rottenness of the labour leaders, and how page after page, month after month — things that I was raised on when I was a kid — would show: you've got gangsterism in your unions, you scoundrels. You've got murder in your unions. You exploit workers. You live off the fat of the land. You get $20,000 income as president, and the worker gets only $20 a week. And what of the Greens, and the Gomperses, and the Hutchesons, and the Lewises? What was their answer to the propaganda of the Trade Union Educational League? What did they answer Earl Browder? "You're attacking the labour movement. You're playing into the hands of the employers. You're playing into the hands of the open-shoppers. They also say the labour movement is rotten. They also say there's racketeering." What did Browder answer? The way I answer him tonight: The truth never hurts the working class! I want to tell the truth about Russia, and I don't want to be told by any paid or unpaid agent of the Stalinists that I can't tell the truth about Russia because it will play into the hands of the reaction! Who has played into the hands of the reaction more than any other single force in the labour movement, who, if not the Stalinists?

"Shachtman doesn't understand" — excuse me — "My opponent doesn't understand — first you have socialism, then you have democracy. That's what I was taught by Marx and Engels," he said.

I quote again from Lenin, just one of the dozen quotes I can get you like that. I not only know them, Browder knows them; he has quoted them in his time. Lenin writes in 1916: "The victorious socialism cannot retain its victory and lead humanity to the stage when the state withers away unless it establishes complete democracy." Now, I stand on that. I stand on that now more than ever before in my life. I stand on that now so much the more firmly after I see what has happened, the degeneration of the Russian Revolution under the Stalinist counter-revolutionary absolutism.

It's plain: if you're moving toward socialism, which is a complicated business, I know, which is difficult, which is beset by a million obstacles, most of them inherited from capitalism, with its rottenness, its corruption, its depravity, you can always tell, however — not every single day, but over periods — you can tell, are we moving toward socialism or away from socialism, by two simple criteria:

One, is the standard of living of the workers going up? Two, is state coercion going down? Is there a trend toward equality?

Nobody but a political idiot — to quote the elegant phrase of "my opponent" — would expect you to have it overnight equality. We're a long way yet. But is it going toward equality, or is it going toward inequality? Isn't that simple? Isn't that an old established criterion for socialist evolution after the proletarian revolution takes place? Browder doesn't even talk about that. Now I say, if you could show me that the Russian workers' standard of living is not only as good as the low standard of living of the American workers, but four times as good — four times as good — and if I should answer, while the standard of living of the worker in Russia has gone to four times as good as the American worker's, at the same time the ruling group — call it what you want — has improved its economic position a hundred times, I say you're moving away from socialism. If you could show me that the working class has more control over the state, if you could show me that state coercion, in the form of this blood-stained GPU, is diminishing, I'd say you were moving toward socialism. But it is not diminishing; the Stalinists announced it twice: the state is being reinforced. We have socialism and the state is being reinforced!

Now (a), you won't find that in Marx or Lenin — that's not important; (b) you won't find that in Russia — and that is important. You'll find a reinforcement of the state such as has never existed. But you won't find a trace of socialism. He imputes to me the position, since he has nothing else to say, that I claim the only test for socialism is the consumption of the masses. When did I say that? Tonight? A year ago? Fifty years? More likely fifty years ago! But not tonight! Not tonight! I say it takes two criteria: Are class lines disappearing? Is there an increase toward equality, or is there, as there is in Russia today, an increase toward inequality? Is the state coercion increasing in intensity or decreasing?

He says, is defence important, or is consumption the immediate task for socialism? God knows that under Stalinism it's not the immediate task, it's not the remote task — consumption for the masses. I don't deny that defence is important. Of course, it's important. It's important in the United States; it's important under Hitler's Germany; it's important in every country. It will disappear when there's world socialism. But that's not the point, is it? I didn't say anything about how much they're spending on tanks. I don't know, Browder doesn't know. It's not important. I leave that aside, I don't want to argue that aspect of it at all. I ask a simple question and I give the simple incontrovertible fact: for the masses, the standard of living declined. That fraction of the production which is available to the people for consumption goes to the bureaucracy first and foremost. That's the fact and that's what's important.

He says I deny the Marxian contention that the expansion of the productive forces is what makes progress possible. I didn't; I don't dream of it. I'm talking about socialism tonight. I want to ask simply, does every expansion of the production of forces, granted all the figures of the Stalinists a hundred times over, does that produce socialism? I say categorically No! Does it make possible socialism? I say categorically Yes! When? How? When, as the *Communist Manifesto*, said 102 years ago, the proletariat is raised to the position of the ruling class, is raised to political supremacy, when democracy is established! That is the first demand in the Communist Manifesto the first: to establish democracy. When the working class democratically takes the destiny of the nation into its hands, then the previous preparation — by capitalism or by bureaucratic collectivism — can and will serve the proletariat in power as the economic or technological basis for the rational order of socialism. That says a good deal for this preparation, but no more.

You have to make up your mind about the fundamental question: is Russia a socialist community? And there I say what I said at the very beginning: if a "socialist community" is to be used to characterise a society where the development of the productive forces, where the control of the productive force, where the control of what Marx calls the conditions of production are entirely and exclusively in the hands of a totalitarian reactionary bureaucracy; if you're going to apply the name of socialism to a regime in which the economic conditions of the working class, which is the only mover toward socialism, the only living motive force toward socialism — where the economic conditions are worse than they are, or worse than they were in the last years of Czarism, where they have not even now reached the development of what I still consider a backward capitalist country — backward as compared with what the USA can and will be some day; at a time when inequality is growing, when all the political privileges, all the economic privileges, are in the hands of this reactionary upper crust, when the precepts and ideas of socialism are banned from the country, when the revolutionists who were the bearers of the socialist ideal are exterminated, only more thoroughly than Hitler exterminated the Social Democratic militants and the Communist Party militants — then I say socialism is lost! Then I say you have given to the reactionary bourgeoisie not only of this but of all other countries a murderous weapon, with which to crush the socialist movement and its aspirations, by saying: here are the socialists themselves claiming this monstrosity, this reactionary society, this new slavery — that's their socialism. Is that what you want? That's the demagogical way of the reaction. We understand it perfectly. And I say that the Stalinist movement in and out of Russia has done more than any other single force in the world, more than any single force in the world's history, to give weapons against socialism, against the working class movement, into the hands of capitalist reaction.

We don't say, as again "my opponent" imputes to us, that Russia is bureaucratic capitalism; we don't contend that Russia is capitalism at all. We distinguish it both from socialism and capitalism by the phrase, perhaps not too elegant, bureaucratic or totalitarian collectivism. The Stalinist bureaucracy represents a new reactionary social order. If you are to argue that this is not provided for in Marx, then you don't understand anything about Marx. Marxism constantly, from the beginning, posited the possibility either of socialism or barbarism. The conditions conforming to that barbarism could not be envisaged by Marx a hundred years ago. We see that barbarism developing in capitalist society in futile wars of extermination, for example. We see it developing in Stalinist society, a new barbarism, a new slavery for the workers and the peasants. They are converted into state serfs, into state slaves. Engels foresaw it, Marx foresaw it, Rosa Luxemburg foresaw it, Lenin foresaw it. They kept warning, as we do to this day, kept warning the working class: You must take over society, remould it, reshape it, in the interests of socialism, on a rational basis; otherwise, society will decay into barbarism. If you do not take over, they said a hundred years ago, and I repeat it tonight, if the working class does not take over, if, for example, as really happened, the working class of Europe did not come to the aid of the Bolshevik Revolution of 1917, there will be decay, and this decay will mean your ruin. It will mean your ruin, that's what Engels repeatedly said to the working class. At that time it was almost only a literary flourish. Today it is a bitter and cruel reality that stares us in the face.

I say again that the Stalin regime has nothing in common with socialism. It represents a form of the new barbarism. It is proof, I repeat, of the prophetic words of Frederick Engels, which I should like to remind you of again:

If the working class itself does not take the leadership of the nation and by its democratic rule reorganise it on a socialist basis, Engels said, it will sink to the level of the Chinese coolie. He says again: if the working class does not take into its own hands the power to achieve the new social order, it will pay the penalty of its own destruction.

Capitalism is dragging us down into the primitive slime of reaction and universal destruction. We don't feel it so acutely here in the United States today. Browder is absolutely right in referring to what it means in Italy, in France, tomorrow or the next day, for all capitalist countries. In that he is absolutely correct. But the Stalinist alternative to capitalism, which he offers us on the same platter with which he must offer his own head, is nothing but a new barbarism. That's why we reaffirm our own faith in the liberation of humanity by socialism, the product of the freed consciousness of the working class. We have seen despotisms like Stalinism before. We have seen them come, we have seen them prevail, and we have seen them go!

We affirm, and we reaffirm it in the teeth of that hideousness which is known as Stalinism, that socialism for us, yesterday, today, tomorrow, still means the end of class rule; the end of class privilege; the freeing of the people from all chains and all coercion, the fullest realisation of democracy, the emancipation of women and of children; the end of slave camps, police terror, frame-ups, butchery of the socialists, abundance for all, and therefore liberty for all.

In spite of the black pall that Stalinism has hung over the heads of the working class in so many countries, despite the mean and cruel shame and discredit with which it has stained the shining shield of socialism, we are confident, now as ever, that socialism will triumph by the power of that invincible force, that irrepressible force, which the young Karl Marx called "the power of the expansion of democratic ideas and humanity's innate thirst for liberty."

New International, May-June 1950

1.

2.

TROTSKY'S WORKS LIVE ON IN HEROIC RED ARMY

The two souls of Orthodox Trotskyism

The two cartoons on these pages show the "two souls" of Orthodox Trotskyism as it evolved after the 1940 split. Above: *The Militant*, "Trotsky memorial issue", 15 August 1942. Left: *The Militant*, 17 March 1945. The Yalta conference was in February 1945. The figure in the lower panel is Stalin.

175

Part 2: The great schism

2. Defend Russia in Hitler-Stalin Poland?

The first two texts are the speeches delivered by James P Cannon and Max Shachtman at the New York membership meeting of the US Trotskyist movement, the Socialist Workers Party, on 15 October 1939. Cannon and Shachtman, the two main leaders of the movement since it was founded in 1928, spoke for opposing sides in this debate, sparked by the invasion and partition of Poland by Stalin and Hitler in September 1939. Contrary to most tellings of the story, the debate was not about how to label the USSR. Shachtman and most of his comrades still accepted the "degenerated workers' state" formula, though with doubts, and they accepted "defence of the USSR" against invasion by a big power. It was essentially about the balance between condemnation of Stalin's invasion and hypothetical defence of the USSR against big-power invasion.

Unconditional defence of USSR

James P Cannon (1939)

THE RUSSIAN QUESTION is with us once again, as it has been at every critical turning point of the international labor movement since November 7, 1917. And there is nothing strange in that. The Russian question is no literary exercise to be taken up or cast aside according to the mood of the moment. The Russian question has been and remains the question of the revolution. The Russian Bolsheviks on November 7, 1917, once and for all, took the question of the workers' revolution out of the realm of abstraction and gave it flesh and blood reality.

It was said once of a book – I think it was Whitman's *Leaves of Grass* – "Who touches this book, touches a man." in the same sense it can also be said, "Who touches the Russian question, touches a revolution." Therefore, be serious about it. Don't play with it.

The October Revolution put socialism on the order of the day throughout the world. It revived and shaped and developed the revolutionary labor movement of the world out of the bloody chaos of

176

the war. The Russian revolution showed in practice, by example, how the workers' revolution is to be made. It revealed in life the role of the party. It showed in life what kind of a party the workers must have. By its victory, and its reorganization of the social system, the Russian revolution has proved for all time the superiority of nationalized property and planned economy over capitalist private property, and planless competition and anarchy in production.

The question of the Russian revolution – and the Soviet state which is its creation – has drawn a sharp dividing line through the labor movement of all countries for 22 years. The attitude taken toward the Soviet Union throughout all these years has been the decisive criterion separating the genuine revolutionary tendency from all shades and degrees of waverers, backsliders and capitulators to the pressure of the bourgeois world – the Mensheviks, Social Democrats, Anarchists and Syndicalists, Centrists, Stalinists.

The main source of division in our own ranks for the past ten years, since the Fourth Internationalist tendency took organized form on the international field, has been the Russian question. Our tendency, being a genuine, that is, orthodox, Marxist tendency from A to Z, has always proceeded on the Russian question from theoretical premises to political conclusions for action. Of course, it is only when political conclusions are drawn out to the end that differences on the Russian question reach an unbearable acuteness and permit no ambiguity or compromise. Conclusions on the Russian question lead directly to positions on such issues as war and revolution, defense and defeatism. Such issues, by their very nature, admit no unclarity, no compromise, because it is a matter of taking sides! One must be on one side or another in war and revolution.

But if the lines are drawn only when political conclusions diverge, that does not at all signify that we are indifferent to theoretical premises. He is a very poor Marxist – better say, no Marxist at all – who takes a careless or tolerant attitude toward theoretical premises. The political conclusions of Marxists proceed from theoretical analyses and are constantly checked and regulated by them. That is the only way to assure a firm and consistent policy.

To be sure, we do not decline cooperation with people who agree with our political conclusions from different premises. For example, the Bolsheviks were not deterred by the fact that the Left SRs were inconsistent. As Trotsky remarked in this connection, "If we wait till everything is right in everybody's head there will never be any successful revolutions in this world" (or words to that effect.) Just the same, for our part we want everything right in our own heads. We have no reason whatever to slur over theoretical formulae, which are expressed in "terminology." As Trotsky says, in theoretical matters "we must keep our house clean."

Our position on the Russian question is programmatic. In brief: The theoretical analysis – a degenerated Workers' State. The political conclusion – unconditional defense against external attack of imperialists or internal attempts at capitalist restoration.

Defensism and Defeatism are two principled, that is, irreconcilable, positions. They are not determined by arbitrary choice but by class interests.

No party in the world ever succeeded in harboring these two antipathetic tendencies for any great length of time. The contradiction is too great. Division all over the world ultimately took place along this line. Defensists at home were defeatists on Russia. Defensists on Russia were defeatists at home.

The degeneration of the Soviet state under Stalin has been analyzed at every step by the Bolshevik-Leninists and only by them. A precise attitude has been taken at every stage. The guiding lines of the revolutionary Marxist approach to the question have been:

See the reality and see it whole at every stage; never surrender any position before it is lost; the worst of all capitulators is the one who capitulates before the decisive battle.

The International Left Opposition which originated in 1923 as an opposition in the Russian party (the original nucleus of the Fourth International) has always taken a precise attitude on the Russian question. In the first stages of the degeneration of which the Stalinist bureaucracy was the banner bearer the opposition considered it possible to rectify matters by methods of reform through the change of regime in the Communist Party of the Soviet Union. Later, when it became clearer that the Communist Party of Lenin had been irremediably destroyed, and after it became manifest that the reactionary bureaucracy could be removed only by civil war, the Fourth International, standing as before on its analysis of the Soviet Union as a workers' state, came out for a political revolution.

All the time throughout this entire period of 16 years the Bolshevik-Leninists have stoutly maintained, in the face of all slander and persecution, that they were the firmest defenders of the workers' state and that in the hour of danger they would be in the front ranks of its defense. We always said the moment of danger will find the Fourth Internationalists at their posts defending the conquests of the great revolution without ceasing for a moment our struggle against the Stalinist bureaucracy. Now that the hour of danger is at hand – now that the long-awaited war is actually knocking at the door – it would be very strange if the Fourth International should renege on its oft-repeated pledge.

Throughout all this long period of Soviet degeneration since the death of Lenin, the Fourth Internationalists, analyzing the new phenomenon of a degenerating workers' state at every turn, striving to comprehend its complications and contradictions, to recognize and defend all the progressive features of the contradictory processes and to reject the reactionary – during all this long time we have been beset at every new turn of events by the impatient demands of "radicals" to simplify the question. Thrown off balance by the crimes and betrayals of Stalin, they lost sight of the new system of economy which Stalin had not destroyed and could not destroy.

We always firmly rejected these premature announcements that everything was lost and that we must begin all over again. At each stage of development, at each new revelation of Stalinist infamy and treachery, some group or other broke away from the Fourth International because of its "conservatism" on the Russian question. It would be interesting, if we had the time, to call the roll of these groupings which one after another left our ranks to pursue an ostensibly more "revolutionary" policy on the Russian question. Did they develop an activity more militant, more revolutionary, than ours? Did they succeed in creating a new movement and in attracting newly awakened workers and those breaking from Stalinism? In no case.

If we were to call the roll of these ultra-radical groups it would present a devastating picture indeed. Those who did not fall into complete political passivity became reconciled in one form or another to bourgeois democracy. The experiences of the past should teach us all a salutary caution, and even, if you please, "conservatism," in approaching any proposal to revise the program of the Fourth International on the Russian question. While all the innovators fell by the wayside, the Fourth International alone retained its programmatic firmness. It grew and developed and remained the only genuine revolutionary current in the labor movement of the world. Without a firm position on the Russian question our movement also would inevitably have shared the fate of the others.

The mighty power of the October revolution is shown by the vitality of its conquests. The nationalized property and the planned economy stood up under all the difficulties and pressures of the capitalist encirclement and all the blows of a reactionary bureaucracy at home. In the Soviet Union, despite the monstrous mismanagement of the bureaucracy, we saw a tremendous development of the productive forces – and in a backward country at that – while capitalist economy declined. Conclusion: Nationalized and planned economy, made possible by a revolution that overthrew the capitalists and landlords, is infinitely superior, more progressive. It shows the way forward. Don't give it up before it is lost! Cling to it and defend it!

On the Russian question there are only two really independent forces in the world. Two forces who think about the question independently because they base themselves, their thoughts, their analysis and their conclusions, on fundamental class considerations. Those two independent forces are:

1. The conscious vanguard of the world bourgeoisie, the statesmen of both democratic and fascist imperialism.

2. The conscious vanguard of the world proletariat. Between them it is not simply a case of two opinions on the Russian question, but rather of two camps. All those who in the past rejected the conclusions of the Fourth International, and broke with our movement on that account, have almost invariably fallen into the service of the imperialists, through Stalinism, social and liberal democracy, or passivity, a form of service.

The standpoint of the world bourgeoisie is a class standpoint. They proceed, as we do, from fundamental class considerations. They want to maintain world capitalism. This determines their fundamental antagonism to the USSR. They appreciate the reactionary work of Stalin, but consider it incomplete, insofar as he has not restored capitalist private property.

Their fundamental attitude determines an inevitable attempt at the start of the war, or during it, to attack Russia, overthrow the nationalized economy, restore a capitalist regime, smash the foreign trade monopoly, open up the Soviet Union as a market and field of investments, transform Russia into a great colony, and thereby alleviate the crisis of world capitalism.

The standpoint of the Fourth International is based on the same fundamental class considerations. Only we draw opposite conclusions, from an opposite class standpoint.

Purely sentimental motivations, speculation without fundamental class premises, so-called "fresh ideas" with no programmatic base – all this is out of place in a party of Marxists. We want to advance the world revolution of the proletariat. This determines our attitude and approach to the Russian question. True, we want to see reality, but we are not disinterested observers and commentators. We do not examine the Russian revolution and what remains of its great conquests as though it were a bug under a glass. We have an interest! We take part in the fight! At each stage in the development of the Soviet Union, its advances and its degeneration, we seek the basis for revolutionary action. We want to advance the world revolution, overthrow capitalism, establish Socialism. The Soviet Union is an important and decisive question on this line.

Our standpoint on the Russian question is written into our program. It is not a new question for us. It is 22 years old. We have followed its evolution, both progressive and retrogressive, at every stage. We have discussed it and taken our position anew at every stage of its progressive development and its degeneration. And, what is most important, we have always acted on our conclusions.

The Soviet Union emerged from the October revolution as a workers' state. As a result of the backwardness and poverty of the country and the delay of the world revolution, a conservative bureaucracy emerged and triumphed, destroyed the party and bureaucratized the economy. However, this same bureaucracy still operates on the basis of the nationalized property established by the revolution. That is the decisive question for our evaluation of the question. If we see the Soviet Union for what it really is, a gigantic labor organization which has conquered one-sixth of the earth's surface, we will not be so ready to abandon it because of pure hatred of the crimes and abominations of the bureaucracy. Do we turn our backs on a trade union because it falls into the control of bureaucrats and traitors? Ultra-leftists have frequently made this error, but always with bad results, sometimes with reactionary consequences.

We recall the case of the International Ladies' Garment Workers Union here in New York. The bureaucrats of this union were about as vile a gang of labor lieutenants of the capitalist class as could be found. In the struggle against the left-wing in the middle twenties they conspired with the bosses and the AF of L fakers. They expelled the left-wing locals and used hired thugs to fight them and to break their strikes. The difference between them and Stalin was only a matter of opportunity and power. Driven to revolt against the crimes of, these bureaucrats the left-wing, under the influence of the Communist Party in the days of its third period frenzy, labelled the union – not merely its treacherous bureaucracy – as a "company union." But, this same "company union," under the pressure of the workers in its ranks and the increasing intensity of the class struggle, was forced to call a strike to defend itself against the "imperialist" attack of the bosses. Workers who had kept their heads supported ("defended") the strike against the bosses. But the Stalinists, trapped by their own hastily-improvised theory, having already denounced the union as a company union, renounced support ("defense") of the strike. They denounced it as a "fake" strike. Thus their ill-considered radicalism led them to a reactionary position. They were denounced, and rightly, throughout the needle trades market as strike breakers. To this day they suffer the discredit of this reactionary action.

To defend the Soviet Union as a gigantic labor organization against the attacks of its class enemies does not mean to defend each and every action of its bureaucracy or each and every action of the Red Army which is an instrument of the bureaucracy. To impute such a "totalitarian" concept of defense to the Fourth International is absurd. Nobody here will deny defense of a bona fide trade union, no matter how reactionary its bureaucracy. But that does not prevent us from discriminating between actions of the bureaucracy which involve a defense of the union against the bosses and other actions which are aimed against the workers.

The United Mine Workers of America is a great labor organization which we all support. But it is headed by a thorough-going scoundrel and agent of the master class who also differs from Stalin only in the degrees of power and opportunity. In my own personal experience some years ago, I took part in a strike of the Kansas miners which was directed against the enforcement of a reactionary labor law, known as the Kansas industrial Court Law, a law forbidding strikes. This was a thoroughly progressive action on the part of the Kansas miners and their president, Alex Howat. Howat and the other local officials were thrown into jail. While they were in jail, John L. Lewis, as president of the national organization, sent his agents into the Kansas fields to sign an agreement with the bosses over the head of the officers of the Kansas district. He supplied strike breakers and thugs and money to break the strike while the legitimate officers of the union lay in jail for a good cause. Every militant worker in the country denounced this treacherous strike-breaking action of Lewis. But did we therefore renounce support of the national union of mine workers? Yes, some impatient revolutionaries did, and thereby completely disoriented themselves in the labor movement. The United Mine Workers retained its character as a labor organization and only last spring came into conflict with the coal operators on a national scale. I think you all recall that in this contest our press gave "unconditional defense" to the miners' union despite the fact that strike-breaker Lewis remained its president.

The Longshoremen's union of the Pacific Coast is a bona fide organization of workers, headed by a Stalinist of an especially unattractive type, a pocket edition of Stalin named Bridges. This same

Bridges led a squad of misguided longshoremen through a picket line of the Sailors' Union in a direct attempt to break up this organization. I think all of you recall that our press scathingly denounced this contemptible action of Bridges. But if the Longshoremen's union, headed by Bridges, which is at this moment conducting negotiations with the bosses, is compelled to resort to strike action, what stand shall we take? Any ordinary class conscious worker, let alone an educated Marxist, will be on the picket line; with the Longshoremen's union or "defending" it by some other means. Why is it so difficult for some of our friends, including some of those who are very well educated in the formal sense, to understand the Russian question? I am very much afraid it is because they do not think of it in terms of struggle. It is strikingly evident that the workers, especially the more experienced workers who have taken part in trade unions, strikes, etc., understand the Russian question much better than the more educated scholastics. From their experiences in the struggle they know what is meant when the Soviet Union is compared to a trade union that has fallen into bad hands. And everyone who has been through a couple of strikes which underwent crises and came to the brink of disaster, finally to emerge victorious, understands what is meant; when one says: No position must be surrendered until it is irrevocably lost.

I, personally, have seen the fate of more than one strike determined by the will or lack of will of the leadership to struggle at a critical moment. All our trade union successes in Minneapolis stem back directly to a fateful week in 1934 when the leaders refused to call off the strike, which to all appearances was hopelessly defeated, and persuaded the strike committee to hold out a while longer. In that intervening time a break occurred in the ranks of the bosses; this in turn paved the way for a compromise settlement and eventually victorious advance of the whole union.

How strange it is that some people analyze the weakness and defects in a workers' organization so closely that they do not always take into account the weakness in the camp of the enemy, which may easily more than counter-balance. In my own agitation among strikers at dark moments of a strike I have frequently resorted to the analogy of two men engaged in a physical fight. When one gets tired and apparently at the end of his resources he should never forget that the other fellow is maybe just as tired or even more so. In that case the one who holds out will prevail. Looked at in this way a worn-out strike can sometimes be carried through to a compromise or a victory by the resolute will of its leadership. We have seen this happen more than once. Why should we deny the Soviet Union, which is not yet exhausted, the same rights?

We have had many discussions on the Russian question in the past. It has been the central and decisive question for us, as for every political tendency in the labor movement. That, I repeat, is because it is nothing less than the question of the revolution at various stages of its progressive development or degeneration. We are, in fact, the party of the Russian revolution. We have been the people, and the only people, who have had the Russian revolution in their program and in their blood. That is also the main reason why the Fourth International is the only revolutionary tendency in the whole world. A false position on the Russian question would have destroyed our movement as it destroyed all others.

Two years ago we once again conducted an extensive discussion on the Russian question. The almost unanimous conclusion of the party was written into the program of our first Convention:

1. The Soviet Union, on the basis of its nationalized property and planned economy, the fruit of the revolution, remains a workers' state, though in a degenerated form.

2. As such, we stand, as before, for the unconditional defense of the Soviet Union against imperialist attack.

3. The best defense – the only thing that can save the Soviet Union in the end by solving its contradictions – is the international revolution of the proletariat.

4. In order to regenerate the workers' state we stand for the overthrow of the bureaucracy by a political revolution.

But, it may be said, "Defense of the Soviet Union, and Russia is a Workers' State – those two phrases don't answer everything." They are not simply phrases. One is a theoretical analysis; the other is a political conclusion for action.

Our motion calls for unconditional defense of the Soviet Union against imperialist attack. What does that mean? It simply means that we defend the Soviet Union and its nationalized property against external attacks of imperialist armies or against internal attempts at capitalist restoration, without putting as a prior condition the overthrow of the Stalinist bureaucracy. Any other kind of defense negates the whole position under present circumstances. Some people speak nowadays of giving "conditional" defense to the Soviet Union. If you stop to think about it we are for conditional defense of the United States. It is so stated in the program of the Fourth International. In the event of war we will absolutely defend the country on only one small "condition": that we first overthrow the government of the capitalists and replace it with a government of the workers.

Does unconditional defense of the Soviet Union mean supporting every act of the Red Army? No, that is absurd. Did we support the Moscow trials and the actions of Stalin's GPU in these trials? Did we support the purges, the wholesale murders of the old Bolsheviks? Did we support the actions of the Stalinist military forces in Spain which were directed against the workers? If I recall correctly, we unconditionally defended those workers who fought on the other side of the barricades in Barcelona. That did not prevent us from supporting the military struggle against Franco and maintaining our position in defense of the Soviet Union against imperialist attack.

It is now demanded that we take a big step forward and support the idea of an armed struggle against Stalin in the newly occupied territories of old Poland. Is this really something new ? For three years the Fourth International has advocated in its program the armed overthrow of Stalin inside the Soviet Union itself. The Fourth International has generally acknowledged the necessity for an armed struggle to set up an independent Soviet Ukraine. How can there be any question of having a different policy in the newly occupied territories? If the revolution against Stalin is really ready there, the Fourth International will certainly support it and endeavor to lead it. There are no two opinions possible in our ranks on this question. But what shall we do if Hitler (or Chamberlain) attacks the Sovietized Ukraine before Stalin has been overthrown? This is the question that needs an unambiguous answer. Shall we defend the Soviet Union, and with it now and for the same reasons, the nationalized property of the newly annexed territories? We say, yes!

That position was incorporated into the program of the foundation congress of the Fourth International, held in the summer of 1938. Remember, that was after the Moscow trials and the crushing of the Spanish revolution. It was after the murderous purge of the whole generation of Bolsheviks, after the people's front, the entry into the League of Nations, the Stalin-Laval pact (and betrayal of the French workers). We took our position on the basis of the economic structure of the country, the fruit of the revolution. The great gains are not to be surrendered before they are really lost. That is the fighting program of the Fourth International.

The Stalin-Hitler pact does not change anything fundamentally. If Stalin were allied with the United States, and comrades should deny defense of the Soviet Union out of fear of becoming involved in the defense of Stalin's American ally, such comrades would be wrong, but their position would be understandable as a subjective reaction prompted by revolutionary sentiments. The "defeatism" which broke out in our French section following the Stalin-Laval pact was undoubtedly so motivated and, consequently, had to be refuted with the utmost tolerance and patience. But an epidemic of "defeatism" in the democratic camp would be simply shameful. There is no pressure on us in America to defend the Soviet Union. All the pressure is for a democratic holy war against the Soviet Union. Let us keep this in mind. The main enemy is still in our own country.

What has happened since our last discussion? Has there been some fundamental change in Soviet economy? No, nothing of that kind is maintained. Nothing happened except that Stalin signed the pact with Hitler! For us that gave no reason whatever to change our analysis of Soviet economy and our attitude toward it. The aim of all our previous theoretical work, concentrated in our program, was precisely to prepare us for war and revolution. Now we have the war; and revolution is next in order. If we have to stop now to find a new program it is a very bad sign.

Just consider: There are people who could witness all the crimes and betrayals of Stalin, which we understood better than anybody else, and denounced before anybody else and more effectively – they could witness all this and still stand for the defense of the Soviet Union. But they could not tolerate the alliance with fascist Germany instead of imperialist England or France!

Of course, there has been a great hullaballoo about the Soviet invasion of Polish Ukraine. But that is simply one of the consequences of the war and the alliance with Hitler's Germany. The contention that we should change our analysis of the social character of the Soviet state and our attitude toward its defense because the Red Army violated the Polish border is even more absurd than to base such changes on the Hitler pact. The Polish invasion is only an incident in a war, and in wars borders are always violated. (If all the armies stayed at home there could be no war). The inviolability of borders – all of which were established by war – is interesting to democratic pacifists and to nobody else.

Hearing all the democratic clamor we had to ask ourselves many times: Don't they know that Western Ukraine and White Russia never rightfully belonged to Poland? Don't they know that this territory was forcibly taken from the Soviet Union by Pilsudski [quasi-fascist Polish head of state] with French aid in 1920?

To be sure, this did not justify Stalin's invasion of the territory in collaboration with Hitler. We never supported that and we never supported the fraudulent claim that Stalin was bringing "liberation" to the peoples of the Polish Ukraine. At the same time we did not propose to yield an inch to the "democratic" incitement against the Soviet Union on the basis of the Polish events. The democratic war mongers were shrieking at the top of their voices all over town. We must not be unduly impressed by this democratic clamor. Your National Committee was not in the least impressed.

In order to penetrate a little deeper into this question and trace it to its roots, let us take another hypothetical example. Not a fantastic one, but a very logical one. Suppose Stalin had made a pact with the imperialist democracies against Hitler while Rumania had allied itself with Hitler. Suppose, as would most probably have happened in that case, the Red Army had struck at Rumania, Hitler's ally, instead of Poland, the ally of the democracies, and had seized Bessarabia [eastern Romania], which also once belonged to Russia. Would the democratic war mongers in that case have howled about "Red imperialism?" Not on your life!

I am very glad that our National Committee maintained its independence from bourgeois democratic pressure on the Polish invasion. The question was put to us very excitedly, point-blank, like a pistol at the temple: "Are you for or against the invasion of Poland?" But revolutionary Marxists don't answer in a "yes" or "no" manner which can lump them together with other people who pursue opposite aims. Being for or against something is not enough in the class struggle. It is necessary to explain from what standpoint one is for or against. Are you for or against racketeering gangsters in the trade unions? – the philistines sometimes ask. We don't jump to attention, like a private soldier who has met an officer on the street, and answer "against!" We first inquire: who asks this question and from what standpoint? And what weight does this question have in relation to other questions? We have our own standpoint and we are careful not to get our answers mixed up with those of class enemies and pacifist muddleheads.

Some people – especially affected bosses – are against racketeering gangsters in the trade unions because they extort graft from the bosses. That side of the question doesn't interest us very much. Some people – especially pacifist preachers – are against the gangsters because they commit violence. But we are not against violence at all times and under all circumstances. We, for our part, taking our time and formulating our viewpoint precisely, say: We are against union gangsterism because it injures the union in its fight against the bosses. That is our reason. It proceeds from our special class standpoint on the union question.

So with Poland: We don't support the course of Stalin in general.

His crime is not one incident here or there but his whole policy. He demoralizes the workers' movement and discredits the Soviet Union. That is what we are against. He betrays the revolution by his whole course. Every incident for us fits into that framework; it is considered from that point of view and taken in its true proportions.

Those who take the Polish invasion – an incident in a great chain of events – as the basis for a fundamental change in our program show a lack of proportion. That is the kindest thing that can be said for them. They are destined to remain in a permanent lather throughout the war. They are already four laps behind schedule: There is also Latvia, and Estonia, and Lithuania, and now Finland.

We can expect another clamor of demands that we say, pointblank, and in one word, whether we are "for" or "against" the pressure on poor little bourgeois-democratic Finland? Our answer – wait a minute. Keep your shirt on. There is no lack of protests in behalf of the bourgeois swine who rule Finland. The *New Leader* has protested. Charles Yale Harrison (Charlie-the-Rat) has written a tearful column about it. The renegade Lore has wept about it in the *New York Post*. The President of the United States has protested. Finland is pretty well covered with moral support. So bourgeois Finland can wait a minute till we explain our attitude without bothering about the "for" or "against" ultimatum.

I personally feel very deeply about Finland, and this is by no means confined to the present dispute between Stalin and the Finnish Prime Minister. When I think of Finland, I think of the thousands of martyred dead, the proletarian heroes who perished under the white terror of Mannerheim [military leader of Whites in Finland's civil war, 1918] . I would, if I could, call them back from their graves. Failing that, I would organize a proletarian army of Finnish workers to avenge them, and drive their murderers into the Baltic Sea. I would send the Red Army of the regenerated Soviet Union to help them at the decisive moment.

We don't support Stalin's invasion only because he doesn't come for revolutionary purposes. He doesn't come at the call of Finnish workers whose confidence he has forfeited. That is the only reason we are against it. The "borders" have nothing to do with it. "Defense" in war also means attack. Do you think we will respect frontiers when we make our revolution? If an enemy army lands troops at Quebec, for example, do you think we will wait placidly at the Canadian border for their attack? No, if we are genuine revolutionists, and not pacifist muddle-heads, we will cross the border and meet them at the point of landing. And if our defense requires the seizure of Quebec, we will seize it as the Red Army of Lenin seized Georgia and tried to take Warsaw. Some may think the war and the alliance with Hitler change everything we have previously considered; that it, at least, requires a reconsideration of the whole question of the Soviet Union, if not a complete change in our program. To this we can answer:

War was contemplated by our program. The fundamental theses on *War and the Fourth International*, adopted in 1934, say:

"Every big war, irrespective of its initial moves, must pose squarely the question of military intervention against the USSR in order to transfuse fresh blood into the sclerotic veins of capitalism ...

"Defense of the Soviet Union from the blows of the capitalist enemies, irrespective of the circumstances and immediate causes of the conflict, is the elementary and imperative duty of every honest labor organization."

Alliances were contemplated. The theses say:

"In the existing situation an alliance of the USSR with an imperialist state or with one imperialist combination against another, in case of war, cannot at all be considered as excluded. Under the pressure of circumstances a temporary alliance of this kind may become an iron necessity, without ceasing, however, because of it, to be of the greatest danger both to the USSR and to the world revolution.

"The international proletariat will not decline to defend the USSR even if the latter should find itself forced into a military alliance with some imperialists against others. But in this case, even more than in any other, the international proletariat must safeguard its complete political independence from Soviet diplomacy and thereby also from the bureaucracy of the Third International."

A stand on defense was taken in the light of this perspective.

The slogan of defense acquires a concrete meaning precisely in the event of war. A strange time to drop it! That would mean a rejection of all our theoretical preparation for the war. That would mean starting all over again. From what fundamental basis? Nobody knows.

There has been much talk of "independence" on the Russian question. That is good! A revolutionist who is not independent is not worth his salt. But it is necessary to specify: independent of whom? What is needed by our party at every turn is class independence, independence of the Stalinists, and, above all, independence of the bourgeoisie. Our program assures such independence under all circumstances. It shall not be changed!

The question of today is Stalin's invasion of Poland

Max Shachtman (1939)

IN ORDER TO have a clear understanding of the present dispute, it is necessary to start with an account of how it originated and developed. It might have been possible to dispense with this aspect of the question if Comrade Cannon had not presented a completely distorted version of it.

Our differences did not develop out of thin air nor as a result of an arbitrary whim on the part of any comrade. It can, therefore, be understood only by a knowledge of the actual circumstances in which it arose.

The question now in dispute originated in reality at our last convention. As will be seen later, it is important to bear this date in mind.

As you know, prior to the convention and during its sessions we had no specific Russian discussion or special resolution. Formally the question was dealt with only to the extent that it was referred to in the program of transitional demands which the convention formally adopted. Apparently nobody deemed it necessary to raise the Russian question in the manner in which it had been discussed in the past.

However, it was raised in a new form, at least in one of its aspects, during the discussion on the international report which I delivered. Comrade Johnson in his speech dwelt on the question of our attitude towards Stalin's policy and towards the Red Army in the event of an encroachment upon or an invasion of Poland, the Baltic countries, and other lands adjacent to the Soviet Union. This question was assuming an urgent character because of the negotiations between Stalin and England and France. Stalin was demanding that he be given the right to "guarantee" the Baltic countries and Poland from German attack. I emphasize the fact that this was at the time of the Soviet alliance with France and what appeared to be an impending alliance with Anglo-French imperialism, that is to say, with the "democracies."

Comrade Carter was the only delegate who took up the discussion on this point, and I referred to it in my summary, As I recall it, I said that it would be necessary to consider the question seriously, especially as it became increasingly pertinent, because the masses in Russia's border states undoubtedly looked with the greatest suspicion, fear and hostility upon Stalin's proposal to "guarantee them from aggression". Nobody else took the floor on this point. I don't know whether Cannon was disinterested in the question or did not consider it important at the time, but he did not say a word about it, either privately or on the convention floor.

Nothing came of this matter in any concrete form at the convention or immediately afterward because the issue was still somewhat vague. It was still in the realm of secret and obscure diplomatic discussion in the European capitals and chancelleries. In any case, it had not taken on such concrete form as to require from us an answer or perhaps even to make it possible for us to give that answer. But at least one important thing to bear in mind is that the very fact that it was raised at that time is sufficient by itself to dispose of the slanderous falsehood now disseminated by Cannon, and repeated in the internal bulletin by Goldman, that our resolution and standpoint implied a rejection of Stalin's policy only because he is linked with fascist imperialism, and an acceptance of the policy if he had been linked with the democratic bandits. The question, I repeat, was first raised in the period of Stalin's alliance with French imperialism, and if we did not present a concrete resolution it then was only because it had not yet assumed concrete form.

It was only after the Stalin-Hitler pact was signed and the invasion of Poland had passed from the realm of possibility and speculation into the realm of living reality that the question assumed the most urgent importance and actuality. It is not correct that everybody took the events in his stride. The fact is all the leading comrades were greatly disturbed. At the August 22 meeting of the Political Committee, I moved, "That the next meeting of the PC begin with a discussion of our estimate of the Stalin-Hitler pact as related to our evaluation of the Soviet State and the perspectives of the future." Nobody argued that there is nothing new in the situation. Nobody proposed a mere reaffirmation of our old line, My motion was carried unanimously, as a matter of course, so to speak. So that the record is given in full and no wrong impressions created among you, I point out that Comrade Cannon was not present at this meeting. His supporters were not so intransigent on the question then as they are now.

The next meeting of the PC took place after I had left on my brief tour on the Pact. That was September 1. The second world war had to all intents and purposes broken out and we were faced with enormous tasks and responsibilities. Comrade Gould, who was acting for a week or two in my place, made a series of motions for an immediate plenum, the aim of which was to put the party on a war footing, on the alert, for speeding the preparations to qualify the party for its multiplied tasks. Some of his motions were perhaps not feasible — that is possible. But the general line of them was absolutely correct and in order. Everybody present was in favour of an immediate plenum. The difference revolved only around the date a week earlier or a week later.

But it is most interesting to note that everybody agreed to put the Russian question on the agenda, and that Comrade Burnham was unanimously assigned to make the report on this question!

Now Burnham's position on the Russian question is no secret to the party, even less so to the PC. It was as well known in the past as it is now. His editorial in the *New International*, about which there has since been so much clamour, was already out. If the PC majority really and honestly thought there was nothing new in the situation, and if they really were ready to defend their old position without further ado, why in heaven's name was Burnham assigned to make the report? It is entirely unprecedented in our movement to act in this way. If, for example, I am known as an avowed critic or opponent of the official party position on the trade union question, I would never be assigned by the Committee to report on this question to a plenum or a membership meeting. The Committee would assign a supporter of its position to report on it, and in a discussion I would be assigned to deliver a minority report. Why was a contrary procedure followed in the case of Burnham and the report on the Russian question?

The talk about our having created a crisis or a panic is completely absurd. In actuality it was these comrades who maintain that their political line is so clear, so unaltered, so uncompromising that they must have an organizational stranglehold on the NC and the PC — it was these comrades who showed themselves completely disoriented and incapable of giving the leadership they boast about. On precisely that question which they now claim marks the dividing line between the hard Bolshevik and the vacillating petty-bourgeois they demonstratively acknowledged their bankruptcy by failing to put forward one of their number to report and assigning it instead to Burnham. Again to keep the record accurate, Cannon was not present at the meeting.

Two days later, a special meeting was held to consider the question, this time with Cannon present. Although I was still on tour, I venture to speak from hearsay because his arguments were subsequently repeated upon my return. Cannon charged that the comrades were creating a panic for nothing, that they were hysterical, that there was nothing new in the situation. As for the plenum, he was against its immediate convocation for the above reasons and because, he said, it had to be prepared documentarily. Good. Two days later, at the September 5 meeting of the PC, Burnham submitted his document on the character of the war and Russia's role in it. Apart from this document, from my resolution, and Johnson's statement, no other document was submitted for the plenum. Cannon submitted nothing, absolutely nothing, in the form of a resolution or thesis on the question, or for that matter on any other question on the agenda of the plenum; nor did anyone else. Was that because other comrades thought there really was nothing new in the situation? In my opinion, no. For on September 3, Cannon moved that Crux [Trotsky] be asked officially "to express himself on the Russian question in the light of recent events." Furthermore, that Crux be familiarized with "the material submitted in the question" and that we "request his opinion before a decision is taken by the plenum."

Now it seems to me that an obvious contradiction is present here. If there is nothing new in the situation, if all that is needed, as Cannon contended, is a reaffirmation of our previous position, then a decision of that kind could be taken without requesting Comrade Crux's opinion and without making it dependant upon this opinion. The opinion would be, as it was, valuable, enlightening and important, it would be what you will, but yet it could not be of such a nature as to necessitate holding up a vote by us on the question.

The fact is that everybody was disturbed by the events and felt that the old line, even if correct, was not adequate. At the very least, something had to be added to it. And that was the only serious meaning contained in Cannon's motions on Crux. It goes without saying that the request for Crux's opinions was adopted unanimously. But I at least voted for the motion precisely because there was "something new" in the situation, and I was very anxious to read Crux's analysis of it. Yet, I say that the motions were in conflict with Cannon's views because at the very next meeting, on September 8, Cannon and his supporters came forward against a discussion of the Russian question — against any discussion. There is nothing particularly new in the situation, said Cannon, in the circular he sent out to the NC members commenting on Burnham's resolution. A discussion at this time is a luxury we cannot afford, he said, in just those words. When Cannon says now that a discussion of a position such as Burnham put forward would be fruitful and educational, it simply does not square with his statements a month ago that a new discussion would be a luxury we cannot afford.

On September 12, at the first PC meeting to be held after my return from the speaking tour, there was a turn about face. My motion on the plenum was carried without objection. I did not propose, as is stated, to call the plenum on the Russian question. The four points I proposed for an agenda — the war crisis, the work of the International, the Russian question, and the organization-press drive — were adopted virtually without discussion. Why? Because, I believe, among other things I reported that every NC member I spoke with on the road was also "panic-stricken". Clarke and Solander in Detroit, comrades in Chicago, all were for an immediate plenum. In Minneapolis I signed a joint telegram with all the local NC members pointing out their readiness to come to a plenum almost immediately. There is not the slightest doubt that every responsible leading comrade outside New York felt that a plenum was urgently required to discuss the questions I mentioned.

In the middle of September the events precipitated the problem directly and concretely without waiting for us to get together a plenum. Stalin invaded Poland in alliance with Hitler. What was the party to say? What was its mouthpiece, the *Appeal*, to say? It is utter nonsense to argue that the membership of the party went blandly about its way, unmoved and uninterested in the events. They were intensely interested in the position the party would take on the invasion and there is not the slightest doubt in the world that the readers of the party press were equally interested. It was, of course, impossible for me to write in the *Appeal* on the basis of my personal opinion alone. I, therefore, called together all the available members of the staff and of the Political Committee. By its very nature the gathering could not be anything but informal, it could not adopt decisions on such a matter of policy and I announced both before and at the end of the meeting that I considered it a consultative body, that is to say, only the Political Committee could decide the line of our articles. After as thorough a discussion of the question as we could have under the circumstances it was generally agreed that an emergency meeting of the PC would have to be held to decide the question, if possible before the *Appeal* went to press.

That same evening, September 18, a special meeting was held. We were of the opinion that whatever the party's basic estimate of the class nature of the Soviet State might be, a specific answer had to be given to the specific question. Comrade Burnham moved that the *Appeal* take the line that through its invasion of Poland the Red Army is participating integrally in the imperialist war, that is to say, that we condemn the invasion. That point of view was rejected by the majority of the Political Committee. Comrade Goldman presented the following motion: "Under the actual conditions prevailing in Poland, we approve of Stalin's invasion of Poland as a measure of preventing Hitler from getting control of all of Poland and as a measure of defending the Soviet Union against Hitler. Between Hitler and Stalin, we prefer Stalin." Comrade Goldman was the only one to vote for his motion. Yet his position was entirely consistent, consistent in particular with the traditional position of the party and the interpretation we had always placed upon it. But with his motion defeated, Goldman voted for the motion of Cannon.

And what was Cannon's answer to the problem raised by the Polish invasion, the answer that the Political Committee adopted? Here is his motion in full: "The party press in its handling of Russia's participation in the war in Poland shall do so from the point of view of the party's fundamental analysis of the character of the Soviet State, and the role of Stalinism as laid down in the fundamental resolutions of the party's foundation convention and the foundation congress of the Fourth International. The slogan of an independent Soviet Ukraine shall be defended as a policy wholly consistent with the fundamental line of defending the Soviet Union."

Now I contend that this was no answer at all, or rather that it made possible a variety of answers. On the basis of this motion, a half dozen members of the Political Committee could write a half dozen different articles. We would repeat time and again that the Soviet Union is a workers' state and that we are for its defence, but that did not answer the question uppermost in the minds of everybody: Do we support the invasion of Poland, or do we oppose it? Cannon categorically refused to give a reply to this question. His point of view was that it is purely a military question and that we were in no position to express ourselves affirmatively or negatively on it. Our task, said Cannon, is merely to explain. In support of this view, Gordon, for example, placed the invasion of Poland in the same category as the invasion of Belgium in 1914, and argued that there, too, we merely "explained" the invasion as an "episode" in the war as a whole but did not say that we were for it or against it. (It might be remarked parenthetically that even in this comparison Gordon was wrong because the internationalists did not hesitate even in the case of Belgium to condemn the invasion by Germany, even though the invasion of Poland by Stalin is not on the same footing.)

At the same meeting I moved that the Committee "endorse the general line of the September 18 editorial" in the *Appeal* which I had written. Cannon and his supporters rejected the motion, Cannon voting against it and the others abstaining. Why? For the simple reason that I condemned the invasion in the very mildest terms. I had characterized the reports that Stalin was moving to the aid of Hitler as a "sinister plan." Cochrane took objection to this phrase. He motivated his abstention on the basis of it. He considered it too strong. The very next day the press carried reports of a statement made by Trotsky in Mexico condemning the invasion as shameful and criminal.

At the meeting we pointed out that the inadequate and evasive motion of Cannon would meet its first test twenty four hours later at the mass meeting which Goldman was scheduled to address and at which questions would undoubtedly be asked about the party's attitude towards the invasion. But the Committee refused to take any steps to deal with this matter. The result was that when Goldman spoke the next day, September 19, he not only declared at a public meeting that there was a dispute in the party on the subject and that we were calling a plenum to settle it, but also that the Political Committee disagreed with Trotsky in condemning the invasion. And as you know, in the article which Cannon was assigned to write for the *Appeal* on the subject, he carefully refrained from characterising or condemning the invasion and confined himself merely to rejecting the Stalinist contention that the result of the invasion would be the liberation of the Ukrainians and the White Russians.

Finally we came to the PC meeting on the eve of the plenum. The document which we awaited from Comrade Crux had not arrived. We had the Burnham resolution on the subject, but the majority, which had insisted on the need of preparing material prior to the plenum, had no resolution whatsoever to offer. I could not subscribe entirely to the Burnham resolution, and I announced that I would offer one of my own on the invasion of Poland. When the question of reporters arose, Burnham announced that he would either write a different resolution or support one that would be introduced. This announcement occasioned no astonishment or criticism at that time. At the same meeting, confronted with the fact that the majority had no document at all to present to the plenum on the Russian question, Cannon presented the following motion as his resolution: "We reaffirm the basic analysis of the nature of the Soviet State and the role of Stalinism, and the political conclusions drawn from this analysis as laid down in the previous decisions of our party convention and the program of the Fourth International." This was the sole contribution made by the majority.

To sum up, therefore, the Political Committee confined itself to a simple-reiteration of the traditional party position not as a basis for giving concrete answers to concrete questions, but as a substitute for these answers; that is, it failed and refused to give an answer to the specific questions posed by the events. To the extent that it tried to give one, it was false and spread confusion or else left matters hanging in the air. Cannon's article in the *Appeal* is one example. Goldman's speech at the New York mass meeting is another. If that is the meaning of revolutionary leadership on the issues of the day, I have nothing in common with it.

Now as to the actual contents of the dispute. One way of approaching the question is from the angle of the so called unprincipled bloc that we have formed. The argument runs about as follows: Burnham says that the Soviet Union is not a workers' state. Shachtman says he does not raise this question. Consequently, the minority is a bloc and an unprincipled one. I regard the charge as unprincipled bunk. While I have not and do not raise the question of revising the party's fundamental position on the nature of the Soviet State, I was and am ready to discuss the question. The fact is that I requested such a discussion and the minority supported me in this request. We proposed that the pages of the *New International*, our theoretical organ, be opened up for such a discussion. This was at first refused and granted only at the plenum. Why am I not in favour of centring the present discussion around that question here? Because I do not think it is necessary. In fact, under the circumstances I do not think it would be fruitful. The way in which the discussion has already been started indicates to me that it would only serve to obscure the real issue and dispute at hand. In what sense do I mean this? (Burnham is new being condemned for having withdrawn his document. But this withdrawal actually occurred on the basis of the advice of Comrade Crux and on my advice).

In a brief letter to the Political Committee which arrived before his main document, Comrade Crux pointed out that in so far as the dispute was "terminological" no practical political question could be altered by changing the formula "workers' state" to the formula "not workers' state" or "bureaucratic caste" to "class". He said, granted that it is not a workers' state: granted that it is a class and not a caste. What change would then be introduced into our political conclusions? The opponents, as Crux pointed out, would have gained an "empty victory" and would not know what to do with it.

I do not begin to deny the importance even of the "terminological dispute" if only because we must strive for the strictest scientific accuracy in our characterizations. But under the circumstances, that is, of the need of answering the questions raised by the Polish invasion, such a dispute could very easily degenerate into a sterile and purely terminological discussion. That can already be seen by the manner in which the question has been presented. A workers' state is defined as a social order based upon nationalized property. On that basis, many comrades conclude that the whole problem is exhausted. That being the definition of a workers' state, the Soviet Union is a workers' state. Thus we do not advance an inch.

Why would such a discussion be sterile at the moment? Because it would not and does not necessarily alter one's political conclusions. Trotsky pointed that out and so do I. The political question is: Will you defend the Soviet Union? whereupon it must be asked: What do we defend? The only remaining conquest of the Russian Revolution is nationalized property. Now there is not a soul in our party who stands for the denationalization of property in the Soviet Union — not Burnham, not Cannon, not Shachtman, not Johnson. The only question that can possibly be in dispute is — How do we defend nationalized property?

Let us take the question from another angle. The fundamental position of the party, no matter how often reiterated, does not provide us automatically with an answer to the concrete questions. For example, Goldman, Cannon, Trotsky, all proceed from the fundamental conception that the Soviet Union is a workers' state. Yet Goldman approved the invasion, Cannon was indifferent to it, considering it a purely military question which we were incapable of judging, whereas Trotsky denounced the invasion. It was for such reasons that Burnham was, therefore, prevailed upon to withdraw his thesis from the present discussion, to withhold it for another and more suitable occasion and place, to confine the discussion of the questions that he and others have raised to the theoretical organ of the party.

In this connection I was challenged by Cannon: Why don't you propose to expel Burnham as a defeatist? I made a motion two or three years ago declaring defeatist views are incompatible with membership in the party, and Cannon supported me in that position. I do not propose such a motion now. Cannon says that I speak equally well on both sides of the question. By the same token, he can speak well on one side of the question at one time and be silent on it at another. Why doesn't he propose the expulsion of the defeatists? But, it is argued, you make a bloc with Burnham against Cannon and Goldman, with whom you are in fundamental agreement. The argument is not valid.

In 1925-26 the Sapronovist group of Democratic Centralists [within the Bolshevik party] declared in its platform that the [Russian] revolution was over. The Thermidor [counter-revolution] had triumphed. Russia was no longer a workers' state. Yet when the opposition bloc was formed in 1926 by the Moscow and Leningrad groups, the Democratic Centralists entered into the bloc. If they broke from it later, it was on their initiative — "artificially", said Trotsky, and not on his initiative. He opposed the break, as he pointed out in 1929 in a letter to one of the supporters of the Democratic Centralist group. If he joined with them in one bloc, it was because all supporters of the bloc jointly gave the right answers to the concrete questions before the party. In my opinion, that is what we have to do now. I could vote a hundred times over, just as Goldman does, for the "fundamental motion" of Cannon. So can Abern and Erber and others. But I cannot give the same answer to the problems that Goldman gave or that Cannon gave. And that makes it impossible for me and all others to join with them just as it makes it mandatory for me and all others to join with these who give the same answer.

But does not that deprive you of a fundamental position from which to derive your policies? Not at all. There are fundamental criteria for a revolutionary Marxist which are just as valid now as they were a year ago and twenty five years ago, even before the Russian Revolution. The first is the fundamental and decisive character of the war in question, and we say that the decisive character of the present war is imperialist. And secondly our policies in all questions must be derived from the fundamental conception of the interests of the world socialist revolution, to which all other interests are subordinate and secondary.

Before I can return to this question I find it necessary to deal again with the point: is there anything new in the situation to cause us to change our policy? Yes! And in reality everybody acknowledges it, if not explicitly then tacitly.

Is it because of the pact with Hitler? If so, then you are a People's Fronter. No, that is a slander. I have already pointed out that the questions we now raise were first raised three months ago, at the time of the Soviet alliance with the democratic imperialists. No, it is not the pact itself that changes the situation. I have pointed out a hundred times in articles and speeches that an isolated Soviet State not only may but often must conclude commercial, diplomatic, and even military agreements with imperialist powers, and that there is not a particle of difference in principle between an agreement with a democratic country, a fascist country or a feudal country. So it is not the pact itself that necessitates a change in our policy. It is the concreteness of the events and it is doubtful that we could have foreseen them in their actuality. And the actuality, if only because of its concreteness, is different from our necessarily limited prognoses, as different as arithmetic is from algebra.

As I understand it, that is how Lenin dealt with the reality of the democratic revolution in Russia. His prognosis about the "democratic dictatorship" did not and could not conform with the concrete reality. He had no hesitation in altering his political conclusions to suit that reality. I can give many other examples. It is argued that there is no need to be surprised at the events and no need to modify our policy because we foresaw them. Before 1914 Lenin foresaw the degeneration of the Second International. But it was only after August 4, when the Second International ranged itself openly and, so to speak, dramatically on the side of imperialism that he proposed a change in policy, that is to say, to withdraw from the Second International to which he had belonged and to call for a Third International.

Another example. Trotsky saw and foresaw the degeneration of the Third International. In Germany [1933] Stalinism betrayed the proletariat and the revolution no more than it had betrayed them in China six years earlier. Yet although we retained our fundamental views on the principles of revolutionary Marxism, we broke with the Comintern not on the occasion of the Chinese betrayal but on the occasion of the German. It is argued against us now that we propose a change in policy only because the alliance is made with the fascist imperialists and that we did not propose such a change when the alliance was made with the democratic imperialists four years ago. One could just as legitimately argue that we considered it all right for the Stalinists to betray Chinese coolies but not to betray the superior white workers of Germany. Both arguments are equally wrong. What was involved in both cases was an accumulation, precipitated in the form of a concrete event or a series of events.

Similarly in the case of the invasion of Poland and the Baltic countries. In the period of the pact with France, the question was essentially theoretical and we could put forward only hypotheses. It is true Stalin was then also an agent of imperialism. But the war and the concrete events attending it had not yet broken out. Years ago the Stalinist regime indicated that it might or would act in the way it has now really acted, just as before the war of 1914 the social democracy indicated that it might or would act the way it finally did when the war broke out.

The challenge to present some fundamental change in the situation is in this case either superficial or irrelevant. As I understand our basic position, it always was to oppose separatist tendencies in the Federated Soviet Republics. Now I ask: what fundamental change occurred, what was the nature of this change, and when did it occur, to cause us to raise the slogan of an independent united Soviet Ukraine, that is to say, a separatist slogan?

Another example: when and why did we decide in favour of a political revolution in Russia? Because of the imprisonment or the shooting of Zinoviev? No. That is so much nonsense. We changed our policy on that question because an accumulation of things dictated that change.

Take the question from still another angle. I do not have to be instructed on the admissibility of a workers' state extending the revolution to other countries, even by military means and without regard for frontiers laid down in imperialist treaties, or for that matter any other kind of frontiers. I have taught that to thousands of people. But I point out that throughout the early years of the Bolshevik movement we hailed the advances of the Red Army into other countries. When the Red Army marched into Poland in 1920, then regardless of whether or not it was tactically correct, we hailed its progress enthusiastically. We called upon them to weaken and destroy the Polish army and to facilitate the victory of the Red Army. We took the same position when the Red Army invaded Georgia [in 1921]; we said then that "democratic" considerations about which international Menshevism howled so much were entirely subordinate (if they were involved at all in the Georgian case) to socialist considerations. We denounced the opponents and critics of the Red Army. We justified the entry of the Red Army into Georgia.

Now, if there is nothing new in the situation, why does not the majority propose to hail the advance of the Red Army into Poland, into the Baltic countries, into Finland? Why don't we call upon the workers and peasants of these countries to welcome the Red Army, to facilitate its victory, to help destroy all the obstacles that stand in the way of this victory?

Again we endorsed Stalin's seizure of the Chinese Eastern Railway in 1929. We defended the action from all varieties of democratic and "revolutionary" critics who pointed out that the railway was Chinese or partly Chinese, and that the Chinese were not consulted about the seizure. Why don't we by the same token endorse the seizure of Poland and other countries by Stalin today? What is new in the situation? The refusal even of the majority to take the same position today that we all took in 1920 and even in 1929 indicates that at least in this respect the burden of proof about what is new in the situation rests upon the majority.

I cannot take seriously the argument of the majority that the only thing really new in the situation is that people in the party are succumbing to "democratic pressure." That there is an enormous democratic pressure being exerted upon the labour movement and even our movement is undeniable. That it is necessary to guard against yielding to that pressure is equally true. But it is necessary not only to guard against that pressure but to fight against it. How? We must first recognise that the whole policy of Stalin facilitates the work of democratic demagogues. As in the past they exploit Stalinist crimes and the resentment against them felt by the working class in order to bring the working class more completely under the sway of imperialist and anti-Bolshevik ideology. We can combat the efforts of the democratic imperialists' agents only by a correct and unambiguous policy of our own and not by mere denunciation. We can combat them only by pointing out that Stalin's course has nothing in common with ours. Only by condemning the Stalinist invasion as an act which is contrary not only to the interests of the international working class but to the interests of the Soviet Union itself. We cannot combat it — the workers will rightly turn their backs on us — if we endorse Stalin's action, if we condone it, or even if we appear to do so.

Now as to the slogan of unconditional defence which we must now abandon, in my opinion, unless we mean to keep the formula and by means of sophistry to fill it with a new content. What did this slogan mean to us in the past? Goldman says now: "I repeat. It was taken for granted that the slogan of defending the Soviet Union applied only in case of war by a capitalist nation against the Soviet Union." Let us grant that for a moment and we shall see who it is that unwittingly yields to the pressure of democratic patriotism and to the pacifist distinction between wars of aggression and of defence.

What we really meant in the past when we said we were for unconditional defence was this: We are for defeatism in the enemy country and patriotism in the Red Army. In the Red Army we are the best soldiers. We are for the victory of the Red Army and for the defeat of its enemy, and that regardless of who "started the war." We never asked who struck the first blow or who first crossed his own frontiers. By Soviet patriotism we also meant that we call upon the soldiers and population of the enemy to give active support to the Red Army; that we call for sabotage in the country and in the army of the Red Army's enemy. Isn't that what we always said and meant in the past by our slogan?

Now why didn't we and don't we say that in the case of Poland, or tomorrow, in the case of Finland? Isn't Poland a capitalist country? Isn't it an imperialist power? Isn't it an ally of the democratic imperialists opposed to Russia? In accordance with our old conception, we should have called upon the Polish masses to welcome the Red Army. Why didn't we? Was it because Russia was the military aggressor? But we have not ever and we should not now draw any basic distinctions between defence and aggression, and Cannon was a thousand times right in pointing out that Marxian platitude, as he so very often is.

Further. Why don't we take that line in the case of the Baltic countries — Latvia, Lithuania, Estonia? They are capitalist countries, they are tools of one or another imperialist bloc. If they are engaged in any kind of struggle — regardless, I repeat, of who fired the first shot or who first crossed frontiers — it is obviously a question of war between the Soviet Union and a capitalist power. In that case, by unconditional defence we must mean, as we always did in the past, that we are for the victory of the Red Army. Surely we never took the position in the past that we gave unconditional defence of the Soviet Union only when the troops of a capitalist power take the initiative in the struggle and cross into the territory of the Soviet Union. By virtue of our old position, we should fight for the victory of the Red Army and simultaneously for the defeat of the opposing armies. The majority is simply not consistent with itself. While holding to the old conception, it has adopted a document which says that we are opposed to the seizures of new territory by the Kremlin. According to Comrade Trotsky, the Stalinist invasion was shameful and criminal, that is to say, we condemn it. Now we would not condemn Russia for invading Germany, would we? And if Poland had first attacked, militarily, the Soviet Union, I do not believe we would condemn Stalin or the Red Army for repulsing this attack and pushing the Polish Army back to Warsaw or further. Why would we? Would it be because in that case Poland was the "aggressor," whereas in the actual case Russia was the "aggressor"?

Again. Comrade Goldman said his error, which he now acknowledges, consisted in supporting the invasion under the impression that it was not done in agreement with Hitler. When he became convinced that it was done in agreement with Hitler, he opposed it. It seems to me that Comrade Goldman replaces here one error with another. If that is his motivation for opposing the invasion, then at the very least we overlooked an important problem in failing to oppose a similar step when Stalin sought to take it in agreement with Daladier and Chamberlain. That was precisely the point that was dealt with by Comrades Johnson, Carter and myself at the last convention. Certainly the reason we failed to act at that time could not have been based upon the fact that Stalin planned his action in alliance with the democratic imperialists.

You give no answer to the concrete questions! Trotsky says: "We were and we remain against seizures of new territories by the Kremlin." Goldman says now: All right, but it's all over now in Poland; consequently, the basis for the dispute has been removed. Unfortunately this is not the case. If we are against such seizures, we are against them not only after they take place but also before. It is radically false to think that Poland was an incidental or accidental episode in the war, an episode of no characteristic importance. Yesterday it was Poland and today the Baltic countries, tomorrow and the day after, Finland, Rumania, Afghanistan, India, China, and other countries. The same problem will arise continually and with it the necessity of giving an answer far more concrete than we were systematically given by the majority of the PC

Do not think for a moment that you can dispose of such questions the way Cannon tried to do today. I was shocked when I heard him say half jokingly, "off the record", that the best thing that could happen to Finland would be to wipe it off the map altogether. That is a piece of first-class political cynicism. I am not a Finnish patriot any more than I am a Polish patriot. But as a revolutionary Marxist I am at the same time a consistent democrat. I am ready to subordinate democratic considerations only to socialist and internationalist considerations. I have no hesitation at all in saying that I am concerned not only with the socialist revolution but also with the national and democratic rights of Finland and the Baltic countries. I am prepared to subordinate even these rights to the interests of the socialist revolution if and where the two conflict. I am not ready to subordinate them to the interests of the Stalinist bureaucracy.

Decisive in politics is not only the "what" but also the "who." I am damned particular as to who "liberates" countries like Danzig [then German-populated city-state in Poland, seized by Germany 1939] or the Sudetenland [then German-populated areas of Czechoslovakia, seized by Hitler 1938]. Under Hitler the right of self-determination "triumphed" in appearance. In actuality reaction triumphed. And when Stalin invades Poland it is the Stalinist counter-revolution that has triumphed.

Your policy or rather your lack of policy makes it impossible for us to talk intelligibly or effectively to the masses of these countries who are threatened by Stalinist seizures or invasion. I want to see the party and the international adopt a policy which enables us to advance the cause of international revolution in these countries. We say in our international program that the anti-Hitlerite patriotism of the masses in the bourgeois countries has something potentially progressive in it. I want to be able to say to the masses of Russia's border states:

"Your anti-Stalinist patriotism has something potentially progressive about it. Your fear of a Stalinist invasion, your hostility to it, is entirely justified. You are not so ignorant that you do not know what Stalin's rule over you would mean. You must resist any attempt, military or political, to establish that rule. You must fight against the Red Army and not for its victory, if it seeks to establish Stalin's domination over you. But I say to you, your present patriotism is only potentially progressive. You cannot and must not fight against Stalinism under the rule of your own bourgeoisie, be it in Poland or Latvia or Finland, because that bourgeoisie is imperialist or the agent of imperialism. You must resist being driven into slavery under Stalin. So fight for power in your land. Win over the army and establish an army of your own, the people's militia, and fight for your own socialist cause."

It is true that by this line I will not succeed in having a revolution in Poland or Finland overnight. But if I reach two workers with it I will have brought them one stop closer to the goal they must attain, and that is what should be the purpose of any political line. The majority says: We will not approve and we will not condemn. We will merely "explain" the invasion. I say: Resist. Fight the Stalinist army under your own independent class banner. Fight them because they have imposed upon them the execution of an imperialist policy.

At this point the majority objects. The term "imperialist policy" cannot be applied to the Stalin regime. Comrade Goldman adds that while the term may be used in a broad or journalistic sense, it is incorrect because it may be deduced from this term that the Soviet Union is a capitalist imperialist state. That may well be. I do not deny it. But it does not necessarily follow, for otherwise many of our characterizations would have to be rejected on the same grounds. In the first place I am not the first one to have used this term in our movement. Only a couple of years ago, in a discussion with a Chinese comrade about the dangers of Stalinist intervention in China, the question was asked by the comrades: does that mean that Stalin can follow an imperialist policy in China? To which Trotsky replied: Those who are capable of perpetrating the Moscow frame-ups are capable of anything. Could not a "capitalist imperialist Soviet State" also be deduced from this entirely correct statement?

We say that Stalin has adopted the political methods of fascism.

Stalin's regime is closer to the political regime of fascism than to any other we have ever known. From this statement, often repeated by us, some people have deduced that fascism rules in Russia. But this has not altered our characterization of the Stalin regime. We say in one and the same breath that Hitler's regime is totalitarian, Mussolini's regime is totalitarian, Stalin's regime is totalitarian. I still believe that this is entirely accurate. The false deductions that some make from these statements do not mean that the statements are wrong.

We say that there is a Bonapartist regime in Germany and in Russia. I recall that when Trotsky first presented the formula of Soviet Bonapartism, he was criticized by many comrades. They argued that his Bonapartism covers too many different things. He replied that while neither Marx, Engels or Lenin had ever applied the term Bonapartism to the workers' state that was not to be wondered at; they never had occasion to, although Lenin did not hesitate to apply terms of a bourgeois regime with the necessary qualifications to the workers' state, as, for example, "Soviet state capitalism." Bonapartism, said Trotsky, is an exact, scientific, sociological characterization of the Soviet regime. Yet it may very easily be objected that it follows from this characterization that the Soviet Union is a bourgeois state.

Again. Trotsky points out — and I think it is right even though Comrade Weber characterized it as stupid — that in one sense the Soviet Union is a bourgeois state just as in another it is a workers' state. Elsewhere he says that the bureaucracy which has the state as its private property is a bourgeois bureaucracy. Shouldn't we reject these characterizations because of what some people may deduce from them as to the nature of the Soviet State?

It is in accordance with this spirit that we say Stalin is pursuing an imperialist policy. In two senses. In the first place, he is acting as a tool of imperialism, an agent of imperialism. To that characterization nobody seems to take objection. Stalin crushed Poland jointly with Hitler. The spoils of their victories are being jointly divided throughout eastern Europe. But also, in another sense, he is pursuing an "independent" imperialist policy of his own. To my characterisation, Comrade Weiss among others answers that there is no such thing and can be no such thing as imperialism except as a policy of decaying monopoly capitalism. That reply is correct only in one sense; namely, that the policy of monopoly capitalism is the modern form of imperialism. But there was imperialist policy long before monopoly capitalism and long before capitalism itself. "Colonial policy and imperialism," said Lenin, "existed before this latest stage of capitalism and even before capitalism. Rome, founded on slavery, pursued a colonial policy and realized imperialism." It is entirely correct, in my opinion, to characterize the Stalinist policy as imperialist, provided, of course, that one points out its specific character, that is, wherein it differs from modern capitalist imperialism. For, as I have insisted on several occasions, I do not identify Stalin with Hitler, Chamberlain or Roosevelt.

Stalin has showed himself capable of pursuing imperialist policy. That is the fact. The Kremlin bureaucracy has degenerated beyond all prediction. When we say it has interests all its own, we do not only mean that they are diametrically opposed to the interests of the proletariat but that these interests are very specific. They also have a specific economic basis. Like every bureaucracy, the Stalinist is interested in increasing the national income not in order to raise the standard of living of the masses but in order to increase its own power, its own wealth, its own privileges. In its struggle for self preservation not only from the living forces of the proletariat and peasantry in the Soviet Union, but also from the consequences of the chronic economic crisis in the country, it is now seeking new territories, new wealth, new privileges, new power, new sources of raw material, new trade facilities, new sources of labour power. A policy of expansion which under Lenin and Trotsky would mean extending the basis of the socialist revolution means under the Stalinist bureaucracy, degenerated and reactionary to the core, a policy of imperialism. That is, it has an imperialist policy peculiar to the Soviet regime in its present stage of decay.

Now, that is as close to a characterization of it as I can come. How do you characterize this policy? What is your political or sociological definition of it? You do not give any. Bonapartism, too, is not 100 per cent exact. The analogy upon which it is based is like all great historical analogies a limited one, but it is close enough; it is an approximation and no improvement upon it has yet been made. Similarly with the term imperialist. Until a better term is found to describe the present Stalinist policy, and you have proposed neither a better one nor any at all, I shall persist in using the one which I have put forward.

These are the considerations which in our opinion make it impossible for us to continue employing the slogan for the unconditional defence of the Soviet Union in the sense in which we construed it in the past. It is that sense which dictated the attitude of the majority, most explicitly, consistently and not accidentally expressed in the position taken by Comrade Goldman.

It is, of course, entirely true that a fundamental line is required for a correct approach to all concrete political problems. That fundamental line must be in general the interests of the world socialist revolution. In so far as the war itself is concerned, we must proceed from the fundamental and decisive character of the war, and judging it by that standard it is necessary to characterize the war as imperialist in its decisive aspects. I say, "in its decisive aspects," because in all modern wars there are, so to speak, conflicting elements. Let me take a well known example: in the last world war, Lenin contended in 1914 that if the struggle had been confined as to a duel between Serbia and Austro-Hungary, on the part of Serbia the progressive element of struggle for national unity would have been decisive, that is, revolutionists would have wished for the victory of Serbia, even of the Serbian bourgeoisie. But scarcely had that war started than it was extended throughout Europe. The progressive element represented by Serbia's national aspirations was lost in the midst of the struggle for imperialist mastery between the two big blocs. That is, the character of the war changed. In its decisive aspects it was imperialist. Serbia was nothing more than part of one of the imperialist camps.

Another example is furnished by the Franco-Prussian War of 1870. Bismarck's struggle against Napoleon III for the establishment of a united German nation was historically progressive. But when Bismarck proceeded to take Alsace-Lorraine, the character of the war changed, so to speak, and was condemned by Marx and Engels. Now the present war may and in all probability will also change. Our resolution foresees that and provides for it. If the character of the war changes into a war of imperialist attack upon the Soviet Union, the position of the revolutionary party must change accordingly. Comrade Cannon notes that this is contained in our resolution, but instead of recognizing it for its real and simple significance, he devotes himself to scathing remarks about the phrase "bourgeois counter-revolution is on the order of the day." For this obviously true statement I am denounced as a pessimist. Why? Trotsky used exactly the same phrase more than two years ago. As far back as then he said that if Franco wins in Spain, the bourgeois counter revolution will be on the order of the day in the Soviet Union. I deeply resent the attitude which accepts without a word a phrase or formula or concept uttered by Comrade Trotsky, and for purely factional reasons condemns those who merely repeat the phrase as pessimists, if not worse. If the character of the war changes, I repeat, and if the bourgeois counter revolution has not triumphed in Russia, we will defend the Soviet Union from imperialist attack.

It may be asked: How can you defend a country that has pursued an imperialist policy? The class struggle is not as simple as it is implicitly represented by that question. Under certain circumstances, we have done that in the past; we will do it in the future. Even in the case of Spain [1936-9], which none of us believed to be a workers' state of any kind, we were for the "defence" of Azana and his regime [i.e. the Republic] in our own way and by our own methods, even though that same regime was openly imperialist and still claimed imperialist domination over the colonies of Spain. With all the greater reason, with all the greater force, will the policy of defence apply in the case of an imperialist attack upon the Soviet Union.

I have said that Stalin is following an imperialist policy in two senses, in that he is a tool of imperialism, rather an agent of imperialism, and that his own policy is imperialist. I have at the same time denied the foolish charge that we consider this policy identical with the imperialism of Hitler or Chamberlain. No, there is imperialism and imperialism, just as there is Bonapartism and Bonapartism.

As a matter of fact I believe that the key to the imperialist policy of the Stalinist bureaucracy is to be found in the historical analogy with Bonapartism. The analogy between the Stalinist regime and the old Bonapartist regime has been used repeatedly by Comrade Trotsky and by our press in general. Given certain limitations, and allowing for the necessary changes, the analogy is both correct and illuminating. Bonaparte came to power to safeguard the social rule of the bourgeoisie by expropriating it politically. The bourgeoisie admitted, in Marx's words, that in order to preserve its social power unhurt its political power must be broken. Yet though Bonaparte came to power to preserve the social rule of the bourgeoisie, Marx pointed out that the third Napoleon represented an economic class, the most numerous in France at that time, the allotment farmer. To be sure, the farmers then as now, were a class only in a limited sense. Like Bonaparte Stalin represents not what is revolutionary but what is conservative in the farmer and in all other groups upon which his regime rests. In order to perpetuate his domination, Bonaparte carried out a policy which Marx characterized as the "imperialism of the farmer class," that is, the policy or hope of opening up new markets at the point of the bayonet, so that with the plunder of a continent the dictator would "return to the farmer class with interest the taxes wrung from them."

Now it may be argued that imperialism is a class policy. In the interests of what class, it may be asked, does Stalin carry out this so-called imperialist policy? Let us assume the legitimacy of this question for a moment. Here, too, we can find illumination in the analogy with the Bonapartist regime. Like the second Bonaparte, Stalin "is forced to raise alongside the actual classes of society, an artificial class, to which the maintenance of his own regime must be a knife and fork question." I do not believe that the Stalinist bureaucracy represents a new class, in any case none comparable with the great historic classes of society like the bourgeoisie and the proletariat. But in the sense in which Marx used the term to describe the Bonapartist bureaucracy, so, too, the Stalinist is an "artificial class." It seeks new resources of labour and of raw materials, markets, seaports, gold stores, and the like. It is compelled in life to recognize what it denies in theory, the impossibility of constructing a socialist society — even that caricature of socialism represented by the present regime — in one country. As a bureaucracy, increasingly separated from the masses because increasingly threatened by them, it is interested in a growing national income only for its own sake. Only in order to enhance its privileges and power — economic, social and political. But its own existence, its own rule, constitutes the greatest brake on the development of the productive forces and consequently on the national income. Hence, its growing urge to expand and to resolve its crisis abroad. And where the earlier Bolsheviks sought to resolve the crisis abroad in a socialist internationalist sense, by spreading the revolution, by raising the spirit of the class struggle abroad, the Stalinist regime seeks to resolve its domestic crisis by a policy which we cannot characterize as anything but imperialist. It is substantially on the basis of this analysis alone that we can consistently oppose what Trotsky calls "new seizures of territories by the Kremlin." It is on the basis of such an analysis that we are able to tell the masses or their vanguard what to do both before and after the Stalinist invasions.

And what policy shall we advance for the Russian masses? There, too, I do not believe we advance very far by the simple reiteration of the formula of unconditional defence. I would say to the Russian worker or soldier: The Stalinist bureaucracy is hurting Russia. It is discrediting the revolution in the Soviet Union throughout the working class of the world, which it is driving into the arms of the imperialist bourgeoisie. It is using you as tools of imperialism. The task that you are performing now under Stalin's command is an ignominious and reactionary one. Unite with the Ukrainian workers and peasants in the territory you have been sent to conquer and jointly overturn the Stalin regime in order to establish a genuine Soviet power. And I would say this to them tomorrow in the case of an invasion of Finland or India.

But I am now asked by Goldman and Cannon: You give no answer in your document to what should be our policy towards the defence of property nationalized by Stalin after the invasion. Is it progressive or reactionary? I cannot characterize this question, considering who are its authors, as anything but impudence. The majority refused to give an answer to any concrete question. We at least tried to give an answer to some of the concrete questions. However, in so far as the question has an independent merit of its own, it presents no difficulties for us. Naturally nationalization of property is progressive as against private property, just as the freeing of the serfs by Alexander III was progressive as against the enslavement of the serfs. I would resist any attempt to reduce emancipated peasants to serfdom again. And it goes without saying that I would defend nationalised property. But I must continue to emphasise that the questions of today are not answered or successfully evaded by necessarily hypothetical questions about tomorrow. However important the latter undeniably are, they do not eliminate the urgency of today's problems and the problem of a Hitler attack against the Ukraine was and is the question of tomorrow.

The question of Stalin's invasion of Poland and of the Baltic countries is the question of today, and that is the one we must answer first and that is the one the majority failed and still refuses to answer.

I find very interesting and important the formulation in Comrade Trotsky's latest document that we subordinate the overthrow of Stalin to the defence of nationalized property and planned economy, and we subordinate the defence of planned economy and nationalized property to the interests of the world revolution. I should like to ask a question about that formula. What is meant in it by "subordinate," especially in the phrase dealing with the subordination of the defence of the Soviet Union, that is, of nationalized property, to the interests of the world socialist revolution? Now my understanding of our position in the past was that we vehemently deny any possible conflict between the two. The defence of Russia was always and unalterably in the interests of the world revolution, and especially against the Stalinists we maintained that the world revolution was the best way to defend the Soviet Union. But I never understood our position in the past to mean that we subordinate the one to the other. If I understand English, the term implies either that there is a conflict between the two or the possibility of such a conflict. If there is a possibility of such a conflict, and I believe there is (it has already been shown in life), that indicates again that we cannot continue maintaining the slogan of unconditional defence of the Soviet Union. By that slogan in the past we meant nothing more than this, that we place no conditions to our defence of the Soviet Union, that is, we do not say we will defend the Soviet Union on the condition that the Stalin regime is first removed. If I understand the meaning of Comrade Trotsky's new formula, it is this: we defend the Soviet Union on the condition that it is to the interests of the world socialist revolution; that it does not conflict with those interests; and that where it does conflict with those interests, the latter remain primary and decisive, and the defence of the Soviet Union is secondary and subordinate.

I should be very much interested in having the comrades of the majority give me concrete examples of conditions under which they would subordinate the defence of the Soviet Union to the interests of the world revolution. Give me one or two, and by an example I do not mean the case of, let's say, a political revolution of the workers and peasants in Russia against the Stalin regime. How can that be interpreted as subordinating the defence of nationalized property to the interests of the world revolution? We have said in the past at least that the political revolution against the Stalin bureaucracy is not a blow against its economic foundations but that it is the best way, and, in fact, the only really sound and fundamental way in which to defend these economic foundations. The two concepts in that case are not in conflict. There cannot be in that case any question of subordinating the one to the other. The interests of both are identical.

Until concrete examples are given by the majority, and until the other questions I have raised are answered, and answered objectively and convincingly, I continue to contend that our slogan of unconditional defence of the Soviet Union has been proved by events, by reality, to be false and misleading, to be harmful, and that therefore it must be abandoned by our party. We must adopt in its place a slogan which is clear, which is defendable, and which makes possible a correct policy in harmony with our revolutionary internationalist position.

I want to turn now in my concluding remarks to other questions raised in the discussion on the Russian question and related to it. We are accused of many things. We create constant crises, we are panic-stricken at every turn of events, and so forth. These charges I have already taken up in my presentation, and upon another occasion I will take them up in even greater detail.

Our charge against the majority, however, is of a different nature and we describe it politically as bureaucratic conservatism. There have been numerous manifestations of this in the past and especially in the recent past. We have found that whenever a proposal is made for implementing the party policy or for establishing a new line of policy or action, we are immediately confronted with the accusation that this creates a "crisis". We had that at the last national convention, where a perfectly normal and proper, and, in my opinion, still necessary proposal to establish an organizational department with an organization secretary was met with a barrage of attack. Instead of a calm discussion on the proposal, the convention was thrown into a turmoil in which we were accused of not understanding the A.B.C. of Bolshevik organization. To the extent that the discussion on the proposal was taken out of this "theoretical" realm, it was rejected on the grounds that no qualified comrade was available for the position in question. Our proposal that Comrade X be considered for the post was condemned, and we were condemned along with it because of our alleged lack of appreciation of the importance of trade union work, work in the field, and so forth. To shift that comrade to direct organization work for the party was allegedly light minded and God knows what else. Less than a month after our proposal was rejected, the same comrade suddenly did become available, and this time the proposal was made not by us but by these who had originally opposed it, and it was hurriedly approved and adopted. It suddenly ceased to be a scatterbrained idea; it suddenly ceased to be the occasion for creating a crisis.

When the war broke out, we confronted a similar inertia. In this case, too, our proposals for immediate action to prepare the party for its tasks were answered with the assurances that there is nothing new, that we had always foretold the war, that we should not be panicky because it broke out, and more of the same. Yet although this was the position of the majority of the Political Committee, I found during my tour that the reaction of the minority to the war [one line of text is missing] crisis, which was described as panic-mongering, was nevertheless the spontaneous reaction of all the non-resident National Committee members with whom I came in contact.

Again, more recently on the question of the Russian invasion of Poland. The record establishes the fact that the majority was not only not prepared to give an answer to the new problems but denied that such an answer was required. And when that which was qualified by the PC as a concrete answer was finally written, it proved to be more of an evasion than an answer. And even this article, which appeared in the *Appeal* over the signature of Comrade Cannon, was and could be only a personal opinion of its author for the simple reason that the motion of the Political Committee on the subject, as I quoted it to you before, was so general as to admit of a variety of purely individual interpretations. The Political Committee simply did not show a serious attitude towards the problem.

At the plenum the majority presented for a vote the document of Comrade Trotsky [*The USSR in War*] which had arrived only a few hours earlier. There could not have been an opportunity for any comrade to reflect on this document. Some of them had not even had a chance to read it. Moreover, it was physically impossible for anybody to have read it in full for the simple reason that one page of the manuscript was accidentally lost in transit. Nevertheless, read or unread, studied or unstudied, complete or incomplete, the document was presented for a vote and finally adopted by the majority on the grounds, as comrade expressed it, of faith in the correctness of Comrade Trotsky's position.

Faith is a very good thing, and a prompt support of Comrade Trotsky's position on various questions has justified itself on more than one occasion in the past. But faith is no substitute for arriving seriously at a thought-out position. This was all the more so the case with this document. Even a hasty reading of it must convince any serious person, as it convinced me, that it is one of the most audacious and breathtaking documents in Marxian literature. In it Comrade Trotsky deals not only with these questions which we have long been familiar with and on which we have had a traditional and thoroughly discussed position, and also with a number of matters and viewpoints which I contend are new to our movement. The question of the inevitability of socialism is not, in my opinion, dealt with in this document as we have dealt with it in the past. In any case, it raises the question from a new angle. Similarly with the question of the nature of our epoch which we have hitherto characterized as an epoch of war and revolution. Similarly with the point raised in the document about the possibility of a new type of state which is neither bourgeois nor proletarian. These are questions which I do not want to deal with here and now but which are, to my view, so obviously a matter for deep reflection and discussion as to exclude so light minded a treatment as is represented by a motion to adopt the document a few hours after it has been given to the members of a party plenum.

When Trotsky raised the slogan of a united independent Soviet Ukraine a few months ago and proposed to submit it to an international discussion, not the slightest objection was raised. When we proposed to open up a discussion on the Polish invasion and problems related to it, the majority raised the most vehement objections. We are not a debating club, they said. The question was settled fundamentally at our last convention, and the convention before, and twenty two years ago. Up to the plenum even our proposal for a theoretical discussion of the questions in the pages of the *New International* was rejected. Discussion had become, in Cannon's words, a luxury that the party could not afford. I point to the fact that even at the Tenth Congress of the Russian Party held under the threat of the guns of rebelling Kronstadt and of peasant uprisings throughout the country which menaced the very existence of the Soviet Republic, the same delegates who condemned the views of the Workers' Opposition as incompatible with party membership, and which prohibited the formation of factions, nevertheless adopted at the same time a resolution which provided amply for the continuation of the discussion on a theoretical plane in special discussion bulletins of the party and at special meetings. Discussion was not a luxury that could not be afforded by the Russian party, even under these acutely dangerous circumstances. For our party we were told it was a luxury we couldn't afford. And in addition, these comrades who insisted on discussion were sneeringly and demagogically dubbed "independent thinkers" who believe that they are wiser than Trotsky.

The political passivity of the party leadership has as its counterpart an organizational rigidity and a super-sensitivity and brusqueness towards all critics, and regardless of the merit of the criticism. This is especially and notoriously the case in its attitude towards the youth. This fact has been observed and commented upon more than once and I will not elaborate on it here except to say that the truth about it cannot and will not be eliminated by repeating the commonplace formula that "we must not flatter the youth".

At the last national convention Cannon and his supporters demanded in their slate an organizational majority on the new national committee. On what political grounds? At the plenum at least the claim was presumably based upon the political differences over the Russian question. What was the political basis for this organizational majority at the convention? There simply wasn't any. At the preceding convention in Chicago two and a half years age, a more or less united leadership was established. Yet Comrade Cannon could come to the convention in New York and declare that he would not assume responsibility for one single member on the Political Committee. We insisted at the convention, as you know, upon including in the new National Committee a number of young comrades. The slate presented by Cannon's friends completely excluded the youth except for the one direct representative to which they are constitutionally entitled. The convention gave the party leadership what was tantamount to a mandate on this point by voting into the NC a number of youth comrades whom we proposed.

After the convention a Resident Political Committee was established by the majority, a committee that was presumably satisfactory to this majority. That was only three months ago. At the last plenum, this committee was drastically reorganized and so reorganized that we refused to take any responsibility for its recasting. The national labour secretary of the party was eliminated from the committee. All the youth comrades elected at the convention were dropped from it, including Comrade Gould and Comrade Erber, as well as Comrade George Breitman. That is, the committee was reorganized on a purely factional basis. I deny that this had an established political basis. I deny that it was reorganized on the basis of positions taken on the Russian Question. I deny that it was reorganized in order that the fundamental position on the Russian question, about which the majority speaks, might prevail in the party leadership. If that was the only ground for the reorganization, why were not comrades like Bern and Erber and others who voted for the original Cannon motion on the Russian question invited to the caucus meeting that was openly convened at the plenum for purpose of deciding on the reorganization? I do not agree with the steps taken for a single minute.

I do not agree either with the conception of leadership growing among the majority and even openly advocated by many of them, at least in informal conversation. I do not agree that any one man must under all circumstances be guaranteed the leadership of the party or the control of that leadership. I do not agree that if you approve that concept you will have a democratic regime in the party. I want a genuinely collective leadership, one that operates, discusses, and decides collectively. And a leader cult which we have had flagrantly expressed by a number of responsible members of the Political Committee is a bad substitute for a collective leadership.

I freely admit that these questions were not brought up, at least not brought up fully, at the July convention. In the first place, the pre-convention meeting of the NC plenum decided against discussing such questions at the convention. The majority argued that "the membership can't settle these questions... They must first be settled by the leadership." There is a kernel of truth in this and that is another reason why I did not bring the matter before the convention in all its amplitude. It has not been my custom because I do not believe it is correct to precipitate every dispute and disagreement among the leadership into the ranks of the party. I am not a professional "rank and file" demagogue who rushes into a membership discussion on the slightest provocation or no provocation at all, and it was with the intention of exhausting the last and remotest possibility of resolving these problems among the leading comrades themselves that I hesitated to bring them before the convention. Yet the situation demanded that the convention be given an opportunity of exercising an influence and pressure on the leadership, if only on a limited scale. That is probably the reason why there was a certain confusion and bewilderment during one part of the July convention. And while I am willing to take my share of the responsibility for it, I cannot take it all or even the major portion of it because it does not belong on my shoulders.

I believe also that it is imperative to change that alien spirit of arrogance and contempt for the membership which is manifested by responsible representatives of the party leadership in organizational and literary posts, which rightly irritates and angers the comrades but which is considered by those responsible for it as a good characteristic of "hard Bolsheviks." Repeated manifestations of this ugly spirit continue to go unrebuked, particularly by these whose main responsibility is to rebuke and eliminate them.

These phenomena and many others that could be referred to create a distinctly unhealthy and harmful situation in the party. The indispensable and preliminary condition for restoring a healthy state in the party is a frank, sober, calm and objective discussion, not envenomed by personal and factional recriminations and insinuations. This alone can create that free atmosphere in the party which will permit an intelligent and fruitful discussion of the multiplicity of questions now raised again so acutely by the war and the new stage of degeneration of Stalinism. Only that way can we arrive at decisions; adopt policies which will be a firm and lucid guide to our party and, through it, to the working class. In that sense and in that spirit, as a contribution to that desirable end, we submit our resolution to the discussion of the party.

Both speeches from SWP Internal Bulletin vol.2 no.3, 14 November 1939.

The real danger is those who identify the USSR with fascist states for the benefit of the USA and UK

Leon Trotsky (1939)

DEAR COMRADE SHACHTMAN:

I received the transcript of your speech of October 15 which you sent me, and I read it, of course, with all the attention it deserves. I found a lot of excellent ideas and formulations which seemed to me in full accordance with our common position as it is expressed in the fundamental documents of the Fourth International. But what I could not find was an explanation for your attack upon our previous position as "insufficient, inadequate and outdated."

You say that "It is the concreteness of the events which differ from our theoretical hypothesis and predictions that changes the situation." But unfortunately you speak about the "concreteness" of the events very abstractly so that I cannot see in what respect they change the situation and what are the consequences of these changes for our politics. You mention some examples from the past. Hence, according to you, we "saw and foresaw" the degeneration of the Third International; but only after the Hitler victory did we find it necessary to proclaim the Fourth International. This example is not formulated exactly. We foresaw not only the degeneration of the Third International but also the possibility of its regeneration. Only the German experience of 1929-1933 convinced us that the Comintern was doomed and nothing could regenerate it. But then we changed our policy fundamentally: To the Third International we opposed the Fourth International.

But we did not draw the same conclusions concerning the Soviet state. Why? The Third International was a party, a selection of people on the basis of ideas and methods. This selection became so fundamentally opposed to Marxism that we were obliged to abandon all hope of regenerating it. But the Soviet state is not only an ideological selection, it is a complex of social institutions which continues to persist in spite of the fact that the ideas of the bureaucracy are now almost the opposite of the ideas of the October Revolution. That is why we did not renounce the possibility of regenerating the Soviet state by political revolution. Do you believe now that we must change this attitude? If not, and I am sure that you don't propose it, where is the fundamental change produced by the "concreteness" of events?

In this connection you quote the slogan of the independent Soviet Ukraine which, as I see with satisfaction, you accept. But you add: "As I understand our basic position it always was to oppose separatist tendencies in the Federated Soviet Republic." In respect to this you see a fundamental "change in policy." But: (1) The slogan of an independent Soviet Ukraine was proposed before the Hitler-Stalin pact. (2) This slogan is only an application on the field of the national question of our general slogan for the revolutionary overthrow of the bureaucracy. You could with the same right say: "As I understand our basic position it was always to oppose any rebellious acts against the Soviet government." Of course, but we changed this basic position several years ago. I don't really see what new change you propose in this connection now.

You quote the march of the Red Army in 1920 into Poland and into Georgia and you continue: "Now, if there is nothing new in the situation, why does not the majority propose to hail the advance of the Red Army into Poland, into the Baltic countries, into Finland..." In this decisive part of your speech you establish that something is "new in the situation" between 1920 and 1939. Of course! This newness in the situation is the bankruptcy of the Third International, the degeneracy of the Soviet state, the development of the Left Opposition, and the creation of the Fourth International. This "concreteness of events" occurred precisely between 1920 and 1939. And these events explain sufficiently why we have radically changed our position toward the politics of the Kremlin, including its military politics.

It seems that you forget somewhat that in 1920 we supported not only the deeds of the Red Army but also the deeds of the GPU. From the point of view of our appreciation of the state there is no principled difference between the Red Army and the GPU. In their activities they are not only closely connected but intermeshed. We can say that in 1918 and the following years we hailed the Cheka in their fight against Russian counter-revolutionaries and imperialist spies but in 1927 when the GPU began to arrest, to exile and to shoot the genuine Bolsheviks we changed our appreciation of this institution. This concrete change occurred at least 11 years before the Soviet-German pact. That is why I am rather astonished when you speak sarcastically about "the refusal even (!) of the majority to take the same position today that we all took in 1920 ..." We began to change this position in 1923. We proceeded by stages more or less in accordance with the objective developments. The decisive point of this evolution was for us 1933-34. If we fail to see just what the new fundamental changes are which you propose in our policy, it doesn't signify that we go back to 1920!

You insist especially on the necessity of abandoning the slogan for the unconditional defense of the USSR, whereupon you interpret this slogan in the past as our unconditional support of every diplomatic and military action of the Kremlin; i.e., of Stalin's policy. No, my dear Shachtman, this presentation doesn't correspond to the "concreteness of events." Already in 1927 we proclaimed in the Central Committee: "For the socialist fatherland? Yes! For the Stalinist course? No!" Then you seem to forget the so-called "thesis on Clemenceau" which signified that in the interests of the genuine defense of the USSR, the proletarian vanguard can be obliged to eliminate the Stalin government and replace it with its own. This was proclaimed in 1927! Five years later we explained to the workers that this change of government can be effectuated only by political revolution. Thus we separated fundamentally our defense of the USSR as a workers' state from the bureaucracy's defense of the USSR. Whereupon you interpret our past policy as unconditional support of the diplomatic and military activities of Stalin! Permit me to say that this is a horrible deformation of our whole position not only since the creation of the Fourth International but since the very beginning of the Left Opposition.

Unconditional defense of the USSR signifies, namely, that our policy is not determined by the deeds, maneuvers or crimes of the Kremlin bureaucracy but only by our conception of the interests of the Soviet state and world revolution.

At the end of your speech you quote Trotsky's formula concerning the necessity of subordinating the defense of the nationalized property in the USSR to the interests of the world revolution, and you continue: "Now my understanding of our position in the past was that we vehemently deny any possible conflict between the two ... I never understood our position in the past to mean that we subordinate the one to the other. If I understand English, the term implies either that there is a conflict between the two or the possibility of such a conflict." And from this you draw the impossibility of maintaining the slogan of unconditional defense of the Soviet Union.

This argument is based upon at least two misunderstandings. How and why could the interests of maintaining the nationalized property be in "conflict" with the interests of the world revolution? Tacitly you infer that the Kremlin's (not our) policy of defense can come into conflict with the interests of the world revolution. Of course! At every step! In every respect! However our policy of defense is not conditioned by the Kremlin's policy. This is the first misunderstanding. But, you ask, if there is not a conflict why the necessity of subordination? Here is the second misunderstanding. We must subordinate the defense of the USSR to the world revolution insofar as we subordinate a part to a whole. In 1918 in the polemics with Bukharin, who insisted upon a revolutionary war against Germany, Lenin answered approximately: "If there should be a revolution in Germany now, then it would be our duty to go to war even at the risk of losing. Germany's revolution is more important than ours and we should if necessary sacrifice the Soviet power in Russia (for a while) in order to help establish it in Germany." A strike in Chicago at this time could be unreasonable in and of itself, but if it is a matter of helping a general strike on the national scale, the Chicago workers should subordinate their interests to the interests of their class and call a strike. If the USSR is involved in the war on the side of Germany, the German revolution could certainly menace the immediate interests of the defense of the USSR. Would we advise the German workers not to act? The Comintern would surely give them such advice, but not we. We will say:

"We must subordinate the interests of the defense of the Soviet Union to the interests of the world revolution."

Some of your arguments are, it seems to me, answered in Trotsky's last article, *Again and Once More Again on the Nature of the USSR*, which was written before I received the transcript of your speech.

You have hundreds and hundreds of new members who have not passed through our common experience. I am fearful that your presentation can lead them into the error of believing that we were unconditionally for the support of the Kremlin, at least on the international field, that we didn't foresee such a possibility as the Stalin-Hitler collaboration, that we were taken unawares by the events, and that we must fundamentally change our position. That is not true! And independently from all the other questions which are discussed or only touched upon in your speech (leadership, conservatism, party regime and so on) we must, in my opinion, again check our position on the Russian question with all the necessary carefulness in the interest of the American section as well as of the Fourth International as a whole.

The real danger now is not the "unconditional" defense of that which is worthy of defense, but direct or indirect help to the political current which tries to identify the USSR with the fascist states for the benefit of the democracies, or to the related current which tries to put all tendencies in the same pot in order to compromise Bolshevism or Marxism with Stalinism. We are the only party which really foresaw the events, not in their empirical concreteness, of course, but in their general tendency. Our strength consists in the fact that we do not need to change our orientation as the war begins. And I find it very false that some of our comrades, moved by the factional fight for a "good regime" (which they, so far as I know, have never defined), persist in shouting: "We were taken unawares! Our orientation turned out to be false! We must improvise a new line! And so on." This seems to me completely incorrect and dangerous.

With warmest comradely greetings, LUND [Leon Trotsky]

CC to J.P. Cannon.

P.S. – The formulations in this letter are far from perfect since it is not an elaborated article, but only a letter dictated by me in English and corrected by my collaborator during the dictation.

From SWP Internal Bulletin vol.2 no.4, December 1939

Champions of Peace and Democracy!

Socialist Appeal, 1 October 1939

3. Finland, Baltics, Romania, Iran. 1939-41: Russian imperialism?

Stalin invaded Finland on 30 November 1939. The war continued until 13 March 1940, when it concluded with limited territorial gains for Stalin. This war inflamed the faction-fight among the Trotskyists: the dispute over eastern Poland had been a dispute about a fait accompli, whereas Finland was an ongoing, undecided issue. Stalin invaded the Baltic states in June 1940 and eastern Romania in June-July 1940 — these were territories "allocated" to him in the Hitler-Stalin pact — and Britain and Russia jointly invaded Iran in August-September 1941.

It is Finnish workers' duty to be Soviet partisans

SWP (1939)

UNTIL A FEW DAYS AGO it appeared that the original demands of the Soviet government upon Finland would be peaceably compromised. Suddenly, however, all indications of compromise seem to have disappeared. Why? What has happened? You cannot tell from the preposterous and wild vituperation in the Soviet press or its repetition in the Stalinist press. Nor can you tell from the anti-Soviet propaganda which dominates the "democratic" press. As in all other questions connected with the Second World War, we in the "third camp" — the camp of revolutionary struggle against the war — must make our analysis independently of both the warring camps.

The general international situation is characterized by continuation of the attempts of Britain to reach an agreement with German imperialism, minus Hitler. Such a peace would be made at the expense of the Soviet Union. The Soviet bureaucracy is aware of the mortal danger which the prospect of a British-German peace would signify for the Soviet Union.

Having no faith in the international working class, the Soviet bureaucracy has placed its fate on pacts with one imperialist power or another. For five years it deluded the workers with slogans for "defense of the democracies." Now that Hitler is the ally, the Stalinist press whines that the British are attempting to assassinate Hitler and replace him by a regime which would agree to turn its guns against the Soviet Union. Therefore — this is plainly indicated by the Stalinist press — Hitler should be defended against assassination or overthrow.

The Kremlin lives in deadly fear of the possibility that, despite all its courting of German imperialism, the latter will make peace with Britain and turn on Russia. It is against that dread day that the Kremlin's moves in the Baltic are calculated. The military and naval outposts secured from the other Baltic countries, plus similar outposts from Finland, would close the defensive circle of the Baltic against Germany. But since the Kremlin is simultaneously wooing Hitler, it cannot very well explain the real meaning of its Baltic moves. Hence one of the most repulsive aspects of its propaganda — its patent fraudulence; as fraudulent as the declaration that the Stalin-Hitler pact would help Poland and the democracies, which the Stalinists were making until the Red Army marched into Poland. This cynical lying confuses and disorients the class-conscious workers everywhere. When, in the days of Lenin and Trotsky, the Soviet power led its armies up to Warsaw and conquered Georgia, the class-conscious workers understood the necessity of these steps and defended them, for the foreign policy of the workers' state was clearly in the interests of the world revolution, was developed and executed before the eyes of the international working class. The methods employed by Stalin in the Baltic are utterly alien to a revolutionary-internationalist policy. Lenin and Trotsky called upon the Polish and Georgian workers to revolt and came to their aid with the Red Army. Stalin calls upon the Finnish people — not the workers — to... change Premiers! Instead of arousing the masses within the Baltic countries to overthrow their capitalist rulers, and establish Soviet Republics which would guard the Baltic against Germany, Stalin prefers pacts with their bourgeois rulers. The only kind of "revolution" he wants in the Baltic is the kind he "made" in backward Polish Galicia [i.e. the area invaded in 1939] — under the direction of the GPU.

In our criticism of the military interventions of the Soviet bureaucracy, we sharply distinguish ourselves from the social-democratic, anarchist and bourgeois critics of the Kremlin. These anti-revolutionary critics denounce the Soviet for using military force and for violating existing borders. For us, however, the borders of the capitalist world are not at all inviolate, and military force in the hands of a revolutionary government may very well serve the revolution. That the Kremlin's military intervention serves only the interests of the Kremlin and its imperialist ally (Hitler in Poland); that it is carried out without consideration of the will and feelings of the workers of the Soviet Union or the occupied territories or the international proletariat; that it compromises the Soviet Union and disorients the world working class — these are our criticisms, which in all fundamentals runs counter to the standpoint of the Kremlin's non-revolutionary critics.

The social-democrats and other lackeys of the "democratic" imperialists call upon the Finnish workers to defend Finland against the Red Army. We, on the contrary, apply to Finland as to every other bourgeois country our fundamental attitude toward imperialist wars. The Finnish government refuses to yield to Soviet demands for military outposts only because Finland is assured of the support of one or more great powers against the Soviet. The *New York Times* makes that plain enough, in its Nov. 28 editorial calling for a holy war against the Soviet Union. We are against the support of any imperialist power in any war, let alone a war against the Soviet Union which remains, despite the Kremlin gang, upon the economic foundations laid down by the October Revolution.

The task of the Finnish workers is to make their own socialist revolution. Nothing else can avail them. They must destroy the Finnish bourgeoisie before they can cope with Stalin's demands upon Finland. If a struggle breaks out between bourgeois Finland and the Soviet Union, it is the duty of the Finnish workers to be Soviet partisans in that struggle.

If the Soviet Union were led by revolutionaries, the Finnish revolution would be made by the Finnish workers with the assurance that they would receive the aid of the Red Army against intervention by the imperialist powers. Instead, however, the brutish and provocative tactics of the Kremlin against Finland drive the Finnish workers into unity with the Finnish bourgeoisie. In this incident as in all others, the tactics of the Kremlin serve to strengthen the imperialist front which will eventually attempt to destroy the Soviet Union.

Here is but the latest proof of our conviction that the defense of the Soviet Union cannot be left in the hands of the Kremlin clique. The armed overthrow by the Soviet workers of the Stalinist bureaucracy — it will not yield its power by any other means — is vitally necessary if the Soviet Union is to be saved and become again what it was under Lenin and Trotsky: drill ground of the world revolution.

"The Kremlin's aims in the Finnish crisis", Editorial, *Socialist Appeal* 1 December 1939 (abridged)

Stalin's reactionary wars

Herman Benson (1939)

THE CRUX OF the dispute taking place in the party at the present time is: is it necessary to amend the party position in order to exclude support to reactionary wars waged by Stalin (e.g., that waged yesterday in Poland; today, in Finland; and tomorrow...)?

The majority of the NC replies that no change whatsoever is necessary. Proceeding from here, it gave an evasive and ambiguous answer to the events in Poland. On the one hand, it applied the term "monstrous" to the invasion of Poland and stated that "we don't support Stalin's invasion of Poland only because he doesn't come for revolutionary purposes". (Cannon in Bulletin No. 3). On the other hand, it resisted all attempts to declare that we oppose all support to that war.

All possible ambiguity has been removed from the position of the majority by the editorial in the *Appeal* (December 1) [i.e. the article above]. Here we are told that if a war breaks out between bourgeois Finland and the Soviet Union it is the duty of the Finnish workers to be Soviet partisans in the struggle. According to the majority, the military intervention of Stalin has the following results:

(1) it serves only the interests of the Kremlin and its ally, Hitler.

(2) it is carried out without consideration of the will of the workers in the Soviet Union, in the world generally, or in the country affected.

(3) it disorients the international working class.

(4) it compromises the Soviet Union.

(5) it drives the Finnish workers into unity with their own bourgeoisie.

Therefore??? Therefore support the military intervention! That is the conclusion of the majority. The majority seems to have discovered a progressive war all of whose implications are clearly reactionary.

We have always recognized the fact that Stalin's foreign policy bore a dual character and could be reactionary or progressive depending upon the precise circumstances. In this particular case we have an example of the reactionary politics of Stalin carried out by war. The war is consequently reactionary. Our policy should be against support to either side.

226

In effect, the majority argues that because the Soviet Union will be fighting a progressive war tomorrow, that therefore it must support its reactionary war today. To revert to the trade union analogy, we would have to say: This trade union is conducting a strike for reactionary purposes (e.g., for the ousting of all Negroes from the shops). But tomorrow, in the course of this strike, the union may be attacked by the bosses. Therefore we must support its reactionary strike today.

Such a policy is suicidal. Support to such a strike would compromise revolutionaries in the eyes of the Negro masses; and would, in their minds, throw all the "white" parties equally in the camp of the Jim Crow elements. Race chauvinism would be strengthened on all sides.

Applied to Finland this policy has the same results. If Stalin's war in Finland tends to make the Finnish workers cling to their own boss class, our support to such a war would make the disease still worse.

However, should the Soviet Union, tomorrow become the victim of a general military offensive conducted by the imperialist powers of either camp who would utilize this or any other reactionary move by Stalin as the pretext for beginning their attack on the USSR, it would be the duty of every worker to rally to the defense of the Soviet Union.

But because Stalin may be fighting this progressive war tomorrow is no reason to support his reactionary war of today. This would be incorrect; just as it would be equally incorrect to conclude that because Stalin conducts a reactionary war today that we must discard our support to his progressive war of tomorrow.

Under the name Ben Hall: "The majority of the NC", SWP
Internal Bulletin vol.2 no.5, December 1939

Finland: for Soviet patriotism!

SWP (1939)

1. THE INVASION OF FINLAND by the Red Army is an incident in the Second World War which is now only in its tentative and initial stages of development.

2. The character of the Second World War is that of an imperialist struggle for the redivision of the earth. Despite present alliances, or future changes in the alignment of the powers, the class antagonism between the imperialist states and the Soviet Union as a degenerated workers' state retains its full force. From this must follow an inevitable attempt on the part of the imperialists of one camp or another, or in a combination, to attack the Soviet Union in order to destroy the economic conquests of the October Revolution and open up the territory of the Soviet Union for capitalist exploitation.

3. Finland is not an independent small state fighting for its independence against an imperialist power. Bourgeois Finland is and always has been a vassal state of the imperialists and an outpost of imperialism on the Russian border.

4. In the present conflict the imperialist powers of the United States and Great Britain stand behind Finland and inspire its foreign policy in relation to the Soviet Union. The diplomatic and propagandistic intervention of the Roosevelt adminstration on the side of bourgeois Finland is not motivated by "humanitarian" considerations but by the class interests and the future military designs of the Wall Street masters of the government.

5. Stalinist policy in the conflict with Finland is characteristic of Stalinist policy as a whole: the protection of the interests and privileges of the bureaucracy in utter disregard of the sentiments and interests of the world proletariat. The means and methods it employs to gain military and strategic advantages repel the sympathy and support of the workers and oppressed peoples, and thus undermine the real defense of the Soviet Union to such an extent as to outweigh by far the immediate military and strategic advantages that may be gained by the conflict with Finland, From this point of view — that is, the real defense of the Soviet Union against the imperialists — the Fourth International has always condemned the foreign policy of Stalinism and condemns it in the present situation. The real defense of the conquests of the October Revolution requires, now more than ever, an unceasing struggle of the workers for the overthrow of the

Stalinist bureaucracy by means of a political revolution.

6. Proceeding from the foregoing points, in accord with the program of the Fourth International, our basic attitude in the present military conflict between the Soviet Union and Finland is as follows:

(a) For the Fourth Internationalists in the United States: Revolutionary defeatism — the main enemy is in our own country! No support, direct or indirect, to the imperialist government of the United States or its Finnish satellite. Expose and denounce the policy of Washington as political and diplomatic preparation for war against the Soviet Union. For the unconditional defense of the Soviet Union. Expose and denounce the methods of Stalinism which compromise the Soviet Union and weaken its defense.

(b) For the Fourth Internationalists in Finland: revolutionary defeatism — the main enemy is in our own country! The first task of the Finnish workers remains an irreconcilable struggle for the overthrow of their own bourgeoisie. Not a man, not a gun, not a cent for the war of the Finnish bourgeois government against the Soviet Union. Work for the defeat of the Finnish bourgeois government in the war. Aim at the creation of an independent Soviet Finland free from the domination of the Stalinist bureaucracy. If that is not possible in the immediate situation because of the unfavorable relation of forces, political unpreparedness, and military weakness — as is almost certainly the case in the present circumstances — utilize the defeat of the bourgeois Finnish Army by the Red Army to arouse the masses to press forward for the complete expropriation of the Finnish capitalists and landlords immediately after the victory of the Red Army. Organize for the maximum independence of the workers from the Stalinist bureaucracy, and thus prepare its future overthrow. In the present military struggle a victory of the Red Army is a "lesser evil" than the victory of the army of the Finnish puppet government of Wall Street and London. The Finnish Fourth Internationalists are partisans of an independent Soviet Finland and the irreconcilable foes of the treacherous and blood-splotched Kremlin bureaucracy and its hand-picked Kuusinen regime in Finland.

(c) For the Fourth Internationalists in the Soviet Union: Soviet patriotism — the main enemy is world imperialism. Unconditional defense of the Soviet Union against the capitalist world. Only agents of imperialism, standing for the restoration of capitalism in the Soviet Union, can desire the defeat of the Red Army by the bourgeois Finnish outpost of the imperialist armies. Irreconcilable struggle for the overthrow of the Stalinist bureaucracy, which betrays the world proletariat and undermines the defense of the Soviet Union. Against the military-bureaucratic annexation of Finnish territory. For the independence of Soviet Finland. Unceasing criticism and exposure of the Stalinist methods of starting and conducting the war, but not the slightest relaxation of material and military support. The Fourth Internationalists in the Soviet Union will be the best soldiers in the Red Army and inspire it to victory over the imperialist bandits and the Stalinist betrayers.

Statement of Policy by the Political Committee of the Socialist Workers Party, *Socialist Appeal*, 9 December 1939

Max Shachtman, early 1960s

Invasion of Finland serves only the Kremlin

SWP minority (1939)

1. THE EDITORIAL ENTITLED, "The Kremlin's Aim in the Finnish Crisis," published in the December 1st issue of the *Socialist Appeal*, expresses openly a political capitulation to Stalinism. The main line of the editorial is concentrated in the sentence: "If a struggle breaks out between bourgeois Finland and the Soviet Union, it is the duty of the Finnish workers to be Soviet partisans in that struggle."

Given this main line, and the concrete circumstances of the invasion of Finland in the context of the present phase of the Second World War, all of the criticisms, modifications and limitations included in the editorial serve only as pseudo-revolutionary embroidery to cover a policy which in its fundamentals is in accord only with the aims and interests of the Kremlin and directly counter to the interests of the world revolution. This fact is indeed implicitly — and unwittingly — admitted by the editorial itself, when it writes "That the Kremlin's military intervention serves only the interests of the Kremlin and its imperialist ally (Hitler in Poland); that it is carried out without consideration of the will and feelings of the workers of the Soviet Union or the occupied territories or the international proletariat; that it compromises the Soviet Union and disorients the world working class..."

If this is the meaning of the invasion, if it serves "only" the Kremlin's interests (in other words, is against the interests of the revolution both in Russia and internationally), on what conceivable grounds, other than piety toward a vague, abstract and out-moded formula of "unconditional defense," is the world proletariat asked to defend and support it?

2. To serve the utterly false policy of the NC majority the *Appeal* of December 1st, as has been consistently the case during the past two months, is compelled to distort and falsify the meaning and direction of current events. As its summary of a period (the last two weeks of November) which witnessed on every front intensification of the struggle between England and Germany (the German sea warfare in a new stage, the drastic British decision to control German exports; and above all the alteration of British speeches and propaganda to attacks on the German people instead of on the German govern-

ment alone as had been the case previously), the *Appeal* sees only a "British Bid to Germany Aimed Against USSR."

It remains true, of course, that the transformation of the present war into a war of combined imperialist assault against the Soviet Union remains possible; and it is undoubtedly the case that certain sections of the ruling class within every power are in favor of such a transformation. But to write as does the *Appeal* that "the nub of the war strategy of the great powers" is to bring about such a transformation is simply silly; since if this were indeed the "nub" of the strategy of the powers — all the powers, the *Appeal* declares — then not the present war, but the war against the Soviet Union would now be going on. The NC majority elaborates an abstract section of an ancient thesis instead of analyzing the actual war.

3. As in the case of Poland, so in the case of Finland, the Soviet Union continues integral participation in the imperialist war, acting on the one side as a partner in the Berlin-Moscow axis, on the other in furtherance of its own imperialist and expansionist aims. Finland, conquered, becomes a necessary strategic base, consolidates the Baltic against future attack both from a defensive point of view and also (if the conquest is speedily and successfully completed) as protection in future expansionist moves either north, into Scandinavia, or west and south into the Balkans and western Asia. The role of the Red Army in the Finnish invasion is reactionary, counter-revolutionary.

4. Reactionary also is the role of the Finnish bourgeois government and its army, a government made up of the murderers of the Finnish workers and the stranglers of the Finnish revolution, a slavish tool of British and US imperialism.

5. From the analysis of the roles of the Finnish and Soviet governments and armies in the conflict follows, just as in the case of Poland or of the lesser Baltic states or of future similar episodes, the practical perspectives and tactical conclusions of the Fourth Internationalists with respect to the conflict. In general: the Fourth Internationalists, internationally, condemn, reject and oppose, both governments and their armies. We call, in this conflict, for the revolutionary struggle of Finnish and Russian workers, against their own governments and the armies of those governments; for fraternization on the fronts, for the right of the Finnish people to genuine freedom and self-determination — a right made impossible alike by their own imperialist-dominated government and by the Kremlin bureaucracy — and for the realization of the objectives of the workers and the masses through the achievement of democratic workers' rule in both countries, and socialism. The realization of the progressive aims of the

workers in both countries will in turn be guaranteed through the Socialist United States of Europe.

6. The presumed difficulty or even impossibility of realizing such a perspective in the immediate present does not in the least militate against the necessity of putting it forward unambiguously and now. Only in the light of such a perspective can the Finnish masses (and this applies only in a less acute degree to the masses of all capitalist and imperialist countries, even those not involved directly in military struggle) be turned from desperate refuge in their own bourgeois governments (toward which they are forced so brutally by the policy of Stalinism, and forced also in less blunt and open fashion by the policy of the NC majority) and the Russian masses guided toward an orientation where they, jointly with the masses of other countries, will regain the road of the revolution. In the application of this perspective, the Fourth Internationalists will, of course, take into account concrete circumstances — the military situation, the moods of the masses, and also the differing economic relations in Finland and Russia. In Finland they will strive wherever possible toward the expropriation of the big landlords and private industry and the establishment of workers' control and the safe-guarding of their rights and conquests from counter-revolutionary Stalinism and its agencies; in Russia they will fight against any tendencies toward reintroduction of private property, and will aim to utilize every occasion for gaining democratic workers' control of the nationalized property. In both countries, they will continue the prosecution of the class struggle on all available arenas, irrespective of the effects upon the military struggle.

7. The collapse of the Finnish bourgeois regime as a result of military reverses will, as in the case of the collapse of the Polish government, produce a movement toward independent workers' power, which can triumph under favorable conditions, primarily, however, on the condition of a rigidly independent class line of the Finnish proletariat. To advocate that the Finnish proletariat act as "Soviet partisans," that is, as assistants of the Stalinist Army, means to urge the strengthening of the forces that will act as the counter-revolutionary suppressor of any independent Finnish working-class movement or power, even if in the most elementary form. On the contrary, the revolutionists must encourage and give support to even the most embryonic tendency toward independent class action and the development of workers' power — directed against the enemy at home (the Finnish bourgeoisie) in the first place, and against the counter-revolutionary Stalinist invaders.

8. Within the United States, the main task of the Fourth Internationalists naturally remains the struggle against the main enemy, the enemy at home. In the case of the Finnish events, this means above all the exposure of the attempts of the administration and all schools of democratic imperialist patriots to exploit these events for the purpose of swinging the people behind the war aims of US Imperialism.

SWP Internal Bulletin vol.2 no.5, December 1939

Natalia Sedova Trotsky

We condemn the invasion; we defend the Soviet Union

Albert Goldman (1939)

STALIN'S INVASION OF BOURGEOIS FINLAND has brought greater clarity into the ideological conflict between the minority and majority of our party. (I hope no one of the minority will accuse me of justifying the invasion because of that). Regretfully we must also admit that it has sharpened that conflict. For, as the issues become clearer, the gulf between the groups grow wider.

Up to now we had to argue about implications of this or that formulation, of the use of this or that word or phrase. Up to now we were confronted by a flood of hypothetical questions and pointless riddles but now we are confronted with an actual situation when everyone is compelled to draw concrete conclusions from his theoretical position. No posing of riddles can help in taking a position in the actual struggle between the Soviet Union and an outpost of world imperialism.

There were comrades who thought that, because both the majority and minority could unite on condemning the invasion of Poland, the differences between the groups were not so serious and could easily be reconciled if only the organizational question could be settled. These comrades must understand now that the reasons given by the two groups for condemning the invasion were all-important and indicated two fundamentally different attitudes to the Soviet Union and to Stalin's activities.

The minority wanted to condemn the invasion because it was an act of imperialism on the part of Stalin. The majority objected to the use of the term imperialism because such an absolutely un-Marxist use of that term could not but lead to absolutely incorrect policies. Condemn the invasion? Yes, but because it violated the cherished principles of socialism, because it confused the masses, destroyed their confidence in the Soviet Union and thus weakened the workers' state.

The important question was: from what point of view should the invasion of Poland be condemned? Sooner or later events were bound to show that the political reasons advanced for condemning the invasion would lead to a different attitude on the question of defending the Soviet Union.

The invasion of Finland brought a new factor into the situation — an actual war between the Soviet Union and capitalist Finland, inextricably connected with the imperialist world, and it is this factor which brought to the surface and made explicit that which was concealed and only implicit in the Shachtman resolution. No longer is it a question of what we meant by unconditional defense, but of defence itself.

It is first of all necessary to understand clearly the issue between the majority and minority on the invasion of Finland. Both groups condemn the invasion. Both groups are for a policy of revolutionary defeatism in Finland, for the overthrow of the Finnish bourgeoisie and establishment of a Finnish Soviet Republic. Both groups also agree that if the Finnish workers should succeed in establishing a soviet republic, they should struggle against Stalin's army for an independent soviet republic.

There is also no difference between the groups on the question of the necessity of continuing the struggle within the Soviet Union for the overthrow of Stalin. We all recognize that it would aid the Soviet Union tremendously if the Stalinist bureaucracy were overthrown by the Russian workers, under the leadership of the Fourth Internationalists.

The question that divides the groups is the question of defeatism or defensism within the Soviet Union, the question as to what position the party should take as to the victory or defeat of the Red Army fighting against the Finnish bourgeois army, before the Finnish workers establish a soviet republic or before the Russian workers overthrow Stalin.

The minority resolution takes a position of defeatism within the Soviet Union. The term defeatism is not found in the resolution but the idea is clearly stated in the last sentence which asserts that within the Soviet Union as well as in Finland the workers should "continue the prosecution of the class struggle on all available arenas, irrespective of the effects upon the military struggle." This is essentially the definition of defeatism adopted by the Fourth International and applied thus far to the policy which workers should follow in an imperialist country when that country is at war. The minority wants to apply it also to the Soviet Union which the Fourth International considers a workers' state.

It is characteristic both of the confusion and the unprincipledness of the minority that it attempts to change fundamental principles of our International incidentally to the adoption of a policy on a particular question. There is nothing wrong in advocating a change of our fundamental principles but one must do so openly and not attempt to introduce such a change via a word or phrase in a resolution which does not in so many words advocate the abandonment of present programmatic principles and the adoption of new ones.

It has, for instance, been the position of the Fourth International that the Stalinist bureaucracy is not a class in the Marxist sense of the term. In one sentence of a short resolution the minority smuggles in the idea that the struggle of the Russian workers against the bureaucracy is a class struggle, in the same sense that the struggle of the workers against the capitalist class in a capitalist country, thus transforming the Soviet bureaucracy into a stroke of the pen.

Until the minority seriously attempts to prove to us that the Soviet Union is an imperialist state in the Marxist sense of the term, and that the bureaucracy is a class in the Marxist sense of the term, we shall not argue the question. We have taken a contrary position on the basis of a very thorough analysis and an exhaustive discussion and it is up to those who want to change our minds to produce some new facts and arguments.

Here it is merely sufficient to note that the minority's position on Finland is based essentially on the concept that Stalin follows an imperialist policy and that therefore our attitude in the Soviet Union should be similar to, if not identical with, the attitude of the workers in any capitalist-imperialist country.

As another justification of the policy of defeatism within the Soviet Union, the minority bases itself on the principle that Stalin is waging a reactionary war. Without any concrete analysis whatsoever the term "reactionary war" is hurled at us by the comrades of the minority in a sort of a triumphant manner, as if the term in and of itself immediately solves all problems.

The argument runs as follows. We support only progressive wars; we do not support reactionary wars; the Soviet Union under Stalin, in invading Finland, is conducting a reactionary war. Hence our policy should be one of defeatism in the Soviet Union. Thus, instead of a Marxist analysis, we have terms thrown at us such as reactionary and progressive.

Is the invasion of Finland by Stalin's Red Army reactionary? We can say: "Yes, it is." But does that solve the problem for us? It does not. For we cannot substitute a word for a Marxist analysis. In what way is it reactionary? Is it reactionary in the same way as the attack of imperialist Italy on Ethiopia or of Japan on China? Is it reactionary because it is an attack of an imperialist country on a colonial or semi-colonial country ? Obviously not. It is reactionary because the invasion goes counter to all the best sentiments of the masses, confuses them and thus weakens the Soviet Union and the world revolution.

But a Marxist cannot stop there. He must take all factors into consideration. What role is Finland playing? What is the actual character of the struggle? What part is world imperialism playing in it? The minority admits that Finland is a tool of British and American imperialism. The majority, taking all factors into consideration, concludes that the war between the Soviet Union and Finland, in spite of Stalin's crime in invading the latter country, is actually a struggle between imperialism and the workers' state.

And once we analyze the struggle as one between the workers' state and imperialist nations our slogan of unconditional defense comes into play; that is, we defend the Soviet Union "from the blows of the capitalist enemies, irrespective of the circumstances and immediate causes of the conflict." (*War and the Fourth International*).

Yes, we are for a Soviet Finland; we are for the overthrow of Stalin but we cannot and dare not be indifferent to the outcome of the actual struggle of the moment. As against the armies of bourgeois Finland fighting the battles of the imperialist world, we prefer and we shall work for the victory of the Red Army which, in spite of everything, is the army of the degenerated workers' state.

Some comrades of the minority point to what they deem to be a gross contradiction in our attitude. We unreservedly condemn the invasion and at the same time we call upon the workers to support the Red Army as against the Finnish bourgeois army. Comrade Ben Hall, in his article "The Majority of the NC", makes a big point of this. After enumerating the criticisms which the majority levels at Stalin's invasion of Finland, he continues in a sarcastic vein: "Therefore? Therefore support the military intervention! That is the conclusion of the majority." No, Comrade Hall. In the first place it is not therefore and in the second place we do not support the intervention. To put it plainly: in spite of Stalin's crime in invading Finland under the circumstances that he did, we shall work for the victory of the Red Army against the Finnish bourgeois army representing imperialism. Why? Because in a war against imperialism, whatever the cause of the war, the consequences of a defeat of the Red Army by an imperialist army can be very grave indeed to the nationalized property. The working masses must at all times reserve for themselves the right and the privilege to destroy the Stalinist bureaucracy. We must, with all means at our disposal, prevent the destruction of that bureaucracy by the imperialists.

The comrades of the minority become exceedingly irritated when we use the analogy of a trade union to illustrate our attitude to the Soviet Union and the Stalinist leadership. It is quite correct that an analogy does not prove anything but it shows how the person using the analogy looks at the whole subject. For us the workers' state is nothing but a very large trade union. That is why we constantly use the analogy. The only valid reason for objecting to the analogy of the trade union is that the Soviet Union is not a workers' state, but once you admit that it is then the trade union analogy is absolutely perfect.

Comrade Hall, however, accepts the analogy and on the basis of the analogy tries to prove that the majority is wrong.

We would not, he says, support a strike of a trade union to exclude Negroes from a factory. That is correct but let us examine the analogy a little further.

What did Stalin, the reactionary leader of the trade union, want from Finland, the little boss representing, in this instance, the big bosses? He wanted certain islands and a peninsula, Hagoe, for the purpose of assuring the defense of Leningrad. The object of Stalin, therefore, is not to exclude Negroes but to get certain positions from the boss in order to be in a better position to ward off a possible attack.

What did Stalin, the reactionary leader, do when the boss refused to grant his request? He did what many reactionary trade union leaders do on many occasions. He attacked the boss in such a way as to alienate the sympathy of everyone including the workers themselves. Therein lies his crime. But once he committed that crime, for which we must condemn him without any reservations, he involved the union in a strike against the bosses and in that strike no revolutionist can possibly be neutral.

Stalin's objective was not bad. The way he attempted to realize it is very bad because even if he achieves the objective he has weakened the union by alienating the sympathy of the workers.

Let us take the analogy from a different viewpoint. Let us consider the objective bad, that is, let us consider that he is actually calling a strike to exclude Negroes, in which case we could not possibly support him. But, whatever his motives may be, the strike actually developed into a struggle between the bosses and the union and the union is in danger of destruction at the hands of the bosses. No revolutionist will permit the bosses to destroy the union, even though the calling of the strike was for a purpose which he could not possibly support. If we are right in considering the Soviet Union a workers' state — though degenerated — and if we are also right that Finland represents an outpost of imperialism, then it follows, as night the day, that in spite of everything we must prevent the defeat of the Red Army at the hands of the Finnish bourgeois army.

There are many comrades of the minority who are playing around with the idea that a defeat of the Red Army is to be preferred because that will lead to a revolution against Stalin. They cite Lenin as authority for the proposition that a defeat of one's own imperialist army is preferable because it will create conditions favorable for a revolution. The difference is that Lenin dealt with a struggle between imperialist camps with the same property relations in both camps and under those conditions the workers can and must be utterly indifferent to the fate of their own imperialist state. The workers must concentrate on the struggle to overthrow their own capitalist government and if this leads to the defeat of their own imperialist army, that risk must be taken.

And after all, it is not such a great risk. Why? Because, even assuming the worst possible variant, that is, assuming that the opposing imperialist army will overrun the country and defeat not only the bourgeoisie but also the revolution, there would be only a change of masters under the same property relations.

It may conceivably happen that a defeat of the Red Army by a bourgeois army would lead to a revolutionary movement among the Russian masses but the far, far greater probability is that such a defeat would give heart to every counter-revolutionary element within the Soviet Union and encourage the imperialists in attempting to smash the workers' state once and for all.

A defeat of an imperialist army creates a revolutionary movement amongst the masses; a defeat of the army of a workers' state — no matter how degenerated — would set the counter-revolutionary elements into motion.

Can anyone point to many cases where strikes have been broken by the bosses and the trade union completely defeated and where as a result the revolutionary elements came to power immediately after the defeat? All the arguments lead to one conclusion. If you believe in the Soviet Union as a workers' state and you analyze the present conflict as one between the Soviet Union and an important outpost of imperialism then the application of our slogan of unconditional defense must apply, regardless of the crimes of Stalin.

The workers and not the imperialists must punish and destroy the Stalinist bureaucracy.

SWP Internal Bulletin vol.2 no.5, December 1939

The hue and cry about poor little Finland

Max Shachtman (1939)

ALMOST EVERYBODY IS JOINING the pack in a hue and cry over Poor Little Finland. Mr. Hoover is collecting funds; President Roosevelt is granting a moratorium on the Finnish debt; Congressmen are yelping for a breaking off of relations with Russia; Alexander Kerensky is stoutly for the independence of Finland; the Finnish White Guards in this country are loading recruits for Finland on to ships; and the liberals and social democrats are pouring out a sea of tears on which to float the ships. The rearguard is brought up smartly by Norman Thomas [of the US Socialist Party] and the editor of his official organ, who are ready to fight it out for Finland to the death.

Without exception, all the "friends of Finland" are serving one objective: the whipping up of a chauvinistic war spirit for the "democratic" imperialists and for American participation in the world slaughter on their side.

As we recall it, Mr. Kerensky, head of the Russian Provisional Government some twenty-two years ago, was then not quite so strenuous in his demand for the independence of Finland from Muscovite rule. In fact, he fought both the Bolsheviks and the Finnish nationalists who demanded the right of self-determination for Finland. We further recall that it was the Bolsheviks under Lenin and Trotsky who, as soon as they were in power, promptly granted Finland its independence. Mr. Kerensky's love for Finland is a little — how shall we say? — belated.

We do not recall any very vigorous activity on the part of Messrs. Hoover, Roosevelt and Co. in behalf of Albania, Ethiopia, Czechoslovakia, Austria, Spain and other victims of reactionary assault.

When the imperialist gangsters were cutting up the world map to suit themselves, and without bothering to inquire of the wishes of those they were carving into greater empires, we heard barely a whisper from all the Congressmen, statesmen and other illustrious citizens of our Great Democracy. They did not then demand the breaking off of diplomatic relations with

Italy or Germany. And for good reasons. Mussolini and Hitler were, after all, only doing what every imperialist nation, the United States included, has done throughout its existence, and continues to do.

But didn't the "liberals" and "socialists" of the *New Leader* and the *Nation* and the Socialist Call protest then? Yes, they protested when the fascist bandits carried out their abominations. But not even from them was there a word of protest against the similar abominations of the "democratic" bandits.

Not a murmur, for example, when France so graciously ceded to Turkey the Syrian province of Alexandretta a short time ago, purely for the purpose of winning Turkey to an alliance with Anglo-French imperialism. The people of Alexandretta, non-Turkish in their majority, were of course not consulted by either the Turks or the French, any more than the Syrians as a whole were ever consulted about being put under the heel of the French army and the French banks.

The protestations of our great American patriots and war-mongers, from Hoover through Roosevelt to Gerry Allard, would sound a spot more convincing if they prefaced their activity by a declaration that their first and main fight is against the violation of national independence and sovereignty which is perpetuated by their own ruling class, that is to say, by American imperialism in Puerto Rico, Samoa, the Philippine islands and elsewhere.

And once they made such a declaration, it would be obligatory for them to add a similar statement with reference to their allies, that is, to those on whose side they are asking us to fight, England and France. They would have to say, it seems to us, that before they presume to say a word in protest against the violation of Finland's independence by Stalin, they denounce the continuing violation of the independence of India, Indo-China, Syria, Algiers, most of Africa and all the other colonies, protectorates and "spheres of influence" of British and French imperialism.

It goes without saying that they will do nothing of the kind. They are too busy working up the campaign for American participation in the war to bother with such trifles. How does the fate of a few hundred million Indians compare with so noble and idealistic a goal as making the world safe for democracy a second time?

It's all very clear and simple. You can commit any crime in the calendar of Stalin or Hitler or Mussolini on one condition: just call yourself a democrat. It will not only sanctify whatever you do, but constitute an unlimited license to condemn your opponent in world politics for doing exactly the same thing.

"In This Corner" column, *Socialist Appeal*, 16 December 1939

In Finland, essentially Stalin was at war with imperialism

Albert Goldman (1940)

OUR PARTY, IN THE RESOLUTION dealing with the invasion of Finland by the Red Army (*Socialist Appeal*. Dec. 9), characterized that invasion as an incident in the Second World War. That is what it turned out to be — an incident which ended by the achievement of peace before it became the beginning of a major conflict between the Soviet Union and Allied imperialism.

That the invasion did not develop into an open conflict between English and French imperialism and the Soviet Union in primarily due to the fact that Stalin's chief aim is to keep from being involved in a major war.

That is what explains the Hitler-Stalin pact. The only enemy Stalin feared was Hitler who, of all the imperialists, had the best chance to attack the Soviet Union. A pact with Hitler would, Stalin thought, do away with the possibility of an immediate war. He was undoubtedly of the opinion that England and France would not go to war over the invasion of Poland and, if they did, he could avoid being involved in such a war.

As his compensation for relieving Hitler of the danger of facing enemy armies on Germany's eastern borders. Stalin received from Hitler guarantees, in the form of territorial concessions in Poland and the Baltic countries, which make the Soviet frontiers more easily defended. [The Hitler-Stalin deal in 1939 included secret clauses agreeing Russian domination in the Baltics. In September-October Stalin pressured those states into accepting Russian military bases. In June 1940 he would invade and annex them].

Why does Stalin want to avoid a major war? Because war threatens the rule of the Stalinist bureaucracy either through revolution or through a successful attack of one or more imperialist countries.

But if he wants to avoid a major war, why did he invade Finland? Because his demands on Latvia, Estonia and Lithuania having been granted, he could not afford to permit Finland to defy him. His prestige was at stake and. besides, he was anxious to take advantage of the general situation to increase his defensive strength. He undoubtedly thought that he could settle matters with Finland very quickly.

Against whom is he trying to defend himself? Primarily against Hitler, for it must not be presumed that Stalin is so stupid as not to see that if Hitler is successful against the Allies, the Nazi war machine will turn to the East.

The creation of the Kuusinen puppet government [for Finland] is evidence of the fact that Stalin at first thought of taking all of Finland. A few days after the invasion, in the early days of December, the Finnish government made a plea through Sweden to the Kremlin to renew negotiations. The Kremlin on Dec. 5 haughtily informed Sweden that there was no Finnish government other than the People's Government of Kuusinen with which the Soviet government had already "made" a treaty.

However, when Stalin found that his army, led by a general staff which he had decapitated and demoralized, could not repeat the exploits of Hitler's army in Poland and that, as a result, there was a real chance of his being involved in war with the Allies, he beat a retreat from his original purpose. After the Red Army cracked the Mannerheim line [of Finnish fortifications] he was willing to call a halt, settle with the same Finnish government which he refused to recognize in December, and thus avoid an attack by the Allied armies. [The Russo-Finnish war ended on 13 March 1940 with a deal in which Finland ceded 11% of its territory to Russia].

Was it merely the Finnish capitalist army that was defeated? In coming out for the defense of the Soviet Union and for the victory of the Red Army as a lesser evil to the victory of the Finnish capitalist army, we took the position that essentially the Soviet Union was at war with the imperialist forces standing behind Finland. It was clear to us that Finland could not have decided to resist Stalin's demands without the encouragement of Chamberlain, Daladier and Roosevelt. It was clear to us that Finland could not have held out so long without receiving substantial aid from the outside. Only when Finland was ready to capitulate did Chamberlain and Daladier reveal how much armament material they had actually sent and how much more material and how many men they were ready to send if Finland would only keep fighting. Our assertion that Finland was fighting the battle for imperialism was completely confirmed.

The cracking of the Mannerheim line would by itself be a sufficient reason for the Finnish government to accept peace terms. True, the Allies offered to send 100,000 men and all the material necessary to withstand the attack of the Red Army. But in view of the time that it would require to get these men over to Finland and especially in view of the refusal of Sweden and Norway to permit transit facilities, the Finnish government saw no possibility of accepting that offer.

And then it was certain, as Prime Minister Ryti informed the Finnish Diet, that to accept the offer of the Allies would mean to invite Germany to send its armed forces into Finland. And they could get there faster than the Allied forces. That meant that Finland would become one of the major battlefields of the war. The Finnish bourgeoisie preferred at this juncture to get peace by surrendering to Stalin the strategical frontiers that he had demanded. They had refused to grant his demands when originally made, only on the mistaken assumption — undoubtedly based on promises made to them by the Allies — that the Allies were going to declare war against Soviet Russia as soon as the invasion began.

Why did not France and England openly declare war on the Soviet Union at the very beginning and immediately send a huge army to aid Finland? It must be recognized that there were serious practical difficulties in the way, chief of which was the attitude of the Swedish and Norwegian governments, unwilling to see their countries become a battle-ground.

Nor must it be forgotten that, while the contradiction between imperialism and the Soviet Union is real and fundamental, there are also inter-imperialist rivalries and, at this particular moment, those rivalries are in the forefront. British and French imperialism are of the opinion that if they can take care of German imperialism they will have no difficulty in settling scores with the Soviet Union.

Of course, if they conclude that, in order to get at German imperialism they must attack the Soviet Union, they will not hesitate to do so and try to kill two birds with one stone. To defend his government against the charge of cowardice in not joining Finland, Christian E. Guenther, Swedish Foreign Minister, showed that the Allied proposal to send troops to Finland was designed more for the purpose of getting at Germany than to assure Finland's independence. To a certain extent Guenther is correct. But another primary motive of the Allies in sending troops to Finland would be to inflict a defeat on the Red Army, if possible, and if not, to keep Stalin busy so that he would not be in a position to help Hitler.

It can be presumed that not only did Hitler agree to peace between the Soviet Union and Finland but he was actually pressing for it. While his general aim is to involve Stalin in a military conflict with the Allies, he obviously is of the opinion that, at this particular moment, Stalin can be of greater service to him if the Soviet Union is at peace. He was also anxious to avoid war in Sweden, for hostilities there meant a chance of having his supply of iron ore and other material cut off.

Nor is he very anxious to see Stalin entrench himself too strongly in the Baltic, for he realizes that any increase in the defensive strength of the Soviet Union makes his future task all the more difficult. However, his all-important problem is to defeat the Allies. He is perfectly willing to grant Stalin defensive positions if thereby the Nazi war machine can only achieve its main purpose at this moment.

It would be folly to deny that the defensive position of the Soviet Union, in a military sense, has been strengthened. But it would be greater folly not to realize that the defense of the Soviet Union depends primarily, not upon military strategic factors, but upon the sympathy of the masses throughout the world. Through the invasion Stalin brought discredit upon the Soviet. Union; he destroyed the sympathy of the masses for the Soviet Union and tied them more firmly to the capitalist world. The loss to the Soviet Union because of that is far greater than the gains achieved in a military-strategic way.

No one except the misled people who blindly follow the Stalinist parties believed the absurd statements made by the Kremlin that Finland threatened to invade the Soviet Union and no one except those same people believe now that the Soviet-Finnish peace treaty is a tremendous victory for peace, as is claimed by Moscow and, of course, by the [Communist Party's] *Daily Worker*.

If and when the Allied imperialists should succeed in defeating Hitler and proceed with settling accounts with Stalin, or if the Allies should decide to invade the Soviet Union before defeating Hitler, it will be a thousand times more difficult to arouse the masses in opposition to such a war. Stalin has destroyed the faith of millions in the Soviet Union and has once more shown that the Stalinist bureaucracy is weakening the Soviet Union.

Millions of workers do not make the distinction that should be made between the Stalinist bureaucracy and the Soviet Union. Stalin acts in the same manner as Hitler and from that they draw the false conclusion that the Soviet Union is the same as Germany. We condemned the invasion because we knew beforehand that no matter what victories the Red Army would gain, the Soviet Union would lose in the esteem of the working masses, because the masses, repelled by the invasion, would tend also to become indifferent or even hostile to the Soviet Union.

But we were staunch in our defense of the Soviet Union and favored the victory of the Red Army against the Finnish capitalist army representing the imperialist world. Recognizing that nationalized property still exists in the Soviet Union we must defend it in any war against a capitalist nation. All that one has to ask is: what would have been the result of a defeat of the Red Army in Finland? Nationalized property would have been endangered and that is what we defend both against imperialism and against the Stalinist bureaucracy.

Has not the Stalinist bureaucracy strengthened itself because of the victory of the Red Army? Perhaps, yes, temporarily. But would not the Soviet Union be in danger if the Red Army had been defeated? We repeat what we have said a thousand times. The task of destroying the Stalinist bureaucracy is a privilege and a duty which the workers must reserve for themselves, and not assign to the imperialists.

How will those profound theoreticians — the Socialist party, the Lovestoneites [a splinter from the Communist Party, former supporters of Bukharin] and their similars — justify their theory of Stalinist imperialism? Undoubtedly they will make all kinds of gyrations to show that they are correct, but anyone who is not blinded by hatred of Stalin can easily see that what he is after primarily is to obtain defensive footholds. It is well-nigh impossible to explain what he has done thus far on the basis of the theory that he has entered into a partnership with Hitler to divide the British Empire or even (some have said it!) the whole world. Of course people do not have to consider facts; they can let their desires and imaginations run away with them. But then these people are not Marxists.

And when the Supreme Council of the Soviet Union will meet it will undoubtedly nationalize industry in that section of Finland ceded to the Soviet Union by the peace terms. It is true that this will be done in a bureaucratic manner and to that extent it is not what we want. But as against permitting industry to remain under capitalism, even bureaucratic nationalization is progressive. Let the middle-class democrats howl about "Stalinist imperialism," but Marxists will continue to make a distinction between imperialism and a degenerated workers' state which, when it annexes territory, takes property away from imperialism and narrows the base of world imperialism.

No one can say with certainty when and under what conditions the Soviet Union will find itself at war. All that our party states is: whenever the Soviet Union will be at war with any capitalist country we shall call upon the workers of the world to defend it because in doing so we are defending the first conquest of the World Revolution. For workers everywhere the main enemy is imperialism. The workers must do their utmost to destroy the power of the Stalinist bureaucracy precisely in order to defend the Soviet Union most effectively.

The Militant, 23 March 1940

Albert Goldman

Taking stock of the Russo-Finnish war

Leon Trotsky (1940)

STALIN'S ALLIANCE WITH HITLER, which raised the curtain on the world war and led directly to the enslavement of the Polish people, resulted from the weakness of the USSR and the Kremlin's panic in face of Germany. Responsibility for this weakness rests with no one but this same Kremlin; its internal policy, which opened an abyss between the ruling caste and the people; its foreign policy, which sacrificed the interests of the world revolution to the interests of the Stalinist clique.

The seizure of eastern Poland — a pledge of the alliance with Hitler and a guarantee against Hitler — was accompanied by the nationalization of semifeudal and capitalist property in western Ukraine and western White Russia. Without this the Kremlin could not have incorporated the occupied territory into the USSR. The strangled and desecrated October Revolution served notice that it was still alive.

In Finland the Kremlin did not succeed in accomplishing a similar social overturn. The imperialist mobilization of world public opinion "in defense of Finland"; the threat of direct intervention by England and France; the impatience of Hitler, who had to seize Denmark and Norway before French and British troops appeared on Scandinavian soil — all this compelled the Kremlin to renounce sovietization of Finland and to limit itself to the seizure of the indispensable strategic positions.

The invasion of Finland unquestionably aroused on the part of the Soviet populace profound condemnation. However, the advanced workers understood that the crimes of the Kremlin oligarchy do not strike off the agenda the question of the existence of the USSR. Its defeat in the world war would signify not merely the overthrow of the totalitarian bureaucracy but the liquidation of the new forms of property, the collapse of the first experiment in planned economy, and the transformation of the entire country into a colony; that is, the handing over to imperialism of colossal natural resources which would give it a respite until the third world war. Neither the peoples of the USSR nor the world working class as a whole care for such an outcome.

Finland's resistance to the USSR was, with all its heroism, no more an act of independent national defense than Norway's subsequent resistance to Germany. The Helsinki government itself understood this when it chose to capitulate to the USSR rather than transform Finland into a military base for England and France. Our whole-hearted recognition of the right of every nation to self determination does not alter the fact that in the course of the present war this right does not have much more weight than thistledown. We must determine the basic line of our policy in accordance with basic and not tenth rate factors. The theses of the Fourth International state:

The concept of national defense, especially when it coincides with the idea of the defense of democracy, can most easily delude the workers of small and neutral countries (Switzerland, partly Belgium, Scandinavian countries.

Only a hopelessly dull bourgeois from a godforsaken Swiss village (like Robert Grimm) can seriously think that the world war into which he is drawn is waged for the defense of Swiss independence.

These words today acquire a special meaning. In no way superior to the Swiss social patriot Robert Grimm are those believe that it is possible to determine proletarian strategy in relation to the defense of the USSR through reliance upon such tactical episodes as the Red Army's invasion of Finland.

Extremely eloquent in its unanimity and fury was the campaign that the world bourgeoisie launched over the Soviet-Finnish war. Neither the perfidy nor the violence of the Kremlin prior to this had aroused the indignation of the bourgeoisie, for the entire history of world politics is written in perfidy and violence. Their fear and indignation arose over the prospect of a social overturn in Finland upon the pattern of the one engendered by the Red Army in Eastern Poland. What was involved was a fresh threat to capitalist property. The anti-Soviet campaign, which had a class character through and through, disclosed once again that the USSR by virtue of the social foundations laid down by the October Revolution, upon which the existence of the bureaucracy itself is dependent, still remains a workers' state, terrifying to the bourgeoisie of the whole world. Episodic agreements between the bourgeoisie and the USSR do not alter the fact that "taken on a historic scale the antagonism between world imperialism and the Soviet Union is infinitely deeper than the antagonisms that set the individual capitalist countries in opposition to each other." Many petty bourgeois radicals, who only yesterday were still ready to consider the Soviet Union as an axis for grouping the "democratic" forces against fascism, have suddenly discovered, now that their own fatherlands have been threatened by Hitler, that Moscow, which did not come to their aid, follows an imperialist policy, and that there is no difference between the USSR and the fascist countries.

Lie! will respond every class conscious worker — there is a difference. The bourgeoisie appraises this social difference better and more profoundly than do the radical windbags. To be sure, the nationalization of the means of production in one country, and a backward one at that, still does not insure the building of socialism. But it is capable of furthering the primary prerequisite of socialism, namely, the planned development of the productive forces. To turn one's back on the nationalization of the means of production on the ground that in and of itself it does not create the well being of the masses is tantamount to sentencing a granite foundation to destruction on the ground that it is impossible to live without walls and a roof. The class conscious worker knows that a successful struggle for complete emancipation is unthinkable without the defense of conquests already gained, however modest these may be. All the more obligatory therefore is the defense of so colossal a conquest as planned economy against the restoration of capitalist relations. Those who cannot defend old positions will never conquer new ones.

The Fourth International can defend the USSR only by the methods of revolutionary class struggle. To teach the workers correctly to understand the class character of the state — imperialist, colonial, workers' — and the reciprocal relations between them, as well as the inner contradictions in each of them, enables the workers to draw correct practical conclusions in situation. While waging a tireless struggle against the Moscow oligarchy, the Fourth International decisively rejects any policy that would aid imperialism against the USSR.

The defense of the USSR coincides in principle with the preparation of the world proletarian revolution. We flatly reject the theory of socialism in one country, that brain child of ignorant and reactionary Stalinism. Only the world revolution can save the USSR for socialism. But the world revolution carries with it the inescapable blotting out of the Kremlin oligarchy.

Manifesto of the Emergency Conference of the Fourth
International, May 1940

Invasion of Baltics: a defensive move against Germany

Felix Morrow (1940)

THE COMPLETE OCCUPATION and transformation into military camps of Lithuania, Latvia and Estonia by Soviet troops last weekend was almost universally recognized as a move inspired by fear of Hitler. With France out of the war, the Nazi armies completely dominated continental Europe, able to turn and rend the partner whose "peace and friendship treaty," freeing Hitler from any worry about a fight on two fronts, had so enormously facilitated the Nazis' speedy victory [in western Europe, in May-June 1940]. Occupation of the tiny Baltic states provided certain strategic advantages in case of hostilities with Germany, but these seemed pitifully paltry as contrasted with the enhanced power of Nazi Germany now as compared with last August when Stalin entered the "peace" pact with Hitler.

From Stockholm it was reported by Otto Tolischus of the New York Times that "Germany makes little secret of her displeasure" at the Soviet move.

Almost the only source that did not characterize the step as a defensive move against Germany was the Stalin regime and its Stalinist press abroad. For Stalin could not admit now, any more than when he sought strategic bases in Finland, that he was seeking protection against the consequences of his "peace" pact of last year. Then, he had justified the pact on the ground that it made impossible a German war against the Soviet Union; the advantage of the pact, Stalinists had argued throughout the world, outweighed all its evil consequences. Now, less than ten months after the pact, Stalin could not admit that he was convulsively adding to his defense to guard against that which this pact with Hitler was to have made impossible.

Since the Stalin cult of infallibility precluded telling the truth the occupation of the Baltic states had to be justified by preposterous lies. The official Soviet communiques solemnly declare that the Lilliputian slates had "prepared an attack on the Soviet garrisons" stationed there.

The Baltic states could very likely play the role of puppets of a great power preparing an assault upon the Soviet Union. But with the Allies cracking under Hitler's blows, the only great power which could be manipulating the Baltic puppets would be Germany — and that Stalin could not admit for it would condemn his entire policy. Hence his absurd lies, which convince no one and which further discredit the Soviet Union in the eyes of the world's workers.

It does not require an admission from Stalin to establish the utter bankruptcy of the Stalin-Hitler pact. When the Nazis marched on Poland, Stalin counted on a second Munich [i.e. British and French acquiescence] as the most likely aftermath. On the day the German troops marched, Molotov, smiled skeptically when the Polish ambassador told him that France and England would fulfill their commitments to Poland; "we shall see," said Molotov unbelievingly. Neither Molotov nor his master had understood that the European crisis had gone too far for a second Munich.

The only other possibility which occurred to the Kremlin minds was that, if war did come, it would be of long duration. Precisely the Stalin-Hitler pact, however, wiping out the possible danger of a war on two fronts, enabled Hitler to concentrate all the war power of German economy in the West to assure a short war. Stalin's intelligence service undoubtedly acquainted him with the fact that Hitler's military machine actually believed in the reality of the blitzkrieg timetable which Hitler was publicly enunciating — with August 15 as the outside date for successful completion of the European phases of the war; but Stalin did not use this information to reorganize his policy. He followed that policy out to its dead end.

And what a dead end! Never in the worst days of the war of intervention of 1918-20 was the infant Soviet republic in a more dangerous position than is the Soviet Union today, thanks to Stalin's strategy.

The European labor movement, which Lenin considered to be the most important bulwark defending the Soviet Union, lies crushed under Hitler's war machine, as the end-result of Stalin's foreign policy. Lenin said the Soviet Union must take advantage of the contradictions between the imperialist powers; instead, Stalin let himself be used, first by one imperialist power, then the other. Lenin said the Soviet Union must take advantage of the con-tradictions between the imperialist powers in order to advance the world revolution, the only real safeguard of the Soviet Union; Stalin permitted him-self to be used by the imperialist powers to crush, one after another, the labor movements of Europe.

In 1936, in the name of the "defense of the Soviet Union" provided by the Franco-Soviet pact, Stalin's French lieutenants prevented the revolution-ary June strikes from culminating in a complete social revolution; instead they told the workers to be good French patriots, to surrender the factories and to obey the coalition with the bourgeoisie, the Popular Front govern-ment of Blum-Daladier. That government and its successors, backed by the Stalinists, broke the back of the French working class. Hounded and de-nuded of its gains and rights, the French workers could scarcely be inspired by the French bourgeoisie to hurl back Hitler.

That same French Popular Front government of Blum-Stalin refused to provide arms to the Spanish Loyalists. Meanwhile the Spanish Popular Front government created by the Stalinists broke the morale of the Spanish work-ers and peasants by forcing them to dissolve their factory, land and soldiers' committees; forced them to limit their struggle against Franco within the im-potent confines of bourgeois democracy. To achieve this foul end Stalin's GPU assassinated the flower of the Spanish revolutionists — all this in Stalin's vain attempt to establish his respectability and to win the good-will of British imperialism. Instead the British facilitated Franco's victory — and another labor movement was wiped off the map.

Having perpetrated all this evil without adding a particle to the security of the Soviet Union, Stalin then sought protection in the pact with Hitler — with what results we have now seen.

Neither to the British workers nor to the American nor to any other labor movement left in the world can Stalin turn with any assurance of aid in this moment of terrible danger to the Soviet Union. Millions upon millions of workers who before that were ready to defend the Soviet Union would not turn a hand for it now, after the Hitler-Stalin pact and the invasions of Poland and Finland. Our prediction that the defensive positions gained by the pact and the invasions would not compensate in any way for the loss among the workers of their former faith and trust in the Soviet Union has been verified. That, and the crushing of the European labor movement by Hitler's victories, leave the Soviet Union bereft of all outer defenses.

The Soviet Union could endure as an isolated workers' state in a capitalist world for 23 years thanks only to the fact that Europe was not a capitalist unity but was divided by imperialist rivalries. Now Hitler is in the process of unifying Europe on the most reactionary basis imaginable. The Soviet Union is confronted by a united capitalist Europe.

This is the end of Stalin's road of "socialism in one country." Stalin and the "realists" who rallied to him turned their back on the dream of world revolution and concentrated on a "practical" task. At every stage the interests of the world revolution, of the world working class, were subordinated, were sacrificed, to the needs of the Soviet Union — so they said. And this is the result.

If Stalin remains at the helm of the Soviet Union, he will bring it to destruction at the hands of the imperialists, we have predicted. The truth is here now for all to see. The masses of the Soviet Union, if they are to save themselves and the nationalized economy from imperialist assault, must overthrow Stalin. The destruction of the Stalinist bureaucracy is an absolute necessity for the Soviet Union. Only a revolutionary internationalist policy and a revolutionary leadership capable of inspiring the world working class to a new effort can save the Soviet Union.

"Stalin moves into Baltic countries", *Socialist Appeal*, 22 June 1940

Baltics: reactionary annexation

Labor Action

THE "GOOD-NEIGHBORLY, FRIENDLY relations between the Soviet Union and Germany are not based on fortuitous considerations of a transient nature," declared Russian Premier Molotov in a speech to the Supreme Soviet on August 1, "but on fundamental state interests of both the USSR and Germany." In a brief review of the past months of the war and the position of the Soviet Union, Molotov endorsed the remarks of Hitler of June 19 that English speculations on conflicts between the two allies were baseless.

He affirmed that the Stalin-Hitler pact of August 1939 "removed the possibility of friction in Soviet-German relations, when Soviet measures were carried out along our western frontier, and at the same time it has assured Germany a calm feeling of security in the East. The developments in Europe, far from reducing the strength of the Soviet-German Non-Aggression Pact, on the contrary emphasized the importance of its existence and further development." Already, Molotov continued, Russia has annexed, "all by peaceful means" (!) territories with a population exceeding 23,000,000 people and has shifted its western frontier to the Baltic coast, "of first rate importance for our country. At the same time we shall have ice-free ports in the Baltic, of which we stand so much in need." The end of the war is not yet in sight, he stated, but "true to its policy of peace and neutrality, the Soviet Union is not taking part in the war." This hypocritical "neutrality" is coupled with further threats against Finland, Iran and Turkey

As to Finland: "Naturally, if certain elements in the Finnish ruling class do not cease their persecution of public circles in Finland (that is, the recently organized Stalinist 'Left Wing' in the Finnish Social Democratic Party) which are striving to strengthen good-neighborly relations with the USSR, then relations between the USSR and Finland may suffer damage."

And the fate of the Baltic countries foreshadows what Stalin and Molotov plan for Finland: reactionary annexation. On the pretext that the Baltic governments had formed a military alliance against Russia, the Soviet Government demanded in the words of Molotov, "changes in the governments of Lithuania, Latvia and Estonia, and dispatched additional Red Army units to these countries." These states, following fraudulent, army-controlled "elections," are now incorporated in the Soviet Union.

Molotov's speech indicated that, despite antagonisms between the reactionary expansionist interests of Russia, and Germany and Italy, about which he was completely silent, the Soviet Union in the next period will continue its foreign policy in accordance with the Stalin-Hitler pact.

From "Molotov says Russia assures Germany of security in East", *Labor Action*, 12 August 1940

Bessarabia: a workers' state has a right and duty to extend its base

Albert Goldman (1940)

TAKING ADVANTAGE of Hitler and Mussolini's preoccupation with their task of dealing a knockout blow to the British Empire, Stalin demanded and obtained the return of Bessarabia, the province which Rumania had seized from the Soviet Union in 1918. The fact that together with Bessarabia Stalin obtained the northern part of Bukovina is almost conclusive evidence that his demands were motivated by a desire to prepare defensive positions against the attack which everyone expects Hitler to launch against the Soviet Union as soon as he is through with or as soon as he makes peace with England. If it is true that Stalin is also demanding control of the mouth of the Danube it would only strengthen the theory that he is trying to seize as many defensive positions as he possibly can while the seizing is good. To gain control of the Danubian estuary would be bearding Hitler in his den.

Did Hitler know of and acquiesce in Stalin's actions? Speculation is rife as to whether there was an agreement between the two permitting Stalin to take Bessarabia and Bukovina, or whether the latter took what he wanted without asking his "friend" Hitler.

The statement issued by the German Legation in Bucharest to the effect that the occupation of Bessarabia was instigated by Cripps, the British ambassador to Moscow, and was nothing but a British trick to involve the Balkans in the war, conflicts with the attitude of the Berlin officials, which is that the whole matter is one entirely between the Soviet Union and Rumania. The inference of this difference between Bucharest and Berlin is that Stalin acted without as much as notifying Hitler. This inference is strengthened by the haste with which the Germans in the occupied territories made their exit.

But the answer to the question as to what extent the move into Rumania was made by Stalin with the knowledge and consent of Hitler does not affect its defensive character, that is, that primarily it constitutes a further preparation of Stalin to defend himself against Hitler. The sudden despatch of tens of thousands of troops into Latvia, Lithuania and Estonia a few weeks ago was clear evidence that Hitler's phenomenal success has Stalin considerably worried.

It is the defensive aspect of the move by Stalin, as against Hitler, that will keep the petty-bourgeois democrats of all varieties from going into hysterics and demanding either that the "democracies" take strong action against the Soviet Union or else that the Bessarabian workers take up arms against the Red Army.

When Stalin sent the Red Army into Finland it constituted an invasion of a "small democratic nation" and the petty-bourgeois democrats reacted so violently that they were willing to take up arms to help defeat the Red Army. Some also claimed an intention to use their arms against the Finnish army, but all were for the defeat of the Red Army.

But the petty-bourgeois democrats cannot get all heated up about Rumania as they did about Finland. Although a small country it can hardly be classed as a democracy. We can therefore expect that the "democrats" of all types, while ceremoniously referring to their theory of Stalinist imperialism and of the partnership between Hitler and Stalin to divide the British Empire if not the whole world will, however not raise much of a howl — all of which indicates the democratic roots of their opposition to the Soviet Union.

As for us we shall continue to state that a workers' state has a right and a duty to take advantage of the conflicts and difficulties of the imperialist world in order to extend its base and strengthen its defensive positions. And we shall continue to attack the bureaucratic methods of the bureaucracy of the degenerated workers' state when these methods alienate the sympathies of the working masses and thus nullify the gains made by virtue of the acquisition of territory and defensive outposts. To the Bessarabian workers and peasants we say: Join your brothers in the Soviet Union in the struggle against imperialism, and against the Stalinist bureaucracy.

And it becomes clearer with the passing of every day that all of the defensive positions acquired by Stalin cannot possibly compensate for his crime in entering into the pact with Hitler. He thereby not only lost the support of millions of workers who considered the Soviet Union as the champion of the struggle against fascism but he also enabled Hitler to gain complete control over Europe, making certain of an attack by him on the Soviet Union without the slightest fear of any interference by France.

The factor of contending imperialist states on the European scene, a factor of tremendous importance to the safety of the Soviet Union, has been wiped out by the pact and by the consequent victory of Hitler.

That Stalin realizes the danger of his situation is evidenced not only by his movement of troops but by a more or less clearly-indicated change of line on the part of the Stalinist parties, a change of line that has a meaning only if Stalin is cautiously preparing a shift towards the "democracies." For the past two months or so the Stalinists have been attacking German imperialism as well as Allied imperialism and now they have launched a campaign against the Munich men in the English cabinet and for a people's government to continue the struggle against Hitler.

It may not be long before the Stalinists will discover that there has been such a change in the constitution of the English government that to support the "democracies" against Hitler will become the sacred duty of the working masses.

"Rumania Move May Herald Stalin's Policy Switch", *Socialist Appeal* 6 July 1940

Stalin seizes eastern Romania for revenues, power, and prestige

Joseph Carter (1940)

WITH THE COMPLETE APPROVAL of Hitler and Mussolini, Russian troops occupied Bessarabia and Northern Bukovina following a twenty-four hour ultimatum to the Rumanian government calling for the ceding of these territories.

Hitler gained control over Rumania and the Balkans, as King Carol accepted the ultimatum and renounced the guarantee of protection pledged a year ago by Anglo-French imperialism. The country is now facing complete dismemberment as Hungary demands the return of Transylvania, a province taken from her after the first world war, and Bulgaria asks for Dobrudja, a province seized from her in 1913. Hitler will decide how and when these demands will be met.

At some points the Russian troops clashed with the Rumanian army because of the rapid occupation of the ceded territory and, according to reports, because they went beyond the frontiers established by the agreement, apparently by mistake. Fighting also broke out between Stalinists released from prison and local police, and as a result of the increased anti-semitic drive in Rumania which caused Jews to flee to Russian-occupied territory.

At the same time there are persistent reports that Stalin has demanded from Rumania naval bases at Constanxa and at the mouth of the Danube; and from Turkey, participation in control of the Dardanelles, the narrow straits linking the Black Sea and the Mediterranean. These reports although not confirmed are in harmony with the general course of the Stalin-Hitler alliance.

The official Russian explanation for its new annexations are given in Molotov's ultimatum-note of June 26. The communique declares that the Soviet Union has never reconciled itself to the seizure of Bessarabia by Rumania at the end of the last world war. It claims that the overwhelming majority of the people of that province are Ukrainians and should therefore be united with the Ukrainian Soviet Republic. This change, it continues, is made both possible and necessary by the new military strength of Russia, and the "present international situation;" and is connected with the need of transferring to Russia Northern Bukovina whose people are bound to the Soviet Ukraine by language and national composition. At the same time the transfer of this province would also be a partial compensation for the 22 year domination of Bessarabia by Rumania. The note concludes by demanding the two provinces within twenty four hours, by June 27...

Hitler permits these seizures of territories by Moscow as compensation for Stalin's "non-belligerent" support of his war against Anglo-French imperialism; and as a means for his own further control of the Balkans, the Mediterranean and the Near East. While Hitler wages war on the Western Front, Russia stands as a threat over Turkey and the Balkan countries, above all Rumania, in case they should decide to join the Allies against Germany. Turkey, whose control over the Dardanelles gives it a unique position in the Mediterranean and the Near East, has been forced to break its alliance with England and France. Rumania had to follow suit. Now Hitler controls that country, and with the aid of Stalin aims to dominate the Dardanelles. While Hitler is conducting his war against the British Empire, Russia will assure the regular flow of goods from the Balkans to Germany.

Stalin's aid to Hitler flows from his own desire to increase the revenues, power and prestige of the reactionary bureaucratic rulers of Russia, whose interests have nothing in common with those of the Russian or world working class. Through his partnership with the most powerful and aggressive imperialist power, German Fascism, Stalin has taken over part of Finland, the Baltics, part of Poland, and now Bessarabia and Bukovina. Like Russian Czarist imperialism, Stalin seeks control over the Dardanelles, and with that, influence in the Mediterranean and the Near East. He is ready to share this expansion with German Fascism, and in order to do so, seeks to make Hitler as dependent on Russia as possible. At the same time these new conquests would become defense outposts in case of a German attack on Russia.

Stalin is working hard for the long term agreement with German Fascism. Hitler has probably promised him such a lasting division of the spoils. Naturally, neither partner trusts the other. And in case of a quick and decisive victory of Hitler over the British Empire, particularly if there is not an immediate war between Germany and the United States, Hitler will turn on Russia, and seek to reduce it to a colony.

Despite apparent strengthening of Russia's defenses, Stalin's entire course has in reality weakened the country. His barbaric dictatorship over the Russian people, the wiping out of the old generation of revolutionists, the suicidal purges of the Red Army officer staff, the economic chaos which has resulted from his bureaucratic economic "planning," his brutal crushing of the national independence of the bordering slates, and his destruction of the growing revolutionary working class movements in Germany in 1932-33, and in France in 1934-39, have all contributed to repelling the masses, and weakening the Soviet Union.

At the same time by his support of Hitler's war against Anglo-French imperialism, Stalin has strengthened German Fascism in its struggle for world domination and has thereby increased the danger of a successful Hitler attack on Russia.

Within Russia itself, new measures were adopted last week for increased production in preparation for large scale military operations. The eight hour working day replaces the seven hour working day; the seven day week is substituted for the six day week, with a revolving rest-day so that while every worker gets one day of rest in seven, factories will operate on a full seven day schedule.

At the same time warnings were issued against the growing trend among workers to leave their places of employment without permission, and heavy penalties decreed. Undoubtedly, the turnover of labor is far greater than officially admitted, and is the expression of an increasing dissatisfaction among the workers with the existing labor standards and terroristic conditions.

Commenting on these decrees *Pravda* (June 26) recalls the words of Stalin that "the whole of our people must be kept in a state of mobilization and preparedness in the face of the danger of military attack so that no single 'accident' and no tricks on the part of our external enemies may take us by surprise..."

However, it should be remembered that every adventure of Stalin, such as in Finland or in the Baltics, was undertaken under the guise of "defense" of the Soviet Union. Stalin is now preparing for large scale warfare — as an ally of Hitler if the German Fuehrer permits, or against him, if and when Hitler decides that he no longer needs Russian collaboration and turns on his ally of today.

Whatever course Stalin takes will be dictated by his own reactionary anti-working class, anti-socialist interests. The Russian workers and peasants, supported by the workers of other countries, can defend their country against Hitler and capitalist imperialism only by the relentless struggle for the overthrow of the Stalin regime and for socialist democracy.

"Russia's Occupation Of Rumania Extends Hitler-Stalin Balkan Hold",
Labor Action, 8 July 1940 (abridged)

Anti-Jewish, anti-Trotskyist headlines from the Mexican Communist Party newspaper, 3 November 1939.

Iran: not all invasions are bad

Albert Goldman (1941)

TO SOME PEOPLE all violence is hateful. The violence of the master against the slave is to be condemned, and also the violence of the slave who attempts to free himself from the master. When British imperialism uses violence in India to keep millions of people in subjection, the moralists who are above the social conflict in society protest. They would also protest if the Indian masses should use force to drive the British rulers out of India. People who argue that way have some abstract standard of good and evil, a standard that ignores classes and class struggles.

The Marxist never evaluates the activities of classes and nations from some abstract moral standard but the needs of classes and nations to achieve their freedom. Are all invasions bad? The Marxist answer to that question is in the negative. He replies: who is doing the invading and who is being invaded; what are the circumstances of the invasion? does it further the interests of the revolutionary working masses?

The Soviet Union invades Iran and British imperialism invade Iran. Middle-class moralists who think every invasion, no matter by whom or against whom or under what circumstances, is an imperialist act, rise in their righteous indignation, to condemn both.

The Marxist says: the Soviet Union is a workers' state, although a degenerated one. It is fighting for its existence against German imperialism; it is under an obligation to take every measure necessary for its defense provided it does not conflict with the interests of the world revolution.

The Soviet Government issued a statement in connection with its invasion of Iran justifying the act on the ground that Article VI of the Soviet-Iranian treaty of 1921 gives it the right to march troops into Iranian territory in order to take necessary military measures whenever the Iranian government is unable to prevent an attack or a threatened attack on the Soviet Union through Iran. The treaty with Iran was made under the regime of Lenin and Trotsky and is significant of the attitude the leaders of the Russian Revolution took to the possibility of marching troops into a territory that did not constitute part of the Soviet Union. In the interests of defending the Soviet Union they demanded and obtained the right to send their armed forces into an adjacent country. The treaty does not require the Soviet Union to obtain permission from Iran before sending troops.

It can be taken for granted that Lenin and Trotsky would have sent troops into neighboring territory even without permission, and even without a treaty, if the interests of the Soviet Union and the world revolution demanded such action.

It is quite true that British imperialism was the enemy that the Soviet

Government had in mind, at the time of the treaty, but the fact that German imperialism is the enemy that now threatens the Soviet Union makes not a particle of difference. And neither is the fact that, because of a particular military situation, the British imperialists are invading Iran at the same time that the Soviet Union is doing so, of the slightest importance insofar as determining the right of the Soviet Government to send its troops into Iran.

But did we not condemn the Stalinist government for invading Poland, Finland and the Baltic countries? Yes, we did, but only because under the circumstances the damage done to the Soviet Union, because the act of invasion alienated the sympathies of millions of people, was greater than any benefits that could be derived from the compulsory annexation of the territories invaded.

Lenin and Trotsky would have been compelled to weigh advantages and disadvantages in undertaking an act like invading another country. They would have made the necessity for such an invasion clear to the workers of the world. And, above all, the masses would have had complete confidence in their motives and in their promises.

No one can deny that Stalin's act in invading Iran is viewed with great suspicion. That is because the policies that he has been and is following have justifiably created suspicion as to his motives and very few people believe in his promises. All his explanations and excuses for invading Poland and. Finland were of no avail. To the vast masses those invasions appeared in the same light as Nazi invasions. Stalin's crime consisted of exactly this: that he made the Soviet Union appear to be in the same category as Nazi Germany.

Although we Trotskyists knew that Stalin had annexed part of Poland and the Baltic countries and part of Finland for military-strategic reasons, to prepare against an attack by Hitler, still we condemned the invasions because the loss of faith in the Soviet Union on the part of millions of people outweighed by far the possible military advantages.

We are not over-confident that Stalin will abide by his promise to withdraw the Red Army from Iran when the necessity for its occupation will have disappeared. That is something to be settled in the future. At present, as far as the Soviet Union is concerned, the class-conscious workers and peasants, including those of Iran, will not permit anything to interfere with the defense of the Soviet Union.

"The Marxist attitude on Iran invasion", *The Militant*, 6 September 1941

Iran: imperialist aggression

New International (1941)

AFTER THE FIRST ROUND of cheers from the liberals for England because she has "finally" adopted Hitler's technique of attacking first and explaining afterward, they have settled down to the more sober and embarrassing problem of elucidating what one of them calls the "ethics" of the invasion of Iran. At bottom, the elucidation is admirable in its simplicity:

When German imperialism does it in the name of self-defense, in the name of preventing the enemy from converting the country in question into a base of war operations, in the name of the "new order" – it is uniformly bad. When British imperialism does it in the name of self-defense, in the name of preventing the enemy from converting the country in question into a base of war operations, and, what's more, in the name of "democracy" – it is uniformly good and deserves to find favor in the sight of the Lord. The modern version of non olet is, "Oil doesn't stink."

In a word, we have here only another of those sordid cases of purely imperialist aggression which requires a copious supply of shamelessness among its apologists. In none of the hundreds of cases that soil the pages of modern history have the invasion and occupation of the weaker and, usually, defenseless country been unaccompanied by assurances that it is all being done for the benefit of the country itself; in most of the cases the imperialists add that if they hadn't done it, some other bandit would have. This is always a great relief to the victim.

The case of Iran, however, is somewhat "complicated" by the Soviet Union's participation in the invasion, as were the invasions of Poland, the Baltic countries, Finland and Rumania in the first stage of the war. At that time, all species of apologists for Stalinism were no less shameless than they are now. Then, it is true, the invasions were effected in concert with German imperialism, but the apologists explained, confidentially, that Stalin was really not sharing the loot with Hitler but preventing him from doing more looting and – this between you and me! – laying the basis for an attack on Hitler. Anyway, Poland was an imperialist state and Mannerheim a butcher of the people (which Stalin is not) [Mannerheim was Finland's military commander in the 1939-40 war, under a Social Democrat/ liberal government. He had also been the military leader of the counter-revolutionary Whites in Finland's civil war of 1918]. Anyway, it is necessary to defend unconditionally the Soviet Union.

In August 1941, the Kremlin apologists feel a little easier – not less shameless, just a little easier. In the first place, Stalin is acting in alliance with a very nice, popular, suave, democratic bandit, instead of with a most unpopular fascist bandit. And in the second place, somebody managed to dig up – glory be! – a sanctifying document, a genuine one this time, not forged or anything like that. It is nothing less than the Russo-Persian Treaty.

Yes, the treaty does indeed exist. It was signed in Moscow on February 26, 1921, by Chicherin and Karakhan for the Russian Soviet Republic and by Moshaverol-Memalek for the Persian (now Iranian) government. The ghost of Lozovsky, who now functions as head of the Soviet Information Bureau, quoted truthfully from Article VI of the treaty which provides that:

"... In the case of attempts made on the part of third countries to pursue an annexationist policy by means of an armed intervention on the territory of Persia, or to transform the territory of Persia into a base for military operations against Russia, and if thereby the frontiers of the Russian Socialist Federated Soviet Republic or the states allied with it should be threatened, and the Persian Government, following a warning on the part of the Russian Soviet Government, should not possess the necessary strength to ward off this danger, the Russian Soviet Government is empowered to direct its troops into the territory of Persia in order to adopt the necessary military measures in the interests of self-defense. After the elimination of the danger, the Russian Soviet Government obligates itself to withdraw its troops immediately from the territory of Persia".

What would Stalin have done if he didn't have this wonderful Article VI from way back in 1921? Why, he would have done exactly what he did in Poland and in the Baltic countries and in Finland and in Rumania, for which he had no Article VI or anything like it. But whatever you say, he does have it now, doesn't he? He does, and every apologist for Stalinism, including most of his allies in the democratic-imperialist camp, are effusively delighted. An imperialist invasion without an Article VI is all right in its way. An invasion with it is almost wonderful.

But before the word there was the deed. And before Article VI of the treaty there was Article II, which Lozovsky, not having sufficient time on the radio, was not able to quote. It reads as follows:

"The Russian Soviet Government stigmatizes the policy of the governments of Czarist Russia which, without the agreement of the peoples of Asia and under cover of guaranteeing the independence of these peoples, concluded treaties relating to the Orient with other countries of Europe whose objective was a gradual annexation. The Russian Soviet Government rejects unqualifiedly this criminal policy, which not only violated the sovereignty of the countries of Asia, but also led to an organized, brutal violation of the living body of the peoples of the Orient by the European robbers.

"Accordingly, and in correspondence with the principles set forth in Articles I and IV of the present treaty, the Russian Soviet Government declares its renunciation of participation in any measures which aim at a weakening or violation of the sovereignty of Persia and declares that all conventions and agreements between the former government of Russia and third states injurious and relating to Persia are abolished and nullified". (Russische Korrespondenz, Vol. II, Sec. 1, No. 5, May 1921, p. 371)

Thus the necessary pre-condition for fulfilling the Russian obligation under Article VI of the treaty in alliance with British imperialism was the violation of Article II, both in letter and in spirit. Iran is only another, and even clearer, proof of the inadmissibility of the cry for "defense of the Soviet Union" in a war in which it is allied with an imperialist camp and, by virtue of its control and direction by the reactionary Stalinist régime, is conducting a reactionary, imperialist war. Imperialist war? Yes. And Iran is an even plainer case than was Poland. It is a war of joint imperialist expansion on the part of Churchill and Stalin, according to the simple and exact description by Lenin, who wrote on February 24, 1918, not of capitalist imperialism alone and in particular, but of imperialism in general: "I characterize here as imperialism the robbery of other countries in general, as imperialist war a war of robbers for the division of the booty."

"Stalin in Iran", editorial, *New International*, August 1941

Labor Action, 10 July 1944.
The political ferment in the British Army. The "8th Army" had fought in North Africa and then from Sicily up through Italy. In response to an outcry in the British press that striking engineering workers were stabbing the fighting soldiers in the back, the Cairo, Egypt "parliament" — an unofficial soldiers' forum for political debate and discussion — passed a resolution insisting that "the right to strike" was an essential part of what they were fighting the war for.

Dividing Up the Booty

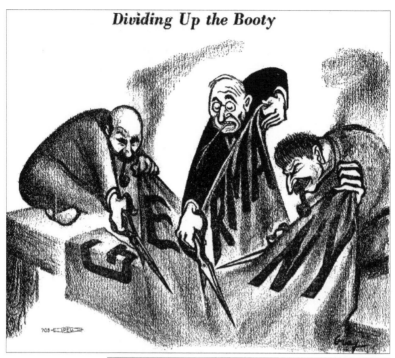

Above: *The Militant*, 11 August 1945. The figures are Attlee, Truman, and Stalin, who divided Germany into their respective "occupation zones" (plus another for France). Right: *Labor Action*, 23 April 1945.

4. A bureaucratic-proletarian revolution?

The idea and the fact of Stalinist-made anti-capitalist revolutions would dominate and shape the Orthodox Trotskyists for decades after 1940. The idea first appeared when Stalin took eastern Poland, the Baltic states, and eastern Romania (and tried to take Finland), assimilating their economic and social structures to that of the USSR. When Max Shachtman and his comrades accused Trotsky of giving credence to the idea of Stalinist "bureaucrat-proletarian revolution" in Poland and Finland, Trotsky denied it indignantly. After Trotsky's death the Orthodox Trotskyists revived the idea in relation to the states of the new Russian empire and independent Stalinist states such as Yugoslavia and China. See also chapter 6 of this volume.

Revolutionary in character, military-bureaucratic in form

Leon Trotsky (1939)

AS I AM WRITING these lines the question of the territories occupied by the Red Army [in eastern Poland] still remains obscure. The cable dispatches contradict each other, since both sides lie a great deal; but the actual relationships on the scene are no doubt still extremely unsettled. Most of the occupied territories will doubtlessly become part of the USSR. In what form? Let us for a moment conceive that in accordance with the treaty with Hitler, the Moscow government leaves untouched the rights of private property in the occupied areas and limits itself to "control" after the Fascist pattern. Such a concession would have a deep going principled character and might become a starting point for a new chapter in the history of the Soviet regime: and consequently a starting point for a new appraisal on our part of the nature of the Soviet state.

It is more likely, however, that in the territories scheduled to become a part of the USSR, the Moscow government will carry through the expropriation of the large landowners and statification of the means of production. This variant is most probable not because the bureaucracy remains true to the socialist program but because it is neither desirous nor capable of sharing the power, and the privileges the latter entails, with the old ruling classes in the occupied territories. Here an analogy literally offers itself. The first Bonaparte halted the revolution by means of a military dictatorship. However, when the French troops invaded Poland, Napoleon signed a decree: "Serfdom is abolished." This measure was dictated not by Napoleon's sympathies for the peasants, nor by democratic principles but rather by the fact that the Bonapartist dictatorship based itself not on feudal, but on bourgeois property relations. Inasmuch as Stalin's Bonapartist dictatorship bases itself not on private but on state property, the invasion of Poland by the Red Army should, in the nature of the case, result in the abolition of private capitalist property, so as thus to bring the regime of the occupied territories into accord with the regime of the USSR.

This measure, revolutionary in character – "the expropriation of the expropriators" – is in this case achieved in a military bureaucratic fashion. The appeal to independent activity on the part of the masses in the new territories – and without such an appeal, even if worded with extreme caution, it is impossible to constitute a new regime – will on the morrow undoubtedly be suppressed by ruthless police measures in order to assure the preponderance of the bureaucracy over the awakened revolutionary masses. This is one side of the matter. But there is another. In order to gain the possibility of occupying Poland through a military alliance with Hitler, the Kremlin for a long time deceived and continues to deceive the masses in the USSR and in the whole world, and has thereby brought about the complete disorganization of the ranks of its own Communist international. The primary political criterion for us is not the transformation of property relations in this or another area, however important these may be in themselves, but rather the change in the consciousness and organization of the world proletariat, the raising of their capacity for defending former conquests and accomplishing new ones. From this one, and the only decisive standpoint, the politics of Moscow, taken as a whole, wholly retain their reactionary character and remain the chief obstacle on the road to the world revolution.

Our general appraisal of the Kremlin and Comintern does not, however, alter the particular fact that the statification of property in the occupied territories is in itself a progressive measure. We must recognize this openly. Were Hitler on the morrow to throw his armies against the East, to restore "law and order" in Eastern Poland, the advanced workers would defend against Hitler these new property forms established by the Bonapartist Soviet bureaucracy.

The statification of the means of production is, as we said, a progressive measure. But its progressiveness is relative; its specific

266

weight depends on the sum-total of all the other factors. Thus, we must first and foremost establish that the extension of the territory dominated by bureaucratic autocracy and parasitism, cloaked by "socialist" measures, can augment the prestige of the Kremlin, engender illusions concerning the possibility of replacing the proletarian revolution by bureaucratic maneuvers and so on. This evil by far outweighs the progressive content of Stalinist reforms in Poland. In order that nationalized property in the occupied areas, as well as in the USSR, become a basis for genuinely progressive, that is to say socialist development, it is necessary to overthrow the Moscow bureaucracy. Our program retains, consequently, all its validity. The events did not catch us unaware. It is necessary only to interpret them correctly. It is necessary to understand clearly that sharp contradictions are contained in the character of the USSR and in her international position. It is impossible to free oneself from those contradictions with the help of terminological sleight of hand ("Workers' State" – "Not Workers' State.") We must take the facts as they are. We must build our policy by taking as our starting point the real relations and contradictions.

We do not entrust the Kremlin with any historic mission. We were and remain against seizures of new territories by the Kremlin. We are for the independence of Soviet Ukraine, and if the Byelo-Russians themselves wish – of Soviet Byelo-Russia. At the same time in the sections of Poland occupied by the Red Army, partisans of the Fourth International must play the most decisive part in expropriating the landlords and capitalists, in dividing the land among the peasants, in creating Soviets and Workers' Committees, etc. While so doing, they must preserve their political independence, they must fight during elections to the Soviets and factory committees for the complete independence of the latter from the bureaucracy, and they must conduct revolutionary propaganda in the spirit of distrust towards the Kremlin and its local agencies.

But let us suppose that Hitler turns his weapons against the East and invades territories occupied by the Red Army. Under these conditions, partisans of the Fourth International, without changing in any way their attitude toward the Kremlin oligarchy, will advance to the forefront as the most urgent task of the hour, the military resistance against Hitler. The workers will say, "We cannot cede to Hitler the overthrowing of Stalin; that is our own task". During the military struggle against Hitler, the revolutionary workers will strive to enter into the closest possible comradely relations with the rank and file fighters of the Red Army. While arms in hand they deal blows to Hitler, the Bolshevik-Leninists will at the same time conduct revolutionary propaganda against Stalin preparing his overthrow at the next and perhaps very near stage.

From "The USSR in War", 25 September 1939

A civil war, and the Red Army is on the side of the workers

Leon Trotsky (1939)

BURNHAM AND SHACHTMAN in January 1939 stood in favor of unconditional defense of the Soviet Union and defined the significance of unconditional defense entirely correctly as "regardless and in spite of the Stalinist regime". And yet this article was written when the experience of the Spanish Revolution had already been drained to completion. Comrade Cannon is absolutely right when he says that the role of Stalinism in Spain was incomparably more criminal than in Poland or Finland. In the first case the bureaucracy through hangman's methods strangled a socialist revolution. In the second case it gives an impulse to the socialist revolution through bureaucratic methods. Why did Burnham and Shachtman themselves so unexpectedly shift to the position of the "League of Abandoned Hopes"?...

In order to punish the Stalinists for their unquestionable crimes, the [minority] resolution, following the petty-bourgeois democrats of all shadings, does not mention by so much as a word that the Red Army in Finland expropriates large land-owners and introduces workers' control while preparing for the expropriation of the capitalists.

Tomorrow the Stalinists will strangle the Finnish workers. But now they are giving – they are compelled to give – a tremendous impulse to the class struggle in its sharpest form. The leaders of the opposition construct their policy not upon the "concrete" process that is taking place in Finland, but upon democratic abstractions and noble sentiments.

The Soviet-Finnish war is apparently beginning to be supplemented by a civil war in which the Red Army finds itself at the given stage in the same camp as the Finnish petty peasants and the workers, while the Finnish army enjoys the support of the owning classes, the conservative labor bureaucracy and the Anglo-Saxon imperialists. The hopes which the Red Army awakens among the Finnish poor will, unless international revolution intervenes, prove to be an illusion; the collaboration of the Red Army with the poor will be only temporary; the Kremlin will soon turn its weapons against the Finnish workers and peasants. We know all this now and we say it openly as a warning.

But in this "concrete" civil war that is taking place on Finnish territory, what "concrete" position must the "concrete" partisans of the Fourth International take? If they fought in Spain in the Republican camp in spite of the fact that the Stalinists were strangling the socialist revolution, all the more must they participate in Finland in that camp where the Stalinists are compelled to support the expropriation of the capitalists...

As for the Kremlin it is at the present time forced – and this is not a hypothetical but a real situation – to provoke a social revolutionary movement in Finland (in order to attempt to strangle it politically tomorrow). To cover a given social revolutionary movement with the all-embracing term of imperialism only because it is provoked, mutilated and at the same time strangled by the Kremlin merely testifies to one's theoretical and political poverty...

From "A Petty-Bourgeois Opposition in the SWP", 15 December 1939

Bureaucratic-proletarian revolution is not desirable and not possible

Max Shachtman (1940)

I CANNOT LEAVE UNMENTIONED your [Trotsky's] references to the "revolutionary" role of Stalinism in its recent invasions. "In the first case (Spain), the bureaucracy through hangman's methods strangled a socialist revolution. In the second case (Poland) it gave an impulse to the socialist revolution through bureaucratic methods". Here again, I find myself compelled to disagree with you. The bureaucratic bourgeois revolution — that I know of. I know of Napoleon's "revolution from above" in Poland over a hundred years ago. I know of Alexander's emancipation of the serfs "from above" — out of fear of peasant uprisings. I know of Bismarck's "revolution from above". I know that Hitler and Mussolini play with the idea of an Arab "national revolution" in Palestine out of purely imperialist and military reasons — directed against their rival, England.

But the bureaucratic proletarian revolution — that I do not know of and I do not believe in it. I do not believe that it took place in Poland even for a day — or that it is taking place or is about to take place in Finland. If Stalin "established" state property in the conquered territories in Poland, it was not at all because, as you imply elsewhere, he was "compelled" to do so on account of the irresistible force of state property in the Soviet Union. Stalin was perfectly willing to "share the power" with the Polish bourgeoisie, as he is doing it with the bourgeoisie of Lithuania, Latvia and Estonia, and on this basis: I will preserve intact your private property and you will turn over to me your political power, which I will assure with my army. This is what the Kremlin proposed during the negotiations with Anglo-French imperialism. The Polish bourgeoisie and landlords refused this "generous" offer for a division of power. The three Baltic countries had the offer imposed on them by force.

When the regime of the Polish Colonels collapsed under the blows of the German army, the bourgeoisie fled in every direction. In the Polish Ukraine and White Russia, where class exploitation was intensified by national oppression (the bourgeoisie of those territories was predominantly Polish), the peasants began to take over the land themselves, to drive off the landlords which were already half-in-flight. Even the garbled and censored reports of those days permit us to see that the workers were beginning to act similarly. In Vilna, a spontaneously formed "Soviet" was reported. The Red Army, entering Poland, encountered no resistance from the Polish bourgeoisie and its Army because there wasn't any to speak of. The Red Army came in as a counter-revolutionary force. Far from "giving an impulse to the socialist revolution" it strangled it (the Vilna "Soviet" was of course violently suppressed).

Just what has since then been "nationalized", how it has been "nationalized" — I do not know and no one has yet been able to say exactly. In any case, I repeat with you that the nationalization, real or alleged, cannot be the decisive criterion for us. The Stalinist bureaucracy is capable only of strangling revolutions, not making them or giving an impulsion to them. To prove the contrary, some evidence must be produced, and I find none in your article.

I find even less for your — how shall I put it? — astonishing remarks about Finland. You say that we do not "mention by so much as a word that the Red Army in Finland expropriates large landowners and introduces workers' control while preparing for the expropriation of the capitalists". True, not by so much as a word. Why? Because the first anyone has heard in our party — anyone! — of the expropriation of the large landowners and the introduction of workers' control in Finland by the Red Army is in your article. Where is this taking place? On what reports do you base yourself? There is no trace of workers' control in the Soviet Union itself; there is even less than that in Finland. That at least so far as my knowledge goes, and on this point I have questioned unavailingly many Cannonites. You continue: "Tomorrow the Stalinists will strangle the Finnish workers. But now they are giving — they are compelled to give (why? why in Finland and not in Spain or Estonia?) — a tremendous impulse to the class struggle in its sharpest form. The leaders of the opposition construct their policy not upon the 'concrete' process that is taking place in Finland, but upon democratic abstractions and noble sentiments".

Where is this "tremendous impulse to the class struggle" in Finland — and "in its sharpest form", to boot? We base our policy on "abstractions"? Let us grant that. On what do you base your statement about the tremendous impulse to the class struggle? No one — no one, I repeat — in our party has seen the slightest sign of it as yet. Perhaps you have seen credible reports about it; in which case such important news should appear in our press. Again, you write: "The Soviet-Finnish war is evidently (?!) already beginning to be completed with a civil war in which the Red Army finds itself at the given stage in the same camp as the Finnish petty peasants and the workers'. You write a little further that the Stalinist policy is "the policy of exterminating finance-capital". And finally, you write: "As for the Kremlin it is at the present time forced — and this is not a hypothetical but a real situation — to provoke a social revolutionary movement in Finland (in order to attempt to strangle it politically tomorrow)". Where is the civil war in Finland which is "evidently already beginning"? Unless you refer to the government of the idiotic scoundrel Kuusinen, we have not yet seen the first traces of that civil war — regardless of how much we should like to see it, no matter how anxious we are to develop a policy that will promote it, no matter how firmly we count upon its eventual materialization. Do you deduce this "civil war" from an abstract and false theoretical estimation of the role of the Kremlin bureaucracy, or is there some objective evidence that this "'concrete' process is taking place in Finland"? Where is the "social revolutionary movement in Finland" that the Kremlin is "forced to provoke"? Is it perhaps the program of the Kuusinen "Democratic People's" government that is provoking it? That program is, formally, the program of a bourgeois "democracy". Since the beginning of the war, one of the reasons why we condemned the Finnish invasion as reactionary was precisely the fact that by it Stalin was driving the Finnish workers and peasants into a bourgeois-patriotic frenzy, into the arms of the Mannerheims, into the "sacred union" and "national unity". What evidence is there that this has changed? We repeat: we know of none, not a scintilla!

It is possible and even likely that, as the Finnish bourgeois regime begins to crumble, the workers and peasants will separate from it and take the first steps on the road to independent class action. But there is every reason to believe that they will not take the road to the Stalinist camp, that they will not, as Cannon tells the Russian workers to do, give "material and military support" to the annexationist invaders. If they did, their tragedy would be no less than that which they are suffering today as the pawns of bourgeois-patriotism. You speak of the Stalinists representing "the policy of exterminating finance-capital". I find it difficult to believe that you mean this literally.

No, the role the Stalinists have played, above all outside the borders of the Soviet Union, has been that of conservative prop of the rule of finance-capital. The Kremlin's agency of finance-capital has not become overnight the latter's exterminator. It does not play a revolutionary role — any more than the Chinese national bourgeoisie played a revolutionary role, any more than Gutchkov [conservative politician, war minister in first Provisional Government] played a revolutionary role in March, 1917 in Russia [the first revolution, which overthrew the Tsar and threw up a bourgeois Provisional Government]; the role of the Stalinist bureaucracy is counter-revolutionary.

Would I tell the Finnish workers to accept arms and ammunition from Stalin? Would I tell the Hindu workers and peasants to accept arms and ammunition from Hitler? That is how you pose the question. My answer is: Of course I would! I would take arms for the revolution from Hitler, or Mussolini, or Stalin, or Daladier, or a Caucasian mountain bandit! If I get them free of charge, so much the better. But it would not follow for me that just because I welcome arms smuggled to me in Palestine by Hitler, that I would welcome Hitler if he sent his army to Palestine, or that I would urge anybody to give that army "material and moral support". The "character" of Hitler's intervention in Palestine would have changed. By the same token, when Stalin is conducting a reactionary, annexationist war in Finland, I would readily accept arms from him if I were a revolutionist in Finland (although, in that case, nine chances out of ten I would receive his "armed aid" in the form of a bullet in the heart or a bayonet in the throat); and under certain conditions, given a favorable relation of forces between his army and the Finnish revolutionary movement, I would even seek a practical military working agreement with him; but it does not follow from this that I call upon anyone now to give him "material and military support" in his reactionary war.

I repeat, I do not believe in the bureaucratic proletarian (socialist) revolution. I do not mean by this merely that I "have no faith" in it — no one in our movement has. I mean that I do not consider it possible. I reject the concept not out of "sentimental" reasons or a Tolstoyan "faith in the people" but because I believe it to be scientifically correct to repeat with Marx that the emancipation of the working class is the task of the working class itself. The bourgeois revolution, for a series of historical and social reasons, could be made and was made by other classes and social strata; the bourgeoisie could be liberated from feudal rule and establish its social dictatorship under the aegis of other social groups. But the proletarian revolution cannot be made by others than the proletariat acting as a mass; therein, among other things, it is distinguished from all preceding revolutions. No one else can free it — not even for a day.

From Max Shachtman's Open Letter to Trotsky, 1 January 1940.
New International, March 1940

Civil war is a fact

Leon Trotsky

MY REMARK THAT the Kremlin with its bureaucratic methods gave an impulse to the socialist revolution in Poland, is converted by Shachtman into an assertion that in my opinion a "bureaucratic revolution" of the proletariat is presumably possible. This is not only in correct but disloyal. My expression was rigidly limited. It is not the question of "bureaucratic revolution" but only a bureaucratic impulse. To deny this impulse is to deny reality. The popular masses in western Ukraine and Byelo-Russia, in any event, felt this impulse, understood its meaning, and used it to accomplish a drastic overturn in property relations. A revolutionary party which failed to notice this impulse in time and refused to utilize it would be fit for nothing but the ash can.

This impulse in the direction of socialist revolution was possible only because the bureaucracy of the USSR straddles and has its roots in the economy of a workers' state. The revolutionary utilization of this "impulse" by the Ukrainian Byelo-Russians was possible only through the class struggle in the occupied territories and through the power of the example of the October Revolution. Finally, the swift strangulation or semi-strangulation of this revolutionary mass movement was made possible through the isolation of this movement and the might of the Moscow bureaucracy. Whoever failed to under stand the dialectic interaction of these three factors: the workers' state, the oppressed masses, and the Bonapartist bureaucracy, had best restrain himself from idle talk about events in Poland.

At the elections for the National Assembly of western Ukraine and western Byelo-Russia the electoral program, dictated of course by the Kremlin, included three extremely important points: inclusion of both provinces in the Federation of the USSR; confiscation of landlords' estates in favor of the peasants; nationalization of large industry and the banks. The Ukrainian democrats, judging from their conduct, deem it a lesser evil to be unified under the rule of a single state. And from the standpoint of the future struggle for independence, they are correct. As for the other two points in the program one would think that there could be no doubt in our midst as to their progressiveness. Seeking to get around reality, namely that nothing else but the social foundations of the USSR forced a social revolutionary program upon the Kremlin, Shachtman refers to Lithuania, Estonia and Latvia where everything has remained as of old. An incredible argument! No one has said that the Soviet bureaucracy always and everywhere either wishes or is able to accomplish the expropriation of the bourgeoisie. We only say that no other government could have accomplished that social overturn which the Kremlin bureaucracy notwithstanding its alliance with Hitler found itself compelled to sanction in eastern Poland. Failing this, it could not include the territory in the Federation of the USSR.

Shachtman is aware of the overturn itself. He cannot deny it. He is incapable of explaining it. But he nevertheless attempts to save face. He writes:

"In the Polish Ukraine and White Russia, where class exploitation was intensified by national oppression ... the peasants began to take over the land themselves, to drive off the landlords who were already half-in-flight," etc.

The Red Army it turns out had no connection whatever with all this. It came into Poland only as a "counter-revolutionary force" in order to suppress the movement. But why didn't the workers and peasants in western Poland seized by Hitler arrange a revolution? Why was it chiefly revolutionists, "democrats," and Jews who fled from there, while in eastern Poland – it was chiefly the landlords and capitalists who fled? Shachtman lacks the time to think this out – he is in a hurry to explain to me that the conception of "bureaucratic revolution" is absurd, for the emancipation of the workers can be carried out only by the workers themselves. Am I not justified in repeating that Shachtman obviously feels he is standing in a nursery?

In the Parisian organ of the Mensheviks – who, if that is possible, are even more "irreconcilable" in their attitude toward the Kremlin's foreign policy than Shachtman – it is reported that "in the villages – very frequently at the very approach of the Soviet troops (i.e., even prior to their entering a given district – L.T.) – peasant committees sprang up everywhere, the elementary organs of revolutionary peasant self-rule ..." The military authorities hastened of course to subordinate these committees to the bureaucratic organs established by them in the urban centers. Nevertheless they were compelled to rest upon the peasant committees since without them it was impossible to carry out the agrarian revolution.

The leader of the Mensheviks, Dan, wrote on October 19:

"According to the unanimous testimony of all observers the appearance of the Soviet army and the Soviet bureaucracy provides not only in the territory occupied by them but beyond its confines – an impulse (!) to social turmoil and social transformations."

The "impulse," it will be observed, was invented not by me but by "the unanimous testimony of all observers" who possessed eyes and ears. Dan goes even further and expresses the supposition that "the waves engendered by this impulse will not only hit Germany powerfully in a comparatively short period of time but also to one degree or another roll on to other states."

Another Menshevik author writes:

"However they may have attempted in the Kremlin to avoid anything which might smack of the great revolution, the very fact of the entry of Soviet troops into the territories of eastern Poland, with its long outlived semi-feudal agrarian relations, had to provoke a stormy agrarian movement. With the approach of Soviet troops the peasants began to seize landlords' estates and to form peasant committees."

You will observe: with the approach of Soviet troops and not at all with their withdrawal as should follow in accordance with Shachtman's words. I cite the testimony of the Mensheviks because they are very well informed, their sources of information coming through Polish and Jewish immigrants friendly to them who have gathered in France, and also because having capitulated to the French bourgeoisie, these gentlemen cannot possibly be suspected of capitulation to Stalinism.

The testimony of the Mensheviks furthermore is confirmed by the reports of the bourgeois press:

"The agrarian revolution in Soviet Poland has had the force of a spontaneous movement. As soon as the report spread that the Red Army had crossed the river Zbrucz the peasants began to share out amongst themselves the landlords' acres. Land was given first to small holders and in this way about thirty per cent of agricultural land was expropriated." (New York Times, January 17, 1940.)

Under the guise of a new argument Shachtman hands me my own words to the effect that the expropriation of property owners in eastern Poland cannot alter our appraisal of the general policies of the Kremlin. Of course it cannot! No one has proposed this. With the aid of the Comintern the Kremlin has disoriented and demoralized the working class so that it has not only facilitated the outbreak of a new imperialist war but has also made extremely difficult the utilization of this war for revolution. Compared with those crimes the social overturn in the two provinces, which was paid for more over by the enslavement of Poland, is of course of secondary importance and does not alter the general reactionary character of the Kremlin's policy. But upon the initiative of the opposition itself, the question now posed is not one of general policy but of its concrete refraction under specific conditions of time and place. To the peasants of Galicia and western Byelo-Russia the agrarian overturn was of highest importance. The Fourth International could not have boycotted this overturn on the ground that the initiative was taken by the reactionary bureaucracy. Our outright duty was to participate in the overturn on the side of the workers and peasants and to that extent on the side of the Red Army. At the same time it was indispensable to warn the masses tirelessly of the generally reactionary character of the Kremlin's policy and of those dangers it bears for the occupied territories. To know how to combine these two tasks or more precisely two sides of one and the same task – just this is Bolshevik politics.

Having revealed such odd perspicacity in understanding the events in Poland, Shachtman descends upon me with redoubled authority in connection with events in Finland. In my article *A Petty-Bourgeois Opposition*, I wrote that "the Soviet-Finnish War is apparently beginning to be supplemented by a civil war in which the Red Army finds itself at a given stage in the same camp as the Finnish petty peasants and the workers ..." This extremely cautious formula did not meet with the approval of my unsparing judge. My evaluation of events in Poland had already taken him off balance. "I find even less (proof) for your – how shall I put it? – astonishing remarks about Finland," writes Shachtman. I am very sorry that Shachtman chooses to become astonished rather than think things out.

In the Baltic states the Kremlin confined its tasks to making strategical gains with the unquestionable calculation that in the future these strategic military bases will permit the sovietization of these former sections of the Czarist empire too. These successes in the Baltic, achieved by diplomatic threat, met with resistance, however, from Finland. To reconcile itself to this resistance would have meant that the Kremlin placed in jeopardy its "prestige" and thereby its successes in Estonia, Latvia and Lithuania. Thus contrary to its initial plans the Kremlin felt compelled to resort to armed force. From this fact every thinking person posed to himself the following question: Does the Kremlin wish only to frighten the Finnish bourgeoisie and force them to make concessions or must it now go further? To this question naturally there could be no "automatic" answer. It was necessary – in the light of general tendencies – to orient oneself upon concrete symptoms. The leaders of the opposition are incapable of this.

Military operations began on November 30. That very same day the Central Committee of the Finnish Communist Party, undoubtedly located in either Leningrad or Moscow, issued a radio manifesto to the toiling people of Finland. This manifesto proclaimed:

"For the second time in the history of Finland the Finnish working class is beginning a struggle against the yoke of the plutocracy. The first experience of the workers and peasants in 1918 terminated in the victory of the capitalists and the landlords. But this time ... the toiling people must win "

This manifesto alone clearly indicated that not an attempt to scare the bourgeois government of Finland was involved, but a plan to provoke insurrection in the country and to supplement the invasion of the Red Army with civil war.

The declaration of the so-called People's Government published on December 2 states: "In different parts of the country the people have already risen and proclaimed the creation of a democratic republic." This assertion is obviously a fabrication, otherwise the manifesto would have mentioned the places where the attempts at insurrection took place. It is possible, however, that isolated attempts, prepared from without, ended in failure and that precisely because of this it was deemed best not to go into details. In any case, the news concerning "insurrections" constituted a call to insurrection. Moreover, the declaration carried information concerning the formation of "the first Finnish corps which in the course of coming battles will be enlarged by volunteers from the ranks of revolutionary workers and peasants." Whether there were one thousand men in this "corps" or only one hundred, the meaning of the "corps" in determining the policies of the Kremlin was incontestable. At the same time cable dispatches reported the expropriation of large landholders in the border regions. There is not the slightest ground to doubt that this is just what took place during the first advance of the Red Army. But even if these dispatches are considered fabrications, they completely pre serve their meaning as a call for an agrarian revolution.

Thus I had every justification to declare that "The Soviet-Finnish War is apparently beginning to be supplemented by a civil war." At the beginning of December, true enough, I had at my disposal only a part of these facts. But against the background of the general situation, and I take the liberty to add, with the aid of an understanding of its internal logic, the isolated symptoms enabled me to draw the necessary conclusions concerning the direction of the entire struggle. Without such semi a priori conclusions one can be a rationalizing observer but in no case an active participant in events. But why did the appeal of the "People's Government" fail to bring immediate mass response? For three reasons: first, Finland is dominated completely by a reactionary military machine which is supported not only by the bourgeoisie but by the top layers of the peasantry and the labor bureaucracy; secondly, the policy of the Kremlin succeeded in transforming the Finnish Communist Party into an insignificant factor; thirdly, the regime of the USSR is in no way capable of arousing enthusiasm among the Finnish toiling masses. Even in the Ukraine from 1918 to 1920 the peasants responded very slowly to appeals to seize the estates of the landlords because the local soviet power was still weak and every success of the Whites brought about ruthless punitive expeditions. All the less reason is there for surprise that the Finnish poor peasants delay in responding to an appeal for an agrarian revolution. To set the peasants in motion, serious successes of the Red Army are required. But during the first badly prepared advance the Red Army suffered only failures. Under such conditions there could not even be talk of the peasants rising. It was impossible to expect an independent civil war in Finland at the given stage: my calculations spoke quite precisely of supplementing military operations by measures of civil war. I have in mind – at least until the Finnish army is annihilated – only the occupied territory and the nearby regions. Today on January 17 as I write these lines dispatches from a Finnish source report that one of the border provinces has been invaded by detachments of Finnish émigrés and that brother is literally killing brother there. What is this if not an episode in a civil war? In any case there can be no doubt that a new advance of the Red Army into Finland will confirm at every step our general appraisal of the war. Shachtman has neither an analysis of the events nor the hint of a prognosis. He con fines himself to noble indignation and for this reason at every step he sinks deeper into the mire.

The appeal of the "People's Government" calls for workers' control. What can this mean! exclaims Shachtman. There is no workers' control in the USSR; whence will it come in Finland? Sad to say, Shachtman reveals complete lack of understanding of the situation. In the USSR workers' control is a stage long ago completed. From control over the bourgeoisie there they passed to management of nationalized production. From the management of workers – to the command of the bureaucracy. New workers' control would now signify control over the bureaucracy. This cannot be established except as the result of a successful uprising against the bureaucracy. In Finland, workers' control still signifies nothing more than crowding out the native bourgeoisie, whose place the bureaucracy proposes to take. Furthermore one should not think that the Kremlin is so stupid as to attempt ruling eastern Poland or Finland by means of imported commissars. Of greatest urgency to the Kremlin is the extraction of a new administrative apparatus from among the toiling population of the occupied areas. This task can be solved only in several stages. The first stage is the peasant committees and the committees of workers' control.

Shachtman clutches eagerly even at the fact that Kuusinen's program "is, formally, the program of a bourgeois 'democracy'." Does he mean to say by this that the Kremlin is more interested in establishing bourgeois democracy in Finland than in drawing Finland into the framework of the USSR? Shachtman himself doesn't know what he wants to say. In Spain, which Moscow did not prepare for union with the USSR, it was actually a question of demonstrating the ability of the Kremlin to safeguard bourgeois democracy against proletarian revolution. This task flowed from the interests of the Kremlin bureaucracy in that particular international situation. Today the situation is a different one. The Kremlin is not preparing to demonstrate its usefulness to France, England and the United States. As its actions have proved, it has firmly decided to sovietize Finland – at once or in two stages. The program of the Kuusinen government, even if approached from a "formal" point of view does not differ from the program of the Bolsheviks in November 1917. True enough, Shachtman makes much of the fact that I generally place significance on the manifesto of the "idiot" Kuusinen. However, I shall take the liberty of considering that the "idiot" Kuusinen acting on the ukase of the Kremlin and with the support of the Red Army represents a far more serious political factor than scores of superficial wiseacres who refuse to think through the internal logic (dialectics) of events.

"From a Scratch to the Danger of Gangrene", 24 January 1940

1940: the Mensheviks split over the USSR

John G Wright (1940)

The Mensheviks opposed the 1917 workers' revolution, believing that Russia then was developed enough only for a bourgeois revolution. They had a sizeable exile organisation and good contacts inside the USSR. In 1940 a group round Theodore Dan split away in a pro-Stalinist direction. Trotsky had taken Dan's reports in the Menshevik press as evidence about what had happened in eastern Poland.

THE "FOREIGN DELEGATION" of the Russian Mensheviks, that is, their leading center, has split on the question of the attitude toward Stalin's regime. Theodore Dan has resigned as chairman and left his post as one of the two editors of *Sotsialisticheskii Vestnik* (Socialist Courier), the Menshevik organ published in Paris. Yugov has resigned as secretary. Abramovich is now provisional chairman and sole editor, B. Dvinov the new secretary.

Abramovich and his friends are "principled defeatists" in relation to Stalin and the Soviet Union. They refuse to draw any distinction whatever between their "defeatist" policy toward Hitler and their policy toward Stalin. Dan, on the other hand, seeks to establish "subtle" distinctions between his attitude toward Hitler as "against Stalin and the Soviet Union". Dan and Abramovich, who remained defensists under the Czar and under Kerensky, have finally become "defeatists". Abramovich wants to go the whole hog. Dan apparently has reservations.

As we shall presently see, Dan's reservations do not at all flow from any deep desire on his part to defend the remaining conquests of the October revolution, but rather from his hopes that a possibility still remains of bringing the Soviet Union back into the orbit of the democratic imperialists. Abramovich thinks the only way to attain this is by "unconditional defeatism." Dan believes the more realistic policy to be that of "conditional defeatism."

Formally speaking, in recent years, the Mensheviks have recognized in Russia "elements of socialism." Insofar as Stalin marched shoulder to shoulder with "democracy," they were "defensists." In other words, they were "defensists" yesterday for the self-same reason that they are "defeatists" today. When Stalin signed his pact with

Hitler on August 30, 1939, Dan and Abramovich concluded it was necessary to re-evaluate their attitude toward Stalin, whom they have always identified with the Soviet Union. There were no disputes among them as to what was involved in this re-evaluation.

As Abramovich writes: There was complete harmony in appraising Stalin's rule as the "rule of a nationalist-imperialist clique, which has completely broken with the proletariat and with socialism and has degraded itself to the level of Hitlerite Nazism." "All of us," complains Abramovich, "have unanimously recognized that his (Stalin's) regime has completely broken with revolution and socialism; that his regime is the greatest enemy of the working class and has become transformed into the rule of a national imperialist Bonapartist clique, on the same plane as Hitlerism, with its fate tied irrevocably to Hitlerism." (*Sots. Vestnik*, March 5.) Unanimity was preserved when the second world war actually broke out. Dan and Abramovich lined up solidly on the side of the "democracies," where they still remain despite their differences.

And the invasion of Finland found both of them unconditional supporters of Mannerheim's "democracy" and "independence." Abramovich reminds Dan that Dan himself "wants with all his heart a debacle and a defeat for Stalin in his brutal assault on Finland."

Why, then, have these good friends split? And after all these years! They have a principled difference. At least Dan claims it is. Abramovich, on the contrary, brands as artificial Dan's "attempt to construct some sort of difference between 'principled defeatism' which he (Dan) advocates towards Hitler, and some other kind of defeatism, apparently 'tactical' defeatism .... in relation not only to the Soviet Union as a country but even towards the Stalinist regime (!) which oppresses the country." (The ironic exclamation is Abramovich's.) Abramovich, it appears, holds that there is only one kind of defeatism. Dan argues there are various kinds. Abramovich is ready to concede to Dan that there is a "difference" between Germany and the Soviet Union as such, i.e., as countries, but that this difference has no bearing on the question of defeatism.

Abramovich's argument in summary form is as follows: (1) if war is the continuation of politics by other means, then "totalitarian war is the continuation of totalitarian politics"; (2) A preliminary condition for the violent overthrow of a totalitarian regime is military defeat; therefore, (3) "We must strive for the most complete and ruthless military defeat of the Stalinist regime." "From this it does not, of course, follow at all," continues Abramovich, "that we want the atomization, dismemberment, bankruptcy or enslavement of our country or any of its various sections. On the contrary, we will fight might and main against this." Lest some innocent reader faint with surprise at Abramovich's conversion to violence and lest he conclude that therein lies the crux of the differences between Abramovich and Dan, we hasten to add that Dan, too, supports the thesis of "violent overthrow" (totalitarian regimes cannot be overthrown in peace-time or peacefully, they both agree).

Furthermore, this "revolution" so ardently supported now by Mensheviks is a "palace revolution." Or, as Abramovich so aptly puts it: "Of all the forms of violent overthrow of totalitarian dictatorship the most probable appears to be that which bears in our literature the highly-qualified label of 'palace revolution'." And Abramovich swears that Dan himself acknowledges that "history, sad to say, has apparently left no other way out save for a palace revolution." A Menshevik sheds tears even when confronted by "history" with such a revolution!

Dan, however, is a pessimist. He warns against any illusions. It would only mean that "another Bolshevik clique will come to power." That is why a different "defeatist" approach is necessary. He does not want to wait for a military defeat but seeks rather to liquidate Stalin's regime "by means of inner forces" and make the "revolution" a lever for the defeat of Stalin's "criminal war policies."

Despite his tears, Abramovich is very optimistic. He lists various "palace candidates" to replace Stalin, and concludes that all of them (including Voroshilov) would be compelled to be very, very progressive. Why? Because a palace revolution, even with Voroshilov at the head, he argues, must unavoidably catapult Russia from the present coalition with Hitler into an alliance with the Allies. And what could be more "progressive" than this to a Menshevik?

Dan does not contest the "progressive" character of such a change. He simply refuses to cherish any illusions that a Voroshilov will behave better than a Stalin. After all, they are both "Bolsheviks" — in Dan's eyes.

P. Garvey, a "principled defeatist", argues as follows against Dan's position: "What we need is clarity! The instrument of the Marxist method must serve us but so as not vainly to obscure controversial issues; so as not to cover up semi-assertions, immediately accompanied by qualifications; so as not to linger and temporize, which only paralyzes action.... Our times demand forthright answers to the accursed questions. It is impermissible under the cloak of 'dialectics' to cover up lapses and irreconcilable contradictions in one's own position... It is impermissible to see in Soviet Russia a totalitarian state....

and at the same time to seek in this social order of state slavery 'elements of Socialism' which must be 'sustained' until the world social revolution. It is impermissible to want the defeat of the Soviet Union in the war against Finland — and at the same time, with glaring inconsistency, to insist on a subtle distinction between the two aggressors.... advocating towards one of them, the Third Reich, principled defeatism, and towards the other, the Soviet Union, a restricted, temporary and conditional defeatism."

What style! What thought!

Socialist Appeal, 6 April 1940 (the issue for the SWP convention of 5-9 April 1940)

Mensheviks hail Stalin's "war-revolution"

Louis Jacobs (1943)

IT IS THE STRANGE FATE of some would-be leaders of the masses to take the wrong road at every turn in history. The October revolution was the greatest event in all history. Despite its degeneration under the dictatorship of Stalin, it has left its stamp on our entire epoch. At its inspired height under the leadership of Lenin and Trotsky, it could attract and kindle into revolutionary flame workers from all lands — but not the Russian Mensheviks! The Abramoviches and the Dans preferred capitalist exile to the living revolution. They were wrong again on the bitter struggle between revolutionary Marxism under the banner of Trotsky, and revisionary "socialism in one country" under the GPU-aegis of Stalin. The Mensheviks interpreted it entirely in the sense of an internal, personal struggle for power. Nevertheless, many Mensheviks found it to their liking to move in the direction of Stalinism. Many, like Vyshinsky, became his henchmen, aiding him to exterminate ruthlessly the Old Bolsheviks who might yet serve to lead the proletarian revolution at its next stage.

One might suppose that the crimes of Stalin in carrying through the bloody purges, his reactionary policies that strengthened a privileged caste in the Soviet Union at the expense of the masses of workers and peasants, his foreign diplomacy that weakened the international proletariat and made capitalism stronger — all this would hardly be likely to attract anybody to Stalinism at this late date. The Menshevik leader Theodore Dan teaches us differently.

Dan from the beginning not only supported the Allies in the war, but agitated that the Soviet Union must enter the war on the side of the "democracies." Dan and his supporters called the second world war not just a war but a war-revolution. Correctly enough in one respect, Dan says that the Soviet Union can play a decisive role in aiding the socialist revolution in Europe. But what about the Stalinist leadership? Ah yes, says Dan, the leaders of the Soviet Union must reform and find a new road.

Let us quote the words that, if given credence and support by the workers, could lead to nothing but new defeats: "The moral-political capital accumulated for twenty-five years of the Russian Revolution is so great that up to now it was more than sufficient to cover all the defects, inherited from the past, but which have long outlived themselves. In the chaos of the military, diplomatic and revolutionary storms which the Soviet Union is facing, it will be ever more difficult to live on the old capital. The coming storms are already making such gigantic demands on it that the creation of new revolutionary and socialist values becomes for it a law of self-preservation. All the elements for creating them exist in Soviet reality, because all those survivals of the past which threaten to press with such a heavy burden on the Soviet Union were not engendered by any creative impotence of the Russian Revolution but merely by the difficulties of its development under the conditions of extreme backwardness and isolation which themselves are receding into the past.

"This suffices to make it easier for the leaders of the Soviet State themselves to begin the liquidation of all that which has lost all rights to existence, and for the issuance to new roads where all the detachments of the working class can meet for a united struggle for peace, freedom and socialism. At any rate, this suffices for us Russian socialists so that with an unshakable faith in final victory we should also invest all our forces, and work in order that in the epoch of the coming storms the Soviet Union should find itself at the height of those gigantic tasks which history places upon it as upon the powerful support of the toilers of the whole world in their struggle to the death against fascism and for socialist democracy." (*Novy Put*, May 1943.) Dan does not enumerate those "defects" that marred the Stalinist leadership of the Soviet Union. Dan's opinion, it seems, is that Stalin in the past twenty-five years "accumulated" moral-political capital instead of completely dissipating it. The tasks of the future are so great that this Menshevik is ready to overlook the peccadillos of Stalin's conduct of the past. Here we see the danger to those workers who may be misled by Dan's complete failure to analyze the real meaning of Stalinism. Dan leaves out the key fact that Stalin was able to gain control of the Soviet Union only in a period of decline and reaction, and that he is wholly incapable of giving leadership in a period of advance, above all in the period that will mark the new rise of the revolutionary wave. Dan has managed after a whole decade to grasp a few ideas of the Trotskyist movement. Give him credit for desiring to defend the Soviet Union against any attack by capitalism, whether of the Axis or the Allied variety. What he still has not learned is one elementary lesson: that Stalinism and the Soviet Union are not only not identical, they are antithetical.

Just ten years ago the Trotskyists created the Fourth International precisely because there remained not the faintest hope that the Soviet bureaucracy could be reformed. The history of those ten years of Hitler's power in Germany has confirmed at every turn the conclusion then reached by the Trotskyist movement. Far from pinning any hope in a reform of the Stalinist bureaucracy, and in the possibility that the gravediggers of the October revolution can become the leaders of the workers in the renewal of October, every worker must learn that Stalinism stands within the working class as the greatest obstacle to achieving socialism.

Dan shares the superficial opinion of the capitalists and their spokesmen, like Davies [Joseph E Davies, former US ambassador to Moscow], that Stalin will emerge from the war with enhanced prestige. We do not share that opinion. The masses of Russia have excited the admiration of the entire world by their grim and steadfast defense of the first workers' state — but they have fought courageously in spite of, and not because of, the Soviet bureaucracy. The fear of war always stood in the way of the opening of a struggle by the masses against the Kremlin bureaucracy. That fear is now gone — or will be with the emergence of a victorious Soviet Union.

> "A Russian Menshevik turns to Stalin". Under the name of A
> Roland, *The Militant*, May 22, 1943

Labor Action was the weekly paper of the Heterodox Trotskyists
from 1940 to 1958

Labor Action, 2 April 1945

5. The USSR at war

Hitler invades Russia

Max Shachtman (June 1941)

WITH CYNICAL BRUTALITY, Hitler has launched his legions into war with the Soviet Union. By signing the Hitler-Stalin pact less than two years ago, in August, 1939, the Kremlin autocracy gave German fascism the green light for unleashing the war in Europe. Moscow hailed the pact as a great victory for Stalin's "policy of peace". It proceeded to divide with Hitler the spoils of imperialist conquest in eastern Europe. It helped plant the black heel of fascism on the people of Poland. In exchange, and by agreement with Hitler, it was allowed to plant the oppressive heel of Stalinist rule upon the peoples of eastern Poland, Latvia, Lithuania, Esthonia, Finland, Bessarabia and Bukovina. It covered the military flanks of German imperialism in the north, east and southeast of Europe. It covered the political position of Hitlerism by concentrating its propaganda attacks exclusively upon the democratic imperialist powers as the ones solely responsible for the war, and by deliberately concealing the equal responsibility of the fascist imperialist powers. In the words of Stalin, uttered in November, 1939, "it was not Germany that attacked France and England, but France and England that attacked Germany, thereby assuming responsibility for the present war." Just as he covered up the war policy of Hitlerism, so, in the same declaration, did Stalin sponsor the demagogic imperialist peace campaign of Hitlerism. Throughout the world, the Stalinist parties, completely servile to the Kremlin bureaucracy, faithfully followed the course of supporting the line of the Berlin-Rome-Moscow Axis in the war.

Now, the Hitler-Stalin pact is shattered to bits. The whole wretched strategy of Stalinism is in collapse. And the Second World War, far from being brought to a close, has been more widely extended than before.

The strategy of German fascism has also collapsed by virtue of the new turn that Hitler has been compelled to make in the war. His fraudulent promises to the German masses that the war would be of short duration have not been kept because they could not be kept. His hope of confining his military strategy to a war on one front at a time has now been dispelled. The British imperialists, fighting desperately to retain their dominion over millions of colonial peoples and their share of the wealth of the world, succeeded, with the growing collaboration of the United States, in withstanding the German offensive. Above all, the passive resistance of the European peoples conquered by Hitler has only emphasized fascism's inability to establish a functioning "new order" in the Old World. Because it does not resolve its multitude of problems by the extension of its rule, but only increases the number of problems to be resolved, German fascism has how found itself forced to plan for a longer and more destructive war. Hitler has now turned upon his ally of yesterday, in the hope of overcoming the effects of the Anglo-American blockade, and particularly of increasing American participation on Britain's side, by seizing the wheat fields, the oil fields and the natural resources of the Ukraine and other Russian territories.

Hitler's latest pretension that the war on Russia is a holy crusade against Bolshevism is another of fascism's transparent frauds, in line with the Fuehrer's notorious dictum that if he tells a big enough lie people will believe it. The fact is that the counter-revolutionary Stalinist bureaucracy has done more than the entire capitalist class of the world to destroy Bolshevism and the great conquests of the Russian Revolution of 1917. No, Hitler is merely continuing and extending the war of German imperialism for the domination of the world. He can accomplish this only by wrecking the British Empire and preventing American imperialism from falling heir to its riches and power.

Stalin's latest pretension, that the war with Germany is a holy crusade against fascism, is no less transparent a fraud. In one country after another, in Germany and Spain in particular, Stalinism carries the chief responsibility for the victory and advance of fascism. As recently as September 1, 1939, when fascism had just launched the war, Molotov was saying that "We have always held that a strong Germany is an indispensable condition for a durable peace in Europe." In the Soviet Union itself, Stalinism is not the banner-bearer of progress but the poisonous carrier of reaction, the wrecker of the revolution, the perfidious oppressor and exploiter of the Soviet masses.

In the first period of the war, the Stalinist bureaucracy fought for its own privileges and power and right to rule, for the extension of its brutal domination over those peoples and countries that fell to it as its share of the plunder of conquest — fought as a subordinate part of the Rome-Berlin camp in the imperialist war.

In the period of the war ushered in by the German attack upon Russia, the Stalinist bureaucracy is continuing its fight for its own privileges and powers and right to rule for maintaining its imperialist rule over the territories it conquered yesterday with German aid or approval, for maintaining its longer-established rule over the Soviet peoples — only this time, it is fighting as a subordinate part of the London-Washington camp in the imperialist war.

The forced shift of the Stalinist bureaucracy — from the camp of German-Italian imperialism to the camp of Anglo-American imperialism — has not changed the fundamental character of the Second World War as an imperialist conflict for the redivision of the world and its wealth among the big bandit powers. Nor has it changed the reactionary role of the Stalinist bureaucracy in the war.

The warmongers and their propagandists in this country and in England have immediately seized upon the fact of Hitler's attack upon Russia to renew their clamorous campaign to drag the United States more deeply into active military participation in the war, and to obtain the support of the American workers for the war.

Churchill and Eden, the spokesmen of the British ruling class, did not lose a minute to proclaim their solidarity with the Stalinist regime in the turn the war has taken. In even less time than it took Hitler to consummate his alliance with Moscow, British imperialism has already formed a military alliance with that same "totalitarian Russia" which it had so piously and hypocritically denounced up to yesterday. It is an alliance which only emphasizes that Russia is an integral part of the imperialist war — now, however, in the other camp — an alliance for the mutual protection of the power and rule of British imperialism and the Stalinist bureaucracy.

Roosevelt and Welles have followed right in the footsteps of their British allies. For all their hasty assurances that they have nothing in common with "Bolshevism" they understand perfectly well the anti-Bolshevik character of the Stalinist regime. And above all, they understand perfectly well that the victory of Anglo-American imperialism in the war now demands the military alliance with Russia, which, up to now, they tried vainly to achieve. They understand perfectly well, too, that just as Stalin was junior partner in the newly broken alliance with Berlin-Rome, so he will be and can only be junior partner in the alliance with London-Washington, albeit a partner, most valuable for the interests of the democratic imperialists.

As always — from the day the Second World War started and before that — our Workers Party remains the irreconcilable enemy of imperialist war, that great destroyer of the peoples.

As always, our Workers Party remains the sworn enemy of all capitalist reaction and above all of blood-stained fascism.

But, as we have never ceased to emphasize, and as recent events in the world have proved over and over again, Hitlerism and Fascism cannot be conquered by the war of the imperialists, or by supporting the imperialist war. For labor to support the imperialist war, no matter on what basis, means in the end to promote the advance of reaction, means to give up the only guarantee against the victory of fascist totalitarianism, namely, a militant, bold and independent working class, with militant and independent working class organizations at its disposal.

For the victory over fascism and reaction, there is only one road. That is the road of the struggle of the working class for itself, for its own interests, for its own aims, which are the interests and aims of all oppressed and suffering peoples. That is the road of the working class struggle for its own government — the government of, for and by the workers. That is the road of the Socialist United States of Europe, the Socialist United States of the World! To travel this road successfully, the working class must not give an ounce of support to any of the warring governments, those government and regimes which have brought such appalling misery and frightfulness to the world.

In order to put an end, once for all, to the barbarism with which the world is threatened, to put an end to capitalism and its periodic wars, to put an end to the "democratic" empires with their millions of colonial slaves, to put an end to fascism with its unspeakable terror and oppression, to put an end to the reactionary pall of Stalinism — the working class and the oppressed peoples of the world must unite their invincible forces against both of the warring camps: Against the imperialist war camp of Berlin-Rome-Tokyo! Against the imperialist war camp of Washington-London-Moscow! On with the fight for the only sacred and just cause — the victory of the Third Camp, the camp of the suffering peoples, the camp of the exploited workers of all lands, of the disinherited and oppressed masses of the colonies! Long live the coming victory of freedom and peace, the victory of the international socialist brotherhood of the peoples!

"Today Germany is in the position of a state which is striving for the earliest termination of the war and for peace." — Molotov, quoted in *World News and Views*, November 4, 1939.

"One may respect or hate Hitlerism, just as any other system of political views. This is a matter of taste. But to undertake war for 'annihilation of Hitlerism' means to commit criminal folly in politics." — *Izvestia*, official Russian government organ, October 9, 1939.

"We have always held that a strong Germany is an indispensable condition for durable peace in Europe." — From speech of Molotov, Foreign Commissar and at that time Premier of Russia, quote in *Daily Worker*, September 1, 1939.

Declaration signed "The Political Committee of the Workers Party, Max Shachtman, National Secretary". *Labor Action*, 30 June 1941

Max Shachtman in 1946

'We call on Stalin to revive soviets and promise liberation to German workers!'

SWP (1941)

WE STAND FOR the unconditional defense of the Soviet Union, as everyone knows who is acquainted with our party's position. The Stalinist leaders are desperately trying to fool their rank and file into believing that the Trotskyists do not defend the Soviet Union. The word "unconditional" is plain enough. It means that we set no conditions whatsoever before we defend the Soviet Union. We do not demand that Stalin make any concessions to us before we defend the Soviet Union.

We defend the Soviet Union because the foundation of socialism established by the October revolution of 1917, the nationalized property, still remains, and this foundation it is necessary to defend at all costs. The Trotskyists in this country, in the Soviet Union, and everywhere in the world, say to the Soviet government: Place us in the most dangerous posts, we are ready and shall unhesitatingly accept. It is to assure victory in the struggle against Hitler that our party presents a minimum program of imperative tasks for the Soviet Union. Whether the Stalinist bureaucracy accepts or rejects this program, we shall defend the Soviet Union. But we insist that this minimum program is vital in order to strengthen immeasurably the fighting power of the Soviet Union.

1. Release all pro-Soviet political prisoners. Restore them to their rightful place in industry and the Red Army.

In the jails and concentration camps of the Kremlin there are tens of thousands of loyal revolutionists who proved themselves in the struggle against the White Guards and imperialist interventionists in the Civil War of 1918-1921 and in the struggle to build industry in the Soviet Union.

In spite of the persecution to which they have been subjected by the Kremlin bureaucrats, the loyalty of these men and women to the Soviet Union cannot be questioned for one moment. Given the opportunity they would immediately rush to the front, prepared to offer their lives in the struggle against Hitler. The release of this great army of pro-Soviet political prisoners, kept in jail solely because Stalin feared their opposition to his false policies, is imperative for the salvation of the Soviet Union.

2. Revive the democratically-elected Soviets. Workers' democracy in the trade unions. The tens of millions of workers and peasants who fought so heroically and self-sacrificingly in the Civil War were organized in the Soviets. The Soviets, constituted by representatives democratically elected in the factories and villages, directly represented the tens of millions of fighters for socialism, gave life to their innermost hopes and were the organisations which were closest to the masses. Without the Soviets, victory would have been impossible in the Civil War. But these Soviets, based on occupational representation, no longer exist. Stalin has destroyed them. The Soviets of Workers' and Peasants' Deputies must be revived. Complete democracy must be granted to the workers and peasants in electing representatives to the Soviets. Within the Soviets, there must be complete freedom of criticism for all pro-Soviet elements. Workers' democracy must be restored in the trade unions which are now merely a department of the apparatus of regimentation and oppression.

3. Legalization of all pro-Soviet political parties. Their right to present their programs to the masses. As part of the restoration of workers' democracy in the Soviet Union, all pro-Soviet political parties must be given legal status. Every political party that is for the defense of the Soviet Union must be given the right to exist as an open political organization, to present its program, and to agitate among the masses for that program. Without these rights, there can be no true democracy.

4. For revolutionary unity with the German working class. For the Socialist United States of Europe. In order to strike Hitler a mortal blow, the Soviet government must issue an appeal to the workers of Germany, calling upon them to destroy Hitler and the capitalist system which gave birth to Hitler. The Soviet government must call upon the workers of Germany to join hands with the Soviet Union to create the Socialist United States of Europe. Hitler is now drawing immeasurable strength from the German workers' fear of the yoke of a foreign invader. The German workers know that the British and American imperialists want, upon defeating Germany, to dismember it and enslave its people. The danger of national oppression at the hands of the "democratic" imperialists haunts the German masses. They must either support Hitler or see themselves subjected once more to the Versailles system — those are the only alternatives offered to the masses of Germany by British and American imperialism.

In this situation the Soviet Union, alone of the existing states, can undermine Hitler by pledging to the German workers that the defeat of Hitler will not mean a second and worse Versailles but will begin the creation of the Socialist United States of Europe. The imperialist states cannot possibly make this pledge to the German workers. Only the Soviet Union, the Workers' State, can thus cement revolutionary unity with the German proletariat.

Capitalist states have refused to state their peace terms. The Soviet Union must clearly state its peace terms — the Socialist United States of Europe, the right of all nations to self-determination.

There is nothing original in this minimum program proposed by our party. The methods it proposes to assure Soviet victory are the methods used by the Soviet government in the Civil War of 1918-1921. By those methods Lenin and Trotsky saved the first Workers' Stale from destruction at the hands of the capitalist world.

By those same method the Soviet Union can assure victory — a victory that will usher in the most progressive epoch that mankind has ever known.

"A Program Of Victory For The Soviet Union", *The Militant*, 19 July 1941

The newspaper of the Spanish Trotskyists, 15 June 1945, and the caption that *The Militant* put on it.

The Revolution in Russia is still alive

James P Cannon (1941)

TWENTY-FOUR YEARS have passed since [1917]. Those who have remained on the fundamental premise of the adherents of the Bolshevik revolution can understand events today better than others, and they can see the prospect of new advances throughout the darkness of the reaction. They understand that the reaction has set back but not yet overthrown the Russian revolution. Those fainthearts, those traitors who said the Russian revolution has been killed, that the Soviet Union is not worth defending, are being answered on the battle fields of Russia today by millions of men in arms. Millions of Soviet soldiers, pouring out their blood, say the revolution still lives and not even Hitler's army can kill it!

That is the meaning of this thing that is inexplicable to all the others, this tremendous Soviet morale. What did they all say? First, they said the two systems — fascism and Sovietism — are so interlocked that Russia and Germany make natural partners against the democratic world. We heard such a monstrous thesis in our own party a little more than a year ago. We were informed by no less an authority than the great Professor Burnham that we Trotskyists were a left cover for Hitler because we wanted to defend the Soviet Union unconditionally. Burnham and his retinue never dreamed of the war that was to burst with full fury two months ago. Then, when it happened, there was one universal expectation, one common prediction. Nobody believed in the fighting capacities of the Soviet army except the Soviet workers themselves — and the Fourth Internationalists.

Stalin didn't believe in the fighting ability of the Red Army which he had beheaded. The only reason he didn't capitulate to Hitler and give him all the concessions he wanted, is that he didn't get a chance. Hitler thought it would be so easy to smash the Red Army, he didn't bother to parley about it.

All the statesmen and military experts expected and freely predicted a Russian collapse on the French pattern in a few weeks. What they all overlooked was the one most important and most fundamental element in war, the one that was elucidated by Comrade Trotsky in our last talks with him in Mexico, fourteen months ago, the element of morale.

In the course of our visit of a week or more — this was at the time when the great battle of France was raging, before Paris had not yet fallen — we asked him more than once to give us his opinion of the military prospects of that fight. And again and again he repeated, "It depends on the morale of the French army. If the French army really has the morale to fight, Hitler cannot win, not even if he comes as far as Paris".

But the French soldiers did not have the morale to fight. That was explained in an article in our magazine, *Fourth International*, as well as by many other correspondents. Our own comrade who was there and had intimate contact with great numbers of French people in the course of his journalistic duties, explained it about as follows: The French workers and the French soldiers, if you asked them if there wasn't some difference between the Hitler regime and the rotting bourgeois-democratic regime in France, would say, "Yes, there is a difference, but the difference is not worth dying for". That was one reason for the catastrophic defeat of the French bourgeois army.

Those who made an equation between Fascist Germany and the Soviet Union could not understand the psychology of the Russian workers and peasants. You can write all the books, wiseacre theses, explaining there is no difference between the degenerated workers' state in Russia and the fascist regime in Germany. But the Russian workers and peasants think there is a difference, and they think the difference is worth dying for. They know better than all the renegades, better than all those who have turned their backs on the Soviet Union in the hour of danger, the hour when people are really tested as to the value of their ideas, opinions, theories and promises.

Trotsky said more than once that the beginning of a war of imperialism against the Soviet Union would undoubtedly arouse a veritable outburst of genuine revolutionary patriotism and fighting spirit in the Russian masses. That is precisely what we have seen there. And as we wait breathlessly from day to day, and even from edition to edition of the newspapers, to see what is the further course, the further fate of the armies locked in combat, we know one thing for sure. We know that by their tremendous demonstration of fighting heroism, the Russian masses have said once again that the revolution in Russia is still alive, and still has the possibilities of reinspiring the world and starting a new upsweep of progress which revolutionary victory alone can bring.

From a speech at a memorial meeting for Trotsky, *The Militant*,
30 August 1941

Only the Russian soldiers have something to fight for

George Breitman (1941)

THE PREDICTIONS of "victory within six weeks" made by the Nazis and echoed by "informed" US generals and military experts have fallen to the ground. They made their estimates on the basis of the weaknesses wrought by the Kremlin bureaucracy through its purges and repressions, and on the slow start of the Red Army in the 1939 Finnish war, a campaign toward which the Soviet masses for the most part had been lethargic. But they completely disregarded the other side of the picture.

Leon Trotsky, because he understood that whole picture, often stated that the outbreak of a capitalist war against the Soviet Union would at the very beginning bring forth the strongest defensist tendencies in the country. In 1934 he wrote in "War and the Fourth International" (and he repeated this thought many times thereafter): "Within the USSR war against imperialist intervention will undoubtedly provoke a veritable outburst of genuine lighting enthusiasm. All the contradictions and antagonisms will seem overcome or at any rate relegated to the background. The young generations of workers and peasants that emerged from the revolution will reveal on the field of battle a colossal dynamic power..."

Trotsky was able to foresee this stubborn resistance chiefly because he understood the class character of the first workers' state and as a result the determination of the workers and peasants, even under the parasitic Stalinist bureaucracy, to hold on to what they have.

Unlike the European armies, the Russian soldiers have something to fight for and they know it! The "European" armies (and this includes the United States and all other capitalist armies as well) have a different morale because they know they have nothing to gain because after the war as well as before, they will be victims of the same depressions, hunger and exploitation. They know that it is not the people who will benefit from the results of the war, but their masters, the imperialists, and that the lives of the worker-soldiers are being thrown away in a cause that is not theirs.

That is why the soldiers in the "democratic" armies do not fight with any conviction. That is why they don't feel ready to sacrifice their lives. That is why their main thought is to get out of the army and go back to their homes. That is why they have no confidence in their military leaders. That is why the French army marched off to war, even against Hitler and everything hateful that he represents, with no cheers or enthusiasm.

It is true that up to this point in the war the Nazis have maintained a certain high discipline in their armies. This morale, however, is only skin deep, and can disappear overnight. It was fostered by Hitler's great successes.

But once the series of Hitler victories is broken and the myth of Nazi invincibility exposed, and once the fear of another Versailles in the event of defeat is removed, discipline and morale in the Nazi army will fall even lower than in the armies of the "democracies." The German army is made up of men who know they are not fighting for their own interests.

The Red soldiers, on the other hand, not only have something to fight against, as do all the other armies (against a semi-slave status under Hitlerism, or a semi-slave status under another Versailles Treaty), but they also have something to fight for. The October revolution of 1917 destroyed the political power of the capitalist class, and then destroyed its economic power. The factories and industries were taken away from the bosses by the state, and the economy was nationalized. The peasants took the large estates away from the landlords and the land went to the peasants who tilled it. In spite of all the crimes and blunders of the Stalinist bureaucracy since then, the economic foundation established by the Russian Revolution still exists. It is this for which the Soviet troops are willing to give their lives rather than capitulate.

When the Red Army soldier fights the Nazi legions, he knows that he is not doing it for the benefit of a gang of bosses who will continue to exploit him after the war just as viciously as before. He knows that he is fighting for himself and his children, to preserve what he has left of the greatest revolution of all time, the nationalized economy which must exist and be extended before society can go ahead to socialism, peace and plenty.

Experience has shown the Russian masses the superiority of living in a workers' state, even though isolated and degenerated under Stalinism. Because they have freed themselves from the bestialization of capitalism and opened up the possibilities for a new life, they are ready against the greatest odds and with inferior military equipment, as in the civil war days following the October revolution, to fight until death to protect what they have already won.

It is not that the Soviet workers live in a perfect state. No one knows better than they what is wrong with the regime. No one knows better than the Soviet workers how this bureaucracy has fastened itself onto the state, sapped its energies and resources and weakened the nationalized economy. They have seen with their own eyes the destruction of the Soviets, the emasculation of the trade unions, the elimination of workers' democracy, and the transformation of the Communist Party from a party of Bolshevism to a mere docile figurehead for the bureaucracy. But in spite of all this, they have something to defend. They know that if imperialism defeats them, not only won't they get back the political rights and workers' democracy usurped by Stalinism, but that they will also lose the economic foundations that they still have.

And when we consider how heroically they are fighting, we can correctly say that in their own language, spoken with the rifle and tank, the Soviet masses show a much clearer understanding of the historic processes of liberation than do the learned professors and lawyers who excel at "socialist" warmongering.

The Soviet masses, living on a progressive economic foundation, even though they have been robbed of their democratic rights, not only rush to the front but continue to fight when it means almost certain death.

It is only the Trotskyists who understand, explain and support the real reasons for the great defensist struggles of the Soviet workers. The Stalinists, who are afraid to speak in class terms, do not give the real reasons because it would offend the imperialists on whom they are placing so much confidence; and because it would open the eyes of the workers in the democracies, whom the Stalinists are urging to support the imperialists in the war, to the fact that they have nothing to fight for until they too establish a workers' state.

Those "radicals" — in reality counter-revolutionists — who are indifferent to the outcome of the military struggle between the Red Army and Hitler also have nothing to say about the reasons for the Soviet workers' fighting enthusiasm, because it ill fits their pseudo-revolutionary theory that the Soviet workers should not defend the Soviet Union.

Nevertheless, the resistance of the Soviet masses by itself cannot insure Soviet victory. For that a program is necessary.

This program must call for (1) the institution of a revolutionary policy toward Germany, and (2) the extension of workers' democracy, control and rights in all spheres of Soviet life.

Such a policy would include the open perspective of revolutionary unity of the Soviet working class with the German working class; a pledge that the Soviet Union would oppose another Versailles Treaty at the expense of Germany; propaganda for the proletarian revolution in Germany and the Socialist United States of Europe.

The morale and strength of the Soviet masses would be raised to the heights by the revival of workers' democracy — the restoration of the Soviets and democracy in the trade unions, the legalization of all pro-Soviet political parties, the release of all pro-Soviet political prisoners and their return to their rightful places in the army and industry.

If the masses are waging such a heroic struggle for a degenerated workers' state, how much more courageously will they strain all their energy and resources when they feel that political power belongs to them and not to the bureaucrats! When they feel that they have the right to determine the important questions, when they feel that their success on the battlefields will not merely bring back the status quo. but will facilitate the extension of the revolution to advanced capitalist countries and result in a socialist world that will forever destroy the possibility of imperialist invasion.

With the adoption of this program, the struggle of the Soviet masses would indeed be transformed from what is still essentially a defensive fight, to maintain what they already have, into an aggressive offensive to gain what they want: workers' democracy inside the Soviet Union and the assistance and collaboration of workers' states in the rest of the world.

"Soviet soldiers fight bravely because they have something worth defending", *The Militant*, 9 August 1941 (abridged)

Hitler's invasion proves Stalin's moves in 1939 were defensive

Albert Goldman (1941)

IT IS A FUNDAMENTAL LAW of politics that a major political error, if persisted in and if not corrected in time, necessarily leads into ever greater and more numerous errors until one is led to adopt a wrong political line on almost all fundamental questions. The Hitler-Stalin pact of August 1939 unnerved and disoriented everyone who did not cling to the fundamental Marxist analysis, made by Trotsky, of the Soviet Union and the Stalinist bureaucracy.

As our readers will recall, a minority in our own ranks (now no longer with us) jumped to the conclusion that the pact indicated a close alliance between Hitler and Stalin for the purpose of conquering and dividing the whole world, at least the British Empire. It was quite common for all the middle-class democrats and also the minority in our ranks to speak of the Berlin-Moscow Axis being pitted against the London-Paris Axis. Their hysteria reached unbelievable heights, at the time of the invasion of "democratic" Finland (now, under the same government, fighting on the side of the Nazis).

As against all of these people our party explained the pact on the basis of Stalin's fear of a major conflict and his anxiety to avoid it at all costs. We were careful to point out, however, that it did not follow from the fact that Stalin wanted to avoid war that war would avoid him. We also contended that one of the aims of the Stalinist bureaucracy in sending the Red Army into Poland, the Baltic countries and Finland was to strengthen its military-strategic position. True, like all bureaucracies, the Stalinist one wanted to increase its power and prestige, but Stalin also had an eye on fortifying his military-strategic position. Against whom? Geography answered that it could be only against Hitler.

England and France had no way by which they could attack the Soviet Union while Hitler was right on the border of the Soviet Union. To those who were not blinded by hate of Stalin it was as clear as daylight that Hitler's designs against the Soviet Union were not given up. The Soviet Union still had raw materials that German capitalism needed and the fundamental antagonism between a Hitler Germany and the Soviet State remained. We did not hesitate to state on innumerable occasions that the Nazis would attack the Soviet Union. It was not possible to predict exactly when and under what circumstances Hitler would attack the Soviet Union. We obviously underestimated, recently, Hitler's urgent need for the raw materials of the Soviet Union in order to prepare for a long war against England and the United States. Unable to bring British imperialism to its knees, Hitler had to turn his guns on the Soviet Union in order to prepare himself for a long war. He certainly had intended originally to conquer England first because that would have left the Soviet Union completely at his mercy but, unable to do so, Hitler shifted his plans.

The democrats and erstwhile Marxists who held the theory that Stalin and Hitler had entered into a partnership for the purpose of conquering and dividing the world, find it completely impossible to explain the sudden attack of Hitler on the Soviet Union.

Let us take, for instance, the statement of the former minority of our party, issued immediately after the attack on the Soviet Union. This document of the "Workers Party" very nonchalantly states that whereas the Soviet Union up to now was part and parcel of the imperialist camp of Berlin-Moscow-Rome-Tokyo, it is now part of the imperialist camp of London-Washington-Moscow. The statement clearly indicates that the Soviet Union was to be considered in the same light as Germany and Italy before Hitler's attack and is now to be considered in the same light as England and the United States.

Having asserted this, the "Workers Party" is then confronted with the necessity of an explanation for such an unusual change in imperialist partnerships. The explanation it gives is as follows: "Because it does not resolve its multitude of problems by the extension of its rule, but only increases the number of problems to be resolved, German fascism has now found itself forced to plan for a longer and more destructive war. This is why Hitler has now turned upon his ally of yesterday, etc. etc."

All this about Hitler is perfectly true — but it does not follow from the "Workers Party" idea of a joint agreement on the part of Hitler and Stalin to divide the world. For, if one claims that such a close partnership existed between Stalin and Hitler, then the fact that Hitler found himself in trouble need not and would not lead to his attacking the Soviet Union. Just as Hitler came to Mussolini's aid when the latter was in trouble, so could Stalin have come to Hitler's aid when such aid was needed. If Stalin had been so intimately connected with Hitler as to have agreed to divide the world with him, the most natural thing would be for Stalin to open the doors to Hitler and offer anything Hitler needed. He would give him more oil, more wheat and more of everything necessary for his partner to win. And if he did not

303

have enough, Hitler would understand the situation and not ask for more than Stalin could give.

Is it possible to show by the example of the shift on the part of France from a partnership with English imperialism to one with German imperialism that such a shift occurred in the case of the Soviet Union? The example of France proves the exact contrary. France had to be defeated and had to establish a completely new government before shifting from one imperialist camp to another. In the case of the Soviet Union there was no defeat and no change of government.

The whole situation becomes grotesque on the basis of the theory that Stalin and Hitler by the pact of August 1939 agreed to conquer and divide the world. But those who leave the firm ground of revolutionary Marxism and persist in their errors must inevitably reach the realms of political stupidity if not of downright betrayal.

"Our Analysis Of The Hitler-Stalin Pact", "Where We Stand", *The Militant*, 5 July 1941

How to explain the USSR's defeats?

SWP (1941)

OUR STRUGGLE against the war program of American imperialism and its consequences is already meeting with interest and response in the ranks of the Stalinists. Our program for revolutionary defense of the Soviet Union has made its way into the Stalinist ranks despite all the frantic attempts of the Kremlin's hirelings to portray us as enemies of the Soviet Union. Only our program explains to the perplexed Stalinist workers why, despite all the heroism and the superior morale of the Red Army and Soviet masses, the German war machine has continued to win victories over the Soviet Union. Trotsky's analysis explains to these workers how Stalin beheaded the Red Army and left the Soviet Union leaderless in industry and agriculture; every day's headlines only confirm the Trotskyist contention that Stalinism is incapable of defending the Soviet Union. Only our analysis of the anti-revolutionary character of Stalinism explains to the workers why the Kremlin has refused to arouse the masses of Europe and undermine Hitler in Germany by the revolutionary weapons which Lenin and Trotsky so successfully employed in 1917-1920.

When the workers now under Stalinist influence realize the extent of the continuous defeats sustained by the Soviet Union, there is great danger that they will fall into despair and passivity, for they will be unable to explain to themselves why the workers' state is unable to defend itself successfully against a fascist regime. Unless these workers are reached in time by us, their

304

disillusionment may lead them to drop out of the revolutionary movement altogether. We have the urgent task of saving these workers for the revolutionary movement by preparing them ideologically in due time.

Our program for the revolutionary defense of the Soviet Union has been confirmed not only against the Stalinists, but also against all the petty bourgeois renegades who denied the Soviet Union its character as a workers' state and who refused to defend it. The unparalleled morale with which the Red Army and the Soviet masses rallied to the defense of the workers' state can be explained only by our analysis of the class character of the Soviet Union. The Soviet masses, despite the oppression which they are under from the Kremlin bureaucracy, proved to be wiser politically than the "cultured," petty bourgeois snobs who abandoned the Soviet Union; the masses were able to distinguish between the Soviet Union and Stalinism even if the Eastmans, Hooks, Burnhams and Shachtmans did not. The Soviet masses threw themselves into the struggle against the Nazi war machine as no "democratic" country — France, England, Czechoslovakia, Norway, etc. — has been able to. The Soviet masses understood that Hitler was attacking, not merely the Kremlin but the nationalized property established by the October revolution.

That this unprecedented upsurge of morale has proved insufficient to halt the Nazi war machine is a tragic confirmation of the fact that only under a revolutionary leadership can the workers' state be saved. But if the Soviet Union should fall, that loss will only crown the crimes of the petty bourgeois renegades who turned their back on the Soviet Union in its hour of danger.

From points 12-14 of a resolution adopted by an SWP "Plenum-Conference", *The Militant*, 18 October 1941

We are the best defenders of the USSR

SWP (1942)

THE EVENTS AFFECTING the Soviet Union during the last year, as well as previously, are incomprehensible except to those who are guided by the Trotskyist analysis of the character of the Soviet Union. We alone have accurately explained the course of the USSR, we alone do not have to conceal what we said yesterday. While Stalin boasted of the "irrevocable victory" of socialism achieved in the Soviet Union, we warned that Germany had become the spearhead of imperialist assault against the workers' state, and that only successful proletarian revolutions in one or more advanced countries could safeguard the Soviet Union. When the League of Nations expelled the Soviet Union and the entire "democratic" world cheered on Mannerheim's Finnish Army against the Soviet Union, petty-bourgeois deserters turned their back on the USSR which they suddenly termed "imperialist", but we remained firm defensists of the workers' state, partisans of its victory over the Finnish outpost of world imperialism. We explained that by the seizures of the Finnish, Polish and Baltic territories the Kremlin bureaucracy was not pursuing imperialist aims but was in its own bureaucratic and reactionary way seeking to safeguard the defenses of the Soviet Union. We condemned the Stalinist bureaucracy for these land seizures precisely because the strategic advantages secured by the seizures were far outweighed by the discredit they brought upon the workers' state in the eyes of hundreds of millions of workers and peasants who considered them joint operations of the Nazi and Red Armies.

Stalin sought to avoid involvement in this war, first by an alliance with France and England against Germany, and then by an alliance with Germany and Japan against France and England. Neither maneuver succeeded in accomplishing its aim of keeping the Soviet Union out of the war. Stalin's diplomatic maneuvers, and all the deceitful propaganda and treacherous actions flowing from them, served only to disorient the workers in capitalist countries, to alienate them from the USSR, and to leave them unprepared for Hitler's inevitable assault upon the USSR. Stalin's foreign and domestic policies did not strengthen the USSR, but weakened it immeasurably.

While Stalin was swearing undying friendship with Hitler, whitewashing the Nazis' crimes, and camouflaging their imperialist aims, Trotsky issued his prophetic warning: "Hitler's war in the West is only a preparation for a gigantic move toward the East — against the Soviet Union." When that move came on June 22, 1941, the workers under Stalinist influence were caught completely off guard. On the eve of the attack, TASS, the official Stalinist news agency, issued a statement from Moscow, denouncing reports of the impending invasion as false rumors inspired by the Anglo-American war mongers. Thus, after shielding Hitler's crimes from the start of the war, Stalin helped to hide from the working class Hitler's preparations for assaulting the USSR. While the Trotskyists warned the workers in advance of the inevitable attack of German imperialism, the "all-seeing" Stalin led them blindfold to the edge of the abyss.

To Hitler's initial advantage of surprise was added the damage to the Red Army wrought by Stalin's purges which had decimated the general staff and officers' corps. The plans and fortifications of Tukhachevsky and his staff had to be put to use by new people. Surprise may have accounted for the first month's German victories. But the German victories of the next months, when both sides were relatively equal in material and manpower, and the Soviet troops superior in morale, can be accounted for primarily by the inferior staff work of the Red Army due to the purges. Hence the loss of the Ukraine, the Dnieper basin, the German advance to the gates of Moscow and Leningrad and the successes of the 1942 German drive into the Caucasus culminating in the assault upon Stalingrad. Thus Stalin and his bureaucratic gang are responsible for the catastrophic defeats of the Red Army, the terrible losses and privations which have brought the Soviet Union to the verge of destruction.

But the Kremlin bureaucracy is not the Soviet Union, any more than Murray, Green and Company are the CIO and the AFL. The vast moral and material resources created by the nationalized property established by the October revolution poured into the breach. The Red Army and war production were free from the fetters which private property imposes upon "national defense" even in wartime; no profiteers existed to limit war orders to monopoly corporations. The "scorched earth" policy could be applied by a land without private property with a determination and planfulness which are impossible to capitalist countries. The moving of industrial plants from endangered areas to places deep in the interior, the building of a second railroad across Siberia — such gigantic economic actions in wartime were made possible only by the system of nationalized property. Bureaucratic mismanagement could dissipate much of the superior resources provided by the nationalized property, but the decisive superiority of this property system was proved in war, as it has already proven itself in peace by the increase in productivity.

Above all, the system of nationalized property provide the basis for the unprecedented morale of the Soviet workers and peasants. The Soviet masses have something to fight for. They fight for their factories, their land, their collective economy. They fight to preserve the remaining conquests of the October revolution against the imperialists who would reestablish private property. After five months of terrible defeats, workers from the factories joined the heroic Red Army warriors at the gates of Leningrad and Moscow and helped recover Rostov in the dark days of last winter, in an outburst of proletarian revolutionary endeavor. There is nothing like this in the imperialist countries.

Those who deny that the Soviet Union is a workers' state cannot explain the unprecedented morale of Soviet workers and peasants. But great sections of the workers throughout the world have grasped the fact that, unlike the people of the imperialist countries and colonies, the Soviet masses are fighting for their own conquests achieved by the October revolution. Soviet resistance has given the workers everywhere renewed strength and hope and has helped restore confidence in their own capacities as a class. These expressions of the strangled and desecrated Russian revolution, fighting for its life under treacherous leaders and the most adverse conditions, indicate what miracles the coming international revolution will achieve as it unfolds its real program and exhibits its full power.

The tremendous advantages of the Soviet Union are not, however, sufficient in themselves to assure victory again the powerful imperialist adversary. The fact remains that the economy at the disposal of Hitler is greater in production than that of the Soviet Union, for despite Stalin's boasts the nationalized production, built on the backward economy inherited from Czarist Russia, could not in its isolation outstrip the imperialist world in efficiency and technique. What the Soviet Union requires to assure victory is the political arsenal by which Lenin and Trotsky saved the young Soviet republic from world war and Trotsky saved the young Soviet republic from world capitalist intervention in 1918-1921. It requires the revival of the Soviets, the organs which mobilized the masses in all spheres and made possible the victory in the Civil War. It requires the release from the jails and concentration camps of the tens of thousands of pro-Soviet political prisoners, restoring them to their rightful place in industry and the Red Army. Workers' democracy in the trade unions! And, as part of the restoration of workers' democracy in the USSR, the legalization of all pro-Soviet political parties and their right to present their programs to the masses. These internal steps would guarantee the maximum mobilization of the energies of the masses for the struggles ahead. Instead, however, the Stalinist bureaucracy is attempting to tighten the hold of its totalitarian apparatus, suppressing the initiative of the masses and striving to restrict their struggles within completely bureaucratic channels.

Stalin's foreign policy is an extension of his reactionary domestic policy. Just as he stifles the revolutionary spirit of the aroused masses at home, so he fears to evoke revolutionary action of the workers in capitalist countries. Yesterday he leaned upon Hitler; today Stalin relies upon the aid and goodwill of Roosevelt and Churchill. Instead of summoning the workers, above all, the German workers, to a joint struggle against their common enemy, world imperialism, Stalin entrusts the defense of the USSR abroad to the Anglo-American section of the imperialist bourgeoisie. But the bourgeoisie are deadly enemies of the working class, concerned with aiding Stalin only insofar as and so long as such aid coincides with their own national aims and class interests. They fear a decisive victory of the Red Army over Hitler far more than Hitler's triumph over the USSR.

Stalin's falsehoods help undermine the defense of the USSR. The Soviet Union cannot be effectively defended unless its real allies and its true enemies are known, recognized and distinguished from one another. The Nazis must be overthrown from within as well as combatted from without. How can Hitler's forces be disintegrated and won over? By arousing the German workers and peasants inside the army and on the home front against Nazism, by calling upon them to struggle in fraternity with their Soviet comrades against the fascist enslavers for their own Soviet Republic. Only the truth, and not Stalinist lies, only a revolutionary program and not a blind dependence upon Anglo-American imperialism, can inspire the German workers to overthrow Hitler and, together with the Russian workers and soldiers, go forward to create the Socialist United States of Europe.

The Stalinist bureaucracy will not and cannot carry out this revolutionary program. The overthrow of this thoroughly degenerated gang has become more urgent than ever. While fighting in the vanguard against the fascists and doing everything possible to strengthen the military front, the Fourth Internationalists in the USSR maintain their irreconcilable hostility to the Stalinist bureaucracy, wage an unceasing struggle against it, and aim at its overthrow by means of a political revolution. The Fourth Internationalists throughout the world stand in full solidarity with their Soviet comrades in this combined struggle.

The beleaguered Soviet workers cannot hold out indefinitely under attack unless the workers of other countries come to their rescue. Unless the revolution rises and conquers in the capitalist world and the Soviet workers throw the Stalinist usurpers off their back, the Soviet Union will inevitably be crushed, either by the Nazi invaders, or by the present imperialist "allies" who remain irreconcilably hostile to the first workers' state, or by a combination of the two. Lenin and Trotsky's program of world revolution and international Socialism which gave birth to the Soviet power and safeguarded the young Soviet Republic against the interventionists on 21 fronts in its first four years is the sole means of saving the USSR for the Socialist future. We Trotskyists remain faithful to that program; we alone propagate its ideas, and work toward its realization. That is why we are today the best defenders of the Soviet Union.

> From points 16 to 27 of "The Imperialist War And The Road To World Socialism: Political Resolution Adopted by Convention of SWP". *The Militant*, 17 October 1942

Defend the socialist achievements in USSR!

George Clarke (1942)

BERLIN BROADCASTING: "More than 1,000,000 Russian troops, aided by thousands of civilian volunteers, are defending Stalingrad with a bitterness unmatched in this war."

"Military observers said the resistance put up by the Russians was so desperate that it was impossible to predict how soon the city would be overcome."

"The Russians... must surrender or fight to the last man and they certainly will not capitulate." (Reported by A.P., Sept. 6.)

Hitler's broadcasters are admitting for the one-hundredth time not only that they could not walk over the Soviet Union as they did Norway, France, Belgium, etc., but that the German legions are being plunged into the buzzsaw of the October Revolution.

The October Revolution is represented in the spirit of the workers and soldiers defending Stalingrad against one of the greatest concentrations of military power and machinery ever hurled against a city. "They certainly will not capitulate," the German High Command admits. Neither did they capitulate in Moscow. Not in Leningrad. Not in Rostov. Not in Sevastopol. Not in Odessa.

The defenders of the October Revolution do not capitulate. Capitalists, bankers, brass hats and the whole run of parasites — they capitulate to foreign invaders to protect their privileges and dividends — and their own hides — against the threat of their own revolutionary working class. They capitulate so that colonial slaves will not achieve their independence. They capitulate so they can share at least part of their profits with the capitalist invader. They did it in Norway, Belgium, Burma and Singapore.

But the workers and Red soldiers of the Soviet Union fight with a "bitterness unmatched in this war" because they are defending the socialist achievements of a workers' revolution. Factories, mines, mills, railroads, workshops belong to those who work them. The soil belongs to those who till it. A man who will not defend such treasures is either a coward or a traitor; a man who fights to the death for them is more than a hero — he is a socialist worker.

The journalists and politicians of the imperialist democracies are at a loss to understand the great heroism of the Soviet worker. They say he gets his courage and morale from the "defense of the great Russian fatherland." Stalin echoes them with his exhortations to defend the "holy Russian soil." Let them explain then why the French, the Poles, the Norwegians, and all the others who fought Hitler on their own soil hardly dented the German armies while the Red Army not only cracked the German armies but annihilated its most effective sections.

They do not explain this contradiction, not because they don't know the answer, but because they are afraid of the answer. The courage of the defenders of Stalingrad fighting with a "bitterness unmatched in this war" knows no country; it is international. A revolution under siege and invasion in Germany, France, England or the United States would evoke heroic actions in no way inferior to that of the Russians.

Roosevelt and Churchill know this, so they talk mystically of "the Russian soil" for fear their own workers might learn the real lesson of Russian resistance.

Hitler knows this so he tells his regiments and the population at home that the Russians are "beasts" and "barbarians."

Stalin knows this but he has betrayed the October Revolution and he fears to arouse its great internationalist power, a power mightier than all Hitler's armies, for fear that a new rise of working class revolution will sweep him and his bureaucrats into the rat-holes along with Hitler and the other capitalist rulers.

The Soviet workers and soldiers show such splendid morale because the revolution is in their hearts and minds. But the Soviet soldiers, despite terrific damage inflicted on the enemy, lose city after city because the revolution is not a weapon in their hands. Stalin has deprived them of the weapon of revolutionary propaganda and for this reason above all others he is principally responsible for the defeats.

The morale of the Russians is international, we repeat. Transformed into conscious, active propaganda it can become the international weapon of working class revolution. Let the Soviet workers once revive this weapon of revolutionary propaganda and victory will be theirs. The German soldiers will then fight not to destroy the October Revolution. They will join with the Russians in a fight to the death against Hitler and international capitalism.

Writing under the name George Collins, "Stalingrad fights", *The Militant*, 12 September 1942

Victories show Russian masses accept Trotsky's view of USSR under Stalin

Albert Goldman (1943)

THE OCTOBER REVOLUTION has stood the test of events under the most adverse conditions. Its enormous vitality has been proved by the terrible test to which it has been subjected in the present war. Where could the Soviet Union have found the power to defend itself against the greatest military machine in history if not for the October Revolution? It is the Revolution with its nationalization of industry and the introduction of a planned economy that enabled the Soviet Union to build a productive machine capable of equipping the Red Army with all the necessary weapons of offense and defense. No matter how great the willingness of an army to fight and die, it is helpless if it does not possess the proper weapons. A great part of the morale of an army depends upon the sufficiency of its equipment. The October Revolution gave the Red Army its equipment.

Where would the Russian masses have found the necessary spirit and stamina to go on fighting desperately after the terrible defeat of the first year if not for the October Revolution? By October 1942 the enemy had seized some of the richest sections of the country, had deprived the masses of huge quantities of food, had destroyed many of the finest industrial centers, had taken millions as prisoners and had killed about twelve million soldiers and civilians. But the army supported by the masses kept on fighting and has achieved victories beyond our fondest hopes. Never in history has such morale existed in a nation.

And one must never forget that the state representing the Revolution is under the control of a bureaucracy to whom the spirit of October is completely alien. The Stalinist bureaucracy constitutes an enormously difficult obstacle in the path of the Soviet masses.

The elimination of workers' democracy in the Soviet Union was the greatest single blow to Soviet industry. The serious problems confronting the workers' state after the revolution can be solved only by the active participation of the masses in their solution. There are enormous resources of initiative and skill in the masses and these can be utilized only if the workers feel free to criticize and to participate freely. The building of socialism without democracy is impossible.

If the Red Army achieved victories subsequent to the murder of Tukhachevsky and other great military leaders, the Stalinists and their fellow-travelers attribute the victories to the executions. But how about the terrible defeats of the first year of the war before a new leadership was developed in the midst of the conflict? The cost of the victories has been terribly high because of the policies of Stalinism.

What a handicap Stalin has placed on the defense of the Soviet Union by substituting the reactionary ideology of Russian nationalism and slavic racialism for the ideas of October! The men who achieved the October Revolution and fought in the Civil War were animated by the ideas of socialist internationalism. They did not think of themselves as Russians fighting for Russia but as workers fighting for the world socialist revolution, for the ideas of Marx and Engels. Stalin has proclaimed the Soviet Union as a champion not or the working masses but of the Slavs.

If the Soviet masses have shown wonderful morale, it is only because they have accepted the position of Trotsky on the Soviet Union and the Stalinist bureaucracy. I do not mean to imply that the Soviet masses have read Trotsky's explanation of the nature of the Soviet Union. Many of the more politically advanced elements have perhaps reached the same theoretical conclusions. But the masses as a whole have been influenced by a very simple and obvious fact. The October Revolution eliminated the capitalist class. The state emanating from the Revolution nationalized the property of the capitalists. Although Stalin has destroyed the freedom and democracy introduced by the Revolution, capitalism has not yet been restored. It is therefore necessary to defend the Soviet Union against all capitalist powers.

The Soviet masses are fighting to the death because they want to prevent the factories from becoming the property of capitalists and the land from returning to the ownership of landlords.

The danger to the Soviet Union is far from over even if we assume, as it is safe to assume, that Hitler's defeat is not far off. Everyone saw how tense the relationship between the Allies and the Soviet Union became when the Red Army began to push the German forces out of the Soviet Union. To the capitalists of the world the Red Army represents a force that guards a state from which capitalism has been eliminated. We have never tired of saying that the fundamental antagonism between the capitalist world and the Soviet Union continues to exist even under the Stalinist regime. The fundamental proposition of Trotsky that so long as the capitalist world continues to exist, the Soviet Union is in danger, remains as true now as it has ever been.

No agreement can eliminate that danger because it is rooted in the fact that capitalism cannot tolerate the danger to it that is implicit in the very existence of a country where capitalism has been destroyed.

According to those who merely look on the surface of things, the Moscow agreement recently signed by Hull, Molotov and Eden assures peace and tranquility both to the Soviet Union and to the capitalist world. But every school boy knows by this time that agreements between states are kept only so long as they coincide with the interests of the respective states. As Marxists we understand that agreements do not determine the relationship between states. Even an agreement between two capitalist states is not to be considered inviolate. How much more so an agreement between a capitalist state and the Soviet Union!

This is not to say that the Moscow agreement [of October 1943, between US, UK, and USSR] has no significance. Its significance lies not in the possibility that it will assure peace between the capitalist states and the Soviet Union but that it presents a serious danger to the Soviet Union. That may sound paradoxical but if one realizes that the agreement necessarily implies concerted action by Stalin. Roosevelt and Churchill against the coming European Revolution, then it becomes clear that it is dangerous to the Soviet Union. For it is only the European Revolution than can save the Soviet Union and any threat to suppress that revolution is a danger to the Soviet Union.

In an article in the magazine section of the New York Times of Oct. 31, C. L. Sulzberger writes: "Many Russians with whom the writer has talked frankly discussed the dangers of a communized Germany. They take the view that this would eventually turn in the direction of Trotskyism and might conceivably begin once again, therefore, to foment dangers for the Soviet Union — a possibility which will at all costs have to be avoided."

Who are the Russians with whom Sulzberger has discussed the matter? Not with revolutionary workers but with bureaucrats. And when a bureaucrat speaks of "danger" to the Soviet Union from a Trotskyist Germany, he means danger to the Stalinist bureaucracy.

The danger which Stalin, Churchill and Roosevelt behold is not illusory. On the contrary it is very, very real. It strikes terror into their hearts. It is the October Revolution lifting up its head and shaking its fist.

From a speech on the anniversary of the Russian Revolution, *The Militant*, 13 November 1943

The amazing unity of the Soviet peoples

Bert Cochran (1943)

THE NEXT GREAT EVENT in the course of this World War, which has affected the whole course of the military struggle and altered the whole relationship of forces, is the amazing and unprecedented victories of the Red Army. And here too, the petty-bourgeois theories of Soviet "imperialism," of the new "acquisitive class" which has taken over in the Soviet Union, here too, the new theories have not stood up very wall under the impact of the events. How is anybody going to explain today that amazing unity of Soviet peoples, that unprecedented vitality and morale which exists throughout the Red Army and the peoples of the Soviet Union, except on the theory that the October revolution, though stifled and degraded, still lives? It is an absolutely unprecedented phenomenon, that after the dreadful defeats that the Red Army suffered, after the unheard of devastation of its industries and its farmlands, the Russian people were able to rally their forces, build up, starting from scratch, a new general staff, rebuild their industries and hurl back the most powerful military machine that exists in the world today, and probably in the whole history of warfare...

The imperialists are well aware of the fundamental contradiction that exists between the economy of the Soviet Union and of the capitalist world. They never permit themselves to forget it. They dread and fear the Soviet Union because it is the bearer of a new and a higher civilization than their own. They reveal their true feelings by their reaction to every Soviet success, their reaction to every advance of the Red Army. Presumably they are allies. Presumably the struggle is one for all and all for one. Presumably every victory on the Eastern front should fill them with elation because it lightens their own burden in winning the final victory over the common foe. But instead, every victory of the Soviet Union is greeted with dismay and horrible foreboding in Washington and London.

The pact that they recently concluded in Moscow [October 1943], based on an agreement of Roosevelt and Churchill with Stalin to join forces against the European revolution — and that is what it is in its essence — that pact has not and could not eliminate the fundamental antagonism that exists between the two systems... Neither Stalin's subservience to imperialism, nor his counterrevolutionary aims in Europe, can abolish this basic contradiction. The contradiction is there, and at a subsequent stage it must again break into the open, and unless the European revolution intervenes, must eventually lead to armed conflict between the USSR and Anglo-American capitalism.

Stalin understands this very well. His constant changes of front, his treachery, his double-dealing, his maneuvering and tacking, which so perplexes the bourgeois commentators — that is explained by us, and we are the only ones who have properly explained it — by the contradictory position of the Stalinist bureaucracy, which conducts its reactionary counter-revolutionary policies upon the foundations of a workers' state, degenerated though it be. Stalin's contradictory position forces him to try to bargain with the imperialists for all kinds of territorial concessions on the periphery of the Soviet Union. For such tenth-rate concessions, he betrays the international revolution and the international working class. But the inevitable consequences of his betrayals always serve to deal another blow against the Soviet Union.

It was demonstrated in his deal with Hitler. As soon as Hitler freed himself in the West, he hurled his awesome might against the Soviet Union. Stalin's new allies will not and cannot act otherwise. If they are established in a dominating position on the European continent, freed of other military struggles, of necessity they must seek to surround and strangle the USSR in order to restore capitalist private property and to open up that one-sixth of the world for capitalist exploitation. Stalin knows this. That is why he tried to find a middle course. On one hand, he sets up "Free German" and "Free Poland" committees. He lends support to the Yugoslav Partisans. He plays around with the idea of reconstituting pseudo-democratic regimes in Germany and elsewhere, all for the purpose of strengthening his hand against the capitalists. On the other hand, he makes deals with the Anglo-American capitalists to cooperate with them in crushing the European revolution and subjugating its peoples.

Stalin's attempts to find a middle course are doomed to failure. Either the socialist revolution is going to conquer in Europe or the continent is going to become the vassal of Anglo-American capitalism. Either the Soviet Union will secure itself by an alliance with a successful Socialist revolution, or eventually it is going to be destroyed and conquered by the capitalists. There are no other alternatives...

We look back today on the last fifteen years of the Trotskyist movement, fifteen years of work, of struggle, of slow, painful growth. And today, as Europe trembles on the verge of great events, we are still not a mass party, nor has the Fourth International yet a mass following. Still we are today more optimistic than ever before. Not because we are professional optimists, hut because the facts do not justify any other conclusions.

The reserves of capitalism are melting away before our very eyes. The peoples of the world hunger for a change and they can't, they won't find any other way out but the way of the socialist revolution. Out of the agony of the battlefields, out of the devastation and the ruins is being shaped the revolutionary anger and determination of the peoples which will erupt in a revolutionary storm. When that awful avenging storm breaks, as break it must, as break it will, it is going to sweep all the old rubbish out of its path. It is going to drive the tyrants and the exploiters before it, like leaves driven before an oncoming gale. The Trotskyist party of the socialist revolution will take its rightful place at the head of the people and will ride that storm. Our party has earned that right. Our cadres have grown hard and firm in adversary. Our cadres stood like a stone wall and never wavered in the times, described by Tom Paine as the "times that try men's souls." Our party, which like a steel spring, has been compressed for so long by its inner force, will, when released, shatter every obstacle in its path by its furious rebound. And the name of Trotsky, which so many times in his lifetime had evoked fear and consternation in the camp of the capitalists, will again strike terror into their hearts, because it is with Trotsky's program that the masses are going to storm the citadel and it is under his banner that they will win the final victory.

From "Labor's Socialist Perspectives and tasks of the Revolutionary Struggle in Europe", under the name E R Frank, *The Militant*, 4 December 1943

The Belgian Trotskyist paper "The Road of Lenin" (31 March 1945), with a headline that got the paper banned by the post-Nazi regime. The Belgians, like the Americans and the French, saw Stalin's "Red Army" as on the side of the working class revolution.

6. "Trotsky's Red Army": bureaucratic revolution II

Stalin enters Poland: an impulse to workers' revolution

SWP (1944)

THE MERE ANTICIPATION of the entry of the Red Armies into the border states has previously provoked grave crises in the relations between the USSR and the Anglo-American allies. Now a new and greater crisis develops as the victorious Red Armies are poised on the old Polish border.

Even though the leaders of the "United Nations" have just concluded a copper-riveted agreement and beat the drums about their concord at Teheran, the Red Army victories again expose the deep and irreconcilable antagonism which divides the Soviet Union and the imperialist powers.

The capitalist press openly expresses its alarm. What are they afraid of? If no more was involved in the successful Red Army offensive than the temporary strengthening of another state power, Roosevelt and Churchill could manage to reconcile themselves to the inevitable and arrive at a compromise agreement regarding territorial limits, spheres of influence, etc. But the conflict between Stalin and his capitalist allies arises out of the class opposition between Soviet and capitalist property relations. Anglo-American Big Business and its representatives remember what happened when the Red Armies marched into Eastern Poland in 1939: how the poor peasants drove out the landlords and nobles and seized the land; how the workers took control of industry; how the ruling caste, the bankers, industrialists, landed proprietors fled in terror before the approaching Soviet forces. They also know what is going on in Yugoslavia, where the insurgent workers and peasants, inspired by the ideas of the October 1917 revolution and the heroic stand of the Red Armies, have been fighting against the Nazis, monarchists, landlords and capitalists for their own Workers' and Peasants' Republic.

What Washington and Wall Street dread is the impetus inevitably imparted by the Red Army advances to these revolutionary moods and movements of the masses and to an overturn in political and property relations. Nothing less is at stake than the fate of capitalism.

That is why the papers have hoisted alarm signals. The New York Times warns Roosevelt editorially on Dec. 30 that, unless "there is a settlement in detail of the Polish-Russian problem before the swiftly moving Russian armies cross the old border into pre-war Poland"... "there are Republican politicians who may find it profitable for purely partisan reasons, to champion the cause of Poland against Russia in the next election." Wm. Philip Simms in the N. Y. World-Telegram (Jan 4), banner bearer of the Scripps-Howard chain, cries out: "What happens when the Red Army crosses into Poland will have epochal importance... will make or mar the chances of a lasting peace."

Simms also points out that neither Washington nor London is now in any position to "get tough" with Moscow. That is another reason why the capitalists are grinding their teeth in chagrin.

The renewed tension over the Polish question demonstrates the insuperable character of the antagonism between the Allied imperialists and the aims and aspirations of the European workers and peasants, including the Soviet peoples. This antagonism will prove more decisive in the final analysis for the fate of the Soviet Union than any understandings arrived at by Stalin with Roosevelt and Churchill. The revolutionary impulses animating the European masses are breaking through all barriers erected against them and will eventually accumulate explosive power enough to blow to bits the counter-revolutionary schemes of Roosevelt, Churchill and Stalin.

"Stalin in Poland", Editorial, *The Militant*, 8 January 1944

Stalinist "liberation" of Poland is an imperialist grab

Max Shachtman (1944)

THE WAR WITH GERMANY was justified by the Allied spokesmen, among other things, on the ground that Hitlerism violates the national sovereignty of nations and peoples, does not allow them to live as they see fit and to rule themselves. There is no need to prove this case against Hitlerism beyond the use of facts which are known to every child. Now that the Allies are beginning to speak of an early victory over Germany the question rises: what is to become of the countries overrun by the Nazis once the latter have been put to the sword? Is their national sovereignty to be restored, at least to the extent that they enjoyed it before the war began?

If we are to judge by the fight developing over Poland, there is no reason to believe that the Allies hold out any such hope. The fight over Poland is not just a battle over the eastern territories of the former Polish Empire, it is a fight for that part of Europe which is, unmistakably and unchallengedly Polish by tradition, common language and culture and all the other recognizable traits of a nation. So far as the eastern territories are concerned, the claims of the [Polish] government in exile [in London] are as notoriously fraudulent as they are old. They are today's remnants of the old dream of a Greater Polish Empire "from sea to sea" — from the Baltic to the Black. Inhabited principally by non-Polish peoples, White Russians, Ukrainians, and Jews, who have neither cultural, linguistic, nor even religious characteristics in common with the Poles, the only claim that the Polish "Pans" [lords] and their colonels ever had to rule over them was the need to sate an imperialist greed. The persecutions these peoples underwent, from the day the Versailles map-makers concocted an "independent" Poland, constitute one of the cruelest and bloodiest chapters in the annals of modern oppression. Nobody can say exactly how many of the people in these lands were murdered, how many sent to rot in prison. What can be said, because it is common knowledge, is that the cultural aspirations of these peoples were trampled under foot with the same cynicism and the same methods employed in the days of the Romanovs, their religious feelings and institutions were systematically offended (the anti-Semitic outrages of the Polish ruling class preceded Hitler's), their political

319

rights were never taken off paper and, above all; their economic status was kept at the lowest possible level. Only the most rabid Polish imperialist could expect any allegiance from these peoples. The blusterings and stutterings of the government in exile, a gang of authentic reactionaries and pupils of the Colonels, plus a handful of social-democratic house-pets, will be pointed out to future generations as typical of imperialist effrontery and hypocrisy.

It does not follow in any way from this that the territories properly belong in what is sardonically known as the "Soviet" "Union." By virtue of what right? The fact that these territories once formed part of the Czarist Empire? Or the fact that they once were part of the Soviet Republics — without quotation marks — and were wrested from the workers' state by the superior force which Pilsudski's armies imposed upon the weak and exhausted Red Army? [Pilsudski was the Polish military leader in 1920, during the war which followed the 1917 revolution].

Such a right would exist and be valid provided the incorporation of these territories into the Union meant the liberation from oppression, or the beginning of such a liberation, of the people inhabiting them. That would have been the case in 1920. It is in no sense the case today. The torments suffered by these peoples under Polish despotism are so widely known that even the bourgeois press refers to them, however discreetly. But they pale beside the organized, systematic, centralized, totalitarian terror against the "blood brothers" of these peoples who have lived for the past decade and more under the rule of the Stalinist autocracy. The Ukrainian and White Russian "Soviet Republics" are nothing but national fiefs of the Kremlin bureaucracy. They have neither independence in the "Union" nor autonomy. Their rulers are picked and unpicked by this bureaucracy, whom they serve in the same capacity and with the same rights and privileges as the Czar's governor-generals. Their economic strength has been sapped so that the bureaucracy might batten on it; their economic position has been reduced to the status of serfs of the regime.

The Polish knout stings no more brutally than the Stalinist knout. The cemeteries of the Western Ukraine are less numerous than those of the "Soviet" Ukraine, filled as the latter are with the corpses of millions of peasants condemned to death in the Stalinist "collectivization drive" alone. It is not without significance that in their initial drive Hitler's legions encountered less resistance from the native population of the Ukraine than from the native people of the northern part of the "Union."

The fact that "even" the Anglo-American ruling class has given its sanction to Stalin's demand should cause only a shrugging of the shoulders and not a bending of the knees. What else could it do? Stalin's "moral" position is flawless, from the imperialist standpoint. What could Churchill, for example, possibly say in reply to a blunt accusation from the Kremlin statesmen: "You want us to give up our Poland, but you cling to India like a leech. You want your colonies? We want ours. You have your amusing elections in India? We have our funny plebiscites in the border states".

More important than the "moral" position is the military position. Neither Churchill nor Roosevelt has as much as a toe-nail on Polish or ex-Polish soil. Mikolajczyk [chief of the wartime Polish government-in-exile based in London, and later, 1944-7, the pro-Western deputy prime minister in a government which was in fact Stalinist-controlled] & Co. are better off only in so far as the Polish underground gives them reluctant and suspicious support. Stalin, however, not only has good, solid boots on more and more Polish (or ex-Polish) soil, but has the power to extend a friendly hand to Hitler if an Allied attempt is made to challenge the rights of his boots.

Stalin is not, however, interested in Western White Russia and the Western Ukraine alone. Those territories are taken for granted, and he leaves it to Eden and Hull to find a convenient formula — diplomatic archives are filled with all kinds of them, like the "Curzon line," which can be tapped for each particular occasion to justify his seizures and to make the Mikolajczyks toe the mark or else. Stalin wants Poland as well, if he can — directly; if he cannot — then indirectly. If he gits thar fustest with the mostest, then Mikolajczyk might just as well retire to Cleveland, like the recently-deceased Smetona of Lithuania [the president of Lithuania who fled to the USA when the Russians invaded in 1940, and died in 1944 in a house fire]. Then, finis Poloniae! There is no question about it: the Polish government in exile is worried far more about Poland itself than about her former eastern territories. More accurately, its apprehensions over the eastern territories are due to its apprehensions over Poland.

The fight over Poland underlies what may be called the two most important ideas of our time: 1. The struggle for national independence and freedom cannot be conducted in a progressive spirit and with consistency and honesty except by the proletariat and its peasant allies. The others are interested in anything but national freedom for all peoples. Conducted by the proletariat, the fight for national freedom must be linked with the fight for social freedom, in which it would find its highest realization. Its highest realization, finally, can come in Europe only in the form of a Socialist United States of Europe, freely entered and equitably and jointly ruled by the independent workers' governments that alone can save Europe from the disintegration, subjugation and chaos to which capitalist barbarism is dooming it.

And second, the seeds of the Third World War are being sown already. World War II is not yet over, decidedly not yet, and the conditions for speeding World War III are being laid. This idea is not peculiar to the revolutionary Marxists. Many capitalists understand it. Many even fear it, for the bourgeoisie does not want war, and especially it does not want the revolutions that come with it. But it is helpless to prevent it, as utterly and completely helpless as it proved to be in 1939. The military struggle between the two big camps is accompanied by a feverish political struggle inside the Allied camp. The attempts made in it to confine to an agreement on the division of the spoils are condemned in advance to the failure which the essentially temporary character of any imperialist agreement bears from the moment it is adopted. They agreed before, once, twice, and ten times. Their very agreements contain the germ of conflict. The agreement over Poland simply injects one of the many germs of tomorrow's conflict.

The two most important ideas of our time are simply the reverse of each other. The continuation of capitalism means war and barbarism. The struggle of the working class, consistently developed, means peace and socialism. The time for the choice was long ago. But even now, it is not too late.

Labor Action, 24 January 1944

The flags of the Red Army will combine with our own red flags

La Vérité (1944)

THE RED ARMY IS ADVANCING towards Romania. It is attacking in force towards Lithuania. It threatens to cut the force of the Reich into two sections. The Red Army is in Poland! This is good news for the workers of the whole world, and in particular for the oppressed people of "fortress Europe". In the bourgeois camps, however, great anxiety reigns.

Goebbels makes call after call to the German people for resistance, and the White Terror intensifies in all the occupied countries. In France, the killer Darnand [leader of the Petain regime's militia] is striving to galvanise a police force which is decaying.

The anxiety is no less in the bourgeois camp in England and the United States. The Red Army is moving a bit too fast for high finance. Standard Oil is at work to keep Hitler's tanks and planes running as long as possible, while Churchill, on his side, activates preparations for landings in Europe and tells us that they will be delayed no longer. The Allies are preparing to replace the failing Nazi gendarme. The capitalist world is trembling, and reaction is feverishly preparing to face the rising revolution.

Stalin has given plenty of pledges to the Allies. He has repudiated the ideas of Lenin, and the bureaucracy is a parasite on the back of the proletariat. Despite that, the USSR is a workers' state where the means of production are socialised. Each victory of the Red Army is a defeat for the international bourgeoisie. Each metre of terrain conquered by it is a metre removed from capitalist exploitation, and, above all, each success of the Soviet soldiers is an encouragement for the workers of the whole world. Resistance becomes more active, and repression more sloppy. Here, strikes break out; there, production falls; elsewhere, clandestine workers' groups develop from day to day.

Everywhere the working class is raising its head, and all across Europe, the bourgeois exploiters of France, of Spain, of Belgium, of Holland, etc. turn their gaze from Berlin towards New York and London who, they hope, will be better able to protect their privileges.

For their part, the transatlantic magnates, while they gear themselves up, while they produce ten times more planes that would be needed for two Wehrmachts, look to Stalin and expect him to kill the coming revolution.

Stalin well knows that the revolution is coming. He knows that with the advance of the Soviet Army a general uprising may explode in Europe. Tomorrow, ten thousand factory soviets may cover Europe. He knows, also, that it is far from certain that these worker and peasant soviets, born in the advanced countries of Europe, will passively obey the parasitic Moscow bureaucracy.

Stalin is not unaware that he cannot be sure of his army for the task of bringing to heel the revolutionary workers of Europe. The USSR's army will not crush the soviets of Berlin, of Budapest, and of Paris. On the contrary, those soviets will make the Russian army remember that it is a soviet army.

The communist revolution in Europe will be the end of exploitative capitalism, and also the end of the parasitic bureaucracy. The Moscow usurpers know that... But the Red Army is advancing.

All those who want to block the Revolution are now resorting to one last trick. They sing the praises of the Red Army. "Wait for it to come and deliver us", they say to the workers. "Meanwhile, all you can do is help it militarily by a few small-scale actions". But the conscious workers will not be caught in that trap. They know that the best way to help the Red Army is to work to overthrow capitalism. They also know that the Red Army cannot "liberate" the working class of other countries unless the working class itself takes its own affairs in hand and itself prepares the revolution against its own bourgeoisie.

By violence from outside one can bring the whip and the terror to a people, not socialist liberation. That is why, as the Red Army advances, the workers become more sure of themselves, and enter greater struggles all across Europe.

Tomorrow, Europe will flare up in revolutionary conflagration, and soldiers will fraternise with the populations of the occupied countries. The flags of the Red Army will combine with ours. In London, in Paris, in Budapest, in Berlin: take power! Form workers' battalions!

Unsigned lead article in the French Trotskyist paper La Vérité, 10 February 1944. This issue of La Vérité came out just after an international conference of Trotskyists in France in February 1944 adopted a document sketching roughly the same perspective. The conference was attended by representatives from the POI-PCI (France), the Revolutionary Communist Party of Belgium, the Internationalist Communist Party of Greece, the Lenin and Trotsky group of Spain, and a group of German Trotskyists living in France.

Stalin aims to subjugate Polish workers

SWP (1944)

NO SOONER DID the Red Army approach the outskirts of Warsaw, than the Warsaw proletariat rose up and, arms in hand, launched a full-scale battle to drive out the Nazi oppressors. The Warsaw proletariat, rich in socialist traditions and revolutionary training, has thereby served notice that five years of Nazi butchery have not tamed its fighting spirit nor destroyed its fighting powers.

Undoubtedly, the Warsaw proletariat expected that the Red Army would hasten its assault on the city, and thus through their joint efforts, from within and without, the Nazi tyrants would be driven out and destroyed. But instead of launching more energetically the military onslaught and redoubling their efforts, the Red Army attack was brought to a sudden standstill, by order of Stalin's generals. Just as Badoglio [general who became head of Italian government after Mussolini was ousted in 1943] had turned the Italian proletariat of the North over to the Nazi invaders a year ago, so Stalin determined to permit the Nazis to crush the uprising of the Warsaw proletariat in blood. Stalin is thus pounding home the lesson (that advanced workers learned, long ago) to the whole Warsaw proletariat: That his aims are counter-revolutionary, that he intends not to liberate the Polish people but to subjugate them again under the yoke of the capitalists, landlords, and Polish "colonels".

After first denying the very existence of the Warsaw revolt, Tass, the Stalinist news agency, now seeks to justify Stalin's latest betrayal by issuing a press release that the Polish government-in-exile in London is alone responsible for the cruel isolation of the embattled Warsaw proletariat. Of course, the government-in-exile, representative of the Polish capitalists, landlords and militarists, undoubtedly seeks to use the insurgent movement of the masses for its own reactionary ends. Of, course, only treachery and reaction can be expected from that quarter. But Stalin cannot hide his crime against the Warsaw proletariat by retreating behind the skirts of the reactionary Polish capitalist-landlord clique in London.

The Warsaw proletariat must draw the lessons. They must organize completely apart from, and in opposition to, the Stalinists. They must mercilessly drive out of their ranks all Stalinist agents, as they would plague-carriers. They must depend only upon themselves, their independent organizations and their independent revolutionary actions. Only in their own revolutionary actions lies the guarantee for protection of the Polish revolution from the Stalinist hangmen. Only through their independent revolutionary actions will they be able to organize fraternization with the Red Army soldiers and help the Soviet masses to settle accounts with the bloody Bonapartist dictatorship of Stalin.

"Warsaw betrayal", editorial, *The Militant*, 19 August 1944

Worker-guerrillas must subordinate to the Red Army command

James P Cannon (1944)

THE AUGUST 19 MILITANT EDITORIAL — Warsaw Betrayed — goes even further afield than the previous editorial we wrote about [see pp.361-2, this volume] in muddling up our line of "unconditional defense of the Soviet Union" in the struggle against the Nazi-imperialist invaders.

To call upon the revolutionary Polish workers to "organize fraternization" with the Red Army soldiers, as the editorial does, is to think in terms of establishing contact with the rank and file of a hostile military force. But the Polish workers must be the allies of the Red Army in its war against Hitler's armies, no matter how reactionary Stalin's policy is. Therefore, the task for the Polish revolutionaries is to organize revolutionary propaganda in the ranks of the Red Army, with which they will be in contact as allies, not to "organize fraternization".

Secondly, the editorial adds that through this "fraternization" the Polish workers will help the Soviet masses to "settle accounts with the bloody Bonapartist dictatorship of Stalin". Our program recognizes the vital necessity of overthrowing Stalinism in the Soviet Union and has always placed this task in order of importance second only to the defense of the Soviet Union against imperialist attacks. However, it is precisely the latter consideration that the editorial slurs over.

Finally, the editorial again fails to put explicitly and unmistakably our slogan "Unconditional defense of the Soviet Union" against all imperialists. The editorial also takes for granted a version of the Warsaw events about which there is little information, none of it reliable, and many uncertainties. A full-scale battle against the Nazis by the Warsaw proletariat is assumed, as is the "order of Stalin's generals" in halting the Red Army attack on the city. The Moscow charge that the London "Polish government in exile" ordered the uprising without consulting the Red Army command is brushed aside without being clearly stated, much less analyzed in the light of the current Soviet-Polish negotiations.

No consideration is given to the question of whether or not the Red Army was able at the moment to launch an all-out attack on Warsaw in view of its long-sustained offensive, the Nazi defensive preparations along the Vistula, the necessity to regroup forces and mass for new attacks after the not inconsiderable expenditure of men and material in reaching the outskirts of Warsaw, the fact that there was a lull along virtually the entire Eastern front concurrent with the halt before Warsaw, etc.

Nor does the editorial take up the question of the duty of guerrilla forces — and in the circumstances that is what the Warsaw detachments are — to subordinate themselves to the high command of the main army, the Red Army, in timing such an important battle as the siege of Warsaw. On the contrary, the editorial appears to take as its point of departure the assumption that a full-scale proletarian uprising occurred in Warsaw and that Stalin deliberately maneuvered to permit Hitler to crush the revolt.

A hasty, sketchy commentary on events, including the badly-limping Badoglio analogy, is then fitted into this arbitrary framework.

We agree, indeed, as to Stalin's counter-revolutionary intentions. Moreover, one has the right to suspect or believe personally that the Warsaw events are just as the editorial pictures them. But we have no right to put in writing in our press, and in an editorial to boot, such sweeping assertions for which we have no proof and to draw conclusions based on such flimsy information. That is not the tradition of *The Militant*. We are deeply concerned about this carelessness in writing about such a crucial question and are anxious to hear the comments on our criticism.

Letter from Cannon (in jail) to be transmitted to the SWP
leadership, August 1944, printed in *New International* March 1945.
This letter is not included in Cannon's *Letters from Prison*, 1968.

Stalin seeks to make Trotsky's Red Army gendarme of capitalism in Romania

James Cowan (1944)

THE ROLE OF THE KREMLIN in the affairs of the European continent is being revealed with complete clarity in the case of Rumania, where Stalin's henchmen have appeared on the scene as the saviors and supporters of the rotted system of capitalist-landlord exploitation and its political regime of oppression and reaction.

At the beginning of April [1944], the Red Army, pursuing retreating German and Rumanian troops, crossed the river Pruth and entered Rumanian territory. This was its first incursion across the Soviet borders. The capitalist world was manifestly nervous and apprehensive. Molotoff, Stalin's foreign commissar, hastened to allay all suspicions and apprehensions with a statement: "The Soviet Government declares it does not pursue the aim of acquiring Rumanian territory or of altering the existing social structure of Rumania. The entry of Soviet troops into the boundaries of Rumania is dictated exclusively by military necessities and the continuing resistance of enemy troops."

Last week, foreign correspondents were taken to the northern corner of Romania, where the Red Army has now been in occupation for three months, and permitted to cable out their findings. What did they discover? Associated Press correspondent Henry C. Cassidy says: "It was the unanimous opinion of American, British and Chinese observers that the Russians are not interfering in any way with the political, economic or social life of Rumania." Which, of course, is confirmation of Molotoff's assurance to the capitalist world that the Stalinist regime will help the Anglo-American imperialists preserve capitalist-landlord rule in the Balkans.

It is, however, the details of the correspondents' findings which afford the most glaring confirmation of the reactionary role of the Stalinist government and reveal the abysmal depths of counter-revolutionary vileness to which it has descended. Wrote Cassidy: "The Russian occupation is administered by military commandants whose sole preoccupation is the maintenance of order... The local officials, including Mayors of the towns and prefects of regions, are left to carry on their usual functions."

Thus all the old reactionary officials, notorious oppressors of the masses, have been confirmed in their offices and "order" is being maintained in the interests of the capitalists and landlords for whom they rule. Stalin seeks to give to the Red Army, the great liberating army of Socialism founded by Lenin and Trotsky, the ignominious role of gendarme of capitalist property.

But this is not the worst of the ignominy. "Local laws," Cassidy tells us, "including those with anti-Semitic provisions, are left unchanged, pending later change by the people themselves. This attitude is applied even to the Rumanian act outlawing the Communist Party, which remains on the books."

The Stalinist ruling clique in this instance goes even further than the Allied imperialists. In an effort to keep up the pretense that this is a war of "liberation," one of the first acts of the Allied Military Government in Italy was to declare null and void the anti-Semitic laws imposed on the country by Mussolini's fascist regime. Stalin, however, preserves all the totalitarian filth of the old semi-fascist Rumanian regime.

In espousing the cause of reaction in Rumania and other nearby countries, in throwing the weight of the Soviet Union to the side of the capitalists and landlords, Stalin is pursuing a twofold purpose. On the one hand, he seeks to hold back the mounting tide of socialist revolution. Such a revolution anywhere, but especially one in a neighboring country, would threaten destruction to the Stalin regime by inspiring the Soviet workers to struggle against it. On the other hand, Stalin hopes that capitalist states like Rumania will become "friendly" to the Soviet Union because of the support given by his regime to their ruling classes. In this way he expects: to build up a counterweight to the great Anglo-American imperialist coalition, which, when Germany has been defeated, will be in a position to exercise enormous pressure on the Soviet Union.

This plan is both utopian and reactionary. It is utopian because it ignores the fundamental antagonism between the Soviet Union and the entire capitalist world, which springs from continuing social ownership of all property in the Soviet Union and will prevail as long as that socialized property remains. It is reactionary because it damages the prestige of the Soviet Union with the exploited masses abroad, sabotages the socialist revolution, and therewith tends to destroy the only sure and dependable support upon which the Soviet Union can rely in a hostile capitalist encirclement.

"Landlord-capitalist rule in Rumania preserved by Stalin", *The Militant*, 15 July 1944 (abridged).

SWP gives Stalin free help

Labor Action

HOW CAN YOU AID Stalinism even if you are against it? How can you spread the worst lies and deceptions of Stalinism while calling yourself a "Trotskyist"? *The Militant*, spokesman of the Socialist Workers Party, gives the answer. Speaking of Rumania and Russia in its July 15 issue, it writes: "Stalin seeks to give to the Red Army, the great liberating army of socialism founded by Lenin and Trotsky, the ignominious role of gendarme of capitalist property." You see, Stalin only "seeks" to give the "Red" Army an ignominious role. He hasn't yet succeeded. You see, the Russian army is not only "Red," but it is still the "great liberating army of socialism."

This is what these self-styled Trotskyists write, and not for the first time. Trotsky, however, back in 1939, declared that "the Red Army... is an instrument in the hands of the Bonapartist bureaucracy." In other words, it is the tool of the Stalinist counter-revolution. It is the tool used by Stalin among the peoples in the territory he conquers "to convert them into his own semi-slaves," as Trotsky said further. That is why, we presume, Trotsky added that "We do not entrust the Kremlin with any historic mission. We were and remain against seizures of new territories by the Kremlin." (All these quotations are from Trotsky's *In Defense of Marxism*.) *The Militant*, which calls itself "Trotskyist," describes this tool of the Bonapartist bureaucracy, of semi-slavery, of the "counter-revolutionary workers' state", as "the great liberating army of socialism." That is how it spreads, or rather continues to spread, one of the fundamental lies of Stalinism.

In the same article, *The Militant* speaks of the "continuing social ownership of all property in the Soviet Union," and declares that "socialized property remains" in Russia. Time and again we have pointed out to *The Militant* that this is not only a lie, violating all the facts and the basic theories of Marxian socialism, but that it is the fundamental lie of the Stalinist bureaucracy and its philosophy. In his book, *The Revolution Betrayed*, Leon Trotsky wrote, as early as 1936: "The new [Stalinist] constitution — wholly founded, as we shall see, upon an identification of the bureaucracy with the state, and the state with the people — says: '... the state property — that is, the possessions of the whole people'. This identification is the fundamental sophism of the official doctrine ... the higher the Soviet state rises above the people, and the more fiercely it opposes itself as the guardian of property to the people as its squanderer, the more obviously does it testify against the socialist character of this state property."

This is not the first time we have called the direct attention of *The Militant* to this quotation. But it is so hell-bent-for-leather to idealize and embellish Stalin's counterrevolutionary state that it continues to ignore Trotsky's view in favor of spreading "the fundamental sophism" of the official Kremlin doctrine. Trotsky speaks accurately of "state property" in Russia. *The Militant*, following the Stalinists, keeps speaking of "socialized property" and the "social ownership of property" in Russia.

"Stalinism gets free help: *The Militant* is at it again", unsigned article, *Labor Action*, 24 July 1944

Socialist Appeal, 2 October 1937, flays CP leader Earl Browder

Stalinism threatens to defeat workers' revolution in Europe

Lewis Coser (1942)

THE RECENT SUCCESS of the Red Army draws our attention to a most-vital problem of the coming European revolution: the danger of a "New Spain"; the danger of a defeat of this revolution, not by the onslaught of the capitalist enemy, but by forces functioning within the working class itself. It is of utmost necessity that this problem be clearly faced now; failure to do so can have only serious consequences later.

It is not merely a matter of academic discussion as to whether the Soviet Union is a workers' state or not. There is more than merely a problem of sociological definition involved here. Regardless of intentions, to speak of Russia as a "workers' state" today is to blind the workers — especially of Germany — to the dangers of tomorrow.

In spite of the tremendous waves of wishful thinking produced during recent years about the definite collapse of the Stalinist parties, it is a fact that in most of the occupied countries the Stalinist Party is the strongest if not the sole mass party of the workers. Facts are stubborn; you have to explain them but you cannot make them disappear merely because your historical analyses want them to. As long as the roots from which Stalinism springs continue to exist. It will remain as a powerful counter-revolutionary factor in Europe.

The reasons for this surprising vitality of Stalinism in Europe are many and complex. The two most important, almost as powerful today as ten years ago, are:

1) The widespread traditional linking of revolutionary action with Moscow, the capital of the first successful working class revolutionary country. The sentiment that, after all, many tactics may be incomprehensible, but still "they know how to do the job." For many years, the Communist Parties had been the gathering place of the revolutionary elite, for many years all those workers who were opposed to opportunism and reformism had been almost automatically drawn to the Stalinists. Every attempt to build a revolutionary mass party outside the CP ranks failed largely because of this attraction. The whole pattern of working class ideas was completely linked with the Soviet Union, even after Stalin had usurped power.

2) The second reason is a socio-psychological one. Craving for leadership, for authority, is a deep-rooted tendency in modern man

and is also present among the workers. It is much easier to transfer one's craving for authority from one powerful force to another than to stand openly in rebellion against existing society. Especially is this true of a working class that has suffered numerous defeats, that is in large measure unemployed and starving. A free trade union worker in a factory who has acquired the feeling of independence is much more difficult to induce into unquestioning obedience toward the rigid structure of Stalinism.

But in Europe today there are millions of unemployed workers who work only occasionally, millions of others near starvation. Recent defeats of the working class in France and Spain, to name but two, have tremendously aggravated this sentiment of despair. Large sections have abandoned confidence in any action arising out of independent class struggle; they are looking for help from outside. (We have recently printed instances of evidence that this sentiment is gradually being overcome, but these are only the first signs.)

If these two reasons for the strength of Stalinism cannot be overcome by the new working class revolutionary movement arising today in Europe, a "new Spain" is inevitable [i.e. a joint bourgeois-Stalinist suppression of workers' revolution, as in Spain in 1936-7]. But how can these two factors be overcome?

Were we here dealing with a problem of "importing" attitudes and ideas to the European working class, our task would be hopeless. But what is rather in question is certain trends already latent in the European masses, certain facts which are the foundation for the new movement. Oppression and semi-slavery, the unlimited reign of bureaucratic authority over the working class as well as over each individual, have created a spontaneous longing for freedom and security. These words are often used in the reports we get from Europe; their concrete meaning is often very blurred; some — certainly not the majority — may think of a return to bourgeois democracy. But for many, these words are linked to the idea of socialism (which is, of course, also thought of as a vague and blurred conception). This is where the tasks of the new movement appear. It is the job of the revolutionary groups in Europe to clarify and define these ideas. Here also — is the basis upon which Stalinism can most effectively be attacked.

It is necessary to point out to the masses that Stalinism (even though it functions on the basis of what can be the form of economic organization of socialism) is not socialism, but rather a totalitarian regime of the most brutal sort. Socialism, it must be pointed out, is conceivable only on the basis of economic planning and nationalized industry — plus democracy, self-determination and initiative from below. Soviet democracy in this sense must be the great idea animating the revolutionary socialists of Europe; only on this basis is it possible to effectively smash once and for all the virus of Stalinism. Class democracy as against bureaucratic authoritarianism, which takes its most vicious form in Stalinism, must become a prime issue of all the political thinking and propaganda of European socialists.

Propaganda alone cannot, of course, change history: theories can only be fertilized in the soil of action. The feeling of powerlessness and the fatal lack of self-reliance which at present characterizes so large a section of the European working class, can only be overcome by the independent action of the class itself.

Independent class action and the concept of democratic, revolutionary socialism are the poles around which the new movement will have to revolve. Without them any hope of overcoming either capitalism or Stalinism is vain.

"The coming European revolution faces a great menace in Stalinism", under the name Europacus, *Labor Action* 9 February 1942

Advert for *New International* in *Labor Action* in March 1947.

"You seem to be hypnotised by the slogan 'defence of the USSR'"

Natalia Sedova, 16 August 1944

I DO NOT CONSIDER MYSELF COMPETENT in political questions to the extent of condemning this or that line of your conduct. But in the given instance your mistaken course is all too clear to me.

Permit me a few words in this connection.

You seem to be hypnotized by the slogan of the "defense of the USSR" and in the meantime profound changes, political as well as moral-psychological, have taken place in its social structure. In his articles, especially the last ones, L.D. [Trotsky] wrote of the USSR as a degenerating workers' state and in view of this outlined two possible paths of further social evolution of the first workers' state: revolutionary and reactionary. The last four years have shown us that the reactionary landslide has assumed monstrous proportions within the USSR. I shall not recount the facts, they are known to you – they bespeak of the complete moving away of the USSR from the principles of October. Soviet literature for the war years (Moscow magazines which I am receiving) confirm these facts; in current Moscow literature there is not the slightest echo of socialistic ideology; dominant in it are petty bourgeois, middle class tendencies; the cult of the family and its welfare. The Red Army, at the basis of whose organization were lodged the principles of the October overturn, and whose (the Red Army's) goal was the struggle for the world revolution, has become transformed into a nationalist-patriotic organization, defending the fatherland, and not against its bureaucratic regime but together with its regime as it has taken shape in the last decade. Do you recall the answer of L.D. to the question put to him in the Politburo in 1927: whether the Opposition would defend the USSR in case of war? "The socialist fatherland – yes; Stalin's regime – no."

The "socialist" has fallen away; the "regime" has remained. A degenerating "workers' state" presupposes that it is moving along the path of degeneration, still preserving its basic principle – the nationalization of private property. But just as it is impossible to build socialism in one country, so it is impossible to preserve inviolate this basic principle, if one pursues the reactionary road, destroying all the other conquests of 1917. It is necessary to explain this tirelessly day by day. It is impermissible to repeat an antiquated slogan by rote.

At the present time there is only one danger threatening the Soviet Union – that is the further development of black reaction, the further betrayal of the international proletariat. This is precisely the direction in which it is necessary to sound the alarm. To defend the Soviet Union against the regime of its "master," mercilessly laying bare the policy of the master who comes to the fore on the international arena in the capacity of a conciliator with bourgeois capitalism and as a counter-revolutionist in the European countries liberated from Hitler. (As far back as 1937 L.D. wrote in the *Bulletin of the Russian Opposition* that not a single serious person believes any longer in the revolutionary role of Stalin.)

You are correctly criticizing the foreign policy of the Marshal, but after all, foreign policy is the continuation of the domestic policy; it is impermissible to separate the one from the other. In your position there is a crying contradiction. It is necessary to hammer away at one point: to warn against the consequences of Russian victories; to warn, to sound the alarm on the basis of the elements that have already been disclosed with complete clarity, as well as to lay bare those elements which are about to be disclosed, and at the same time to point the way out.

"The main danger for the USSR is Stalin"

Natalia Sedova, 23 September 1944

FROM YOUR REPLY I CONCLUDE that my letter was written far too generally. I shall try to concretize it. I do not propose that we take off the slogan of defense of the USSR, but I find that it must be pushed back to the second or third rank. In the process of war and especially of victories its content has sharply altered. It is necessary to lay this bare tirelessly. The slogan of the defense of the USSR comprised in it a two-fold aim: a) the struggle with the internal enemy, Stalin's regime; and b) the struggle against foreign intervention. The final goal of the defense of the USSR is the world revolution.

"I consider that the main source of the dangers for the USSR in the present international situation is Stalin and the oligarchy headed by him. The struggle against them in the eyes of public opinion is indivisibly connected for me with the defense of the USSR." (L.D.'s article on Stalin after the Finnish experience).

The unconditional defense of the USSR was always for us a factor of a merciless struggle against the Bonapartist bureaucracy right up to its overthrow and the re-establishment of Soviet democracy.

The military triumphs have strengthened the position of the Soviet bureaucracy (the internal enemy); reaction is growing — from this it is necessary to draw the conclusion with regard to the slogan of the defense of the USSR. You write that it is necessary to take our starting point from that which is, base ourselves on facts. Absolutely correct. But after all this means that the slogan of the military defense of the USSR withdraws to the background in the face of new events.

The Soviet land stands on the threshold of revolution or counter-revolution. To carry through the counter-revolution under the conditions of encirclement by the revolutionary ferment in Europe is as difficult as to intrench the basic conquests of the October revolution in the reactionary encirclement of the Stalinist regime. When you underscore in your letter the meaning of that which is and the facts on which one must base oneself in his judgements — you apparently have in mind the still unliquidated nationalized sector of property and planned economy. But after all it is impermissible to analyze this most important fact outside of the general present Soviet conditions which could not have failed to find their reflection also in this fact. The nationalization which was carried out in the epoch of revolution had as its goal the equality and raising of the living standards of the masses. In the conditions of advancing reaction and in the hands of the Bonapartist bureaucracy it has still been preserved, but has moved away from its initial task (as has the Red Army). The Bonapartist bureaucracy has used the greatest conquests of the revolution for its own personal interests. In addition to facts it is necessary to take into account the tendency of the development of this or that political phenomenon. Without such an accounting it is impossible to lead, or to prepare or to carry on propaganda, or to sketch out perspectives etc. etc. In the pre-October epoch the Mensheviks, basing themselves on facts, predicted the crushing of the October Revolution, assigning to it a two week period of existence. The Bolsheviks, basing themselves on facts, conducted a confident agitation for the overturn. How is it then? The evolution of the tendencies of political events must take into account, analyze, discuss from different standpoints right up to sharp polemics, right up to differences of opinion. In this consists the living creative work of the organization, its preparation for the impending events; otherwise it is doomed to inaction.

The Soviet bureaucracy, the most reactionary in the world, is pushing planned economy not in the direction of socialism but of capitalism. With the termination of the war the question of planned economy will be posed in all its sharpness. There is ripening a clash of planned economy with the Bonapartist bureaucracy which has strengthened its positions by the victories. The contradictions may become unbearable and the break with planned economy can confront the bureaucracy as a vital necessity. Socialism or the restoration of capitalism? This most important problem of the USSR must be put in the center of our attention. A mortal danger is threatening the Soviet land, and the source of this danger is the Soviet bureaucracy (the internal enemy).

The war is not ended; the external enemy still exists. But at the beginning of the war we viewed it as the most dangerous one and the struggle against the bureaucratic regime ceded its place to the military struggle; at the present time matters must be put just the other way. It is necessary to explain this to the Soviet workers as well as to the workers of the whole world. We must with all the necessary clarity warn them about the threatening danger to the first workers' state.

Military victories of the Red Army cannot assure the overthrow of the Stalinist bureaucracy; military defense does not lead to the revolutionary struggle against the Stalinist regime. The military defense of the USSR in the present world situation has become transformed into the problem of struggle against Stalinism.

A few words about Soviet literature. In your opinion it does not reflect Soviet reality. This is correct, but not entirely, not wholly but only to a certain degree. And this certain degree must be taken into account. The war propaganda could not have failed to have its effect on the Soviet masses. The war, what was lived through — not only the sufferings but also the experience — has taught Soviet citizens a great deal. They are feeling more confident of themselves, more independent, more demanding and this has already found its expression in the local correspondence in *Izvestia* and *Pravda* despite the bureaucratic vice and "command". But this is not all. In the same papers also is reflected the watchfulness and alarm of the bureaucracy in this connection and it is already issuing out calls for the restoration of order.

Natalia is right!

James P Cannon, 26 September, 28 September, and 1 October 1944

NATALIA'S LETTER DRAWS ATTENTION to the accelerated pace of the Stalinist degeneration in the conduct of the war. The political policy of the bureaucracy is the most vulgar nationalism. There is abundant evidence on this side of the question, and the facts cited by Natalia add more concrete instances to fill out the picture whose outlines we have long known. We do not know, however, what sentiments animate the Soviet masses in their unprecedented struggles and sacrifices. I personally am strongly convinced that the conquests and the memories of October play a bigger part than the Stalinist appeals to the past glories of Czars and Czarist generals. And, I do not for a minute forget that the objective logic of the Red Army achievements in the war against the Nazis, regardless of the officially declared aims, is profoundly revolutionary.

We know, and we have always said that the Soviet Union cannot be carried through the transition period from capitalism to socialism without workers' democracy. That is the reason we call for the revolutionary overthrow of the bureaucracy and the reinstatement of workers' democracy. By this formula we sharply distinguish our position from that of the fetishists of democracy who regard it as an end. For us it is a means to an end, i.e. the construction of the socialist society by the creative efforts of the masses and international collaboration between them. We are no less convinced that the transitional period which has assumed the form of a degenerating workers' state dominated by a nationalistic bureaucracy cannot be "permanent", or even long-lived.

The fundamental alternative confronting the Soviet Union is and remains: forward to socialism, or back to capitalism. By this formula we draw a line between ourselves and all the profound "theorists" of a new bureaucratic "class". We have less reason than ever to reconsider our conclusions on these two basic propositions.

The bankrupt bureaucracy was capable of producing only the one evil which it promised to avoid, and to avoid which, it sold out the international revolution — a war on Soviet soil.

The "theory" of a new "bureaucratic" class interposing itself between defeated capitalism and unrealized socialism was given a certain superficial plausibility only by its bolder representatives, such as Bruno R., who assimilated the regimes of Mussolini, Hitler and

Stalin into one homogeneous system. The sorry fate of Italian and German fascism, after a brief rule of 20 years in one case and 10 years in the other, seems to me to have knocked the props out from under Bruno R's "theory" of *La Bureaucratisation du Monde*. It is not necessary even to speak of his half-hearted imitators and their anaemic new, nationally-limited class of "bureaucrats" in one country.

The national-reformist policy of the bureaucracy, in its degenerating course of reaction against the October revolution, can only unless it is overthrown pile quantity upon quantity, and this in turn must, at a certain point, result in a qualitative change in the state inherited from the great revolution, I think we must look for signs of such a change in the field of Soviet economy. Politically the bureaucracy seems to have done all it can do to erase the revolution. By their politics they brought the Soviet economic system to the very brink of overthrow by Nazi militarism, and now leave it exposed, in a terribly weakened position, to the still mightier and as yet unspent military power of the Anglo-American bloc.

The same type of superficial thinking, characterized by the attempt to form political conclusions without reference to economics — the type of thinking which determined an attitude toward the Soviet Union in war without any prior estimation of its class character; which, in another version, light-mindedly assumed that the Stalin-Hitler pact would be long-lasting because of the "affinity" of the two regimes — is now quite convinced of the durability of the Anglo-American-Soviet pact of Teheran. In reality the irreconcilable conflict of economic systems completely excludes the possibility of an Anglo-American toleration of the Soviet economic system over one-sixth of the earth any longer than it is compulsory by reason of necessity, i.e., the relation of forces and the disunity in the imperialist camp. If we leave aside the prospect of workers' revolutions in the capitalist states, or such a state of unrest and insurgence as that which followed the first world war, and it is just these details that are omitted in all varieties of literary politics, then there is no room to doubt that an economic, and, if necessary, a military offensive of the allies against the Soviet Union is predetermined as soon as accounts are finally settled with the Nazis and the Japanese; perhaps even before.

Of course, there are all kinds of difficulties and complications, but — again, if we eliminate the detail of workers' revolution — the only serious question is whether the required economic concessions, opening up the Russian market to Anglo-American exploitation and, thereby, the overthrow of the Soviet economic system, is to be accomplished by war or by economic pressure and threats of war. Have such fatal concessions already been tentatively agreed upon? What was the real meaning of Eric Johnston's visit to the Soviet Union? [Eric Johnston was a US businessman who visited the USSR for a month in 1944 on Stalin's invitation and with Roosevelt's approval].

There is ample ground for the deepest suspicion flowing from the inexorable logic of the situation even if we disregard such surface indications. But so far we do not knew of any basic infringements on the Soviet economic system made during the war, and we therefore have no reason to change our attitude toward it in its relation to the capitalist world.

On the other hand, we do know that the nationalized property system permitting state planning and control (even though it is monstrously distorted and crippled by bureaucratic mismanagement and privilege), revealed an enormous power under conditions of war. We Trotskyists had more confidence in the vitality of Soviet economy than anyone else, including the conservative and cowardly bureaucracy, but all our calculations were far surpassed. The results of the Soviet-Nazi war must have had profound effects on the Russian masses.

We are shut off from every scrap of authentic information on this score. But how can anyone doubt that their self-confidence has been raised and that the returning soldiers will demand something from their victories bought at such a heavy price? What will they do when the bureaucracy offers them nothing but a still more odious oppression and an even sharper division between the privileged caste and the mass of the people? We had better not assume, prematurely, that the Russian workers have said their last word. We had better wait and see what is going to happen before we even think of playing with the idea of changing or modifying our policy which, of all schools of thought on the Russian question, is the only one that turned out to be based on the realities of the situation; the only policy that stood up under the test of such a devastating war that, as Churchill rightly said, no other regime in history could have survived it.

Our "Russian" policy, however, is only one section of a complete program based on a fundamental class concept and a world view. Our active political slogans of the day must always be consistent with our general program and express that phase of it which has the greatest urgency at the moment. It is important always to keep in mind this subordinate relationship of active slogans to the program as a whole and not to identify the one with the other. Serious politics is impossible without a firm program of Marxist internationalism; those who dispense with this chart produce nothing, as we have seen, but speculation, guess work and irresponsible experimentation.

We do not change our program. No amount of criticism and impatience can modify our "conservatism" in this respect. But to stand firmly by the program, naturally, does not authorize us to repeat the same active political slogans all the time with the same degree of emphasis. That would reduce the art of politics to memory work, and as the Old Man once remarked, make every sectarian a master politician. The art of politics consists in knowing what to do next; that is, how to apply the program of Marxism to the specific situation of the day. We do not change any of our slogans insofar as they represent, each in its own way, the various sections of our complete program. But if we are alive to the complexities and quick changes in the world political situation, as well as that at home, we must always be ready to change the emphasis with which we advance one or more slogans while holding others more or less in reserve, as the situation may require.

We think Natalia's letter must be considered from this point of view. When the Nazi military machine threatened the destruction of the Soviet Union, every communist had to put the slogan of the defense of the Soviet Union in first place. Those who denied this defense were then no longer comrades having a different opinion on a theoretical question, as Morrison still wants to treat them, as if nothing had happened, but people on the other side of the barricade with whom comradely arguments were out of season. But this fight for the defense of the Soviet Union against Nazi militarism has been decisively won. The problem will most probably arise again, with another power in place of the Nazis, but that will take some time.

The political reality of the present day is: The military, economic and moral collapse of the Hitler "new order in Europe" which some people even in our own ranks took far too seriously; the military occupation of the continent by Anglo-American and Soviet troops; the indicated beginning of a workers' revolutionary movement and the conspiracy of the imperialists to crush it with the active aid of the Stalinists. Our active slogans, the slogans which we put in first place and emphasize in all our agitation, must correspond, with this political reality.

In our opinion there can be no question of abandoning the slogan of the defense of the Soviet Union; in principle it retains all its validity and will most likely acquire burning urgency again at a later stare of events. But to continue to shout this slogan in the present situation would be the greatest political ineptitude, putting us out of tune with events. All our emphasis now must be placed on the defence of the

European Revolution against the conspirators. Our program gives us all the guidance we need, first to evaluate the problem theoretically and, on that basis, to deduce the appropriate active political slogans of the day.

"For you, the slogan of military defence of the USSR is fixed once and for all"

Natalia Sedova, 6 November 1944

I SHALL NOT DWELL on the section of your letter [a letter from the SWP office, not the previous letter from Cannon] which contains information, limiting myself to a grateful acknowledgement, I must tell you, however, that it supplied me with hardly anything new. The tireless work of our friends and its successes are a guarantee of its viability and we have all the more grounds for a fearless review of our slogans. I must come to the defense of those friends whom you condemn in connection with differences of views, for having altered the character of the mutual (personal) relations, coloring them with sharpness, hostility and impoliteness. This is quite human. We are united by unity of ideas. Whenever this is disrupted, the internal interrelations, and together with them also their external forms, become altered.

After an exposition contained in the informational section in your letter, you pass on to the controversial question of the defense of the USSR; and you begin with a declaration of your complete agreement with me in the evaluation of the Soviet bureaucracy. I never entertained the slightest doubts about it. This has been firmly established through the greatest experience over many years; this was and remains the basis of our successive conclusions. Your declaration, as well as, incidentally, the exposition in the informational section (of your letter) was necessary in order to facilitate for you the road of further discussion. But, after all, the criticism of the Russian bureaucracy does not exist of and by itself, no more than does the slogan of the defense of USSR. One must not incessantly repeat one's condemnation of Russian bureaucracy, without drawing corresponding conclusions from it. Criticism may undergo change during this or that segment of time, corresponding with the changes in the conduct of the bureaucracy itself; we criticize with greater force now one, now another of its sides. It is impermissible to confine oneself to an absolute adjustment once and forever. Criticism of this sort becomes transformed into a worthless, lifeless trinket which serves to lull oneself and to shut one's eyes to the occurring changes. By your declaration — and thereby you seek to bring about appeasement — you rid yourself of any genuine living criticism of the situation that has been created.

"Yes, yes, I am in agreement with the criticism of the Soviet bureaucracy," you say to yourself, and by this lamentation you free yourself from the analysis of the current events, current facts which are bound up with the deeds of the bureaucracy.

You behave similarly with the slogan of the defense of the USSR. You ignore the profoundest changes both in the domestic and foreign situation or the Soviet land. For you the slogan of the military defense of the USSR is fixed once and for all. You do not notice changes that have been introduced into the concept of defense by the general surrounding background; that the direct need of it has fallen away and that in view of the altered conditions now comes to the fore with all its force not the military defense of the USSR but its defense against the internal enemy, the mightiest and most dangerous one.

You forget the essence of the slogan of the defense of the USSR. It includes at one and the same time the military defense against foreign intervention and internal (defense) against the usurping bureaucracy — the latter conditions the former. I do not propose as I have already — not once — written to take off the slogan of the defense of the USSR. But in view of the altered general situation I did propose to remove military defense to the background in view of its needlessness in the present conditions and to advance to the forefront with full force that on which military defense is grounded: the struggle against the Stalinist regime.

Once again, the slogan of defense contains a two-fold meaning and depending upon the circumstances of the general political situation its center of gravity shifts now to one side, now to the other. It is you and not I who reduce to zero the meaning of the slogan of defense as a whole, when you incessantly repeat it in a situation in which the first part of the slogan does not find application; I say as a whole, because the actual situation with its full force demands a stress on the second part. By continuing in uncorresponding conditions to advance the slogan of military defense, you wholly annul the slogan of defense. Whereas I propose to preserve it by removing its first part to the third plan, saving thereby its most important ground (the second part).

"Whither the USSR?" This question must be placed in the center of our attention, of our propaganda, of our agitation. It is impermissible to plead lack of knowledge concerning what is taking place in Russia, (to cite) lack of information, Russian censorship, and so on. With respect to information, the conditions at the present time are much more favorable than was the case a few years ago, which did not prevent us (at the time) from analyzing the internal situation of the USSR, determining the character of the first workers' state in this or that period of time, analyzing the tendencies of its development, and drawing conclusions and sketching out perspectives.

Recall the numerous articles of LD on this subject — articles elucidatory, persuasive, and outlining the possible perspectives. His variant of the revolution in the USSR which would overthrow the bureaucracy, clearing the road for the defense of the Soviet Union against the onslaught of the capitalist environment, rallying the international proletariat to its aid. And the other variant: the military successes of the bureaucracy, its temporary strengthening, the mighty entrenchment of its position, but its inevitable fall, all this notwithstanding.

You recall the caution with which LD [Trotsky] each time analyzed the political condition of the workers' state in order to determine its further evolution. Absolutely correct. But caution served him for a definite aim: to carry out the analysis on the basis of carefully selected material. Caution in and of itself, just as criticism of the Soviet bureaucracy in and of itself, just like the slogan of defense in and of itself, becomes transformed into something just the opposite, something harmful, and incautious (it is at least incautious in the given conditions not to deal with burning questions), into a fear of seriously undertaking the analysis of the most important Russian question: this "bad" caution prompts you to adduce such arguments as lack of information concerning the USSR, absence of materials for arriving at judgments, and so on. And the result is that we, with excessive lack of caution have kept silent over the Russian question in the course of four years.

In your letter, you absolutely correctly take note in your letter of this most onerous omission. Unjustified caution obstructs the road to a review (an analysis) of the slogan of the defense of the USSR. We have delayed exceedingly with it, too.

You write that "the Russian proletariat has not yet spoken its final word." To whom do you address this assertion? Precisely because the Russian proletariat has not spoken its final word. I proposed to review the question of military defense by transferring the center of gravity to the internal struggle against the most dangerous and, at the given time, the one and only enemy of the Russian proletariat — the Soviet bureaucracy, summoning it (the Russian proletariat) daily and hourly to "speak its final word."

In *The Militant* No. 34 [19 August 1944] there appeared a very good article ["Warsaw Betrayal", condemned by Cannon in his letter from prison] on the actions of the Red Army (the Soviet bureaucracy) in Poland, with this exception, that, in my opinion, it is incorrect to consider partisan detachments as revolutionary. Both in their origin and in their composition they bear a purely nationalist character. If one takes into account the point of view expressed in your letter, it is possible to conclude that your attitude to the article is a negative one. Is that the case? In this connection I can adduce a quotation from the *Bulletin of the Russian Opposition* No. 72, 1938:

"Those who under the pretext of the war danger recommend the cessation of war against Stalinism (the Kremlin) are actually deserting revolutionary tasks, covering themselves with loud phrases about a world catastrophe. We have nothing in common with this utterly false view."

You pose the questions: (1) What is the degree of degeneration reached by the workers' state? (2) How long can the period of degeneration endure? (3) What form can it take? (The first two questions are scholastic.) Into the first question it would be possible to introduce greater precision: has the development of the tendencies of the workers' state to the side of capitalism been deepened in the last four years? The time terms of its degeneration can hardly be indicated with precision, and essentially this is not important. The third question is determined by the first — complete degeneration can lead only to capitalism. Regeneration is possible through revolution which will overthrow the bureaucracy and lead to socialism. The questions posed by you ought to be combined into a single one: "Forward to Socialism or back to Capitalism?" And a number of articles should be written on this subject. It is also necessary to pose the question of the Red Army; it must enter into the above-mentioned unified question, but one ought to deal in greater detail with it in a special article or pamphlet. Because there are among us the greatest errors on this score. Here is what was written as far back as May-June 1938 in the *Bulletin of the Russian Opposition* Nos. 66-67:

"The transition from a barracks army to a militia army was systematically prepared for over a decade. But from the moment when the bureaucracy completely crushed all manifestations of independence by the working class, it proceeded openly to transform the *army into an instrument of its rule.* The militia system was completely set aside. An officer caste with generals and Marshals has been reinstituted. *From an instrument of socialist defense the army has become the instrument for the defense of the privileges of the bureaucracy."* (My emphasis.)

This was written, as I have already said, in 1938. But what has happened since then? You are acquainted with it. The example of Bulgaria which you adduced in your letter, undoubtedly indicates the revolutionary spirit of the Bulgarian masses, seeking the Red Banner. But not the revolutionary spirit of the Red Army,

To all your questions, you can already now receive answers from the articles in the *Bulletin of the Russian Opposition.* They wholly retain their actuality. The anti-revolutionary tendencies of the USSR, outlined in them, have been and are deepening year by year; they have deepened catastrophically in the recent war years. I cite still another quotation from the same source:

"The evolution of the Soviet state therefore proceeds in complete contradiction with the principles of the Bolshevik program. The reason for it is that society, as has already been said, is evolving not toward socialism, but toward social contradictions. If in the future the process continues along this same road (and it is proceeding along this road — N), it will inevitably lead to the regeneration of classes, the liquidation of planned economy and the restoration of capitalist property. The state regime will in that case inevitably become fascist".

Permit me still another quotation; "Thus, while it is impermissible to reject in advance in rigidly specific cases the possibility of a 'united front' with the Thermidorian section of the bureaucracy [the text has 'bourgeoisie', obviously a slip] against the open offensive of capitalist counter-revolution, the chief political task in the USSR still remains: the overthrow of the Thermidorian bureaucracy itself. (This appears in bold face — N.) Every additional day of its rule shakes apart the socialist elements of economy and increases the chances of capitalist restoration".

Articles from the *Bulletin of the Russian Opposition* on this subject could be very instructive now. It is incomprehensible why they have remained unutilized in the course of four years. Not only were they not read in their entirety, but they were never quoted, nor referred to — this is very indicative. Only our Spanish friends have occupied themselves with this question. While the articles are being written on the subject treated by us: "Whither the USSR?" I would propose that a number of articles from the *Bulletin of the Russian Opposition* be translated both for the magazine and for the paper; and that they be carried from issue to issue. One could begin say with the article "Does the Soviet Government still continue to follow the principles adopted 20 years ago?" (*Bulletin of the Russian Opposition*, Nos. 66-67). The Bulletin ought to be studied and everything necessary taken from it.

Finally, a few more words about the Russian masses. There cannot be any doubts that the Russian masses are dissatisfied; that there exist oppositional elements and illegal organizations in the USSR. The Master of the Soviet land cannot pass over to capitalism without a counter-revolution, failing this he will not be able to tear away from the peasants the land for which they struggled for ages. It is still more difficult to perform this operation at a time when Europe is seized by a revolutionary movement. "There cannot be any reason to doubt that the overwhelming majority of the communists as well as of the population do not want a return to capitalism, especially now that capitalism has plunged mankind into a now war." (*Bulletin of the Russian Opposition*, Nos, 82-83). From this flows the vital need of intensified propaganda on the above-described subject. Let us warn against the mortal danger threatening the Russian proletariat, let us explain to them the causes of it, let us summon them to a struggle against the usurpers and gravediggers of the great revolution, basing ourselves on the European revolutionary movement.

One additional comment: the article, "Does the Soviet government still continue to follow the principles adopted 20 years ago?" should be supplemented with detailed notes, pointing out the road of further degeneration 1938-1944, and corroborated with the corresponding (enormous) materials which are at our disposal; and this should be done as quickly as possible.

First letter from Sedova: *New International*, March 1945 (in article "From the Bureaucratic Jungle, part 2"). Second letter from Sedova, and letter from Cannon: SWP Internal Bulletin vol.6 no.9 (October 1944). The letter from Cannon, written in sections because of prison regulations, is undated in the SWP Internal Bulletin but dated in *Letters from Prison*, Pathfinder, 1968. Third letter from Sedova: SWP Internal Bulletin vol.6 no.13 (December 1944)

"Revolutionary" Stalinism and "Trotsky's Red Army"

Louis Jacobs (1944)

THE [16-19 NOVEMBER 1944 SWP] CONVENTION has before it a resolution on the European revolution and the tasks confronting the advanced workers. So far as I am aware, this resolution will be adopted unanimously with possible amendments which are unlikely to affect its "line". A separate resolution, not unrelated to be sure, will deal with the question of our attitude on defense of the Soviet Union. Here again we will most likely arrive at unanimity, I have not seen this resolution, but I base myself on the published letters of Natalia [Sedova Trotsky] and Martin [James P Cannon] and on what I know went on in the PC [Political Committee of the SWP].

Here, one would suppose, is an ideal convention for the fundamental education of the party. Unfortunately, this is far from the case. Actually, the Committee is trying to avoid any kind of real education of the membership, due to its unusual hypersensitivity to criticism. The very resolutions adopted should have been the occasion for some open self-criticism, as I propose to show.

Let me explain here that what is involved is not at all mere polemics that went on inside the precincts of the PC. It is perfectly natural that differences should exist on questions that arise inside the Committee. What concerns me is not how we arrived at a line through discussions of the Committee itself. No. I am concerned with a line arrived at without discussion at all (except on my part), without any motions made in the Committee "officially"; a line that appeared in the press of the party on the initiative of the editors with the consent of a committee within the committee, as a "fait accompli". I am concerned with a line that was wrong not in the Committee alone, but in the public press, one that has since been "corrected" after the lapse of months of incorrectness without so much as informing the party. I am concerned with the attempt to hide this patent fact from the Convention and to place, not organizational criticism, but political criticism, in a virtual strait-jacket under the guise of "discipline."

The question of line in respect to the European events first arose in connection with Poland and Yugoslavia. It was I who raised the problem of Yugoslavia twice more on the agenda, each time criticizing the attitude already adopted in the press without any authorization. The line was in fact adopted as a fait accompli. My criticism was never even discussed, but was met by complete, frigid silence. Let the Committee now read to the convention one single scrap of evidence authorizing the line taken in the press! Instead we have a line thrust into the press over my sole protest.

But was there any change in line? We must how examine this question. We turn to an editorial in the April 1943 issue of *Fourth International*.

"As John G. Wright explains in 'The Civil War in Yugoslavia', in this issue, Stalin himself is being driven to take steps which may well go beyond his control and in the end undermine the Kremlin bureaucracy and unleash the European Revolution."

Wright raised the question of our attitude towards the Partisan movement on the one side, and towards Stalin's grabs of territory on the other. Wright was encouraged in this matter by Comrade Cannon. But when I challenged the new line, Cannon refrained from participation in the discussion. No motion was made at all, and it was more or less understood that the matter would be discussed further.

From Wright's article we quote the following:

"But the same fundamental forces arising out of the irreconcilable clash between Soviet economy and world imperialism are driving the bureaucratic caste to measures... which are revolutionary in their objective consequences... The Stalinist bureaucracy depends for its own existence upon the maintenance of the workers' state created by the October Revolution. In desperation and as a last resort this bureaucracy has proved itself capable of so acting in self-defense as to stimulate revolutionary developments."

Bethinking himself of our previous line, Wright adds a caution that:

"The record of Stalinism warns that the Kremlin clique at a later stage will try to restrain within its bureaucratic strait-jacket and to suppress the self-action of the revolutionary workers and peasants."

He continues, however:

"But given continued successes of the Red Army and a favorable relationship of forces vis-a-vis London and Washington, the Sovietization of Yugoslavia along with sections of Poland and Eastern Europe is, even under Stalin, by no means excluded."

Far from being excluded, this became more and more the line followed by the editors of both the *FI* and *The Militant*.

Wright laid the basis for his thesis on Stalinism becoming "objectively" revolutionary, like it or not, in earlier issues of *FI*. This we shall see in connection with his theory on the Red Army. The February 20, 1943 issue of *The Militant* contains an article on "Military Aspects and

Political Roots" by Wright. This begins to set the foundations of the idea that military necessity forces Stalin to use revolutionary means. No wonder Wright (and with him the PC) was willing to support every fait accompli of Stalin's. This political support was given each time on the grounds of defense of the Soviet Union. Speaking of the attempted Federation proposed by Poland, in reality directed against the Soviet Union, he writes:

"Such a coalition would obviously not be directed primarily against Germany, which would have to be defeated before a Federation could be established; its chief purpose would be to block off and isolate the Soviet Union from the rest of Europe, to function as an organized obstacle to the spread of revolution."

The spread of the revolution is here clearly to come from Stalin and the Red Army.

To be sure, Wright thought that he was basing himself on Trotsky's views on Poland and Finland, views concerning which he miseducated the party quite badly.

"Just as in the period of the Stalin-Hitler pact Leon Trotsky used the events in Poland as the key to the Finnish developments, so today we can use the events in Finland, the northern flank of the USSR to understand the civil war in Yugoslavia and the meaning of Stalinist intervention there... Stalin took preparatory steps for the Sovietization of Finland by trying to provoke a civil war and by establishing his puppet Kuusinen government."

Thus Stalin was preparing the ground for the Sovietization of Yugoslavia (*The Militant*, April 3, 1943). This same issue contains another article by Wright on the "Civil War in Hitler's Rear Spreads to Poland."

"The successes of the Red Army and the heroic defense by the Soviet masses of the remaining conquests of the October Revolution have added new explosive power to the irrepressible conflict in Yugoslavia and have spread it beyond the boundaries. Poland is now aflame. This inspiring news can no longer be concealed by the 'democratic allies' of the Kremlin."

What remained concealed to Wright was that these same allies would shortly recognize the regime he was so busy hailing. But, had his analysis been correct, that recognition need not have so abruptly changed his mind about Yugoslavia.

The January 29, 1944 Militant contains Wright's article "Red Army Victories Alarm Stalin's Allies". He quotes [US Communist Party General Secretary] Browder as openly declaring Stalin's intent to prevent any revolution. Browder was interpreting the Teheran agreement and he said in his speech:

"British and American ruling circles had to be convinced that their joint war together with the Soviet Union against Hitlerism would not result in the Soviet socialist system being extended to Western Europe under the stimulus of the victorious Red Army."

"But the whole point is", says Wright, "that the capitalists refuse to reconcile themselves to the price that Stalin needs and demands, that is, the strengthening of the Soviet Union in Eastern Europe. Stabilization of capitalism in Europe is impossible without a capitalist Poland as a 'buffer' in order to keep the Soviet system isolated in preparation for its eventual destruction. Churchill and Roosevelt know this and are working to this end... Furthermore implicit in the Kremlin's territorial demands is the extension of Soviet property forms to the whole of Poland. That this threat is not distant is borne out by the latest pronouncement by Stalin's Union of Polish Patriots calling not only for the inclusion of Silesia, Pomerania, East Prussia and Danzig in a 'New Poland', but also for the seizure of Polish landed estates, their division among the peasants and the nationalization of industries and mines taken from the Germans. Inasmuch as Polish industry is almost wholly in the hands of the Germans, the realization of this program would signify the complete destruction of Polish capitalism and a giant step in the inevitable extension of Soviet property forms far beyond the frontiers of 1939. In its turn, this carries a twofold threat to capitalism: first, in addition to strengthening the USSR immeasurably, it would greatly hamper further attempts to isolate it; second, the revolutionary wave in Europe, especially in Germany, would receive so mighty an impulsion from such developments in the territories of former Poland, let alone Silesia, East Prussia, etc., that the attempt to drown the coming European Revolution in blood would be rendered well-nigh impossible."

How did this line prepare the party for later events? How did it prepare for our present revived Trotskyist line on the role of Stalinism? Where was Cannon with his warning against speculation? The line of Wright, quite different indeed from that of Trotsky, was filled with illusions, could lead only to surprises, gave credit to the Stalinists "despite themselves" as pursuing policies which would "immeasurably strengthen" the USSR, and would, practically automatically, through the victories of the Red Army, spread the Revolution throughout Europe.

This line was in complete contradiction to all the warnings of the Old Man. It gave first importance to the "nationalized property" under Stalinism, treating this nationalized property as a fetish.

Trotsky said: "The primary political criterion for us is not the transformation of property relations in this or another area, however important these may be in themselves, but rather the change in the consciousness and organization of the world proletariat, the raising of their capacity to defend former conquests and accomplishing new ones. From this one and the only decisive standpoint, the politics of Moscow, taken as a whole, completely retains its reactionary character and remains the chief obstacle on the road to the world revolution."

Trotsky warned again and again that the extension of territory dominated by the bureaucracy, even when "cloaked" by socialist measures, might augment the prestige of the Kremlin, and "engender illusions concerning the possibility of replacing the proletarian revolution by bureaucratic maneuvers." Wright (and not alone Wright) tended to engender precisely all the illusions that Trotsky tried so unremittingly to dispel. Said Trotsky: "We do not entrust the Kremlin with any historic mission. We were and remain against seizures of new territories by the Kremlin."

But that is hardly the only sphere in which illusions were created. I must be pardoned for going back to the *FI* for 1941, because the formulations there are completely in line with what Wright had to say later concerning the Red Army. At the time it appeared as exuberant exaggeration. The August 1941 issue contains his article "Soviet Union at War". Here we have the beginnings of a very "special" theory concerning the place and role of the Red Army. To make perfectly clear the offense in attitude revealed on the part of Wright and his collaborators, it is only necessary to see what Trotsky wrote as far back as 1936 in *The Revolution Betrayed*.

The section on the Red Army shows how the degeneration of the Soviet Union is most clearly of all indicated in the changes in the Red Army. Theoretically this would naturally be so. Practically it is indubitable. Trotsky says:

"The army is a copy of society and suffers from all its diseases, usually at a higher temperature."

Further, in discussing the restoration of caste and rank worship, he says:

"No army, however, can be more democratic than the regime which nourishes it. The source of bureaucratism with its routine and swank is not the special needs of military affairs, but the political needs of the ruling stratum. In the army these needs only receive their most finished expression. The restoration of officers' castes eighteen years after their revolutionary abolition testifies equally to the gulf which already separates the rulers from the ruled, to the loss by the Soviet Army of the chief qualities which gave it the name of 'Red', and to the cynicism with which the bureaucracy erects these consequences of degeneration into law."

This was in 1936-7 when the purges took place in this very army to bend it completely to Stalin's will.

Now Wright in 1941, carried quite away by his "Soviet patriotism":

"It is not Stalin's Red Army that has successfully resisted the first two Nazi offensives. It is the Red Army of the October Revolution. It is Trotsky's Red Army, which was built in the fire of the Civil War, built not from the wreckage of the old Czarist armies but completely anew — unlike any other army in history."

One must believe in ghosts to write this after all that had happened. By October Wright had hypnotized himself completely with words. His article on "Trotsky and the Red Army" performs what might be termed a mighty service for Stalin. Degeneration hasn't gone so far after all. The Stalinists were saying that the purges had actually strengthened the Red Army. Victories, it seemed, went to Wright's head like wine.

"Without the essential organ of the Red Army the workers' state could not have endured for more than a few months. It could never have survived the years of Stalinist rule. Again this should not be understood in a purely military sense. In the life of the workers' state the army plays a role that is qualitatively different from the role played by military forces in a class society ruled by an exploiting minority."

Is there perhaps hidden in those words the idea that the Red Army, despite Stalin, fights for the international working class?

"The Kremlin is of course trying to usurp credit for the heroic resistance of the Red Army, but Stalin will not succeed in this. We Trotskyists link up the present heroic resistance of the Red soldiers directly (!) with the Russian October and the Civil War. Whoever is astonished by the power of Soviet resistance is unaware that only the revolution unleashes forces capable of overcoming insuperable obstacles. This is being demonstrated in the battlefields today.

"This was most graphically illustrated in 1918 in the organization of the first victorious army of the proletarian revolution... Terrible as were the blows dealt by Stalin to the Red Army, it remains the one institution least affected by his degenerated regime. This extraordinary development (note: extraordinary indeed) which no one could have foreseen, may well play a vital role in determining the future not only of the Soviet Union but of mankind."

One could pursue this theme right up to the present moment in the writings not only of Wright but of almost all comrades of the Committee. The Red Army apparently is something totally different from the other institutions of Stalin. Yes, our resolution now "corrects" this view somewhat by magisterially laying down that the Red Army is just another instrument of Stalinist policy. Stalin does really control the army and runs it on nationalist lines. But where is the criticism of the kind of "Soviet patriotism" that engendered illusions concerning this instrument of Stalinist policy?

Trotsky taught that there were no guarantees concerning the use of the Red Army. He refused to guarantee that it would never be used for reactionary purposes. Wright gave somewhat of a guarantee by declaring that the institution most affected by degeneration was least affected. Wright helped create an illusion that when it came to a final show-down and the Red Army might be ordered to drown a workers' revolution (say the German workers) in blood, the Red Army would refuse and would turn its arms against the Stalinist bureaucracy. There can be no guarantee at all on this score, one way or the other. We can only watch to judge tendencies and evaluate events. But certainly one can say that if at some stage the Red Army should reach the stage of disobedience of reactionary orders (so far it has carried out completely the will of Stalin) then this will be no simple process in which the Red Army itself remains intact. A vast section of the officers' caste will undoubtedly be found on the side of the bureaucracy. A political revolution is no palace affair. It will mean civil war with every institution involved, not at all excluding the Red Army by some magic of Wright's.

Our party had been the most consistent and correct regarding phenomena connected with the USSR. We prided ourselves on our ability to grasp every nuance of Stalinist degeneration and expose it to the working class. How does it come then, that we have now to devote such length in our resolution to variations on the theme of the reactionary role of Stalinism? That very fact shows that we consider this (certainly no new line) essential at this time, it is essential because it is a necessary corrective of a false line that was pursued in our press. But the resolution tries to hide this fact. It contains criticism in a completely hidden form known only to the initiate at the top. Let us for a moment look at the one paragraph that indulges in such "distant" criticism. It is contained in what was Paragraph 51 in the first draft.

"All those who are propagating the idea that the Kremlin bureaucracy intends to 'Sovietize' Europe under Stalin's Bonapartist dictatorship misunderstand both the class nature of the Soviet Union and the meaning of Stalinist foreign policy. Their theory, which can only disorient the European proletariat and divert it from its necessary tasks, represents in essence a theoretical 'justification' for their own abject surrender to Allied imperialism. The European Revolution cannot be harnessed by any bureaucracy".

When I inquired in the Committee as to whom this was directed at (a not altogether naive question on my part) I was informed that it was meant for the Social Democrats who were warning the "democracies" against Stalinism because it had this aim. But I had taken up in the Committee some time before the common attitude expressed by Wright and by Dan, the Menshevik. Both were in favor of the grabs of territory by Stalin on the ground that they served to spread the proletarian revolution over Europe. Dan and Wright had in common the views that Stalin despite himself would be forced to resort to revolutionary measures to save himself. I brought in quotations from Dan's magazine *Novy Put* which could not have been in any way distinguished from Wright's line, except that Dan thought it possible to reform Stalinism.

The truth is that Wright had been "hauled over the coals" for his whole line when events had broken over the head of the Committee and shown how disastrous that line was. M. Stein [then national organisation secretary of the SWP] informed me concerning this fact and was himself taken aback when I expressed astonishment that this should be done in hidden form among a group of friends, not even in the PC. Naturally in that case there could be no question of criticizing Wright openly in the party or in the convention. But what becomes then of the political education of the party membership? Are they permitted to know what is correct and what is incorrect? Or is it sufficient in a centralized party for the leadership to be educated? The paragraph remains inexplicable except for its indirect and implied criticism of Wright and Warde.

[In] the October 30, 1943 *Militant* appear two articles by Wright on the Red Army victories. They are veritable paeans of victory, without a single trace of warning that these victories by the Red Army do not necessarily lead to the revolution, but with continued Stalinist domination would lead to reaction. The theme underlying these hosannas remained that the Red Army was not the same as Stalin at all, that its victories would inevitably bring the revolution; in fact, the very advances of the Red Army were part of the revolution. Wright says:

"Militarily the Soviet Union is beginning to assert itself as a dominant power. The revolutionary forces in Europe threaten to explode with unprecedented force. Under the impact of the war, the masses who suffered one defeat after another for more than two decades are clearly preparing to reenter the political arena. The altered relationship of forces greatly narrows down Stalin's field for diplomatic maneuvers and agreements. The more this relationship of forces alters in favor of the USSR, all the more decisively must the laws of the class struggle assert themselves, bringing to the forefront what has temporarily been submerged: that is, the fundamental antagonism of our epoch between the decayed system of capitalism, and the new social order which the Soviet Union still represents despite its degeneration under Stalin... Stalin and his allies are seeking a common solution for problems which can be resolved in life only through mortal struggle".

The very next issue of *The Militant*, alas, had to devote itself to an explanation of the Moscow Deal [the agreement reached at the 18 October-11 November US-UK-USSR conference]. The victories in short gave Stalin more scope than ever before for agreements on his own terms. The prestige of the Kremlin, we must reluctantly admit, grew among the workers also. Instead of warning against the effects of this growing prestige, Wright was lulling the workers with soporifics.

Let us sum up the theses followed explicitly or implicitly by Wright and the editors of our press.

(1) the advance of the Red Army creates automatically a revolutionary wave in the occupied lands.

(2) Stalinism against its own will, due to the exigencies of military defense, is forced to resort to revolutionary measures. Its objective role is therefore progressive and worthy of support.

(3) To the Red Army in particular must go the credit for the extension of the Revolution through Sovietization and the nationalizing of property, since this institution is the least of all tainted by Stalinist degeneration.

Our resolution on the European Revolution contains an excellent old truism: "To be forewarned is to be forearmed. The advanced workers of Europe must sound the alarm! They have the clear duty of warning the working class of the counter-revolutionary schemes of Stalin and his native henchmen. The working class must be prepared to combat Stalinist treachery and sell-outs." How could our editors forewarn, or our Committee? In fact, how did they act when a forewarning was attempted (by myself)? Let us see.

The name Tito Broz was given wide publicity from the very first in connection with the Partisan movement. We traced this name back in the literature on the Yugoslav workers' movement. It appeared in no loss a place than *The Militant* itself, in the articles by Ciliga (1936). Those articles referred to the double-dealing Stalinist agent and police spy Brezovich. It was only a short time later (this occurred in December 1943) that positive proof was obtained that this Tito Broz and Brezovich were one and the same. I requested that at least the information contained in *The Militant* be reprinted, first under the title "Is this Tito?

Later in the early part of January, 1944 an article was presented exposing Tito completely as a GPU agent of Stalin. This news was in its way sensational, but our purpose was hardly more sensationalism. To us it was self-understood that a GPU agent could only act to betray the movement led by him in the interests of his boss in the Kremlin. The manner in which this material was handled was shameful. The editors took literally months to "verify" what was stated. A motion was finally adopted to publish the material. But Martin [Cannon] wrote that "we are not social democrats" (meaning I presume that it is not germane or material that the head of a movement we were supporting in our press was a GPU agent.) The editors finally sabotaged the whole issue by reprinting (two months later) a garbled account on the back cover of the *FI* in small print. Nobody understood what was involved. And, of course, this was the intention in so printing the material.

Why was this done in such fashion? The role of Tito became increasingly clear during the time the editors (and the Committee) were pondering on how to avoid printing the exposé. If at the start their line prevented the Committee from printing material that could only appear counterposed to this line (as indeed was my intention), later, after matters began to clarify "obviously", the Committee played the politics of prestige. It wished to cover up its previous line and give itself time to switch over to new rails. Had the material appeared in time, the later events in Yugoslavia would have been well prepared for in advance. Workers would indeed have been forewarned. Was not Martin, in his way, shielding Tito from exposure by calling the attitude of denouncing a GPU agent in our press social-democratic? What is social-democratic about it? The real trouble was that Comrade Martin was apparently still holding to Wright's line on Yugoslavia and the Stalinist role there.

Comrade Martin was present in the Committee whom the Yugoslav line was first broached by Wright. His failure to carry through a thorough and earnest discussion not only on that question but on the matter of Poland and the Stalinist grabs of territory, made him a "victim" when the Committee later changed its line without having as yet convinced him.

We are far from having exhausted the Yugoslav issue. There is no worse politics than that which gives its support to a movement (in this case the Partisans) which later turns out to be reactionary due to its leadership, without having warned in time against that leadership. Tito duped the workers and peasants. Wright gave approval, unwittingly, during the process. To yell "Betrayal" afterwards against the betrayer hardly puts one in position to give advice to the masses. "To support the hangman in every action directed against the workers is a crime, if not treachery."

The attempt to cover up the line later without criticism and discussion not only does not educate anybody. It miseducates — but only leads to the same or to new errors. Warde, in the process of correcting the line of uncritical support to Tito's movement, repeats the very error which caused the trouble in the first instance. He wishes us to understand that the Partisan movement was a real mass movement. Wright and Warde are virtually hypnotized when it comes to mass movements. The question is what kind of mass movement, what program does it follow, who leads it?

Our theoretic stand on the problem of national liberation combined with the Spanish experience, and above all our knowledge that the Stalinists were in control of the movement — these should have made interpretation of Yugoslav events relatively easy. But we have seen the line followed in our press, a line which, in the main, gave uncritical support to the Partisans; which failed to warn of the real nature of this national liberation movement in time; which spoke of the fusing of the national liberation struggle with the class struggle even after all efforts in the direction of class struggle had been suppressed; which failed to expose Tito and his real aims so that his later openly reactionary steps came as a surprise. It was a line whose tendency was to keep the workers and peasants enslaved, rather than to help free them.

We have seen what Wright and Warde said about Stalinism in Yugoslavia after its role became clear. Let us now go back to what was said earlier in the press. The April 1943 issue of the *FI* has Wright's article on "Civil War in Yugoslavia". He says:

"Generally speaking, all movements in society and all the key problems including those of 'National Liberation' are governed by and solved through the mechanism of classes and the dynamics of the class struggle. In occupied Europe the national question is fused intimately with the social. In the case of Yugoslavia the struggle against the occupying armies could not unfold without entering immediately into a head-on collision with the Axis collaborationists headed by the native landlords and capitalists and their central and local bureaucracy. The Stalinists inside and outside the USSR have sought to hide the inspiring fact that, while ostensibly operating within the framework of 'national liberation', the guerrilla movement no sooner acquired a mass character than it inexorably proceeded to assume class struggle forms... the policy of the guerrillas even under Stalinist domination has gone far beyond partial seizures... The wording of the Stalinist dispatch is a euphemistic way of describing agrarian revolution. The Yugoslav peasantry, land hungry for centuries, have seized the opportunity to divide the landlords' estates... It is a fact that the Stalinist-controlled leadership of the Partisans has tried, if not to foster, then at least to supply a legal cover for some of these land seizures".

Wright goes on:

"The Kremlin must secure the southern Balkan flank not only against Hitler but against the present allies just as, in the period of the Stalin-Hitler pact it was driven to protect the northern flank in Finland against its then 'ally'. Just as Leon Trotsky used the Polish experience of 1939 as the key to the Finnish events that followed, so can we use the Finnish experience as the key to the current situation in Yugoslavia... The Kremlin is seeking to exploit the civil war in Yugoslavia — where the Communist Party still retains a mass following — through the establishment of a central government with a program which virtually duplicates that of Kuusinen's puppet government".

There is not a single trace of any attempt to analyze or evaluate the forces involved, their leadership, their policies. Instead we have the worst kind of illusions. "Every success of the Red Army adds new explosive power to the irrepressible conflict in Yugoslavia and spreads it beyond the boundaries". The entire Wright thesis is then transferred to Poland. There follows a kind of ritualistic phrase: "It requires a clear conception of the class nature of the Soviet Union and the parasitic role of the Stalinist bureaucracy to analyze correctly this seemingly unprecedented situation." Just how the parasitic bureaucracy fits in is most unclear, unless one is to understand that mechanically and automatically the working class nature of the Soviet Union determines the merging of the war into revolution, with the parasites (even though in control) carried along willy-nilly. And in fact this distorted concept was precisely the one held: "But the same fundamental forces arising out of the irreconcilable clash between Soviet economy and world imperialism are driving the bureaucratic caste to measures which are revolutionary in their objective consequences...

The Stalinist bureaucracy depends for its own existence upon the maintenance of the workers' state created by the October Revolution. In desperation and as a last resort this bureaucracy has proved itself capable of acting in self-defense so as to stimulate revolutionary developments."

The not by any means consistent line of the editors and the Committee based itself on formulas treated mechanically as fetishes, as quantities fixed once for all. The world may wax, the world may wane, but the formulas are unchanging and go on forever.

The unconditional defense of the Soviet Union – that which differentiated us from the petty-bourgeois Shachtmanites – at least that was handled properly in our press, was it not? This, to be frank, was if anything our weakest side. You will find in *The Case of Leon Trotsky* his answer to a question on this score:

"Trotsky: it is a very complicated question. I believe that during the war the allies can impose on the Soviet Union such concessions, social and economic concessions, that the Soviet Union can become a bourgeois state. It is, in connection with bourgeois states, all alone. At the end of the war it is possible we will have a capitalist Soviet Union. If the Soviet Union will oppose the pressure of its allies, then I believe the allies will come together with its enemies to stifle the Soviet Union at the end of the war... But in the Soviet Union, I would support the Soviet Union, the Red Army, the Soviet State against all its enemies. Because...

"Finerty: One way you would try to sustain or support the Soviet Union would be by fomenting revolutions in Germany and Japan?

"Trotsky: By both means. In the Soviet Union, I would try to be a good soldier, win the sympathy of the soldiers, and fight well. Then, at a good moment, when victory is assured, I would say: 'Now we must finish with the bureaucracy'."

Trotsky later makes the analogy between this situation and the Kerensky period of the Revolution.

Our press, up to May 1944, did not follow this line at all. We had always interpreted the unconditional defense as meaning that while the Soviet Union was in immediate danger, we would not demand as a condition for our support the removal of Stalin. Yet, in *The Militant* you will find things quite in reverse. During the period of defeats, we demanded the removal of Stalin, without the removal the Soviet Union was bound to be defeated. Then when Stalin began to be victorious we hailed the victories no end and, forgetting completely that we were for a political revolution against Stalin, spoke in the most glowing terms of the wonderful unity of the Russian people.

Trotsky had explained so many times that our defense of the Soviet Union had nothing in common with the politics of the totalitarian regime, that: "While arms in hand they deal blows to Hitler, the Bolshevik-Leninists will at the same time conduct revolutionary propaganda against Stalin, preparing his overthrow at the next and perhaps very near stage."

Did Frank make a political concession to Stalinism or not when he wrote on December 4, 1943 in "Labor's Socialist Perspectives and Tasks of the Revolutionary Struggle in Europe": "The next great event in the course of this world war, which has affected the whole course of the military struggle and altered the whole relationship of forces, is the amazing and unprecedented victories of the Red Army... How is anybody going to explain today that amazing unity of Soviet peoples, that unprecedented vitality and morale which exists throughout the Red Army and the peoples of the Soviet Union, except by the theory that the October Revolution, though stifled and degraded, still lives... The contradiction is there, and at a subsequent stage it must again break into the open, and unless the European Revolution intervenes, must eventually lead to armed conflict between the USSR and Anglo-American capitalism."

The complete unity of the Soviet peoples — under the totalitarian regime of Stalin! How could one possibly call for political revolution in that case? The unity of the Soviet peoples amidst the growth of inequality and an almost complete indifference of the bureaucracy to the lot and fate of the people during the war. The unity of the Soviet peoples — and the imprisonment even during the war not of tens of thousands, or hundreds of thousands, but of millions in the concentration camps of the Kremlin! Could Stalin have wished for better propaganda in his favor? Stalin could have pointed to our press and asked what further proof was necessary that his killing off of all the oppositionists had united and strengthened the USSR.

Do you want further proof as to the attitude towards Stalinism? Martin remarks in his letter (on which more anon) "The results of the Soviet-Nazi War must have had profound effects on the Russian masses. We are shut off from every scrap of authentic information on this score." By chance Stanley happened to obtain the report of a doctor who had escaped into Russia from Poland when the Nazis invaded his country. He traveled to the far North, to Moscow, to Siberia, He saw in particular the life of the refugees and of the working masses. This report was made available to *The Militant* editors in the form of an article reporting verbatim, questions and answers. Invaluable material. It was refused publication! On what ground, you will ask in utter astonishment? Were the facts questioned? No. Warde and Frank (the same Frank who had written on Russian unity at exactly the same time the article was submitted) did not question the article at all. They agreed as to its complete authenticity. But it painted too black a picture. Too black a picture for whom, may one enquire? For the workers who believed that everything was hunky dory in the Soviet Union? For the editors who were painting up the revolutionary consequences of the Red Army victories? This reason was later modified — you will hardly believe it. The second reason was that the article was not political enough! It would serve to discourage workers.

Today the article of the doctor would be printed. The false line which virtually forced the editors to exclude them has been modified enough to permit this.

The article would have shown the utter emptiness of speaking of the "unity" of the masses of Russia, suffering under the whiplash of a criminally-hardened, utterly indifferent bureaucracy, a gang interested solely in its own future, its own power, its own privileges.

How then can we speak of having, in our press, laid the basis, when it became clear that the USSR would be victorious, for the overthrow of Stalinism? What understanding did the Committee show on the entire meaning of our defense of the Soviet Union?

The touchstone of this question came with the events in Poland, particularly in Warsaw. The line followed in our press on the entire question of Stalin's grab of the eastern part of Poland, was one of support, political support, on the ground that this would mean the nationalizing of more property and, thereby, the strengthening of the USSR. Read, if you please, the editorial on Stalin and Poland in the February 8, 1944 issue of *The Militant*. I have already quoted Wright's article in the January 29, 1944 issue on "Red Army Victories Alarm Stalin's Allies". These articles violated the clearly stated programmatic line of Trotsky that we take no political responsibility for Stalin's grabs of territory, that the bureaucratic extension of nationalized property to this or that bit of land is secondary to us, the primary thing being the world revolution to which the defense of the Soviet Union is subordinated. The Moscow and Tehran agreements had, however, already raised many misgivings in the Committee. It is this that explains how my article got into the press as an editorial in the February 5, 1944 issue of *The Militant*. This "Program for Poland" was intended as a corrective of the line previously followed on Poland. It places reliance, not on Stalinism, not on any automatic or bureaucratic spread of the Revolution, but rather on the independent action of the Polish workers and peasants.

The role of Stalinism was being demonstrated in event after event that shattered the line the press had previously pursued. You would look in vain for any open correction there, or even any educational discussion in the party. The February 12, 1944 issue contains the editorial "Stalinism and the Danger to Europe's Coming Revolution".

Here, after discussion in the Committee, we find:

"It is this haunting fear of the European Revolution, it is their common determination to crush it that brought the Anglo-American imperialists together with Stalin, first at Moscow, then at Tehran... The Stalinist bureaucracy, itself panic-stricken before the revolutionary specter, likewise wants to crush the revolution in its desperate attempt to preserve its criminal regime by maintaining the capitalist status quo in Europe".

The Committee corrected itself, but only in part and without deigning to answer my sharp attacks on the previous line. Speaking of the Polish underground, the February 12, 1944 editorial says: "They understand that Stalin's Kremlin gang came into Poland not as liberators but as oppressors". But the Stalin gang came into Polish territory in the form of the Red Army! This fact did not strike the editors. Later they would have to say that the Red Army is but the instrument of Stalinist policy.

The May Day Manifesto returns to a correct line without, however, understanding its full import, "inseparable from the real defense of the Soviet Union is the irreconcilable fight against Stalinism, its regime and its policies." It says, this time quite correctly: "Down with Stalinism!" What was not understood was that this very call meant a change of emphasis on the slogan of unconditional defense of the Soviet Union. The USSR was clearly going to be victorious. Hence the danger had lessened, our unconditional defense must begin to retire to the background. But by this time the Committee was treating the formula of defense in purely fetishist fashion, as something unchanging and irrevocable.

The truly pathetic culmination on the question of defense, and on the question of national liberation, came in August 1944. The August 5th issue contained the editorial "Dangers and Tasks Facing the Workers of Poland". This declares :

"Moscow's declaration explicitly states: The Soviet Government declares that it does not pursue aims... of a change of social structure in Poland..."

What has happened to the theory that Stalin must spread the Revolution all over Europe despite himself? What has happened to the Wright-Warde theory concerning the Red Army? The editorial speaks of the Polish workers and says:

"They must seek to enlist in their common cause the rank and file soldiers of the Red Army, and forge bonds of solidarity with the millions of Soviet workers who remain true to the internationalist ideas and revolutionary traditions of 1917. Through their independent struggle the Polish workers will inspire the Soviet masses to settle accounts with the hated Stalinist bureaucracy."

Those members of the Committee who still held to the old line, who did not know what had transpired at the center, immediately recognized that there had been a change, one with which they disagreed. Martin [i.e. Cannon] thereupon wrote a letter to the Committee. This letter, written on August 16, 1944, and a later letter I propose to quote in full. I know that wild accusations will be hurled at me as a violator of discipline of the Committee. This too I propose to answer, and to leave to the convention and to the party who truly violates the discipline of a Trotskyist party.

Excerpt from a letter from Martin's collaborator [i.e., in fact, Cannon again]:

"In our opinion, the editorial on Poland in the August 5 Militant falls into error through a tendency to leap over the incompleted stage of European events – the Soviet Union's life and death struggle against the armies of Hitler. 'With their own armed forces they (the Polish workers) must continue their independent revolutionary struggle' the editorial states, and adds in a later paragraph 'against all the agents....of the counter-revolutionary Stalinist bureaucracy.' This sweeping statement can be understood as implying armed struggle against the Red Army, which is the effective controlling force under Stalin's command in Poland. Nothing is said elsewhere in the editorial to negate this implication. We must not forget that as long as the Red Army remains locked in combat with the armies of a capitalist Germany, our slogan 'Unconditional defense of the Soviet Union' retains its full content, regardless of Stalin's counter-revolutionary policies in occupied areas beyond the Soviet borders.

"Furthermore, this slogan must at all times be emphasized, especially in editorials such as the one on Poland. We should outline a revolutionary program for Poland, as the editorial does. But we must make it explicitly clear that in the struggle for this program there is to be no sabotaging of the Soviet Union war against Hitler. A workers' revolution in Germany will drastically alter the character of the military struggle in Europe. Events will have reached a new, higher revolutionary stage. Then we will approach all questions in the light of the changed circumstances. But Hitler is still in power. Germany remains capitalist. Its imperialist assault on the Soviet Union is not yet totally defeated. We must keep our policy carefully attuned to the situation as it is right now. Because of the present dispute on the European question, we must be doubly careful in thinking these problems through to the end before writing about them. Great care should be taken in treating the Polish and similar questions in the convention's resolution. We must never forgot that our party statements and editorials are now regarded as programmatic documents and taken with the greatest seriousness by the revolutionary workers of the entire world, This imposes upon us a stern responsibility to be careful what we say. This carefulness, this aversion to the practice of going off half-cocked, this habit of waiting to think things through before we speak, has been denominated 'conservatism' by light-minded feuilleton writers, who imagine themselves to be master politicians. But it is this very 'conservatism' that has given all our previous resolutions since the death of the Old Man their thought-out character and made them stand up from year to year as supplements logically flowing from one unchanging program, and like the program itself, needing no fundamental revision".

[Jacobs then cites Cannon's letter of 23 August 1944, p.322 this volume, and Natalia Sedova's letter of 16 August 1944, p.331].

The Committee decided, in the light of its correction of line, to write to Martin giving its views. I participated in the discussion on the letter and explained my view, which was that the time had long since come when it was necessary to shift emphasis on the slogan of unconditional defense of the Soviet Union. It was now necessary to lay the political basis in the light of all the openly reactionary policies of Stalin, for speaking more and more loudly for his overthrow. It was now clear that the Soviet Union would be victorious in the war. We must now follow the line of Trotsky and counterpose the proletarian revolution to Stalinism.

There then appeared in our press the editorial on the Warsaw uprising... [p.321, this volume]. Without question, the revolutionary socialist workers had participated in it. Stalin betrayed it precisely in order to permit the Germans to annihilate these independent non-Stalinized workers on the one hand, and the nationalist Poles who opposed his territorial demands on the other.

The next meeting of the Committee saw a second letter of protest from Martin and his collaborator [i.e. from Cannon: the 23 August letter]. This letter... protests against calling the act of Stalin a betrayal. It calls for unchanging unconditional defense of the Soviet Union. It is truly difficult to take up all the mistakes in this lamentable letter.

The Committee would like to hide this letter from the party. Again it sums up all the previous errors that had appeared in the press.

Let us look a little more closely at the letter. The character of the Warsaw uprising? Martin's collaborator [i.e. Cannon: p.322, this volume] says "Nor does the editorial take up the question of the duty of guerrilla forces — and in the circumstances that is what the Warsaw detachments are — to subordinate themselves to the high command of the main army, the Red Army, in timing of such an important battle as the siege of Warsaw". Let us take this point of view for a moment. Suppose there were Polish worker-guerrilla fighters alone involved. Why must they subordinate themselves to the reactionary Stalinist high command of the Red Army? Why should they not aid the Red Army but, as revolutionary Polish workers, constitute their own independent force?

Actually the answer is not that there is any principle against their doing so, but on the contrary, the Red Army high command would never permit them to do so; those militant workers who are suspected of such designs are arrested and shot! As a matter of fact, Martin's collaborator took the entire matter on a purely military basis. He had a mechanical conception. Unconditional defense, that immutable formula, comes first, before everything else. Stalin uses the Red Army for his own political aims, Martin's collaborator would subordinate the Polish workers to the Red Army high command; that is, to the Stalinist aims.

You may believe personally that Stalin committed an act of betrayal. But that must not appear in the press. And it need not in the least affect your advice directed to the Polish workers. How can this be? Martin's collaborator enters into precisely the kind of defense of Stalin's act that the "friends of Stalin" gave (read Upham Pope in the [New York] Times). No. The evidence is absolutely clear: Stalin deliberately betrayed Warsaw into the hands of the Nazis. Where are the Polish workers of Warsaw who are to subordinate themselves to the high command? They are either dead, or they are imprisoned by the Nazis to whom they were handed over by Stalin. Even if we wanted to obey your advice, says the Polish socialist worker, we couldn't do it, because Stalin and his Red Army don't permit us to do so. How can this be just a matter of personal opinion? Has it no effect on the advice that you will give, say, to the German workers? Will you tell them to place themselves under that high command which will carry put the policies of Stalin and send millions of them to Russia as slave labor? Isn't it clear that your fetishist thinking gets you into an utter impasse? The conclusion is inevitable: your thinking is wrong!

You say: "But the Polish workers must be the allies of the Red Army in its war against Hitler's army, no matter how reactionary Stalin's policy is". We understand that here you base yourself on a statement of the Old Man, but let us quote him to you on this score: "It is one thing to solidarize with Stalin, defend his policy, assume responsibility for it — as does the triply infamous Comintern — it is another thing to explain to the world working class that no matter what crimes Stalin may be guilty of we cannot permit world imperialism to crush the Soviet Union, reestablish capitalism and convert the land of the October Revolution into a colony. This explanation likewise furnishes the basis for our defense of the Soviet Union."

All that you forgot was that this "formula" applies when the menace of imperialism stands ready to crush the Soviet Union. When the menace recedes we do not at all pursue the same policy. Our emphasis becomes different and we cannot wait till the last gasp of the war to make our position clear to the working class. That would be fatal indeed. The greatest menace today is no longer defeat by imperialism of the Red Army. It is rather that if Revolution does not appear in Europe, then the Stalinist bureaucracy will carry the downsliding of the October to completion, and will yield to imperialist pressure to begin the restoration of capitalism in the USSR. That means that now the European Revolution assumes first place and the defense formula recedes to the background. Events may even cause it to disappear completely, if reaction succeeds in its aims.

We listened in the Committee to Wright and Warde defend the unchanging formula of defense, now and forever, even after Natalia's first letter arrived at the same time as the second letter of Martin's collaborator. Natalia's first letter was dated August 16th. The accents of those members, these editors, who thought they were defending Martin's point of view, were clearly the accents of sectarianism and fetishism. The first letter of Natalia (with whose views I was completely in accord long before I saw her letter) contained one sentence of condemnation of the line that the Committee had pursued. That sentence reads: "I do not consider myself competent in political questions to the extent of condemning this or that line of your conduct. But in the given instance your mistaken course is all too clear to me". The Committee is determined apparently — or was — to prevent the party from seeing this criticism. Frank put it that he did not want unnecessary polemics. The Committee sent Natalia's letter to Martin and the others [in jail] (not, however, to Morrison [Goldman] and Cassidy [Morrow]). It is here that was demonstrated the completely hierarchic attitude of the Martin group. There was nothing new in the situation. The letter of Martin's collaborator and that of Natalia's were dated the same day. The Martin group changed its mind. Martin then wrote a letter to the Committee with his new point of view, without so much as taking the trouble to officially withdraw the letter of his collaborator! I proposed that a new section be added to the Resolution on the change in emphasis on defense of the Soviet Union. To motivate this I proposed to put in the internal bulletin both Natalia's two letters and those of Martin's collaborator. I explained that evidently the letter of Martin's collaborator had been withdrawn, since these comrades had changed their point of view. This was certainly permissible, but on one condition; that we educate the party by a full criticism of the previous errors. The Committee delayed acting on this motion, and then finally decided to put over another accomplished fact. Without meeting so that I could be present, the second letter of Natalia's and Martin's letter were rushed into the Bulletin by the Committee.

Let us see what purposes the Committee is serving. Natalia's letters are not the private property of the PC. They were written for the party and for its education. The Committee however wanted to cover up its previous course and so did not want Natalia's criticisms to appear. They adopted her political conclusions — but rejected her criticisms. After the receipt of Natalia's first letter, Wright wrote to Natalia asking for a further clarification of her point of view. Natalia then wrote the letter which appears in the Bulletin. When I proposed that both letters appear, Stein advanced the specious argument that the first letter had been written hastily and that he wanted to save Natalia's prestige! It might be necessary, he said, to secure her permission to print the first letter! I informed Stein that this was unprecedented and would no doubt astonish Natalia, but that I would certainly agree to have the Committee write to "request her permission". My agreement with this proposal disturbed the Committee no end. They then proposed to keep the entire matter in abeyance (that is, to caucus on the situation after the meeting!). Thereupon, for the first time in our movement, so far as I am aware, the Committee acted in the manner of the old CP when it used to send telegrams to Moscow — with the object of "putting something over". Without informing me, they sent a telegram to Natalia, asking her whether her second letter did not express her views more clearly than her first. Natalia's reply must have caused a very distinct burning of the ears of the Committee. She understood very well what was involved. The Convention should demand that this telegram and the reply be produced and read! Natalia agreed that her second letter gave her entire point of view better than the first one. But she went on to remind the Committee that it was necessary for it to listen to the criticism of members with more attention. She reminded them (please tell us in what connection, Comrade Stein) of an incident way back in 1927 in which the Old Man and a Stalinist bureaucrat were involved. The Old Man was criticizing the Stalinists in the Executive Committee. One of them asked "Where is the party?" and Trotsky replied: "You have strangled the party". Natalia recounted this incident in a vain attempt to bring the Committee to its senses in its extremely nervous attitude towards criticism.

One must ask: if Natalia's criticisms are suppressed — even after those who suppress them have adopted the ideas of Natalia (they were hardly prepared to do so when the same, exactly the same, criticisms emanated from me) — what chance has any ordinary member of getting a hearing?

The letter of Martin on the question of defense of the Soviet Union that appears in the Bulletin is undated. The reason for this is quite simple. The letter of Natalia's that appears in the Bulletin is dated August 23rd, 1944. Her first letter was written August 16th. Martin's first letter in reply was written in between. To hide the fact that a first August 16th letter had been written, the editors are forced to suppress the date on the first Martin letter.

The publishing in this fashion of the Natalia and Martin letters serves, does it not, to make it appear that both together were motivating a turn in our course, with a new emphasis, a different one on the European Revolution and the question of defense of the USSR. It is this false face before the party that makes it necessary to publish, under my name, the letters of Martin's collaborator.

Those letters were also the letters of Martin. They are all the more significant because they are the first documents of this kind to appear under the name of Martin and his collaborator in a period of years. We cannot quote from the articles of Martin on the tremendous political events of the past several years. Not one has appeared. Not one! We can quote only from the articles of those to whom he gave full support — Wright, Warde, Frank. Martin never wrote to criticize the distortions of these comrades. He never cautioned them against speculations which have indeed proved to be the inventions of a warped point of view. Martin's first documents (the letters from his collaborator) show him lagging behind the Committee after it had already begun to correct itself, Why then should it now be attempted to make it appear that Natalia and Martin have set the party on a new line? Natalia's letters were in actuality a polemic against Martin's and the Committee's point of view. The answer, in view of the fact that the Committee wants to hush up necessary educational criticism of its past course, not just in the letters of Martin's collaborator, but in the open press, is that the Committee is not concerned too deeply with the political questions; it is absorbed in apparatus politics, in votes that will determine the membership of the next Committee. The letters of Martin's collaborator are important, not in themselves, but precisely because they throw an illuminating light on the past course of the PC in the press.

Glance for a moment at the Martin letter, written without so much as mentioning the letters of his collaborator which therefore still lay on the table before the Committee. It states: "And I do not for a minute forget that the objective logic of the Red Army achievements in the war against the Nazis, regardless of the officially declared aims, is profoundly revolutionary". This sentence serves as a "bridge" from the old course to the new. It is correct only in a certain sense. If it is intended to testify to the correctness of the line previously pursued — namely, that Stalinism, in its defense of itself, and therefore in defense of the Soviet Union with its nationalized property, was forced against its own will to use revolutionary methods which "objectively" aided the European Revolution — then it is false. It is true in one sense only; namely, that the success of the Red Army means the defeat of the Nazi and Fascist armies, that this leaves a highly fluid situation in which the capitalist class has been critically weakened by its complete identification with Fascism. It gives rise to the Revolutionary Situation, during which, if the workers find the proper road and the proper leadership, they have the possibility to come to power.

But to point to the "objective logic" is precisely completely inadequate at such a time. Comrade Frank tells us that we have a complete and unchanging program which we present to the working class, and we leave it to those advanced militants in the European movement ("with all their stores of experience") to pick out from the program what they consider best at the given time. That attitude (the attitude of the "objective logic") means the avoidance of the entire problem, not its solution. ("Once burned, twice careful").

It is precisely in the pre-revolutionary and revolutionary situations that the subjective factors become far more important than the objective. Without the subjective factors, the objective situation can pass on without leading to anything. Need I quote on this score from Trotsky, who repeated it to us so many times?

"But as soon as the objective prerequisites have grown to maturity the key to the whole historic process is handed to the subjective factor, that is, the party and its revolutionary leadership... In all these cases, as well as in others of lesser importance, the opportunistic tendency expressed itself in the fact that it relied solely upon the masses and completely neglected the question of a revolutionary leadership. Such an attitude, which is false in general, operates with positively annihilating effect in this epoch."

It is part of the duty of the "subjective factor" to warn the workers of the obstacles and dangers in their path. It is part of the duty of the "subjective factor" to say what is, to characterize events correctly, to indicate the tendencies involved in every major situation so as to guide the working class along the correct road. The plenum was a small instance of making an unexpected and abrupt leap in the characterization of the Badoglio regime as a regime of prevention of the proletarian revolution. Cannon told us then that we need not "speculate" on what goes on among the "tops" that is, as between Churchill, Roosevelt and Stalin — it was sufficient to follow the course of the masses. To keep your eyes solely on the masses, that was revolutionary optimism, to speculate on the dangers from the tops, that could lead only to pessimism.

The optimistic attitude led at once to declaring the Italian Revolution "defeated" when it had hardly started. The word was deleted from the resolutions of both "majority" and "minority" at my instance. I tried to teach the Harry Frankels, the youths of our movement, that it was necessary to keep in mind all factors, all tendencies, in order to warn workers in time of the dangers in their road, in order to help them avoid those dangers and win to firm ground. Do you remember my disagreement with you on "tempo"? You had comrades believing that the Italian Revolution was two weeks, at most two months, off. What could such an "incautious" attitude lead to except pessimism when it had to "let down" those comrades who had been "keyed up" by your "optimism"?

The party is paying now (it will not realize it until after the convention, which will not take up the really burning issues, that I warrant) for its incredible attitude towards Stalinism. Now, mind you, we need a lengthy Resolution to persuade "ourselves" that Stalinism is a frightful menace to the world revolution. The "subjective factor" is working at extremely slow tempo in a period when it should be geared for the most flexible functioning. We are told that the party must if anything be more centralized. Why? In order that the Committee may become even more separated from the membership than it already is? In order that the PC may make its decisions (some of which we see here) completely behind the scenes, only to have them changed abruptly and then covered from the view of the party? In order to create the kind of discipline in which the editors are allowed to put over a line by "accomplished facts"? In order to build up a theory of an infallible leadership? In order to make it impossible to exercise criticism, the only form of control?

A further word on "discipline". Haven't I broken all the discipline of the decalogue in this lengthy article? No, comrades, I am only carrying on the best kind of discipline in our movement. That discipline must be based first and foremost on loyalty not to persons nor to committees nor to an apparatus, but to the basic principles of our movement. In final analysis, our kind of discipline depends on ideas, correct ideas. Before a convention, the ordinary discipline to carry out decisions of the various party bodies relaxes and is partially dissolved so that the convention can make all its decisions on the basis of all facts, laid freely before it. But even the ordinary discipline in between conventions is being misinterpreted by some comrades. Our discipline is based on the freest possible discussion inside the movement, so as all the better to carry out our decisions in "iron discipline" in actions outside the party.

Comrade Martin speaks of "literary politics" in his letter. I urge him to turn his attention to editor Wright in this connection. Wright can tell us (and we are hardly yet in a Civil War!): "No statement on the war has been issued in the name of that party which under Lenin held congress after congress under conditions of complete democracy in the very midst of the civil war". Are we striving to emulate Lenin and the party in his time, or some more centralized party? It does not do to make a parade of democratic centralism just before and even, perhaps, during a convention, only to violate its real spirit all the year round. The attitude of the Committee towards critics (and I include here those who are right in their criticisms as well as those who are wrong) is a completely apparatus attitude. It simply will not brook the slightest criticism. Isn't there an "anxiety complex" involved here? Instead of infinite patience in order to educate members, there is utter impatience, a real "baiting" of critics, a split spirit.

Lenin gives you his views on discipline, and Trotsky quotes them with complete approval. "We have defined more than once our view in principle on the significance of discipline and on the meaning of discipline in a working class party. Unity of action, freedom of discussion and criticism, that is our definition." Then he adds: "Discipline without ideas is an absurdity which transforms the workers in practice into miserable appendages to the bourgeoisie in power.

Therefore, without freedom of discussion and criticism the proletariat does not recognize unity of action".

Trotsky explains this quotation more fully in *The Case of Leon Trotsky*: "Because even in the Bolshevik Party, with its very severe discipline, Lenin first emphasized that the essence is more important than the form; that the ideas are more important than the discipline; that if it is a question of fundamental importance, we can break the vows of discipline without betraying our ideas."

This is the attitude I take on discipline. I violate no statute of our party, no principle of our movement, by bringing loyally to the convention my open criticisms of the leadership. On the contrary, I am carrying out an elementary principle of our party, to say what is, to help preserve a correct line. But, if I were violating the narrow interpretation that the Committee falsely places on its discipline, then I do it completely in the Trotskyist spirit and tradition. And I say categorically that the effort of the Committee to "put something over on the party" completely violates every concept of loyalty to principle and Bolshevik discipline. Had the Committee been willing to enter into a wee bit of self-criticism, the outcome would have been entirely different and far more beneficial. The party would have experienced a real impetus in its education.

I must repeat what Trotsky said. It cannot be stated often enough: "In politics not even the smallest mistakes pass unpunished, much less the big ones. And the greatest mistake of them all is when the mistake is veiled, when one seeks mechanically to suppress criticism and a correct Marxist estimate of the mistake". You think to correct yourselves without discussion. Enough of discussion; we are tired of it! You will accuse me of wanting interminable discussion, and no action. All I can say to you is, action based on the wrong ideas will harm the party sooner or later. The only way to assure correctness is to listen carefully to all points of view in discussion before arriving at decisions, not to precipitate ideas into the open press as accomplished facts.

From "We arrive at a line", under the name of A Roland, SWP
Internal Bulletin vol.6 no.12, December 1944

"Defence of the USSR"? A defence quite unlike Trotsky's

Eugene Shays and Dan Shelton (1946)

"IT IS INDISPENSABLE to warn the masses tirelessly of the generally reactionary character of the Kremlin's policy, and of those dangers its bears for the occupied countries." (Trotsky, *In Defence of Marxism*)

The purpose of this article is to demonstrate the complete deformation and distortion which the concept of the "Defence of the Soviet Union" has undergone at the hands of the present SWP leadership.

We have made a detailed and systematic study of *The Militant* from the end of the European war (May 1945) until the present moment (June 1946). By direct references to each article dealing in whatever form with the Kremlin's role and policies, we shall prove by *The Militant*'s own record that:

1. Except in formal resolutions, the defence of the Soviet Union in the party press has turned into a capitulation to Stalinism.

2. *The Militant* has consistently and bureaucratically violated our 1944 convention resolution which relegates the defence of the SU into the background and pushes to the fore the defence of the European revolution against all its enemies including the Stalinists.

The method used to establish these two key criticisms will simply consist of (a) an enumeration of the main crimes committed against the socialist revolution by Stalin in the course of the year since the end of the European war (as reported in the world press), and (b) the record of *The Militant* on each of these crimes. [This record surveys only the *articles* in *The Militant*. Laura Gray's *cartoons* were sometimes more sharply anti-Stalinist].

1. The USSR and the dismantling of factories

A large part of the industries in countries occupied by the USSR have been stripped, dismantled and shipped to Russia. In Czechoslovakia, the official figure is over 20% of all industry; in Poland, over 30%. These are "allied" countries. In Austria and German (now Polish) Silesia, the figures are correspondingly higher. In Manchuria (containing 70% of China's heavy industries), heavy industry in the Mukden area is almost 100% stripped; the Fushun mining area is stripped of all its electrical and modern mining equipment. In Germany more than 50% of all productive capacity in the USSR zone has been removed. The same policy was followed in Romania, Hungary and Korea.

The objective resultant has been the de-proletarianisation of large parts of the working class, the lowering of the standard of living of the masses, the condemnation of the country to social and political stagnation and, thus, the creation of grave obstacles in the path of the coming socialist revolution.

The bourgeois press, for its own reasons, has carried literally thousands of documented items of reporting on this question. What has *The Militant* carried?

With the exception of three articles by the SWP minority (one by Goldman, two by Morrow) in 50 issues of *The Militant*, there appeared only the following:

July 14 1946: Allied Looting of Germany (unsigned) deals with both US and USSR; very brief, factual only, a rewrite job from bourgeois newspapers, no interpretation.

Aug. 25, 1945: NC Statement on "USSR in China" has not a single reference to the USSR's looting of China and Manchuria!

Aug. 18, 1945: International News; Austrian factories looted by USSR; brief, factual only, no interpretation.

Dec. 8, 1945: Austrian Election (unsigned) correctly relates losses of CP at polls to Stalin's policy which includes looting of factories. Reference is thus nothing more than incidental to the main argument of the article on losses of CP at elections.

There is not a single reference to any looting of factories in the 1946 *Militant*; no reference in either 1945 or 1946 to looting of factories in Manchuria, Hungary, Romania, Korea, etc.

2. USSR and forced labour

Millions of physically fit men and women, war prisoners and nationals of "defeated enemy nations" have been deported to the USSR and put to forced labour in concentration camps. Among them are tens of thousands of political opponents of the Stalin regime.

Inside the USSR, whole peoples have been declared "collaborators" and shipped to Siberia (Tartars, Volga-Germans, etc.) Torture and malnutrition has resulted in the deaths of literally hundreds of thousands of these modern slaves.

In addition to impeding the revolutionary upsurge by removing, demoralising and killing off millions of workers and peasants, and alienating the rest of the working class, this Stalinist crime must be opposed by socialists as the most cruel and brutalised form of human slavery yet perfected. The enslavement of man, and socialism, the freeing of man, are mutually exclusive.

In 56 issues of *The Militant*, except for two of the above mentioned articles by Goldman and Morrow, there is not a single reference to forced labour. There is no reference ever to forced labour of war prisoners and political opponents in all the countries occupied by the USSR.

3. USSR and the seizure of territory

The following countries were occupied and were incorporated into the USSR: Lithuania, Latvia, Estonia, Eastern Poland, Bessarabia, Bukovina, Moldavia, Carpatho-Ukraine, Eastern Prussia, Karelo-Finland, Petsamo, Tanno-Tuva, Southern Sakhalin, Kuerlies.

In addition, through occupation troops and police rule, the following areas have been occupied: Romania, Hungary, parts of Austria and Germany, Czechoslovakia, Bulgaria, Yugoslavia, Poland and half of Korea.

As Marxists, we must oppose this violation of the right of self-determination of the countries involved.

In 56 issues of *The Militant*, the following references appeared:

June 2, 1945: Relations between US and USSR (Li Fu-jen). In passing calls Stalin's aims "counter-revolutionary" but there is no condemnation whatsoever of Stalin's seizure of territories!

Aug. 25, 1945: NC Statement on USSR and China "explains" Stalin's "defensive expansionism" (!), opposes it only (!) because of – "bad results"!

Sept. 1, 1945: Editorial condemnation of Stalin's seizures in the Far East. But the "expansionism" is explained solely as a "defensive" one.

May 11, 1946: Carsten states that "the extension of USSR domination prevents the stabilisation of capitalist relations and powers". This unqualified statement leads the reader to think that these seizures are to be welcomed. Further, Stalin wants spheres of influence only as a defensive measure, but (according to Carsten) no effective defence can thus be built. Presumably, this is Stalin's crime — a crime in military logistics!

May 18, 1946: "Korean Labor Pleads for Aid Against Brutal US rule" (unsigned) – but presumably not against brutal USSR rule, for the USSR is not even mentioned! Whoever relies exclusively on *The Militant* for his news does not even know up to the present moment that the USSR occupied half of Korea.

This is the entire record of *The Militant* on Stalin's seizures of territory.

4. USSR and reparations

The USSR has demanded and was granted by the Allied imperialists reparations from Germany in the form of machinery. Entire industries have been made inoperative by the loss. The Soviet Union has demanded $100,000,000 in reparations from Italy and has just been granted payments out of current Italian production. Crushing reparations have been imposed on Romania, Hungary and Finland.

Marxists are opposed to the very concept of reparations, which holds the people of a country responsible for the crimes of the capitalist class. Reparations are a blow at internationalism. Our slogan must be the Bolshevik slogan of "No annexations, no reparations!"

In 56 issues of *The Militant*, there has appeared nothing whatsoever on this question.

5. USSR and economic aggrandisement

In the spring of 1944, a secret treaty was concluded by the USSR with Churchill, assigning special spheres of influence in Southeastern Europe to Russia and to England.

Throughout the Nuremberg trials there has been constant references to secret economic treaties between the USSR and Hitler Germany, assigning spheres of influence in Eastern Europe and Asia Minor, agreements concerning machinery to be delivered by the USSR and other help to be extended to Germany. These references have been diligently suppressed by the Russian prosecutor.

377

Joint stock companies have been and are being created in Manchuria, Romania, Austria, Hungary, etc. under the pressures of the USSR, giving the latter control over the wealth falling under these agreements.

Marxists are opposed to such imperialist acts as the establishment of spheres of influence, exploiting the peoples, deciding the fate of peoples without their consent. These are characteristic methods of the imperialist division of the world.

In 56 issues of *The Militant*, there appeared nothing on this topic.

6. The USSR's terror-rule in the occupied countries

The USSR enforces its rule everywhere through the agency of the NKVD; through fraudulent elections; by imposing CP-dominated governments upon people whose vote was overwhelmingly opposed to CP rule (Hungary, Romania, Germany); by the re-opening of concentration camps (Buchenwald, Sachsenhausen); by deportation and arrests; by suppressing and demoralising opponents; by postponing elections (Bulgaria, Romania); by lawless evictions; by torture, murder and the third-degree; by the ever-present threat of the "Red" Army; by the threat of loss of ration cards.

Such police dictatorships are but a reflection of the internal regime in the USSR and must be mercilessly exposed before the working class.

In 56 issues of *The Militant*, except for the above mentioned article on Poland by Goldman, *The Militant* carried this single reference:

July 28, 1945: International News: Tito — a police dictatorship, no freedom.

There was nothing further in either 1945 or 1946.

7. USSR and forced migrations

The Kremlin has mercilessly carried through forced migrations in various European countries. These migrations have caused millions upon millions, mostly peasants and workers, unspeakable sufferings and degradations. Involved were and are: Germans who within 24 hours had to evacuate Poland; Poles who had to move into German territories, annexed to Poland; Sudeten Germans who had to leave Bohemia; Hungarians who had to leave Czechoslovakia and Transylvania; peoples within the USSR; and innumerable "minor" migrations, involving other nationalities, especially those of the Baltic states.

This brutal violation of the right of self-determination of these people must be opposed and denounced by the socialist movement.

In 56 issues of *The Militant* there appeared the following:

Oct. 6, 1945: 4 million Germans expelled from Eastern Germany by — (says *The Militant*) — Poles!!! (not by order of the Kremlin, by any chance!); even this is one paragraph only, buried in an article on a different topic, facts only, no comment or condemnation!

No other references, either in 1945 or 1946!

8. The USSR's role in preparing the next war

By its policy of armed aggression, intimidation and supporting the suppression of small nations; by its nationalist-chauvinistic terror-rule in occupied countries; by its police-state methods and dictatorial acts in its vassal states and the labour movement, the Kremlin, as much as the imperialists, is laying the foundations for the next world war.

In 56 issues of *The Militant*, the following appeared.

June 2, 1945: Relations between the US and USSR (Li Fu-jen) denounces US at length; then makes passing references to Stalin's "counter-revolutionary" aims in Europe.

Dec. 15, 1945: Sen. Wheeler attacks the USSR (Hansen); a re-write job on Wheeler's speech, written to defend the USSR — Not a single reference or mention of any of Stalin's crimes.

March 9, 1946: Hansen explain that (a) Workers must oppose US imperialism. (b) Workers must oppose the Stalinists — "in the labour movement". (c) The workers must defend the USSR in case of war. A big sub-head reads: "Defend the USSR". Not a word of condemnation!

March 16, 1946: US prepares war (Hansen). Correctly opposes US. Then: "In the fact of this unbridled assault on the SU, the Kremlin is at an extreme disadvantage." Why? — because it always denied the danger of a third war, thereby disorienting the workers. Presumably Stalin's alarms have corrected this previous omission.

March 23, 1946: "Wall St. Hurls Reactionary Barrage at USSR" (Carsten). In a long and detailed article, there is a single paragraph on Stalin, buried in the text.

March 30, 1946: Preparations for anti-Soviet war (Carsten); 25 paragraphs directed against the US, one paragraph against Stalin's "brutal policy of aggression". Except for this generality, not a single detailed charge or condemnation is made.

April 6, 1946: Iran used to further war on USSR (Wright), first page, lead article. Exposes US. Stalin not mentioned, except for his "crime" — what crime? "Painting up the United Nations as peace instrument." Nothing further.

April 13, 1946: Long article on War danger; (unsigned); no reference to Stalin's role or crimes.

April 20, 1946: US prepares war (Carsten), not a single word on Stalin.

May 4, 1946: Carsten refers to US's building a ring of steel around the USSR. Exposes US. Not a single word against Stalin.

May 11, 1946: Paris Foreign Minister Conference (Carsten). Sub-head: "Imperialists Blame USSR". "Imperialists are attempting to lay the entire blame for deadlock on the USSR." No attempt made to show Kremlin shares the blame.

May 18, 1946: Carsten finds US "blaming" USSR for breakdown of peace negotiations. Except for one abstract statement — Stalin engaging in "power politics" — there is nothing else on Stalinist policy.

In none of the articles mentioned is there so much as a hint that Stalin may carry at least part of the responsibility of bring on the next war. On the contrary, the entire onus for World War III is placed on the imperialists. To clinch this charge, one need only mention Gray's cartoon (March 16, 1946) on "Preparing for World War III" showing Truman, Churchill and Bevin playing with the Atom Bomb. Stalin is absent. Apparently he is the innocent victim of that bomb.

9. USSR and Iran

The Big Three forced a treaty on Iran in 1942 permitting their troops to be stationed there until six months after the end of the war. After this date, Russian troops remained giving a vague pretext ("elucidation of the situation"). They also charged that Iran was threatening war on the USSR (!!). Stalin manufactured a carefully planned "revolt" against the Tehran government, put pressure on it with the help of troop movements and reinforcements, and finally compelled it to grant important economic concessions, spheres of influence, monopoly of its northern oil resources.

In 56 issues of *The Militant*, there appeared the following:

March 23, 1946: Wall St. Hurls Reactionary Barrage at SU (Carsten). The entire article is devoted to Iran: headline suggests that whatever may be said against Stalin is reactionary poppycock. This impression is heightened by the absence of any reference to Stalin's crimes in Iran except for a small paragraph, buried in the text.

March 30, 1946: Iran (Carsten) 25 paragraphs against US, one against Stalin.

April 6, 1946: Wright, on the first page, lead article — Iran used for war preparations against the USSR. Exposes US; refers ironically to the "pitiful plight of 'Poor Little Iran'" (!!) This reference to "Poor Little Iran" is in quotation marks in Wright's text to show that he is making fun of the imagined complaints in Iran. What, then, is Stalin's crime in this connection? "To paint up the UNO as a peace instrument." (!!!) Not a single word more!

April 13, 1946: (unsigned) one line: "Stalin exerts pressure on Iranian government" in a long article. No condemnation. Nothing further.

May 4, 1946: (Carsten) once again refers to "Poor little Iran" (quotation marks his!) Not a single word against Stalin.

The above is the complete record *The Militant* on the Iranian issue.

10. The USSR's rule in Germany

The USSR, as much as its imperialist accomplices, has brought misery and starvation to its zone in Germany. It has looted machinery, dismantled entire factories. It dragged off millions to slave labour. It kept the country at starvation levels and rules by brute dictatorial force. These undeniable crimes of the Kremlin must be exposed in our press.

In 56 issues of *The Militant* there appeared the following:

May 26, 1945: (Hansen) "Allies impose Barbarous Rule on Germany" contains 1) one passing reference to Allies' "Kremlin accomplices", 2) all of long article devoted to denunciation of US and England. Not a single word more on Stalin!

July 7, 1945: CP opposes Soviets in Germany (Abbott), but not a single reference to Stalin's policies in Germany.

Oct. 6, 1945: "Allied Rule in Germany" — generalities only.

Nov. 10, 1945: "Allied Rule in Germany" (Varlin) exposes US, not a single reference to the USSR!

April 6, 1946: Starvation in Germany (unsigned) eloquent about US and England, completely silent about USSR!

April 27, 1946: an especially odious example of an almost explicit capitulation to Stalinism: Two articles on the same page.

1) "Kremlin Policy in Germany" — under this comprehensive title, the "Kremlin's policy" is outlined as: a) bringing Soviets (incidentally contradicting Abbott's July 7th article: "CP opposes Soviets in Germany"!) b) creating factory democracy c) workers' seizure of factories. Nothing further.

2) "US Imperialism Brings Starvation to Germany" (Varlin). The juxtaposition of such two articles on one page is tendentious in the extreme. Apparently one of the occupying powers brings factory democracy; while the other powers bring starvation!

This is the complete record of *The Militant* on this topic.

11. USSR and the merger of the German CP and SDP

As in Eastern Europe and Korea, so in its zone in Germany, the SU has compelled the merger of the Social-Democratic parties with the CP, resulting in the dominance of the CP. The merger in Germany was attended by an overwhelmingly vote of the SDP members against the merger (7:1) and by the last-minute prevention of the balloting in the Soviet sector of Berlin, in which half the SDP membership reside. It was further attended by the reactivation of the concentration camps of Buchenwald and Sachsenhausen where actual and potential opponents of the merger were imprisoned, as well as by the terror of the NKVD and police.

Imposed by brute force, the merger strengthens the hands of the Stalinists, puts a party based on totalitarian principles at the head of the masses, and thereby adds to the difficulties of the German workers in creating the preconditions for a struggle.

We must oppose such a merger.

In 56 issues of *The Militant*, there appeared nothing on this issue.

12. USSR and political asylum

The USSR has taken a definite stand against the granting of political asylum in the post-war period. In the UNO, the SU demanded that persons not wanting to return to their countries of origin should receive international assistance only with that country's consent; that "no propaganda" be allowed against the idea of return home (a limitation of political freedom) and that no aid should be given to any refugee hostile to any of the United Nations. The Soviet Union has advocated forced repatriation of its political opponents who come from Eastern Europe. (The Czech government was forced to return 50,000 refugees from the Carpatho-Ukraine.)

The Soviet Union's shameful betrayal of this elementary human right of asylum — ever defended by Marxists — must be exposed in our press.

In 56 issues of *The Militant*, there was not a single reference to this problem.

13. The conduct of the Red Army

Twenty years of life under Stalinist barbarism have left their mark on the "Red" Army soldiers. Fed on the reactionary ideology of chauvinism and revenge, they entered into new territories as rapacious conquerors. Brutalities against the population, plunder, rape and widespread looting are on the order of the day. Living off the countryside like locusts, confiscating the peasant's produce and land, and thereby further depleting already catastrophically low food supplies, the Soviet soldier incurs to an ever greater degree the wrath of the population. As a policing agent of the Stalinist bureaucracy — by crushing opposition, suppressing workers' uprisings, etc. — the "Red" Army's ideology is chauvinistic and reactionary; its tasks are counter-revolutionary and anti-internationalist.

In 56 issues of *The Militant*, there was not a single reference to this topic.

14. USSR and the food problem

With food being the first and last issue confronting the peoples of Europe and Asia, the SU has its occupation troops live off the land. The SU has offered no plan by which even a minimum ration of food can be guaranteed to these people. In Austria, the Kremlin exacted first a levy of 60,000 tons of wheat. It then confiscated vast areas of the richest agricultural section for the cultivation of the Army's food supply. While the masses in the SU and in all Soviet-occupied countries starve, the SU shipped cereals to France amidst great publicity to strengthen its agents there. It bribes potential political adherents with food and allows extra rations to CP members. By dismantling industries vital to the production of agricultural machinery and machine parts, it forces the peasants of Eastern Europe into virtual idleness, further aggravating both present and future food shortages.

In 56 issues of *The Militant*, there is, except for one article by Morrow, not a single reference whatsoever to the problem.

15. USSR and Turkey

In an even more brazen and undisguised manner than in Iran, the USSR demanded from Turkey the cession of large parts of territory (Kars and Ardahan) and the establishment of spheres of influence in Northern Turkey. The pretext given was the preparations by Turkey for an "anti-Soviet" war. As in Iran, such policies must be opposed.

In 56 issues of *The Militant*, there was not a single reference to this topic.

Conclusions

An objective perusal of the above record of *The Militant* from May 1945 to June 1946 constitutes the most damning indictment of our party policy at the present moment. The Kremlin has entered upon the European scene as a ruthless conqueror, a bloody oppressor, a grandiose looter and a robber par excellence.

It rules by terror and assassination. By its criminal policies, its rapacious conduct and its Genghis Khan-like demeanour, it has dealt and is dealing terrible blows to the European and, ultimately, the world revolution. It denied the right to self-determination to all its conquered peoples.

It demanded and extracted spheres of influences, "bilateral" trade agreements, raw material concessions in the best imperialist style.

It drowned the independent working-class movements in blood and "convinced" its political opponents by means of the NKVD and the hangman's noose.

It added untold millions of war prisoners, workers and peasants, political opponents of all nationalities, to its vast reservoir of forced labour.

It looted the countryside, bringing starvation to the masses, as much as it looted the factories in the cities, undermining the economic foundations of the very class destined to lead mankind out of chaos — the proletariat.

It trampled democratic and political freedoms underfoot.

It denied the most fundamental rights to political refugees and demanded their forcible return to their home countries.

In short — it brought the reality of Soviet Russian life today to the masses of Europe and the Far East.

In the face of this almost unending list of crimes against the socialist revolution, the record of *The Militant* is both pitiful and criminal indeed. *The Militant* has failed in its revolutionary task to tell the truth.

The attacks on the Kremlin in whatever few manifestos or resolutions appeared in *The Militant* were purely perfunctory and hence, meaningless, since the line was not carried out in the party's propaganda or press.

The objective resultant of the party press's failure to in any way adequately deal with the Kremlin's crimes thus becomes, at least implicitly, or by omission, a capitulation to Stalinism on the part of the Trotskyist movement.

What remains is to uncover the roots of this terrible record of the party press. There is probably no comrade in the party, be they majorityite or minorityite, who is not aware of the fact that — without a resolution to signal a change of line — the majority leadership in its dealings with Stalinism is proceeding from the fundamental premise that an Anglo-American war against the USSR is imminent. Hence, the defence of the USSR is placed again in the foreground of our propaganda.

Further proof of this contention is to be found in the fact that *The Militant*'s record on the Soviet Union is slightly better for 1945, and gets progressively worse in 1946 when the SWP majority began to be convinced of the "imminence" of war. The Convention resolution on the Soviet Union (October 1944) — accepted only under the pressure of Comrade Natalia and the SWP minority and proclaiming the receding into the background of the slogan of defence of the Soviet Union — has now been buried quietly in the backyard. Bureaucratically, without consent or knowledge of the party, the line was changed.

Given the "imminence" of a new war, the slogan of defence of the Soviet Union is suddenly back in the foreground; the slogan of the defence of the European revolution against all its enemies has receded into the background.

Presumably, as far as the majorityites are concerned, the European revolution is off the agenda for the moment and is to be preceded by the war against the USSR. For if it was not, how could the "imminence" of a war against a trustworthy accomplice in putting down the revolution be otherwise explained?

We shall not enter here into a discussion of the SWP majority's ludicrous position on the "imminence" of war, for such discussion is irrelevant to the subject. Regardless of the majority's position on the present world situation, their concept of defence of the SU still has nothing in common with Trotsky's concept of the defence of the SU. Let us recall certain key formulations of his interpretation of defence of the SU and counterpose to them *The Militant*'s role during the past year.

1. However progressive, the statification of industry in Soviet-occupied territory, "this does not alter the reactionary character of the Kremlin's policy", which it is "indispensable to tirelessly warn the masses against". (*In Defence of Marxism*)

When has *The Militant* ever "tirelessly" pointed this out?

2. "The defence of the USSR coincides for us with the preparation of world revolution. Only those methods are permissible which do not conflict with the interests of the revolution. The defence of the USSR is related to the world socialist revolution as a tactical task to a strategic one. A tactic is subordinated to a strategic goal and in no case can be in contradiction to the latter." (*In Defence of Marxism*)

When did *The Militant* point out to the masses that the Kremlin's occupation of Eastern Europe, Germany and the Far East is "in contradiction" to the strategic goal of world revolution?

3. "The primary political criterion for us is not the transformation of property relations in this or another area, however important those may be in themselves, but rather the change in the consciousness and organisation of the world proletariat, the raising of their capacity for defending former conquests and accomplishing new ones. From this one — and the only decisive standpoint — the policies of Moscow, taken as a whole, completely retain their reactionary character and remain the chief obstacle on the road to world revolution." (*In Defence of Marxism*)

When did *The Militant* point this out?

4. "The statification of the means of production is a progressive measure, but its progressiveness is relative; its specific weight depends on the sum total of all the other factors. Thus, we must first and foremost establish that the extension of the territory dominated by bureaucratic autocracy and parasitism, cloaked by 'socialist' measures, can augment the prestige of the Kremlin, engender illusions concerning the possibility of replacing the proletarian revolution by bureaucratic manoeuvres and so on. The evil by far outweighs the progressive content of Stalinist reforms." (*In Defence of Marxism*)

When did *The Militant* "first and foremost" point this out?

5. "We were and remain against the seizures of new territories by the Kremlin." (*In Defence of Marxism*)

When did *The Militant* point this out?

For more than one entire year, the party press, under the compulsion of a completely distorted concept of the defence of the Soviet Union, has objectively, both by what it said and what it omitted, defended Russian foreign policy. It has done so, furthermore, in violation of the party's own 1944 resolution on the Soviet Union. It is high time that the party press began to espouse a Trotskyist interpretation of the USSR's role in Europe and the Far East instead of objectively capitulating to a Stalinist interpretation.

"*The Militant*'s Record on Stalinist Foreign Policy", SWP Internal
Bulletin vol.8 no.11, October 1946

Some Fourth International publications at the end of World War
Two. Graphic from *The Militant*.

The eruption of bureaucratic imperialism

Jean van Heijenoort (1945)

THE RUSSIAN ARMIES, after their victory over Germany, have occupied Eastern Europe and, in great part, Central Europe. Nobody, of course, expected that they would stop at the borders of the USSR, and the mere fact of crossing borders, in the last act of a gigantic war, has no independent political significance in itself: its military necessity is obvious. The problem to be examined is not the mere crossing of borders, but the policy followed by the occupying authorities.

The first point to be noted in this policy is the total absence of internationalism. The Soviet authorities sow and cultivate with great care blind chauvinism, a spirit of revenge. Internationalism and even every elementary human compassion are trampled. This fact alone would be sufficient for our condemning Stalinist policy in Europe. But in this there is nothing new. Only illusions about Soviet reality could have made one expect something else.

As the second point, it is necessary to mention the conduct of the Soviet soldiers. There is no reason to embarrassedly keep silent on this repulsive aspect of the occupation, provided that the cause of it is properly explained and the responsibility placed where it belongs. Twenty years of Stalin's political barbarism have not passed without leaving their mark. The Soviet soldier, constantly inoculated with strong doses of chauvinist hatred, treated as cattle by his officers, compensates himself by brutalities against the local population, by plunder and rape. Cars full of plundered goods were recently crossing Poland, according to an American journalist, decorated with the Soviet star (!) and with inscriptions like this one: "We belong to a nation of conquerors." This moral depravity is a direct product of the brutal regime of the bureaucracy. To keep silent on this aspect of the occupation is to keep silent on one of the most monstrous crimes of Stalin.

However, when everything has been said about the reactionary chauvinist policy of the bureaucracy, about the corruption of the Soviet army, there remains a series of facts, such as the truly fantastic indemnities, the dismantling of factories, the forced labor on a grand scale, etc., that cannot be explained except by deeper economic and social causes. The dismantling of factories, systematically practiced from Austria to Korea, is not merely due to the depravity of some Soviet general or bureaucrat. We have here a series of phenomena whose social and economic roots are to be looked for in the bureaucratic management of Soviet economy. This last aspect of the occupation I propose to name imperialism, more precisely bureaucratic imperialism, for a series of reasons that I will try to present.

Still more precisely, it is more correct to speak of elements of imperialism.

386

We have observed these new phenomena only during a period that, historically, is still very brief. They have been until now explosions, violent indeed, but concentrated in an interval of time still very short. These elements of imperialism are playing in Soviet economy a role still secondary; they are still very far from having engendered a whole system, such as the British Empire. However, as elements, their existence is undeniable.

The imperialism that now dominates the world is finance imperialism. Bureaucratic imperialism is obviously not finance imperialism. Quite the contrary. Finance imperialism has its inner spring in a superabundance of capital, previously accumulated, in quest of investments. The distinctive feature of Soviet economy is still the low degree of industrialization, and the problem that confronts it does not at all resemble the one that confronts mature capitalism, but rather the one that nascent capitalism had to solve, namely the problem of primitive accumulation.

The country that came first in capitalist development, England, solved the problem of primitive accumulation through barbaric methods which Marx has so vividly described in the next to last chapter of the first volume of Capital: the laws against paupers and vagrants, the kidnapping of children, etc. In the countries that followed England on the road of capitalism the same methods were combined to various degrees, with the investment of British capital, previously accumulated, which permitted solving the task more easily.

Soviet economy is still far from having realized an industrialization of the country comparable to that of the advanced capitalist countries. However, Stalinist bureaucracy manages Soviet economy in such a way that the yearly fund of accumulation is greatly reduced. Not only does the bureaucracy appropriate a disproportionate share of the national income, but also – and that is the more important point – by its methods it retards the increase of the productivity of labor, multiplies losses and, in general, increasingly hampers the development of the economy. Thus, the bureaucracy finds itself forced, lest the rate of accumulation fall to a ridiculously low level or even become negative, to plunder means of production and labor power, everywhere it can, in order to cover the costs that its management imposes on Soviet economy. The parasitic character of the bureaucracy manifests itself, as soon as political conditions permit it, through imperialist plundering.

The policy of the Soviet bureaucracy outside the USSR is but the continuation of its policy inside. From this fact, incontestable in itself, some may conclude that the eruption of bureaucratic imperialism hardly deserves any special attention and that it is merely a geographical extension of an already existing system; therefore, nothing politically new. This means to simplify the problem too much, for the action of the bureaucracy, inside and outside of the USSR, does not operate in the same milieu.

Russian armies have occupied in Europe regions that are much more advanced than the USSR in the development of the productive forces and of technique, in the cultural level of the workers and of the working population in general (the extreme cases are those of the industrial regions of Czechoslovakia, Germany, and Austria).

The bureaucracy found its historical raison d'être in the USSR in the barbaric condition of the country, in the necessity of transplanting foreign technique. It fulfilled these tasks in its own way, that is, very badly, and, to the extent to which it partly fulfilled them, it became a greater and greater brake on the further development of industrialization, of technique, of culture.

The extension of the power of the Kremlin bureaucracy to a backward country, such as Outer Mongolia for instance, may still signify for such a country a quicker industrial development. (Even in this case one may now be skeptical after the dismantling of factories in Manchuria and in the part of Korea occupied by the Russian army.) But in the highly industrialized parts of Central Europe, Soviet occupation has directly and terribly reactionary consequences.

The "abolition of the kulaks as a class," fifteen years ago, did not lack in horrors. According to a testimony cited by Trotsky, the troops of the GPU took away boots of young "kulak" children. However, whatever may be our indignation at such methods, the expropriation helped fulfill the first Five Year Plan.

The present situation in Europe is very different. When the Soviet bureaucrats dismantle factories in Vienna, they condemn the Viennese worker to a death more terrible than just physical death; it is the death of his class, his social death. It means to condemn the country not to get out of economic, social, political and cultural stagnation. It means to instigate the disintegration of the proletariat, the only class from which the salvation of Europe can come. It means to deal a blow at the very heart of the perspective of socialism.

According to official figures, the Kremlin bureaucracy had already last September dismantled and shipped to Russia twenty per cent of Czech industry, thirty per cent of Polish industry. These are "allied" countries. What has happened in Austria, in Silesia, etc.? And these figures are merely quantitative: the bureaucrats have certainly not taken the least modern material. Moscow has claimed the privilege of seizing in the occupied countries, "friendly" or enemy, every machine of German make; in fact, it means to claim the right to grab all the industrial equipment of these countries. The economy of the enemy countries is, moreover, crushed by tremendous war indemnities for an indefinite period.

To the dismantling of factories must be added forced labor. War prisoners, Polish and Baltic exiles of 1939-40, political prisoners, German minorities deported from the Volga or from Rumania, etc., form a herd of unfortunate forced laborers, the number of which is certainly higher than eight millions and maybe not lower than fifteen or twenty. [1] The fate of these unfortunates is below that of slaves, for the owner of slaves ordinarily provides conditions that allow their indefinite reproduction. But the Soviet bureaucrat, because of his own situation, thinks only of drawing from the forced laborers all the possible labor in the shortest possible time. From one group of 100,000 German prisoners, six thousand were still alive three months ago, after three years of captivity, according to one of these unfortunates who had escaped.

Forced labor has occupied, in Soviet economy, a place which is far from being negligible compared to wage-labor. With eight to twenty millions of forced laborers side by side with the Russian working class, forced labor has not only a political, but also an economic importance. With the bureaucratic management of Soviet economy, the problem of manpower and efficiency is insoluble. The most immediate result of such management, with its uncontrolled command and its arbitrariness, its iniquities and brutalities, is to keep the productivity of labor at an extremely low level. The worker, deprived of every right and every protection, hardly feels inclined to produce more, to take better care of his tools and of his machines, etc. [2]

The bureaucrat tries to solve this problem by his methods: Stakhanovism, extreme differentiations in wages and, finally, forced labor on a great scale. The latter penetrates the more easily into the system since the efficiency of wage-labor is very low, often hardly higher than that of forced labor, and therefore there are many works which are less costly to execute with forced labor than wage-labor, especially when these forced laborers are deprived of all social life and reduced to being mere givers of labor-power until their death. It would be economically impossible to use forced labor on such a great scale in the United States, for instance, where the labor-power of well-paid workers, equipped with modern machinery, usually would be cheaper than the labor-power of forced labor with a very low efficiency. Thus the bureaucratic management of the economy, while keeping the productivity of labor at a low level, calls for, and at the same time makes possible, the use of forced labor on a great scale.

The most vivid manifestations of bureaucratic imperialism – plunder, requisitions, dismantling of factories, forced labor – are thus the direct consequences of the bureaucratic domination of the Soviet economy and not the product of Zhukov's caprice, or Stalin's thirst for power, or the depravity of Soviet soldiers. The whole bureaucratic management of the economy calls for such methods. In this sense, it is fully legitimate to speak of bureaucratic imperialism as a system growing out of definite economic needs.

Every imperialism springs from difficulties in the economy of the country. What this imperialism seeks reveals what these difficulties are. Finance imperialism, in quest of investments, reveals in the metropolis a superabundance of capital that does not find a sufficient rate of profit. Bureaucratic imperialism, with its millions of forced laborers and its carrying away of machines, reveals the need of an economy suffocating under the bureaucratic management.

At this point someone will probably remark that war has destroyed so much in the USSR that this destruction is sufficient to explain the needs of Soviet economy, independently of the disorder and waste of the bureaucracy. This remark remains too abstract. Soviet economy does not start from scratch. In the years immediately preceding the war, in 1938-40, the existence of the bureaucracy weighed more and more heavily on the economy. The rates of development of the key industries had very much decreased in those years. War, with the poverty it has wrought, has deepened, materially and spiritually, the gulf between the bureaucracy and the people. Feeling itself surrounded everywhere by the hatred, the bureaucracy can less and less appeal to emulation, to enthusiasm, to voluntary sacrifice, in order to get out of a terribly difficult situation. How could a bureaucrat ask the Czech or Hungarian peoples to voluntarily collaborate with the Soviet people for the building of a better future? Such appeals coming out of the mouth of a parvenu do not have the accent of truth and remain ineffective. The bureaucrat, in his own way, knows that very well. Nothing remains but the way of violence and plunder.

Does the appearance of elements of imperialism imply the revision of the theory that the USSR is a degenerated workers' state? Not necessarily. The Soviet bureaucracy feeds in general on an appropriation of the work of others, and we have already, long ago, recognized this fact as part and parcel of the degeneration of the workers' state. Bureaucratic imperialism is only a special form of this appropriation.

If they do not necessarily imply a revision of the theory, the various manifestations of bureaucratic imperialism force us, nevertheless, to see how far the degeneration has advanced. It is not possible any more to simply speak of workers' state and to add, as if between parenthesis, degenerated. Of the two attributes, "workers" and "degenerated," it is the latter that we must now underline with greater emphasis. The degeneration has made such an advance and the impact of this degeneration on Europe has such terribly reactionary consequences that it is impossible to automatically apply to the USSR of today propositions that would be valid for a "normal" workers' state. The Soviet Union is as far from being a "normal" workers' state as a rotten apple is a "normal" apple, and nobody would think of biting into a rotten apple. With the present imperialist plundering, the degeneration has reached the last stage of rottenness.

As the result of historical circumstances, which we have very often analyzed, a social formation has appeared which really is a monster of history. As the biologists explain to us, a monster is due to disturbances occurring during the development of the embryo; likewise the isolation of a proletarian revolution in a barbaric country has engendered a society not only without any precedent, but also very different from all the outlined norms.

To repeat today that "fundamentally" the USSR is a workers' state because the means of production are nationalized is to dupe oneself with words. If it were so, the Poland of Bierut would be a good approximation of the dictatorship of the proletariat! If an economic form is separated from the social and political context in which it is immersed, it becomes an empty abstraction. Trotsky saw much more clearly than all these amateurs of empty phrases when, as early as 1936, he wrote that in the USSR "the character of the economy as a whole depends upon the character of the State power."

If the Soviet Union still remains today, in my opinion, a degenerated workers' state, it is because, from that monstrous society, nothing new and stable has yet come out. In the rotten apple no germ has appeared. The personal position of each bureaucrat still remains very precarious. The manifestations of imperialism that we can now observe reveals precisely the parasitic character of a bureaucracy that lives from day to day by plunderings and expediencies. If the monster would reveal itself capable of reproducing itself, it would not be a monster any more, but a new species. If the system of political absolutism combined with state-ownership of the means of production were to extend over the world, the Soviet bureaucracy would already today be, of course, the prototype of this system. But history has not yet proven that from the Stalinist bureaucracy can emerge a social system of an historical scope, in the full sense of the word. To accept today that the proof has been given means, it seems to me, to overlook all that is monstrous, exceptional, parasitic and unstable in the Stalinist bureaucratic regime.

The various features of bureaucratic imperialism which we now observe are a new phenomenon and, like any new phenomenon, it is difficult to label them. We have to create a new term or use a term already applied to other phenomena. To create a new word is easy, but to create a new word that would be understood by everybody, that could be used in our daily propaganda and agitation, is much more difficult, and until now, nothing of that kind has been proposed. We are, therefore, reduced to using a term already used for other phenomena, that is to say, to extend its meaning to a certain degree. Two names have already been used: expansionism and imperialism, and the question of choosing between the two would be very paltry if very often deeper disagreements were not hiding behind that choice. Let us weigh a moment the relative advantages and disadvantages of the two terms.

The term "imperialism" is used most of the time to designate the finance imperialism of advanced capitalist countries. (Not only, however. Trotsky, describing Tsarist imperialism, discovers in it many features which do not belong at all to classical finance imperialism.) If we want to use the term for the Soviet bureaucracy, we are then obliged, in order to avoid confusion, to state clearly what are the economic and social roots of bureaucratic imperialism, and that is what I have tried to do above. This task once accomplished, there remains the formal argument that to speak of bureaucratic imperialism means to identify the USSR with the capitalist countries, for it means to use the same word for the two camps. But, the same objection, if it were valid, would equally invalidate the term "expansionism" (and many other terms too, such as oppression, plunder, etc.) for the great capitalist powers also practice expansionism (and oppression, plunder, etc.). Thus, every formal argument directed against the word imperialism strikes also the word expansionism. If the disadvantages are the same, the term imperialism is the better under the heading of advantages. For, what constitutes the difference? Expansionism is a much more neutral term, equally applicable, for instance, to a peaceful expansion into a virgin continent. Imperialism designates much more precisely the oppression and exploitation of foreign peoples and is much more charged with opprobrium, considerations which, in face of the monstrous crimes of the Soviet bureaucracy, should decide us to adopt the term in our propaganda and agitation.

In October 1939, after the occupation of eastern Poland, Trotsky wrote:

"Can the present expansion of the Kremlin be termed imperialism? First of all it is necessary for us to agree on the social content which we put in this term. History has known the imperialism [3] of the Roman state based on slave labor, the imperialism of feudal land-ownership, the imperialism of the Tzarist monarchy, etc. The driving force behind the Moscow bureaucracy is indubitably the tendency to extend its power, its prestige, its revenues. This is the element of 'imperialism' in the widest sense of the word which was a property in the past of all monarchies, oligarchies, ruling castes, medieval estates and classes. However, in contemporary literature, at least Marxist literature, imperialism is understood to mean the expansionist policy of finance capital which has a very sharply defined economic content. To employ the term 'imperialism' for the foreign policy of the Kremlin, without explaining exactly what one means by it, means simply to identify the policy of the Bonapartist bureaucracy with the policy of monopolistic capitalism on the basis that both one and the other utilize military force for expansion".

From this citation it appears dearly that Trotsky is irritated with those who employ the term imperialism in regard to the USSR as a simple insult in order to vent their indignation, but "without explaining exactly what one means by it." However, to demand that one explains is to accept implicitly that it is possible, once the demand is satisfied, to extend to the Soviet Union the term imperialism.

In 1940 we were entering a gigantic war that would bring an answer to many questions, and it was legitimate to hesitate at that moment to introduce a theoretical innovation. Moreover, the territories occupied then were economically insignificant, their occupation had almost entirely a military meaning on the eve of an imminent war, the few dismantlings of factories which were then carried out were not known abroad at the time Trotsky was writing. Today, however, it is a question of half of Europe, plus large territories in Asia. A little before the war we were still criticizing the Kremlin for its actions in the League of Nations, for pacifism, pacts, etc. All this appears today almost like child's play compared to the regime of violence and pillage which has been extended over Europe. Countries with advanced working classes are being condemned to economic, social and cultural disintegration. In the eyes of large masses, communism is being discredited. The parties of petty bourgeois democracy suddenly recover prestige and votes. The very perspective of socialism is placed in jeopardy.

The oppression and exploitation, pillage on a grand scale, the millions of forced laborers, the hopeless situation of the occupied countries – all these facts are undeniable. I have tried to show that it is not a matter of simple political episodes but that it results from the bureaucratic management of Soviet economy and that it is therefore legitimate to speak of bureaucratic imperialism. The reality is so complicated that there is room for discussions on this point. But even on the exact mechanism of finance imperialism the discussions have never ceased among Marxists during a half century! With much greater reason the teratological character of the Soviet Union impels us to a constant reexamination of our conceptions. What is necessary to ask of anyone who takes part in this discussion is, rather than immediate agreement, a desire to learn, a willingness to weigh all arguments, a firm decision to reduce to silence those who want to fetter the analysis by considerations foreign to the discussion. It is only thus that we will be able to advance.

Footnotes

1. Official statistics are, of course, silent on this sector of "socialist" (!) economy. Light is thrown on a small bit of the reality by information which the Mensheviks have just published on one colony of the GPU. In northeastern Siberia, near the river Kolyma, there are gold deposits so rich that they can be exploited without a great amount of machinery. The whole region, an area about that of France, was given to the GPU. It exploits the deposits with the help of five million forced laborers, Poles deported in 1939-40 or German war prisoners, reduced to a regime of bread and water, deprived of all social life, treated, in the strictest sense of the word, as cattle, in a region with the most inclement weather in the world.

2. This well known aspect of Soviet economy was again underlined recently in a report of a delegation of the Iron and Steel Trades Conference at its return from the USSR: "The workers are competent, but 'in spite of the stories about fabulous increases in production, we believe that their output per man-hour is considerably lower than ours.' The delegates were unfavorably struck by the 'little importance attached to the care of the machine'." (New York Times, November 17, 1946.)

3. In the English translation (*In Defence of Marxism*, p.26) the term imperialism is at this point placed between quotation marks, which is not the case in the original Russian. The American translator has taken upon himself the right to "correct" (and here is where it is necessary to use quotation marks) Trotsky, who had dared mention Roman imperialism without quotation marks. What breadth of view!

"The Eruption of Bureaucratic imperialism: A Contribution to the Discussion on the Russian Question", written under the name Daniel Logan. Written December 1945, published in *New International*, March 1946

The Red Army is a friendly proletarian force

SWP (1946)

IN THE EUROPEAN ZONE occupied by the Red Army, our sections, while taking first place in the struggle for completing the agrarian reform and for state-ization of large industry, banks, transportation, as well as for the realization of our democratic slogans... also demand the right of each people to self-determination and the defense of national minorities. They oppose the forced integration and federation of other peoples with the peoples of the USSR, as well as the forced transfers of populations, and every measure of national oppression.

They demand the right for free development of the workers' movement in these countries, guaranteed by the free constitution and free functioning of workers' parties, trade unions and Soviets. They tolerate the presence of the Red Army only to the extent that it is a friendly proletarian armed force having as its objective to guarantee the fulfillment of agrarian reform and the state-ization of the means of production against imperialism and against national reactionary elements, without hindering in any way whatsoever the free development of the working class movement.

In all cases where the Red Army, obeying the reactionary orders of the Soviet bureaucracy, opposes insurrectionary movements of the masses and their struggles for the overthrow of capitalism and the installation of the proletarian dictatorship, our sections will be for the defeat of the Red Army and the victory of the workers. They will work for this defeat by resorting simultaneously to military means and to propaganda for fraternization addressed to the soldiers of the Red Army, inviting them to revolt against every executant of the reactionary orders of the Soviet bureaucracy and to join the masses struggling for the proletarian revolution.

"Tasks in the Countries Occupied by the USSR", in "The New imperialist 'Peace' and the Building of the Parties of the *Fourth International*", SWP Internal Bulletin vol.8 no.3, February 1946

Socialist Appeal, 31 October 1939.

Socialist Appeal, 29 January 1938

7. Stalinist Russia: degenerated workers' state or exploitative class society?

This exchange, in 1944, was the main one in the formative period of the 1940s in which the Orthodox explicitly debated the nature of the USSR with the Heterodox. It came after Shachtman's "Heterodox Trotskyist" group published an English translation of Trotsky's *The New Course* (1923), with a long commentary by Shachtman. That was Shachtman's reply to *In Defence of Marxism*. Harry Braverman (1920-1976: pen-name Frankel) is best known today as the author of the book *Labour And Monopoly Capital*. From 1937 to 1953 he was a member of the "orthodox Trotskyist" organisation led by James P Cannon; then in 1953 split away with a faction characterised by the other SWP leaders as pro-Stalinist. He became a central figure in the magazine *Monthly Review*.

Property forms define the workers' state

Harry Braverman (1944)

THE COLLECTION OF articles entitled *The New Course* was Trotsky's opening gun in the struggle against the Stalinist bureaucracy. In 1923, the year of the writing of these articles, the Russian Bolshevik Party was passing through a profound internal crisis. It was not the first struggle inside the Bolshevik Party which had grown and developed through many previous internal disputes over questions of program, strategy, and tactics. The 1923 conflict, however, differed from all the previous ones in culminating in the triumph, not of the proletarian-Leninist tendency, but the Stalinist tendency of capitulation to alien class influences that were pressing heavily upon the party. After 1923 the European revolutionary wave began to recede, leaving as a deposit moods of pessimism, exhaustion and despair which enveloped the proletarian vanguard and which found their expression through the weakest section of the party. It was in this atmosphere that the Stalinist vice began to close upon the Bolshevik Party, squeezing out its democratic life and transforming it into an instrument of the narrow, opportunist, and eventually counter-revolutionary clique of Stalin. It was this growing bureaucratisation of the party against which Trotsky took up the cudgels in 1923. With *The New Course*, he began his fight, lasting almost two decades, against the degeneration of the first workers' state.

A new edition of this famous series of articles has been put on sale by Max Shachtman who deserted Trotskyism and broke with the Trotskyist movement in 1940. Attached to Trotsky's 112 page classic, there is a 128 page "explanatory" document by Shachtman. We have here another instance of that common, current black-market device, the tie-in sale, which compels a buyer to purchase inferior, shoddy or worthless goods in order to obtain the articles he really desires. In order to get beef these days a working class housewife is often obliged to buy tripe as well. Trotsky's essays supply Marxist insight and are a matchless example of consistent and principled polemic; Shachtman's essay is the antipode: it is tripe.

One reads occasionally in the Stalinist, or Social Democratic press that there are "two Trotskyist papers" or "two wings" of the Trotskyist movement in this country. This deliberate misrepresentation is akin to references often made in the bourgeois press to "two kinds of communism." In reality, of course, there is only one "kind of communism" just as there is only one party in this country which teaches and applies the program of Trotskyism. Trotsky himself made sure in his lifetime that there would be no confusion on this point. On more than one occasion he took the opportunity to explain what he thought of Shachtman's politics and program. "Our old Mensheviks were real heroes in comparison with them," he wrote of the Shachtmanites. After the split with the petty bourgeois opposition led by Burnham and Shachtman, Trotsky took particular pains to clarify his attitude toward these people. He wrote:

"Only the other day Shachtman referred to himself in the press as a 'Trotskyist!' If this be Trotskyism, then I, at least. am no Trotskyist ... Had conscious agents of the class enemy operated through Shachtman, they could not have advised him to do anything different from what he himself has perpetrated."

No one can deny Shachtman the right to abandon Trotsky's ideas, any more than ex-colleague Burnham could be denied the right to abandon the Socialist movement, after he together with Shachtman split with American Trotskyism. The "right" of betrayal and renegacy has always been freely exercised by petty bourgeois intellectuals, particularly in periods of reaction. But then, they should not masquerade, like Shachtman, in the trappings of Trotskyism while propagating the polar opposite of the program of Trotskyism. Lenin pointed out that the enemies and opponents of the great Marxist teachers have invariably sought after their death to "emasculate and vulgarise the real essence of their revolutionary theories and to blunt their revolutionary edge." Shachtman is merely another recruit to this legion of emasculators, vulgarisers and falsifiers. With typical impudence, Shachtman pretends that Trotsky's class analysis of the Soviet Union as a degenerated workers' state "is not even a decisively important part" of Trotskyism. This is like saying that a man could function without a heart.

In addition, Shachtman states: "Our criticism of Trotsky's later theory of the 'workers' state' introduces into it an indispensable correction. Far from 'demolishing' Trotskyism, it eliminates from it a distorting element of contradiction and restores its essential harmony and continuity."

Every word here is false. The truth is that Trotsky devoted the main energies of the last period of his life to analysing the various stages of the development of the Soviet Union. His study of the degeneration of the Stalin regime ranks among his greatest theoretical contributions to Marxist thought. Even a conscientious opponent will admit that it is an integral part of Trotsky's theory of the permanent revolution and of the Trotskyist program. He affirmed and reaffirmed this literally in scores of articles and books. Thus, in the programmatic document *The Soviet Union and the Fourth International* it is flatly stated:

"The condition for further successes is the correct evaluation of the world situation, including the class character of the Soviet Union. Along this line, the new [Fourth] International will be subjected to tests from the very first days of its existence."

Leon Trotsky properly attached crucial importance to the class nature of the Soviet Union. It is only necessary to recall that the entire struggle against the Burnham-Shachtman faction as well as their break with the Trotskyist movement revolved in the main around the question of the USSR. Answering at that time the attempts of Burnham (supported by Shachtman) to smuggle into the program of the Fourth International the anti-Marxist notion that the regime of Stalinism represented the rule of a new exploiting class, Trotsky wrote that "the perspective of a non-worker and non-bourgeois society of exploitation, or 'bureaucratic collectivism,' is the perspective of complete defeat and the decline of the international proletariat, the perspective of the most profound historical pessimism." (Leon Trotsky, *In Defence of Marxism*)

The revisionist theory that a new social formation can come to replace capitalism concerns not only the USSR. Trotsky made this quite clear. He wrote: "It concerns the whole fate of the world proletariat and mankind." And he asked: "Have we the slightest right to induce ourselves by purely terminological experiments in a new historic conception which occurs to be in an absolute contradiction with our program, strategy and tactics?"

Burnham's theory of "bureaucratic collectivism" (borrowed from Bruno [Rizzi: see glossary] is now coolly offered as an "indispensable correction" to Trotskyism. Shachtman tries to palm off as a restoration of the "essential harmony and continuity (of Trotskyism)" what was flung back in Shachtman's face by Trotsky himself as an absolute contradiction of "our program, strategy and tactics," or, if you prefer, the "whole of Trotskyism." Small wonder that in 1940 Trotsky characterised Shachtman and his tendency as that of "ideological charlatanism," "petty-bourgeois counterfeits of Marxism," "outright theoretical betrayal."

Let us review briefly the ABC of Marxism. Marxists view classes as the product of historical development, in other words, all classes have a past and a future, as well as the present. Shachtman's "new exploitive class" is, in Shachtman's own words, "without a past and without a future." (Max Shachtman, *The Struggle for the New Course*.)

Lenin insisted that the roots of all class rule are to be found in the productive foundations of society. He said: "The rule of the class is determined only by the relationship to property." To explain the rule of his "new class" Shachtman points not to the foundation but to the political superstructure. It thus turns out that Shachtman's "indispensable correction" applies not only to Trotsky but to Lenin and Marx as well. But Shachtman simply forgets to mention such trifles.

"Wherein does the rule of the class (the proletariat) express itself?" asked Lenin. And he answered: "The rule of the proletariat expresses itself in the abolition of landed and capitalist property." Not the introduction of nationalised property and planning but the abolition of the old property forms sufficed for Lenin.

How does Shachtman get around this? Very simply. He denies that his new class needs either to abolish previous property forms or institute new ones of its own. Shachtman's class that has no past and no future possesses for its "fundament" not property relations but the "ownership" of "political power." Needless to add, this "ownership" in its turn has neither a past nor a future. Such tripe is, according to Shachtman, "the veriest commonplace of Marxism."

According to Marxists the historical justification for every ruling class is the ability under its particular system of exploitation to raise the development of productive forces of society as a whole to a new level. Does Shachtman grant this ability to Stalinism, i.e., his own "new exploitive class"?

What then remains of the Marxist conception of class? The gist of Shachtman's 128-page argument boils down to a representation of the crimes of Stalinism as the birthpangs that marked the rise of a new class to power. No more, no less. It is an elementary principle of Marxism that ruling classes rise in society through the operation of forces beyond the control of men's consciousness, reason or will. The rise of new ruling classes can be retarded or facilitated but never prevented – until and unless these classes have exhausted their historic mission. In the light of this, what is Shachtman's version of the evolution of the Soviet Union if not an attempt to supply an historical justification not for the ascendancy of a new class but actually for the abominations of the Kremlin?

It is not for nothing that Trotsky told Shachtman in 1940 that an attempt to revise the principled position of the Fourth International on the class nature of the USSR was a mockery of Marxism. In fact, according to Trotsky, to say that the Stalinist bureaucracy was a new exploitive class is to declare that the class struggle for socialism was only a Utopian dream. Here is what Trotsky wrote:

"The historic alternative, carried to the end, is as follows: either the Stalin regime is an abhorrent relapse in the process of transforming bourgeois society into a socialist society, or the Stalin regime is the first stage of a new exploiting society. If the second prognosis proves correct, then, of course, the bureaucracy will become a new exploiting class. However onerous the second perspective may be ... nothing else would remain except only to recognise that the Socialist program, based on the internal contradictions of capitalist society, ended as a utopia."

Shachtman's choice of the 1923 writings of Trotsky as the springboard for his polemic against Trotsky's position on the USSR is deliberate. The very date of the writing of these essays and the circumstances surrounding their publication precluded the possibility of their containing a fundamental analysis of the Stalinist degeneration in the Soviet Union. In 1923 Thermidor was still in the year of its birth. Lenin was still alive. The fate of the German revolution still hung in the balance. Moreover, the major political differences between the Stalinists and the Left Opposition had not yet ripened. Stalin had not yet promulgated the theory of socialism in one country, which was to form the crux of the epic struggle. The events of the Chinese Revolution of 1925-27 and the Anglo-Russian Committee were still in the future.

It is no slur upon the value of Trotsky's 1923 writings to say that they do not contain a finished analysis of events which had not yet occurred at the time. Shachtman, however, finds *The New Course* indispensable for his purposes not for what it does say, but primarily for what it does not and could not of necessity say. Could Shachtman have published *The Revolution Betrayed* and attempted to refute it? Or perhaps *The Soviet Union and the Fourth International*, and attempted to refute that? He might at least have attempted to review *In Defence of Marxism* which contains the most finished and the most recent analysis of the Soviet Union made by Trotsky, and is, in addition, addressed in person to Shachtman and Co. Shachtman's perspicacity, lamentably limited though it may be, extends at least far enough for him to foresee the consequences of such foolhardy enterprises. Discretion is indeed the better part of valour, for Shachtman.

The Trotskyist movement holds that the Soviet Union remains a degenerated workers' state, basing that analysis upon the property forms of the Soviet Union: the existence of nationalised property and monopoly of foreign trade. This position is a line of demarcation between Trotskyism and all hostile and alien tendencies in the labour movement.

In order to give a picture of the Soviet Union to advanced workers, Trotskyists have often drawn an analogy between the first workers' state and a trade union. Just as trade unions have become corrupted and degenerated, losing their internal democracy and giving up militant struggle in defence of the interests of the membership, just so, the Soviet Union, subject to far more enormous pressures, has been altered. But the degenerated workers' state and the degenerated trade union remain class organisations and a struggle must be conducted to reform them and to defend them against the capitalists. Shachtman discusses the trade union analogy only to abandon this time the Marxist position on trade unions. We quote Shachtman verbatim:

"The trade unions remain trade unions, no matter how bureaucratised they become, so long as they fight (ineptly or skilfully, reformistically or militantly) in the defence of the workers' share of the national income, or at least against its diminution. Once they give up that fight, they may call themselves what they will, they may have ever so many workers in their ranks (as many company unions have), but they are no longer class organisations. John L. Lewis' [US mineworkers' leader] organisation is still a trade union; Robert Ley's [leader of Hitler's 'Labour Front'] is not."

This point of view is clear, it is consistent, it is harmonious with the Shachtmanite point of view on the Soviet Union. It likewise happens to be the traditional position of the ultra-leftists. Lenin polemicised against it in *The Infantile Disease of Left-Wing Communism*. It is precisely on this theory that the Stalinists constructed their thesis of "social fascism," and their designation of the AFL as a "fascist" organisation.

"The trade unions remain trade unions, no matter how bureaucratised they become, so long as they fight (ineptly or skilfully, reformistically or militantly) in the defence of the workers share of the national income or at least against its diminution." But what of those unions that have abandoned the fight? What of those bureaucratised leaderships which have offered their co-operation to the war administration and fight for the diminution of the workers' share of the national income? What of the Stalinist controlled unions? Shachtman's answer is clear: "They are no longer class organisations." By this criterion, the trade union movement of the United States (and not only the United States) has all but disappeared!

Notice the examples given: "John L. Lewis' organisation is still a trade union: Robert Ley's is not." A typical Shachtmanite evasion! In order to find an example of a union that is "still a union" Shachtman cites the one union which has conducted four general coal strikes in the midst of the war! Shachtman is willing to admit it is still a union. This generous fellow would give ice away at the North Pole. Somebody should inform him that any schoolchild would readily agree that the United Mine Workers is "still" a union, while the Nazi Labour Front is not. But the question remains: what is the Hod Carriers Union, which holds conventions every 99 years? Or the Stalinist-run UE, which fights for incentive pay, not against it? Or anyone of a dozen others.

When a union is involved in a strike against the bosses, all labour must rally to the defence, even though a bureaucracy dominates the particular union. People who advocate defeatism for the striking union are traitors to the labour movement. That is the role of Shachtman, who denies defence to the Soviet Union in its struggle against Nazi imperialism. Among the primary results of the Nazi-Soviet war has been the elucidation of the attitude of the Soviet masses towards the state which emerged from the October revolution. Of the attitude of the Soviet workers and peasants to the Stalinist bureaucracy there can be no doubt. Stalin has betrayed their democratic hopes by making a prison house of the Soviet Union. He has betrayed their revolutionary aspirations by his continual abasement before world imperialism. The hatred of the masses for the Stalinist caste, so long expressed through the struggle of the advanced workers under the banner of the Trotskyist Left Opposition, will break out into the open at the first decisive turn in the European situation. But what of the attitude of the masses towards the Soviet state? The remarkable spirit and fighting energy, not only of the Red Army, but of the whole people, demonstrate their conviction that something important remains in the Soviet Union which must be defended; something which they feel belongs to them. The morale of the Red Army is the envy of the putrefying bourgeois military staffs everywhere. None of them can duplicate it because its secret lies in that event which they all hate so thoroughly; the October revolution of 1917.

Shachtman attempts to dismiss the morale of the Soviet peoples as of little significance. In 1940, during the Soviet-Finnish war, he was quite concerned about it. At that time, the Soviet workers, repelled by Stalin's counter-revolutionary policy, by the spectacle of the friendship and collaboration between Stalin and Hitler, and more important, not yet actually feeling the pressure of the bourgeois military intervention against the first workers' state, prosecuted the war with indifference. At that time, Shachtman, like any shyster lawyer, considered testimony relating to the morale of the Red Army to be perfectly admissible evidence as to the "character of the war." He and his followers quoted derisively Trotsky's prediction as to the morale of the Soviet people in the event of war. That forecast is well worth repeating now.

"Within the USSR war against imperialist intervention will undoubtedly provoke a veritable outburst of genuine fighting enthusiasm. All the contradictions and antagonisms will seem overcome, at any rate relegated to the background. The young generations of workers and peasants that emerged from the revolution will reveal on the field of battle a colossal dynamic power. Centralised industry, despite all its lacks and shortcomings, will reveal great superiority in serving war needs. The government of the USSR has undoubtedly created great stores of food supplies sufficient for the first period of war. The general staffs of the imperialist states clearly realise, of course, that in the Red Army they will meet a powerful adversary, the struggle with whom will require long intervals of time and a terrific straining of forces."

These are the words at which Shachtman scoffed during the

Finnish events. Where is the "genuine fighting enthusiasm?" he then taunted. Have you seen that spirit yet? The Soviet masses have given their answer.

During the factional struggle in the SWP in 1939-1940 Shachtman's petty-bourgeois opposition insisted that its sole political point of difference with the majority of the party was over the unconditional defence of the Soviet Union. The class nature of the Soviet Union, they explained, was no concern of theirs "at the moment", and was only dragged into the dispute by Trotsky for "factional, demagogic purposes." "Is it not demagogy for Trotsky to direct polemics against Eastman and Hook, or Bruno instead of against our ideas?" claimed Burnham and Shachtman. Today, Burnham writes from the standpoint of an avowed enemy of Marxism, while Shachtman espouses the former position of Burnham, who in turn borrowed it from Bruno. Today Shachtman even adduces as his main "proof" of the existence of a new class the argument adduced originally by Bruno, namely, Stalin's purges and frame-up trials of 1936-38. A modest disciple never fails gratefully to acknowledge his teacher. Shachtman ungraciously ignores his true preceptors: Burnham and Bruno.

Equipped with the compass of Marxism, Trotsky charted in the struggle of 1939-40 not only our own course, but the future course of the Shachtmanites. That is why he was able to write an annihilating answer to Shachtman's "theoretical" document long before Shachtman set it down on paper! Trotsky's writings *In Defence of Marxism* require no "corrections." Trotsky's characterisations of Shachtman as a "charlatan" and a "betrayer" are as true today as when Trotsky wrote them in 1940.

Fourth International, May 1944

Stalinist state property defines a new exploitative class society

Max Shachtman (1944)

LEON TROTSKY'S NAME will be forever linked with the Russian Revolution, not of course as a Russian revolution but as the beginning of the international socialist revolution in Russia. He fought for this revolution with pen and sword, from his study and from his armoured train in the Red Army. Between the start of his fight, under Czarism, and its end, under Stalinism, there is a continuous line, the line flowing from Trotsky's great contribution to Marxism, the theory of the permanent revolution.

Except for the first period of the Bolshevik revolution, when the theory was not — and could not be — attacked, it might be said that all of Trotsky's literary-political activity revolved around the elaboration of his theory, and its defence from critics. Which critics? The guide in choosing the objects of his polemics was not always their prominence or importance, the extent of the front along which they attacked Trotsky's views, the weightiness of their criticism. Wherever Trotsky was given an opportunity to elucidate his views, to expand upon them from a new angle, to fortify them in a new way, he seized upon it. The critic did not need to be Stalin or Radek. Even if he was so obscure, and his criticism so trivial or absurd, that the mere mention of his name by Trotsky sufficed to save him from oblivion, Trotsky did not for that reason disdain to deal with him. Ample evidence of this is to be found throughout Trotsky's writings. The evidence relates not only to polemics about his theory of the permanent revolution but more generally to any of the important views he held.

Similarly with those who were his students and his followers in every country. One example is *The New International*, which, month in and month out, from its first issue onward, emulated Trotsky by its systematic defence of the principles and program of Marxism against all critics, honest or mendacious, big or small, partial or total. It is, after all, only by this method that the Marxian movement can maintain theoretical alertness, preserve its pre-eminence over all other currents in the working class, and imbue its followers with informed confidence, in contrast to the blind faith, nurtured ignorance or confusion, and slick demagogy that hold together other movements.

What is said above applies not only to debate of Marxists with non- or anti-Marxists, but to discussions within the Marxian movement itself. There we have too often heard that a discussion is a "luxury." It is as much a luxury to the movement as the circulation of the blood is a luxury to the human body.

In the 1939-40 discussion in the Socialist Workers Party, Trotsky repeatedly challenged the then opposition (now the Workers Party) to debate first and foremost the question of the class character of the Soviet Union, he taking, as is well known, the standpoint that Russia is a degenerated workers' state. It goes without saying that he did not for a moment consider it a "closed question" precluding all discussion, although it is no less true that on this question his own position was firm and aggressive. For reasons that were then, and often since, advanced, the opposition did not wish to debate on this ground.

If the writer may speak personally for a moment: I not only did not wish to debate the view that Russia was still a workers' state, but I could not if I would. Like so many other members of the opposition (and not a few of the majority), I had developed some doubts (as an otherwise dull commentator correctly observed) on the correctness of our traditional position, without being able to say to myself, and therefore to others, that this position was fundamentally false and that an alternative position had to replace it. Inasmuch as only a dilettante, but not a serious politician, can be "sceptical toward all theories," or engage in a dispute on the basis of "doubts," let alone make them a polemical platform, it was manifestly impossible for me, and not me alone, to take up Trotsky's challenge.

Doubts are a bridge you cannot stand on for long. Either you go back to the old views or move on to new ones. Along with several other comrades who sought to probe the question seriously, thoroughly and in an unclouded atmosphere, I helped work out, in 1940-41, a critique of Trotsky's theory of Russia as a degenerated workers' state. We arrived at an analysis and conclusions of our own, summed up in the phrase "bureaucratic collectivism," a new class, exploitive state in Russia which is neither bourgeois nor proletarian but is basically different from any other class regime preceding or contemporary with it. We proceeded to set forth our views in dozens of articles in our press. Stalin's assassin deprived Trotsky of the opportunity, which he would undoubtedly have taken, to subject these views to criticism. But the "official" Trotskyist press, *The Militant* and the *Fourth International*? For three years it maintained complete silence. It did not, you see, deign to reply, unless a reply means repeating that we are "petty bourgeois," "counter-revolutionists," "enemies of the Soviet Union," "renegades from Marxism... common thieves" and the like — "arguments" which had failed to convince us when they originally appeared in the *Daily Worker*.

Yet not only we, but all those interested in Trotsky's views, especially those who supported them, had a right to expect an objective reply to our point of view from the SWP spokesmen. Our theory is the first serious attempt to present a rounded analysis of the Stalinist state from the Marxian standpoint, which, while basing itself in many respects on the invaluable contributions of Trotsky, is at the same time a criticism of Trotsky's conclusion. Our theory, furthermore, is a unique contribution to the question and not a rehash of old, refuted and discredited doctrines. We do not contend that it cannot be successfully disputed, only that it has not been. The SWP did not even make an attempt to do so.

When we finally published the first English edition of Trotsky's classic, written in 1923, *The New Course*, and added to it, as is our custom, an essay by the editor, it explained to the new reader the historical circumstances of the work, its significance in the light of subsequent events, plus a critical re-examination of Trotsky's later theory of the "workers' state." We felt that the SWP would now have to reply. Some of us thought it would assign a responsible, theoretically and politically equipped spokesman, to review the book as it deserves to be reviewed. Others thought that at most it would assign the job to some unschooled lad equipped with an advanced case of psittacosis and a penchant for abuse. Obviously, some of us were wrong. Under the characteristically restrained title, "A Defamer of Marxism," a review of the book appeared at last in the May, 1944, issue of the *Fourth International*, over the signature of Harry Frankel. This is, as we shall see, the literal equivalent of saying: Since the soup is too hot to handle, we might as well spit in it.

Frankel wastes only a few indifferent words on the section of the book written by Trotsky. He concedes, it is true, that *The New Course* is "beef," whereas "Shachtman's essay is the antipode: it is tripe." But he leaves the impression in the few sentences he devotes to *The New Course* that it is merely an initial, immature and dated effort by Trotsky. This is in the order of things.

Trotsky's *The New Course* is even more timely today than when it was first written. It is one of his most durable works. It is a classic socialist statement on workers' democracy. It is perhaps the clearest exposition ever written of what democracy means in a centralised, revolutionary proletarian party. It is, of course, a specific analysis of the problem of a specific party, after it has taken power, in a specific country and under specific conditions. This does not detract from its general applicability. What Trotsky says there about party democracy, about a free and vibrant internal life, about the role of tradition and the need of constantly enriching it, about critical and independent party thought, about Leninism, about discussions and how they should be conducted, about loyalty in discussion and in leadership, about the relations between leaders and ranks, between "young" and "old," about bureaucratism and conservatism, about factions and groupings, and a dozen other vital problems of any revolutionary party amounts to an annihilating criticism of the inner-party regime of the SWP today, of its leaders and their methods. Frankel's silence on all this, his generally deprecatory remarks, are in the order of things. Had he spoken commendatorily and at length about the ideas Trotsky puts forward in *The New Course*, he could only have brought a wry smile to the lips of every thinking member of the SWP.

Perhaps we do him an injustice. Perhaps he is so eager to work on the tripe that he has no time for the beef. The tripe he divides into five important parts. He deals with the parentage of our theory; the question of its significance in the "whole of Trotskyism"; the question of the roots of class rule; the question of the historical place of the Stalin bureaucracy; the question of the analogy between Russia and a trade union. If we pursue him through his often dreary and never bright abuse, it is because the task, though thankless, is not without profit.

Frankel writes:

Today, Burnham writes from the standpoint of an avowed enemy of Marxism, while Shachtman espouses the former position of Burnham, who in turn borrowed it from Bruno. Today, Shachtman even adduces as his main "proof" of the existence of a new class the argument adduced originally by Bruno, namely, Stalin's purges and frame-up trials of 1936-38. A modest disciple never fails gratefully to acknowledge his teacher. Shachtman ungraciously ignores his true preceptors: Burnham and Bruno.

And elsewhere:

Burnham's theory of "bureaucratic collectivism" (borrowed from Bruno) is now coolly offered as an "indispensable correction" to Trotskyism.

About Burnham, our readers know something, and so, presumably, does Frankel. But who is this sinister Bruno? All we know of him is that just before the war he wrote a big book in France on the "bureaucratisation of the world." This book we never read. Neither did Frankel. The only thing he knows about Bruno, about whose views he speaks with such impressive familiarity, is the reference to it made by Trotsky in 1939 in a few sentences. It takes a high grade of impertinence or transoceanic vision, one of which Frankel certainly possesses, to speak with such assuredness about views elaborated in a book you have neither seen nor read, and about which all you know is a dozen paraphrasing sentences written by a critic.

But can't it be assumed that the sentences in which Trotsky sums up the views of one of the "parents" of our theory are adequate? We are ready to do so. According to Trotsky's summary, Bruno seems to hold the theory that "bureaucratic collectivism" or the bureaucratic state is a new, unprecedented exploitive social order, with a new ruling class, which exists not only in Russia but also in Germany and in a less developed form in "New Deal" America, and is, in a word, sweeping the world. According to this theory, there is no class difference between the German-US type of state and the Russian type. As is known, Burnham's latest theory is similar, apparently, to Bruno's.

What, however, has such a theory to do with ours? In every article we have written on the subject, in the official resolution of our party, we have repeatedly emphasised the unique class character of the Russian state, its fundamental difference not only from a workers' state, but from all the bourgeois states, be they fascist or democratic. Time and again we have polemised against the theory that Russia and Germany, for example, have the same class state or social system or ruling class — against those who, like Burnham and Macdonald, held that both countries were "bureaucratic-collectivist," as well as against those who held that both were capitalist. Our party has formally rejected both these standpoints. If our cavalier is aware of these facts, he is practising a fraud on his readers by concealing them. If he is unaware of them, he is practising a fraud on his readers by dealing with matters he is ignorant of. Take your choice.

In *The New Course*, Trotsky lays the greatest stress on loyalty in discussion, on the importance of an honest presentation of your opponent's views, on the reprehensibility of amalgamating one view with views that are essentially alien to it. No wonder Frankel thinks so little of the book.

Where does our theory have its roots? Primarily in the writings of Trotsky! More accurately, in the resolving of the two basic, irreconcilable theories about Russia as a "degenerated workers' state" which are to be found in Trotsky's writings. For a long time Trotsky rightly based his theory that Russia is a degenerated workers' state on the view that, to one degree or another, in one form or another, the Soviet proletariat still retained political power, that it could yet submit its bureaucracy to its control, that it could regenerate the state by means of a profound reform. Indeed, Trotsky repeated that the proof of the working class character of the Soviet states lies in the fact that the regime could still be changed by reform. This theory he later abandoned, substituting the point of view that, although the proletariat had lost all semblance of political power and control, and an uncontrolled, counter-revolutionary bureaucracy had complete possession of the state power, and that it could not be removed save by means of a violent revolution, the state was nevertheless proletarian by virtue of the existence of state property. Only Trotsky's immense authority in the movement made possible the acceptance by it of a theory which, up to that time, had never been held by any Marxist.

In numerous articles we have pointed out the contradiction between the two theories. We have pointed out how Trotsky abandoned the one for the other without so much as a link between them. We have showed how Trotsky was compelled to abandon his original theory because events refuted the essential predictions about Russia's evolution which he based on it. The voluminous quotations we have adduced from Trotsky's writings are simply irrefutable. Enough of them are again cited in our essay on *The New Course*. Frankel does not even hint at their existence (we are making the audacious assumption that he actually read the book). With consummate native skill, he plays dumb on this point. And not on this point alone.

This is not all. Frankel knows — and if he does not know, why does he venture to blacken so much innocent white paper? — that our press, the present writer in particular, has called attention to the fact that the first man (so far as we know) in the Trotskyist movement who put forward the theory that the Stalinist bureaucracy is a new ruling class, based on a new "property form," was neither Shachtman, Burnham, nor, God help us, the mysterious Bruno, but Christian Rakovsky. More than a decade ago, Rakovsky, next to Trotsky the outstanding leader of the Opposition, presented this view in a theoretical document of his own, which was circulated throughout the Russian Opposition. Trotsky, although he obviously did not share this view, printed it in the organ of the Russian Opposition without comment and certainly without denunciation — he was not made of the same stern and intransigent stuff as his eminent theoretical successor, Frankel. There is enough evidence, moreover, in letters of Oppositionist exiles and in the testimony of A. Ciliga, that Rakovsky's theory was shared by a considerable number of Russian Trotskyists. Poor devils! They had no Frankel to explain to them that they were "defamers of Marxism," purveyors of tripe, and belonged, as he so delicately puts it, to the "legion of emasculators, vulgarisers and

411

falsifiers" of Trotskyism.

We do not hesitate for a moment to say that this or that element of our theory as a whole is taken from numerous other sources, including, if you please, Burnham (the Burnham of 1937-38, of course, and not the Burnham of 1940 or today). If our critics derive satisfaction from this readily-made acknowledgement, it is either because they do not know anything about the "alien" origins and components of the entire theoretical system of Marxism, or because they do not care. For the construction of our theory, for its synthesis, for the ideas of others and of our own incorporated into it, for the manner in which they are incorporated and interlinked, we and we alone are responsible.

"With typical impudence," says Frankel, to whom impudence of any kind is as foreign as a bad odour to a sty, "Shachtman pretends that Trotsky's class analysis of the Soviet Union as a degenerated workers' state 'is not even a decisively important part' of Trotskyism. This is like saying that a man could function without a heart."

We thus learn for the first time, but from an authority, that the "heart" of Trotskyism is the theory of the "degenerated workers' state." Which of the two theories Trotsky held on this subject is the "heart" of Trotskyism, the authority does not say. After all, what does it matter?

In our own confused way, we have always though that the "heart" of Trotskyism is the theory of the permanent revolution and the struggle for it. Frankel, we regretfully record, has not changed our opinion. For if the theory that Stalinist Russia is still a degenerated workers' state is the "heart" of Trotskyism, then obviously Trotskyism was without a heart, and consequently non-existent, before the Russian Revolution and during the early years of the revolution. It seems equally obvious that if Russia should tomorrow cease to be a "degenerated workers' state," either by virtue of its regeneration or its transformation into a capitalist state, the "heart" of Trotskyism would thereby be removed, leaving only a lifeless carcass which Frankel would not consider worthy of decent burial. To put it differently, the restoration of the Russian revolution to full life would produce the instantaneous death of Trotskyism. Or, to strain fairness toward our inimitable dialectician to the groaning point, if the "degenerated workers' state" were replaced by a revolutionary workers' state, Trotskyism would have a new "heart" grafted into it, its old one being removed to a bottle of formaldehyde labelled: "This was the heart of Trotskyism when Russia was a degenerated workers' state. Remove only in case of similar contingency — Dr. Frankel, M.D."

Only one other thing need be said about this nightmarish idiocy. We consider ourselves Trotskyists because we are partisans of the theory of the permanent revolution, because Trotskyism incarnated the tradition and principles of revolutionary Marxism, of socialist internationalism, above all in a period when these principles were being trampled under every foot. We are not idolators, precisely because we are Trotskyists. We know how easy it is, as Lenin used to say, sardonically, to "swear by God," and we have only pitying contempt for those who substitute the quotation for the living idea, worshipful parrotry for critical thought. We are Trotskyists, but we do not "swear by God." But if it can truly be demonstrated that the very "heart" of Trotskyism is the belief that Russia today is a "degenerated workers' state" and that all the other organs and limbs of Trotskyism live from the bloom pumped to them by this heart, then the present writer, at least, would promptly cease calling himself a Trotskyist. At the same time, however, he would have to conclude that Trotskyism and Marxism are not reconcilable. Fortunately, no such conclusion is indicated, or necessary, or possible.

We come now to the third of Frankel's five points. Here we must admonish the reader. He must resolve in advance not to laugh himself sick. On this he must be firm, for Frankel offers more temptations than the unforewarned reader can possibly resist.

The reader is surely acquainted with the point: An analogy is made between the bureaucratised trade unions, with their bourgeois-minded leaders, and bureaucratised Russia. "Just as trade unions have become corrupted and degenerated, losing their internal democracy and giving up militant struggle in defence of the interests of the membership, just so, the Soviet Union, subject to far more enormous pressures, has been altered," writes Frankel. But the degenerated workers' state and the degenerated trade union remain class organisations and a struggle must be conducted to reform (!) them and to defend them against the capitalists." (According to Trotsky, the "degenerated workers' state" cannot be reformed; according to the heart specialist, it can and must be reformed. Frankel does not know the difference between revolution and reform, but in every other respect he is an authority on Trotskyism and above all on what lies at its heart.)

The "trade union analogy" has long been a favoured argument of the defenders of the theory that Russia is a degenerated workers' state. Following Trotsky, the present writer used the "analogy" more than once. Along with others, he accepted it uncritically from Trotsky. This acceptance was eased, so to speak, by the fact that the analogy has a long and worthy standing dating back to the earliest days of the Russian Revolution. But if it is traced back clearly to those days, it will be seen that the analogy was entirely legitimate in its time. It was not employed to prove that Russia was a workers' state, however. It was employed to show why the workers' state did not always operate as the ideal program indicated. Between the two uses of the analogy, there is a world of difference.

Whatever may have been our errors on this point in the past, they look like downright virtues in comparison with what Frankel does with it. We beg the reader to follow very closely. It would be a pity to miss any part of it. "Shachtman discusses the trade union analogy only to abandon this time the Marxist position on trade unions," says our relentless Spartan. Shachtman, it is clear, has left very little of Marxism, and Frankel has left very little of Shachtman. But even if there were less, it would still suffice for what follows.

Wherein lies this new "abandonment"? Read carefully the quotation from Shachtman which Frankel cites:

The trade unions remain trade unions, no matter how bureaucratised they become, as long as they fight (ineptly or skilfully, reformistically or militantly) in the defence of the workers' share of the national income, or at least against its diminution. Once they give up that fight, they may call themselves what they will, they may have ever so many workers in their ranks (as many company unions have), but they are no longer class organisations. John L. Lewis' organisation is still a trade union; Robert Ley's is not.

Now read just as carefully Frankel's comment on this definition, part of which we ourselves emphasise:

This point of view is clear, It is consistent, it is harmonious with the Shachtmanite point of view on the Soviet Union. It likewise happens to be the traditional position of the ultra-leftists. Lenin polemicised against it in The Infantile Disease of Left-Wing Communism. It is precisely on this theory that the Stalinists constructed their thesis of "social fascism," and their designation of the AFL as a "fascist" organisation.

What's right is right; our view on the trade unions is clear, consistent and harmonious with our views on Russia. Every thing else in this quotation, except for the spelling and punctuation, is — if we may be forgiven the abusiveness provoked by snarling, stubborn ignorance — wrong and stupid.

Frankel thinks I cited the Lewis union because it is "the one union which has conducted four general coal strikes in the midst of the war ... This generous fellow would give ice away at the North Pole." A heart specialist, a trade union expert, and a wit to boot. The fact is the United Mine Workers was cited by me not because it "conducted

414

four general coal strikes in the midst of the war," but because it is one of the most bureaucratically constructed, managed and controlled unions in the country, and yet is a proletarian organisation. Our wit is persistent: "But the question remains: what is the Hod Carriers Union, which holds conventions every ninety-nine years? Or the Stalinist-run UE, which fights for incentive pay, not against it? Or anyone of a dozen others."

The answer to these questions must be given, we fear. Frankel is old enough to be told the truth, at least in a whisper. The members of the Hod Carriers Union are among the highest-paid workers in the United States. The union leaders are despots, some are even said to be gangsters, grafters and corruptionists, some have made a mighty good thing for themselves out of unionism. But, by terroristic methods, if you will, by bureaucratic and reactionary methods, and with the aim of feathering their own nests, they work and must work "in the defence of the workers' share of the national income, or at least against its diminution." If they did not, the union would disappear and so would the very basis on which their autocratic power and privileges are built up. The Stalinist-led unions are, of course, somewhat different, but fundamentally the same. Take even incentive pay. The Stalinists put it forward, and are compelled to put it forward, as a means of increasing the workers' income. We say that the incentive-pay system, while it would increase the income of some workers, or of all of them temporarily, would do so at the expense of the muscles and nerves of the workers, at the expense of their long-range interests, at the expense of the solidarity and fighting power of the union, etc., etc. How mortifying the thought that the ABC's have to be explained to a Marxian theoretician of such height, breadth and weight.

Four times we read Frankel's comment on our definition. But nowhere did we find a word to indicate how he defines a trade union, how he would distinguish even the most reactionary trade union from a company union or from Ley's "Labour Front." What standard would he employ? That it was originally formed by workers? That it is composed of workers? That it claims to speak for workers? What? What?

If instead of comparing Russia with a union, we would compare a union with Russia, then by Frankel's standards, a union would still deserve the name: if the "union" bureaucracy had all the power, if it had an army and police at its disposal to oppress the members, if it could be removed from office only by violent insurrection, if it ran prisons for recalcitrant members, if it made an alliance with U. S. Steel for joint picket lines against Republic Steel, if we opposed the organisation of the unorganised ("against the seizures of new territories by the Kremlin" — Trotsky), if we favoured the withdrawal, say, of its Negro members to form a separate union ("independence of the Ukraine" — Trotsky), and so forth. Ley's "union" could easily fit into such a definition.

Disappointed by Frankel's failure to define a union, we seek elsewhere. Perhaps the following definition will prove acceptable:

The character of such a workers' organisation as that of a trade union is determined by its relation to the distribution of the national income. The fact that Green & Co. defend private property in the means of production characterises them as bourgeois. Should these gentlemen in addition defend the income of the bourgeoisie from the attacks on the part of the workers, should they conduct a struggle against strikes, against the raising of wages, against help to the unemployed, then we would have an organisation of scabs and not a trade union. However, Green & Co., in order not to lose their base, must lead within certain limits the struggle of the workers for an increase — or at least against diminution — of their share in the national income. This objective symptom is sufficient in all important cases to permit us to draw a line of demarcation between the most reactionary trade union and an organisation of scabs. Thus we are duty-bound not only to carry on work in the AFL, but to defend it from scabs, the Ku Klux Klan, and the like.

Is this the "traditional position of the ultra-leftists"? Is this what Lenin polemised against? Is this "precisely" the theory on which "the Stalinists constructed their thesis on "social fascism"? Is this clear? Is it consistent? Is it, too, "harmonious with Shachtman's point of view on the Soviet Union"?

Doesn't every one of Frankel's strictures against Shachtman's definition apply equally to this definition? Absolutely! No more, no less! Who is the author of this second definition? Shachtman? No! Shachtman is guilty only of having copied it, in some places word for word, in all places meaning for meaning. It is Trotsky who is guilty of writing it! Our "authority" will find it in the December, 1937, Internal Bulletin of the Socialist Workers Party, No. 3, page 4.

Trotsky says you recognise the difference between a scab outfit and a union by the fact that the latter, even under Green and Co., "must lead within certain limits the struggle of the workers for an increase — or at least against diminution — of their share in the national income."

Shachtman, frankly "plagiarising" from Trotsky, says you recognise the difference between a fascist "front" and a union by the fact that the latter, even under Lewis and Co., "fight (ineptly or skilfully, reformistically or militantly) in the defence of the workers' share of the national income, or at least against its diminution."

The thought and even the language are identical, and not by accident, for both are dealing, Mr. Authority, with the ABC's of Marxism; both are dealing, Mr. Trade Union Expert, with the ABC's of trade unionism. And what does the Expert-Authority say about these definitions — not the stupid things about Lenin and social-fascism, but the unwittingly intelligent things? He says, let us remember, that "this point of view... is harmonious with the Shachtmanite point of view on the Soviet Union." Agreed! No complaint!

We could complain, however, if we were given to indignation over such things. If we were, then we might say: Have we really committed such unforgivable crimes that in a discussion of this importance you send against us a zero who does not know what the "heart" of Trotskyism is, where the roots of our theory lie, what the difference is between revolution and reform in Russia, or even what a common, ordinary trade union is — not even what Trotsky said it is — and who argues that Trotsky's definition of a union is harmonious with Shachtman's definition of Russia?

Inasmuch as indignation is really not called for here — pity is the more appropriate emotion — we do not make this complaint. It seems to us, however, that the membership of the SWP does have grounds for energetic complaint — Does our party have to discredit itself so ridiculously? Is this the only way we have of replying to the views of the Workers Party? These questions will gain greater poignancy when we examine the last two points dealt with by the Authority. We fear he will not fare too well under the examination. We invited honest, sober and informed criticism of our position. Instead, we got Frankel. The fault is clearly not ours.

We have already seen that our critic does not know what the "heart of Trotskyism" is, what are the sources of our criticism of Trotsky's theory of the "degenerated workers' state," and that he does not even know what a trade union is. We have also established that by Frankel's involuntary admission, Trotsky's conception of a trade union (which Frankel attributes to Shachtman alone) "is clear, it is consistent, it is harmonious with the Shachtmanite point of view on the Soviet Union." There remain two of the original five points to deal with: the question of the roots of class rule and the question of the historical place of the Stalin bureaucracy.

Marxists view classes as the product of historical development, in other words, all classes have a past and a future, as well as the present. Shachtman's "new exploitive class" is, in Shachtman's own words, "without a past and without a future." (Max Shachtman, The Struggle for the New

417

Course) *Lenin insisted that the roots of all class rule are to be found in the productive foundations of society. He said: "The rule of the class is determined only by the relationship to property." To explain the rule of his "new class," Shachtman points not to the foundation but to the political superstructure. It thus turns out that Shachtman's "indispensable correction" applies not only to Trotsky but to Lenin and Marx as well. But Shachtman simply forgets to mention such trifles. "Wherein does the rule of the class [the proletariat] express itself?" asked Lenin. And he answered: "The rule of the proletariat expresses itself in the abolition of landed and capitalist property." Not the introduction of nationalised property and planning but the abolition of the old property forms sufficed for Lenin. How does Shachtman get around this? Very simply. He denies that his new class needs either to abolish previous property forms or institute new ones of its own. Shachtman's class that has no past and no future possesses for its "fundament" not property relations but the "ownership" of "political power." Needless to add, this "ownership" in its turn has neither a past nor a future. Such tripe is, according to Shachtman, "the veriest commonplace of Marxism." (Fourth International*, May, 1944.)

This is typical Frankel: x parts ignorance (principal ingredient), x parts falsification (never omitted), x parts insolence (the style is the man), and x parts plain, ordinary, anhydrous muddleheadedness; the solvent is not even tap-water. This chemical analysis requires demonstration. Here it is.

1. *For Lenin, the roots of class rule are to be found in the productive foundations of society; Shachtman, however, who simply forgets to mention (note: "forgets to mention") such trifles, points not to the foundation but to the political super-structure.*

That Shachtman, who is in his way as human as Frankel, may forget to mention one trifle or another, is more than possible. But the trifle of which Frankel speaks with that mastery of sarcasm which marks him out from a world of dullards, was not forgotten by Shachtman. Not only was it not forgotten, but it is to this very trifle that the origin of the new ruling class in Russia was traced. In *The Struggle for the New Course* it says:

At bottom, classes have risen and come to power throughout history in response to the developing needs of production which preceding classes were unable to satisfy. This is the case, also, with the new ruling class in Russia. The Russian bourgeoisie had ample opportunity to prove that it could not, or could no longer, develop the productive forces of the country. It came upon the scene too late to play the historically progressive role it played in the Western countries....

But if the bourgeoisie came too late, the proletariat of Russia came to power, so to speak, "too early." It is of course more proper to say that the rest of the European proletariat did not come to power early enough. The results of this retardation of the world revolution are known. The isolated Russian proletariat, in a backward country, could not satisfy the needs of production, either. It could not satisfy them on a socialist basis. That was the quintessential point made by Trotsky in his theory of the permanent revolution. It was with this conviction in mind that he combatted the bureaucracy's theory of "socialism in a single country." The bureaucracy won, the revolution degenerated. But not in accordance with the predictions of Lenin or Trotsky. The revolution did not turn to capitalism.

The reader, we think, is getting some idea of who it is that simply "forgets to mention" the "trifles." Let us continue.

"All modern nations," we noted, *"experience the need of an economic organisation and strength that will enable them to survive."* The Russian bourgeoisie, however, was unable to develop the productive forces, an inability which conditioned its social impotence and the triumph of the Russian revolution under the hegemony of the proletariat. (A contrary view is a capitulation to Menshevism.) The proletariat, in turn, was able to develop the productive forces — in Trotsky's words, make possible an "authentic rise of a socialist economy" — only with the state aid of the victorious Western proletariat. (A contrary view is a capitulation to Stalinism.) The old prediction said: Without the world revolution, Russia will inevitably stagnate and then succumb to capitalism in the form of foreign imperialist exploitation; also, Stalinism is turning the country in that direction. The prediction, however understandable, was erroneous. A tremendous economic advance was made under Stalin's "planning." It was not a socialist advance — this prediction of Trotsky was absolutely borne out. But neither was it capitalist! It was not accomplished by restoring private ownership in the means of production and exchange or by abolishing the monopoly of foreign trade.

The productive forces were not developed by way of socialisation (which implies a trend toward socialism) but by way of bureaucratic collectivism. The new bureaucracy was born, grew, and took power in response, not to the needs of society as a whole — the world proletariat is sufficiently capable of satisfying those — but to the organic needs of a backward, isolated country, existing in unique and unprecedented world conditions.

Let us temper the verdict with charity, and say: Frankel "simply forgets to mention" that he wrote his review before reading the book. Impossible! the reader may protest. Impossible or not, the statement has the virtue of mercifully avoiding the right name for Frankel.

2. For Lenin, the rule of the class is determined only by the relationship to property; Shachtman, however, tries to get around this by arguing that "his new class" establishes no new property forms of its own, and does not have property relations but the ownership of political power as its fundament.

That looks bad — but only if there lingers in you a faith that Frankel understands what he reads, or even reads what he reviews and condemns. It does not look so bad when you understand that the rule of the class is determined in the same way in Lenin's conception and in Shachtman's. The latter wrote in *The Struggle for the New Course*: "It is of the ABC of Marxism that the fundament of all social relations (that is, relations of production) are property relations. That holds for the old slaveholding societies, for feudal society, for capitalist society and for the proletarian state." "How," asked Frankel, "does Shachtman get around" Lenin's conception? Very simply: by sharing it.

But it is necessary to know what conception it is we share. Lenin speaks of property relations, of the relationship of a class to property, that is, to the means of production and exchange. Let us present a little more of the speech by Lenin at the 9th Congress of the Russian party in 1920, from which Frankel takes his quotations.

When the question of property was decided in practice, the rule of the class was thereby assured: thereupon the constitution wrote down on paper what life has decided: "There is no capitalist and landed property," and it added: "The working class has more rights than the peasantry, but the exploiters have no rights at all." Therewith was written down the manner in which we realised the rule of our class, *in which we bound together the toilers of all strata, of all the little groups....*

The rule of the class is determined only by the relationship to property. That is precisely what determines the constitution. And our constitution correctly sets down our attitude to property and our attitude to the question of what class must stand at the head. (My emphasis — M. S.)

"And it added" — what Frankel failed to add: The working class has more rights than the peasantry, but the exploiters have no rights at all. "Therewith was written down the manner in which we realised the rule of our class." Class rule is determined only by the relationship to property. "Our constitution correctly sets down our attitude to property and our attitude to the question of what class must stand at the head." Today, the working class does not have "more rights than the peasantry." The capitalist exploiters have no rights at all in the Stalinist state, but neither have the workers or the peasants. The working class does not "stand at the head." It is in the prison house that — so Frankel says — Stalin has made out of Russia.

In Russia in 1917, the proletariat first took political power. Then, the proletariat-in-power "did abolish property and abolished it completely." The "rule of the class was thereby assured." The constitution then gave the proletariat ruling rights; it provided that the proletariat "must stand at the head." The means of production and exchange became the property of the workers' state. The setting up of a new class state by the Stalinist counterrevolution was accomplished by wiping all this out, by establishing fundamentally different property relations.

All wiped out? This is where Frankel is baffled. Isn't it a fact that property is still nationalised, still state property? Do not the property forms set up by the Bolshevik revolution still remain? Isn't it a fact that "the abolition of the old [capitalist] property forms sufficed for Lenin"? and that these old forms have not yet been restored by the counterrevolutionary bureaucracy? Here we approach the nub of the problem.

The "abolition of the old property forms" would not have "sufficed for Lenin" if these forms (capitalist private property) had been burned out in a fire, inundated in a storm, or bombed into rubble by Flying Fortresses. The abolition sufficed because it was accomplished by the proletariat-in-power which converted capitalist property into the property of a proletarian state. By this action, the proletarian state completed (the first stage of) the transformation not only of the old property relations. What is the meaning of this distinction between "forms" and "relations"? Does it exist in reality or is it purely verbal?

Under capitalism, property exists in the form of capitalist private property. This simple sentence already shows what are the property relations under capitalism. Regardless of the political regime (be it monarchical, democratic, militarist, Fascist or even semi-feudal), the capitalist class owns the property (means of production, etc.) and the proletariat works, as Marx would say, "with conditions of labour belonging to another." That is how we find the relationships of the classes to property. The state exists to maintain these relationships. The minute, therefore, you say "capitalist property forms" you have already said "capitalist property relations." Similarly, under slavery and feudalism, and in general wherever property is privately owned. The class that owns the property is the ruling class.

But what about the society in which property is not privately but state-owned? Trotsky wrote about the Stalinist bureaucracy that "the very fact of its appropriation of political power in a country where the principal means of production are in the hands of the state, creates a new and hitherto unknown relation between the bureaucracy and the riches of the nation" (*Revolution Betrayed*). Let us re-emphasise: a new and hitherto unknown relation. This thought, however, needs supplementation: the seizure of political power by the proletariat in a country where it turns over the principal means of production to the hands of the state also creates a new and hitherto unknown relation between the rulers and the property. For the third time we emphasise: a new and hitherto unknown relation.

Why new? Why hitherto unknown? Because the proletariat, its revolution, and the social order whose establishment is its historic mission, differ fundamentally from all preceding classes, their revolutions and their social orders. The proletariat is not a property-owning class under capitalism; and it does not become a property-owning class when it takes power. When it takes state power, it turns the property over to its state. Its relations to property are then expressed only through its state. It "owns" the property only inasmuch as it rules the property-owning state. That is the only way the proletariat ever did own property, ever will own it and ever can own it. It owns it through its state, the workers' state, through its political power!

That is why there is such lamentable ignorance in the sarcastic question: "Since when did a ruling class have for its fundament not property relations but the ownership of political power? Are the Fascists a new ruling class? Is an absolute monarch a new ruling class?"

No, the monarch was not a ruling class; the feudal lords were, because they owned the landed property. The fascists are not a ruling class; the bourgeoisie is, because it owns the means of production and exchange. The proletariat, however, is not merely "another" class, but a fundamentally different one: It does not and cannot own property. It can only "own" the state when it takes power. By that "ownership" it establishes state property which it organises and operates so that it ceases to be state property and becomes social property. The state itself ceases to be.

The complete expropriation of the political power of the working class by the Stalinist bureaucracy only makes this point clearer. The property forms seem to be the same as they were before: property exists in the form of state property. Therefore, cries Frankel triumphantly, it is still a workers' state, even if politically degenerated.

But hold on a moment: What are now the property relations in Russia? That is, what are the relations of the various classes (or, let us say, the various social groups) to the state property? We have been told by Lenin, through Frankel, that the rule of the class is determined only by the relationship to property. Granted. But just how shall we now determine what the relationship is?

In a society where property is privately owned, the question answers itself: this class (or social group) owns the property, this class does not. Such an answer is obviously impossible in a society where property is not privately owned but state owned. To determine then the relations to property of the various social groups, is it not clear that we must first find out what are their respective relations to the state-which-owns-the-property?

"From the point of view of property in [ownership of] the means of production," wrote Trotsky, "the differences between a marshal and a servant girl, the head of a trust and a day labourer, the son of a people's commissar and a homeless child, seem not to exist at all." (*Revolution Betrayed*).

That's just the point, although Trotsky did not draw the right conclusion. If you look at Russia from the standpoint of ownership of the means of production in the same way you look at a society in which these are privately owned — the trust head and the labourer have exactly the same property relations. Yet, in reality, their respective relations to property are as fundamentally different as the respective relations to property of the bourgeois and the proletarian under capitalism (except that in Russia the gap between the classes is so much greater). The bureaucracy is the ruling class. It has all the political power, the proletariat has none.

That is why Frankel's "irony" about Shachtman because the latter "points not to the foundation but to the political superstructure," is so utterly out of place. He does not understand the historically unprecedented nature of the proletarian state power, the peculiarity of the proletariat as a ruling class. He does not understand what is unprecedented about the class rule of the Stalinist bureaucracy. He derides its "ownership" of "political power" as something quite secondary, because he cannot grasp the simple idea that where property belongs to the state, the "ownership" of the state power means the monopolisation of all economic and social power. The bureaucracy is the ruling class because its "mere" political power makes it the owner of the conditions of production. It is always the relation of the owners of the conditions of production to the actual producers that shows us the real basis of a class society and establishes the true class character of the state. The Stalinist state is no exception to this rule.

This is the nub of the problem, we said. Without understanding this essentially simple idea, the Stalinist counter-revolution will remain an enigma and a source of confusion. We wrote that our criticism of Trotsky's theory "introduces into it an indispensable correction." The key to this correction is given by Trotsky. If we quote Trotsky himself, this may be of help to Frankel, whose Marxism consists, in Lenin's excellent phrase, of "swearing by God."

In the *Revolution Betrayed*, Trotsky shows how bourgeois society has maintained itself and developed in spite of different political regimes and bureaucratic castes. *"In contrast to this, the property relations which issued from the socialist revolution are indivisibly bound up with the new state as their repository.* The predominance of socialist over petty bourgeois tendencies is guaranteed, not by the automatism of the economy — we are still far from that — but *by political measures* taken by the dictatorship. *The character of the economy as a whole thus depends upon the character of the state power."* (My emphasis — M.S.)

Our whole difference with this basically unassailable statement of the problem lies in the fact that we draw the consistent conclusion. The new state is the repository of the property relations and is indivisibly bound up with them! The character of the economy depends upon the character of the state power! And that in contrast to bourgeois society! Once this is understood, the rest follows.

It is this conception that lay at the heart of Trotsky's first theory of Russia as a degenerated workers' state: the state is the repository of the property relations; the character of the economy depends upon the character of the state power. In this first theory, Trotsky, as Frankel would put it, "pointed not to the foundations but to the political superstructure." That is why Trotsky used to repeat and repeat that Russia is still a workers' state because the political power can be reformed, "that the proletariat of the USSR has not forfeited the possibility of submitting the bureaucracy to it, of reviving the party and of mending the regime of the dictatorship — without a new revolution, with the methods and on the road of reform." (*Problems of the Development of the USSR.*)

With the abandonment of the program of reform and the adoption of the view that the Stalinist bureaucracy can be overthrown only by a revolution, Trotsky was compelled also to abandon his first theory and to develop an altogether different one, namely, Russia is still a workers' state because property is still nationalised. This complete change has been demonstrated by us in detail and in several places, including *The Struggle for the New Course.* Frankel just acts as if he never heard of the point. His silence encourages the belief that our demonstration is irrefutable.

The second theory of Trotsky is radically different from the first. Originally, the state was the repository of the property relations; now the "property relations" (nationalised property) are the "repository" of the state. Originally, the character of the economy was determined by the character of the state power (Frankel's "political superstructure"); now the character of the state power is determined by the character of the economy.

If you understand and hold to the first, and only correct, conception of Trotsky, you understand why the counter-revolutionary bureaucracy, in conquering state power and establishing itself as the new ruling class, did not need "to abolish previous property forms or institute new ones of its own," at least not in appearance. By completing its conquest of state power, the bureaucracy established new property relations. Thereby (will Frankel ever understand this?) it established property forms of its own, if by that is meant social property forms. When the proletariat was in power, property existed and was exploited in Russia in the form of property-of-the-workers'-state. With Stalinism in complete power, property exists and is exploited in the form of property-of-the-bureaucratic-collectivist state. Stalinism has wiped out all the conquests of the proletarian revolution.

The trouble with Frankel, at bottom, is that he accepts and his party repeatedly disseminates the fundamental sophism of the Stalinist doctrine, which, in the new Russian constitution, legalises the lie that state property equals "the possessions of the whole people."

3. A ruling class without a past and without a future? In a terse, but all the more devastating reply, Frankel says: "Such tripe is, according to Shachtman, 'the veriest commonplace of Marxism'." Neither the commonplaces nor the complexities of Marxism are made up of tripe. This we will grant. But only if we are allowed to add that discussions of Marxism should not be made up of forgeries.

In the chapter on the bureaucracy as a new ruling class, Shachtman analyses the hopeless contradiction into which Trotsky's theory drove him in 1939 when he presented us with a proletarian revolution carried out in Russian-occupied Poland by the "counterrevolutionary workers' state." (Brave Frankel, like his friends, has not one word to say in defence of Trotsky on this point.) *At the end of his analysis, Shachtman writes that "In comparison with this, our theory of the Stalinist bureaucracy as a new and reactionary exploitive class, and of Russia as a bureaucratic-collectivist class state, neither proletarian nor bourgeois, is the veriest commonplace of Marxism". Several pages later, at the end of the volume, Shachtman writes, in an entirely different connection, about "the new bureaucracy, without a past and without a future".*

Frankel, who belongs to the "only moral people," simply cuts away the couple of thousand words that separate the two quotations, pastes together the two unrelated clauses with a little trip, and passes it off on the public as a genuine check written "according to Shachtman." Following right after this clumsy little forgery appears a subheading over another one of Frankel's stern indictments of us. It reads (O Coincidence!): "A Petty Bourgeois Counterfeit." The only comment this requires is two punctuation marks: !!

However, we did speak of the Stalinist bureaucracy as being without a past and without a future. It is a question that is best dealt with — in so far as it can be adequately treated in an article — in connection with the final point raised (i.e., muddled up) by Frankel:

According to Marxists, the historical justification for every ruling class is the ability under its particular system of exploitation to raise the development of productive forces of society as a whole to a new level. Does Shachtman grant this ability to Stalinism, i.e., his own "new exploitive class"? ...

The gist of Shachtman's 128-page argument boils down to a representation of the crimes of Stalinism as the birthpangs that marked the rise of a new class to power. No more, no less. It is an elementary principle of Marxism that ruling classes rise in society through the operation of forces beyond the control of men's consciousness, reason or will. The rise of new ruling classes can be retarded or facilitated but never prevented — until and unless these classes have exhausted their historic mission. In the light of this, what is Shachtman's version of the evolution of the Soviet Union if not an attempt to supply an historical justification not for the ascendancy of a new class but actually for the abominations of the Kremlin?

Ex ungue leonem — you know the lion by his claws. Another species of animal, however, you know by its bray. From the braying, we gather that Shachtman is not only trying to provide an historical justification for Stalinism, "but actually for the abominations of the Kremlin." Obviously a detestable creature this Shachtman. Much deeper he cannot sink.

However, if we fumigate the air a little and reflect a little, things look more cheerful. In the first place, the two accusations are in conflict: Shachtman says the bureaucracy has no past and no future, and he gives the bureaucracy an historical justification. If it is historically justified, it has both an historical past and an historical future. In the second place, Shachtman nowhere speaks of an historical justification of Stalinism, nor does he suggest that it has one. Here we have not a forgery, but an invention. And in the third place, the only one in our movement who ever spoke of an historical justification of the Stalinist bureaucracy was — Leon Trotsky. As in the case of the definition of a trade union, Frankel does not know where Trotsky ends and where Shachtman begins (this is his only qualification for writing on either one of them).

On December 28, 1934, Trotsky wrote: "Indeed, the historical justification for the very existence of the bureaucracy is lodged in the fact that we are still very far removed from socialist society." (*The Kirov Assassination*.) Further, he notes that the Stalinist dictatorship is both a heritage of past class struggles and an instrument for preventing a new class struggle. "In this and in this alone rests the historical justification for the existence of the present Soviet dictatorship." (Ibid.) Again, in the same work: "It would be criminal to deny the progressive work accomplished by the Soviet bureaucracy." (This Trotsky pamphlet was translated by J. G. Wright. Wright is editor of the *Fourth International*. Without a murmur, he prints Frankel's ignorant and venomous observations on "historical justification." What does it matter? Who will read the answer to it? Is it against the "petty bourgeois opposition"? Is it true and harsh and tough and vicious? Well, so much the better! That's how we rough-and-tumble proletarians (i.e., J G Wright! i.e., H Frankel! i.e., J. Hansen!) write, and if you don't like it you can lump it. Let's print it, damn it all.)

In a sense, we are able to accept Trotsky's characterisation of the bureaucracy. That is why we are able to speak of the new class without a past and without a future — that is, without an historical past or future. If Frankel had resisted his penchant for tearing phrases out of their context, the meaning would have been clearer. We say the Stalinist bureaucracy is a new ruling class because it is the "owner of the conditions of production." Despite similarities in certain aspects with other class societies (the capitalist, for example), it differs basically from all of them in its own unique mode of production, in the "specific economic form in which unpaid surplus labour is pumped out of the direct producers," in the distribution of the means of production and of the products of economy. As a result of unforeseen historical circumstances, it arose out of "the needs of production"; it did develop the productive forces in a way that no other class could under the given conditions.

We say this class is without a past. We seek thereby to distinguish it from the great and durable classes of history which, for various objective reasons (economic, geographical, etc.), went through a long evolution and decisively directed the course of social development. What Frankel says about "every ruling class" is true only in a manner of speaking, that is, with the necessary historical limitations. In other words, it is not true as an absolutely valid dogma. History is studded with the record of classes under whose rule society stagnated and which could not be fitted into Frankel's rigid formula. Whoever does not know this had better rush to a serious history before he even pretends to speak about Marxism. Marxism does not say that the world, and everything in it, marches straight from primitive communism to slavery, then to feudalism, then to capitalism, then to the proletarian dictatorship and communism, with no reversions, sideleaps, combinations or "oddities" whatsoever. This is an utterly primitive conception of Marxism.

"My critic," wrote Marx to the Russian Populist, Danielson, "must needs metamorphose my outline of the genesis of capitalism in western Europe *into a historic-philosophical theory of the general course, fatally imposed upon all peoples, regardless of the historical circumstances in which they find themselves placed*, in order to arrive finally at that economic formation which insures with the greatest amount of productive power of social labour the most complete development of man. But I beg his pardon. He does me too much honour and too much shame at the same time....

"... Strikingly analogical events, occurring, however, in different historical environments [lead] to entirely dissimilar results. *By studying each of these evolutions separately and then comparing them, one will easily find the key to these phenomena, but one will never succeed with the master-key of a historico-philosophical theory whose supreme virtue consists in being supra-historical.*" (My emphasis — M. S.)

Marx often repeated the same thought. All classes and all ruling classes are not the same and do not always have the same characteristics. They cannot always be measured by the same criteria. The same obviously holds true of all societies, for in each of them, as Marx points out, the "prevailing element" is a different one. To apply the same criteria to the present ruling class and the present social order in Russia as is applied, for example, to feudalism, simply makes no sense from the Marxian or any other standpoint. "By studying each of these evolutions separately, and then comparing them, one will easily find the key to these phenomena." This is what we have sought to do in our analysis of Stalinist Russia. A suprahistorical master-key does not exist. Not even a thinker of Frankel's stature can, if we may say so, forge one.

We say, further, that this new class has no future. Why? Because it arose at the stage of the final decay and crisis of class society. It has given no sign of an ability to resolve the crisis which the combined forces of world capitalism have failed to resolve. It is historically conditioned by the concrete circumstances of its origin. One of these circumstances is the existence of its origin. One of these circumstances is the existence of a modern proletariat which, on a world scale (but not on a national scale), is capable of breaking the fetters on the productive forces, on social development, on freedom, and thus resolving the last social crisis of humanity.

That is how it stands historically. Theoretically, it is conceivable that this new class may have "a future" and that on a world scale. Such a perspective might open up for it if, for example, it was conclusively demonstrated that the proletariat is organically incapable of resolving the crisis, of taking and holding power and employing it to inaugurate a classless society. Nothing of the sort has yet been demonstrated, much less demonstrated conclusively. There are some dilettantes and ex-radicals who confine themselves to just such speculations, and even make them their program of "action." We for our part find little interest in them, and less need for them. Our task is the mobilisation of the working class for the revolutionary assault against decaying capitalism. Our task is not ponderation over the growth and "future" of Stalinism, but the struggle against it for the future of the proletariat.

Successful struggle against a foe requires an understanding of his nature. That Frankel and his like do not understand, is already bad. That they refuse to understand — and a precondition of understanding is intelligent and loyal discussion, be it ever so vigorous — is worse. Frankel is only a minor epigone of Trotsky. Trotsky's whole *New Course* is an instructive protest against the type of methods, outlook, procedure that Frankel and his friends represent. That is why Frankel speaks so cavalierly of Trotsky's work. That is why he does not give the reader as much as an inkling of its contents. We have already suggested that he does not know much. But he knows enough to see that what Trotsky wrote in 1923-24 is a timely and thorough indictment of what he stands for. In this sense, a reading of *The New Course* may be recommended all over again as an excellent preparation for a fruitful discussion of "the Russian question."

New International, August 1944 and October 1944

Max Shachtman (left) and James P Cannon in Paris,
in 1938, at the entrance to a cul-de-sac.

8. Petty-bourgeois opposition, proletarian party?

A charge against the minority in the dispute among the Trotskyists over Poland and Finland in 1939-40, one still accepted even by many who no longer think that the Stalinist USSR was a workers' state, was that they were a "petty-bourgeois opposition". Three chief bits of evidence for this charge have been repeated over the years. One, that Burnham and Shachtman led the minority, and they both ended up "choosing the West" in the Cold War. (But no political tendency can be judged by its renegades, or by its activists' vagaries in demoralised old age. Least of all when its texts give the most cogent refutations of those vagaries or renegacies. Moreover, the majority of 1939-40 slid into "choosing the East" quicker). Two, that their arguments on Poland and Finland reflected the pressure of bourgeois-democratic public opinion. (But the Shachtmanites' stance in World War 2 affronted bourgeois-democratic public opinion more than the Cannonites' "proletarian military policy" and "defence of the USSR"). Three, that the minority's leaders had a long record of "petty-bourgeois" slidings over the years before 1939. The third argument came with the authority of Leon Trotsky himself.

A record of petty-bourgeois slidings

Leon Trotsky (1940)

COMRADE SHACHTMAN INVITES ME to present proof of the existence of a "petty-bourgeois tendency" in the party during the past year; or even two-three years. Shachtman is completely justified in not wishing to refer to the more distant past. But in accordance with Shachtman's invitation, I shall confine myself to the last three years. Please pay attention. To the rhetorical questions of my unsparing critic I shall reply with a few exact documents.

I.

On May 25, 1937, I wrote to New York concerning the policy of the Bolshevik-Leninist faction in the Socialist Party [i.e. the Trotskyist group which would become the SWP, which was then active as a minority in the Socialist Party]:

"... I must cite two recent documents: (a) the private letter of 'Max' about

the convention, and (b) Shachtman's article, Towards a Revolutionary Socialist Party. *The title of this article alone characterizes a false perspective. It seems to me established by the developments, including the last convention, that the party is evolving, not into a 'revolutionary' party, but into a kind of ILP, that is, a miserable centrist political abortion without any perspective. The affirmation that the American Socialist Party is now 'closer to the position of revolutionary Marxism than any party of the Second or Third Internationals' is an absolutely unmerited compliment: the American Socialist Party is only more backward than the analogous formations in Europe – the POUM, ILP, SAP, etc. ... Our duty is to unmask this negative advantage of Norman Thomas and Co., and not to speak about the 'superiority (of the war resolution) over any resolution ever adopted before by the party ...' This is a purely literary appreciation, because every resolution must be taken in connection with historical events, with the political situation and its imperative needs ..."*

In both of the documents mentioned in the above letter, Shachtman revealed excessive adaptability toward the left wing of the petty-bourgeois democrats – political mimicry – a very dangerous symptom in a revolutionary politician! It is extremely important to take note of his high appraisal of the "radical" position of Norman Thomas in relation to war ... in Europe. Opportunists, as is well known, tend to all the greater radicalism the further removed they are from events. With this law in mind it is not difficult to appraise at its true value the fact that Shachtman and his allies accuse us of a tendency to "capitulate to Stalinism." Alas, sitting in the Bronx, it is much easier to display irreconcilability toward the Kremlin than toward the American petty bourgeoisie.

II.

To believe comrade Shachtman, I dragged the question of the class composition of the factions into the dispute by the hair. Here too, let us refer to the recent past. On October 3, 1937, I wrote to New York:

"I have remarked hundreds of times that the worker who remains unnoticed in the 'normal' conditions of party life reveals remarkable qualities in a change of the situation when general formulas and fluent pens are not sufficient, where acquaintance with the life of workers and practical capacities are necessary. Under such conditions a gifted worker reveals a sureness of himself and reveals also his general political capabilities. Predominance in the organization of intellectuals is inevitable in the first period of the development of the organization. It is at the same time a big handicap to the political education of the more gifted workers ... It is absolutely necessary at the next convention to introduce in the local and central committees as many

workers as possible. To a worker, activity in the leading party body is at the same time a high political school... The difficulty is that in every organization there are traditional committee members and that different secondary, factional and personal considerations play a too great role in the composition of the list of candidates."

I have never met either attention or interest from comrade Shachtman in questions of this kind.

III.

To believe comrade Shachtman, I injected the question of comrade Abern's faction as a concentration of petty-bourgeois individuals artificially and without any basis in fact. Yet on October 10, 1937, at a time when Shachtman marched shoulder to shoulder with Cannon and it was considered officially that Abern had no faction, I wrote to Cannon:

"The party has only a minority of genuine factory workers ... The non-proletarian elements represent a very necessary yeast, and I believe that we can be proud of the good quality of these elements ... But ... Our party can be inundated by non-proletarian elements and can even lose its revolutionary character. The task is naturally not to prevent the influx of intellectuals by artificial methods, ... but to orientate practically all the organization toward the factories, the strikes, the unions ... A concrete example: We cannot devote enough or equal forces to all the factories. Our local organization can choose for its activity in the next period one, two or three factories in its area and concentrate all its forces upon these factories. If we have in one of them two or three workers we can create a special help commission of five non-workers with the purpose of enlarging our influence in these factories. The same can be done among the trade unions. We cannot introduce non-worker members in workers' unions. But we can with success build up help commissions for oral and literary action in connection with our comrades in the union. The unbreakable conditions should be: not to command the workers but only to help them, to give them suggestions, to arm them with the facts, ideas, factory papers, special leaflets, and so on.

"Such collaboration would have a tremendous educational importance from one side for the worker comrades, from the other side for the non-workers who need a solid re-education. You have for example an important number of Jewish non-worker elements in your ranks. They can be a very valuable yeast if the party succeeds by and by in extracting them from a closed milieu and ties them to the factory workers by daily activity. I believe such an orientation would also assure a more healthy atmosphere inside the party. One general rule we can establish immediately: a party member who doesn't win during three or six months a new worker for the party is not a good

party member. If we established seriously such a general orientation and if we verified every week the practical results, we will avoid a great danger; namely, that the intellectuals and white collar workers might suppress the worker minority, condemn it to silence, transform the party into a very intelligent discussion club but absolutely not habitable for workers. The same rules should be in a corresponding form elaborated for the working and recruiting of the youth organization, otherwise we run the danger of educating good young elements into revolutionary dilettantes and not revolutionary fighters."

From this letter it is obvious, I trust, that I did not mention the danger of a petty-bourgeois deviation the day following the Stalin-Hitler pact or the day following the dismemberment of Poland, but brought it forward persistently two years ago and more. Further more, as I then pointed out, bearing in mind primarily the "non existent" Abern faction, it was absolutely requisite in order to cleanse the atmosphere of the party, that the Jewish petty-bourgeois elements of the New York local be shifted from their habitual conservative milieu and dissolved in the real labor movement. It is precisely because of this that the above letter (not the first of its kind), written more than two years before the present discussion began, is of far greater weight as evidence than all the writings of the opposition leaders on the motives which impelled me to come out in defense of the "Cannon clique."

IV.

Shachtman's inclination to yield to petty-bourgeois influence, especially the academic and literary, has never been a secret to me. During the time of the Dewey Commission I wrote, on October 14, 1937, to Cannon, Shachtman and Warde :

"... I insisted upon the necessity to surround the Committee by delegates of workers' groups in order to create channels from the Committee in the masses ... Comrades Warde, Shachtman and others declared themselves in agreement with me on this point. Together we analyzed the practical possibilities to realize this plan ... But later, in spite of repeated questions from me, I never could have information about the matter and only accidentally I heard that comrade Shachtman was opposed to it. Why? I don't know."

Shachtman never did divulge his reasons to me. In my letter I expressed myself with the utmost diplomacy but I did not have the slightest doubt that while agreeing with me in words Shachtman in reality was afraid of wounding the excessive political sensibilities of our temporary liberal allies: in this direction Shachtman demonstrates exceptional "delicacy."

V.

On April 15, 1938, I wrote to New York:

"I am a bit astonished about the kind of publicity given to Eastman's letter in the New International. The publication of the letter is all right, but the prominence given it on the cover, combined with the silence about Eastman's article in Harper's, *seems to me a bit compromising for the New International. Many people will interpret this fact as our willingness to close our eyes on principles when friendship is concerned."*

VI.

On June 1, 1938, I wrote comrade Shachtman:

"It is difficult to understand here why you are so tolerant and even friendly toward Mr. Eugene Lyons. He speaks, it seems, at your banquets; at the same time he speaks at the banquets of the White Guards."

This letter continued the struggle for a more independent and resolute policy toward the so-called "liberals," who, while waging a struggle against the revolution, wish to maintain "friendly relations" with the proletariat, for this doubles their market value in the eyes of bourgeois public opinion.

VII.

On October 6, 1938, almost a year before the discussion began, I wrote about the necessity of our party press turning its face decisively toward the workers:

"Very important in this respect is the attitude of the Socialist Appeal. It is undoubtedly a very good Marxist paper, but it is not a genuine instrument of political action ... I tried to interest the editorial board of the Socialist Appeal in this question, but without success."

A note of complaint is evident in these words. And it is not accidental. Comrade Shachtman, as has been mentioned already, displays far more interest in isolated literary episodes of long-ago-concluded struggles than in the social composition of his own party or the readers of his own paper.

VIII.

On January 20, 1939, in a letter which I have already cited in connection with dialectic materialism, I once again touched on the question of comrade Shachtman's gravitation toward the milieu of the petty-bourgeois literary fraternity.

"I cannot understand why the Socialist Appeal is almost neglecting the Stalinist Party. This party now represents a mass of contradictions. Splits are inevitable. The next important acquisitions will surely come from the

Stalinist Party. Our political attention should be concentrated on it. We should follow the development of its contradictions day by day and hour by hour. Someone on the staff ought to devote the bulk of his time to the Stalinists' ideas and actions. We could provoke a discussion and, if possible, publish the letters of hesitating Stalinists. It would be a thousand times more important than inviting Eastman, Lyons and the others to present their individual sweatings. I was wondering a bit at why you gave place to Eastman's last insignificant and arrogant article ... But I am absolutely perplexed that you, personally, invite these people to besmirch the not so numerous pages of the New International. The perpetuation of this polemic can interest some petty-bourgeois intellectuals, but not the revolutionary elements. It is my firm conviction that a certain reorganization of the New International and the Socialist Appeal is necessary: more distance from Eastman, Lyons and so on; and nearer the workers and, in this sense, to the Stalinist Party."

Recent events have demonstrated, sad to say, that Shachtman did not turn away from Eastman and Co. but on the contrary drew closer to them.

IX.

On May 27, 1939, I again wrote concerning the character of the *Socialist Appeal* in connection with the social composition of the party:

"From the minutes I see that you are having difficulty with the Socialist Appeal. The paper is very well done from the journalistic point of view; but it is a paper for the workers and not a workers' paper. As it is, the paper is divided among various writers, each of whom is very good, but collectively they do not permit the workers to penetrate to the pages of the Appeal. Each of them speaks for the workers (and speaks very well) but nobody will hear the workers. In spite of its literary brilliance, to a certain degree the paper becomes a victim of journalistic routine. You do not hear at all how the workers live, fight, clash with the police or drink whiskey. It is very dangerous for the paper as a revolutionary instrument of the party. The task is not to make a paper through the joint forces of a skilled editorial board but to encourage the workers to speak for themselves. A radical and courageous change is necessary as a condition of success.

"Of course it is not only a question of the paper, but of the whole course of policy. I continue to be of the opinion that you have too many petty-bourgeois boys and girls who are very good and devoted to the party, but who do not fully realize that their duty is not to discuss among themselves, but to penetrate into the fresh milieu of workers. I repeat my proposition: Every petty-bourgeois member of the party who, during a certain time, let us say three or six months, does not win a worker for the party, should be demoted

to the rank of candidate and after another three months expelled from the party. In some cases it might be unjust, but the party as a whole would receive a salutary shock which it needs very much. A very radical change is necessary."

In proposing such Draconian measures as the expulsion of those petty-bourgeois elements incapable of linking themselves to the workers, I had in mind not the "defense" of Cannon's faction but the rescue of the party from degeneration.

X.

Commenting on skeptical voices from the Socialist Workers Party which had reached my ears, I wrote comrade Cannon on June 16, 1939:

"The pre-war situation, the aggravation of nationalism and so on, is a natural hindrance to our development and the profound cause of the depression in our ranks. But it must now be underlined that the more the party is petty-bourgeois in its composition, the more it is dependent upon the changes in the official public opinion. It is a supplementary argument for the necessity for a courageous and active re-orientation toward the masses. The pessimistic reasonings you mention in your article are, of course, a reflection of the patriotic, nationalistic pressure of the official public opinion. 'If fascism is victorious in France ...' 'If fascism is victorious in England ...' And so on. The victories of fascism are important, but the death agony of capitalism is more important."

The question of the dependence of the petty-bourgeois wing of the party upon official public opinion consequently was posed several months before the present discussion began and was not at all dragged in artificially in order to discredit the opposition.

.....

Shachtman, as we have already seen, persistently demands the citation of precedents: when and where in the past have the leaders of the opposition manifested petty-bourgeois opportunism? The reply which I have already given him on this score must be supplemented here with two letters which we sent each other on the question of defensism and methods of defensism in connection with the events of the Spanish Revolution. On September 18, 1937, Shachtman wrote me:

"... You say, 'If we would have a member in the Cortes he would vote against *the military budget of Negrin.' Unless this is a typographical error it seems to us to be a* non-sequitur. *If, as we all contend,* the element of an imperialist war *is not dominant at the present time in the Spanish struggle, and if instead the decisive element is still the struggle between the*

437

decaying bourgeois democracy, with all that it involves, on the one side, and fascism on the other, and further if we are obliged to give military assistance to the struggle against fascism, we don't see how it would be possible to vote in the Cortes against the military budget ... If a Bolshevik-Leninist on the Huesca front were asked by a Socialist comrade why his representative in the Cortes voted against the proposal by Negrin to devote a million pesetas to the purchase of rifles for the front, what would this Bolshevik-Leninist reply? It doesn't seem to us that he would have an effective answer ..." (My emphasis)

This letter astounded me. Shachtman was willing to express confidence in the perfidious Negrin government on the purely negative basis that the "element of an imperialist war" was not dominant in Spain.

On September 20, 1937, I replied to Shachtman:

"To vote the military budget of the Negrin government signifies to vote him political confidence ... To do it would be a crime. How we explain our vote to the anarchist workers? Very simply: We have not the slightest confidence in the capacity of this government to conduct the war and assure victory. We accuse this government of protecting the rich and starving the poor. This government must be smashed. So long as we are not strong enough to replace it, we are fighting under its command. But on every occasion we express openly our non-confidence in it: it is the only one possibility to mobilize the masses politically against this government and to prepare its overthrow. Any other politics would be a betrayal of the revolution."

The tone of my reply only feebly reflects the... amazement which Shachtman's opportunist position produced in me. Isolated mistakes are of course unavoidable but today, two and a half years later, this correspondence is illuminated with new light. Since we defend bourgeois democracy against fascism, Shachtman reasons, we therefore cannot refuse confidence to the bourgeois government. In applying this very theorem to the USSR it is transformed into its converse – since we place no confidence in the Kremlin government, we cannot, therefore, defend the workers' state. Pseudo-radicalism in this instance, too, is only the obverse side of opportunism.

Excerpts from Trotsky's "From a Scratch to the Danger of Gangrene", January 1940

Errors of the whole SWP, not just us

SWP minority (1940)

IN HIS OPEN LETTER to Comrade Trotsky, Comrade Shachtman, repeating the challenge issued by the Minority since the moment it was accused of representing a petty-bourgeois tendency in the party, declared:

"... it is first necessary to prove (a) that the Minority represents a deviation from the proletarian Marxian line, (b) that this deviation is typically petty-bourgeois, and (c) that it is more than an isolated deviation — it is a tendency. That is precisely what has not been proved."

Comrade Trotsky has been the only one thus far to take up this challenge and to attempt to answer it. Before we deal with his answer, a preliminary observation is necessary.

Our challenge was addressed in the first place to the Cannonites. If there were a petty-bourgeois tendency which had been developing gradually but unmistakably in the party for the past year or two or three (time enough for any tendency to manifest itself), the ones who would be in an excellent, if not the best, position to discern and describe it would be the Cannonites. They know the records of the party directly and intimately. They know, in particular, the political records of the representative spokesmen of the Minority. Shachtman wrote of the record of these comrades:

"They have one and, as said above, it is easily available. There are the records of the Political Committee, containing the views of all the comrades on every question; there are our articles in the press, there are our programs and manifestoes; there are our brochures and speeches. Let them be cited! There has been no lack of bourgeois-patriotic, anti-Soviet, reformist pressure upon our party in the past. Show us from the record when and where any of our leading comrades yielded to this pressure! I say confidently: It cannot be done."

Indeed, it was not done. What is more, Cannon, Goldman and the other Majorityites replied that it need not be done – because they knew it could not be done. Hundreds of comrades who heard him at membership meeting debates recall Cannon's statement that he did not charge the Minority with having or representing a petty-bourgeois tendency prior to the outbreak of the present dispute. In fact, Cannon gave the following "analogy" with the present fight: Zinoviev and Kamenev had been flawless Bolsheviks, the closest collaborators of Lenin, up to April 1917, and suddenly, overnight, so to speak, they broke from Leninism and became "strike-breakers." We leave aside here the question of Cannon's ignorance of the historic basis for the petty-bourgeois tendency represented in 1917 by Zinoviev and Kamenev (Trotsky devoted most of his *Lessons of October* to explaining the political roots of what Cannon thinks had no roots in the past), and emphasize merely the fact that in Cannon's view the "petty-bourgeois tendency" had no roots in the past, that it was a sudden, so to speak, an accidental (or episodic) phenomenon – as sudden and accidental (in his presentation of the analogy) as the 1917 action of Zinoviev and Kamenev. In other words, it was not a tendency at all. In other words, again, Cannon met our challenge up to recently by denying its validity, by declaring in effect that until the present Minority adopted its position on the Russian question there was no petty-bourgeois tendency in the party. He was compelled to put forth this view because he knows that the records of the party and of the Minority spokesmen cannot possibly substantiate any other view.

The merit of Trotsky's reply lies, first in his recognition of the validity of our challenge, and, second, in his attempt to substantiate the political characterization of the Minority in the only possible and permissible way, namely, by producing documentary material dealing with political questions of the past period and the political position taken by various comrades on these questions. In doing so, he adduces eleven pieces of evidence aimed to prove his point. Before we take up the evidence, it is well to bear in mind what it is that has to be proved:

To establish that, as against the Majority, the political tendency of the Minority is petty-bourgeois, it is necessary to show, concretely and not by mere assertion, that in a whole series of political questions in the past period the representative spokesmen of the Minority tended to take or did take a petty-bourgeois position, while the representative spokesmen of the Cannon faction tended to take or did take the contrary position, that of revolutionary Marxism.

With this important point in mind, it will be easier to judge the value of the evidence Trotsky adduces against the Minority. We will take it all up, point by point, in the order in which it is presented.

1. The policy in the Socialist Party

Trotsky quotes a letter to our faction center in the Socialist Party criticizing the estimate of the situation represented by "(a) the private letter of 'Max' about the convention, and (b) Shachtman's article Towards a Revolutionary Socialist Party." At best, this is calculated to prove that Shachtman made an opportunist mistake in 1937. But let us see what this has to do with the political position of the present Minority and that of the Majority.

The "private letter" signed "Max" was a circular letter sent out to all the Trotskyist groups in the Socialist Party under instructions and with the approval of the entire Political Committee of our tendency at that time. The same is true of the article by Shachtman in the SP monthly magazine. Let us grant for the moment that the line of these two documents was erroneous and opportunistic. But this line represented the unanimous opinion of the entire faction leadership, with the exception of Burnham. More important, it was the line initiated by Cannon. Here are the facts:

On the eve of the Chicago convention of the SP, a violent campaign was launched by the right wing to expel us from the party. Cannon was then in California. He hastened to New York to confer with the Political Committee. He advanced the policy that it was necessary to retreat before the right wing offensive in order to avoid expulsion, to moderate our tempo and our line. Rightly or wrongly, our Political Committee agreed with this line, except, we repeat, Burnham, who advocated what may be described as a more aggressive policy. In the PC, and on the basis of PC discipline, Burnham was not granted his request to present his own view to the New York membership meeting of the faction. Cannon's main slogan, reporting for the PC at that meeting, was: "We must make a 'second entry' into the SP." Every New York comrade who belonged to our group at that time will remember the meeting and the slogan very vividly. Shachtman and the others bore the same responsibility as Cannon for this line, not less, but not more. It was Cannon who initiated the conversations with Norman Thomas at that time, with the aim of establishing a sort of "truce" which would prevent the right wing from carrying through its drive against us. At the Chicago convention itself, our delegates' fraction was directed mainly by Cannon and Shachtman, for the Political Committee. Still following the line initiated by Cannon, our delegates were constantly held in check. This was true especially of some of the "natives," who wanted to make a stiff political fight against the right wing and the Clarityites. The PC line was to evade the political fight. Our delegates were even instructed to vote for the Clarityite war resolution if our own failed of adoption, as it did. Our delegates were instructed not even to raise the question of the Moscow Trials or the endorsement of the American Committee's work. Our delegates were instructed not to make a serious fight for representation on the National Committee of the SP. And so on.

Wherein did the spokesman of the "proletarian Marxist wing" differ from the spokesman of the "petty-bourgeois tendency"? Only in that the former initiated the policy pursued, was its principal and most vigorous protagonist, while the latter supported the policy. Using Trotsky's method of proof and criterion, a much better case could be made out to "prove" that Burnham represented the intransigent Marxist line while Cannon and Shachtman "revealed excessive adaptability towards the left wing of the petty-bourgeois democrats."

The letter and article of Shachtman were only a continuation of the official policy of the Political Committee. Trotsky, who opposed it, sought to have it changed, as indicated by the letter of May, 1937, which he quotes. Although he does not quote them, his letters to Cannon, who returned to California after the Chicago convention, also pursued this aim. Cannon subsequently proposed a change in the policy – his own policy! – and a new line was finally adopted by the whole Political Committee, which finally led to the split in the SP.

These are the facts. If Trotsky was unaware of them, it was his duty to acquaint himself with them. Cannon, who was aware of them, has taken good care to make no reference in the present dispute to the question of our SP policy in 1937. The same is true of Goldman, who also knows the facts cited above, as well as a number of other facts. Like every other informed comrade, they know that Point 1 in Trotsky's evidence does not even begin to prove his contention about the Minority. For, remember, Trotsky's task is to prove the existence of a certain tendency in the Minority which distinguishes it from the "Marxist" wing of Cannon.

2. The Question of Workers in The Leadership

Trotsky's second point deals with the question of introducing workers into the local and national leadership. "To believe Comrade Shachtman, I dragged the question of the class composition of the factions into the dispute by the hair." To prove that he did not, he quotes a letter to New York dated October 3, 1937. Read the letter: by what single word does it deal with the "class composition of the factions?" It does speak of the need of electing more workers to leadership and points out that "in every organization there are traditional committee members" and that "different secondary, factional and personal considerations play a too great role in the composition of the list of candidates." Quite correct. Conclusion: "I have never met either attention or interest from Comrade Shachtman in questions of this kind." From whom has Comrade Trotsky met with attention and interest in questions of this kind? If not from Shachtman or the Minority, then perhaps from Cannon? Let us see. At the Chicago founding convention of the SWP, the list of candidates for the National Committee was prepared mainly by Shachtman, with the knowledge and approval of most of the other leading comrades. At the July 1939 convention, two lists were presented, Shachtman's for one group of comrades, and Dunne's for the Cannon faction. Which one was oriented towards the conception of "traditional committee members"? In which one did "secondary, factional and personal considerations play a too great role"? An examination of the list can give only one answer: Dunne's slate. Shachtman's slate proposed to introduce new and fresh elements into the National Committee – worker-militants like Breitman and qualified youth comrades like Gould and Erber. There being no important or visible political differences in the party, the slate did not aim at any faction majority. Dunne's slate aimed first and foremost at a majority for the Cannon clique, and, towards that end, of retaining some of the "traditional committee members." Dunne and Lewit were the two spokesmen of the Cannon group for their slate. Who were the only four individuals on their slate for whom they spoke by name? Clarke, Cochran, Morrow and Stevens – not a single one of them a proletarian, and one of them, in particular, distinguished by his petty-bourgeois intellectualism, rudeness and snobbery which repelled any workers' milieu into which he was placed.

The July convention dispute was not without significance. The Cannonites talk a good deal about "proletarians in the leadership," especially on ceremonial occasions or for what they consider are good factional ends. The reality is quite different. The actual, functioning leadership of the Cannon faction, even though it does not live in the Bronx but in Greenwich Village, does not show any special "interest or attention" in introducing proletarians into its ranks – unless (we except such comrades as Lewit and Breitman) Gordon, Cochran, Clarke, Morrow, Wright, Hansen, Goldman, etc., are to be written down as workers.

3. The Social Composition of the Party

In Point 3, Trotsky quotes a letter in 1937 to Cannon concerning the poor social composition of the party. He stresses the need of orienting the party membership towards the factories, having each branch, or groups in each branch, concentrate all its forces on one, two or three factories in its area. In this way, it would be possible to alter the composition of the party in favor of the proletarian instead of the non-proletarian elements. Good.

This letter was addressed to Cannon. Why does not Trotsky conclude on this point, as he did on point 2, that "I have never met either attention or interest from Comrade Cannon in questions of this kind"? What single proposal did Cannon make in the past two-and-a-half years with reference to orienting the party and its membership towards the factories? Wherein was the leader of the "proletarian Marxist wing" distinguished in this respect from other comrades? When Trotsky wrote to the Political Committee, some time back, that a rule should be adopted providing that any non-worker who does not bring a proletarian into the party within six months shall himself be reduced to the rank of probationer, McKinney supported the proposal, but no one else, not even Cannon. The latter proposed to send a copy of the letter to the branches without a word of comment, and that is all that was ever heard of the letter, of the proposal, or of Cannon's position on it.

Where does the letter quoted by Trotsky indicate that there was in the party, in his opinion, a petty-bourgeois tendency peculiar to the present Minority? That is what he has set out to prove, but the letter does it in no wise. The social composition of the party as a whole is very poor from the standpoint of a proletarian organization. That is incontestable. But both factions in the present dispute represent, to a somewhat greater or lesser extent, cross-sections of the party as a whole. The contention that the Cannon faction represents all the proletarian elements in the party, or the bulk of them, and the Minority all or most of the non-proletarian elements, will not stand the test of investigation for a single minute. An objective examination of the social composition of the two factions will not show any class preponderance in the ranks or the leadership of either one of them – especially if the party is taken not in an isolated city but as a whole, nationally. A similar examination of the social compositions of the New York organization, which is indeed far from what it should be, would help to dispel many of the consciously and unconsciously fostered exaggerations and even myths, many of which are so "cleverly" disseminated by the Cannonites in order to arouse unhealthy prejudices especially among the newer comrades in the outlying branches.

It is true that the Cannonites now show both "attention and interest" in the question of the social composition of the party. But only because they believe that by falsifying the relative composition of the two groups and by demagogical speeches this "issue" can be utilized for their factional advantage, especially since they, who show an interest in theoretical questions about once every two years, have been qualified, so unexpectedly to themselves, as the "Marxist" wing of the party. Their "attention and interest" have been displayed before in this question, and in the same way. If it seems to suit them as a factional football, they make very solemn speeches about it. As soon as it no longer has a value as a factional issue, it is forgotten by them ... until the next time.

4. The Dewey Commission

Shachtman's failure to "surround the (Dewey) Committee by delegates of workers' groups" is cited as another piece of "evidence" that the Minority represents a petty-bourgeois tendency. This proposal by Trotsky two years ago was supported in the Political Committee by one comrade, McKinney. No other member did, neither Shachtman, nor Burnham, nor Cannon, nor Lewit. Under the circumstances, the Committee considered it from the standpoint of practical possibilities and effectiveness, and decided that it was not feasible to undertake the formation of such workers' groups.

Wherein was the Minority distinguished in this question from the Majority, or from Cannon in particular? Trotsky does not say, and that for the good reason that he cannot say. The letter from which he quotes was addressed to Cannon, Shachtman and Novack. What was Cannon's answer to the proposal?

The work of the party, and especially of the party leadership, in connection with the Moscow Trials and the Dewey Committee, was not, to be sure, flawless. There are many lessons to be learned from our experience in this campaign, especially with respect to the liberal democrats with whom we cooperated. We did not always take advantage of the revolutionary possibilities offered us by the situation. At the same time, let it be borne in mind that the problem of the Dewey Committee was not a simple one, and only special reasons which every comrade will understand prevent us from going into the details of the problem. Yet, with all its defects, the campaign we launched around the Moscow Trials (at a time when we were half-tied and half-gagged in the Socialist Party!) was the most successful we ever undertook – a real triumph for the party and the International. Comrade Trotsky played an invaluable part in working out the campaign, and in its success; that goes without saying. But the daily work – elaborating the not always simple policy, directing the work in general, the writing, speaking and organizing – that had to be done on the spot under the leadership of the Political Committee. We have no hesitation in saying that a good eighty per cent of that work was done by comrades of the present Minority. They feel no reason to be ashamed of or apologetic for that work – quite the contrary – either organizationally or politically. To ignore all that was accomplished, especially the political gains for our movement, and to reduce everything to the comparatively trifling question of whether or not we carried through the organization of the workers' groups, is to abandon all sense of proportion.

Here, as in all the other cases mentioned in Trotsky's "evidence," we are prepared, without exempting ourselves from responsibility for mistakes, to match the main line against the incidental error, the great achievement against the episodic shortcoming, the record of political line and activity of our comrades which is known to the party as a whole, and even to the radical public, against the obscure trifles which constitute most of Comrade Trotsky's "proofs" of our "tendency."

5. Eastman in *The New International*

Point 5 is also supposed to prove that the Minority represents a petty-bourgeois tendency whereas the Majority represents revolutionary Marxism. What is this proof? Not the publication of Eastman's open letter to Corliss Lamont on the Moscow Trials, for that "is all right, but the prominence given it on the cover, combined with the silence about Eastman's article in *Harper's*."

The "proofs" for Trotsky's contention must be scarce indeed to mention this one among them. The size of type used to announce Eastman's article on the cover of The *New International* was too large; presumably the Cannonites proposed to use a smaller type, or would have proposed it if they could ever be gotten to display any interest in the theoretical organ of the party. But perhaps the prominence given the article on the cover is not the most important point; it is the "silence about Eastman's article in *Harper's*." In that case would it not have been better, if only in order to complete the point, to indicate that a reply was written to Eastman's article? Who wrote the article? Burnham. On whose direct personal request? Trotsky's. Trotsky knows then, as well as he knows now, Burnham's position towards Marxian dialectics. He knew then that Eastman's *Harper's* article on *The End of Socialism in Russia* had as its point of departure Eastman's particular criticism of Marxian dialectics. In his article on *A Petty-Bourgeois Opposition in the SWP* Trotsky declares that without a Marxian criticism of the opponents of dialectics, it is impossible to expose the essence of the false political position of Eastman, Hook and others. If that is so, why did Trotsky propose to Burnham, in 1938, that he write a polemical reply to Eastman's *Harper's* article? Why did he not propose that Cannon or Weber or Wright or Gordon or Cochran or Morrow write the reply? And why was there no criticism of the reply (and the counter-reply to Eastman's rebuttal) after Burnham had written it? If it was a satisfactory reply from the standpoint of the party program, should not Trotsky have mentioned this fact in his Point 5? If it was unsatisfactory, why was nothing heard about it, either from Trotsky or anyone else in the party? And above all, where were the spokesmen of the Majority in all this, of the Cannonites who represent themselves today as the exclusive defenders of Marxism and dialectics?

6. Eugene Lyons and the Banquet

Another point to prove that the Minority represents a petty-bourgeois tendency is made by Trotsky when he refers to the fact that "you are so tolerant even friendly towards Mr. Eugene Lyons. He speaks it seems at your banquets; at the same time he speaks at the banquets of the White Guards." To whom does the "you" refer? To the Minority perhaps? To Shachtman? What are the facts in this case? The Pioneer Publishers organized a banquet to which a number of people were invited as speakers in a symposium on the Russian Revolution and Marxism. Lyons, [the anarchist Carlo] Tresca, Hook and others were among them. The Political Committee knew nothing about the details of the affair. When the advertisement for the banquet appeared in the *Socialist Appeal*, Cannon and Shachtman discussed the question and took a critical attitude towards the speakers' list; the other leading comrades did likewise. The main objection was to the fact that the list was "weighted" heavily against representatives of revolutionary Marxism. It was decided that Shachtman be designated to take the floor at the banquet for the party point of view and, after the brief speeches of the critics of the Russian Revolution, to present the views of the Marxists. This is exactly what he did, to the satisfaction, politically, of every one present, except, of course, the Lyonses and the Hooks. The composition of the speakers' list at the banquet was a mistake, for which no member and no group of members of the Political Committee was responsible.

To adduce this miserable incident, not for its actual worth, but in order to demonstrate that the Minority represents a petty-bourgeois tendency, only shows with striking force the weakness, or more accurately, the baselessness of the case which Trotsky is trying to make against us.

As against such trivialities which could be dug up by the dozen if one were interested, can and should be placed the vigorous, effective and intransigent political campaign in defense of revolutionary Marxism, of the Fourth International and of the party, and against precisely that type of critic represented by the Eastmans and the Lyonses. Trotsky mentions only a yellow leaf here and there and makes no reference to the big green forest. The defense of the party and its program from the Lyonses, the education of wide circles of radical workers and intellectuals to the true meaning of the "democratic" backsliders and renegades — have the representatives of the Minority been behindhand in this work in the past? If anything, they have been in the forefront.

It is not necessary to institute an objective re-examination of the record as a whole, instead of taking up isolated, insignificant incidents of fugitive importance. The party needs no such re-examination for the simple reason that the record is already common knowledge.

And if there were such a re-examination, it would reveal that it is the Cannonites, more than anyone else, who showed a complete indifference to the defense of the party program and of Marxism on the theoretical front. Except for one article by Goldman and another by Wright, the Cannonite leadership is represented by a blank space in the past two-three years of struggle against precisely that tendency in and around the radical labor movement which is represented variously by Hook, Eastman, Lyons, Stolberg, etc., etc.

Has Trotsky failed to notice this fact? Has he failed to call attention to it in the proper quarters? In any case, the party in general has noticed it and has drawn the necessary conclusions: Except for factional considerations, the "normal" interest of the Cannonites, Cannon in particular, in theoretical questions of Marxism, is distinguished by its absence.

The "practical" leader leaves that to the "intellectuals."

7, 8, 9. The *Socialist Appeal*

It is not necessary to dwell on the defects of the *Socialist Appeal* in this document. They are not unknown to the party. On the basis of criticisms of the *Appeal* made by Trotsky and comrades in the American party, on the basis of many direct experiences, on the basis of criticisms of many readers of the paper, these criticisms, with proposals for improving the paper, were incorporated in the report to the July Convention delivered by Comrade Abern, in the remarks of Morrow, Shachtman and many other delegates.

However, to refer to the defects of the *Appeal* for the purpose of characterizing either one of the factions in the party, or any group of comrades, or any individual comrade, is totally absurd. The problem of the *Appeal* is, and always has been, and most likely always will be, the problem of the party itself. The official organ of the party can, so to speak, rise above the party to a certain extent, as has been pointed out on more than one occasion, but it cannot reflect the class struggle in the country to a radically different degree than the one to which that struggle is participated in by the party itself.

On more than one occasion, the editorial staff made efforts to organize a network of worker-correspondents for the *Appeal*, and it succeeded in a modest measure. If the success was far from what is desirable and necessary, it is, as was recognized by all comrades in many discussions, due basically to the detachment of the party as a whole (with isolated exceptions) from the political life and the life of the working class of the country. It is at bottom only to the extent that the entire party enters into the political life of the country, into the life and movements of the working class, that the "face" and the contents of the *Appeal* will be altered in the right direction.

But it is precisely at this point that the criticism of the Minority shows its validity — the criticism of the bureaucratic conservatism that characterizes the Cannon faction. The analysis of the Minority, "War and Bureaucratic Conservatism," replete with facts that are easily verifiable where they are not already common party knowledge, has not been refuted to the present day. The attempt to dispose of the indictment of the Cannon regime by a few sarcastic remarks in passing, will not serve as a refutation.

10. Again, the social composition

Trotsky quotes also from a letter to Cannon on June 16, 1939, on the poor social composition of the party and its consequent greater liability to the pressure of "official public opinion". Wherein is this a point of proof of the charge that the Minority group represents a petty-bourgeois tendency? In quoting his letter to prove his charge, Trotsky assumes that which he is attempting to prove, namely, that the Cannon group is the group of the proletariat in the party, and the Minority the group of the petty-bourgeois. But this is just what it is impossible to demonstrate on the basis of the facts.

In the first place, even if this division corresponded to the reality — and we deny it — it would be necessary to emphasize that it would not have the same significance in our tiny organization that it has in a mass party of tens or hundreds of thousands which, because it is deep in the turbulent streams of the class struggle, is directly affected by the changes of the prevailing current. In general, the smaller the organization, the less rooted it is in the classes — the less accurately it reflects social forces and pressures.

In the second place, even if this division corresponded to the reality — again, we deny it — it would be necessary to examine the actual situation not so much in terms of generalities, not so much in terms of what holds true "in the long run, in the final analysis," but in terms of what is demonstrable in the given dispute, of what is shown by concrete experience.

The social composition of the revolutionary party is decisive in the long run, for the quite obvious reason that the working class is the decisive and only consistently progressive class in modern society, that the working class alone can lead the struggle for socialism. The social composition of the revolutionary party is decisive immediately, in this sense, that the revolutionary party, regardless of its social composition at its formation or at any given stage, must constantly strive to become a proletarian party, it must orient itself mainly towards the working class.

It would, however, be erroneous to make the arbitrary deduction from this that at any given stage, and in any political dispute, that party or group in a party which is predominantly proletarian in its composition, is correct in its political standpoint, as against another party or group whose social composition is, from the proletarian viewpoint, inferior. Such a conclusion would have meant, as we know from the past, the capitulation, on more than one occasion, of the revolutionary Marxist tendency to the reformist tendency, specifically in the Russian Social Democratic party, where the Mensheviks at times had by far the greater number of proletarians in their ranks, compared with the Bolsheviks.

The problem then boils down, as it always does fundamentally, to the question of the political position, as it does in the present dispute. And there it is necessary to decide, objectively, on whether victory of Stalin's annexationist army in Finland, for example, or the struggle for the development of the independent class activity of the Third Camp, is the correct position, the one that really represents the interests of the proletarian revolution.

The triumphant reference of the Cannonites to the fact that the Minneapolis branch, for example, supports the Majority — with such remarkable unanimity, too — does not decide for a minute the correctness or incorrectness of their political position. There is no smaller number of proletarian militants in other sections of the party who support the standpoint of the Minority.

But even if this were not true (and its truth is easily demonstrated), it would not be as decisive, precisely from the standpoint of social

450

composition and class pressures, as the fact which we consider to be much more decisive and significant in the present dispute, namely, the fact that the overwhelming majority of the Youth comrades support the Minority. The Youth, with all the deficiencies that characterize them, are precisely the ones who, more than any other single stratum in the party, are the best barometer in the present discussion.

The young comrades who make up our Youth movement are, by and large, quite different from the elements who made up the revolutionary youth organizations in the past, say, ten-fifteen years ago. They are literally the vanguard of the "locked-out generation". In the past, many of the youth aspired (and even had the possibility) to "lift" themselves out of the working class, to become part of the bourgeois or petty-bourgeois world — lawyers, doctors, teachers, members of the "liberal professions" or even "better". Their conduct in the movement corresponded to this aspiration. Thus, their constant conflicts with the party (we speak of the early days of the CP in the USA) were most often based on their resistance to the party's demands for activity in the class struggle, in the political life of the country, to the party's demands for sacrifices, etc.

The Youth of our party differs radically in every respect. With few exceptions, they have no illusions about the possibilities for "rising in the world" of American capitalism today. They have a deep attachment to the movement, based on far more than intellectual reasons. It is not comfort they seek but struggle. The war question to them is not an abstraction but a reality. It is most significant that their conflicts with the party in the past two years have been based precisely on their criticisms — substantially if not always justified — of the party leadership's tendency to do-nothingness, to routinism, to lack of initiative, to lack of planned and systematic activity.

It is most significant that in Cannon's pre-convention articles in the *Appeal*, he attacked the Youth comrades not for "petty-bourgeois dilettantism" or for "opportunism" or for "inactivity" or for "refusing to get into action," but rather in the opposite sense, for their alleged "adventurism" and "leftism."

The Youth of our movement in this country are immature in many respects. They have not gone through many indispensable experiences. They have not passed all the tests. But in the present party dispute, they passed the test of the war crisis and the problems posed by it, far, far better than did the Cannon clique. To try to pass off the strong support which the Youth have given to the Minority with the argument that it is most susceptible to "bourgeois-democratic and patriotic pressure," can be put down either to ignorance of the real composition and sentiments of the bulk of our Youth, or, at best, to sheer rationalization.

One last point may be made here. The self-styled "proletarian" wing of the party claims Minneapolis and the seamen's fraction as its citadels. Let us grant that for the moment it is correct. It claims also that the Soviet Union has been under the attack of imperialism for the past six months, and particularly now, in the war in Finland; claims, too, that the United States is also engaged in an imperialist attack on the Soviet Union. What social pressure has thus far prevented the Majority, completely in control of the party apparatus, from issuing a single leaflet to the American seamen, to the longshoremen, calling upon them to refuse to load or sail ships with material for Finland and its backers and to load and sail ships with material for the Soviet Union? What social pressure has prevented the raising of this concrete slogan even in the columns of the *Appeal* since the war began?

What social pressure has prevented the comrades in Minnesota, heavily populated by Finnish and Scandinavian workers, from issuing a leaflet explaining in simple but clear terms that we are not only for the defeat of the Mannerheim army in Finland but that we are for the victory of the Red Army? The Minority has asked this question for months. The answer is still to be heard.

11. Negrin's military budget

One of Trotsky's trump cards, so to speak, is the exchange of letters between him and Shachtman on the question of voting for the military budget of Negrin in the Loyalist Cortes. Let us grant that Shachtman's position on this question was entirely wrong.

But in whose name did Shachtman write his letter of inquiry? The letter speaks of "we" and "us". The "we" and "us" referred to most of the comrades of the Political Committee. Upon receiving Trotsky's 1937 article in which he said that we would not vote for the Loyalist military budget, Cannon and Shachtman, among others, could not believe that this was Trotsky's position. This may not speak well for their political development, but it is the fact.

It was decided that Shachtman write Trotsky about it, not in his name alone, but in the name of Cannon and the others. The "opportunist position" which Trotsky attributes to Shachtman alone, in an attempt to prove a continuity of line of the Minority, was the position of Cannon and other leading comrades of the party. In this as in so many of the other cases noted above, Trotsky tries in vain to separate that which was inseparable.

It may be argued, after all this, that Trotsky does nevertheless prove that for the past two-three years he constantly called attention to the dangers and mistakes of a petty-bourgeois tendency that existed in general in the party, and that by its present position in the Russian question, the Minority shows itself to be the clearest expression of this tendency.

In the first place, what it was necessary to prove was that the Minority, on a series of political questions in the past, took or tended to take a petty-bourgeois position on these questions as against the Cannonites, who took or tended to take the Marxist position. Even if Trotsky is granted all his points, they would at best show that on the whole the position of both the Majority and the Minority was the same in the eleven cases he mentions.

The distinction between the two groups first occurs clearly on the Russian question. It is therefore necessary to demonstrate how, on this question, the position of the Minority is petty-bourgeois. But this is no easy matter. At least, it has not yet been done and, in our opinion, it cannot be done.

In the second place, we contend that by Trotsky's method of selection, one could "prove" almost anything about the tendency of the two groups. Out of two-three years of the political record of the party and its leadership, Trotsky has taken a number of isolated instances in which he adopted a critical attitude, and then quite arbitrarily, and after the fact, he makes the present Minority the object of that criticism.

Trotsky writes: "Let Shachtman not object that the lapses and mistakes in which the correspondence is concerned likewise can be brought against other comrades, including representatives of the present Majority. Possibly. Probably. But Shachtman's name is not repeated in this correspondence accidentally."

But why should we not object? Whether or not Cannon's name is mentioned as often as Shachtman's (it is), is besides the point. What is important is that, as has been demonstrated above, what applied to one comrade applied at least as well to many others, to the Majority as well as the Minority.

Why is it not just as legitimate to say today. "Cannon's present position on the Russian question is the logical flowering of the petty-bourgeois tendency he showed on the question of Negrin's military budget, of the S.P. tactic, of the Eastman letter, of the *Socialist Appeal*, etc." To answer: "But it is not, it is the Marxian position!" is merely an assertion, which is made just as vigorously by the Minority. The conflicting assertions have to be examined objectively; the arguments have to be judged on their merits. The fact that Cannon and Shacht-man, or Goldman and Burnham, took the same position on political questions in the past, does not prove that one of them represents a different tendency today.

In the third place, even if it were granted that in every one of the eleven cases Trotsky's criticism was valid, and that it applied to Shachtman, or even to all the leaders of the Minority exclusively, as against the Majority leaders, it would still be necessary to ask: What importance have all these cases, including the invitation of Lyons to the Pioneer banquet and the prominence given to Eastman's article on the cover of The *New International*, in comparison with the known record of these comrades on all the other political problems facing the party in the past period? The struggle for the Fourth International and its program, their defense from all varieties of democrats, social-democrats, Stalinists, sectarians and others, did not begin a couple of months ago, when Cannon discovered that Burnham was not a defender of dialectics. It has been going on in the party for some time.

We repeat: the record of the leaders of the Minority in the struggle to build the Fourth International and to defend its program, above all in the question of war and bourgeois-patriotism, is well-known, and it is not worse than the record of the other comrades. Can it so easily be forgotten, or wiped out, even by all the eleven "proofs" cited by Trotsky, even if they were multiplied by two? That, too, will not be so easy. For the party to try to deny this record would be to deny itself.

Our characterization of the political tendency represented by the Cannon clique has only been denied, but never refuted. Not even the attempt has been made. To our challenge to show the development of the "petty-bourgeois tendency" from the political record of the Minority in the past, only Comrade Trotsky replied, although one would suppose that our most immediate collaborators, the Cannonites, who know that record intimately, should have been the first to meet the challenge by drawing on that knowledge.

Not a single one of Trotsky's eleven "proofs" have been evaded in our answer, which shows the utter groundlessness of the political characterization which he has attempted to attach to the Minority. The charge remains unproved because there is no proof for it.

New International, June 1940 (dated 9 March 1940)

Class struggle within the party?

Martin Abern, Paul Bern, James Burnham, Max Shachtman
(1940)

THE [FOURTH] THEORY OF CANNON is as follows: The present dispute in the party is the expression of a conflict between the petty-bourgeois, middle-class elements (the minority) and the proletarian elements (the majority). A luscious and satisfying theory indeed! What we — the majority says to itself, licking its chops — have in the party is: the class struggle. Thus the majority can get compensation by participation in "its own" class struggle for the party's inadequacies in the real struggle which is proceeding in its own way in the outside world.

This theory also is not political, but sociological. If it were true — and significant — it would still be necessary to characterise the position reached by the "petty-bourgeois current" politically. It is not enough just to call it "petty-bourgeois".

Now, in the first place, this theory — even if it were significant and relevant as it is not — is not true even as a description of the facts, quite apart from their interpretation. We do not miss "petty-bourgeois elements" prominently in the Cannon faction in many localities from Boston to the Pacific Coast to, above all, the national centre. If we really think it worth while to speak of social status, we must remember that it is not altered by learning to speak out of the side of one's mouth, to smoke large cigars, or to sprinkle one's speeches with resounding cuss words.

We are the first to admit that the social composition of our party, above all its lack of genuine proletarians, is a tragic weakness, and that all justifiable means must be used to overcome this weakness. We find, however, that this has been a weakness of the entire Fourth Internationalist movement, and in fact of wide sections of the revolutionary movement from its inception. We do not expect, therefore, to solve it in a day or by an easy formula. "Pursue a correct Marxian policy, translate our views into terms understandable by the masses, participate directly in the mass movement along this line" — that is the only "formula" we know and it is not an easy one.

The revolutionary program is not the spontaneous or automatic product of the proletarians themselves; the "natural" proletarian policy is reformist or syndicalist. Indeed, from at least one most important point of view, the most radical influence in our party is the youth, the disinherited generation who above all have "nothing to lose but their chains" and their hopeless social situation. And the youth is in its overwhelming bulk against Cannon and his policies and his regime.

Cannon's "class struggle" theory of the party crisis is a very dangerous fraud. Its concrete meaning is to encourage the trade union comrades to free themselves — not from "petty-bourgeois elements" — but from political control by the party. The talk about "petty-bourgeois elements" serves them as a rationalisation to excuse rejection of political control by the party when that control seems to (and sometimes, necessarily, does) interfere with local or temporary advantages in trade union work. In this fundamental respect it is identical with the "theory" and agitation of the Foster faction in the CP years ago, often condemned by our movement in the past and meriting the same condemnation today.

From the 1939-40 opposition document "The War and Bureaucratic Conservatism", SWP Internal Bulletin vol.2 no.6, January, 1940,

The front page of *Labor Action*, August 26 1940

456

Trade unionists and revolutionists

James P Cannon (1953)

In 1953 the SWP had a faction-fight after which it expelled at least a third of the organisation, including Bert Cochran, George Clarke, Harry Braverman and most of the SWP's more established trade-unionists. This article is an abridged transcript of a speech by Cannon to a majority faction meeting, in which he shows that political groupings in a revolutionary socialist party cannot be evaluated just by tagging them as "petty bourgeois" or "proletarian".

THE REAL SOCIAL COMPOSITION of the party is by no means uniform; it reflects some of the changes which have taken place in the American working class. This has been strikingly demonstrated by the line-up of the party trade unionists in our factional struggle. The revolutionists among them – the big majority – on the one side, and the conservatised elements – a small minority – on the other, have chosen different sides instinctively and almost automatically.

Since the consolidation of the CIO unions [the mass industrial unions dating from the 1930s: before then, unions in the USA were mostly craft unions of more skilled workers] and the 13-year period of war and postwar boom, a new stratification has taken place within the American working class, and particularly and conspicuously in the CIO unions. Our party, which is rooted in the unions, reflects that stratification too. The worker who has soaked up the general atmosphere of the long prosperity and begun to live and think like a petty bourgeois is a familiar figure in the country at large. He has even made his appearance in the Socialist Workers Party as a ready-made recruit for an opportunist faction.

In our 1952 convention resolution, we explained the situation in the American working class as a whole in the two sections "The Causes of Labour Conservatism and the Premises for a New Radicalisation" and "Perspectives of a New Radicalisation". In my report at the national convention, I called those two sections "the heart of the resolution" and centred my report around them.

It appears to me now, in the light of the conflict in the party and its real causes, which are now manifest, that those sections of the convention resolution dealing with the class as a whole require further elaboration and amplification. We need a more precise examination of the stratifications within the working class, which are barely touched there, and of the projection of these stratifications in the composition of the unions, in the various inner-union tendencies, and even in our own party. This, I believe, is the key to the otherwise inexplicable riddle of why one proletarian section of the party, even though it is a small minority, supports a capitulatory opportunist faction against the proletarian-revolutionary line and leadership of the party.

This apparent contradiction – this division of working class forces – in party factional struggle is not new. In the classical faction struggles of our international movement since the time of Marx and Engels, there has always been a division, in the party itself, between the different strata of workers. The proletarian left wing by no means ever had all the workers, and the opportunist petty-bourgeois wing was never without some working-class support, that is, working class in the technical sense of wage workers. The revisionist intellectuals and the trade union opportunists always nestled together in the right wing of the party. In the SWP at the present time, we have a repetition of the classical line-up that characterised the struggle of left and right in the Second International before the First World War.

Trotsky told us on one of our visits with him – I think he also wrote it somewhere – that there was a real social division between the two factions of the original Social Democratic Party of Russia, which later became separate parties. The Mensheviks, he said, had nearly all the intellectuals. With a few exceptions, the only intellectuals Lenin had were those whom the party had trained, a good deal like our own worker-intellectuals for the greater part. The intellectual – I mean the professional intellectual of the Burnham type, the man from the professor's chair, from the universities – was a rarity on Lenin's side, whereas the Mensheviks had shoals of them.

In addition, the Mensheviks had most of the skilled workers, who are always the privileged workers. The printers' union was Menshevik even through the revolution. The railroad workers' bureaucracy tried to paralyse the revolution; it was only by military force and the aid of a minority that the Bolsheviks were able to prevent the Menshevik railroad workers' officialdom from employing their strategic position against the revolution.

Trotsky said that the Mensheviks also had most of the older workers. Age, as you know, is associated with conservatism. (In general, that is, but not always; there are exceptions to the rule. There are two different ways of measuring age. In ordinary life you measure it by the calendar, but in revolutionary politics you measure it by the mind and the will and the spirit – and you don't always get the same result.)

On the other hand, while the older workers, the skilled and the privileged, were with the Mensheviks, the unskilled workers and the youth were with the Bolsheviks; that is, those of them who were politicalised. That was the line of division between the factions. It was not merely a question of the arguments and the program; it was the social impulses, petty-bourgeois on one side, proletarian on the other, which determined their allegiance.

The same line-up took place in Germany. The prewar German Social Democracy in its heyday had a powerful bloc of opportunist parliamentarians, Marxologists who utilised their scholastic training and their ability to quote Marx by the yard to justify an opportunist policy. They were supported not merely by the petty shopkeepers, of whom there were many, and the trade union bureaucrats. They also had a solid base of support in the privileged stratum of the aristocracy of labour in Germany. The trade union

458

opportunists in the German Social Democratic Party supported Bernstein's revisionism without bothering to read his articles. They didn't need to read them; they just felt that way. The most interesting facts on this point are cited by Peter Gay in his book on Bernstein and his revisionist movement, entitled *The Dilemma of Democratic Socialism*.

All through the prewar fight over revisionism, then through the war and postwar days, through 1923 and 1933, the skilled, privileged trade unionists were the solid base of support of the opportunist Social Democratic leaders – while the communist revolutionaries, from the time of Liebknecht and Luxemburg all the way down to the fascist catastrophe in 1933, were the youth, the unemployed, and the unskilled, less privileged workers.

If you will go back and read Lenin again, in case you've forgotten it, you will see how Lenin explained the degeneration of the Second International, and its eventual betrayal in the First World War, precisely by its opportunism based upon the adaptation of the party to the conservative impulses and demands of the bureaucracy and aristocracy of labour.

We had the same thing in the US, although we never had a Social Democracy in the European sense and the working class was never politically organised here as it was there. The organised labour movement, up to the 30s, was largely restricted to a privileged aristocracy of labour – as Debs and De Leon used to call it – of skilled craftsmen, who got better wages and had preferred positions, "job trusts", and so on. The chief representative of this conservative, privileged craft union stratum was Gompers.

On the other side, there was the great mass of the basic proletariat, the unskilled and semiskilled, the mass production workers, the foreign born, and the jobless youth. They were without benefit of organisation, without privileges, the outcasts of society. It was not without reason that they were more radical than the others. Nobody paid any attention to them except the revolutionists and radicals. Only the IWW of Haywood and St. John, Debs, and the left Socialists voiced their bitter grievances, did the organising work, and led the strikes of the mass production workers in those days. If the official labour bureaucracy intervened in the spontaneous strikes of the unorganised it was usually to break them up and sell them out.

The officials of the skilled unions did not welcome the great upsurge of the unorganised workers in the 30s. But they could not prevent it. When the spontaneous strikes and drives for organisation could no longer be ignored, the AFL began to assign "organisers" to the various industries – steel, rubber, auto, etc. They were sent however, not to lead the workers in a struggle but to control them, to prevent the consolidation of self-acting industrial unions. They actually wouldn't permit the auto workers in convention to elect their own officials, insisting that the AFL appoint them "provisionally". The same with the rubber workers and other new industrial unions.

These new unions had to split with the conservative labour fakers of the AFL before they could consolidate unions of their own. The drives behind the 1934-37 upsurge were the bitter and irreconcilable grievances of the workers; their protest against mistreatment, speedup, insecurity; the revolt of the pariahs against the pariah status.

This revolt, which no bureaucracy could contain, was spearheaded by new people – the young mass production workers, the new, young militants whom nobody had ever heard of. They were the real creators of the CIO. This revolt of the "men from nowhere" reached its high tide in the sit-down strikes of 1937. The workers' victory in these battles definitely established the CIO and secured stability of the new unions through the seniority clause.

It is now 16 years since the sit-down strikes made the new CIO unions secure by the seniority clause. These 16 years of union security, and 13 years of uninterrupted war and post-war prosperity, have wrought a great transformation in the unprivileged workers who made the CIO.

The seniority clause, like everything else in life, has revealed a contradictory quality. By regulating the right to employment through time of service on the job, it secures the union militant against arbitrary discrimination and layoffs. It is an absolute necessity for union security. That is the positive side of the seniority clause. But, at the same time, it also gradually creates a sort of special interest in the form of steadier employment for those unionists who have been longest in the shop. That is its negative side.

In time, with the stretching out of their seniority rights and their upgrading to better jobs, a process of transformation in the status of the original union militants has taken place. In the course of 16 years, they have secured more or less steady employment, even in times of slack work. They are, under the rules, the last to be laid off and the first to be rehired. And in most cases, they have better jobs than newcomers to the shop. All of this, combined with war and postwar prosperity, has changed their material position and, to a certain extent, their social status.

The pioneer militants of the CIO unions are 16 years older than they were in 1937. They are better off than the ragged and hungry sit-down strikers of 1937; and many of them are 16 times softer and more conservative. This privileged section of the unions, formerly the backbone of the left wing, is today the main social base of the conservative Reuther bureaucracy. They are convinced far less by Reuther's clever demagogy than by the fact that he really articulates their own conservatised moods and patterns of thought.

But these conservatised ex-militants are only part of the membership of the CIO, and I don't think that our resolution at the convention deals specifically and adequately with that fact. In these mass production industries, which are real slave pens and hell holes, there are many others. There is a mass of younger workers who have none of these benefits and privileges and no vested interest in the piled-up seniority rights. They are the human material for the new radicalisation. The revolutionary party, looking to the future, must turn its primary attention to them.

If we, counting on a new upsurge in the labour movement, look to those who led it 16 years ago, we could indeed draw a gloomy picture. Not only are they not in a radical mood now; they are not apt to become the spearhead of a new radicalisation. That will take youth, and hunger, and raggedness, and bitter discontent with all the conditions of life. We must look to the new people if, as I take it, we are thinking in terms of the coming American revolution and not limiting our vision to the prospect of a new shake-up in the bureaucracy and of caucus combinations with slick "progressive" fakers for little aims.

This new stratification in the new unions is a feature which the party can no longer ignore. All the more so, since we now see it directly reflected in our party. A number of party members in the auto union belong to this privileged upper stratum. That's the first thing you have to recognise. Some of the best militants, the best stalwarts of the party in the old times, have been affected by the changed conditions of their own lives and by their new environment. They see the old militants in the unions, who formerly cooperated with them, growing slower, more satisfied, more conservative. They still mix with these ex-militants socially, and are infected by them. They develop a pessimistic outlook from the reactions they get on every side from these old-timers, and, unknown to themselves, acquire an element of that same conservatism.

That, in my opinion, is the reason why they support a crudely conservative, pessimistic, capitulatory tendency in our internal faction fight. This, I am afraid, is not a misunderstanding on their part. I wish it were, for in that case our task would be easy. The miserable arguments of the Cochranites cannot stand up against Marxist criticism – provided one accepts the criteria of revolutionary Marxism.

But that's the rub. Our conservatised trade unionists no longer accept these criteria. Like many others, who "used to be radicals themselves", they are beginning to talk about our "Theses on the American Revolution" as a "crackpot" idea. They don't "feel" that way, and nobody can talk them out of the way they do feel.

That – and perhaps a guilty conscience – is the true explanation of their subjectivity, their rudeness and factional frenzy when one tries to argue with them from the principled standpoint of the "old Trotskyism". They do not follow Cochran out of exceptional regard for him personally, because they know Cochran. They simply recognise in Cochran, with his capitulatory defeatism and his program of retreat from the fighting arena to a propaganda circle, the authentic spokesman of their own mood of retreat and withdrawal.

Just as the older, more skilled and privileged German trade unionists supported the right against the left, and as their Russian counterparts supported the Mensheviks against the Bolsheviks, the "professional trade unionists" in our party support Cochranism in our fight. And for the same basic reasons.

I, for my part, must frankly admit that I did not see this whole picture at the beginning of the fight. I anticipated that some tired and pessimistic people, who were looking for some sort of rationalisation to slow down or get out of the struggle, would support any kind of an opposition faction that would arise. That happens in every faction fight. But I didn't anticipate the emergence of a conservatised workers' stratum serving as an organised grouping and a social basis for an opportunist faction in the party.

Still less did I expect to see such a grouping strutting around in the party demanding special consideration because they are "trade unionists". What's exceptional about that? There are 15 million trade unionists in this country, but not quite so many revolutionists. But the revolutionists are the ones who count with us.

The revolutionary movement, under the best conditions, is a hard fight, and it wears out a lot of human material. Not for nothing has it been said a thousand times in the past: "The revolution is a devourer of men." The movement in this, the richest and most conservative country in the world, is perhaps the most voracious of all.

It is not easy to persist in the struggle, to hold on, to stay tough and fight it out year after year without victory; and even, in times such as the present, without tangible progress. That requires theoretical conviction and historical perspective as well as character. And, in addition to that, it requires association with others in a common party.

The surest way to lose one's fighting faith is to succumb to one's immediate environment; to see things only as they are and not as they are changing and must change; to see only what is before one's eyes and imagine that it is permanent. That is the cursed fate of the trade unionist who separates himself from the revolutionary party. In normal times, the trade union, by its very nature, is a culture-broth of opportunism. No trade unionist, overwhelmed by the petty concerns and limited aims of the day, can retain his vision of the larger issues and the will to fight for them without the party.

The revolutionary party can make mistakes, and has made them, but it is never wrong in the fight against grievance-mongers who try to blame the party for their own weaknesses, for their tiredness, their lack of vision, their impulse to quit and to capitulate. The party is not wrong now when it calls this tendency by its right name.

People often act differently as individuals, and give different explanations for their actions, than when they act and speak as groups. When an individual gets tired and wants to quit, he usually says he is tired and he quits; or he just drops out without saying anything at all, and that's all there is to it. That has been happening in our international movement for 100 years.

But when the same kind of people decide as a group to get out of the line of fire by getting out of the party, they need the cover of a faction and a "political" rationalisation. Any "political" explanation will do, and in any case it is pretty certain to be a phony explanation. That also has been going on for about 100 years.

The present case of the Cochranite trade unionists is no exception to this rule. Out of the clear sky we hear that some "professional trade unionists" are suddenly against us because we are "Stalinophobes", and they are hell-bent for an orientation toward Stalinism. Why, that's the damnedest non-sense I ever heard! They never had that idea in their heads until this fight started. And how could they? The Stalinists have gotten themselves isolated in the labour movement, and it's poison to touch them. To go looking for the Stalinists is to cut yourself off from the labour movement, and these party "trade unionists" don't want to do that.

The people in Michigan who are hollering for us to make an orientation toward the Stalinists have no such orientation on their own home grounds. And they're perfectly right about that. I don't deny that people like Clarke, Bartell, and Frankel [Braverman] have heard voices and seen visions of a gold mine hidden in the Stalinist hills – I will discuss this hallucination at another time – but the Cochranite trade unionists haven't the slightest intention of going prospecting there. They are not even looking in that direction. What's amazing is the insincerity of their support of the orientation toward the Stalinists. That's completely artificial, for factional purposes. No, you have to say the orientation toward Stalinism, as far as the Michigan trade unionists are concerned, is a phony.

What is the next thing we hear? That they are full of "grievances" against the party "regime". I always get suspicious when I hear of grievances, especially from people whom you didn't hear it from before. When I see people revolting against the party on the ground that they've been badly treated by this terrible regime in our party – which is actually the fairest, most democratic and easy-going regime in the history of the human race – I always remind myself of the words of J. Pierpoint Morgan. He said: "Everybody has at least two reasons for what he does – a good reason and the real reason." They've given a good reason for their opposition. Now I want to know what the hell is the real reason.

It can't be the party's hostility to Stalinism, as they say – because the Cochranite trade unionists wouldn't touch the Stalinists with a 10-foot pole, not even if you stood behind them with bayonets and lighted firecrackers under their coat-tails.

It can't be the Third World Congress [of the Fourth International, in 1951] concerning which they are suddenly working up a lather. These comrades in Michigan have many admirable qualities, as has been shown in the past, but they're by no means the most internationalist-minded section of the party; not by far. They're not that section of the party most interested in theoretical questions. The Detroit branch, sad to say, has been most remiss in the teaching and study of Marxist theory, and is now paying a terrible price for it. This branch hasn't got a single class going; no class in Marxism, no class in party history, no class on the Third World Congress or anything else. So when they suddenly erupt with the demand that the Third World Congress be nailed to the party's masthead, I say that's another good reason, but it's a phony too.

The real reason is that they are in revolt against the party without fully knowing why. For the young militant, the party is a necessity valued above everything else. The party was the very life of these militants when they were young and really militant. They didn't care for jobs; they feared no hazards. Like any other first-class revolutionists, they would quit a job at the drop of a hat if the party wanted them to go to another town, wanted them to do this or that. It was always the party first.

The party is the highest prize to the young trade unionist who becomes a revolutionist, the apple of his eye. But to the revolutionist who becomes transformed into a trade unionist – we have all seen this happen more than once – the party is no prize at all. The mere trade unionist, who thinks in terms of "union politics" and "power blocs" and little caucuses with little fakers to run for some little office, pushing one's personal interest here and there – why should he belong to a revolutionary party? For such a person the party is a millstone around his neck, interfering with his success as a "practical" trade union politician. And in the present political situation in the country, it's a danger – in the union, in the shop, and in life in general.

The great majority of the party trade unionists understand all this as well as we do. The vulgar "trade unionist" appeal of the Cochranites only repels them, for they consider themselves to be revolutionists first and trade unionists second. In other words, they are party people, as all revolutionists are.

Fourth International, spring 1954 (abridged)

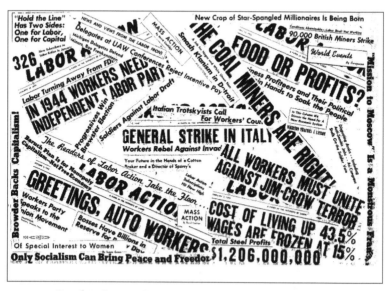

Graphic from Labor Action displaying its coverage of labour struggles

Part 3: Angels, devils, political folklore, and historical falsification

A Workers Party demonstration, 1945: left to right at front, Reva Craine, WP New York organiser; Emanuel Garrett; Ernest Rice McKinney

Ernest Rice McKinney, national secretary of
the Workers Party, 1946

9. Legends of the fall

Resisting an assault on Marxism

Joseph Hansen and George Novack (1942)

The introduction to *In Defence of Marxism*, a selection of Trotsky's writings from 1939-40 published in December 1942 by the SWP. See introduction, pp.70-71

I.

FOR MORE THAN 40 years Leon Trotsky defended and developed the ideas and methods of Marxism. In early manhood he undertook their defence against the czarist regime and the whole bourgeois world. During the First World War he defended revolutionary internationalism against the social-patriots and revisionists of the Second International. In the Russian Revolution, side-by-side with Lenin, he defended the program of Bolshevism against the Mensheviks and Social-Revolutionaries. After the victorious October 1917 revolution, as the leading Soviet propagandist, he defended Marxist principles in the field of political polemics as vigorously and brilliantly as he had the defence of the workers' state on the military fronts. With Lenin he founded the Third International to spread the ideas of Marxism throughout the world.

Trotsky's greatest battles in defence of Marxism came after Lenin's death. When the first signs of bureaucratic reaction appeared within the Russian Communist Party, Trotsky organised the Left Opposition which sought to maintain the Bolshevik program against the backsliding towards petty bourgeois politics of the Stalin-Zinoviev-Kamenev block. Despite his deportation to Alma-Ata he continued the struggle of the Russian Communist Left Opposition against the growing revisionist tendencies of the degenerating Stalinist clique. In exile in Turkey he organised the Communist Left Opposition on an international scale. When the Third International capitulated to fascism without a struggle in Germany in 1933, Trotsky founded the Fourth International to carry on the struggle for socialism.

During the last decade of his life Trotsky defended Marxism against fascism, against bourgeois-democratic public opinion, against all varieties of petty-bourgeois politics from the virulent Stalinism of the Third International and the social-reformism of the Second International to impotent centrism, ultra-leftism, and anarcho-syndicalism. There was no significant anti-Marxist tendency which did not have to reckon with Trotsky and which he did not analyse in his writings. In the universal reaction culminating in the Second World War, Trotsky stood forth as the foremost champion of revolutionary socialism.

At the beginning of the Second World War, Trotsky was again called upon to give battle in defence of Marxism. This time the struggle took place in the ranks of the American section of his own Fourth International. Unbalanced by the impact of the war in Europe and the pressure of alien class influences and ideas, a group of leaders within the Socialist Workers Party made what Trotsky characterised as "an attempt to reject, disqualify and overthrow the theoretical foundations, the political principles and organisational methods of our movement."

They and their followers failed. They failed because Trotsky, basing himself upon the experiences of the Bolshevik party and its predecessors, had forewarned the Trotskyist movement that the outbreak of another imperialist war would inevitably precipitate a crisis in its ranks; that under the onslaught of bourgeois public opinion the petty bourgeois elements in the party would become disoriented; that the proletarian wing must prepare itself against the dangers of this degeneration. They failed because when that crisis did break out, Trotsky detected its first symptoms, diagnosed the nature of the disease and prognosticated its further development. They failed because Trotsky was able to lead the proletarian majority in the ensuing factional conflict.

This volume is the most valuable product of that struggle which tested and tempered the ranks of our party. Here are many of Trotsky's most mature contributions to Marxist thought. To this last battle in defence of Marxism, Trotsky devoted the best energies of the last year of his life. He wrote the final item in this collection on August 17, 1940 – three days before the Stalinist assassin struck him down.

II

As Trotsky demonstrated in his article *From a Scratch to the Danger of Gangrene* the elements of a petty-bourgeois deviation had long been germinating within the American Trotskyist movement. This tendency did not dare assert itself in an organised and open political shape until it was impelled to do so by the events leading up to and directly following the outbreak of the Second World War.

The immediate occasion for the formation of the petty-bourgeois

468

opposition and its assault upon Marxism revolved around the question of the USSR. This was no accident. Since November 7 1917, the question of the Russian Revolution – and the Soviet state which is its creation – has drawn sharp dividing line through the labour movement of all countries. The attitude taken towards the Soviet Union throughout all these years has been the decisive criterion separating the genuine revolutionary tendency from all shades and degrees of waverers, backsliders and capitulators to the pressure of the bourgeois world – the Mensheviks, Social Democrats, anarchists and syndicalists, centrists, Stalinists. The development of the discussion quickly revealed that all the fundamental issues were involved.

On August 22, 1939 came the announcement of the Soviet-German pact. Thereupon a great wave of anti-Soviet propaganda swept through the "democracies". The petty-bourgeois wing of the Socialist Workers Party was shaken to the core. The same day at the meeting of the SWP Political Committee, Shachtman made the following motion: "That the next meeting of the Political Committee beginning with a discussion of our estimate of the Stalin-Hitler pact as related to our evaluation of the Soviet state and the perspectives for the future." Shachtman still affirmed defence of the USSR. But his motion indicated that he was now approaching James Burnham's views on the nature of the USSR which he had previously opposed. In several documents written before, Burnham – like Shachtman a member of the Political Committee – had already questioned the fundamental principle of the Fourth International that the Soviet Union is a workers' state which, although degenerated under the Stalinist regime, must be unconditionally defended against imperialist attack by the world working class. Thus the pact which ushered in the war likewise ushered in our inner-party crisis.

A week later the Second World War began. The pent-up petty-bourgeois tendency now broke the bonds. At the September 3 Political Committee meeting Burnham made a motion to convene a full session of the National Committee the following week and to place on its agenda a reconsideration of the Russian question. The majority agreed and demanded that the opposition first put its new ideas in written form. The majority also asked for sufficient time to invite Trotsky to acquaint us with his views. Characteristic of the opposition's hostility to Trotsky from the outset was the fact that it voted against this proposal.

On September 5 Burnham submitted his document *On the Character of the War* for the plenum meeting of the National Committee. Its essence is in the following sentences: "it is impossible to regard the Soviet Union as a workers' state in any sense whatsoever.... Soviet intervention (in the war) will be wholly subordinated to the general imperialist character of the conflict as a whole; and will be in no sense a defence of the remains of the socialist economy". A week later, in the letter with which this volume begins, Trotsky began laying bare the real implications of Burnham's doctrine: "that all the revolutionary potentialities of the world proletariat are exhausted, that the socialist movement is bankrupt, and that the old capitalism is transforming itself into 'bureaucratic collectivism' with a new exploiting class."

Trotsky expanded upon Burnham's position in his first important document of the faction struggle, *The USSR in War*, which arrived in time for discussion at the plenum. Since the petty-bourgeois opposition had not yet openly constituted itself as a faction, Trotsky utilised arguments similar to theirs which had been advanced by the Italian ex-Communist, Bruno R. and others, and developed their logical conclusions. This document constituted a stern warning to Burnham and his followers that, in challenging the program of the Fourth International on the Russian question, they thereby actually challenged the basic postulates of scientific socialism.

Three different groupings came together in the petty-bourgeois opposition. Burnham was its ideological leader, expressing most completely its anti-Marxist character. Abern's clique ostensibly agreed with Trotsky's views and disclaimed Burnham's. Shachtman, occupying an intermediate position, was beset with doubts and reservations which he applied indiscriminately to both Trotsky's and Burnham's positions. These last two tendencies in the bloc – those of Abern and Shachtman – were not yet ready to take the stand on Burnham's ground. They still pretended allegiance to the programme of the Fourth International. How did they get around these contradictions in their position in order to form a common faction which Burnham? They conspired with Burnham to suppress his real views. Then they found a common formula for their unprincipled combination by refusing to consider basic principles and demanding that the discussion be limited to immediate "concrete" issues.

At the plenum which convened on September 30, when the time came for Burnham to speak by his document, he blandly announced that he had withdrawn it! Instead, his attorney Shachtman produced a resolution as the joint platform of the opposition which attempted to evade and postpone discussion of the fundamental dispute on the class nature of the Soviet state by limiting the struggle to "immediate answers to the concrete questions raised by the Hitler-Stalin pact".

The resolution nevertheless failed to adhere to its own aims and conditions. The Red Army invasion of Poland was termed an act of "imperialist policy" which necessitated a "revision of our previous concept of the 'unconditional defence of the Soviet Union'."

The Abern clique exposed its unprincipled character by voting for both Shachtman's resolution and the motion of the party majority to "reaffirm our basic analysis of the nature of the Soviet state and the role of Stalinism" and to "endorse the political conclusions" of Trotsky's *The USSR in War*.

From all appearances, at this stage of their flight from Marxism, the opposition simply differed with Trotsky's interpretation of current events and the "organisational manners" of the leadership of the Socialist Workers Party which they attributed to Cannon. But Trotsky and his co-thinkers discerned the anti-Marxist tendency concealed within this entire unprincipled combination. The ideological parentage of Shachtman's resolution was clear. Its question mark over the class nature of the Soviet Union was a bridge leading to Burnham's answer. That answer was foreshadowed in these characterisation of the Red Army's actions as "acts of imperialist policy". As Trotsky explained in his first letter to Sherman Stanley and in his article, *Again and Once More on the Nature of the USSR*, "imperialism" is a term Marxists reserve for the expansionist politics of monopoly capitalism. The plenum accordingly condemned the resolution of the opposition "as an attempt in part to revise the fundamental position of the party, and in part to shield the position of those who aim at revision of our policy on the question of the Soviet Union in a fundamental sense," and accepted the position put forward in Trotsky's article *The USSR in War*.

The opposition organised on a national scale and sought support in other national sections of the Fourth International. As a series of membership meetings in New York, the majority continued its efforts to bring the fundamental issues to the surface.

In his next article *Again and Once More on the Nature of the USSR*, Trotsky dealt more specifically and sharply with the arguments being circulated by Burnham's followers, warning those who care to heed: "if we are to speak of a revision of Marx, it is in reality the revision of those comrades who project a new type of state 'non-bourgeois' and 'non-worker'". Stenograms of a speech by James P Cannon in support of the Fourth International position and of a speech by Shachtman which tried to cover up Burnham and maintain the highly unstable position of his plenum resolution were sent to Trotsky. Upon receipt of the two stenograms, Trotsky immediately dictated a letter to Shachtman, answering in detail the revisionist ideas which Shachtman had up to this time try to palm off as being in agreement with Trotsky's *The USSR in War*.

The majority printed articles in the Internal Bulletin of the Socialist Workers Party during the next weeks following, clarifying the deep going character of the differences, but the opposition stubbornly refused to accept battle on this principled basis. Trotsky decided that the time had come to cut through the rationalisations of the minority and to open up the abscess from which the infection was flowing – Burnham's ideological leadership. In the famous first paragraph of his next article, *A Petty Bourgeois Opposition in the Socialist Workers Party*, he declared: "It is necessary to call things by their right names. Now that the positions of both factions in the struggle have become determined with complete clearness, it must be said that the minority of the National Committee is leading a typically petty bourgeois tendency. Like any petty-bourgeois group inside the socialist movement, the present opposition is characterised by the following features: a disdainful attitude toward theory and an inclination toward eclecticism; disrespect for the tradition of their own organisation; anxiety for personal 'independence' at the expense of anxiety for objective truth; nervousness instead of consistency; readiness to jump from one position to another; lack of understanding of revolutionary centralism and hostility towards it; and finally, inclination to substitute clique ties and personal relationships for party discipline..."

These words cut like a scalpel through the pretensions of the mentality. The full implications of the faction struggle had now been posed point-blank by the leader of the Fourth International. The article, mainly directed against Burnham, brought forward before the entire Fourth International the question of Burnham's method in arriving at his theoretical and political conclusions. Trotsky showed that Burnham and Shachtman's rejection of dialectics and their substitution of the pragmatic method had inexorably led to incorrect political conclusions. For the benefit of workers unacquainted with dialectical materialism, Trotsky outlined the elementary ideas of the method in lucid terms.

Trotsky followed up his analysis of the petty bourgeois opposition with *An Open Letter to Comrade Burnham*. This was designed as a deliberate challenge to force Burnham into the open and compel him to defend his real views. Burnham did not dare remain silent any longer under Trotsky's concentrated fire for fear of losing influence over his personal following. Moreover, Trotsky's thrusts had hit him in the vitals. As Burnham subsequently confessed in his letter of resignation,

Trotsky dealt with the very beliefs that were determining Burnham's course and of which he was conscious long before his public break with the Fourth International.

Why did not a large part of the opposition leave Burnham and return to Marxism at this point? The answer can be found in the social pressure bearing down upon them as the war encircled the globe. This was the period when Baron Mannerheim's "poor little Finland" was the object of commiseration and the Soviet Union the object of hatred in England and the United States.

Shachtman came out in defence of Burnham in an open letter attacking Trotsky. In line with Burnham's contention that the method of dialectical materialism – the message implied by Trotsky – was of no use in answering the political problems of the day, it utilised the Polish and Finnish events to cast aspersions upon Trotsky's interpretation of current events.

Trotsky answered Shachtman in *From a Scratch – To the danger of Gangrene*. In this article Trotsky's attack on Burnham – always his main attack throughout the fight – is supplemented by a powerful and devastating analysis of Shachtman's past and his role as Burnham's attorney. Burnham now came out in his own defence. He replied to Trotsky's open letter with his notorious document *Science and Style* which has been appended to this volume.

Science and Style was the crassest expression of the anti-Marxist character and tendency of the opposition. Trotsky's success in smoking Burnham out and forcing him to divulge his real views was the turning point in the struggle. With Burnham's answer the struggle became clearly defined for the whole Fourth International. Here was empirical proof that the fight centred between revisionism and Marxism! Burnham's document, which appeared on the crest of the wave of Anglo-American war hysteria against the Soviet Union, rendered explicit what Trotsky and others with a dialectical understanding of the deep structures of the party had seen as implicit for a long time.

Trotsky had achieved his main aim: to prove to the Fourth International that the heavy proportion of petty bourgeois elements in its membership has thrown the SWP into a crisis with the outbreak of the Second World War and that this crisis concerned the most fundamental propositions of scientific socialism. When *Science and Style* appeared, Trotsky explicitly stated in his letter of February 23: "The abscess is open. Abern and Shachtman can no longer repeat that they wish only to discuss Finland and Cannon a bit. They can no longer play blind man's buff with Marxism and with the Fourth International. Should the Socialist Workers Party remain in the tradition of

473

Marx, Engels, Franz Mehring, Lenin and Rosa Luxemburg – a tradition which Burnham proclaims 'reactionary' – or should it accept Burnham's conceptions which are only a belated reproduction of pre-Marxian petty-bourgeois socialism?" He invited Abern and Shachtman to speak up: "what do you think of Burnham's 'science' and of Burnham's 'style'?... Comrades Abern and Shachtman, you have the floor!" They remained silent.

When Abern and Shachtman refused to disavow Burnham and his doctrines, including his "science" and his "style", it became obvious that they were preparing to split from the Fourth International. The majority endeavoured to maintain unity, acting under the conviction that the unity of the revolutionary party and the inculcation of party patriotism are among its most precious assets. The majority likewise had two objectives: (1) to keep wavering elements in the minority under the maximum influence of our program; (2) to prove conclusively to the other sections of the Fourth International that is matters came to a split the responsibilities of the split rested wholly with the minority. "We must do everything in order to convince also the other sections that the Majority exhausted all the possibilities in favour of unity", Trotsky explained. "The happenings in the Socialist Workers Party have now a great international importance... You must act not only on the basis of your subjective appreciations, as correct as they may be, but on the basis of objective facts available to everyone."

All the objective facts demonstrate that the minority's break with Marxism was the primary reason for the split. The discussion – which continued for more than six months – was the fullest ever undertaken in our movement. There was complete freedom from every viewpoint to express itself. The opposition was given every opportunity to win a majority and leadership in the party. "Even as an eventual minority," Trotsky wrote to the majority on December 19, "you should in my opinion remain disciplined and loyal towards the party as a whole. It is extremely important for the education in genuine party patriotism, about the necessity for which Cannon wrote me one time very correctly". At the convention where Trotsky's followers succeeded in winning a majority of the party to their position, they did not expel the minority from the party, deprive them of a share in the leadership, of responsible posts, or demand that they renounce their beliefs. On the contrary, representation corresponding to their actual strength was offered on all the bodies of the party; only observance of the principle of democratic centralism was demanded, that the minority abide loyally by the decision of the majority and confine its activity to further attempts to win the party to its position. The convention majority even agreed to a continuation of the discussion in the internal bulletin.

The conduct of the majority in this respect, guided at every step by Trotsky, serves as a model of correct Bolshevik tactics in building the proletarian party. Trotsky draws the balance sheet of this aspect of the struggle in his article, *Petty-bourgeois Moralists and the Proletarian Party*.

At the SWP convention which concluded on April 5, 1940, the majority of the party reaffirmed its support of the Fourth International programme. On April 16 the Political Committee met and moved: "That the committee accepts the convention decisions and obligates itself to carry them out in a disciplined manner." The minority bloc leaders refuse to vote for this motion. Instead of expelling them, as would have been wholly justified, the majority still waited. The record was made clear to the other sections of the Fourth International to the very end. Burnham and his followers were simply suspended until they would indicate "their intention to comply with the convention decisions."

The minority, however had already rented a separate headquarters. They set up a separate organisation which they named the "Workers Party," began printing a public newspaper, and stole the party's theoretical organ, the *New International*. These actions of the minority are characterised in Trotsky's article, *Petty-Bourgeois Moralists and the Proletarian Party*, which, together with the *Balance Sheet of the Finnish Events*, tersely sums up the political lessons of the struggle. Such was the sequence of events in the factional struggle from August 1939, when the minority leaders started to attack and revise the Fourth International program, to April 1940, when they broke away from the Socialist Workers Party.

III

Burnham was far from an isolated figure. He not only had followers inside the Socialist Workers Party; he had a host of kindred spirits outside amongst the ex-radical petty-bourgeois intellectuals. Most prominent amongst them were Sidney Hook, Max Eastman, Lewis Corey, Louis Hacker. These forerunners of Burnham had already revised Marxism all along the line, beginning with its theoretical foundations and ending with its politics. They constituted the American section of an international brotherhood of renegades from Marxism headed by Souvarine, Victor Serge, Bruno R., etc.

As Trotsky pointed out in *A Petty-Bourgeois Opposition in the So-*

cialist Workers Party, Burnham and Shachtman had endeavoured to analyse this tendency in an article in the January 1939 issue of the *New International*: *Intellectuals in Retreat*. Their analysis proved inadequate for the same reasons that later induced them to join this procession of fugitives from the revolutionary movement. Hook, Eastman, Corey blazed the trail for Burnham and Shachtman. Indeed, the petty-bourgeois opposition drew their arguments and ideas and received moral encouragement and inspiration from this "League of Abandoned Hopes" which they had previously criticised.

Most of these renegades had begun their careers as revisionists with a *philosophical* struggle against materialist dialectics. To conceal the extent and profundity of their opposition to Marxism from themselves as well as from others, one and all protested that their differences were "purely philosophical" and that such abstract differences in theory need not affect their specific political ideas and actions. Logic and philosophy in general, they held, had no necessary connection with politics. Consequently, they argued, the Marxist philosophy of dialectical materialism had no bearing on concrete political parties, programs and struggles. Burnham and Shachtman first enunciated this attitude in their article *Intellectuals in Retreat*. They jointly maintained it during the faction struggle. Burnham disclosed his irreconcilable hostility to Marxist theory in *Science and Style* when he accused the Trotsky of dragging dialectics into the political controversy as a "red herring". "There is no sense at all", declared Burnham, "in which dialectics... is fundamental in *politics*, none at all." Burnham and Shachtman had simply taken over this position from Eastman and Hook. Eastman had long contended that Marxism should purge itself of dialectical materialism which, he alleged, was nothing but a remnant of religion and Hegelian metaphysics, and adopt his "common-sense" approach. Hook, echoing these arguments, scoffed at "the fancied political implications of the doctrine of dialectical materialism."

This divorce of logic from politics, this rejection of dialectical materialism as the theoretical foundation of Marxism, is alien to Marxist thought and tradition. Marxism is a unified, consistent and comprehensive world conception. Its method of thought, the materialist dialectic, is an integral part of its doctrines. Marx, Engels and their disciples arrived at their political conclusions and formulated their political programmes by means of this method. Trotsky said "... Marxism without the dialectic" is "a clock without a spring".

Trotsky several times in these pages defines dialectics as the logic of evolution. It is the highest form of logic yet developed by the scientific thought. The materialist dialectic, as distinguished from Hegel's idealistic dialectics, is essentially the logic of *revolutionary* change. The principal laws of this logic rationally explain not only the course of gradual changes in natural, social and mental processes but also the sharp breaks and qualitative leaps whereby things are transformed into their own opposites.

Why are bourgeois thinkers repelled from the materialist dialectic? Mainly because as a logic of history, it recognises the seeds and roots of social revolutions within gradual changes in social life. At a certain stage in the accumulation of these changes, a qualitative leap occurs, a great break with the past, a revolution. Thus, according to the dialectic, social and political revolutions are not accidental aberrations or avoidable detours in history but materially caused and lawfully determined stages in the cycle of development of class societies. Finally – and to bourgeois ideologists and their petty-bourgeois shadows, this is its most horrifying feature – the materialist dialectic explains the logical evolution of the class struggles of our own epoch. It demonstrates why progressive capitalism becomes transmuted into reactionary monopoly capitalism with its imperialist politics and wars; it demonstrates the inevitability of the overthrow of monopoly capitalism by the social revolution of the international working class, and the transformation of dying capitalism into living socialism.

The materialist dialectic cannot be severed from social life or political thought because it formulates those general laws of social movement which give rise to the class struggle, govern its course and determine its outcome. When Lenin remarked and Trotsky in these writings reiterated, "There can be no revolutionary practice without revolutionary theory", they meant specifically: there can be no consistent revolutionary proletarian politics without the materialist dialectic which is the essence of scientific socialism.

This is the key to the significance of materialist dialectics to the revolutionary socialist movement and to the opposition it arouses among such enemies of that movement as the renegade petty bourgeois doctrinaires. To accept the logic of Marxism, to study, master and use it, is to embrace and advance the revolution. Indifference or opposition to the logical foundations of Marxism, if consistently developed, most often led, as it did in the case of Burnham, Shachtman, Hook, Eastman and other high priests of "common sense", to a repudiation of Marxism, not simply in philosophical theory but in political practice. Their desertion of socialism and a prostration before bourgeois thought was implicit from the beginning, as Trotsky foresaw, in their hostility toward materialist dialectics. The antagonism to Marxism they first manifested in the apparently unrelated field of philosophical controversy reached fruition in their political program. Obviously logic and philosophy are not so far removed from practical reality is they claimed.

History itself speaks most strongly against such attempts to split Marxist method from practical politics. Under Lenin and Trotsky the Bolshevik Party realised in social and political action what Marx and Engels with the aid of their dialectical method had explained and forecast in *The Communist Manifesto* and *Capital*. What the Bolsheviks proved in the most positive practical manner in the Russian Revolution of 1917 – the harmonious integration of Marxist theory and revolutionary action – Burnham, Hook and Eastman have amply proved in a negative way by their own renegacy. Today these deserters openly espouse bourgeois ideas in politics as well as in philosophy; and from the camp of the class enemy they conduct a spiteful struggle against the movement with which they once identified themselves.

Burnham's flight into the camp of the bourgeoisie was the most precipitate and complete of all. One month after he and his followers departed from the Trotskyist movement he disdainfully resigned from his new "party". Burnham's resignation and his letter of apology to his dupes involuntarily confirmed all that Trotsky had said about Burnham in the course of the controversy. This letter is republished in the appendix for the information and enlightenment of students of the dialectic.

A few months later Burnham expanded his ideas on world politics in a book, *The Managerial Revolution*. This book enjoyed wide popularity in Big Business, bureaucratic and petty-bourgeois intellectual circles until Hitler's attack upon the Soviet Union exploded its chief "concrete" political thesis: that Hitler and Stalin, the chief representatives of the future managerial society, had joined forces in the August 1939 pact to "drive death wounds into capitalism." From the theoretical standpoint this wretched book was essentially literary preparation for a nascent fascist movement in this country. The logic of contradiction revenged itself upon Burnham and thus this "witch-doctor", as Trotsky called him, who would not on logical grounds admit the inevitability of anything, and especially the inevitability of socialism, ended up with preaching the inevitability of – the totalitarian state.

Burnham's orphans have also gone from bad to worse. A month and a half before the split convention the majority predicted that "because of its internal contradictions" the group would disintegrate, "part going over to the bourgeoisie, part moving over to the 'sidelines' and part returning to Marxism..." This prediction has since in large measure been fulfilled. A section of the minority, realising that they had been deluded by Burnham's leadership, returned to the SWP. Many others have entirely given up any pretence of political activity. Following Burnham, a group of youth inclining toward social-patriotism left the minority to join the moribund Socialist Party. Those remaining act as political parasites, attempting to masquerade as "Trotskyists" while defaming Trotsky and rejecting his most fundamental ideas. This remnant, however, is steadily zig-zagging in the direction already taken by Burnham.

Since the split their program has undergone a series of changes along the line of political degeneration. Revising the Marxist theory of the state, they have officially adopted Burnham's viewpoint that the Soviet Union is no longer a degenerated workers' state but a "bureaucratic collectivist state", neither capitalist nor proletarian in character. They have abandoned the defence of the Soviet Union in its hour of mortal peril. Since Pearl Harbor, they have abandoned support of China's war against Japan and evade any clear statement of position on India's present struggle against British imperialism. Rejecting Trotsky's proletarian military policy, they have adopted a sectarian semi-pacifist attitude toward the military training of the working class. All these frenzied jumps from one position to another are given an extremely "radical" coloration with quotations from Lenin thrown in for good measure. But Lenin himself long ago demonstrated that "petty-bourgeois revolutionism" is only the other side of the coin of petty-bourgeois opportunism.

As events unfold, the irreconcilable cleavage between the Trotskyists and these petty bourgeois pretenders reveals itself on every important issue. What appeared at the beginning of the struggle to be remote differences regarding the relations between logic and politics and a slight dispute over the Russian question has turned out to be a fundamental opposition in methods of thought, class theory and political programme.

IV

The Trotskyist movement in the United States gained far more than it lost in the struggle and split with the petty-bourgeois opposition. The proletarian majority of the party demonstrated in action its understanding of Marxism together with its ability to defend these ideas. Since the split it has become in composition as well as in programme a genuine proletarian organisation

In November-December 1941 the political and trade union leaders of the Socialist Workers Party stood up in the capitalist court at Minneapolis where they were on trial for "sedition" and defended against the government of the American bourgeoisie the same programme which they and Trotsky had defended against the petty- bourgeois opposition. They now face prison terms for their refusal to recant. Since the trial, despite the war hysteria, the American Trotskyists have registered significant gains in membership.

All the sections of the Fourth International which were able to learn of the struggle in the United States supported Trotsky's position. How well the Fourth International absorbed the lessons and methods of Marxism is proved by the Bolshevik-Leninist Party of India, which, independently and without direct knowledge of the faction struggle of the documents written in that struggle (due to the war and the British censorship), published a pamphlet, *Whither the Soviet Union*, which presents with absolute precision our position on the character of the workers' state and the necessity for its unconditional defence.

World events have confirmed Trotsky's analyses and revealed the utter bankruptcy of the minority's estimates. At that time Trotsky warned of the impending assault by Hitler's armies and girded the class-conscious workers for the defence of the Soviet Union. Burnham held that the defence of the Soviet Union constituted ipso facto support of Hitlerism! As for their analyses of the Polish and Finnish events, Burnham's followers are the last ones in the world today who want to speak about that!

The petty-bourgeois bloc counted on exploiting the theoretical deficiencies of our party, which reflected the traditional theoretical backwardness of the American working class. By repelling this assault upon dialectical materialism and the political programme flowing from it, the Socialist Workers Party thereby showed that it had taken a great step forward in mastering the fundamental method of Marxism. This was just the beginning, even in our own ranks, of understanding the importance of the materialist dialectic, of studying it, of using it, of teaching it to the advanced workers. Today in our party and in the Fourth International this task remains among the foremost. Trotsky's writings during the factional struggle, gathered here in one volume, are an indispensable aid for accomplishing this great historical work.

December 1942
Introduction to *In Defence of Marxism*, a selection of Trotsky's polemics from 1939-40 published by the SWP in 1942

The Workers' Party: a petty-bourgeois tendency

Leon Trotsky (1940)

QUESTION: IN YOUR OPINION were there enough political differences between the majority and the minority to warrant a split?

Trotsky: Here it is also necessary to consider the question dialectically, not mechanically. What does this terrible word "dialectics" mean? It means to consider things in their development, not in their static situation. If we take the political differences as they are, we can say they were not sufficient for a split, but if they developed a tendency to turn away from the proletariat in the direction of petty-bourgeois circles, then the same differences can have an absolutely different value; a different weight; if they are connected with a different social group. This is a very important point.

We have the fact that the minority split away from us, in spite of all the measures taken by the majority not to split. This signifies that their inner social feeling was such that it is impossible for them to go together with us. It is a petty-bourgeois tendency, not a proletarian. If you wish a new confirmation of this, we have an excellent example in the article of Dwight Macdonald.

First of all, what characterizes a proletarian revolutionary? No one is obliged to participate in a revolutionary party, but if he does participate, he considers the party seriously. If we dare to call the people for a revolutionary change of society, we carry a tremendous responsibility, which we must consider very seriously. And what is our theory, but merely the tools of our action? These tools are our Marxist theory because up to today we have not found better tools. A worker is not fantastic about tools – if they are the best tools he can get he is careful with them; he does not abandon them or demand fantastic non-existent tools.

Burnham is an intellectual snob. He picks up one party, abandons it, takes up another. A worker cannot do this. If he enters a revolutionary party, addresses the people, calls them for action, it is the same as a general during a war – he must know where he is leading them. What would you think of a general who said he thought the guns were bad – that it would be better to wait for ten years until they had invented better guns, so everybody had better go home. That is the way Burnham reasons. So he abandoned the party. But

481

the unemployed remain, and the war remains. These things cannot be postponed. Therefore it is only Burnham who has postponed his action.

Dwight Macdonald is not a snob, but a bit stupid. I quote:

"The intellectual, if he is to serve any useful function in society, must not deceive either himself or others, must not accept as good coin what he knows is counterfeit, must not forget in a moment of crisis what he has learned over a period of years and decades."

Good. Absolutely correct. I quote again:

"Only if we meet the stormy and terrible years ahead with both skepticism and devotion – skepticism towards all theories, governments and social systems; devotion to the revolutionary fight of the masses – only then can we justify ourselves as intellectuals."

Here is one of the leaders of the so-called "Workers" Party, who considers himself not a proletarian but an "intellectual." He speaks of skepticism toward all theories.

We have prepared ourselves for this crisis by studying, by building a scientific method, and our method is Marxism. Then the crisis comes and Mr. Macdonald says "be skeptical of all theories," and then talks about devotion to the revolution without replacing it with any new theory. Unless it is this skeptical theory of his own. How can we work without a theory? What is the fight of the masses and what is a revolutionary? The whole article is scandalous and a party which can tolerate such a man as one of its leaders is not serious.

I quote again: "What is the nature of the beast (fascism), then? Trotsky insists it is no more nor less than the familiar phenomenon of Bonapartism, in which a clique maintains itself in power by playing one class off against another, thus giving the State power a temporary autonomous character. But these modern totalitarian regimes are not temporary affairs; they have already changed the underlying economic and social structure, not only manipulating the old forms but also destroying their inner vitality. Is the Nazi bureaucracy a new ruling class, then, and fascism a new form of society, comparable to capitalism? That doesn't seem to be true either."

Here he creates a new theory, a new definition of fascism but he wishes, nevertheless, that we should be skeptical toward all theories. So also to the workers he would say that the instruments and tools they work with are not important but they must have devotion to their work. I think the workers would find a very sharp expression for such a statement.

It is very characteristic of the disappointed intellectual. He sees the war, the terrible epoch ahead, with losses, with sacrifices, and he is afraid. He begins to propagate skepticism and still he believes it is possible to unify skepticism with revolutionary devotion. We can only develop a revolutionary devotion if we are sure it is rational and possible, and we cannot have such assurances without a working theory. He who propagates theoretical skepticism is a traitor.

We analyzed in fascism different elements:

1. The element which fascism has in common with the old Bonapartism is that it used the antagonisms of classes in order to give to the state power the greatest independence. But we have always underlined that the old Bonapartism was in a time of an ascending bourgeois society, while fascism is a state power of the declining bourgeois society.

2. That fascism is an attempt of the bourgeois class to overcome, to overstep, the contradiction between the new technique and private property without eliminating the private property. It is the "planned economy" of fascism. It is an attempt to save private property and at the same time to check private property.

3. To overstep the contradiction between the new, modern technique of productive forces within the limited borders of the national state. This new technique cannot be limited by the borders of the old national state and fascism attempts to overcome this contradiction. The result is the war. We have already analyzed all these elements.

Dwight Macdonald will abandon the party just as Burnham did, but possibly because he is a little lazier, it will come later.

Burnham was considered "good stuff" at one time? Yes, the proletarian party in our epoch must make use of every intellectual who can contribute to the party. I spent many months on Diego Rivera, to save him for our movement, but did not succeed. But every International has had an experience of this kind. The First International had troubles with the poet, Freiligrath, who was also very capricious. The Second and Third Internationals had trouble with Maxim Gorki. The Fourth International with Rivera. In every case they separated from us.

Burnham was, of course, closer to the movement, but Cannon had his doubts about him. He can write, and has some formal skill in thinking, not deep, but adroit. He can accept your idea, develop it, write a fine article about it – and then forget it. The author can forget – but the worker cannot. However, so long as we can use such people, well and good. Mussolini at one time was also "good stuff"!

Coyoacan, D.F. August 7, 1940

Fourth International, October 1940

No conciliation with renegades

SWP (1941)

IN THE NEXT PERIOD our party must be more than ever absolutely unrelenting in its warfare against any existing or arising centrist groups (Shachtmanites, etc.). Lenin, never much of a unity shouter, became especially intransigent during the first world war as the fundamental cleavage between the Bolsheviks and the Mensheviks revealed itself more clearly. So now must we maintain the cohesion of the genuine revolutionists during this war. Trotsky said the fight between the proletarian majority of the party and the petty bourgeois opposition was similar in many respects to the historical struggle between the Bolsheviks and the Mensheviks in the Russian movement. In justice to the Russian Mensheviks, Trotsky also said, they appear as revolutionary heroes in comparison with the wretched faction of Burnham, Shachtman and Co.

We must educate cadres who are not afraid of isolation and who do not seek fictitious strength through numbers at the expense of programmatic clarity... The condition for a fruitful intervention on our part in a revolutionary development among the Stalinist workers, or the political awakening of any other group of serious workers, is the prohibition in our own ranks of any sentiment of conciliation toward the degenerate petty bourgeois clique of Shachtman and Co.

From points 12-14 of a resolution adopted by an SWP "Plenum-Conference", *The Militant*, 18 October 1941

The Workers Party after five years

Max Shachtman (1945)

THE WORKERS PARTY WAS ORGANISED as a result of the factional struggle that broke out in the American Trotskyist movement (the Socialist Workers Party and its youth organisation) when the second world war began, and ended in a split. Those who founded the new party had reason to be confident. First, they had better than held their own in the debate. Difference of opinion and even factional struggle were not new in the Trotskyist movement. But never before had the leadership of any section of the International shown such poverty of ideas, such bewilderment and downright helplessness when confronted by a new situation, a new problem and a critical opposition.

In face of the joint partition of Poland by Germany and Russia, followed by the invasion of Finland and the annexation of the Baltic countries by Stalin, we proposed the abandonment of the traditional position of "unconditional defence of the USSR" in war. We argued that Russia was playing a reactionary role in the war, having joined one of the imperialist camps in order to share in the booty; and that to support Russia meant supporting the imperialist war in violation of the interests of the international working class and socialism. The majority had no other reply save the repetition of the formula, "Russia is a degenerated workers' state; therefore, we are for its unconditional defence in the war." Its attempts to give more specific answers to the political situation were sorry models of confusion: witness the fact that it produced three mutually contradictory documents on the war in Finland in less than that number of weeks. In effect, it took its political courage into its hands and retired from the debate. Its task was taken over by Trotsky and by him alone.

Never in the history of the movement did we have what followed. Trotsky found himself obliged to lead and carry on the fight for the paralysed majority all by himself. One document by him followed another, sometimes in almost daily succession. He found it necessary to write at length on the tiniest questions, or aspects of a question, in dispute, and even questions that were very doubtfully related to the disagreement. One of his principal documents he even sent directly to the branches of the party, without the normal intermediary of the central party committee. The least that can be said about him is that he more than discharged his obligations as a political leader.

The American party leadership could not have been more heavily indicted for political helplessness than it was by the very thoroughness with which Trotsky was compelled to assume the burden that properly belonged to it. The majority confined itself to acting as Trotsky's phonograph. In the days between the arrival of records, it was astutely and firmly silent. To be sure, a phonograph that does no more than reproduce an eloquent voice performs a much more valuable service than a man from whose throat emerges only unharmonious gibberish. Still, if it continues to play the records a thousand times over, it will never develop a voice itself. It will always remain a phonograph that needs a record in order to articulate. The man with the throat has the advantage after all. He cannot only listen to the recorded voice but can, by persistent application, develop a clear voice of his own.

Trotsky enjoyed a tremendous authoritative (authoritative, not authoritarian) standing among the members of the minority. Only the greater strength of their arguments enabled them to continue the debate with him. When the debate ended, they had held not only to their views, but to their forces. In the final vote, the minority had more than forty percent of the votes; if the Trotskyist movement is taken as a whole in this country (party and youth organisations together), the minority had well over fifty percent of the votes. It was a distinct victory for us. As for the Cannonites, it was an utterly crushing defeat from every standpoint. There is no doubt that if Trotsky had not intervened (he had, of course, both the right and duty to intervene), the Cannonites would simply have been inundated in the fight.

In the second place, the way in which the split took place enhanced our confidence. The split, to our knowledge, simply has no precedent in the working-class movement. To this day, the Cannonites have carefully guarded against making public even to their membership the full text of the resolution that split the SWP. The first part of the resolution provided for acceptance of the decisions of the convention that had just taken place (April, 1940) and a commitment "to carry them out in a disciplined manner." This "clever" motion, characteristic of the little mind that conceived it, merely meant that the minority should vote to gag itself in the working-class public on the most vital question of the day, the war, and approve of handing over its inner-party rights to the mercies of a majority that had gone out of its way to prove that it was entitled to no such confidence. We therefore abstained in the vote on this motion.

The second part of the resolution provided that those not voting for the first part shall, for that reason alone, be deprived of all party positions, responsibilities and rights! In their introduction to Trotsky's *In Defence of Marxism* Hansen and Warde describe the occurrence. They quote the first part of the resolution, and add: "The minority bloc leaders refused to vote for this motion. Instead of expelling them, as would have been wholly justified [!!], the majority still waited."

Two points: 1. The decisive second part of the motion is not quoted. Why? Are our bold men so ashamed of their... innovation?

2. The majority did not "still wait," for the simple reason that, as stated above, the second part of the motion provided for our expulsion in every respect except pure form, namely, for removal from all posts and for disfranchisement in the party and deprivation of all rights of party membership. That is how the disciples of the "historian of American Trotskyism" write its history.

A unique contribution to revolutionary party procedure! We had not violated a single disciplinary provision. We were not even charged with any such violation. We were expelled, in effect, merely for abstaining from the vote on the majority's motion, providing that we "accept" convention decisions which among other things branded us as "petty-bourgeois." The whole procedure lasted, as the party boss gleefully noted to a crony at the meeting, exactly four and three-quarter minutes. We knew well in advance what and whom we were dealing with. We knew, in so far as it is possible to be certain in politics, that the leading clique was determined to get rid of the opposition, especially because it was not prepared to proclaim the omniscience and omnipotence of ignorance and impotence. So we were well prepared. The Workers Party was publicly proclaimed and our *Labor Action* and *New International* [1] were issued shortly after the expulsion ukase.

Fear of our views, and of our ability and determination to defend them, prompted our expulsion, and nothing else. The consciousness of this only fortified us in our actions.

Thirdly, we had won to our side the overwhelming majority of the youth. In itself, this may not be "proof" of anything, but in such situations it is almost invariably an excellent sign. The history of the revolutionary movement shows exceedingly few, if any, exceptions to the rule that in such disputes the youth takes the side of the left-wing against the right or conservative wing. How reconcile this fact with the accusation that we were a "petty-bourgeois opposition"? The majority simply never made a serious attempt to reconcile the two, except, perhaps, by repeating some of the "explanations" made by the Socialist Party right-wingers when the socialist youth joined with the Trotskyists in 1936, or else by repeating the accusation in a louder voice.

And lastly, the development of the war confirmed our position on Russia's role in it, and not that of the majority, which found itself compelled with each new event and turn to explain away the arguments it had given for its position the day before. The political question around which the dispute revolved was the question of Russia. Far from a "foreign question," for the whole world and the whole labour movement finds itself forced, more and more each day, to discuss and decide it! In politics, nobody has the right to rest on an adopted position without constantly submitting and re-submitting it to the test of events, to the test of honest self-criticism and the criticism of opponents. Only lead-bottomed and brass-headed smugness can speak in the revolutionary movement of "our finished program" (finished: exsanguinated and embalmed, waxed and polished, shrouded, crated and consecrated, entombed and headstoned). This phrase is now the favorite shibboleth of the SWP. If Marx and Engels had so much as thought in such terms, even after writing the program of the communists which we know as the Communist Manifesto, we would not have the Marxian theory of the state today, to say nothing of a few other trifles in our arsenal, like the theory of the permanent revolution.

How have the positions taken in 1939-1940 stood up under the test of the years that followed? In a word, we have strengthened ours; they have had to abandon theirs and they will have to abandon more before long. Our opposition to the defence of Stalinist Russia in the war was explained by the Cannonites as due to "bourgeois-democratic pressure." How? It appears that we had left Russia to fight single-handed against Poland and Finland. The bourgeoisie of the democratic countries had launched a big campaign against Russia for the alliance with fascist imperialism; and to this campaign, we succumbed.

However, nowhere, in any of our writings of the time or since, did we motivate our position on the grounds that Russia had made an alliance with wicked Fascist imperialism instead of with benevolent democratic imperialism. The Cannonites, completely off the track, worked themselves into the belief that this was our motivation, and nothing else. Predictions were freely made that if and when Russia switched to the camp of Anglo-American imperialism, and the "bourgeois-democratic pressure" would be exerted in the other direction, we would make a turn in our course.

Naturally, nothing of the sort occurred. More exactly, it did occur in the case of about a dozen party members who had taken our position in 1939 but who proposed to reverse it in favour of support of Russia in the war once Hitler attacked in the East and Russia joined the camp of the democratic imperialists. It is interesting to note that it was this group of comrades, who failed to win any support for their position in our party, that thereupon returned to the SWP, where it was welcomed with enthusiastic cheers! The accusation against us on the score of "bourgeois-democratic pressure" obviously made no sense.

It makes even less sense, and stands out as the factional invention that it was from the outset, when the record of the Workers Party on the imperialist war in general is examined. If, as "petty-bourgeois," we had succumbed to the pressure of bourgeois democracy even before this country was in the war, and in connection, after all, with mother country, it stands to reason that we would certainly succumb to this pressure when it was exerted in the direct interests of American imperialism, namely, when the United States itself entered the war. And as Trotsky once remarked, there must be some reason even in slander. Yet, to put it with restraint, there was not and is not the slightest evidence of our "succumbing." On the contrary. The Workers Party was the only working-class organisation, with no exception, which took a forthright, unambiguous position in public in opposition to American imperialism in the war. Our manifesto in *Labor Action* on this score was the only one to appear in the labour movement immediately after the Pearl Harbour events. In this, we did our elementary duty. It was our political demonstration against American imperialism, and under the circumstances, the best that could have been (certainly the least that should have been) made. The SWP did not follow suit. This fact cannot be talked away, although efforts have not been lacking. And since Pearl Harbour, as before it, our position has been equally forthright and unambiguous. It has formed part of our work of awakening the consciousness of the American working-class, of arousing it to its class interests, of imbuing it with the spirit of socialist internationalism.

We did not change our position on Russia but, as stated, we did strengthen it. Unlike the Cannonites, we sought to learn from the 1939-1940 discussion. If Trotsky was the only one we could learn from, that was neither his fault nor ours. He was the only one who contributed to his side of the debate. Trotsky never succeeded in freeing himself from the basic contradictions of his position. He could not (nor did he attempt to) explain how the counter-revolutionary, anti-socialist, anti-Soviet, Bonapartist bureaucracy, as he rightly called it, could nevertheless establish in the capitalist countries (Poland, the Baltic lands) what he called the foundations of a workers' state, i.e., carry out a social revolution "via bureaucratic military means." He could not explain why, if Stalinist Russia is like a big trade-union in power whose army is to be supported, he is nevertheless opposed to this "union" gaining in membership and strength, so to speak, by extending its frontiers ("We were and remain against seizures of new territories by the Kremlin," he wrote). But he did succeed in pointing out many of the contradictions in our position as it was developed and defended at that time. At least, that is the opinion of the present writer.

The untenability of Trotsky's basic position, and the defects and contradictions he revealed in our original position, only stimulated us to further and deeper analysis of the question. The result, a product of genuinely collective thought and elaboration by the leading comrades of our party, was worked out and presented (not, thank God, as a "finished program") in our theory of Stalinist Russia as a bureaucratic collectivist state. Our theory has been put forward in great detail elsewhere. Here it is necessary to point out only two things. One is that our theory not only made possible a more harmonious relationship to our practical policy than before, but enabled us to eliminate the weaknesses contained not so much in the policy (i.e., refusal to defend Russia in the war), as in some of the motivations for it. Two is that the Cannonites, once so insistent on discussing the "class character of the Soviet Union," have shrewdly avoided dealing with this question from the moment that we presented our own systematic position on it.

The question itself is so momentous, however, that it will not tolerate silence. One way or another, the silence had to be broken, and it has been. Stalin's spectacular successes in the defence of the "degenerated workers' state" have now imposed a "turn" in policy upon the SWP. It is one of the most remarkable "turns" in the history of the movement. The slogan of "unconditional defence" of Russia in the war was what distinguished the SWP from the rest of the world. So it said repeatedly during the war, and in just those words. Whoever did not work for the victory of the Russian army in the war, thereby placed himself on the other side of the barricades. That too was said in those words, and more than once. It would seem now that this slogan has been favoured by truly rich success. The Russian armies are victorious on every front. Now, if ever, is the time for the bearers of the slogan to cheer their victory, and to express a justified pride in themselves and in the modest contribution they made to the victory.

It is almost the very opposite that has happened. Near the very pinnacle of overwhelming victory, it has been discovered that the slogan which aimed to bring about this victory must now be abandoned! Slogans have been abandoned and policies changed before now, and so it will be in the future. This is the first case we know of, however, where a slogan has been abandoned because it proved to be too successful! An indispensable addition to this is the fact that it has been abandoned with an accompanying insistence that the only reason ever given for advancing it in the first place still holds, namely, that Russia is a workers' state.

To be sure, "abandoned" is a strong, simple and forthright word, and above all, in the present case, a most embarrassing word. A substitute, of the requisite delicacy, equivocalness and face-saving quality had to be found, and it was. The slogan is not really "abandoned." No. It merely "recedes to the background" (like a coffin "receding" to the grave); it is merely that we "are shifting our emphasis" to another slogan. Priceless formulas! Classics of their type! Their author should somehow be rescued from modest anonymity. He may not be worth a damn as a revolutionary party leader, but what a diplomat he would make in Monaco! What slogan do the Cannonites "push to the fore"? To which one do they shift the emphasis? To the "defence of the European revolution ... against the Kremlin bureaucracy, against all its agents and agencies," presumably including the "Red Army" which has suddenly become "an instrument of the counter-revolutionary bureaucracy."

Good. Very good. But just why is it necessary to push and to shift right now? Because... because... because the slogan of the past five years was too good — it suffered from an over-abundance of success! How did it come about that the European revolution is so perilously threatened by the Russian army? Because... because... because the Russian army has been so victorious, as a result (in microscopic part, to be sure) of the slogan that was just "receded." We read in the SWP press today that "the attitude of the revolutionary vanguard toward the Red Army occupation troops in eastern Europe is thus essentially no different than its attitude toward Anglo-American troops in western Europe." But the very reason why it is necessary today to adopt this "attitude," is that for five years the SWP has urged everyone to be the "best soldier in the Red Army" in order that it might be victorious, i.e., so that it might become the "occupation troops in Eastern Europe." There you have the balance-sheet after five years: The old line must "recede" because it was such a success.

Honest and open abandonment of the fatal policy, with honest and open self-criticism, is the very pre-condition of educating the party and the workers around it. The SWP leadership is not concerned with education; it is concerned only with face-saving, with bureaucratic prestige. Honest self-criticism would show that virtually every point on which Trotsky assailed the Chinese policy of Stalin in 1925-1927 applies to the Cannonite policy on Russia in the war. Like Stalin in China, they embellished their "ally"; they confused the banners; they urged capitulation to Stalin by those who were rising independently. Proof? Here it is: The Fundamental Sophism. They disseminated glibly what Trotsky called the fundamental sophism of Stalinism, namely, that the Russian workers own the factories and the land. This sophism is contained not only in numerous articles in the SWP press but in a unanimously-adopted convention resolution. It has yet to be repudiated. They disseminated glibly the declaration that the army they now call counterrevolutionary was "Trotsky's Red Army." They proclaimed that this army of counterrevolution, which is now to be treated like the other imperialist armies, is bringing socialism to Europe. (Now, the revolution in Europe must be defended from the army that was... bringing socialism to Europe. A real "shift in emphasis" if we ever saw one!) They advised the rebellious peasants of Iran not to impede the progress or damage the interests of the "Red" Army (by the way, they still call "the instrument of the counterrevolutionary bureaucracy" a Red Army; the shift has not yet been made in full, it seems). And only yesterday, their leader, who still thought the background was the foreground, advised the Warsaw revolutionists to put themselves voluntarily at the disposal of the Stalinist hangmen.

This is no shift in emphasis, it is a rout. It is the collapse of a policy. They are not even trying to save the fragments, but only their faces. Here too the comparison with Stalin in 1927 is striking. Old, previously obscured and never-used quotations are dug up to show that they really "foresaw everything" and were not caught unawares. They even have the coolness to say that they made the "shift" a long time ago, when every child in the party now has the documents that prove how they resisted a change in line and adopted it at the very last minute under the pressure of the "outside" comrade who has been called an Eminent Interventionist. The new tactic, says the loudest of the party's empty barrels, was made "some nine months ago [by] our committee." And "the discerning reader will have noticed that we conducted our propaganda in this spirit for a good many months." But since hellishly few readers are discerning, and since those that are would have needed a microscope; and since, after all, a turn in policy ought to be made for the information and guidance of every reader including those with less "discernment"; and since the empty barrel has discerned that it requires little discernment to see through his dodges — he adds, "We propose now to incorporate this tactical prescription in our resolution, in order to make unambiguously clear to all the nature of our tactical adjustment and the reasons for it." (*Fourth International*, Feb. 1945. [The article was by Bert Cochran]) Push? Shift? Adjustment? No, a first-class rout.

The rout is not yet complete. What we are also witnessing in the SWP after five years is the collapse of its basic theory on Russia. Unable to speak any longer with enthusiasm or conviction for the theory that Russia is still a workers' state, and dogmatically refusing to examine objectively the theory we have put forward, they have nothing left to do but hunt feverishly for signs that Stalin is restoring capitalism in the form of private property. In the hunt, Wright, with the inevitable aid of *Pravda*, has already turned up the usual kulak with the usual extra cow in the usual mountain village. Of more significant signs in Russia, there are none. The huntsmen have a long search in store for them. Outside of Russia, in the occupied countries, they have noticed that Stalin has yet not nationalised property everywhere. They have not reflected that for the time being, the Russian bureaucracy can very well exploit these countries as semi-colonies without in the least changing the social and economic structure of its own regime. It will not be the Rumanian economy that will determine the Russian, but the other way around. The hunt for "capitalism" in Russia is, so far as the Cannonites are concerned, a desperate search for a way of abandoning their untenable theory without losing their dearest possession, face. He who lives, will see.

The Workers Party never had the need for such gyrations. From the beginning of the war, we repeated that the victory of the armies of the Stalinist counterrevolution did not coincide with the interests of the working class. Whatever errors we may have made in detail, our basic policy was clear and correct, and is now fully confirmed. We warned the workers that Russia was playing a reactionary and imperialist role in the war, that it was participating in the imperialist division of the spoils — now on the side of Germany, now on the side of England-America. We urged that the workers and colonial peoples declare their independence of both imperialist camps, and form their own movement: and that organisation of this "Third Camp" was the first step toward real peace and freedom.

Now, the Cannonites who derided the idea of the "Third Camp," are compelled to advance it themselves, but of course without using the same term. Now they no longer repeat that Russia is part of the camp of the proletariat and the colonial peoples. They laughed themselves wet at the idea that Russia was following an imperialist policy for its share of the spoils — it was merely defending itself, you see, by bureaucratic methods. Now, in their shamefaced "shift," they make their involuntary retractions. We now read that Russian "foreign policy has lost every vestige of its former isolationism and defensiveness and is becoming aggressively expansionist and adventurist." Imperialist? Good Lord, no! That term is petty-bourgeois heresy. Russia is merely... "aggressively expansionist and adventurist." Apparently a whim on Stalin's part.. We read further that the allies "accept Stalin as a third partner and in a business-like manner arrange with him a division of spoils." (*Fourth International,* March, 1945.) Imperialist? My God, no! It is simply a case of the poor little workers' state, in sheer self-defence, getting a share of the... spoils. It is to be regretted that there are people who begrudge it even so modest an award for its efforts to bring socialism to Europe on the bayonets of Trotsky's Red Army.

Five years have sufficed for the test on the "Russian question." There is incontrovertible evidence to show who survived the test.

The dispute on the Russian question was important, and so it will continue to be. But far more important is the question of participation in the class struggle in the United States. In this field, the work of our party has been valuable and fruitful.

We founded the Workers Party with a membership composed for the most part of youth. The preceding years of crisis and depression had deprived many of them of the opportunity of entering industry and taking part in the trade-union movement. The war gave those who were not drafted the opportunity they sought. Before long, virtually our entire membership was concentrated in important industries and active in the labour movement, acquiring experience not only from the older party members but also from the militants in the labour movement with whom they established friendly contact.

The difficulties encountered in carrying on militant activities in the trade unions during the war need little elaboration. There is the powerful pressure exerted on all sides for "national unity," so that the ruling class may increase its power and carry out its reactionary policies without interference by the workers acting in defence of their class interests. There are the conservative trade-union leaders, tied to the imperialist machine, and exerting every ounce of their strength against effective independent action by the workers and against the militants who urge it. There are above all the Stalinists, ready and eager to pounce upon every progressive and every genuine socialist, to frame him up, to hound him and drive him out of the labour movement. And there is always the unholy combination of the employers, trade-union bureaucrats and draft boards which does not hesitate to use its power to ferret out militants and get rid of them. All in all, not the easiest conditions for the activities of militants.

Yet, apart from considerations of socialist duty to the working class, there were also favorable conditions. The measure of our activity in the labour movement was not determined, as some would like to put it, by arbitrary considerations. Before the war, we had all declared in our analyses that once the war got under way, the political differences between the totalitarian and the democratic countries would dwindle rapidly. We also foresaw a working class swept by a mighty chauvinistic wave with the beginning of the war in this country. Neither prediction proved correct. In the United States, the working class soon showed that while it supported the war, above all in the sense of not wanting to see the country defeated by Germany or Japan, its support was reluctant, mingled with healthy suspicion of imperialism and the class intentions of the capitalists. Without the opportunity to express itself in organised form, it nevertheless showed growing hostility to all attempts to lower its living standards or deprive it of political rights. The labour movement was bent to its knees by the union leaders, but they could not prostrate it; they could not even prevent it from rising repeatedly to its feet and fighting for its interests. The existence of a powerful labour movement, plus its barely suppressed mood of militancy, undoubtedly slowed down enormously the tendency toward totalitarianism in the United States during the war. Refusing to be guided by disproved assertions of yesterday, we established these facts early in the war and proceeded to orient our activities accordingly. In this respect, too, our analysis was justified by the results.

We set ourselves the goal of bringing the militant moods of the workers to the surface, of stimulating them to more conscious action in defence of their class interests, of awakening them to independent political action. We did not retire to a storm cellar for the duration, "until it blows over," and if we did not, it was not out of intemperate brashness or heroism. We rightly judged both the needs and the possibilities.

Our party during the war constituted the principal and the clearest center of the militant movement in the trade unions. It is absurd to think that the progressive forces revolved around our small party, and it is far from our mind to say any such thing. Literally thousands, even tens of thousands, of workers in the unions did not allow the outbreak of the war to stop the struggle for a progressive labour movement. Many times they would put forward ideas and launch campaigns on their own initiative which our party thereupon decided to champion. This is true not only of many of the nameless rank and file, but of better known rank-and-file union leaders, too. If our party was distinguished from them, it was not necessarily in degree of aggressiveness, but primarily in the fact that we sought to harmonize the fight for all the progressive measures, to explain their fundamental significance in the class struggle, to show their connection with the imperialist war, and to relate them to the need for independent political action and socialism. It could be summed up saying that our party sought to imbue the American workers with class consciousness.

We were among the front-rank fighters, as we still are, against the paralyzing "no-strike pledge," urging the labour movement to reclaim its power to resist the encroachments of war-swollen capitalism. Toward the same end, we called upon labour to withdraw its representatives from the War Labor Board, which we characterized as the cemetery of labour's grievances. Our party carried on a persistent propaganda in favour of labour breaking from the capitalist parties and forming a Labor Party of its own, based on the representative mass organisations of the workers.

Unquestionably, thousands of progressives developed these ideas on their own. Our contribution was to provide the best reasons for these demands, an unceasing agitation for them, an organised centre from which the movement for these demands could be systematically maintained, stimulated and clarified. We sought, furthermore, to connect up these demands with a far broader, more significant Program of Action to be adopted as the fighting platform for the American working class. The central aim of this program still is: the mobilisation of the American working class as a unified, conscious political force, the struggle against the capitalist class and its government, the defence of labour's interests at every step of the road and at the expense of capitalist profit and capitalist power, and the establishment of a party of labour and a workers' government.

In this campaign, we had from the outset an invaluable instrument, *Labor Action*. Our party is exceptionally proud of this paper. To publish it, we had to break with a long tradition. But the break did not prove to be difficult, and the results more than justified it. We decided to issue, for the first time in the history of the revolutionary movement in this country, a popular socialist agitational weekly addressing itself primarily to the progressive trade-unionist. It was to be written in simple language, with an absolute minimum of the special jargon familiar in the radical movement and only in it. It was not to be written on the assumption that its readers already agree with every political and theoretical idea of the editors, but rather on the assumption that the readers agree only with a very few of the more elementary ideas of the editors. It was to appeal to the readers on the basis of his daily experiences, of his immediate problems, of those views which the editors, the party and most if not all the readers already had in common. Only by having this as its point of departure, as its main emphasis, could the paper then bring the attention of the reader to the fundamental principles of socialism, to the more advanced political conceptions, for which the paper stood, and develop his understanding and sympathy. Above all, it was to be an active participant and guide of the militant workers in the labour movement.

If *Labor Action* has not always succeeded in achieving every detail of its original purpose, it has nevertheless come so much closer to it that no other radical paper even merits serious comparison with it. The type of paper *Labor Action* aimed to be dictated a mass distribution among workers. The popularity and influence of the paper among tens of thousands of workers exceeded our most ambitious hopes. Indirectly, through the agitation and activity of its readers, its ideas reach additional tens of thousands. It is no exaggeration to say that in some of the largest working-class concentrations of the country, the weekly arrival of *Labor Action* is eagerly awaited. Lunch-time in many plants finds thousands of workers with their copies of the paper opened before them. Factory walls are decorated with articles, editorials and cartoons clipped from its pages. Time after time, and in city after city, unaffiliated militants have collected subscriptions to *Labor Action* from fellow-workers, and done it completely on their own initiative.

The influence exerted by the ideas of the Workers Party has not been limited for its source to the written word. In plant and in union, the members of our party have not been missing from the fight for progressive and militant policies. Our paper has not called upon the workers in general to do what our members have refrained from doing. From the beginning, the activities of our party members has been directed toward the formation of broad progressive groups of all the militants in the trade unions who agree on a minimum program of action to restore the fighting capacity of the labour movement. Where such groups already exist, we have worked to unite them on a national scale in order to increase their effectiveness. Our activities have yielded fruit.

The rabid concentrated fury of the Stalinists, in particular, against what they call Trotskyism in the labour movement, is a notable tribute to these activities.

It goes without saying that we do not deserve one-tenth of the compliments paid us by the Stalinists. The activities they denounce as Trotskyist are due only in small part to the work of our party. But the significance of their denunciations cannot be overrated. There is a good deal of truth even in their frenzied falsehoods and calumny. Under Trotskyism, they include every policy, every act, calculated to strengthen the working class, to retrieve its independence and freedom of movement, to advance its economic and political interests. If by this they mean to convey the idea that Trotskyism is the most consistent, most clear-headed, and most aggressive advocate of such policies, they are involuntarily telling the truth. The falsehoods consist in their declarations that everyone who takes a progressive position on any question confronting the labour movement — be it John L. Lewis or Norman Thomas, Thomas de Lorenzo or Jesse Ferrazza, Samuel Wolchok or David Dubinsky — is thereby a Trotskyist or in a "conspiracy" with the Trotskyists. The falsehoods become calumny when they associate every progressive or militant or revolutionist with Fascists like Coughlin, or with their own blood-ally of yesterday, Hitler.

We readily accept another involuntary tribute the Stalinists pay us. Wherever they attack the work not of those they try to label as Trotskyists, but of real Trotskyists, in four cases out of five it is the activities of the Workers Party they have in mind. We of the "petty-bourgeois opposition" are proud of the fact that we are a thorn in the side of the totalitarian gangsters in the labour movement. We are proud of the fact that in the past year, for example, the brunt of the fight for progressive and class-struggle policies in some of the most important unions of the CIO, in so far as it was borne by organised and conscious revolutionists, was borne by militants of the Workers Party and their close friends, and by no other party. We do not hesitate to say that it was our comrades and other trade-union militants working with them who led, or helped to lead, the fight for a regenerated labour movement in the conventions of the shipbuilding workers, the rubber workers, the auto workers, the electrical workers, the steel workers, and in such movements as the Michigan Commonwealth Federation. The Socialist Party played no part in these movements, lined up with the conservatives, or else its members acted in an individual manner as each saw fit. The Cannonites were conspicuous by their absence. Or by their silence, or, in some cases, by their factional sabotage of progressive movements which they could not dominate.

The policy of the Cannonites in the trade unions during these five years is worth an added comment, if only to contrast it with the policy we pursued. They did not follow a policy cautiously; caution was their policy. And by "caution," they meant abstention from any notable activity in the unions. The policy their leadership imposed upon the members was argued as follows: This is wartime: the workers are not in motion; we must lie quiet until they do get into motion; then we will offer them our leadership; meanwhile, we must confine ourselves to "preserving the cadres." A more specious opportunism is hard to find. It became disgusting when it was coupled with sneers at the "adventurism" of those who did their revolutionary duty.

This policy was not swallowed by all the SWP members. In Detroit, at first, and elsewhere later, protests were made against it; but in vain. One of the protests of recent date correctly attacked the policy as follows: "We cannot lay low and abstain from any substantial leadership now while awaiting the upsurge itself and expect the workers to follow us once it comes... when the workers do begin to move on a mass scale, why should they follow anyone who did not previously supply some type of leadership? How would they know that we are even capable of this leadership? How would a young comrade ever gain his leadership experience and confidence while sitting it out?" (SWP Bulletin, October, 1944.) It is interesting to note in passing that Trotsky warned us all against such an interpretation of the formula, "preserve the cadres." The question was raised by the SWP boss in our discussion with Trotsky early in 1938 about the party in the coming war. Trotsky answered in effect: Naturally, if we do nothing but "preserve the cadres" during the war, the workers will treat us like preserves and put us on the shelf! That last phrase of his I remember word for word: "They will treat us like preserves and put us on the shelf." The warning was not heeded by Cannon. A contrary course was imposed and the SWP kept itself on the shelf.

For our part, we operated in the trade union movement on the basis not only of what was possible but what was necessary. We understood that the class-consciousness and cohesion of the revolutionists cannot be "preserved" without continuous activity to awaken the class-consciousness and strengthen the cohesion of the working class as a whole. To break this link can only have pernicious consequences.

It is impossible to deal here with every aspect of the work and life of our party in these five years. But a balance-sheet of losses and gains should be cast up. Our losses have been of different kinds, and not easy to bear. Our first loss was Burnham. He betrayed everything he had stood for, including the movement that nurtured him intellectually. Ever since he turned coat, he has cut a sorry figure. People wonder how can such transparent drivel flow from such an intelligent mind?... The explanation is easier than is generally assumed. He feels driven to attribute his own betrayal to the betrayal of others. It was Trotsky that betrayed him; Marxism betrayed him; socialism betrayed him; the proletariat betrayed him. It is all false, but it is comprehensible. Incomprehensible is the fact that he continues to speak authoritatively (and in the very pools into which he used to spit so eloquently!) on politics. Surely a man who insists that he was so easily, so systematically and so thoroughly fooled on the most important political questions of our time, disqualifies himself as a political thinker by that very admission. If a lady kept moaning that for ten years running she was unable to walk along a lighted street without surrendering enthusiastically to every gay blade she met, she might be entitled to sympathy, or to a guardian, or to seclusion in a convent. She might pose as a martyr and do penance far from the sight of men. But if, instead, she remained at large, posed as an authority on how to resist temptation, and blamed her eager fall on the blandishments of the blades, even though there were always enough wiser ones at hand to warn her against them — people might very well say: Lament and repent in silence, teach aesthetics if you wish, but in heaven's name do not speak about virtue.

Burnham's defection lost the party a talented intellect. We have not the slightest interest in denying this. The Cannonites, for unworthy factional reasons, tried to present Burnham as the political leader of the opposition, and the opposition itself as "Burnhamite." There was no truth in this, as our comrades knew and as was soon proved clearly. What is true is that the leading comrades made every reasonable effort to keep Burnham in the movement, where his talents would have a fertile field and not be sterilised as they are now. The efforts, entirely justified in themselves, proved vain. To say that his defection is part of a much more general political or social phenomenon, is correct. But it does not suffice to explain every individual case. Most of the radical intellectuals collapsed. But some, like James T. Farrell and Dwight Macdonald, did remain loyal to their basic principles. It was Burnham's character that was inadequate to the task; he could not bring himself to make a thorough break with a bourgeois

500

existence. Everything else was rationalisation, and still is.

Other losses were inevitable, and we reckoned with them from the outset. If there are "laws of split," they include this one: Not all those who vote with you in a dispute go along with you in the final division. Some stay behind. Others use the turmoil of the split to drop away in the hope that they will not be noticed. We had that experience when the Trotskyists were expelled from the Stalinist party, and during the split in the Socialist Party, and again in the split of 1940. Nothing can be done about it, except write them off in advance. Another law is this one: Whenever a political fight is connected with a fight against bureaucratism, the opposition inevitably attracts to its side people who have the most peculiar notions about organisational questions and who have little in common with the opposition politically. In the showdown, they often prove to have been "against bureaucratism" only to the extent that they were against democratically-organised discipline and responsibility in the movement. Or else they think that the "anti-bureaucrats" are fighting for the policies that the bureaucracy maliciously attributes to them. When they learn differently, they too drop away, often very bitter over the fact that they listened not to what the opposition really stood for, but to what the bureaucracy said it stood for. For example, Trotsky's fight against Stalinism actually attracted some dilettantes and anti-Bolsheviks who thought Stalin was right in charging that Trotsky wanted a party of dilettantes and anti-Bolsheviks. The mistakenly attracted were soon... disillusioned. Thereafter they denounced not Stalin, but Trotsky! In the SWP split, we had our modest quota of such people — for a while.

Their defection, as well as Burnham's, was not one-hundredth as serious as our real loss. Our party was composed overwhelmingly of people of draft age. It is doubtful if there is another political organisation in the country which has had such a high percentage of its membership taken into the armed forces as our party. Being a militant working-class organisation, and not a group of pacifists, our people claimed no exemptions on grounds of conscience. They did not simply talk about taking on the responsibilities and tasks of their generation; they took them on, even if it meant severing relations with party activity. Among those who went off were some of our ablest and most experienced men, our indispensables; and we know that not all of them will be returned to us. Our corps of organisers, speakers, writers was cut into heavily, and that from top to bottom. It was an oppressive blow, and we suffer from it yet.

Their departure laid a heavier burden on those who remained.

What has been done by those who remained, especially by our magnificent female comrades, is perhaps the most inspiring and encouraging thing in our movement. Comrades have taken on doubled and trebled responsibilities and labours. Distributions of literature before and after a working day that often lasts ten hours; meetings of branches and committees piled on to meetings of their unions and union committees; organisation of classes for their own education and classes for sympathising workers; hours spent every week in personal agitation and propaganda among fellow-workers; systematic and generous financial contributions to the party's work on a scale higher than that of any other movement — these are the marks of conviction, zeal and devotion that are seldom found elsewhere. They are a guarantee of our future and the future of socialism.

There are also gains to record.

We have won to our party some of the best militants in the labour movement. They have learned, from studying our program and observing how our deeds conform to our words, that the best trade union activity in the world is incomplete and, in the long run, ineffectual, unless it is coupled with political organisation, rendered coherent and consistent by a fundamental political program and political direction. The popularity of our program is an assurance that we will succeed in recruiting more of these militants in the future.

The party has gained tremendously in the clarity of its program. What has been contributed to our political strength by the development of our position on Russia has already been dealt with. On the basis of this position, we have been able to deal more thoroughly with the problem of Stalinism as the greatest menace to the integrity and future of the labour movement. The importance of this question cannot be stressed too heavily. Among revolutionary socialists, it was long argued that the Stalinists and the conservative or reformist labour officialdom are equally dangerous to the working class. This point of view is no longer valid; to try to maintain it in practice can only lead to grave blunders and even to disaster. Reformism in the labour movement means the weakening of the working class, but even the most reformist bureaucracy is vitally concerned with maintaining the organised labour movement, for it cannot exist without it. Stalinism means the totalitarian strangulation and destruction of the labour movement. Wherever class-conscious militants are unable to challenge both in a directly independent form, and are obliged to choose between the two evils, there is no question of which is the lesser evil of the two. A consciousness of this fact has enabled our party to function more effectively and more progressively in more than one fight in the labour movement. Maximum clarity on the problem of Stalinism in the labour movement is possible, however, only as a result of complete clarity about Stalinist Russia. The Cannonites are anything but alone in their confusion on this score. It is shared and multiplied many times over not only by the labour movement in general, but in particular by the leading men in it. Among our tasks is the dissipation of this dangerous confusion.

Our party was the only one in this country to analyse and appraise correctly the great significance of the revolutionary "national movements" that sprang up throughout Europe under the rule of German imperialism. Along with our German comrades, who developed their standpoint independently of ours but in harmony with it, we have made a contribution on the "national question" whose value will not diminish in the period ahead. In contrast, the futile wordmongering and sterile dogmatism of the Cannonites on this question has been typical of their helplessness when confronted with a new problem or an old problem in new form. They have so thoroughly disaccustomed themselves from critical, independent thought, and gone so far in converting Trotskyism from a guide to action, and a means of arriving at a guide to action, into a body of scriptural revelation, that the most important revolutionary movement in the last ten years could develop and shake all Europe without producing anything more than a stereotyped and utterly false reaction from the SWP. Like the Socialist Labour Party, which answers all problems, big and small, with the mouth-filling demand for the "unconditional surrender of capitalism," the SWP avoids taking a position on the most urgent problems of the day by repeating, in season and out, its demand for the "Socialist United States of Europe." The struggle for democracy and for national freedom, which is increasingly the key to the struggle for socialism, is simply not grasped by the Cannonites. They are paralysed by some obscure fear that, somehow or other, the struggle for democracy, carried on in a working-class way, with a working-class program, makes you a "bourgeois democrat" who has given up the fight for socialism. That means, so far as the SWP is concerned, that at least four men have worked in vain: Marx, Engels, Lenin and Trotsky.

The last thirty years have been rich in events and in lessons for the working class, if not in victories. If we were asked to tell what makes us believe that the final victory will go to socialism, we would answer: Capitalism has shown conclusively that it cannot advance society and civilization, but only drive it further along the road of exhausting conflict, human degradation, barbarism and ruin. It no longer has a capacity for stability, order, peace and progress. The working class, even those sections of it that have been most cruelly oppressed, has shown a power of recuperation from defeat and resources of resistance to capitalist decay that amply justify our confidence in its eventual triumph. It has proved repeatedly that the conditions for its existence and progress is the struggle against the conditions of its existence. That is how it has been and that is how it must be.

Although the connections between conscious socialism and the working class were broken once by the old social-democracy and again by Stalinism, they have not been destroyed. They exist in the form of our movement and its program, and they will be strengthened. The firmness of our party and the confirmation of its program by events justify the confidence we have in both. They justify also our confidence that the revolutionary International of the working class — a most important matter that cannot be dealt with briefly because it requires and deserves a chapter for itself — will be restored and solidified.

What makes the struggle for socialism and freedom seem more difficult, also makes it more urgently necessary. It simply makes no sense to us when we are told that encroaching capitalist barbarism is destroying the prospects of socialism and it is better to give up the fight. That is the talk of demoralized and spiritually vanquished serfs. It is precisely the fact that decomposing capitalism is filling the air with its poisonous fumes, that imposes upon us the redoubling of our efforts to bury the putrid beast.

Let the cowards flinch and the traitors sneer. Our minds are incapable of absorbing the truly monstrous idea that humanity, which has shown so often an irresistible passion for liberty and an inexhaustible capacity for achieving it progressively, will, now, at the historic pinnacle of its intellectual and social development, finally yield to the yoke in permanence, like brute cattle. We reiterate our faith in the people, in the working class, and dedicate ourselves again, on this fifth anniversary, to the socialist emancipation.

[1] The moralistic hue-and-cry that was raised when we continued to issue the *New International* under our own auspices is hard to imagine. It is only deplorable that Trotsky added his own voice to it. We had not only been the responsible editors and manager of the magazine, but generally speaking, it was our comrades who were most active in promoting it and who evaluated it properly. For the most part, the Cannonite leaders either ignored it or sneered at it openly as superfluous to the party and of interest only to

a "little gang of petty-bourgeois intellectuals," as one of the Cannonite spokesman said in our 1939 convention. The contempt these people really had for "theory" was notorious in the party. In the long list of contributors to the magazine's many rich years, Cannon's name stands, characteristically, at the very bottom, as the author of two-or-three journalistic articles. Except for a couple of comrades in his entourage, the names of the others are not even on the list. In his recent *History of American Trotskyism*, the *New International* is mentioned a couple of times in the most casual way. Once, with reference to one of the rare articles by Cannon; a second time, with reference to its suspension upon our entry into the SP. In other words, he has nothing whatsoever to say about the magazine which, if we may be permitted, played such a decisive role in the development of the Trotskyist movement both here and abroad.

This did not prevent him, in 1940, from threatening us with court action to get back the "stolen" magazine! A precedent for this threat (very wisely not carried out) was the action of the right-wing socialist Ward Rogers, in sending a sheriff's notice to the Trotskyists who, in the SP split, had taken with them some of the chairs belonging to a party local in the West. As for ourselves, we felt in perfectly good conscience about the *New International*, not only for the reason given above, but also because it represented a very modest part of what so large a section of the party as we constituted was entitled to have. We recommend to the attention of the protesters a reading of what Cannon wrote about Ward Rogers in the *Socialist Appeal* some seven years ago.

"Five Years of the Workers Party". New International, April 1945. Another passage from that text has been extracted and included at p.593

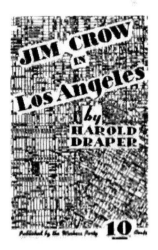

A Workers Party pamphlet published in Los Angeles in 1946.

Why and how the 1940 split happened

Max Shachtman and Ernest Rice McKinney (1946)

THE TROTSKYIST MOVEMENT in the United States split into two parts immediately after the national convention of the Socialist Workers Party in April, 1940. The two principal differences which caused the split were, first, the slogan of "unconditional defense of Russia" in the war, upheld by the then majority and rejected by the Minority, and, second, the regime in the SWP which the Minority criticized as bureaucratic conservatism.

Rightly or wrongly — that is not the question at the moment; we shall return to it later — the Minority was profoundly convinced of the tremendous harm that would be inflicted upon the movement by the exclusive presentation of the position of the majority on the Russian question. It was just as much convinced of the correctness of its own position and the need of presenting it to the radical working class public. That is why it insisted upon the right of publishing an organ of its own, after the convention, which while defending the party and its line in every sphere would diverge from it on the question of defense of Russia. This demand, while extraordinary, was not, however, unprecedented. The convention majority rejected it.

Under ordinary circumstances and given a normal party regime, the Minority would undoubtedly have submitted to the decision of the Majority. However, the Minority believed that the circumstances were not ordinary and the party regime not normal. In its view, the avowedly exceptional demand which it made was being converted by the Majority into a convenient pretext for ridding itself of a substantial body of inconvenient and very embarrassing critics. The events that followed immediately after the convention only served to confirm the opinion of the Minority.

At the very first meeting of the PC after the convention — after the newly elected National Committee had assigned the various comrades of the Majority and Minority to their various posts and responsibilities — the Majority confronted the Minority with a resolution which has no precedent whatsoever in the history of our movement. To find its equal you must look in the annals not of the early Stalinist movement but of the Stalinist movement in its worst period. This resolution did not charge the Minority with any overt act against the party, not even with any act of indiscipline, not even the violation of the most insignificant rule or statute of the party. The first part of the resolution of April 16, 1940, provided "that the Committee accepts the convention decisions and obligates itself to carry them out in a disciplined manner." We did not vote for this resolution and we did not vote against it — we abstained from the vote.

It is not necessary for us to justify our abstention here. You may consider that we were entirely wrong in abstaining. But who can contest our inviolable right to have voted on this motion as we saw fit? Any member of the party at all times has the right to vote for or against a proposition or to abstain in the vote. If a majority can at any time dictate to a minority that the latter must vote for any proposition of the former, then obviously you no longer have a party but a mechanical voting machine operated from above.

Yet it was precisely this elementary right that was contested by the majority at the same meeting of the PC. The second part of the resolution it submitted provided that anyone who fails to vote "for" is automatically suspended from all party posts and rights in such a manner as to make the "suspension" equivalent, to all intents and purposes, to an expulsion — an expulsion or "suspension" without so much as a trial or hearing! And inasmuch as the Minority in the PC failed to vote "for" the first proposition it was declared automatically suspended from all posts and rights in the party. The same procedure was immediately practiced against all the supporters of the Minority in the party branches. The SWP was effectively split!

Have you ever heard of such a procedure in all the history of our movement? Have you even ever been told by the party leadership that this is the procedure it followed toward the Minority in 1940? You know the answer to both questions. The first part of the infamous resolution was finally made public by the SWP leadership in the introduction to Trotsky's *In Defense of Marxism* by Hansen and Warde. Why did they stop with the first part? Why didn't they make public the text of the second part in that introduction? Why has it never been made public anywhere else? Does your leadership feel a sense of shame at this blatant aping of the Stalinist principle that the price of membership in the party is a vote "for"? Does it feel that the publication of the second part of the resolution would give a truer picture of how the split in 1940 actually came about? That its publication would help dispel many of the legends which it has woven around the circumstances of the split?

Your PC statement speaks at great length about the 1940 split. Why does it not give all the facts? Why does it not quote from its April 16, 1940 resolution, or even refer to it? He who does not have the whole of the relevant facts cannot reach the whole of a relevant judgment. Demand that the resolution be made available to you in full! You are entitled to it.

We have already spoken of the two main causes of the split. But it was the April 16, 1940 resolution which actually precipitated the split. The plan of the Majority to get rid of the critics of the party regime was clearly evident before then. The course and tone of the Majority reflected a predetermined line for our expulsion. This required no special perspicacity on our part to anticipate an attempt to get rid of us on one pretext or another, although, we admit, we did not anticipate that the measure would take such an outrageous form. We have no desire, therefore, to conceal the fact that we prepared for any eventuality so that no measure taken against us would catch us by surprise. Nevertheless, it must be emphasized that this effective expulsion of the Minority took place without any charge whatsoever of indis-

507

cipline; that it took place before we had published the first issue of *Labor Action*; that it took place before we published the first issue of The *New International* under our own auspices. Our expulsion was clearly the result of a plan to get rid of critics of the party regime on one flimsy pretext or another.

As we saw it, and as we said at that time, an expulsion or split of the party should have and could have been averted if the Majority had been genuinely and intelligently concerned with maintaining unity. That is the case even if every characterization of the Minority held true — that it was "petty bourgeois," that it was "yielding to the pressure of bourgeois public opinion," etc.

During the Brest-Litovsk period of the Russian Revolution, the so-called Left Communists, headed by Bukharin, Radek and others, published their own independent press and attacked the party and its leadership in the most violent and unrestrained terms. That was at a time when the fate of the revolution literally hung by a hair. Lenin characterized the Left Communists as "petty bourgeois phrase mongers" and the like. He had good "petty bourgeois phrase mongers" and the like. He had good grounds for this designation. They formed a bloc, for all practical purposes, with the Left SRs, a non-Marxist, petty bourgeois current. He spared them as little as they spared him, but he proposed no organizational measures against the clear violation of the party statutes by the Left Communists. He did not propose a formal banning of their independent press and party committees. Although not an advocate of unity-at-all-costs, Lenin was sincerely and wisely concerned with unity. He had confidence in the power of his own views, confidence that they would persuade at least the bulk of the Left Communists in good time. When Bukharin refused to serve on the Central Committee because of the differences, Lenin insisted that he remain a member, right in the face of the fact that Bukharin had set up a "rival" press and "rival" party committees. Before too long not only did Lenin's views triumph but his method triumphed as well. The breach was healed; party unity was restored; the crisis was overcome with a minimum of damage.

Naturally, the situation in the SWP in 1940 was not identical with that of the Bolshevik Party in 1918. Everything must be examined with due regard for the differences in proportion. But if anything, Lenin's method was even more clearly indicated for 1940 in the United States than for 1918 in Russia. The fate of the revolution in the United States did not hang by a hair in 1940!

Extracts from an open letter to the convention of the SWP, *Labor Action*
11 November 1946

Why we wanted our own periodical

Max Shachtman and Ernest Rice McKinney (1946)

WHY WAS THE MINORITY so insistent in its proposal that, if defeated at the convention, it should have the right to publish a periodical of the kind we have described? In a letter of February 20, 1940, to the Cleveland conference of the opposition, Comrade Trotsky wrote us that "the future Minority can ask for certain reasonable guarantees for its ideological existence and we believe that the future Majority should grant these reasonable guarantees in order to prevent a premature and not unavoidable split." The difficulty, however, lay in the fact that the Minority believed that the presentation of its point of view on the vital question of the Russian defense slogan to the radical working class public was necessary in order to moderate the disastrous consequences of the Majority position on this question; that only in that way could the Minority remain loyal to its ideas and the interests of the working class and thereby to the Fourth International itself. But not only that. The trouble lay further in the fact that the Majority not only offered no "reasonable guarantees," but that our bitter experience during the dispute in the party had already removed any grounds that we may have had for placing confidence in any "guarantees" of genuine party democracy that the Majority might give us. The reason for this conclusion cannot be better stated than by quoting from a document issued by the Minority on March 9, 1940:

"Is there the slightest ground for believing that the Cannonites would grant us, if we prove to be in the minority at the convention, those 'reasonable guarantees for ideological existence' of which Trotsky speaks? For what reason should any party member place the slightest confidence in the loyalty or in the adherence to the principles of party democracy of the Cannon clique? It sought at the very beginning to prevent a discussion entirely, calling it a 'luxury we cannot afford'. When it was finally compelled to open a discussion, Cannon moved that it be confined to one membership meeting of the New York local. Although the last Political Committee meeting steamrollered through a motion ' recommending' another discussion-debate membership meeting of the New York local (we proposed to refer the question to the City Committee, whose record in organising the fullest and most democratic discussion is flawless, and which has since organised the meeting 'recommended' by the PC), the same Cannonite PC has never voted to 'recommend' the holding of a discussion-debate membership meeting of the Minneapolis or Flint locals. Just the contrary. The Cannonite controlled Michigan-Ohio District Committee has just sabotaged to death the district membership meeting at which official representative of the two groups were to debate before the Youngstown-Cleveland-Toledo-Detroit-Flint membership. The Internal Bulletins have been progressively 'weighted' against the

Minority's documents and articles, especially in the latest issues. Now the *Bulletin* is, in effect, completely suspended. The *Socialist Appeal* was denied to the Minority in the pre-convention period on purely Stalinist grounds. Instead of a discussion in its columns, the Cannonites have devoted themselves in editorials and articles to a dirty, insinuatory, underhanded and disloyal polemic against us without our having the opportunity to reply.

"A petty, typically Stalinist censorship of articles has been introduced against the Minority in the *Appeal*, specifically against the column of Comrade Macdonald, who was not even allowed to quote the official Stalinist statement that the Kremlin does not aim to Sovietize Finland.

"Even the *New International* was closed to the Minority, on the most hypocritical and demagogical grounds. The last issue was filled with the Cannonite position without a word appearing from our side. At the last minute, a decision is made to make the coming issue of the *New International* a 'discussion' number, which will appear just in time to greet the delegates after they have been elected. In this 'model' discussion number, at least two-thirds of the space is to be given the Majority position. This decision is presented as a 'concession' to the Minority. Fraudulent claim! Its purpose is not the preservation of the democratic rights of the Minority, but the preparation of the split. On the eve of driving us out of the party, the Cannonites are preparing the sympathisers of the party by making public, among other documents, Trotsky's fierce attack on the Minority, 'From a Scratch to the Danger of Gangrene.' Trotsky's authority and prestige are being used in the hope of 'discrediting' the Minority, of psychologising the party sympathizers into accepting the already-prepared expulsions.

"Who can seriously ask the Minority to place the slightest confidence in the Cannonites after this? What are the 'reasonable' guarantees they offer? Their reply to our resolution on Party Unity simply does not offer any. Trotsky speaks of the 'exceptional' situation. Cannon replies: Submit and shut up! That is one of the main reasons why that Minority insists on the right of either group, if it is not victorious at the convention, to publish a political organ if it so desires".

No, we did not contend then and we do not say now that the regular statutes of the party provide for the issuance of any public organs by a Minority of the party. Statutes, however, do not exist as an end in themselves. They should be enforced, at all times, but enforced intelligently and always with an eye to the best interests of the party. To grant any group of comrades the right to a public organ of its own and every time it decides that it wants one, merely in order to try to preserve party unity or some measure of party unity, in contrast to a definitive split, would obviously be absurd. We take no such position, and we never did. It is necessary to weigh the choices with the most scrupulous objectivity.

To go by the pure party statutes in a case where a Minority insists on its special demand, and the Majority rigidly insists upon the letter of the statutes, obviously means a definitive split, probably of long duration. Obviously, this is an evil. To yield on the formal aspects of the statutes in the same case certainly means a loosening of the party cords. Here too obviously there is an evil. But such a loosening may, given a wise and politically self-confident majority, avoid a complete disruption of those bonds and lay the basis for re-examining them at an early stage. The weighing of the two must be undertaken in order to arrive at a scrupulous decision on which is the greater evil and which is the lesser.

Can any serious and objective comrade say now — especially now in the light of the six years' development of the two groups — that the 1940 majority arrived at a scrupulously objective decision? On the one side there was a decision which could have healed the breach in a round-about and even painful way; on the other side was the split of the Trotskyist movement into almost two equal parts. Surely, you cannot deceive yourselves into really believing that the Minority was composed of "worthless petty-bourgeois scum." Naturally, we had some petty-bourgeois riff-raff in our ranks. Every minority that launches a fight against, among other things, bureaucratism attracts to its side a certain amount of petty-bourgeois or dilettante camp followers. Whoever knows the history of the Trotskyist struggle against Stalinist bureaucracy knows this to be a fact. We got rid of these camp followers without much difficulty. But the overwhelming bulk of the Minority was made up of devoted revolutionists, capable of enduring struggle against the class enemy and for revolutionary Socialist principles; it was made up of comrades who played no small role in founding and building up the Trotskyist movement in this country and elsewhere and in acting as its most loyal and not least competent defenders. It had the support of what your PC now acknowledges to have been almost 50 per cent of the party — and even a greater percentage of the youth, a support which it was not easy to gain in the face of the great authority enjoyed by our only real opponent, Comrade Trotsky. Faced with a choice of trying to retain unity with this considerable and important section of the Trotskyist movement, on the one hand, and a split with "a line of blood between us," as your leader said, on the other hand, the Majority did not hesitate. It decided on the cold, calculated split.

Those are the facts of the split, for which we are ready to take our share of the responsibility, even though it is now a more or less outlived question — but only our share.

Extract from an open letter to the convention of the SWP, *Labor Action*
11 November 1946

We must deepen the split with the WP

James P Cannon (1945)

IN DISCUSSING EVERY DIFFERENCE of opinion and every proposal we should aim to carry our thoughts through to the end and draw the whole party into our thinking. For this it is necessary not only to explain to the party what is proposed but why it is proposed. The characteristic defect of all eclectic thinking is that it is only half-thinking. It is marked by the failure to carry a thought through to the end; the tendency to jump to conclusions and formulate proposals midway in the consideration of a subject.

Take the question of the Shachtmanites, for example. We witness an attempt, direct or implied, to revise our estimate of the petty-bourgeois opposition. But the question is not ended with our estimate of the Shachtman party; it is only started. What follows from this estimate, or the proposal to revise it? To what end is it pointed? If we keep thinking without stopping half-way we must recognize that our estimate inexorably leads us either (1) toward reconciliation and unity, or (2) toward a deepening of the split. The discussion is not completed until that question is decided and reasons given for the decision.

We, on our part, assume that the course toward deepening of the split is necessary and correct; our attitude flows from that. Naturally, if someone has a different proposal, we are ready to discuss it. But if that is the case, let us discuss fully and properly, in logical order, from premise to conclusion. Let us go back to the internal struggle and the split in which it culminated, and put the following questions as a basis for the discussion.

(1) Was the analysis of the petty-bourgeois opposition which we together with Trotsky made at that time correct or not?

(2) Was the attitude which we took toward them properly based on the analysis?

(3) Was our action in expelling them when they refused to accept the convention decisions the proper action?

(4) What changes have taken place in the meantime? Has the Shachtman party come closer or gone farther away from us?

(5) Do these changes provide the logical ground to reassert and strengthen our original decision, or to change or modify it?

Do I hear an answer to these questions? By all means let us discuss the "Workers Party" if anyone really wants to discuss it. But let us not nibble at the proposition. Let it be discussed fully — to the end.

From "Reflections on the 11th Party Convention", SWP Internal Bulletin vol.7, no.2, April 1945

Answers to Comrade Cannon's questions on the Workers Party

Albert Goldman (1945)

IN THE INTERNAL BULLETIN OF APRIL 1945, Comrade Cannon poses five questions dealing with our past and present estimate of the Workers' Party. A sixth question is added by Cannon in a tone of triumph as if no one will dare take up his challenge. That question is: "Do I hear an answer to these questions?" I hope Comrade Cannon "hears" the answers that I am giving to his questions.

Question 1. "Was the analysis of the petty-bourgeois opposition, which we together with Trotsky made at the time, correct or not?"

Answer: Yes.

Question 2. "Was the attitude which we took toward them properly based on that analysis?"

Answer: What attitude does Cannon mean? Did the party adopt a resolution officially indicating the proper attitude towards the minority that split from us? Did the party adopt a resolution designating the members who were expelled as renegades? If such a thing was done I am completely unaware of it.

As far as I was concerned our attitude toward the minority was one of struggle against them on the basis of their incorrect theory on the defense of the Soviet Union and their criminal conduct in splitting from the party when they were given the right to have their own faction and factional organ. I probably wrote at least as many articles against Shachtman as any other member of the party. True, I did not call him names. I let Comrade Hansen and other comrades do that. I merely presented arguments.

Question 3. "Was our action in expelling them when they refused to accept the convention decisions the proper action?"

Answer: A thousand times yes.

Question 4. "What changes have taken place in the meantime? Has the Shachtman party come closer or gone farther away from us?"

It is obvious that the answer to this question touches the heart of the problem and should indicate to us what attitude we should take to the former minorityites. It must be divided into several sections.

a) The important event that occurred after the split was the entry of the United States into the World War. Thereupon, from a revolutionary Marxist standpoint, every party and every group pretending to march under the banner of revolutionary socialism was subjected to the most serious test. Next to the revolution itself the best and most serious test for any party claiming to base itself on the principles of revolutionary Marxism is an imperialist war on the part of its own bourgeoisie. The attitude of a party towards its own imperialist bourgeoisie during a war is a decisive test of the seriousness with which such a party takes its convictions.

In his polemic against Burnham, Trotsky remarked that should any of the American opponents of the dialectic reveal a self-sacrifice and independence from patriotism, similar to that of Karl Liebknecht, we shall render what is due him as a revolutionist. Lenin was ready to applaud all socialists who adopted a revolutionary position in the First World War.

When the Workers Party refused to support the American bourgeoisie in this war, we should have been the first to give it the credit it deserved. One does not need to be a profound student of Lenin and Trotsky to know how scrupulous they were in giving an opponent credit for a correct position on an important question. The attitude of Cannon in failing to do this is the very opposite of this. Because of the circumstances under which the Burnham-Shachtman group refused to defend the Soviet Union during its war with Finland, we asserted that it yielded to the pressure of the democratic bourgeoisie. Although the minority refused to defend Finland, its attitude to the Soviet Union resembled the attitude of the petty-bourgeois democrats, and the conclusion was plausible that it yielded to the pressure of that social layer in society.

But the bourgeois democratic pressure exerted on all socialist groups was infinitely greater after the United States entered the war. Norman Thomas yielded to that pressure immediately and went over to a war position. If a group had actually become part of the democratic world it could not possibly have withstood the pressure and would have gone over to a pro-war position. In fact to be against the defense of the Soviet Union, an ally of American imperialism, became more difficult than to favor its defense.

On the basis of our assertion that the minority had yielded to democratic pressure during the Finnish-Soviet conflict, some comrades predicted that the Shachtmanites would go over completely to the side of the bourgeois democrats. That was of course a complete vulgarization of the Marxist method and, as was to be expected, Comrade Hansen took first prize among the vulgarizers. In an article published in the *Fourth International* of February 1941, the prophet Hansen gave Shachtman a few months in which to catch up and outstrip Burnham. (I presume Hansen will answer that his error is one of tempo).

Even such a serious crime as splitting from the Fourth International can be partly expiated by taking a revolutionary position during an imperialist war.

b) In our present estimate of the WP one must not ignore the important fact of the separation of Burnham and his followers from that party. It was Burnham who largely set the tone of the minorityites of 1939-40. From the fact that Burnham left the WP soon after it was organized the conclusion can justifiably be drawn that Burnham worked for a split during the factional struggle and, once the split was achieved, left the new party in the lurch. His leaving the new group was an important factor in keeping the Shachtmanites on the road of the proletarian revolution. With his departure the members of the minority who had devoted many years to the revolutionary movement freed themselves from an anti-revolutionary element.

Instead of prophesying, as Comrade Hansen did, that Shachtman would follow Burnham, an intelligent Marxist would have expressed the hope that Shachtman and the others, having gotten rid of Burnham, would find it easier to remain on the path of revolution.

Dwight Macdonald's dissociation from the WP, while not having the important influence that Burnham's leaving had, was an indication that those who were consciously anti-Bolshevik were finding it difficult to remain in the new party.

c) A large proportion of the minority of 1939-40 consisted of non-proletarian youth. Their separation from the problems actually confronting the workers created an unhealthy atmosphere, where the necessity for discussion tended to be over-emphasized. On the basis of the fact that the WP had no roots in the trade union movement, some comrades predicted that, at best, it would never be more than a propaganda group, and most comrades prophesied an early demise for the new party.

The expansion of industry as a result of the war, plus an undoubted policy of proletarianization, transformed a good many of the de-classed youth of the minority into workers. My judgment, based on a reading of the WP press, is that the WP has made some gains from the activity of their members in the trade unions. I know that this runs contrary to the assertions of most of our comrades, but none of these comrades has taken the trouble to explain how a disintegrated party can continue to publish a weekly and a monthly. It is impossible to explain this fact if one accepts the picture of disintegration that some of our comrades give us of the WP. That they have not made the gains we have made is certain, but it is not certain that they have lost in membership.

Because the minority had a proportionately larger number of youth than we did, it is very likely that they lost a proportionately larger number to the armed forces. Without recruiting some new members it is unlikely that they could have continued to publish a weekly and a monthly theoretical organ. Furthermore the fact that *Labor Action* consciously attempts to orientate itself to trade union workers is additional evidence that the WP is active in the trade unions and has made some gains.

The question of the nature of the activities of the WP in the trade unions and the correctness of their policies is completely irrelevant. Even if the WP members were as adventurous as some comrades claim they are (and that is difficult to believe, judging by their press) I would not be impressed by such an argument. Most young and inexperienced revolutionists tend towards leftism in trade union work. I shall not hold youth and inexperience against any revolutionist.

Some comrades who are in a position to know claim that the Shachtmanites are stronger than we are in the trade unions of the New York area. They have played a larger role than we have in the recent conventions of some important trade unions. That is of course because of our "policy of caution". Nevertheless it proves that they are active in the trade unions.

What is important is that the non-proletarian youth whom we justly criticized at the time they were in our party have shown a seriousness of purpose which we did not expect. Because they are very articulate, intellectual youth in the trade union movement are very valuable once they are cured of ultra-leftism and adventurism. In judging the character of the WP, and in determining our attitude to the membership of that party, we must by all means take into consideration that the group which we thought would never have anything to do with trade union work has made serious attempts to orientate itself to such work and in some instances has achieved some success.

d) Certain aspects of the present program of the WP have undoubtedly, in a formal sense, widened the gulf between us and the former minorityites. It is necessary to analyze each one of these aspects to determine the essential question whether or not the WP cannot be considered a revolutionary Marxist party because of their differences with us on some important questions. Of course some comrades will contend that refusal to defend the Soviet Union immediately transforms one into an anti-Marxist. But if this is so why were we willing to permit "anti-Marxists" to remain in the party and grant them the right of a faction? There are very important questions upon which Marxists can differ and even split without ceasing to be Marxists. Some comrades should remember that Trotsky and Lenin differed on the very important question of dictatorship of the proletariat versus democratic dictatorship of the proletariat and peasantry, but it occurred to neither one to call the other an anti-Marxist, because of their differences on this question.

The WP considers the Soviet Union a bureaucratic collectivist state. Only Burnham and Carter had that viewpoint at the time of the split. [See *The Fate* vol.1 p.292 for a different account]. Undoubtedly the official position of the WP on that question means that the minorityites are farther away from us now than they were at the time of our struggle with them. But it is necessary to remember that Burnham and Carter were members of our party for several years while they held to that view of the Soviet Union and it occurred to no one to suggest that they be expelled.

It may well be that after capitalism should be restored in the Soviet Union, the Shachtmanites will still consider it to be a bureaucratic collectivist state. It would be downright insanity if, all other factors permitting, two groups would refuse to unite because one considers the Soviet Union a capitalist state and the other a bureaucratic collectivist state.

e) If, on the question of the nature of the Soviet Union, the gulf between us and the WP, has been deepened, this is not true at present in the case of the more important question of the defense of the Soviet Union. For the time being we all agree that the military defense of the Soviet Union has receded into the background. According to Comrade Munis it is hardly probable that the question of the defense of the Soviet Union will come up again in as sharp a form as it confronted us in 1939. Be that as it may there is not a single voice in opposition to the view that all of our efforts must now be concentrated on the defense of the European Revolution against Stalin. And on this question there is no difference between us and the WP.

Nevertheless, if reuniting the two parties were to be proposed, the question of the defense of the Soviet Union would still be the most important question. For, so long as we believe in defending the Soviet Union in case of any imperialist attack, there is still the possibility of our using the slogan. What sense would there be in uniting if, to-morrow, the same struggle that took place in 1939-40 were to be renewed? Personally I do not believe that unity is a practical proposition so long as there is a fair probability that the defense of the Soviet Union will once more be placed by us on the order of the day.

Nevertheless it must not be taken as absolutely certain that the former minorityites would not be willing to return to the party under the same conditions that we offered them in 1940 in order to keep them from splitting the party. Had they agreed to accept discipline in action we would have given them proportionate representation on the various leading committees, with the right to have a faction and a factional organ. It is now five years since they have split; they have had their experience outside of the party; the slogan of the defense of the Soviet Union is not the burning question that it was in 1940. It Is therefore necessary for us to ask the WP members to return to the party and accept the same conditions that we proposed to grant them in 1940.

Such an offer would serve the interests of our party either in case of acceptance or rejection. Should the former minorityites accept, our forces would be strengthened by the addition of about four hundred members, many of whom are able people with long experience in the revolutionary movement. Their return to the party would eliminate a group which confuses many workers who cannot see the difference between us and the WP, Should they, however, reject our offer we would have a powerful argument to disprove their contention that our party is a "bureaucratic jungle". They would be in an exceedingly difficult position to defend their organizational criticism of our party, and the likelihood is that they would lose many of their members to us.

It should be clear, however, that our estimate of the WP is not to be determined by the fact that unity is impossible because of our differences on the question of the defense of the Soviet Union. It does not follow that, because unity is impossible, the members of the WP are renegades. It does not follow, because unity is impossible at present, that we should not collaborate with the WP, wherever and whenever possible, on the trade union and on the political field. To harbor a permanent grudge because of our differences on the defense of the Soviet Union and because of the split is infantile.

f) Since the split, three questions have arisen upon which we took a position contrary to that taken by the WP. We decided to continue giving material support to China in its struggle against Japanese imperialism, after the United States entered the war, while the WP took a position against material support. The WP favored raising the slogan of national liberation for the countries occupied by Hitler's armies. We opposed that slogan. Whereas our party adopted the slogan of military training under trade union control, the WP rejected that slogan.

All of these questions are such that differences could be expected with reference to them in the same party. Recently the majority of the Fourth Internationalists in India took a position against supporting China. On the national question there are differences in our own ranks. The same is true of the slogan for military training under trade union control. Some English comrades are strenuously opposed to the slogan. Undoubtedly our differences with the WP on the three questions mentioned above are important but they are not at all of a nature, which, in the course of a party discussion, could not be solved by a majority decision with the acceptance by the minority of the decision of the majority...

May 7, 1945

SWP Internal Bulletin, vol. 7, no. 5, June 1945

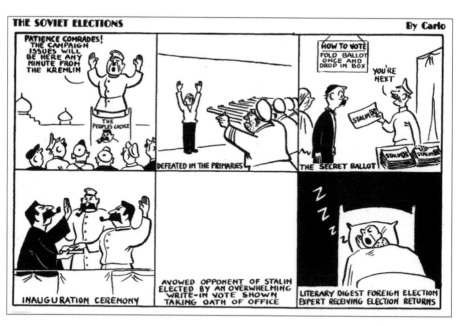

Socialist Appeal, 4 December 1937

518

What we said would happen and what did happen

Albert Goldman, Felix Morrow, and Oscar Williams (1945)

1. IT IS NOW MORE than five years since the groups which we designated as the "petty-bourgeois opposition" left the party. Immediately after the split they organized the Workers Party under the leadership of comrades with many years of experience in the revolutionary movement. After five years, we note that their activities in the labor movement continue unabated. They publish a weekly agitation paper, *Labor Action,* and a monthly, *New International*; put up candidates in elections; conduct fraction work in trade unions, etc. They took with them in the split 40 percent of our membership; their present activities indicate that they have retained a substantial portion of this number and recruited new elements.

2. Assuming that the Workers Party is but one-third the size of our party, we cannot ignore the possibility of reunification of the two forces on the ground of their allegedly sparse numbers. Unification would result in a 25% increase of our forces. More important, unification would return to the party cadre elements who are the product of decades of Marxist training and experience and whom we cannot hope to recruit elsewhere.

3. Our attitude toward re-unification must be based on a political estimate of the Workers Party. This means not to repeat what we said about the minority at the time of the split, but to analyze without prejudice the history of the Workers Party and the character of its program and present activities.

4. With the exception of the important questions of the nature and defense of the Soviet Union, the Workers Party remains on the fundamental programmatic basis of the Fourth International. Its propaganda, agitation and activities are based in the main on the program of transitional demands adopted by the Founding Conference of the Fourth International.

5. The acid test of a workers' party is its attitude toward imperialist war. Without the slightest hesitation and with no opposition in its ranks, the Workers Party took a Leninist position toward its own imperialist bourgeoisie. It has maintained that position throughout the war. Some comrades deny that this is an acid test of the revolutionary character of the Workers Party; they point to the anti-war position of Martov in World War I and of the Young People's Socialist League in this war, as examples of centrists and/or non-revolutionists who oppose imperialist war. The speciousness of this argument is that it ignores the fact that Martov and the YPSL remained in parties dominated by social-chauvinists, whereas the Leninist character of the Workers Party's position includes its recognition of the principle that Leninists must have their own party and cannot remain in one party with social-chauvinists.

6. The comrades of the Workers Party have shown that they remain loyal to the proletarian revolution. On the American scene the Workers Party has followed the same general course as our party: against the no-strike pledge and against class collaboration through the War Labor Board, for a Labor Party, etc. On questions of the European revolution, it has likewise followed the same course as we, and similarly on tasks of liberation of the colonies, etc. Today the similarity of the two parties' programs and activities has become still closer, with the disappearance into the background of the question of the defense of the Soviet Union, and the appearance in the foreground of the urgent need to defend the European revolutions against Stalin, a question on which the Workers Party is in complete agreement with us. It is inevitable that militant workers will not understand our separation into parties which they deem to be similar in fundamental program and immediate aim. Nor can we justly deny to these militant workers the essentially revolutionary character of the Workers Party.

7. The Workers Party position on the Soviet Union is that it is a bureaucratic-collectivist state. However, this does not constitute an insuperable obstacle to unity. Within the Fourth International there have for some years been currents rejecting the concept that the Soviet Union is a degenerated workers' state. Nobody has claimed that the Fourth International must expel comrades who believe that the Soviet Union is a bureaucratic-collectivist state or a state of capitalist restoration.

8. Yet there are comrades of the Political Committee who, while agreeing to the principle that differences on the Soviet Union are no bar to unity within the Fourth International, nevertheless argue that the comrades of the Workers Party do not belong in the Fourth International because they are "revisionists." But revisionists in the classical sense refers to reformists of the type of Bernstein, who distort Marxism for the purpose of giving up the class struggle and the proletarian revolution. The "revisionism" of the Workers Party is obviously not to be confused with Bernsteinian revisionism; the former is a revision of the Marxist theory of the state in the sense that the WP theory of bureaucratic-collectivism is not compatible with the Marxist theory of the state; but we must recognize that the Workers Party agrees with us against Bernsteinian revisionism on the necessity of carrying on the class struggle to proletarian revolution, and denies that it has abandoned the Marxist theory of the state, whereas revisionists make no bones about their abandonment of it. Only those bewitched by words can fail to distinguish between Bernsteinian revisionism which has no place in the Fourth International, and the "revisionism" of those who differ with us on the Soviet Union but who do have a place in the Fourth International and actually have a place in several of the parties of the Fourth International.

9. Another argument against unity is that the "petty-bourgeois" opposition has continued to move further and is further away from us since the split. This abstract spatial metaphor is not a valid political proposition. It is true that several political differences have arisen in the past five years be-

tween the position of our party and that of the WP, but neither singly nor together are they a bar to unity. There are differences on the question of material aid to China; on some phases of our military policy; on our attitude to the Stalinist parties; differences on the national question in Europe during the Nazi occupation may also still exist to a certain extent. But differences on all these questions must be expected with comrades in our own or sister parties of the Fourth International. They are not questions upon which difference of opinion can be expected to lead to a split, assuming the disputants to be genuine Bolsheviks and sensible. On some of these questions we had differences in our own ranks and no serious factional struggle resulted. Moreover, many of those in the WP who differ with us on these questions would be influenced by our arguments were they to be in our party; much of these differences can be laid to the existence of two separate parties. Perhaps also many of our comrades would be influenced by the arguments of the Workers Party comrades if they returned, but this is natural and to be expected. He who objects to unity on the ground of these differences and possible future differences will only find satisfaction in a monolithic party, a party without differences, which in reality would not be a party at all.

10. Another argument against unity is that the very fact that the "petty-bourgeois opposition" split from us shows they do not belong in the same party with us. This argument amounts to saying that once we have split there should never be unity again. It is completely alien to the method of Trotsky, who so often attempted to heal splits in the parties of the Fourth International. Following earlier unsuccessful attempts by Trotsky, our French comrades have recently succeeded in healing a nine-year split with the Molinierists. Our Belgian comrades have again offered unity to the Vereecken group, with whom they have more long-standing and far deeper differences than we have with the Workers Party. The fact that the comrades of the WP split from us is irrelevant to the question of unity now.

11. The Political Committee insists on continuing to characterize the WP as "petty-bourgeois" and to use that as an argument against unity. "When did they change?" is the argument against those who say that unity is possible now. A date is demanded of us. We cannot give it, but we can indicate precisely in what the change consists.

(a) Our characterization of them as "petty-bourgeois" was based mainly on the fact that we considered they had yielded to bourgeois-democratic pressure in abandoning the defense of the Soviet Union during the period of the Stalin-Hitler pact when bourgeois-democratic public opinion was hostile to the Soviet Union. But had they continued to yield to democratic public opinion, they would not have adopted a Leninist position on the war, a position which indicated that the comrades of the WP were capable of resisting far greater pressure than was exerted during the Stalin-Hitler pact.

(b) In the split Burnham was the ideological leader of the petty-bourgeois opposition. But Burnham left the WP and with him also a small group influenced by his anti-Marxist theories; likewise, Macdonald, an anti-Bolshevik, did not find himself at home in the WP. The departure of these elements was an important factor in permitting the group to remain on the fundamental position of the Fourth International instead of taking the path first indicated by Burnham.

(c) During the war the petty-bourgeois elements in the WP found jobs in industry and many of them had their first experience in fighting in the ranks of organized workers. They undoubtedly made many mistakes because of inexperience, but we cannot deny their seriousness of purpose and their devotion to the labor movement. We can also expect that the large number of their members drafted into the army have undergone a significant transformation through their experience with masses in the war.

These are the specific changes which answer the formalistic question as to when the WP ceased to be a petty-bourgeois group.

12. Even if it had remained a petty-bourgeois group, that would be no principled obstacle to unity, for even when we characterized them as a petty-bourgeois opposition the party was willing to keep them in its ranks. Although the organizational question was raised in the form of an indictment of the Cannon regime as a bureaucratic-conservative tendency, and although that question played an important role in the struggle culminating in the split, the basis of the struggle was the question of the defense of the Soviet Union. Under the guidance of Trotsky, we took the position that a split on this question was not justified; that it was possible and desirable for the minority to accept discipline in action and to strive further to win the majority of the membership to its point of view. Trotsky proposed that the minority be given guarantees that factions would not be prohibited; that no restrictions would be imposed on factional activity other than those dictated by the necessity for common action; that the minority could choose to have an internal bulletin of its own or a common one with the majority. The minority demanded the right to publish a public newspaper agitating against the party position. This right the majority rejected as irreconcilable with Bolshevik procedure. The split occurred because the minority violated the convention decision denying it permission to publish a public organ.

13. It is clear from the facts that led to the split that either the elimination by history of the question of the defense of the Soviet Union or a willingness on the part of the comrades of the WP to accept the conditions proposed by Trotsky to avoid the split should lead to a serious attempt at re-unification.

14. The question of the defense of the Soviet Union has not been eliminated by history, but it is no longer the burning question that it was in 1940. The burning question today is the defense of the European revolution from Stalin, on which both parties agree. This creates the possibility of working together again in one party. No one can say if and when we are likely to bring to the fore again the slogan of defense of the USSR. The variant of a fairly long term of peace between the imperialists and Stalin is more likely to occur than the variant of war. At any rate, it is necessary to invite the WP comrades to re-enter our ranks, offering them the same conditions that we were willing

to offer them in order to avoid the split.

15. How the WP will react to such an invitation is not certain. The important thing is to work out a correct line for our party on this question: to invite the WP to unite with us on the same conditions we offered in 1940. We shall benefit no matter what attitude the WP takes. A refusal on its part can be utilized to tear away some of their supporters within and outside their party. Acceptance means increasing our membership by several hundred among whom are capable comrades with many years of experience in the revolutionary movement. It means eliminating a party whose existence side by side with ours causes much confusion.

16. An attitude which condemns those who split to permanent separation from the party, regardless of their loyalty to the revolution, is incompatible with the true spirit of Bolshevism. In the course of building a Bolshevik party, sharp differences of opinion, even bitter struggle and splits, are almost unavoidable. Unification after a split, when tempers have cooled, when events have eliminated or pushed to the background the cause of the controversy, is just as obligatory as refraining from splitting. We correctly characterized the split as a criminal blunder against the movement, but that does not justify us in forever barring the door to those who left us.

17. The unwillingness to unite with comrades who have different opinions has nothing in common with Bolshevism. Such unwillingness bases itself on the concept of a monolithic party whose leaders, while granting formal democratic rights of discussion, do not in reality conceive differences of opinion and discussion of the differences as a method of building a healthy Bolshevik party. They do not have confidence in their ability to convince intelligent revolutionists: they depend upon blind followers. Building the party to them is to create a machine with a membership that is docile and accepts unquestioningly the directives of the leaders. The question of unification with the comrades of the WP is thus of enormous symptomatic importance in determining the kind of party we want to build. The party's decision will be a touchstone indicating the direction in which we shall henceforth move.

New International, September 1945

I was unready in 1940

Max Shachtman (1943)

DURING THE RUSSIAN DISCUSSION prior to the split in the SWP, there were two more-or-less definitive standpoints on the class character of the Soviet state. There was Trotsky's view, supported by the Cannonites; there was also the Carter (or Carter-Burnham) point of view that Russia was not a workers' state. As some comrades know, the war and Russia's role in it helped to upset my own views on the working-class character of Russia. I did not, at first, adopt the standpoint that Russia was not a workers' state. I simply began to have doubts about the old position, to be uncertain of it. The only correct word Hansen ever said in that factional fight was that Shachtman represents the "doubtist faction" on this question. He was essentially correct. But I took my responsibility as a leader seriously enough, if I may say so, not to engage at that tine in a discussion of the class character of the Russian state. What could I contribute to a discussion on that question between Burnham and Cannon, or Carter and Trotsky? Only one thing: I am in doubt; I am not sure of my position. How would such nonsense have helped make a discussion on the class character of the Russian state fruitful? The membership would have been 100 percent right in telling me: If you don't know, if you have nothing but doubts, then be silent and don't mess things up until you know where you stand. I didn't wait for anyone to give me this counsel. I deliberately avoided that discussion; I refused to be dragged into it, at least so far as I was concerned. (There were, of course, other reasons of a more general group nature which indicated to us the wrongness of such a discussion at that time, but they had nothing to do with my personal case.) I waited. I discussed time and again with comrades holding all sorts of views on the question. I reexamined the question to the best of my ability by studying all the available material, re-studying it, checking and re-checking. If I finally appeared before the party membership with a position of my own, it was only after I knew where I stood and that I could defend (or try to defend) my views before the party membership and the radical workers in general. I like to think that this procedure and conduct helped to make the fundamental discussion that ensued a more fruitful and positive one. In this personal reference, the reader will surely understand there is no element of boastfulness, or self-commendation. I, least of all, feel like boasting about having conducted myself, in such a matter, in accordance with the ABC rules of the movement, which I always assume are the common knowledge and property of all. It is a source of the keenest disappointment to realize that there are among us leading comrades who either never knew and understood these rules that make for intelligent and profitable discussion, or who, having long known them, unlearn them overnight.

From a Workers Party bulletin, circa summer 1943

Labor Action, 29 April 1946

The Militant, 15 May 1943. "Mission to Moscow", a film made by Warner Bros, one of the main Hollywood studios, tried to justify the Moscow Trials, and so did the on-screen introduction to the film by Joseph E Davies, a former US ambassador to Moscow...

10. Leon Trotsky is dead? Long live Trotsky!

"In answer to the 'independent thinkers' Cannon used to say 'Trotsky is my brain'." — Felix Morrow, Minority Report, 1946

To the memory of the Old Man

James P Cannon (1940)

COMRADE TROTSKY'S entire conscious life, from the time he entered the workers' movement in the provincial Russian town of Nikolayev at the age of eighteen up till the moment of his death in Mexico City forty-two years later, was completely dedicated to work and struggle for one central idea. He stood for the emancipation of the workers and all the oppressed people of the world, and the transformation of society from capitalism to socialism by means of a social revolution. In his conception, this liberating social revolution requires for success the leadership of a revolutionary political party of the workers' vanguard.

In his entire conscious life Comrade Trotsky never once diverged from that idea. He never doubted it, and never ceased to struggle for its realization. On his deathbed, in his last message to us, his disciples — his last testament — he proclaimed his confidence in his life-idea: "Tell our friends I am sure of the victory of the Fourth International — go forward!"

The whole world knows about his work and his testament. The cables of the press of the world have carried his last testament and made it known to the world's millions. And in the minds and hearts of all those throughout the world who grieve with us tonight one thought — one question — is uppermost: Will the movement which he created and inspired survive his death? Will his disciples be able to hold their ranks together, will they be able to carry out his testament and realize the emancipation of the oppressed through the victory of the Fourth International?

Without the slightest hesitation we give an affirmative answer to this question. Those enemies who predict a collapse of Trotsky's movement without Trotsky, and those weak-willed friends who fear it, only show that they do not understand Trotsky, what he was, what he signified, and what he left behind. Never has a bereaved family been left such a rich heritage as that which Comrade Trotsky, like a provident father, has left to the family of the Fourth International as trustees for all progressive humanity. A great heritage of ideas he has left to us; ideas which shall chart the struggle toward the great free future of all mankind. The mighty ideas of Trotsky are our program and our banner. They are a clear guide to action in all the complexities of our epoch, and a constant reassurance that we are right and that our victory is inevitable.

Trotsky himself believed that ideas are the greatest power in the world. Their authors may be killed, but ideas, once promulgated, live their own life. If they are correct ideas, they make their way through all obstacles. This was the central, dominating concept of Comrade Trotsky's philosophy. He explained it to us many, many times. He once wrote: "It is not the party that makes the program [the idea]; it is the program that makes the party." In a personal letter to me, he once wrote: "We work with the most correct and powerful ideas in the world, with inadequate numerical forces and material means. But correct ideas, in the long run, always conquer and make available for themselves the necessary material means and forces."

Trotsky, a disciple of Marx, believed with Marx that "an idea, when it permeates the mass, becomes a material force." Believing that, Comrade Trotsky never doubted that his work would live after him. Believing that, he could proclaim on his deathbed his confidence in the future victory of the Fourth International which embodies his ideas. Those who doubt it do not know Trotsky.

Trotsky himself believed that his greatest significance, his greatest value, consisted not in his physical life, not in his epic deeds, which overshadow those of all heroic figures in history in their sweep and their grandeur — but in what he would leave behind him after the assassins had done their work. He knew that his doom was sealed, and he worked against time in order to leave everything possible to us, and through us to mankind. Throughout the eleven years of his last exile he chained himself to his desk like a galley slave and labored, as none of us knows how to labor, with such energy, such persistence and self-discipline, as only men of genius can labor. He worked against time to pour out through his pen the whole rich content of his mighty brain and preserve it in permanent written form for us, and for those who will come after us.

The whole Trotsky, like the whole Marx, is preserved in his books, his articles, and his letters. His voluminous correspondence, which contains some of his brightest thoughts and his most intimate personal feelings and sentiments, must now be collected and published. When that is done, when his letters are published alongside his books, his pamphlets, and his articles, we, and all those who join us in the liberation struggle of humanity, will still have our Old Man to help us.

He knew that the super-Borgia in the Kremlin, Cain-Stalin, who has destroyed the whole generation of the October Revolution, had marked him for assassination and would succeed sooner or later. That is why he worked so urgently. That is why he hastened to write out everything that was in his mind and get it down on paper in permanent form where nobody could destroy it.

Just the other night, I talked at the dinner table with one of the Old Man's faithful secretaries — a young comrade who had served him a long time and knew his personal life, as he lived it in his last years of exile, most intimately. I urged him to write his reminiscences without delay. I said: "We must all write everything we know about Trotsky. Everyone must record his recollections and his impressions. We must not forget that we moved in the orbit of the greatest figure of our time. Millions of people, generations yet to come, will be hungry for every scrap of information, every word, every impression that throws light on him, his ideas, his aims, and his personal life."

He answered: "I can write only about his personal qualities as I observed them; his methods of work, his humaneness, his generosity. But I can't write anything new about his ideas. They are already written. Everything he had to say, everything he had in his brain, is down on paper. He seemed to be determined to scoop down to the bottom of his mind, and take out everything and give it to the world in his writings. Very often, I remember, casual conversation on some subject would come up at the dinner table; an informal discussion would take place, and the Old Man would express some opinions new and fresh. Almost invariably the contributions of the dinner-table conversation would find expression a little later in a book, an article, or a letter."

They killed Trotsky not by one blow; not when this murderer, the agent of Stalin, drove the pickax through the back of his skull. That was only the final blow. They killed him by inches. They killed him many times. They killed him seven times when they killed his seven secretaries. They killed him four times when they killed his four children. They killed him when his old coworkers of the Russian Revolution were killed.

Yet he stood up to his tasks in spite of all that. Growing old and sick, he staggered through all these moral, emotional, and physical blows to complete his testament to humanity while he still had time. He gathered it all together — every thought, every idea, every lesson from his past experience — to lay up a literary treasure for us, a treasure that the moths and the rust cannot eat.

He was a great man of action, to be sure. His deeds are incorporated in the greatest revolution in the history of mankind. But, unlike the opportunists and leaders of a day, his deeds were inspired by great ideas, and these ideas still live. He not only made a revolution; he wrote its history and explained the basic laws which govern all revolutions. In his *History of the Russian Revolution*, which he considered his masterpiece, he gave us a guide for the making of new revolutions, or rather, for extending throughout the world the revolution that began in October 1917.

Trotsky, the great man of ideas, was himself the disciple of a still greater one — Marx. Trotsky did not originate or claim to originate the most fundamental ideas which he expounded. He built on the foundations laid by the great masons of the nineteenth century — Marx and Engels. In addition, he went through the great school of Lenin and learned from him. Trotsky's genius consisted in his complete assimilation of the ideas bequeathed by Marx, Engels, and Lenin. He mastered their method. He developed their ideas in modern conditions, and applied them in masterful fashion in the contemporary struggle of the proletariat. If you would understand Trotsky, you must know that he was a disciple of Marx, an orthodox Marxist. He fought under the banner of Marxism for forty-two years! During the last year of his life he laid everything else aside to fight a great political and theoretical battle in defence of Marxism in the ranks of the Fourth International! His very last article, which was left on his desk in unpolished form, the last article with which he occupied himself, was a defence of Marxism against contemporary revisionists and sceptics. The power of Trotsky, first of all and above all, was the power of Marxism.

Do you want a concrete illustration of the power of Marxist ideas? Just consider this: when Marx died in 1883, Trotsky was but four years old. Lenin was only fourteen. Neither could have known Marx, or anything about him. Yet both became great historical figures because of Marx, because Marx had circulated ideas in the world before they were born. Those ideas were living their own life. They shaped the lives of Lenin and Trotsky. Marx's ideas were with them and guided their every step when they made the greatest revolution in history.

So will the ideas of Trotsky, which are a development of the ideas of Marx, influence us, his disciples, who survive him today. They will shape the lives of far greater disciples who are yet to come, who do not yet know Trotsky's name. Some who are destined to be the greatest Trotskyists are playing in the schoolyards today. They will be nourished on Trotsky's ideas, as he and Lenin were nourished on the ideas of Marx and Engels.

Our movement was built firmly from the very beginning and has remained firm because it was built on Trotsky's ideas.

In the sections of the Fourth International throughout the world. Only a very few individual comrades have ever met Trotsky face to face. Yet everywhere they knew him. In China, and across the broad oceans to Chile, Argentina, Brazil. In Australia, in practically every country of Europe. In the United States, Canada, Indochina, South Africa. They never saw him, but the ideas of Trotsky welded them all together in one uniform and firm world movement. So it will continue after his physical death. There is no room for doubt.

Trotsky's place in history is already established. He will stand forever on a historical eminence beside the other three great giants of the proletariat: Marx, Engels, and Lenin. It is possible, indeed it is quite probable, that in the historic memory of mankind, his name will evoke the warmest affection, the most heartfelt gratitude of all. Because he fought so long, against such a world of enemies, so honestly, so heroically, and with such selfless devotion!

Future generations of free humanity will look back with insatiable interest on this mad epoch of reaction and bloody violence and social change — this epoch of the death agony of one social system and the birth pangs of another. When they see through the historian's lens how the oppressed masses of the people everywhere were groping, blinded and confused, they will mention with unbounded love the name of the genius who gave us light, the great heart that gave us courage.

Of all the great men of our time, of all the public figures to whom the masses turned for guidance in these troubled terrible times, Trotsky alone explained things to us, he alone gave us light in the darkness. His brain alone unravelled the mysteries and complexities of our epoch. The great brain of Trotsky was what was feared by all his enemies. They couldn't cope with it. They couldn't answer it. In the incredibly horrible method by which they destroyed him there was hidden a deep symbol. They struck at his brain! But the richest products of that brain are still alive. They had already escaped and can never be recaptured and destroyed.

We do not minimize the blow that has been dealt to us, to our movement, and to the world. It is the worst calamity. We have lost something of immeasurable value that can never be regained. We have lost the inspiration of his physical presence, his wise counsel. All that is lost forever. Trotsky still lived in the hearts of the Russian people. They didn't believe the lies. They waited and hoped for his return. His words are still there. His memory is alive in their hearts.

Just a few days before the death of Comrade Trotsky the editors of the Russian Bulletin received a letter from Riga. It had been mailed before the incorporation of Latvia into the Soviet Union. It stated in simple words that Trotsky's *Open Letter to the Workers of the USSR* had reached them, and had lifted up their hearts with courage and shown them the way. The letter stated that the message of Trotsky had been memorized, word by word, and would be passed along by word of mouth no matter what might happen. We verily believe that the words of Trotsky will live longer in the Soviet Union than the bloody regime of Stalin. In the coming great day of liberation the message of Trotsky will be the banner of the Russian people.

The English historian Macaulay remarked that apostates in all ages have manifested an exceptional malignity toward those whom they have betrayed. Stalin and his traitor gang were consumed by a mad hatred of the man who reminded them of their yesterday. Trotsky, the symbol of the great revolution, reminded them constantly of the cause they had deserted and betrayed, and they hated him for that. They hated him for all the great and good human qualities which he personified and to which they were completely alien. They were determined, at all cost, to do away with him.

We saved him for eleven years! Those were the most fruitful years of his whole life. Those were the years when he sat down in full maturity to devote himself to the task of summing up and casting in permanent literary form the results of his experiences and his thoughts.

Their dull police minds cannot know that Trotsky left the best of himself behind. Even in death he frustrated them. Because the thing they wanted most of all to kill — the memory and the hope of revolution — that Trotsky left behind him.

At the hour Comrade Trotsky was finally struck down, I was returning by train from a special journey to Minneapolis. I had gone there for the purpose of arranging for new and especially qualified comrades to go down and strengthen the guard in Coyoacan. On the way home I sat in the railroad train with a feeling of satisfaction that the task of the trip had been accomplished, reinforcements of the guard had been provided for.

Then, as the train passed through Pennsylvania, about four o'clock in the morning, they brought the early papers with the news that the assassin had broken through the defences and driven a pickax into the brain of Comrade Trotsky. That was the beginning of a terrible day, the saddest day of our lives, when we waited, hour by hour, while the Old Man fought his last fight and struggled vainly with death. But even then, in that hour of terrible grief, when we received the fatal message over the long-distance telephone: "The Old Man is dead" — even then, we didn't permit ourselves to stop for weeping. We plunged immediately into the work to defend his memory and carry out his testament. And we worked harder than ever before, because for the first time we realized with full consciousness that we have to do it all now. We can't lean on the Old Man anymore. What is done now, we must do. That is the spirit in which we have got to work from now on.

He was the world's exile in the time of reaction. No door was open to him anywhere except that of the Republic of Mexico.

The capitalists — all kinds — fear and hate even his dead body! The doors of our great democracy are open to many political refugees, of course. All sorts of reactionaries; democratic scoundrels who betrayed and deserted their people; monarchists, and even fascists — they have all been welcomed in New York harbor. But not even the dead body of the friend of the oppressed could find asylum here! We shall not forget that! We shall nourish that grievance close to our hearts and in good time we shall take our revenge.

The great and powerful democracy of Roosevelt and Hull wouldn't let us bring his body here for the funeral. But he is here just the same. All of us feel that he is here in this hall tonight — not only in his great ideas, but also, especially tonight, in our memory of him as a man. We have a right to be proud that the best man of our time belonged to us, the greatest brain and strongest and most loyal heart. The class society we live in exalts the rascals, cheats, self-seekers, liars, and oppressors of the people. You can hardly name an intellectual representative of the decaying class society, of high or low degree, who is not a miserable hypocrite and contemptible coward, concerned first of all with his own inconsequential personal affairs and saving his own worthless skin. What a wretched tribe they are. There is no honesty, no inspiration, nothing in the whole of them.

They have not a single man that can strike a spark in the heart of youth. Our Old Man was made of better stuff. Our Old Man was made of entirely different stuff. He towered above these pygmies in his moral grandeur.

Comrade Trotsky not only struggled for a new social order based on human solidarity as a future goal; he lived every day of his life according to its higher and nobler standards. They wouldn't let him be a citizen of any country. But, in truth, he was much more than that. He was already, in his mind and in his conduct, a citizen of the communist future of humanity. That memory of him as a man, as a comrade, is more precious than gold and rubies. We can hardly understand a man of that type living among us. We are all caught in the steel net of the class society with its inequalities, its contradictions, its conventionalities, its false values, its lies. The class society poisons and corrupts everything. We are all dwarfed and twisted and blinded by it. We can hardly visualize what human relations will be, we can hardly comprehend what the personality of man will be, in a free society.

Comrade Trotsky gave us an anticipatory picture. In him, in his personality as a man, as a human being, we caught a glimpse of the communist man that is to be. This memory of him as a man, as a comrade, is our greatest assurance that the spirit of man, striving for human solidarity, is unconquerable. In our terrible epoch many things will pass away. Capitalism and all its heroes will pass away. Stalin and Hitler and Roosevelt and Churchill, and all the lies and injustices and hypocrisy they signify, will pass away in blood and fire. But the spirit of the communist man which Comrade Trotsky represented will not pass away.

Destiny has made us, men of common clay, the most immediate disciples of Comrade Trotsky. We now become his heirs, and we are charged with the mission to carry out his testament. He had confidence in us. He assured us with his last words that we are right and that we will prevail. We need only have confidence in ourselves and in the ideas, the tradition, and the memory which he left us as our heritage.

We owe everything to him. We owe to him our political existence, our understanding, our faith in the future. We are not alone. There are others like us in all parts of the world. Always remember that. We are not alone. Trotsky has educated cadres of disciples in more than thirty countries. They are convinced to the marrow of their bones of their right to victory. They will not falter. Neither shall we falter. "I am sure of the victory of the Fourth International!" So said Comrade

Trotsky in the last moment of his life. So are we sure.

Trotsky never doubted and we shall never doubt that, armed with his weapons, with his ideas, we shall lead the oppressed masses of the world out of the bloody welter of the war into a new socialist society. That is our testimony here tonight at the grave of Comrade Trotsky.

Farewell to our greatest comrade and teacher, who has now become our most glorious martyr. We do not deny the grief that constricts all our hearts. But ours is not the grief of prostration, the grief that saps the will. It is tempered by rage and hatred and determination. We shall transmute it into fighting energy to carry on the Old Man's fight. Let us say farewell to him in a manner worthy of his disciples, like good soldiers of Trotsky's army. Not crouching in weakness and despair, but standing upright with dry eyes and clenched fists. With the song of struggle and victory on our lips. With the song of confidence in Trotsky's Fourth International, the International Party that shall be the human race!

Abridged from speech at the Leon Trotsky Memorial Meeting in New York on August 28, 1940. *Socialist Appeal*, 6 September 1940. This speech was also published as a pamphlet.

Trotsky as depicted by Carlo,
cartoonist for *Socialist Appeal*
and then *Labor Action*

What is Trotskyism?

Max Shachtman (1943)

OUR CRITICISM OF Trotsky's later theory of the "workers' state" introduces into it an indispensable correction. Far from "demolishing" Trotskyism, it eliminates from it a distorting element of contradiction and restores its essential inner harmony and continuity. The writer considers himself a follower of Trotsky, as of Lenin before him, and of Marx and Engels in the earlier generation.

Such has been the intellectual havoc wrought in the revolutionary movement by the manners and standards of Stalinism, that "follower" has come to mean serf, worshipper, or parrot. We have no desire to be this kind of "follower." Trotsky was not, and we learned much of what we know from him. In *The New Course* he wrote these jewelled words, which are worth repeating a hundred times:

"If there is one thing likely to strike a mortal blow to the spiritual life of the party and to the doctrinal training of the youth, it is certainly the transformation of Leninism from a method demanding for its application initiative, critical thinking and ideological courage into a canon which demands nothing more than interpreters appointed for good and aye. Leninism cannot be conceived of without theoretical breadth, without a critical analysis of the material bases of the political process. The weapon of Marxian investigation must he constantly sharpened and applied. It is precisely in this that tradition consists, and not in the substitution of a formal reference or of an accidental quotation. Least of all can Leninism be reconciled with ideological superficiality and theoretical slovenliness.

"Lenin cannot be chopped up into quotations suited for every possible case, because for Lenin the formula never stands higher than the reality; it is always the tool that makes it possible to grasp the reality and to dominate it. It would not be hard to find in Lenin dozens and hundreds of passages which, formally speaking, seem to be contradictory. But what must be seen is not the formal relationship of one passage to another, but the real relationship of each of them to the concrete reality in which the formula was introduced as a lever. The Leninist truth is always concrete! ...

"Leninism is orthodox, obdurate, irreducible, but it does not contain so much as a hint of formalism, canon, nor bureaucratism. In the struggle it takes the bull by the horns. To make out of the traditions of Leninism a supra-theoretical guarantee of the infallibility of all the words and thoughts of the interpreters of these traditions, is to scoff at genuine revolutionary tradition and transform it into official bureaucratism. It is ridiculous and pathetic to try to hypnotise a great revolutionary party by the repetition of the same formula, according to which the right line should be sought not in the essence of each question, not in the methods of posing, and solving this question, but in information ... of a biographical character."

There are "followers" who seem to think that the whole of Trotskyism (that is, the revolutionary Marxism of our time) is contained in the theory that Russia is still a workers' state and in the slogan of "unconditional defence of the Soviet Union." They merely prove that they have retired from a life of active and critical thought, and from the realities of life in general, and confine themselves to memorising by heart two pages of an otherwise uncut and unread book. They would be the first to deny, by the way, that the whole of Leninism is contained in Lenin's theory of the "democratic dictatorship of the proletariat and peasantry" or in his strictures against Trotsky and the theory of the permanent revolution.

The whole of Trotsky, for the new generation of Marxists that must be trained up and organised, does not lie in his contradictory theory of the class character of Russia; it is not even a decisively important part of the whole. Trotskyism is all of Marx, Engels and Lenin that has withstood the test of time and struggle — and that is a good deal! Trotskyism is its leader's magnificent development and amplification of the theory of the permanent revolution. Trotskyism is the defence of the great and fundamental principles of the Russian Bolshevik revolution and the Communist International, which it brought into existence. Trotskyism is the principle of workers' democracy, of the struggle for democracy and socialism.

In this sense – and it is the only one worth talking about – *The New Course* is a Trotskyist classic. It was not only a weapon hitting at the very heart of decaying bureaucratism in revolutionary Russia. It was and is a guide for the struggle against the vices of bureaucratism throughout the labour and revolutionary movements.

Bureaucratism is not simply a direct product of certain economic privileges acquired by the officialdom of the labour movement. It is also an ideology, a concept of leadership and of its relationship to the masses, which is absorbed even by labour and revolutionary officialdoms who enjoy no economic privileges at all. It is an ideology that reeks of its bourgeois origin. Boiled down to its most vicious essence, it is the kind of thinking and living and leading which says to the rank and file, in the words Trotsky once used to describe the language of Stalinism: "No thinking! Those at the top have more brains than you."

We see this ideology reflected in the every-day conduct of our own American trade union bureaucracy: "We will handle everything. Leave things to us. You stay where you are, and keep still." We see it reflected throughout the big social-democratic (to say nothing of the Stalinist) parties: "We will negotiate things. We will arrange everything. We will manoeuvre cleverly with the enemy, and get what you want without struggle. You sit still until further orders. That is all you are fit for." We even see it in those smaller revolutionary groups which are outside the reformist and Stalinist movements and which consider that this fact alone immunises them from bureaucratism. We repeat, it is a bourgeois ideology through and through. It is part of the ideas that the bourgeoisie, through all its agencies for moulding the mind of the masses, seeks to have prevail: "Whatever criticism you may have to make of us, remember this: The masses are stupid. It is no accident that they are at the bottom of the social ladder. They are incapable of rising to the top. They need a ruler over them; they cannot rule themselves. For their own good, they must be kept where they are."

The New Course does more than dismiss this odious ideology that fertilises the mind of the labour bureaucracy. It analyses its source and its nature. It diagnoses the evil to perfection. It indicates the operation needed to remove it, and the tools with which to perform the operation. It is the same tool needed by the proletariat for its emancipation everywhere. Its name is the democratically organised and controlled, self-acting, dynamic, critical, revolutionary political party of the working class.

The counter-revolution in Russia was made possible only because Stalinism blunted, then wore down, then smashed to bits this indispensable tool of the proletariat. The bureaucracy won. "If Trotsky had been right," says the official iconographer of Stalin, Henri Barbusse, "he would have won." How simple! What a flattering compliment to ... Hitler. The bureaucracy not only won, but consolidated its power on a scale unknown in any country of the world throughout all history. Stalin himself is now the Pope-Czar of the Russian Empire.

But that is only how it seems on the surface; that is how it is only for a very short while, as history counts. "Any imbecile can rule with a state of siege," said Rochefort. Only the really powerful and confident can rule by establishing peaceful relations in the country. That, the new bureaucracy, without a past and without a future, cannot do. The combined efforts of world capitalism cannot do that nowadays, still less the efforts of the Stalinist nobility. The latter has succeeded in establishing "socialism," for itself and "in a single country." It will not live long to enjoy it. Together with all modern rulers, it is doomed to perish in the unrelenting world crisis that it cannot solve, or to perish at the hands of an avenging socialist proletariat.

Cromwell's Roundheads marched with Bibles in their hands. The militant proletariat needs no divine revelations or scriptural injunctions, no Bibles or saviours. But it will march to victory only if its conscious vanguard has assimilated the rich and now-more-timely-than-ever lessons to be learned from the classic work of the organiser of the first great proletarian revolution.

From *The Struggle for the New Course*, preface to an edition of
Trotsky's *The New Course*, 1943

Antoinette Konikow had been a member of the first Russian marxist group "The Emancipation of Labour" organisation of George Plekhanov, Pavel Akselrod, Vera Zasulich and Lev Deutch. A physician, she was a campaigning pioneer of birth control and an early militant feminist. In Boston she and a few others formed a Trotskyist group before the Communist Party leaders Cannon, Shachtman and Abern declared for Trotsky (1925). She died in 1946, a member of the Socialist Workers Party.

What is Leninism?

Leon Trotsky (1923)

LENINISM CANNOT be conceived of without theoretical breadth, without a critical analysis of the material bases of the political process. The weapon of Marxian investigation must be constantly sharpened and applied. It is precisely in this that tradition consists, and not in the substitution of a formal reference or of an accidental quotation.

Least of all can Leninism be reconciled with ideological superficiality and theoretical slovenliness. Lenin cannot be chopped up into quotations suited for every possible case, because for Lenin the formula never stands higher than the reality; it is always the tool that makes it possible to grasp the reality and to dominate it. It would not be hard to find in Lenin dozens and hundreds of passages which, formally speaking, seem to be contradictory. But what must be seen is not the formal relationship of one passage to another, but the real relationship of each of them to the concrete reality in which the formula was introduced as a lever. The Leninist truth is always concrete!

As a system of revolutionary action, Leninism presupposes a revolutionary sense sharpened by reflection and experience which, in the social realm, is equivalent to the muscular sensation in physical labor. But revolutionary sense cannot be confused with demagogical flair. The latter may yield ephemeral successes, sometimes even sensational ones. But it is a political instinct of an inferior type.

It always leans toward the line of least resistance. Leninism, on the other hand, seeks to pose and resolve the fundamental revolutionary problems.

Leninism is, first of all, realism, the highest qualitative and quantitative appreciation of reality, from the standpoint of revolutionary action. Precisely because of this it is irreconcilable with the flight from reality behind the screen of hollow agitationalism, with the passive loss of time, with the haughty justification of yesterday's mistakes on the pretext of saving the tradition of the party.

Leninism is genuine freedom from formalistic prejudices, from moralising doctrinalism, from all forms of intellectual conservatism attempting to bind the will to revolutionary action. But to believe that Leninism signifies that "anything goes" would be an irremediable mistake. Leninism includes the morality, not formal but genuinely revolutionary, of mass action and the mass party. Nothing is so alien to it as functionary-arrogance and bureaucratic cynicism.

A mass party has its own morality, which is the bond of fighters in and for action. Demagogy is irreconcilable with the spirit of a revolutionary party because it is deceitful: by presenting one or another simplified solution of the difficulties of the hour it inevitably undermines the next future, weakens the party's self-confidence.

Swept by the wind and gripped by a serious danger, demagogy easily dissolves into panic. It is hard to juxtapose, even on paper, panic and Leninism.

Leninism is warlike from head to foot. War is impossible without cunning, without subterfuge, without deception of the enemy. Victorious war cunning is a constituent element of Leninist politics.

But, at the same time, Leninism is supreme revolutionary honesty toward the party and the working class. It admits of no fiction, no bubble-blowing, no pseudo-grandeur.

Leninism is orthodox, obdurate, irreducible, but it does not contain so much as a hint of formalism, canon, nor bureaucratism. In the struggle, it takes the bull by the horns. To make out of the traditions of Leninism a supra-theoretical guarantee of infallibility of all the words and thoughts of the interpreters of these traditions is to scoff at genuine revolutionary tradition and transform it into social bureaucratism. It is ridiculous and pathetic to try to hypnotise a great revolutionary party by the repetition of the same formulae, according to which the right line should be sought not in the essence of each question, not in the methods of posing and solving this question, but in information of a biographical character.

This character of the revolutionary tradition is bound up with the peculiar character of revolutionary discipline. Where tradition is conservative, discipline is passive and is violated at the first moment of crisis. Where, as in our party, tradition consists in the highest revolutionary activity, discipline attains its maximum point, for its decisive importance is constantly checked in action. Thence, the indestructible alliance of revolutionary initiative, of critical, bold elaboration of questions, with iron discipline in action. And it is only by this superior activity that the youth can receive from the old this tradition of discipline and carry it on.

We cherish the tradition of Bolshevism as much as anybody. But let no one dare identify bureaucratism with Bolshevism, tradition with vacuous routine.

From *The New Course*, 1923

Platforms and events

Leon Trotsky (1930)

YOU SAY THAT in all this time you have not departed by an iota from the platform of 1925, which I had called an excellent document in many respects. But a platform is not created so as to "not depart from it," but rather to apply and develop it. The platform of 1925 was a good document for the year 1925. In the five years that have elapsed, great events have taken place. In the platform there is no answer whatever to them. To attempt replacing answers to questions which flow from the situation in 1930 by references to the 1925 platform is to uphold a policy of vagueness and evasiveness...

> From a letter "To The Editorial Board Of Prometeo" (the magazine of the Italian communists with allegiance to the ideas of Amadeo Bordiga). 19 June 1930. *Fourth International*, September-October 1947

Suppressed Belgian Trotskyist Paper

Nouvelle série. — No 21
Cinquième année.   Prolétaires de tous les pays, unissez-vous !   31 Mars 1945
                                                                   PRIX : 2 FRANCS

LA VOIE
DE LENINE

Organe central (bi-mensuel) du Parti Communiste Révolutionnaire (trotskyste)
section belge de la IVe Internationale

Solidarité avec le
Prolétariat Allemand!

This advocacy of class solidarity with the German workers (31 March 1945) led to the banning of the Belgian Trotskyist paper by the administration installed by the Allies after the Nazis retreated from Belgium.

Trotsky's predictions triumph!

Joseph Hansen (1940)

FOURTEEN MONTHS AGO, upon the invasion of Poland from the west by Hitler and from the east by the Red Army, the social democrats and those clinging to their coat tails were thrown into complete confusion by the complex events. With the disappearance of the Polish bourgeois government and the advance of Soviet troops, they were utterly incapable of foreseeing what might be expected to occur in the eastern occupied territories. Among our own ranks certain elements raised the question of changing our slogan of unconditional defense of the Soviet Union because of the Red Army invasion of Poland.

Leon Trotsky analyzed the Polish events on September 25, 1939, in an article, *The USSR in War*, in the following lucid words:

"It is more likely, however, that in the territories scheduled to become a part of the USSR, the Moscow government will carry through the expropriation of the large land owners and statification of the means of production. This variant is most probable not because the bureaucracy remains true to the socialist program but because it is neither desirous nor capable of sharing the power, and the privileges the latter entails, with the old ruling classes in the occupied territories. Here an analogy literally offers itself. The first Bonaparte halted the revolution by means of military dictatorship. However, when the French troops invaded Poland, Napoleon signed a decree: 'Serfdom is abolished.' This measure was dictated not by Napoleon's sympathies for the peasants, nor by democratic principles, but rather by the fact that the Bonapartist dictatorship based itself not on feudal but on bourgeois property relations. Inasmuch as Stalin's Bonapartist dictatorship bases itself not on private but on state property, the invasion of Poland by the Red Army should, in the nature of the case, result in the abolition of private capitalist property, so as thus to bring the regime of the occupied territories into accord with the regime of the USSR."

Trotsky in his next paragraph explains that this change in property relations could not however cause us to favor the invasion of Poland by the Red Army, since it would be "achieved in military-bureaucratic fashion" and hence lower the capacity of the proletariat to defend the old conquests and to make new ones through socialist revolution. Trotsky's conclusion was that class-conscious workers should condemn the invasion of Poland by the Red Army but continue their unconditional defense of the Soviet Union including the new territorial gains. Trotsky saw the invasion as providing a remarkable demonstration of the analysis of the Fourth International that the Soviet Union is still a workers' state but suffering from bureaucratic deformations.. He concluded that there was nothing "new in the situation" which should cause us to change our position of unconditional defense of the Soviet Union". This analysis by Trotsky drew derision from all sides especially among those under the influence of the bourgeois war pressure. They declared that the invasion of Poland proved that there "was something entirely new in the situation," and that the Soviet Union had become an "imperialist" state seeking imperialist territorial gains.

James Burnham, for example, declared that the policy of the Soviet state had become "imperialist or quasi-imperialist." Max Shachtman declared in a resolution dated September 28, 1939, that "Stalin and the Red Army thus played a flatly counter-revolutionary role in Poland. The bitter realities of the recent events, most particularly of the events in Poland, dictate a revision of our previous concept of the 'unconditional defense of the Soviet Union'."

Now it is possible to ascertain just who was right and who wrong in their analysis of the events in Poland — not that we expect either Burnham or Shachtman to acknowledge themselves wrong!

In an article in the press, Ludwig Lore [see glossary] reports that private capitalist property has been entirely abolished in the occupied territories of Poland.

"The nationalization of big industrial enterprises and banks... was the first," he states. Then came other important financial institutions. "The small and middle-sized industries were a difficult matter," he continues. "No immediate nationalization was attempted. The owners remained in possession of their enterprises and were merely ordered to submit statements to the workers' delegates regarding the cost of production, wages paid, hours employed and working conditions generally. For every branch of industry and again for the individual concerns, councils consisting of representatives of the employees and the employers were established, which jointly fixed a 'just rate of profit' and supervised working and wage conditions.

"However that was a transitory situation. After seven months complete state ownership was established. According to a government statement, the dual regime of employers' and employees' control over production was 'ineffective and working to the disadvantage of state and industry,' wherefore abolition of private ownership in small and medium industries, was decreed.

"A similar situation was created in the trades. Wholesalers and retailers were given a period of grace in which to wind up their enterprises and to sell out their old stocks. After that the Soviet state trusts refused to sell them supplies and private trade died."

Already the Stalinist bureaucracy has purged the local organizations in the occupied territories of any elements who might prove anti-Stalinist. This was likewise predicted by Trotsky, when he warned that the workers of Poland must organize resistance against the crushing totalitarian hand of Moscow. With nothing but the meager details furnished by the bourgeois press dealing mainly with the bare fact of the invasion by the Red Army, Trotsky was able from his analysis of the Soviet Union as a workers' State with bureaucratic deformations to predict with absolute accuracy the course which history actually took. A remarkable triumph of Marxian analysis.

"Go Forward" column, *The Militant*, 16 November 1940

The revolution is very near

James P Cannon (1943)

THE PLENUM OF THE NATIONAL COMMITTEE of the Socialist Workers Party, meeting for the fifth time during the Second World War, reaffirms the basic program of Trotskyism.

Our analysis shows that Europe is now on the verge of proletarian revolution, that already the beginning of this revolution can be seen in Italy. In the very near future full confirmation will be given to Trotsky's theses that for the oppressed toilers the Socialist United States of Europe will prove the only road out of totalitarianism and war.

Despite the worst efforts of our enemies, despite their lies and slanders, their prisons and their assassins, our party has become firmer and stronger.

In extending greetings to you, dear Natalia, our Plenum also salutes all our friends and co-thinkers in other lands who have borne the brunt of cruelest blows. We assure them that the long period of reaction is rapidly drawing to a close and that their day is now dawning, the day of a great world-wide upsurge of the working class.

Nothing can stop the development of our movement. Ideas cannot be slain. As Trotsky predicted, the program of Marxism will prove invincible.

"Telegram To Natalia Trotsky, from a Plenum and Banquet of the Socialist Workers Party", *The Militant*, 6 November 1943

Labor Action, 1946

Careless thinkers say the war is over

James P Cannon (November 1945)

LENIN AND TROTSKY LINKED their revolution directly to the German Revolution. They said: "We live in a beleaguered fortress until the European revolution comes to our aid." None of the leaders of the Russian Revolution believed it could last very long if it remained by itself, alone and isolated in a capitalist world.

But the Russian Bolsheviks built better than they knew. The Revolution proved to be stronger than they or anyone else ever dreamed it could be. The Russian Revolution could not complete itself within the national borders of a single country, but in spite of that, in spite of the drawn-out delay of the European revolution to which they had looked with such hope, the revolution in Russia didn't die. It survived and struck deep roots into the soil. The property foundations laid down by the revolution — the nationalization of industry and the planned economy — proved to be far stronger than any previous calculations, even the most optimistic.

But the isolated revolution, encircled by a hostile capitalist world, could not escape the ravages of a terrible reaction which set in on Russian soil. This reaction led to the renunciation of the international perspective and a nationalistic degeneration all along the line. The regime of workers' democracy based on the Soviets was replaced by a brutal totalitarian tyranny. The Revolution was beheaded, and a whole generation of Bolsheviks was massacred. The political rule of the workers was overthrown, but the economic conquests of the Revolution displayed a great vitality. Thanks to that, the Revolution survived twenty years of bureaucratic degeneration and betrayal and revealed an enormous power on the field of battle in the war with Nazi Germany, as Trotsky had predicted it would.

Trotsky alone analyzed and explained this phenomenon, hitherto unknown and unforeseen, unique in history, of an isolated workers' state in a capitalist encirclement, mutilated and betrayed by a usurping bureaucracy, but surviving nevertheless, although in a horribly degenerated form.

Trotsky — and we following him — had far more confidence than others in the reserve powers which the Soviet economic system would display in the war. But even we underestimated it by far. Even we underestimated the tremendous resources of power that were lodged in the basic achievements of the workers' revolution of 1917 when they swept away capitalist private property and reorganized production on a nationalized and planned basis. The frightful bureaucratic degeneration proceeded at an accelerated pace during the war. How far it has gone, and how far it is yet to go before the upswing begins again, we do not know. But we are firmly convinced that the destiny of the revolution of 1917 is not yet decided. It will be decided in the further course of the war which they call "the peace".

The accusation has been made against us — and not for the first time — that our theory is a religion with which we console ourselves; that our analysis of the Soviet Union, of what has been lost and what has been saved and what is still worth defending, is a religion. Those who made that accusation in the past — and there have been many, of them — nearly always ended by placing their own faith in "democratic" imperialism. We want nothing to do with that kind of religion in any case.

Marxism and the Russian Revolution represent the union of theory and practice; the union of the word and the deed. Every tendency toward capitulation to the class enemy which we have known in the past — and we have known many — every one began with a revision of the theory and ended in repudiation of the deed. After the first flush of victory in 1917, each and every setback of the struggling Revolution, every difficulty, every defeat, brought new waves of disillusionment, and with them new experiments and new revisions of theory: and, finally, new capitulations in principle to the class enemy. The case of Professor Burnham is only the latest example.

The case of Professor Burnham is recent enough to be remembered. He began with a revision of the Marxist theory of the state and the Marxist analysis of the Russian Revolution, and ended in the camp of American imperialism. That is the most disgraceful and shameful capitulation that one can make. It represents a real betrayal of humanity because American imperialism is the enemy of humanity. One who goes over into that camp has a "religion" which no self-respecting worker ought ever to become infected with.

Stalinism itself began as a revision of Marxist theory and ended in class betrayal. Trotsky began his struggle against Stalin in the realm of a theoretical dispute over the revisionist theory of "socialism in one country" and the renunciation of the international character of the Russian Revolution. The Trotskyists understood the nature of Stalinism better, and explained it earlier, and fought it longer and harder than any others. Therefore nobody needs to incite us against Stalinism. But vulgar "anti-Stalinism" is no more revolutionary and no more attractive to us. We know where this "anti-Stalinism" leads. Up to now it has always led to the camp of "democratic" imperialism.

We can have no quarrel whatsoever with those who denounce Stalinism for its bloody crimes against the workers — and they are legion. But excessive zeal in criticizing and denouncing the Soviet Union and those who still defend it — that part of it which is worthy of defense — against imperialism — is subject to suspicion. The unbridled antagonism bordering on Russophobia — which one can notice in the atmosphere these days — is a very dangerous sentiment, especially at the present time. Because it is perfectly clear to everybody that before any peace is concluded, the mobilization for the next stage of the war, a war against the Soviet Union, is already taking place, and proceeding at a feverish pace. Why, the preparations are going forward openly on all fronts. Who can be so blind as not to see them and understand them? On the diplomatic front American imperialism is mobilizing its forces and lining up allies. On the economic front American imperialism is granting or withholding loans and credits to serve its diplomatic aims. On the propaganda front, why, the American people are being bombarded by a calculated campaign of prejudice to prepare them for another war of "democracy" — God help us! — against the Soviet Union. And even on the military front we read the brazen announcements in the papers every day now that the armies of Chiang Kai-shek engaged in the civil war in Northern China, are armed, equipped, and even partly trained by American militarists.

A tremendous wave of public sentiment against Russia, reminiscent of the early days of 1917-19, which some of us remember, is being set into motion. The present agitation recalls again the days of the Soviet-Finnish war when every democrat, every liberal, every Russophobe, every anti-Stalinist, was waving the flag for war against the Soviet Union in the service of American imperialism. It was a little difficult, and it took some courage and independence of judgment, to stand up against that terrific anti-Russian wave of sentiment and propaganda at the time of the Soviet-Finnish war. We see the same thing developing again today, helped along, as before, by the bestial crimes of Stalin. The crimes of Stalin inside the Soviet Union, in Poland, in Eastern Europe, and now in Korea, deal mortal blows to the prestige of the Soviet Union. In the occupied territories the Red Army, under Stalinist leadership, behaves in such a way as to tear the heart out of the workers and disillusion them with the Soviet Union, and weaken their allegiance and friendship for it, and thus open the way for a more effective eventual mobilization of the capitalist world against it.

Denouncing these crimes with all our souls, we must still strive to keep our balance, to see the picture whole, to see behind the crimes and filth of Stalinism the Soviet Union and the stake which the workers of the world still have in it. Trotsky predicted that the fate of the Soviet Union would be decided in the war. That remains our firm conviction. Only we disagree with some people who carelessly think that the war is over. The war has only passed through one stage and is now in the process of regroupment and reorganization for the second. The war is not over, and the revolution which we said would issue from the war in Europe, is not taken off the agenda. It has only been delayed and postponed, primarily for lack of leadership, for lack of a sufficiently strong revolutionary party. The Fourth Internationalists all over the world are working to build that leadership, to build that party.

From a speech at a meeting to mark the 28th anniversary of the Russian revolution, 4 November 1945, published in *The Militant*, 17 November 1945

Is World War 2 really not over?

Felix Morrow; SWP (1945)

Motion on Comrade Cannon's Speech on the Russian Revolution, by Felix Morrow

THE POSITION OF THE PARTY on defense of the Soviet Union was fixed at the last convention, the resolution of that convention recognizing that the slogan of defense was no longer to the fore; that "the fight for the defense of the Soviet Union against the military forces of Nazi Germany has essentially been won"; that "the present reality is... the conspiracy of the imperialists and the Kremlin bureaucracy to strangle the revolution. We therefore push to the fore and emphasize today that section of our program embodied in the slogan: Defense of the European Revolution Against All its Enemies."

Today, just as at the time of the November 1944 convention, the present reality remains the conspiracy of the Big Three against the revolution. The pushing to the fore of the slogan "Defense of the European revolution against all its enemies" and the receding into the background of the slogan of defense of the USSR remains correct and will in all probability continue to be correct for a whole historical period. War is inevitable under capitalism and therefore if the revolution is not successful a war among the Big Three is certain eventually; just as preparations for World War II began immediately after World War I, so war preparations have begun already now for World War III. But before World War III can take place, a whole series of economic and political pre-conditions must first come into existence which do not now as yet exist.

Party policy on this all-important question was stated in Comrade Warde's article, "The Big Five at London", in the November 1945 *Fourth International*: that Washington is in no mood for war; that the tide of events is now running in the opposite direction; that the growing revulsion against war since the atomic bomb bridles the war-mongers; that Washington now seeks to cash in on its war gains and therefore has material reasons for wishing peace; that the Big Three are held together by their common fear of revolution and hence Stalin remains a firm ally of the Anglo-American imperialists for this reason.

Entirely contrary to party policy, therefore, was Comrade Cannon's speech (*Militant*, November 17). Equally, his speech was in flagrant violation of the obvious facts. Particularly we condemn the following central passages in his speech:

"A tremendous wave of public sentiment against Russia, reminiscent of the early days of 1917-19, is being set into motion. The present agitation recalls again the days of the Soviet-Finnish war when every democrat, every liberal, every Russophobe, every anti-Stalinist, was waving the flag for war against the Soviet Union... we see the same thing developing again today... Trotsky predicted that the fate of the Soviet Union would be decided in the war. That remains our firm conviction. Only we disagree with some people who carelessly think that the war is over. The war has only passed through one stage and is now in the process of regroupment and reorganization for the second. The war is not over, and the revolution which we said would issue from the war in Europe is not taken off the agenda..."

We condemn the above passages for the following reasons:

1. There is no analogy between the present reality and the situation in 1917-19 or during the Soviet-Finnish war. Were there an analogy, our whole party press and activity would have to undergo a decisive change. Our principal slogan would become "Defense of the Soviet Union," our press would be devoted to that task, etc., etc. What is at issue here is not a mere matter of prediction concerning when the next war will come, but what should be the content of our political work during the whole next period.

2. Comrade Cannon's line plays into the hands of the Stalinists who are raising a hue and cry about the war danger precisely in order to cover up the fact that the Big Three remain united in their attempts to strangle the revolution. Our emphasis must be the opposite of that of the Stalinists, namely that both the Kremlin and the Stalinists abroad continue their counter-revolutionary collaboration with the bourgeoisie.

3. World War II is over. Our prediction that during the course of the war the Soviet Union would either be regenerated or would become capitalist proved erroneous. It is far better to recognize our error than to insist on our previous prediction and thus be led to the fantastic position of denying that the war is over, as Comrade Cannon has done.

4. Likewise it is better to recognize the erroneousness of the prediction of a great revolutionary wave emerging in the course of the war. A correct understanding of the slow tempo of the class struggle today in Europe provides a correct selection of the tactics necessary for today, particularly the extreme importance of such democratic demands as the republic in Belgium and Italy, the Constituent in Italy, immediate elections in Holland and Belgium, the adoption of a democratic constitution by the French Constituent, etc. Without these democratic slogans as points of departure, demands for nationalization of economy today become empty propaganda. But if Comrade Cannon's line is followed — that the war isn't over and out of it is coming the revolution — then we would have to go back to the line of the November 1945 Plenum resolution which predicted a speedy revolutionary tempo in which democratic demands would play an entirely subordinate role. But to do so would be to abandon everything which the European parties of the Fourth International have painfully had to learn during the past two years concerning the central importance today of democratic demands.

In view of the publication of the full text of Comrade Cannon's speech in the press as if it were party policy, an editorial shall be published in *The Militant* stating that the speech was not party policy and correcting the errors made by Comrade Cannon.

November 30, 1945. Motion lost; Morrow voting for.

Counter-Motion to Morrow's Motion on Comrade Cannon's speech on the Russian Revolution, adopted by the SWP Political Committee

COMRADE MORROW'S MOTION on Comrade Cannon's speech on the Russian Revolution is factionally motivated and the object of it is to "outlaw" any public party advocacy of our policy of defense of the Soviet Union against imperialist attack. It is designed to serve the minority faction as a basis for a political rapprochement with the Shachtmanites, which they have been seeking so desperately. While the resolution of the 11th Party Convention pushed to the fore "the defense of the European revolution against all its enemies," it also stated that "our policy of unconditional defense of the Soviet Union against imperialist attack retains all its validity..." From this point of view Comrade Cannon's speech was entirely within the framework of party policy.

If Comrade Morrow wishes to "re-evaluate" the Russian Question, as he indicated in his speech at the New York membership meeting, and to challenge the principled position of the party from the viewpoint of Shachtmanism, as he indicated in private conversation, let him quit playing hide and seek with the party and write a resolution and submit it to the party for discussion.

December 4, 1945. Motion carried; Morrow voting against.

SWP Internal Bulletin vol.7 no.13, December 1945

My theoretical principles of Marxism

Arne Swabeck (1946)

COMRADE GOLDMAN SPOKE in debate with Comrade Larson in Chicago August 19th. Anticipating questions over his proposal to explore the possibility of fusion with the WP, he attempted to answer them in advance. He maintains that the question of defense of the Soviet Union has receded into the background. It is not to be considered an obstacle to unity because it is unlikely to become an issue in the next five years. Further in regard to theory, he said that theory must finally be settled by history and even the theory of a socialist society will only be settled by the establishment of a socialist society. He then raised the question of what we would do if a bureaucratic form of government similar to that in Russia should be established in the United States, a socially advanced country. Would we not be forced to reconsider our theory?

There is a weakness of theoretical principle here which no one who calls himself a socialist should ever permit. This is not criticism of theory by testing it with reality, but is an unscientific attitude toward the theoretical foundations of Marxism. Marxism is scientific socialism and the only socialist movement which has remained loyal to its principles. The theory of Marxism, like theories in other fields where careful analysis and exact fidelity to material reality is necessary, is the result of lifetimes of investigation and participation in the movement of society. They are the necessary consequences of it, and the only explanation which can be given for these facts. A theory is not "only a theory" which can be treated lightly. Advancement in scientific knowledge is not possible where a light opinion is held of the scientific theory which is its foundation. At best it could only advance amid the greatest confusion. Many things such as radio waves, planets, etc. have been predicted before they were ever known because they were the necessary conclusions to the principle of science. Theory flows logically from reality and explains it. When further advance is made it takes as its point of departure the theory out of which it grows. Advance is made from it, not apart from all that has happened in the past. Marxism derives its great power from its historical necessity. It analyzes the component parts of society and points out the driving forces, the class character of it. In spite of the organized opposition, Marxism will not be destroyed. It is being forced into existence by the nature of material reality. We accept its theoretical principles as something — not which may come into existence — but which must come. When you desert Marxist theory you must inevitably lose the historical necessity for your organization. This is what has happened to many groups in the past.

Contrary to what Comrade Goldman may expect, we are not worried about disagreement with the WP over defense of the Soviet Union in the next five years. That may or may not be true. What is important is that the WP betrayed the theoretical principles of Marxism in 1940. Comrade Goldman says he agrees to this — that he was right in 1940. Then instead of seeking peace with the WP, it is they who must make their peace with Marxism. Nobody can do that for them. It is not enough to push all that has happened to one side and go on from here, even if that were possible. There must be a crystal clear understanding of the principles involved. Goldman raises the objection that it is not necessary for them to come publicly beating their breasts and confessing their errors. No one expects them to publish it in the *Chicago Tribune*, but if there has been any change they must at least tell us.

What is the WP position on the nature of the state? What is their concept of party organization? Do they still accept as part of their theoretical principle that the bureaucratic government of Russia is a new class? These differences are not "possible within one party" when that party accepts Marxist theory as necessary to its very existence. Far more fundamental than insisting that they do not publish a "separate public organ" is the necessity of coming to theoretical understanding which will eliminate the need for one.

It is true that even the theory of a socialist society will only be settled by the establishment of a socialist society. It is precisely because history settles the fate of theories that we take such an exacting and careful attitude toward Marxist theory. It must first be correct, then we must conduct our activity on the basis of it. The future of the Workers Party will be affected by its theoretical foundation. If that is incorrect they cannot possibly be the party of the proletarian revolution.

"The Minority's Attitude Toward Theory", dated 17 November 1945, and written under the name S Simmons. SWP internal Bulletin vol.8, no.1, January 1946

What kind of party should we build?

Felix Morrow (1945)

RUMORS ARE CIRCULATING concerning my relation to our faction. It is being said I never did agree with Goldman on the "organization question" and that I now wish to abandon the fight for inviting the WP to return to the party. I take this opportunity not only to set the rumors at rest but also to indicate in brief my basic views on the situation in the party.

In Trotsky's lifetime, one felt free to try to make contributions to the ideas of the movement, I well remember with what a sense of freedom I wrote my Spanish pamphlets. If I were wrong on one question or another, I was assured that when Trotsky would examine it he would do so in all comradeliness and seek to prove I was wrong without impugning my motives, character or revolutionary integrity. Trotsky created an atmosphere of free exchange of ideas, of hospitality to attempts to find what is new in a situation, of striving to add something to what has already been said.

After his death, however, the PC majority tended more and more to create a very different kind of atmosphere. Comrade Cannon calls it a conservatism justified by the fact that our resolutions since 1940 "stand up". But, as I demonstrated in "The Balance Sheet of the Discussion on Europe", repetition of formulas in the face of new events leads to flagrant violations of the traditions of our movement. The fact that the PC majority sincerely thinks it is clinging conservatively to the "fundamentals" of Trotskyism does not prevent it from throwing overboard much of the political methodology of Trotskyism. I think that Logan, Goldman and I have demonstrated that in our articles of the past year.

I shall not repeat here a summary of the political errors of the PC majority. My point is that more important than these errors is the attitude which causes them, which also leads the PC majority never to admit its errors, and which leads it to resent bitterly all differences of opinion. It is this attitude which is the foundation-stone of the false conception of the party held by Comrade Cannon and his associates.

Their attitude can be summarized as follows: to refuse to consider any difference as being a legitimate difference of opinion as between comrades who remain equally revolutionary; to dub the difference "fundamental" and fight it in the spirit of war to the death; not to argue by reason against the ideas of the opponent, but to try to discredit him by amalgams which equate the opponent with renegades and class enemies.

It is true that at times they are compelled to retreat from this attitude. Thus after more than a year of fulminations against the minority's ideas on the European situation as being fundamental differences, revisionist, etc.,, the PC majority switched to saying that the differences were secondary, matters of emphasis, etc. But within a few weeks, the PC majority reverted to its fulminations, this time against the slogan of the republic in Italy and Belgium. At this moment again we are witnessing a partial retreat of the PC majority, in connection with the minority proposal for unity negotiations with the WP, which yesterday the PC majority was condemning as conciliationism with Menshevism, disloyalty to the party, etc. But it is all too clear that the PC majority considers such retreats as tactical maneuvers and has not changed its attitude toward opponents in the party.

I consider the method of the PC majority as alien to the conception of the party of Lenin and Trotsky. Trotsky taught us that: "It is in contradictions and differences of opinion that the working out of the party's public opinion inevitably takes place." Trotsky taught us that "there should be no oversimplification and vulgarisation in the understanding of the thought that party differences, and this holds all the more for groupings, are nothing but a struggle for influence of antagonistic classes... It frequently happens that the party is able to solve one and the same problem by different means, and differences arise as to which of these means is the better, the more expeditious, the more economical. These differences may, depending on the question, embrace considerable sections of the party, but that does not necessarily mean that you have there two class tendencies."

Where Trotsky sometimes, after the most thorough discussion and after the most indubitable evidence, finally concluded that an opponent reflected the pressure of alien classes, Comrade Cannon practically always, and at the beginning of a dispute, sets the tone by declaring it is a class struggle and then, logically enough, conducts the "discussion" with the opponent in the spirit of civil war. Comrade Cannon is guilty precisely of the "oversimplification and vulgarization" that Trotsky warned against and Cannon has carried it so far that it has become a veritable system alien to the Bolshevism of Lenin and Trotsky.

I have agreed in all essentials with Goldman's criticisms of this Bolshevism-à-la-Cannon. The one point on which I disagree with Goldman is his use of the terms "Stalinist germs" and "Stalinist attitude" to describe Cannon's attitude toward differences of opinion. These terms are too easily manipulated by the Cannon group, who pretend that they could not object to our speaking of a false tendency but that they object to the term "Stalinist" because it confuses phenomena belonging to very different causes. Imputing to Goldman and myself the idea that we are saying that this is a Stalinist party, they claim that we of course will not remain in a Stalinist party and that we are making our farewell speeches to the party. Both imputations are untrue. We do not believe this is a Stalinist party, but that Bolshevism-à-la-Cannon is a false tendency which is making dangerous inroads into the authentic Bolshevik traditions of our party.

Goldman and my other associates, just as much as I, are ready to join with the PC majority in any reasonable ways and means of guaranteeing the maximum functioning of the party during this dispute. But in takes two to make such a bargain. The Cannon group, instead, embarked on the hoary but still-useful trick of creating a crisis atmosphere in the party and then blaming the minority for precipitating a crisis which interferes with the functioning of the party.

As part of this trick, the Cannon group shouted that the minority means to split, and refused to discuss the question of unity with the WP on its merits until the "split danger" is warded off. In my debate with Comrade Collins in Detroit, I stated that the minority would find ways and means to assure the party membership that we are neither splitters nor agents of the WP in order to attempt to got the Cannon group to discuss unity with the WP on the merits of the question. I was ready to go to the length of dissolving our faction.

Upon reflection, however, it is all too clear to me that such a step would not serve the interests of the party. It would not succeed in its immediate aim of getting a calm and conscientious discussion of unity with the WP. It was before we formed our faction that Comrade Cannon had already denounced Goldman and me as agents of the WP. Had we dissolved our faction, Cannon's fire would then have concentrated on our talks with Shachtman. Had we stopped talking to Shachtman, Cannon's fire would have concentrated on the "anti-Bolshevism" of Morrow and Goldman — in short, on anything but rational discussion of the resolution on unity. We would have dissolved our faction without gaining the aim of a conscientious discussion.

Far more important, however, is the fact that dissolution of the faction would only lead at best to a postponement of the question of which our resolution on unity with the WP is only a part: the contending conceptions of a Bolshevik party. Our resolution on unity is merely one example of how a really Bolshevik leadership would conduct itself. Our resolution flows from our basic conception of a Bolshevik party as one in which differences of opinion, such as those between us and the WP, are compatible with membership in one party; our conception of the party as a broad unity of the proletarian vanguard and not a tight-knit faction as the PC majority conceives the party.

It is better to accept this fight for what it is, a single fight in which all disputed questions are interrelated.

I now see that one of the most important of these questions is the nature of a faction and the right to form a faction. The Cannon group has made this question important by distorting it beyond recognition, and the minority has the duty to pose it correctly and explain it. Here I limit myself to recalling what, Trotsky warned, is the end-result of such a hue and cry against factions as the Cannon group is now conducting: "If factions are not wanted, there must not be any permanent groupings; if permanent groupings are not wanted, temporary groupings must be avoided; finally, in order that there be no temporary groupings, there must be no differences of opinion, for wherever there are two opinions, people inevitably group together." Cannon's fight against our having a faction is in the last analysis a fight against any right of differences of opinion in the party. To dissolve our faction would tend to give credibility to Cannon's conception, and would go a long way to fastening Cannon's conception irrevocably on the party. This result would be a hundred-fold worse for the party than any possible immediate gain for the discussion of the unity resolution which would result from dissolution of our faction.

To conclude, I repeat it is better to accept the present dispute for what it is, a single issue in which all questions in dispute are interrelated. What kind of party do we want? That is the issue, and on it I was and remain in complete solidarity with my associates in our faction. August 29, 1945

Socialist Workers Party Internal Bulletin vol.8 no.5, September 1945

You cling to outworn formulas

Felix Morrow (1946)

WITH EACH SUCCEEDING DAY it will become more and more impossible to repeat the outworn formulas of the pre-conference resolution. This mad clinging to outworn formulas — that is the source of all the disputes between us. What Comrade Cannon calls our "unchanging program". There is the heart of the dispute. For Cannon and his followers the program must not have rude hands laid upon it; it is sacred, inviolable. Comrade Cannon described his method well-enough in a letter of August 16, 1944. He wrote:

"This carefulness, this aversion to the practice of going off half-cocked, this habit of waiting to think things through before we speak, has been denominated 'conservatism' by light-minded feuilleton writers, who imagine themselves to be alter politicians. But it is this very 'conservatism' that has given all our previous resolutions since the death of the Old Man their thought-out character and made them stand up from year to year as supplements logically flowing from one unchanging program, and like the program itself, needing no fundamental revision."

"Unchanging program". "No fundamental revision". This is the method of Cannon and of the Pre-conference resolution. According to their method, it is more virtuous to say the earth is flat than to go off half-cocked and say it's round. I must confess that Cannon used to scare me with his thunderous proclamations against changing the program. I accepted the implication that the onus, the burden of proof, was on the one who wanted to change something. But that's a lot of nonsense. There is no burden of proof in these matters; those who want to stand still and those who want to change are equals, equally responsible for defending their positions.

What hair-raising nonsense the majority has defended in the name of the unchanging program. In the name of the unchanging program, Comrade Cannon, you taught the following things: That our proletarian military policy means that we should telescope together overthrow of capitalism and defense of the country against foreign fascism. That the Polish revolutionists should subordinate themselves to the Russian Army. That there is an objectively revolutionary logic brought about by the Russian victories. That naked military dictatorships are the only possible governments in Europe because it is impossible to set up a new series of Weimar republics in Europe. That American imperialism is at least as predatory as Nazi imperialism in its methods in Europe. That it is theoretically impossible for America to help rebuild or feed Europe. That there are no democratic illusions in Europe. That there are no illusions about American imperialism. That amid the revolutionary upsurge it is reformist to call for the republic in Greece, Italy and Belgium or the Constituent Assembly. That to speak of a Stalinist danger to the European revolution is only possible for a professional defeatist. That the fate of the Soviet Union would be decided by the war but only careless people think the war is over. What happened to those planks in your unchanging program, Comrade Cannon? I notice they aren't in the International Resolution. Is their disappearance, to use your expression, a typographical error?...

It is fruitful, comrades, to look back and see how this dispute began. Central to our understanding of the dispute is to understand the situation created by the death of Trotsky. The death of Trotsky was bound, sooner or later, to lead to a political crisis of the Fourth International, and that is what we are confronted with — a political crisis on an international scale. It was bound to happen because Trotsky's death created a gap which nobody could fill either individually or collectively.

In answer to the "independent thinkers" Cannon used to say "Trotsky is my brain." When the brain died. Cannon and Gabriel [Michel Pablo, or Raptis] tried to freeze the program as it stood. That is the source of the political crisis. In Trotsky's lifetime, his genius and authority made the necessary process of change relatively easy. There were of course disputes and splits but they were reduced to a minimum not only by Trotsky's authority but also by his readiness to change when change was indicated.

One example in the history of our own party will indicate what I mean. In 1938 the Republican Congressman Ludlow introduced a proposed constitutional amendment for a referendum on war. I was then in Minneapolis editing the *Northwest Organizer* of the teamsters' movement. I was for critical support of the Ludlow amendment and proceeded to show in the pages of the *Northwest Organizer* how revolutionary Marxists could make revolutionary propaganda through critical support of the referendum on war. The question came up in the Political Committee. Burnham supported my position. Comrade Goldman opposed me sharply. Comrade Shachtman howled for my reformist head. Comrade Cannon, if I recall, took the same position as Comrade Goldman. The PC voted overwhelmingly against supporting the referendum on war. Trotsky saw the decision in the Political Committee minutes. He understood the error immediately, brilliantly demonstrated the transitional character of the slogan of a referendum on war. His arguments and his authority swiftly mustered unanimity in the PC. That is how the referendum on war was borrowed from Congressman Ludlow and became part of our transition program.

It is easy to imagine what would have happened had the referendum on war first arisen as a problem after Trotsky's death. What profound arguments would have been offered against it! Comrade Warde would show that it isn't in our transition program, and it is not an accident that it isn't in there. Comrade Wright would marshal scores of quotations from Trotsky to show that war can be prevented only by overthrowing capitalism. Comrade Cannon would prove conclusively that it is another petty-bourgeois deviation.

I shudder to think what would have happened had Trotsky died before he switched positions on the Labor Party, leaving behind all the bad arguments he used up to 1938 against advocating a Labor Party. How those quotations would have been poured over the head of anyone daring to propose a change in position on the Labor Party. Spoon-fed the pap about "unchanging" program, how many of the new members of the party — and they are now the majority — know that we changed our position on the war-referendum and the Labor Party as recently as 1938?

Trotsky's death made inevitable a great political crisis in the Fourth International, it was bound to start just as soon as new questions confronted the movement, as new questions will always rise as the years pass. Especially the political crisis was bound to come after World War II and its aftermath confront us with new questions...

The majority was blindly determined to cling to the unchanging program, while Logan, Goldman and I were trying to come to grips with events which more and more failed to fit into the prognosis with which we entered the war. What was that prognosis? The Manifesto of the Pre-conference dares to say that that prognosis has been confirmed. It can do so only by tailoring its quotations and leaving out the heart of the matter. For the first time in the history of the Trotskyist movement we can't say about our documents that we have nothing to unsay and nothing to conceal. What must be unsaid and what the Manifesto and the resolution try to conceal are the two main ingredients of our prognosis of 1940.

1. That in the course of the war the Soviet Union would either collapse into capitalism or be regenerated and victorious. In either case we would be through with the problem of Stalinism. Soviet victories, bringing the Red Army into Europe, would inspire a wave of revolution which would in turn topple Stalinism.

2. That, galvanized by the ravages of the war and freed of the incubus of Stalinism, the European proletariat would surge forward in a wave of proletarian revolution (the first revolution, Trotsky thought, would come early in the war) on a greater scale than in 1917-1921. This did not necessarily mean immediate establishment of Soviet power throughout Europe, but certainly meant the emergence of great mass parties of the Fourth International. (By 1948, Trotsky was sure, the Trotskyist membership would number in the millions.)

Trotsky tried to teach us to understand that it is necessary to make a prognosis but equally necessary to understand that it is impossible to guess the tempos in advance for a prolonged period and hence one must introduce the necessary correctives into it in the course of experience. This is what the minority tried to do since 1943. The majority answer was that the real issue was not one over tempo but over fundamental perspective and program. Now, in the International Resolution, the majority explains that the only mistakes it made were mistakes about tempo. But the term tempo has been rendered in the course of this dispute so meaningless that it is better to say; yes, we have profound differences in perspective and program, meaning by these terms the estimate of what is to come during the next few years and what is to be done about it. Please take note that we are talking of the short-term perspective and not what is to come in a decade or more.

We definitively parted company in July 1943. The dispute began with estimating the significance of the fall of Mussolini. The majority proceeded to take it as a complete confirmation of our 1940 prognosis. It wrote along its line in *The Militant*, and I wrote along a very different line in *Fourth International*, True, I didn't yet understand the full implications, but comrades who want to understand the roots of this struggle could fruitfully go back and compare the two lines at that time.

You won't find the majority's line about the fall of Mussolini in the International Resolution although one might think at least a passing estimate of that event ought to be in the first International Resolution of the Fourth International in six years. You will find it, however, in a speech of E. R. Frank published as late as the February 1945 *Fourth International*. There, slandering the German comrades, falsely attributing to them the idea that "They consider the European revolution already defeated," he refutes them by the following:

"We base ourselves on the rising working-class revolution. They consider the European revolution already defeated. We knew that out of the war would come a gigantic revolutionary explosion, above all in Europe, and we were confidently preparing for it. And less than a year after our 1942 convention, Italian fascism crashed to the ground. We saw in the downfall of Mussolini and the beginning of the Italian revolution the most striking confirmation of our analysis and program, and by the same token, an annihilating refutation of all the theories and speculations of our enemies. We immediately proceeded in our press to subject the Italian events to a thorough-going analysis and point to the road ahead."

The alleged thorough-going analysis to which E. R. Frank refers was based on a false, arbitrary, obviously factually untrue idea: the idea that Mussolini had been directly overthrown by a revolutionary uprising of the masses. That idea was necessary in order to claim the Italian events as a confirmation of our 1940 prognosis. But it was not true.

Recently our Italian section's Central Committee adopted a resolution on the situation in Italy. It makes clear that no one can understand what has happened in Italy unless he understands that Mussolini was not overthrown by the masses but by a palace coup d'etat. I saw a translation of this resolution the other day on Comrade Carsten's desk; I trust it will be published.

In the months between July and the October 1943 Plenum, the Italian experience unfolded and mirrored the future of western Europe: the development of bourgeois democracy; the revival of the dominance of the traditional reformist workers' parties; the central role of such democratic questions as the republic and the Constituent Assembly; illusions about American imperialism. I tried to explain this at the Plenum and was met with a vicious slander campaign. All this is presumably what the International Resolution now admits to have been correct criticisms of leftist exaggerations.

The Italian experience showed what had happened to our 1940 prognosis of a wave of proletarian revolution in the course of the war. Instead of the masses overthrowing fascism as we had expected, fascism was being over- thrown by its imperialist opponents, not only in Italy but in Germany and occupied Europe as well. Such a purely imperialist conclusion to the war would mean continuation of European capitalism. The one chance to prevent this was the transformation of the ideology of the resistance movement. But to do this one had to be in it. Our comrades weren't in it thank to the sectar- ian prejudices which they shared with the SWP majority.

These sectarian prejudices were buttressed by their theory of the revolu- tionary consequences of Russian victories. What a terrible tragedy! They ig- nored the revolutionary movement which was everywhere about them, the armed proletariat and peasantry of western Europe, and instead saw the coming revolution being brought by the Russian Army. Instead of preparing to play a role in the coming Paris insurrection, they looked to the East for the Red dawn. There is irony, pitiful irony, in this awful error...

Try to realize what were the consequences of it in Europe... Here, for ex- ample, is a typical-enough issue, *La Vérité* [French Trotskyist paper] of Feb- ruary 10, 1944. Its main headlines read as follows: "The flags of the Red Army will join themselves with our red flags." I am reading from the main article:

"Stalin knows that with the advance of the Soviet Army a general upris- ing can break out in Europe. Tomorrow, ten thousand factory Soviets can cover the old continent. He knows also that it is less than certain that these workers' and peasants' Soviets created in the advanced European countries will passively obey the parasitic bureaucracy of Moscow. Stalin cannot ig- nore the fact that he cannot count upon his army to put down the revolu- tionary workers of Europe. The army of the USSR will not wipe out the Soviets of Berlin, of Budapest and of Paris. It is these Soviets on the contrary that will remind the Russian army that it is a Soviet army. The communist revolution in Europe will be the end of exploiting capitalism and also the end of the parasitic bureaucracy. The Moscow usurpers know it. But the Red Army continues to advance..."

Was this idea, that the Russian army was bringing the socialist revolution, that the Russian army was not the instrumentality of the Stalinist bureau- cracy, that its red flags were still the flags of revolution, was this idea some awful aberration of the isolated French comrades in the Paris underground? Or was it, as some people pretend, an aberration of John G. Wright?

No comrades, it was the common idea of the Fourth International. Parties of our international divided by oceans and without contact for many years were simultaneously repeating the same idea. Seven months after the issue of *La Vérité* that I have quoted, the very able leadership of the Bolshevik- Leninist Party of India met in conference, in September 1944, and adopted a resolution on "The Red Army in Eastern Europe" which stated:

"...particularly the entry of the Red Army will give a powerful impetus to the revolutionary movement. For these reasons proletarian revolutionaries will not in any way modify the unconditional support given hitherto to the Red Army in its actions against the forces of imperialism, as the Red Army leaves Russian territory in pursuit of the German army. The entry of the Red Army into these territories will release latent forces and give such an impetus to the revolutionary movement as to create a pre-revolutionary situation in Eastern Europe, the heightening of which is of inestimable importance for world revolutionary perspectives."

The Indian comrades went on to warn that "it is certain that the Red Army will be brought into conflict with the developing revolution, either to crush it completely or to bureaucratise the social conquests made." Their revolutionary understanding made it impossible for them to blind themselves to what the Red Army is. What is important, however, is that in spite of this they were saying, as our French comrades, that the entry of the Red Army into Europe would give an impetus to the revolutionary movement. Four months later, the organ of our Belgian party, *La Voie de Lénine* of February 4, 1945, gave as its main headline, "The new soviet victories, are they preparing the German revolution?" it answered the question affirmatively, the first paragraph saying:

"Scarcely have the soviet troops penetrated into (German) Silesia than outbreaks take place at Ratibor, Gleiwitz and Beuthon. The tremendous advance of the Red Army can play a capital role in the uprising which is preparing little by little in Germany against Hitler".

Three months later, in the May Day 1945 issue of the organ of our comrades in Chile, *El Militante*, the headline reads: "Will Europe be Soviet?," and the question is answered affirmatively, the first paragraph reading:

"When *El Militante* arrives on the street, making its homage to the first of May, Berlin, the capital of German imperialism, the centre of fascism, will already be in the hands of the Red Army and of the German workers who have risen writing epic pages against their totalitarian oppressors."

This was the universal theory of the Fourth International. Abler and more educated comrades advanced it in India with more intelligent reservations than the crude formulas of the leadership in Chile, but they shared with all other Trotskyists — except the Workers Party — the idea that Russian victories, the entry of the Russian army into Europe, would give an impetus to social revolution.

What is the source of this theory? Trotsky's writings of 1939-40 on the occupation of Poland and the war in Finland. It seemed to Trotsky that when the Russian army entered new territory and sought to turn private property into state property, it can do so only by methods of civil war. Hence he wrote that the bureaucracy "gives an impulse to the socialist revolution through bureaucratic methods" in its occupation of Poland. Hence he wrote of the Kremlin's "appeal to independent activity on the part of the masses in the new territories — and without such an appeal, even if worded with extreme caution, it is impossible to constitute a new regime". And even more categorically he wrote about what would have happened if the Finnish war had continued: "Occupation presupposed a social overturn which would be impossible without involving the workers and poorer farmers in civil war."

Trotsky sharply distinguished this first stage — the uprising of the masses — from the second in which the Stalinist bureaucracy attempts to crush the masses. The distinction meant: Stalin can achieve the second stage in godforsaken Galicia, but if victorious Red Armies occupy advanced countries in western Europe the, socialist revolution, to which the bureaucracy is compelled to give this impulse, will get beyond the control of the bureaucracy and overthrow it.

After Trotsky's death, and especially after the USSR survived the first year of war, this idea that the bureaucracy is compelled against its will to "give an impulse to the socialist revolution through bureaucratic methods" became the main justification for Soviet defensism in the Fourth International. The quotations I have already given from the world Trotskyist press show that.

This theory has proven completely false. In eastern Europe the Soviet occupation took place without risings of the masses; it is now clear that the 1939 rising in Poland was not, as Trotsky thought, a necessary "interaction between the masses, the workers' state and the bureaucracy." In 1939 the illusions of the masses about the "liberating" Red Army played a great role; there was also deliberate staging by the bureaucracy which, allied then to Hitler, needed the "rising" to show the masses in the democracies that the USSR was different from its ally. In 1945 there were fewer illusions in Eastern Europe about the Red Army; still more important, the bureaucracy had to consider its present democratic allies. The point is that the will of the bureaucracy was sufficient to prevent risings, rather than risings being dictated to the bureaucracy by statification of property. As to risings which could get out of the control of the bureaucracy, the very possibility did not arise.

Comrade Natalia saw this very clearly, and wrote in this vein to the party in 1944. Under her pressure, and appalled by the debacle of our theory of the revolutionary consequences of Soviet victory, the SWP majority yielded at the last moment and inserted in the convention resolution one of those famous "literary and clarifying amendments" which the membership had never seen or discussed — the idea that defense of the USSR has receded into the background in the face of the Stalinist danger to the European revolution.

Comrade Natalia's proposal was new and unprecedented. It was based on what was new: the reactionary consequences of Soviet victory. Comrade Natalia's proposal to relegate the slogan of defense to the background was, in my opinion, a half-way house to dropping the slogan of the defense altogether from the program. One cannot defend (fight for) victories which bring reactionary consequences. The consequences of Russian victory in World War Two demonstrate irrefutably that they would be the same consequences in any foreseeable war conducted by the Stalinist bureaucracy. That is why I shall shortly present theses on the Russian question in which I shall propose not only, as Comrade Natalia originally proposed, to withdraw the slogan of defense from the foreground, but to withdraw it altogether from the program of the Fourth International.

If further proof were necessary as to the imperative need for withdrawing the slogan of defense, it is provided by the horrible example of what Russian defensism is doing to the press of the Fourth International. To limit myself only to *The Militant*, and only to a few passing examples:

Try to find out from *The Militant* the Trotskyist position on the Chinese student demonstrations before the Soviet consulates against Russian imperialism in Manchuria. Try to find out what Trotskyists should say about the Polish student demonstrations in Cracow on Polish Independence Day (May 3) against Stalin's puppet government. Try to find out what Trotskyism says about the Stalinist attempts to force the German Socialists into a totalitarian "united" party, or about the profound significance of the overwhelming vote of those Socialists against the "unity".

You won't find these things and a hundred like questions in *The Militant*. But you will find an article on the "Kremlin's policy inside Germany" sent special to *The Militant* (April 27 issue) from the International Secretariat which approvingly quotes "an important article" from the *Economist*: that in the Russian zone there exists "a fair amount of resemblance to the factory democracy of the early years of the Russian revolution." As if to underline this, this article appears side by side on one page with one headed: "Rule of US Imperialism brings starvation to people of Germany."

Let me repeat. That article about factory democracy in the Russian zone was not something cooked up in *The Militant* office to fill a hole in the paper, it was sent by the International Secretariat.

How can such madness be? The answer is the same as the answer to all the disputes we have had during these three years. The majority leadership blindly clings to outworn formulas, to the unchanging program, and hence must distort, must falsify what is being revealed by the changing reality. Our theory said there must be revolutionary consequences to Soviet victory and, by God, the majority will find them even if it has to invent them. Out of ten thousand press clippings on the terrible consequences of Soviet occupation of Germany, the International Secretariat picks the rare exception which talks nonsense about factory democracy.

And to what terrible, terrible, reactionary positions the Russian defensists are led by their theory! I confess, I did not anticipate that the Pre-conference resolution would go so far as to oppose the withdrawal of the Russian troops from the countries it has occupied. I never dreamt that in a resolution of the Fourth International would appear this paragraph: "In the oppressor countries (USA, Great Britain, France insofar as Germany is concerned) the Fourth International actively defends the right of the occupied nations to independence and demands the recall of the occupation troops."

Russia is thus deliberately left out of the list of the powers which are oppressing Germany! The other troops must leave but not the Russian troops!

Our Russian party is not to tell the Russian workers that the Russian army must get out of the countries it is holding against the will of the occupied peoples! And this foul line, this capitulation to Stalinism, is proclaimed in the name of Trotsky!

Here we can see the profoundly reactionary character of the majority's line not only on the Russian question but also on the national question. The national struggle for independence of the occupied peoples is not a radical-enough struggle for Cannon and Gabriel, they want nothing less than the proletarian revolution. Therefore? Therefore no struggle to throw the Russian armies out of the countries they are oppressing.

The facts are now so clear that the majority must admit that there is national oppression in eastern Europe, But they admit it only to deny the need for the national struggle today. They do so in the following paragraph of the resolution: "Just like the German occupation, the present occupation of Europe by the Anglo-American, French and Russian armies is also the cause of a certain national oppression. Given the perspective of a definite decline in the revolutionary movement, the prolongation for several years of this occupation could throw certain nations back to the level of colonial countries and open a new era of national struggles and wars".

This nonsense is proclaimed in the name of the unchanging program. But it has nothing whatsoever in common with Leninism. Leninism teaches that the national struggle of oppressed countries is our struggle, and that is true even when it is merely called "a certain national oppression." Leninism teaches us that the national struggle is not a separate stage arising after a decline of the revolutionary movement, but is inextricably part of the revolutionary movement. That is how it happened in the Russian Revolution and that is how it will happen again in the European revolution: national struggles occurring simultaneously with and intermingled with the development of the proletarian revolution. Yesterday it was still the ABC of Leninism that the October revolution succeeded because it supported all national struggles. Today this ABC is condemned as the revisionism of the "Three Theses."

What is the national question? it is the struggle for democracy against the foreign invader. The revolutionary party demands from the occupying power all the democratic rights, including the right of the people to choose its own government freely, which can only be done, isn't that clear, comrades, by ridding the country of the occupying troops. He who does not demand the recall of the Russian troops can spout words about being for the democratic rights and freedom of the occupied peoples, but his words are empty, they are lies. That's what Lenin taught us about the Austro-Marxists who were for autonomy, for complete democracy, for everything you please to be granted to the subject peoples of the Austrian Empire but not far the ousting of the Austrian troops. The right of self-determination is the right to throw out the foreign invader.

Themselves not a little frightened at where their line is carrying them, the majority tries to cover it up by phrases and formulas borrowed from the classical centrist position on the national question. Here is just one example, in the section of the resolution on "Tasks in the Countries Occupied by the USSR": "In the European zone occupied by the Red Army, our sections... tolerate the presence of the Red Army only to the extent that it is a friendly proletarian armed force having as its objective to guarantee the fulfillment of agrarian reform and the State-ization of the means of production against imperialism and against national reactionary elements, without hindering in any way whatsoever the free development of the working-class movement."

What is this centrist ambiguity doing in a Trotskyist resolution? This is the most classical centrist formula: "we support... only to the extent that." Bolshevism scorns such claptrap. Bolshevism answers the question: is the Red Army "a friendly proletarian armed force... without hindering in any way whatsoever the free development of the working-class movement"? The answer, written in the blood of tens of millions of German, Austrian, Romanian, Yugoslav, Bulgarian, Polish workers and peasants — in their blood spilled by the GPU or drained from them in slave labor — is that the Red Army is no Red Army, is not a friendly proletarian force, is instead the main enemy of the proletariat of the countries it occupies and oppresses. He who can talk about the Red Army as a friendly proletarian force has lost his head as a Marxist, has lost his feeling for proletarian democracy, and has objectively capitulated to Stalinism.

Why does the International Resolution oppose recall of the Russian troops from the countries they oppress? A terrible answer is indicated in the section on the Soviet Union (pages 6-7) in the following paragraphs:

"In order that Soviet economy rise again, in order that this revival be accomplished without resorting to the exclusive or principal aid of American imperialism, which would take advantage of this opportunity to destroy the USSR's independence, in order that the USSR gain a certain protective cover against the pressure of world imperialism, the Soviet bureaucracy finds it necessary to extend its strategic zones and to draw on the economic resources of other countries, in Europe and Asia alike...

"In its defense against both the external pressure of imperialism and of the internal reactionary elements, and in its efforts to rapidly revive the Soviet economy, the bureaucracy's best chances for success lie in the economic contribution of the countries now under Soviet control."

What does this mean, except to justify what you call Soviet expansionism and what I call bureaucratic imperialism? And this you dare do in the name of the unchanging program which still, let us hope, says that we are not in favour of seizures of new territory by the Kremlin bureaucracy.

To justify its continuation of Russian defensism, the International Resolution is compelled to pretend that what we based Russian defensism on in the past has now happened, namely that the entry of the Red Army gave an impetus to the socialist revolution by bureaucratic methods. But we didn't in 1940 mean by this the statification of property. That wasn't the basis of our revolutionary hope. Our hope was based on the idea that in order to statify the property the bureaucracy, against its will, would have to precipitate an uprising of the masses. And now, in spite of all that has happened, the International Resolution dares to say that this happened. It says it on page 8: "The Soviet occupation and control have given an impetus, although in varying degrees, to civil war and the development of a regime of dual power... the promotion of organs of dual power (committees for the control of production and trade, committees of poor peasants to carry out the agrarian reforms)."

So, comrades, the Trotskyist world movement is to proclaim that Stalin's Potemkin villages are the real thing — that the farcical pseudo-committees he sets up are veritably organs of dual power. What is dual power? It is a regime in which the formal power is still in the hands of a bourgeois or Stalinist government but the essence of real power is already in the hands of the rising proletariat organized in Soviets or the equivalent of Soviets. That is what "a regime of dual power" has meant in the dictionary of our movement. Is that what exists in the Russian zone? So you say on page 8. But ten pages later (p. 18) we read: "In the part of Europe controlled by the USSR, the working class movement has in several places attained the level of dual power, but it has experienced at the same time the bureaucratic straitjacket and the demoralization which are provoked by the Stalinist bureaucracy."

Dual power in a bureaucratic straitjacket: that is certainly a novel terminological contribution to Marxism, no doubt in the name of the unchanging program.

The International Resolution is enabled by such mumbo-jumbo to proclaim the European situation more revolutionary than ever before. By turning the minus of the Russian occupation into the plus of dual power by such a mad method one can call anything revolutionary.

More revolutionary than ever before. Please ask yourselves a simple question. When was the situation in western Europe more revolutionary — in August 1944 when the proletariat was armed or today when it has been disarmed?

The Manifesto of the Pre-conference lists the factors whose existence defines a revolutionary situation, and asserts they exist in Europe. Time presses, I shall limit myself to one of them: that the petty-bourgeois masses are following the workers' parties. But what is the meaning of the French referendum results, in which the proletariat voted one way and the petty-bourgeoisie (the peasantry) the other way? Or of the Belgian elections in which the same division took place? Again, the same thing in the Dutch elections? But enough.

One final word: The International Resolution correctly says: "Our European sections, having for a long time prior to the war lived on general propaganda, and then during the war having lived isolated from the masses, inexperienced and in the strictest illegality, are today finding it difficult to break with obsolete ideas and methods of organization and activity." Correct, but very significantly it appears in the resolution in the wrong place, under the wrong heading, "Organizational Tasks." The obsolete ideas that the European sections are finding difficult to break with are not in the first instance organizational ideas, but political ones, and they come precisely from the people who are complaining about it. The fish stinks from the head, as always. The chief culprit is the international leadership, whose theory of the revolutionary situation bars from aiding the sections in formulating programs of action with which to go to the masses.

Just one fantastic example: not a word in this very, very long document about the question of food. The famine is upon Europe, not for a day or a month but for years to come, it is the question which preoccupies every man, woman and child in Europe, it is the question which defines the relations between Europe and America, it is the political question, and it isn't even mentioned in this document, much less is it submitted to a program of action for struggle against the famine. That alone is enough to characterize the bankruptcy of the political line of this document.

"Minority Report to Plenum", May 19, 1946. SWP internal Bulletin
vol.8 no.8, July 1946

Socialist Appeal,
12 March 1938

11. War and the USA

The USA entered World War 2 on 8 December 1941. The Japanese bombing of Pearl Harbour on 7 December 1941 was only a trigger; the US had helped the UK from early in the war, applied economic sanctions on Japan since 1940, and since August 1941 imposed a potentially crippling oil embargo on Japan.

World in Flames

Workers Party (1941)

THE UNITED STATES IS NOW at war with the Axis powers. Only twenty-two years after the signing of the Versailles Peace Treaty, which brought an end to the "war to end all wars", the United States finds itself a full-fledged participant in the Second World War, a war that is more destructive, more futile and hopeless than the war of 1914-1918.

All the peace treaties, all the disarmament agreements, all the non-aggression acts have been torn to shreds. All the solemn assurances that peace would be preserved, all the pledges that the United States would not enter the war have been flouted and discarded by the very statesmen who made them. Like the people of the rest of the world, the people of the United States too have yearned only for peace and freedom, and security; now all their hopes have been shattered and their faith betrayed.

Every worker, every person who cherishes liberty and despises oppression, is a sworn enemy of the Axis powers. The infamous regime of Hitler is justly hated for its cruel destruction of the labor movement in Germany, its bloody persecution of freedom of thought and organization and action; for its hideous oppression of the people of Austria, Czechoslovakia, Poland, Norway, Holland, France and most of the other lands of Europe whom it has deprived of all national independence and over whom it rules with the iron heel and the lash. The regime of Mussolini is justly hated for its oppression of the people of Italy, for its cynical ravishment of Ethiopia. The regime of Japanese imperialism is justly hated for the bitter sufferings it has imposed upon the people of its own land, no less than for the bestial appetite which has led to even greater sufferings for the people of Korea, Manchuria and China.

This noble hatred of tyranny has been cunningly exploited by the imperialist statesmen of the so-called democracies for the purpose of whipping up a pro-war sentiment among the masses of the people. The people have been systematically stuffed with lying assurances and hypocritical pretensions that this will be, this is, a war against fascism and for democracy and national freedom.

When the Second World War broke out in 1939, and long before it broke out, the Workers Party warned the working class and the people as a whole against the monstrous deception being practiced upon them. We declared, from the very beginning, that the Second World War, like the First, was a war between two great imperialist comps to decide, with the blood and misery of the people, which of the imperialist groups shall dominate the world, which of them shall oppress and exploit the hundreds of millions of colonial slaves, which of them shall bestride the commercial lanes of the earth, which of them shall control the sources of raw materials and cheap labor that guarantee a continuous flow of profits to the capitalist monopolists, which of them shall be master of the fields of capital investment. We declared, from the very beginning, that Hitler is fighting to replace the British Empire with the World Empire of Germany; that England is fighting to preserve the World Empire which she has sucked of its wealth for centuries; that Japan is fighting to drive its rivals out of the Orient in order to become undisputed master of an Empire of Asia and the Pacific; that the United States will inevitably enter the war in order to challenge all competitors and to assert its imperialist rights to mastery of the world and its wealth. We warned, from the very beginning, of the lies and deceptions of all the governments — against the falsehood of the Axis that it is fighting for "national socialism" and against "plutocracy" in its fighting for "national socialism" and against "plutocracy" in its drive for imperialist power; against the falsehood of the Allies that they are fighting for "democracy" and "national sovereignty" and against fascism in their drive for imperialist power.

The Workers Party, whose very existence and principles and life are bound up with a great tradition of struggle throughout the world against all despotism and oppression, against exploitation in any form which has an unbroken and proud record of opposition to fascism everywhere, now feels called upon to reiterate its fundamental position.

We know that the government of the United States, for its own imperialist reasons, is determined to carry through the war to a victorious conclusion against its rivals. We know also that the majority of the working class and the people of the United States are at present supporting the government in the successful prosecution of the war. We cannot but acknowledge this reality. Yet, our loyalty to the principles and interests of the working class, of the exploited and oppressed in this country and in every other country, our attachment to the principles of socialism and of international solidarity of the people, compels us to restate our position now, especially when the war has finally broken out in this country and when we shun more than ever before any concealment of our program.

This is not a war for democracy and against fascism It is the very same statesmen who thus designate the war that bear their full share of responsibility for the rise to power of Hitler and Mussolini. It is the very same statesmen who are responsible for the systematic undermining of all democratic rights and democratic institutions in their own countries. It is the very same statesmen who made possible the shipments of oil to Japan to power the death-dealing seacraft and aircraft of Tokyo, the shipments of scrap-iron converted into the very bombs that brought destruction to China, to Hawaii and the Philippines.

This is a war for the mastery of the world, and not for national independence. Japan's oppression of China has its counterpart in the three centuries of British oppression of India. In these two cases is symbolized the imperialist reality behind all the pretensions of the democratic spokesmen on the one side and the Axis on the other. This is a war of finance capital; this is a war for oil and steel and coal; this is a war for rubber and tin and tungsten; this is a war for stocks and bonds and profits; this is a war for rule over countless millions of colonial slaves. This is a war conceived and bred by world capitalism — not by this or that country alone, not by this or that statesman alone, but by the rotten, decaying, poisonous reaction of the capitalist system which these statesmen represent and defend.

That is why the Roosevelt government has so easily obtained the unanimous support of all the representatives of capitalism now that the war is actually and formally on. That is why the spurious opposition of the so-called "isolationists" and "non-interventionists" collapsed overnight. That is why the Lindberghs and Wheelers and Nyes and Hoovers, why even the rabid *Chicago Tribune* and *New York Daily News*, rushed to take a position behind the government and for full support to the prosecution of the war. And that is also why the whole labor bureaucracy, from Green through Murray to Lewis, the representatives of capitalism inside the labor movement, also rushed to assure the government of servile support.

The Workers Party, however, as the uncompromising foe of capitalism and capitalist war, cannot and does not give any political support to the government and the war. The Workers Party declares openly that it does not place a single iota of confidence in the Roosevelt government, in its war, or in its conduct of the war. As a minority in the country, the Workers Party is naturally obliged to adapt and adjust its actions to the views of the majority of the people. Yet we are convinced that the views we hold as a minority today will be the views of the majority of the people tomorrow.

The Workers Party is not indifferent to the struggle for national independence. It is, on the contrary, an intense partisan of national freedom, as it is a partisan of people's freedom in general. But this is not a war for national defense; it is a war of imperialist rivalry. The interests of national defense, like the interests of internationalism of the peoples, therefore demand, now more than ever, the unremitting struggle to defend the interests and rights and standards of the masses of the American nation — the workers and poor farmers of this country — from the attacks of the capitalist ruling class. It is to this struggle that our party rededicates itself today.

We call the attention of every worker to the dangers that threaten him in the war.

Under the cry of "national unity," of "sacrifice for the war," the ruling class, which has again begun to amass fabulous war profits, is seeking to place the terrible and mounting war burden upon the shoulders of the workers and poor farmers. At the same time, the drive is on to deprive the working class and the labor movement of the fundamental rights they acquired in the course of long years of bitter struggle. Congress is filled with bills aimed at depriving labor of its basic defensive weapon, the right to strike — a right without which the right to organize becomes an empty formality. The right of free speech and free press has already been given the first blow by the indictment and conviction, in Minneapolis, of the leaders of the Socialist Workers Party. The blows directed at the most militant sections of the labor movement are meant for the labor movement as a whole in the days to follow.

Labor must be on its guard. Precisely during the war, it must be doubly vigilant, doubly jealous in the protection of its interests.

The Workers Party therefore calls upon the working class to rally around a fighting program of self-defense. Unitedly and resolutely, let us demand:

Hands off the right to organize, and the right to strike!

Hands off the right of free speech, free press, free assembly!

Hands off the standards of living of the working class!

No sweating of labor to the point of exhaustion, says the Workers Party. Double pay for all overtime work.

The people are being conscripted into the army — conscript the war industries! Let the government take over all the big industries, nationalize them, and put them under workers' control.

A capital levy on all the corporations, and confiscate the great private fortunes of the "Sixty Families." Let the profiteers and capitalists carry the war burden; it is on their shoulders that it belongs.

Wipe out, root and branch, all social, economic and political discrimination against the Negro people in the United States — in industry and in the armed forces.

Grant full political rights to the men in the Army who must do the fighting and dying in the war.

Workers, let us organize our own National Labor Party, of, for and by labor, founded on its powerful organizations, the unions, and authorized to speak and act for labor in the political field. Labor must have its own ticket in the 1942 elections!

Workers, let us work with all our strength for our own government, of, for and by labor — the rule of the workers through a workers' government, in the United States.

This is the program to which the Workers Party is pledged in the war. It is a program representing the interests of the working class. It is the program that leads to a world of durable peace, freedom for all peoples, security in abundance.

"Statement Of National Committee, Workers Party", *Labor Action*, 15 December 1941 (first issue after Pearl Harbour)

The Militant of 3 January 1942 offers recommendation on "how labor can strike Hitler a mortal blow", before it has made any statement of its attitude to the USA entering World War Two on 8 December 1941. See page 32.

SWP's first comment on US entry into war

The Militant (1941)

The article excerpted below was the SWP's only comment for several weeks after the USA entered World War 2.

THE DECLARATION OF WAR on Japan by Congress on Monday [8 December 1941] brought automatically into operation the war-time legislation known as the "Espionage Act", first enacted June 15, 1917.

In his letter of April 25, 1917, President Wilson promised that "I shall not expect or permit any part of this law" to "be used as a shield against criticism". What followed, however, scarcely bore out Wilson's words...

> "War reinstates 1917 Espionage Act", *The Militant*, 13 December 1941

The strange silence of *The Militant*

Max Shachtman (1942)

IMMEDIATELY AFTER THE DECLARATION of war in this country, the National Committee of the Workers Party made public a statement of its opinion which appeared in *Labor Action*. In doing so, it merely complied with the elementary duty of a wording-class socialist organization. With the outbreak of the war, it acquitted itself of its first responsibility — the solemn and unambiguous reaffirmation of its internationalist stand against imperialist war. The Thomasite Socialist Party issued a statement at about the same time according to its lights. Even the ghost of the Socialist Labor Party let itself be heard from in an official declaration on the war.

The Socialist Workers Party, however, made no statement of its position, either when the war broke out or in the more than four weeks period that has elapsed since then. Neither has *The Militant*, spokesman of the Cannonites, had a single word to say about its position on the war in the past month. In fact, it has talked about everything else except what every radical worker has rightfully looked for it to say. What is the explanation of this strange silence? What does it mean?

Unofficially, it seems, spokesmen of the SWP have stated that its position is too well known to require another statement and that, besides, its position was already stated in the course of the Minneapolis trial. This is true in so far as its position before the declaration of war is concerned. But that is not the point. What is involved is precisely the question of its position after the declaration of war, now that the war is a fact in this country and not merely a prospect.

Another thing that remains unexplained is the failure of the SWP to reply to a communication sent it by the Workers Party. On December 11, 1941 the Workers Party wrote the National Committee of the SWP proposing the drafting of a joint statement against the imperialist war, to be signed by the two organizations. The letter said: "It is neither necessary nor possible, as you know, for us to arrive at an agreement on all the aspects of the Second World War. However, it is our opinion that sufficient agreement does exist between us on the decisive questions of the United States in the Second World War to make both possible and urgently necessary a joint declaration".

This letter, as stated, has not been answered; not even its receipt has been acknowledged. The strained and haughty attempts of the Cannonites to "ignore" our existence, so pathetically comical in the past, are not a sufficient explanation for their failure to respond this time. There is more than this, involved, and not a few comrades — supporters of the SWP — are insistent on establishing just what is involved.

Can there be any connection between the singular silence of the SWP on the one side and the notorious theory advanced months ago by its leader, according to which the SWP would "telescope" the two tasks of fighting for socialism and at the same time defending the capitalist fatherland?

Labor Action, 12 January 1942

Statement on the USA's entry into World War 2

James P Cannon (1942)

JAMES P. CANNON, National Secretary of the Socialist Workers Party, issued a "Statement on the War" in the January issue of *Fourth International* monthly magazine, which went on the news-stands last week.

The statement recalls that up to Dec. 8. "We considered the war upon the part of all the capitalist powers involved — Germany and France, Italy and Great Britain — as an imperialist war." Then it says:

"This characterization of the war was determined for us by the character of the state powers involved in it. They were capitalist powers in the epoch of imperialism; themselves imperialist — oppressing other nations or peoples — or satellites of imperialist powers. The extension of the war to the Pacific and the formal entry of the United States and Japan change nothing in this basic analysis."

The statement then goes on to emphasize that its attitude toward the Soviet Union and China is entirely different than its attitude toward the great capitalist powers. It says:

"We make a fundamental distinction between the Soviet Union and its 'democratic' allies. We defend the Soviet Union. The Soviet Union is a workers' state, although degenerated under the totalitarian-political rule of the Kremlin bureaucracy. Only traitors can deny support to the Soviet workers' state in its war against fascist Germany. To defend the Soviet Union, in spite of Stalin and against Stalin, is to defend the nationalized property established by the October revolution. That is a progressive war.

"The war of China against Japan we likewise characterize as a progressive war. We support China. China is a colonial country, battling for national independence against an imperialist power. A victory for China would be a tremendous blow against all imperialism, inspiring all colonial peoples to throw off the imperialist yoke. The reactionary regime of Chiang-Kaishek, subservient to the 'democracies', has hampered China's ability to conduct a bold war for independence; but that does not alter for us the essential fact that China is an oppressed nation fighting against an imperialist oppressor. We are proud of the fact that the Fourth Internationalists of China are fighting in the front ranks against Japanese imperialism."

The real war against fascism, the statement says, can only be waged by a Workers' and Farmers' Government. "When the people of Germany can feel assured that military defeat will not be followed by the destruction of Germany's economic power and the imposition of unbearable burdens by the victors, Hitler will be overthrown from within Germany. But such guarantees against a second Versailles cannot be given by Germany's imperialist foes". Such guarantees can be given only by a Workers' and Farmers' Government.

The statement concludes with a section on the conduct of the revolutionary minority in wartime. It says:

"Our program against Hitlerism and for a Workers' and Farmers' Government is today the program of only a small minority. The great majority actively or passively supports the war program of the Roosevelt administration. As a minority we must submit to that majority in action. We do not sabotage the war or obstruct the military forces in any way. The Trotskyists go with their generation into the armed forces. We abide by the decisions of the majority. But we retain our opinions and insist on our right to express them.

"Our aim is to convince the majority that our program is the only one which can put an end to war, fascism and economic convulsions. In this process of education the terrible facts speak loudly for our contention. Twice in twenty-five years world wars have wrought destruction. The instigators and leaders of those wars do not offer, and cannot offer, a plausible promise that a third, fourth and fifth world war will not follow if they and their social system remain dominant. Capitalism can offer no prospect but the slaughter of millions and the destruction of civilization. Only socialism can save humanity from this abyss. This is the truth. As the terrible war unfolds, this truth will be recognized by tens of millions who will not hear us now. The war-tortured masses will adopt our program and liberate the people of all countries from war and fascism. In this dark hour we clearly see the socialist future and prepare the way for it. Against the mad chorus of national hatreds we advance once more the old slogan of socialist internationalism: Workers of the World, Unite!"

22 December 1941

Published *The Militant*, 7 February 1942 (but see page 32)

The Workers Party: Against the Boss War! For A Workers' Government!

Max Shachtman (1940)

Max Shachtman's election manifesto as candidate for US Congress in the Bronx, spelled out the politics of the Workers Party.

WORKERS OF THE BRONX! The elections this year are taking place under conditions which are of the most vital importance to us all. The issues are more than local or state-wide in importance. The main issues facing us are international in scope.

Against The War! Against Fascism!

The entire world now faces the twin scourges of capitalism — Fascism and War. One country after another has been dragged into the Second Great World War. The few who still remain outside are not even "neutral" but only "non-belligerents" who merely await the proper moment to join the murderous conflict. One country after another has come under the heel of totalitarian dictatorship, imposed upon the working people by their enemy at home, or by an enemy invader.

What is left of freedom and democratic rights is threatened by Fascism. What is left of life and civilization is threatened by War.

Every worker who loves liberty, who wants a decent standard of living that will enable him to exist as a comfortable human being, looks with alarm at the growth of Fascism throughout the world, at the speedy advances of the Fascist hordes, and at the spread of war from one continent to another.

Labor Must Crush Fascism

Every worker knows what Fascism means: the crushing of all independent labor organizations, be they economic, political or cultural; the wiping out of every vestige of democratic rights; the reduction of the standard of living until every workingman is a slave; the suppression of all cultural and scientific progress; the violent sharpening of racial and religions antagonisms. We share the feeling of horror and hatred of Fascism. We want to see this pestilential reptile crushed before it crushes all of us.

We know that isolationism cannot smash Fascism. Isolationism is an illusion — or a fraud. No country today can isolate itself from the rest of the world and the problems of the world. No country today is isolated!

We know that pacifism cannot smash Fascism. Fascism attacks armed to the teeth. It can be met and defeated only if the real enemies of Fascism are properly armed, properly trained, and properly led against it.

Shall we therefore support the war of the Democracies against the Axis Powers? Shall we therefore support the program of militarization of the United States today? Shall we therefore support those who are rushing this country into the World War? No!

A War For Profits And For Profiteers

This is not a war against Fascism! This is not a war for Democracy! These are only clever phrases aimed to dupe the people into suffering and dying so that one imperialist gang may triumph over another and take over the world and its wealth for itself.

The present war is like the war of 1914-1918 — a war for imperialist plunder, for profit, for colonies, for sources of raw materials, for fields of capital investments, for control of cheap labor.

Before the war started, England, France and the United States had most of these. Germany, Italy and Japan wanted them. The Axis Powers want to take them for their own exploitation. The Democratic Powers want to keep them, to continue benefiting from them.

You can see this most clearly in the colonies. England and Italy are fighting in and around the Mediterranean in order to determine which of the two empires shall rule over the slaves of Africa. Why should we fight and die in order that a boot "Made in England" instead of a boot "Made in Italy" should grind down the neck of Africa's peoples?

The Pretense of "Democracy"

England calls for support in the war in order to restore the independence and national sovereignty of Poland and Czechoslovakia and Norway, in order to drive the foreign, German troops out of these countries. Why does not England establish full national sovereignty for Ireland, for Egypt, for India, for Palestine, for all her other colonies and dominions? Why does not England withdraw her troops from these long-oppressed countries?

Because the story that this is a war for democracy, for national freedom, is a lie, an imperialist lie!

The leading statesmen of the United States say that they are preparing to fight for democracy and against totalitarian dictatorship. Then why are Roosevelt and the United States government allied with, and why do they support the bloody, totalitarian dictatorships in Latin America — Getulio Vargas in Brazil, Somoza in Nicaragua, Batista in Cuba? Why do they support, and take support from, the reactionary dictatorship below the Mason-Dixon line, which keeps millions of American Negroes in a state of political and economic semi-slavery ?

Their "fight for democracy" is a sham and a lie. They are interested in something else entirely.

The "New Deal" Has Become The "War Deal"

After more than seven years in office, the New Deal has proved to be a failure so far as the masses of the people are concerned. It has not kept any of its promises except one: it has restored the big profits of the bankers and industrialists. Roosevelt rightfully boasts about this. But the standard of living of the workers has not been lifted. Unemployment has not been wiped out. There are still 12,000,000 unemployed in the United States. Housing conditions are basically as bad as ever. The real crisis remains unsolved.

American capitalism now wants to take the opportunity to solve it on a world scale — by plunging the country into war. The armies of death will now solve the unemployment problem! Coffins for the millions will take the place of the housing program that was necessary! Blood profits for the arms and munitions industries will expand the wealth of the imperialists. Already the United States has obtained, almost for nothing, England's naval bases in the Atlantic. Tomorrow, it will be Singapore and other bases and colonies in the Pacific. The loot is rich — not for the people, but for the parasitic ruling class. And if the war is won, American imperialism will take the lion's share of the loot.

Wall Street Wants War

Like the Axis Powers, the United States is fighting to dominate the world. What will American workers and farmers die for? So that American business may exclude Germany, Italy, Japan and England from the rich markets of Latin America and garner the profits for itself. So that Germany is prevented from dominating Europe and the investments and loans of American bankers thereby lost. So that Japanese imperialists are driven out of China and their places taken by no less avaricious American imperialists. So that the United States may become master of the Dutch East Indies, with its vast resources of and profits in rubber, tin and other raw materials.

And what happens to democracy at home while this fake "war for democracy" is going on abroad?

War Means The End Of Democratic Rights

The first victim of the "war for democracy" is democracy itself! The first things to be sacrificed are the democratic rights of the people!

Precisely because we hate Fascism with every fibre of our being, we raise the cry of warning: The closer and deeper we get into this war, the closer we bring totalitarianism and Fascism to this country. The first steps have already been taken in the United States; the next steps will not be long in following.

Beginning in September, 1939, Congress, preparing America's road to war, began a wholesale enactment of anti-labor legislation. Under the hysterical cry of "Fifth Column", the LaFollette "Civil Liberties Bill" was turned into a vicious anti-labor, union busting bill. The "Alien" bill was passed providing for the registration and finger printing of all aliens in the US. The FBI, and the Attorney General's office were converted into a veritable Gestapo or GPU — a political police directed against labor and its organizations. The right of free election and petition is being turned into a mockery by a thousand little "tricks" of coercion and intimidation employed by the Federal and State police.

Conscription Is A Step Toward Totalitarianism

The adoption of military conscription, in the face of the decisive opposition of the majority of the people, is being coupled in Washington with the idea of labor conscription in industry.

Tomorrow, workers will be toiling in war industries, and then in the other industries, under military discipline, and for the low army wages. Tomorrow, the workers will be deprived of their powerful weapon for righting economic wrongs — the right to strike.

Already, before the United States has formally declared war, the demand for an improvement in wages and working conditions is being attacked as "pro-German" and "Fifth Columnist". What will the war-mongers, the war-profiteers and their government say when the country is at war?

War today is totalitarian! It can only be carried on in a totalitarian way. The deeper we get into the war, the closer we come to a totalitarian regime!

That is exactly what happened in France. The people trusted the capitalist politicians, the self-styled "democrats". The people trusted the capitalist army and the reactionary officers' clique that ran it. In the crisis, it was precisely these "democrats" who made an alliance with the Nazis against the French people, and then set up a totalitarian regime over them. How long shall we wait for the same thing in England, and then in the United States?

If the people continue to follow the capitalist politicians and parties and. their tools, the victory of War and Fascism is assured. All of them are turning the present elections into a sinister farce.

Roosevelt And Willkie Are Both For War

The difference between Roosevelt and Willkie is the difference between Tweedledum and Tweedledee. Both of them are for the war program. Both of them are for the conscription and militarization program.

Both of them are for the murderous armaments race which is rushing the people towards impoverishment and death. Never before has there been so little difference between the two main parties of American capitalism, between, their respective candidates. The Roosevelt-Willkie contest is a sham and a fraud from start to finish.

The American Labor Party, which was a promising beginning of independent working-class political action, is now torn in two by two pro-war factions — the right-wing labor bureaucrats and the tools of Stalin.

The labor bureaucrats, instead of fighting labor's battle against the war and the war-mongers, are singing the praises of Roosevelt and doing their bit to regiment the labor movement for the "democratic" war.

No Support To The Lackeys Of Stalin

The Stalinists are working might and main to bring the labor movement under the control of the Moscow tools of Hitler. They are not concerned in the slightest with the interests of the workers in this country or any other. Their one objective is to protect the interests of the bloody bureaucracy of the Kremlin. When it was to the Kremlin's interest to get an alliance with American imperialism, the Communist Party in this country shouted for Roosevelt and for war. Now that the Kremlin's interests are bound up with the camp of the Axis Powers, the Communist Party shouts against Roosevelt. If Stalin should shift to American imperialism again tomorrow, the American Stalinists will again work to tie American labor to the war machine.

To support any of these parties means to further the paralysis of the working class, to bring closer the day of war, and to smooth the way for oncoming reaction and Fascism. There is only one road out of the crisis — the road of independent working class action.

For Peace, Freedom And Security

The toiling people must rely on their own strength. They must rely on their own arms and leadership. They must take over the reins of government and run it in the interests of the people, in the interests of peace, and freedom, and abundance for all.

The Workers Party calls upon all workers to rally to its banner in the election — the banner of the only consistent and uncompromising enemy of war and Fascism! The Workers Party, as the party of world peace and international socialism, calls upon all workers to join with it in a struggle for a program of action.

We stand for:

A Job And A Decent Living For Every Worker In The Country

End unemployment by: Thirty-thirty — a $30-a-week minimum wage and a 30-hour-a-week maximum working week.

Houses — Not Coffins

A twenty-billion dollar Federal housing and public works program. The government spends billions for death and destruction and is ready to spend many more. We want houses, not coffins. We demand playgrounds, not graveyards. We want highways, not trenches.

Adequate Relief For The Unemployed!

According to the 1940 census, there are still 14,000,000 unemployed workers in the United States. Jobs must be provided for the unemployed. But until they are, the government must provide adequate relief for the unemployed.

Congress and the President have refused consistently to increase the appropriations for relief and WPA. Pointing to the overwhelming national debt, the government succeeded in keeping millions of workers and their families on starvation rations.

Congress however did not find it embarrassing to the national debt to appropriate $15,000,000,000 for purposes of National Defense. It is apparent that funds are available. We demand therefore a sharp increase in the federal appropriations for relief and WPA, to afford every unemployed worker and his family a living allotment until employment is provided.

Confiscate The Wealth Of The Parasites!

Expropriate the Sixty Plutocratic Families! The government does not hesitate to confiscate millions of lives by conscription and war. We demand the confiscation of the wealth of the handful of parasites who rule the economic and political life of the country. Nationalize American industry and run it under workers' control. Under private capitalist ownership and control, industry has experienced one crisis after another, resulting in intense suffering for millions. Let the workers manage and control industry! They produce all the wealth, let them control and manage this production.

For A Workers' Government!

A workers government! If Roosevelt or Willkie or the other capitalist politicians do not accept these demands, and they do not and will not and cannot, because they are bound hand and foot to Big Business and its system — let the workers take over and run the government themselves!

For Democratic Rights, Against Fascism!

In the present war crisis, the Workers Party stands for:

A people's army! The government says we are threatened by foreign invasion, by an attack from Fascism: Then let the people be armed! We did not support conscription and fought bitterly against conscription. We opposed the adoption of the draft legislation.

We have no confidence in the capitalist government — we know only too well its aims in this war. We have no confidence in the present army and the reactionary officers' clique that runs it — we saw only too clearly how it acted in France.

The arming of the people must take place under the complete control of the workers' organizations, the trade unions. They will train and organize the people's army. A people's army will not be an imperialist force interested in acquiring domination over foreign people and colonies. It will not be used to crush labor and labor's rights. It will not be used to smash strikes. The masses can have confidence in such an army, for it will not only resist invading Fascism but also Fascism and all other reactionary forces at home, right here in the United States.

Democratic Rights For Conscripts

Full democratic rights for all conscripts and enlisted men! All soldiers, conscripted or enlisted, must be given the right to vote in all elections, local, state or federal. Soldiers must have the right of free speech, free press and free assembly in the army itself — the right to meet freely to discuss any and all questions, the right to receive or to publish any periodical they desire. Soldiers must have the right to organize and elect freely their rank and file committees to represent them in the presentation of all demands and grievances, and in any other negotiations with their officers. Workers have fought for that right in the factories; the same workers should have the same right in the barracks.

Repeal the anti-labor, strike breaking clauses of the draft bill ("Selective Military Service Bill") ! Repeal the conscription bill!

The selective military service bill gives the boss of the factory the right to decide whether a worker in question for the draft is to be deferred from the draft or not. He can decide upon who is "indispensable" to the industry and who is not. This guarantees that the bosses' relatives and "loyal" workers will be deferred, while active unionists (especially in strike actions) will be rendered "non-essential", and thus drafted. This right must be taken from the bosses. Trade Union committees must be given the right to represent the interests of the workers before the draft boards.

Similarly, the threat of conscription directed at striking workers must be removed by a categorical clause granting the right of workers to strike without the penalty of being conscripted on grounds of "unemployment".

"Conscript" The War Industries

Nationalize the war industries and place them under workers' control! The Government says this is not a war for profit. The bosses of the war industries, however are not only demanding fabulous profits but they are getting them. These profits will come out of the oceans of workers' blood shed in the war. The government "nationalizes" millions of workers by conscription. We demand the nationalization of the war industries. And since it is the workers who are called upon to die in the war, let them be the men in control of the industries of war.

Let The People Vote Against The War

A people's referendum on war! The government says this is a democratic war, a people's war. Then let the people vote on war! The people must have the right to say whether the government shall declare war or not. If it is, as they say, "their war," let them decide whether or not to declare it. The right to vote must be extended to everyone from the age of 18 onward.

Abolition of Secret Diplomacy!

No secret negotiations, no secret commitments, no secret treaties behind the backs of the people! Throw open the diplomatic archives of the government. It was only after the last World War that we were told of some of the secret documents that led the United States into the war without the knowledge of the people. We demand that we know the truth, the whole truth, now, before the United States is led into the war.

Preserve And Extend Democratic Rights

No restrictions on the greatest exercise of the right of free speech, free press, free assembly, the right to organize and to strike! If this is a "war for democracy," why should democratic rights be the first to be sacrificed? Labor must guard these rights zealously, and fight every inch of the way to preserve them, to make them more genuine, to extend them in every direction.

Against Lynching, And "Jim Crow"

Full social, political and economic equality for the Negroes! It is miserable hypocrisy to talk about "democracy" or a "war for democracy" when 14 millions of our fellow-citizens, the Negroes, are almost completely deprived of their democratic rights in this country. Complete abolition of any and every form of discrimination, of Jim-Crowism, is on the order of the day.

The Negro workers are Jim-Crowed, lynched, kept from the election polls by poll taxes, barred from unions and jobs, segregated into slum areas. The discrimination against the Negroes takes place not only in civil life, but also in the army. The Negroes are segregated into special army units, and their opportunity for promotions as well as fields of service are restricted by reactionary laws and the officer corps.

We demand:

1. The immediate passage of the anti-lynch bill.
2. The immediate and unconditional abolition of all poll taxes.
3. Jobs for Negroes. No discrimination against the Negro on the job.
4. No segregation of the Negro in the army or in civilian life.

Repeal The Anti-Alien Legislation

No discrimination against foreign-born workers! We demand the immediate repeal of all discriminatory anti-alien legislation. It is aimed at dividing the workers, at pitting foreign-born against native-born.

Unite Against War And Fascism! Unite For Socialism And Peace!

The workers of the Bronx have an opportunity in this election to voice their protest against the warmongers, the profiteers, the capitalist politicians.

Vote For The Workers Party

The Workers Party, which has no interests separate from the interests of all the workers, has put its own candidate in the field for Congressman, for the member of the House of Representatives in the 23rd Congressional District. Our candidate is Max Shachtman, National Secretary of the Workers Party, last year candidate for Councilman from the Bronx, a revolutionist with a record of twenty unbroken years of service to the working class movement.

The Workers Party calls upon all workers to cast their vote for its candidate, the candidate of the working class itself, Max Shachtman.

A vote for the candidate of the Workers Party is not a vote for an individual. It is a vote for a program. The program of the Workers Party is the program of militant struggle: Against war and Fascism! For socialism and peace! World reaction has divided the globe into two camps, we are told. One is the camp of Axis imperialism; the other the camp of Democratic imperialism. The victory of either of these camps means the further decay of society and civilization. All they have to offer is deception, broken promises, wretchedness, suffering and death.

There is another camp! It is the Third Camp! The Third Camp is the camp of the independent working class movement throughout the world. It is the camp of every worker, in every land, who yearns for an end to the nightmare of war, for peace, for security. It is the camp of every colonial slave who longs for the day when the heel of imperialism will be removed from his trampled-down body.

The victory of this camp over all the imperialist bandits means Peace — peace in permanence — and Security — abundance for all. It means an end to oppression and exploitation of all sorts. It means a new order, the order of world socialism!

Workers! Rally to this great inspiring struggle for freedom!

Support the campaign of the Workers Party!

Cast your ballot for Max Shachtman for representative of the 23rd Congressional District.

Election Platform of the Workers Party for the Bronx Congressional election in which Max Shachtman ran. *Labor Action*, 14 October 1940

Move this anti-war resolution!

Labor Action

A GROUP OF PROGRESSIVE workers, members of the Social Service Employees Union, a local of the United Office and Professional Workers of America, have submitted the following resolution to the SSEU for adoption and presentation to the Constitutional Convention of the UOPWA to be held in Chicago, August 31-Sept. 6.

Whereas, the Second World War is not a struggle for democracy but for the re-division of the world for markets, raw materials, colonies and, for the domination and oppression of the peoples of the world,

Whereas, the war is a struggle between Anglo-French imperialism and German-Italian imperialism with the support of Moscow which joined Hitler in conquest of Poland and conquest of Finland, Latvia, Esthonia and Lithuania,

Whereas, the working people have nothing in common with the imperialist aims of the belligerents but are only victims of their bloody conflict,

Whereas, the defeat of German-Italian Fascism, barbaric destroyers of the labor movement and all civil liberties, cannot be entrusted to the allied ruling classes who financed and helped Hitler come to power and re-arm, and who themselves exercise a brutal, dictatorial rule over 500 million colonial peoples of Africa and Asia, the condition of whose lives is no better than that of the Jews under Hitler and Mussolini, but can be achieved only by the unity and joint action of the working classes of all lands.

Whereas, President Roosevelt, in defiance of the expressed will of the overwhelming majority of the American people, has taken and is taking steps to support the Allied imperialists and oppressors and involve the US in the reactionary predatory war.

Whereas, such an act would mean the slaughter of the youth of the country, the regimentation of our unions, the destruction of our labor standards and social legislation, and the blackout of civil liberties and political democracy in the United States.

Whereas, President Roosevelt in defiance of the expressed will of the overwhelming majority of the American people, has taken and is taking steps to support the Allied imperialists and oppressors and involve the US in the reactionary predatory war.

Whereas, such an act would mean the slaughter of the youth of the country, the regimentation of our unions, the destruction of our labor standards and social legislation, and the blackout of civil liberties and political democracy in the United States.

Resolved, that the SSEU stands instructed to cooperate with other labor organizations for a concerted drive against the war mongers, against compulsory military training; against anti-alien legislation; against the denial of all civil rights; for a referendum of the people before the US enters any war; for the defense of the unions, social legislation, and democratic rights, and for a job and decent living for every worker.

Labor Action, 8 July 1940

Conscription? Yes, but...

Leon Trotsky

DEAR CHRIS: I VERY MUCH ENJOYED your appreciation of the anti-pacifist position accepted by the party. There are two great advantages to this position: first, it is revolutionary in its essence and based upon the whole character of our epoch, when all questions will be decided not only by arms of critics, but by critiques of arms; second, it is completely free of sectarianism. We do not oppose to events and to the feelings of the masses an abstract affirmation of our sanctity.

The poor *Labor Action* of August 12th writes: "In his fight against conscription we are with Lewis 100 per cent." We are not with Lewis for even a single per cent, because Lewis tries to defend the Capitalist Fatherland with completely outdated means. The great majority of the workers understand or feel that these means (professional voluntary armament) are outdated from a military point of view and extremely dangerous from a class point of view. That is why the workers are for conscription. It is a very confused and contradictory form of adhering to the "arming of the proletariat." We do not flatly reject this great historical change, as do the sectarians of all kinds. We say "Conscription? Yes. But made by ourselves." It is an excellent point of departure.

With best greetings, I am,

Fraternally,

YOUR OLD MAN [Leon Trotsky]. August 17, 1940

Fourth International, October 1940

LONG LIVE THE THIRD
COMMUNIST INTERNATIONAL!
EVVIVA IL TERZA
INTERNAZIONALE COMUNISTA!
VIVE LA TROISIEME
INTERNATIONALE COMMUNISTE!
ES LEBE DIE DRITTE
KOMMUNISTISCHE INTERNATIONALE!

Тов. Ленин ОЧИЩАЕТ
землю от нечисти.

"Comrade Lenin cleans the world of filth"

12. The revolutionary party

The minority's charge that the majority practised "bureaucratic conservatism", and the majority's charge that the minority were lightweight "petty bourgeois intellectuals", played a large part in the 1940 split. Even before the split, Cannon proclaimed it as a decisive step "from a loosely organised propaganda circle and discussion club to a centralised and disciplined proletarian party". After the split, the Orthodox developed a new regime, and a new conception of what Marxism and a revolutionary socialist party were and had to be.

"A military organisation"

James P Cannon, Leon Trotsky (1940)

CANNON: I THINK that the party in the eyes of the leading militants should be considered as a military organization. The party forms should be much more considerably formalized in a deliberate form of hierarchical organization. A strict record of grades of authority in the party...

Trotsky: It is necessary to create an elastic relationship between democracy and centralism. We have enough hundreds of members who have passed through enough experiences who now require more centralized organization. These people in another ten years will be the old guard. These cadres in a new phase can give the possibility of some hundreds of thousands of members of different origin. These people can introduce new tendencies of criticism. To assimilate them it can't be done by centralism. It is necessary to enlarge the democracy, to let them find that the old guard is more experienced. So after a period of very centralized existence, you can have a new period of wide discussion, then a more normalized centralized period.

Our growth will be a convulsive growth. It can introduce into its ranks some half-raw human material. It is a tremendous advantage to have the support of the cadres. They will explain to the new comrades. At the same time it is dangerous to impose centralism too soon on new members who don't have this tradition of esteem for the leadership which is based by and large on experiences of the past...

During a severe war [i.e. the Russian civil war] the party relations

589

indicated a severe and military organization. In spite of all the party equilibrium was preserved. Even at the front we had closed party meetings, where all party members discussed with complete freedom, criticized orders, etc...

Discussions with Trotsky, 12-15 June 1940.
Writings 1939-40, p.286-7

Fourth International newspapers from around the world in 1938.

Our Bolshevik party already exists

James P Cannon (1946)

THE DECISIVE INSTRUMENT of the proletarian revolution is the party of the class conscious vanguard. Failing the leadership of such a party, the most favorable revolutionary situations, which arise from the objective circumstances, cannot be carried through to the final victory of the proletariat and the beginnings of planned reorganization of society on socialist foundations. This was demonstrated most conclusively – and positively – in the 1917 Russian Revolution. This same principled lesson derives no less irrefutably – even though negatively – from the entire world experience of the epoch of wars, revolutions, and colonial uprisings that began with the outbreak of the First World War in 1914.

However, this basic conclusion from the vast and tragic experience of the last third of a century can be and has been given a reactionary interpretation by a school of neo-revisionism, represented by the ideologues, philosophers, and preachers of prostration, capitulation, and defeat. They say in effect: "Since the revolutionary party is small and weak it is idle to speak of revolutionary possibilities. The weakness of the party changes everything." The authors of this "theory" reject and repudiate Marxism, embracing in its place the subjective school of sociology. They isolate the factor of the revolutionary party's relative numerical weakness at a particular moment from the totality of objective economic and political developments which creates all the necessary and sufficient conditions for the swift growth of the revolutionary vanguard party.

Given an objectively revolutionary situation, a proletarian party – even a small one – equipped with a precisely worked out Marxist program and firm cadres can expand its forces and come to the head of the revolutionary mass movement in a comparatively brief span of time. This too was proved conclusively – and positively – by the experiences of the Russian Revolution in 1917. There the Bolshevik Party, headed by Lenin and Trotsky, bounded forward from a tiny minority, just emerging from underground and isolation in February to the conquest of power in October – a period of nine months.

Numerical weakness, to be sure, is not a virtue for a revolutionary party but a weakness to be overcome by persistent work and resolute struggle. In the US all the conditions are in the process of unfolding for the rapid transformation of the organized vanguard from a propaganda group to a mass party strong enough to lead the revolutionary struggle for power.

The hopeless contradictions of American capitalism, inextricably tied up with the death agony of world capitalism, are bound to lead to a social crisis of such catastrophic proportions as will place the proletarian revolution on the order of the day.

In this crisis, it is realistic to expect that the American workers, who attained trade union consciousness and organization within a single decade, will pass through another great transformation in their mentality, attaining political consciousness and organization. If in the course of this dynamic development a mass labor party based on the trade unions is formed, it will not represent a detour into reformist stagnation and futility, as happened in England and elsewhere in the period of capitalist ascent. From all indications, it will rather represent a preliminary stage in the political radicalization of the American workers, preparing them for the direct leadership of the revolutionary party.

The revolutionary vanguard party, destined to lead this tumultuous revolutionary movement in the US, does not have to be created. It already exists, and its name is the Socialist Workers Party. It is the sole legitimate heir and continuator of pioneer American Communism and the revolutionary movements of the American workers from which it sprang. Its nucleus has already taken shape in three decades of unremitting work and struggle against the stream. Its program has been hammered out in ideological battles and successfully defended against every kind of revisionist assault upon it. The fundamental core of a professional leadership has been assembled and trained in the irreconcilable spirit of the combat party of the revolution.

The task of the Socialist Workers Party consists simply in this: to remain true to its program and banner; to render it more precise with each new development and apply it correctly in the class struggle; and to expand and grow with the growth of the revolutionary mass movement, always aspiring to lead it to victory in the struggle for political power.

From "Theses on the American Revolution", *Fourth International*, January 1947

The kind of party we are building

Max Shachtman (1945)

PERHAPS OUR GREATEST GAIN is in the kind of party we have succeeded in building. In it, we have living proof that a Bolshevik party does not mean the totalitarian prison so many people have been led to believe it always was and must always be. The democratic character of our organisation is not merely our boast. Militants and radicals outside our party know the facts and acknowledge them. Our party is intolerant of any attempts to curb the intellectual freedom and critical independence of its membership. All it demands is rigid discipline in action and a high degree of responsibility in building up the party. It is able to make and enforce this demand not only because its main policies have proved to be correct, but because there is no bureaucratic regime, "benevolent" or otherwise, in the party.

Without ever descending to the futility of a "debating society," our party has repeatedly had the freest discussions of political and theoretical questions. Some have been confined to the party ranks, but the more important ones have also been discussed in public, in the pages of our *New International*. Some of them have been extremely ardent, even sharply polemical. Groups, ideological formations, of different kinds have existed in the party and continue to exist; in one form or another, on one question or another, they will probably always exist. But we have no resolutions calling for the "dissolution of factions," and if good Bolshevik practice continues to prevail, we shall never have such resolutions. We have established in our party such a relationship between leaders and members and of all members with each other, and between adopted program and criticism of it, that there is no air in the party for a bureaucratic or clique regime. And there, after all, lies the secret of the absence of permanent factions, as distinguished from ideological groupings. There are no such factions because there is no soil — a bureaucratic regime — for them to grow in.

It might be said that the kind of party we have built up is our richest possession. In itself, it does not guarantee against making political mistakes, including serious ones. But it makes possible a speedy correction of such mistakes if they are made, a correction without the convulsive crises to which bureaucratized parties are doomed whenever a serious difference of opinion forces its way past the lid. From

593

this standpoint, it might be added in passing, the big obstacle to the union of the two Trotskyist organisations in this country is not so much the political differences that exist. Although some of these differences are greater than they were five years ago, others have become less acute. In any event, people with even greater political differences could live and work side by side in a single party provided it were a normal party. It is no secret, for example, that in our own party close cooperation is possible between comrades who, on some questions, have greater differences between themselves than our party as a whole has, on other questions, with the SWP.

The principal obstacle (as this writer sees it) lies precisely in the sterile, bureaucratic regime which the Cannonites have imposed upon and continue to maintain in the SWP, a regime which the new minority in the SWP rightly describes as Stalinist in its trend. Unity is a precious thing. The kind of party that would result from unity is, however, far more important. Our comrades are not disposed for a minute to trade off what they have built up for any regime that smacks of Cannonism.

The last thirty years have been rich in events and in lessons for the working class, if not in victories. If we were asked to tell what makes us believe that the final victory will go to socialism, we would answer: Capitalism has shown conclusively that it cannot advance society and civilization, but only drive it further along the road of exhausting conflict, human degradation, barbarism and ruin. It no longer has a capacity for stability, order, peace and progress. The working class, even those sections of it that have been most cruelly oppressed, has shown a power of recuperation from defeat and resources of resistance to capitalist decay that amply justify our confidence in its eventual triumph. It has proved repeatedly that the conditions for its existence and progress is the struggle against the conditions of its existence. That is how it has been and that is how it must be. Although the connections between conscious socialism and the working class were broken once by the old social-democracy and again by Stalinism, they have not been destroyed. They exist in the form of our movement and its program, and they will be strengthened. The firmness of our party and the confirmation of its program by events justify the confidence we have in both. They justify also our confidence that the revolutionary International of the working class — a most important matter that cannot be dealt with briefly because it requires and deserves a chapter for itself — will be restored and solidified.

What makes the struggle for socialism and freedom seem more

difficult, also makes it more urgently necessary. It simply makes no sense to us when we are told that encroaching capitalist barbarism is destroying the prospects of socialism and it is better to give up the fight. That is the talk of demoralized and spiritually vanquished serfs. It is precisely the fact that decomposing capitalism is filling the air with its poisonous fumes, that imposes upon us the redoubling of our efforts to bury the putrid beast.

Let the cowards flinch and the traitors sneer. Our minds are incapable of absorbing the truly monstrous idea that humanity, which has shown so often an irresistible passion for liberty and an inexhaustible capacity for achieving it progressively, will, now, at the historic pinnacle of its intellectual and social development, finally yield to the yoke in permanence, like brute cattle. We reiterate our faith in the people, in the working class, and dedicate ourselves again, on this fifth anniversary, to the socialist emancipation.

From "Five Years of the Workers Party", *New International*, April 1945

A homogeneous party

SWP (1946)

THE ORGANIZATION QUESTION, our concept of the party and how to build it, was the second big issue in dispute between ourselves and the Burnham-Shachtman faction in 1939-40. The discussions on this question, recorded in two books *In Defense of Marxism* by Leon Trotsky and *The Struggle for a Proletarian Party* by James P. Cannon have in truth exhausted the differences between our two concepts of the party. As a matter of fact, very little fundamentally new has been said on this subject since Lenin wrote his memorable work, *One Step Forward, Two Steps Back*, which comprises the record and an analysis of the struggle between the Bolsheviks and the Mensheviks at the 1903 convention of the Russian Social-Democratic Party.

The Shachtmanites, who show an organic tendency toward-opportunism in every political question, naturally display the same tendency in the organizational sphere, in their concept of the character of the party, in their methods of building the party. The six-year struggle between ourselves and the Workers Party has imparted to our differences on this question a finished character. We want a party of workers, a party that has discipline both for the leaders and the rank-and-file, a party of action and struggle, a party that is Marxist to the marrow of its bones, a party which shrugs off with contempt all alien ideologies and pressures, a party so constituted that it can seriously contemplate leading the workers in the revolution.

That is why we believe in a homogeneous party, a party built solidly upon a common program and common methods. We reject any concept of a party of fundamentally different tendencies. Such a party can never forge a genuine discipline and is destined to fly apart in opposite directions when confronted with the first serious test. We are firm believers in party democracy and we practice it. But we insist that democracy be combined with centralism not just in name, but in fact. We insist that once a decision has been taken, the discussion shall cease and the minority subordinate itself to the will of the majority.

Despite all their protestations to the contrary, the Shachtmanites want, and have constructed, a "discussion club" party, a petty-bourgeois "madhouse," a perpetual talking shop. They are still hunting for the fourth dimension of party democracy. Their every instinct and their most deep-rooted characteristics force them to want and to do everything they can to create a party which will forever be a happy hunting ground for "litterateurs," "independent spirits," "free souls." They want a party which has an accommodating attitude toward every perversion of Marxism, a party where one feels free to "experiment."

The SWP resolution on "Organizational Principles," adopted by the founding convention in 1938, declares:

The revolutionary Marxian party rejects not only the arbitrariness and bureaucratism of the Communist Party, but also the spurious and deceptive "all-inclusiveness" of the Thomas-Tyler-Hoan Socialist Party, which is a sham and a fraud. Experience has proved conclusively that this "all-inclusiveness" paralyzes the party in general , and the revolutionary left wing in particular... The SWP seeks to be inclusive only in this sense, that it accepts into its ranks those who accept its program and denies admission to those who reject its program.

The Shachtmanites fought against this concept of a homogeneous Bolshevik organization in the faction struggle and split of 1939-40. Thus by implication they adopted the principle of an "all-inclusive" talking-shop party. Today the Workers Party has explicitly embraced this opportunist concept of organization... Shachtman declares:

We are unlike these previous movements (the Bolsheviks before 1917, the Communist Party of America at any time in its history, or the Communist League of America at any time in its history) in that our composition is much broader than was theirs at any time. Our program and theories are not less clearly and strictly defined than were theirs. Our party, however, takes in, makes room for, and allows the free functioning of people who have such differences with our party's theories and policies as were never tolerated or possible in the movements before. Do you have any doubts about it? If so, tell me of one revolutionary Marxist party which allowed for such a wide range of differences in its ranks as we allow in our party. If you go through the histories with a glass you will not find one, because there never was one... Such a wide range of differences in a reformist party? Yes, and even a wider range at one time or another. But never before in a revolutionary party! I think it was Erber who coined the phrase that our party is an all-inclusive revolutionary party (the underlined word sufficiently distinguishes us from Norman Thomas's all-inclusive reformist party). Properly understood, I am ready and proud to refer to ourselves by this formula. (Workers Party Internal Bulletin, Vol. 1, No. 14, May 15, 1946.)

From "Revolutionary Marxism or petty-bourgeois revisionism: statement of the Political Committee of the SWP", SWP Internal Bulletin vol.8 no.10, August 1946

Your party is Zinovievist, not Leninist

Max Shachtman and Ernest Rice McKinney (1946)

WE CAN BE AND ARE in favor of unity, in spite of the differences that exist between our parties, because we have a different conception of the party than your leadership has. We do not deny it. On the contrary, we want to underline this difference. We are consciously trying to build a party which is based firmly on the principles and traditions of revolutionary Marxism and which, precisely because of that, provides for the most genuine and not merely formalistic party democracy. Party democracy, from our point of view, and we consider that point of view to be in absolute harmony with the best traditions of the authentic Marxian movement, calls for the strictest observance of discipline in action precisely because, given the firm principled foundation of the party, it provides for the freest interplay in the party of all opinion which stands on the basic principles of Marxism, and consequently provides for genuinely free and critical expression, discussion and debate.

We reject categorically and indignantly all those who hold that Bolshevism was not democratic, that the genuine Bolshevik Party was in the remotest way comparable to its present day Stalinist antithesis. That is why we aim to build a Bolshevik party, for only in a Bolshevik party is it possible to have that free and fruitful interplay of ideas even when those ideas take the form of tendencies and even factions. That is all that is meant by those of our comrades who employ the term an "all-inclusive revolutionary party," that is, an utterly Bolshevik party in which true party democracy is cherished with the same passion that monolithism is abhorred.

Your leadership, on the other hand, is opposed to unity with us precisely and above all because of our conception of the party which, we do not hesitate to say, we would seek to instill into the very blood of the united party if it came into existence. It is nonsense to think that the opposition to unity is based on the differences between us on the Russian question, the national question, or the other questions which are dealt with in the statement of your PC. We do not say this because these questions are not important. They are of tremendous importance, they are of vital importance, but in the eyes of your leadership they fade into unimportance compared with the question of its conception of the party. It has the conception of a monolithic party. That is what it means when it speaks of a "homogeneous" party. That conception acquired currency and supremacy in the Communist movement after the usurpation of leadership in it by the Zinoviev-Stalin faction, after the death of Lenin, after the launching of the reactionary struggle against "Trotskyism." The Zinovievist preachment of a "homogeneous" and "monolithic" party marked and symbolized the beginning of the end of Bolshevik Party democracy and what that end is we all know. [After its 4th Congress in 1924, the leadership of the Communist International, around Zinoviev, launched a drive for "Bolshevisation", for "monolithic" organisation, and against political "deviations", notably "Trotskyist" or "Luxemburgist"].

We cannot consider it a mere coincidence that the leader of your party, the one who sets its tone and course, was one of the principal "Bolshevisers" in the Zinovievist style in the Communist movement of a score of years ago. It is not his course then that is so reprehensible; it is his repetition of his course today in the Trotskyist movement that is reprehensible.

The statement of your PC continually sneers at our party for being a "discussion club", not because it is against a discussion club but because it is against discussions which upsets the comfortable routine of the party bureaucracy. It sneers at the fact that we "tolerate" so many differences of opinion in our ranks, because its ideal is a rank and file which has no differences with the leadership and a leadership which "arranges" its disagreements by clique decisions. It sneers at the fact "there is no dearth of answers" to the many problems that beset a living revolutionary party like ours because its ideal is a party in which there is not and cannot be more than one "answer." Your leadership betrays its bureaucratic Zinovievist monolithism in every line of its attack on our conception of a revolutionary party.

That is why your leadership is so obdurate in its opposition to unity. It knows the consequences to its own concepts and its own regime that would follow from living and working inside one party with hundreds of devoted, serious, able, thoughtful and critical revolutionists, who have views of their own and know how to advance them.

That these are the reasons why we have no confidence in your leadership from the standpoint of protecting the principles of genuine party democracy, we have always said forthrightly. We must repeat it here. We want no misunderstanding on this score. Unity is desirable. Unity is necessary and unity is possible only if it is imposed upon the leadership that has stood and still stands in the way. Unity imposed upon a reluctant membership would not be worth a scrap of paper; but unity can be achieved by imposing it upon a reluctant leadership, whose bureaucratic concepts must be subjected to the needs and interests of the united revolutionary movement in this country.

What could be done toward the accomplishment of this task, we have done and will continue to do. On the unity question we do not withdraw a single proposal that we have made. Now it is up to the members of the SWP and of the whole International to assume their responsibilities in the accomplishment of this task. That is how the matter stands today.

Your PC statement has set up new criteria for membership in the Trotskyist movement. They are calculated to perpetuate and deepen the split in the United States. But that is not all. If your leaders seek, as they will, to impose these criteria upon the Fourth International as a whole, we are in for a period of splits and disaggregation in the world-wide movement. A serious application of these new utterly sectarian and authentically bureaucratic criteria means immediately splitting the British, the French, the Spanish, the German, the Italian, the Greek and other sections of the International. It means the reconstruction of the International in the image of a narrow-minded faction, at the best, and clique, at the worst.

This is a warning, and a warning that every serious comrade will reflect upon twenty times before he commits himself or allows his party to commit itself to these new criteria aimed at preventing the unity in this country and of inducing the split into others.

For the sake of unity we were ready to sacrifice a good deal. These sacrifices we are still prepared to make. But under no conditions were we prepared yesterday, are we prepared today, or will we be prepared tomorrow, to abandon our political and theoretical views and our right to advance them and above all sacrifice our conception of a revolutionary Marxist party based on real party democracy. That conception is the only conceivable basis upon which unity with us is possible. We cannot state this more categorically. As with all our views, this one too we shall hold to and fight for to the end.

Labor Action, 11 November 1946

The history of Bolshevism can be found in our own deeds

James P Cannon (1944)

OUR TENDENCY IS THE ONLY ONE in the labor movement that analyzes the role of Stalinism in the capitalist countries correctly, that is, as an agency of capitalist imperialism in the labor movement seeking to buy concessions for the nationalist bureaucracy of the USSR at the expense of the world proletariat and the colonial peoples. In this they are like any other group of privileged bureaucrats and aristocrats of labor who ally themselves with the exploiters against the deprived and oppressed masses — only magnified a thousand times. This is the little secret which explains the phenomenon which mystifies and baffles the professional "democrats" — the "hearty", if temporary, accord between the Stalinist bureaucracy and the Anglo-American imperialists. Those who do not understand that Stalinism, as represented by the bureaucracy in the Soviet Union as well as by its foreign agencies, is a tendency, a section, of the world labor movement, cannot begin to understand it, or the reason it wields such a great influence, and consequently cannot fight it effectively. On the contrary, the opportunists of all shades, all those who look for some way of compromise with capitalism, are at bottom no different from the Stalinists and sooner or later co-operate with them in one form or another when the vital interests of the capitalist order imperiously require it.

It is the degree of acuteness of the class struggle, not the "ideology" of the different varieties of imperialist agencies in the labor movement, that decides whether they quarrel among themselves or work together against the revolutionary masses. Witness the Anarchist and Socialists in Spain, the French people's front, the Socialist-Stalinist co-operation in Italy. Here at home we have already seen the Hillman-Browder amity in the PAC, the no-strike pledge bloc at the auto convention and the Stalinist-Tobin combination against us.

When the masses really take the road of resolute struggle in their own interests they are compelled to turn against Stalinism because they come up against its malign policy at every step. They can wage this struggle only under our leadership, and no other. We, however, can lead this struggle only if we insist upon irreconcilable programmatic clarity on the question of the Soviet Union, and hence of Stalinism; sternly reject any kind of unity with other groups who bring confusion into this question; and tolerate no taint of conciliationism in this respect.

We firmly believe that the cadres of the Fourth International which are again emerging in Europe can grow and prosper, and come to the leadership of the revolutionary struggle of the workers against imperialism and its Stalinist agents, only insofar as they follow this line. We believe that the tendencies in our own ranks in the US toward conciliation with the petty-bourgeois opposition, represented by the present opposition to the party leadership, is an anti-Trotskyist tendency.

The incident of the New York membership meeting (where several members were censured for conducting political discussions with WP members without the knowledge of the party) appears to have touched off a debate in which some fundamental questions, on which the party has more than once spoken decisively, are again called up for review. That is strange, for even at a distance, without knowing the details of the affair, it is difficult for one to misunderstand the simple issue involved. The New York organization wants to control and direct all the political activity of its members, and took this method of asserting its will in this respect. A Leninist can only applaud this attitude. Of course, one may hold the opinion, since it is our traditional practice to go very slow with organizational measures, that a pedagogical explanation of this elementary principle, without a formal censure, would have been sufficient. If the grievance were confined to this secondary, organizational side of the affair, redress of the grievance could undoubtedly be obtained. A big discussion over such a small matter would not be worth while. The article of Comrade Morrison, however, raises larger issues. This was the case also, as I am informed, in the discussion at the New York membership meeting. These issues require discussion and clarification.

In appealing to the party against the procedure of Local New York, Morrison resorts to arguments which are far-reaching in their implications. A discussion of these arguments is decidedly in order and necessary, since, whether so intended or not, they represent an assault against the traditions of Bolshevism all along the line, in the name of the traditions of Bolshevism. This anomaly can be explained on only one of two hypotheses: either Morrison has neglected to inform himself of the traditional practices of Bolshevik organization; or, he is again indulging his well-known penchant for underestimating the intelligence of other people — this time, of people who know something about the tradition which he invokes, the tradition of Bolshevism. Morrison's arguments have a tradition, but it is not the tradition of Bolshevism.

What does Morrison mean when he refers to the history of Bolshevism? Doesn't he know that it is our own history? What have we been doing for the part sixteen years but writing the continuing history of Bolshevism in life? Bolshevism is not a mummy preserved in a Russian museum, but a living movement which long ago crossed the borders of the Soviet Union and became world-wide in its scope. The Russian part of the history of Bolshevism was never definitively written; and although its main outlines are well known, there is a sad lack of documentation in the English language available to the modern student. Our part of this history, however — the history of the Fourth International in general and our party in particular — has been written and documented. The history of our party is a chapter of the history of living Bolshevism. And not the poorest chapter, either, for it was written in sixteen years of reaction, defeats and uphill struggle all the way from the beginning up to the present day.

We have waged an unceasing and irreconcilable theoretical and political fight against the Stalinist degeneration. But not only that. Our record is also a record of struggle against all other anti-Marxist tendencies as well. Our fight against sectarianism was conducted on classic lines. Our fight on all fronts — theoretical, political and organizational — against the petty-bourgeois revisionists recapitulated the whole historical struggle of Bolshevism and Menshevism. In building our party we employed, from the beginning, the organizational methods of Lenin, and successfully fought off every attempt — and there were many — to replace them by anarcho-Menshevik substitutes.

The older members of our party know its history as a part of the authentic history of Bolshevism. They do not need to be told that Morrison's arguments are not drawn from this arsenal. The younger party members who want to know what the traditional practice of Bolshevism are have not far to seek. They need only study the history of their own party. There is no lack of material.

The contentions of Morrison can find no support in this history, but on the contrary are directed against it. In a published letter, written while at work on the pamphlet which forms the first section of *The Struggle for a Proletarian Party*, I remarked that the pamphlet was not designed to influence the course of the inner-party struggle then drawing to its end, but was, rather, being "written for the future." The arguments of Morrison transform this "future" into the present. The answer to these arguments, written in advance, appears in polemics directed against the organizational conceptions of the petty-bourgeois opposition.

When it comes to organization we follow Lenin, and nobody is going to talk us out of it. Lenin always paid far more attention to the "organization question", was far stricter, firmer, more definite about it, precisely because he really aimed to build a party to lend a revolution. The Mensheviks only dabbled with the idea, but Lenin was in earnest; he had it in his blood. This difference — and what a difference — manifested itself even before any political differences were formulated. So it has always been. "Hard" and "soft" approaches to the organization question have marked every conflict of the two opposing tendencies from the very first preliminary skirmishes at the Russian party congress of 1903, up to the present time. The documents of our party history testify to the role this question played in the last great party fight against the petty-bourgeois faction of Burnham and Shachtman. It is a historic fact that the 1903 split between the Bolsheviks and Mensheviks — a premature split, to be sure — took place over the formulation of the first paragraph of the party constitution defining party membership. [In fact, it did not. Lenin was in the minority on that question at the congress, but did not split over it. The split came through the Mensheviks refusing to accept the editorial board for the party paper *Iskra* elected at the congress.] Even there, says Trotsky in his autobiography, "the two divergent tendencies were unmistakable. Lenin wanted clear-cut perfectly defined relationships within the party. Martov tended toward diffuse forms." The debate which has arisen over the affair of the New York membership meeting in the year 1944 sounds like an echo of these words.

Insisting on "perfectly definite relationships within the party", Bolshevism — all the outraged howling of its opponents to the contrary notwithstanding — has nevertheless always been, and is now, completely free from any trace of dogmatic rigidity, fixity or finality in its organizational forms and procedures. Our organizational methods are designed to serve political ends, are always subordinated to them, and are readily amended, changed or even turned upside down to suit them. Democratic centralism, for example, is not a dogma to be understood statically as a formula containing the unchanging quantities of 50% democracy and 50% centralism. Democratic centralism is a dialectical concept in which the emphasis is continually being shifted in consonance with the changing needs of the party in its process of development. A period of virtually unrestricted internal democracy, which is normally the rule during the discussion of disputed questions under legal conditions, can be replaced by a regime of military centralism for party action under conditions of external persecution and danger, and vice versa; and all conceivable gradations between these two extremes can be resorted to without doing violence to the principle of democratic centralism.

What is essential is that the right emphasis be placed at the right time. Bolshevism, far from any dogmatic rigidity ascribed to it by superficial critics, is distinguished by the great flexibility of its organizational forms and methods. This does not signify, however, that there are no definite rules, no basic principles. These principles, in fact, are unchanging in their essence no matter how flexibly the party may see fit to apply them in different situations. Two of these basic principles, which are recognized by every Bolshevik but which appear to need reassertion in the light of the dispute over the New York incident, may be set down as follows:

(1) The party is conceived as a combat organization destined to lead a revolution. It is not a free-thinkers' discussion club, not a mere forum for self-expression and self-improvement imposing no personal obligations on its members. The party is not an anarchist madhouse where everyone does as he pleases, but an army which faces the outside world as a unit.

(2) Following from this, it is an unchanging party law that the party has the right to control and direct the political activity of each and every member; to be informed about and regulate and supervise the relations, if any, of each and every member with political opponents of the party; and to demand of each and every member disciplined compliance with party decisions and instructions, and 100% — not 99% — loyalty to the party.

Anyone who disputes these principles does not talk our language. Anyone who disputes these principles must seek support for his arguments from some other source than the history of our party. He will not find it there.

Morrison discerns evidence of "Stalinism" in the procedure of the New York organization, and other incidents, and is greatly disturbed by symptoms of "degeneration" which he sees, or thinks he sees, on every side. He says: "Since the terrible Stalinist degeneration, every serious person in the Marxist movement fears and thinks of possible degeneration". Again: "Let not one single Stalinist germ penetrate into our ranks." And so on and so forth. Such warnings have a familiar ring. We have heard them many times before. But up till now our party has successfully resisted all dangers of Stalinist degeneration, with or without benefit from the numerous warnings, which their authors, unfortunately, were not always equally successful in resisting other forms of degeneration no better than the Stalinist variety. The history of our party contains some instructive lessons on this point also.

The danger of degeneration in a revolutionary party comes from the pressure of its environment. The founding cadres of our party came exclusively from the Communist Party; and for the first five years of our existence we maintained the position of a faction, seeking to reform the parent organization and disclaiming any desire to form an independent party. Our most immediate environment, therefore, was the Communist Party in which the process of Stalinist degeneration was in full swing, Moreover, the successes of the Soviet industrialization at that time — the period of the first Five Year Plan — contrasted to the destructive crisis in the capitalist world, were lending great prestige to the Stalinists. The CP was rapidly expanding in membership and influence; its domination of the progressive labor movement and of the radical intellectual circles was complete. The pressure upon our small dissident group was very strong at that time. It is a historic fact worth noting that the great majority of the original cadres of the Left Opposition throughout the world succumbed to this pressure. "Capitulation" to the Stalinist regime decimated the ranks of the Opposition like a plague in one country after another.

How did the young Trotskyist organization in America fare under these hard conditions? Nothing of the kind happened here. A few casual individuals of no special influence who had joined us on "democratic" grounds — perhaps half a dozen all told — gave up the fight and went back to the Stalinist camp as capitulators; "democracy" alone is not an adequate platform for a serious and protracted political fight. But not a single leader, not a single American Trotskyist of influence, nationally or locally, then or ever made peace with Stalinism.

From this fact, which speaks louder than anybody's words, one is entitled to infer that the American section of the International Left Opposition, the predecessor of the Fourth International, was pretty well inoculated against the Stalinist degeneration from the start. And that inference would be 100% correct. We educated our cadres (and ourselves) to fight the theoretical and political positions of Stalinism, not only its organizational methods and techniques.

Yes, it may be said once again, you thoroughly exposed Stalinism and taught the advanced workers to despise it. But in waging this fight you yourselves, adopted the "methods" of Stalinism. Of course, of course. We know all about that. We have heard all about that before. And we answered them as we answer now: Stalinism is not a system of "methods", as its superficial critics imagine, but a political tendency with a definite social basis, the social basis of a privileged bureaucracy in the Soviet Union and its hired agents throughout the world. The "methods" are the result, not the cause. These methods — bureaucratic violence, lying, falsifying, double-dealing, betraying — are needed by a bureaucracy serving special interests in forcing through a policy which violates the doctrines and traditions of Bolshevism.

But what need have we of these methods? What special interests do we serve which conflict with the interests of the rank and file of the party and the working class? What false policy do we have to impose on them by violence and fraud? Burnham and Shachtman are still trying to find a plausible answer to these questions. Morrison will have no better success.

It is not much of an answer to say that this or that individual is by nature a Stalinist who perversely employs methods in a small party dedicated to the struggle against Stalinism. Why has the party, which is anti-Stalinist to the core, tolerated such individuals and even placed them in central positions of leadership? Better yet, why have such Stalinists by nature, if they have any sense at all, and if they are not simply Stalinist agents in our ranks — why have they wasted their time in a small persecuted party whose internal democracy has always been a model for the whole world? Why haven't they gone back to the Stalinist party where they would feel more at home? Such questions have never seriously arisen for the simple reason that Stalinist influence in our party has existed only in the imagination of people who have exaggerated its dangers and overlooked other and far greater ones to which they themselves were yielding.

The danger of degeneration in a revolutionary party comes from the pressure of its environment. The environment which our party has operated in, especially since our definitive break with the Comintern in 1933, is the bourgeois society in the strongest and richest of all bourgeois countries. This pressure has been real, not imaginary; it has claimed not a few victims in the past; and today, with the reaction engendered by the war, it presses against us more heavily than ever. If one is seriously looking for signs of "degeneration" he should turn his attention in the direction of the real danger. He should quit babbling about Stalinism for a while and become more sensitive to evidences of weak-willed yielding to the powerful influences of the class enemy.

Stalinism itself, properly understood, is not at all an independent force, but one of the forms of adaptation to the material and moral terror of the bourgeoisie; and, thereby, it is one of its agencies in the labor movement. There are other forms of adaptation and capitulation. We have had enough experience with them already to be able to identify them at first sight. In their finished form they all seek to oppose a petty-bourgeois program to the program of Bolshevism, but they almost invariably begin by revolting against its irreconcilable spirit and its organizational methods. Such tendencies, wherever they appear in the party, reveal the real danger of degeneration as unfailingly as the holes where water seeps through show the weak spots in a dike. Since the earliest days of our movement in the United States nobody has gone over to Stalinism. But deserters to the camp of "democratic" capitalism have been rather numerous. What is to be guarded against, on the basis of this experience, is any tendency of conciliationism toward these deserters in any stage of their degeneration. Such conciliationist tendencies are the real, not imaginary, "danger of degeneration in our ranks."

Morrison rejects the idea that the party has the right and duty to be informed about, and to regulate and control, any and all relations which party members may have with political opponents. This idea, concretely demonstrated by the ruling in the case of the four New York comrades, impresses him as "having a resemblance to Stalinist procedure."

When the party leadership insists on strict rules in this regard, it indicates, to Morrison, only that "the leadership thinks it is impermissible to discuss questions with members of the WP"; that they lack pride and confidence in their ideas. In contrast to the party leadership's attitude toward opponent organizations, Morrison proceeds to lay down some rules of his own. Relating what his own practices have been, he recommends them to the party members as a guide. Morrison sees nothing abnormal in a member of our organization shopping around at the meetings and affairs of other political organizations, fraternizing with their members and discussing political questions with them, formally or informally, on their own responsibility. Whether such activity should be reported to the party or not — that, says Morrison, is up to the individual member to decide. On this point, he again refers to Lenin and the Bolsheviks.

It would have been better to leave Lenin out of it. Morrison's view of this matter is not new, to be sure, but it has no right to represent itself as a Leninist conception of normal relations between rival political organizations and their members. This question also has a history, which apparently has made no impression on Morrison.

The formulas he offers would take us back to the primitive conceptions of party organization which dominated American labor radicalism before the First World War; that is, before the movement grew up and learned the meaning of a program and a party. It was precisely what we learned from Lenin that enabled us to discard those outmoded and entirely inadequate conceptions a full quarter of a century ago. And in this, as in so many other fields, experience corroborated Lenin's theory and, in turn, supplied its own instructive lessons along the same line. Morrison's formulas contradict the theory and disregard the experience. Before the First World War the dominating sentiment among the various social protest organizations and groups, despite all their differences and quarrels, was that of fraternity — the feeling of one-ness, the opinion that all the groups were part of one and the same movement, and that all would, sooner or later, "get together." As a rule, a definite distinction was made between the terms "organization" and "the movement". One's own particular organization, be it the Socialist Party, the IWW, any one of the numerous anarchist groups, local forums, or even a club of Single Taxers [followers of Henry George's program for a "single tax" on land values to replace all others], or an independent socialist educational society, was thought of as a party; the "movement" was the whole. It was common practice for the "radicals" of different affiliations to patronize each other's meetings and affairs, to participate in common forums, reading clubs and purely social organizations. In Kansas City and San Francisco, to my knowledge, "Radical Clubs" were deliberately organized to promote fraternization at monthly dinners. Radicals of all tendencies mingled socially and inter-married without thought of personal incompatibility arising from a conflict of ideas.

Nor did the separate organizations draw sharp lines in their admittance of members. With the exception of De Leon's Socialist Labor Party, which stood aloof and was with some justice regarded as intolerant and sectarian, they were all rather catholic in their composition. Reformists and revolutionists, "ballot boxers" and "direct actionists", belonged to one and the same Socialist Party. Christian socialists and professional Christ-killers, prohibitionists and partisans of the open saloon, kept them company. The propaganda branches of the syndicalist IWW extended their hospitality alike to socialists and anarchists. Anarchism was thought by many to be more radical, more revolutionary, than socialism; and anyone who was against "authority" was free to call himself an anarchist. Freelance radicals, whose name was legion, were regarded as part of "the movement" on even terms with all the others.

In Europe, the pre-war social democracy was an "all inclusive party". Unity was fetishized; the left wing shrank from the thought of split. Luxemburg and Liebknecht were party comrades with Kautsky, Noske and Scheideman. In Russia Lenin resolutely carried through the split [between Bolsheviks and Mensheviks, actually definitive only in 1912], but Trotsky insisted on the unification of the Bolsheviks and Mensheviks [he made a failed attempt at unification with a congress in 1912].

The state of affairs in American labor radicalism prior to the First World War is related here without intention either to praise or to blame. It was due to circumstances of the time; the organizations, in their membership composition and in their relations with each other, could not rise above the level of their own understanding. This was the period of the infancy of the American revolutionary movement. Neither theory nor experience had yet taught us any better. The differences between the theories and tendencies, and their respective organizations, had not been fully thought out. None of the tendencies had yet been put to great historic tests. Great events shattered this idyll. The war, and then the Russian revolution, put all theories and tendencies to the test and drew them out to their ultimate conclusions. Reformist socialism was revealed as class treachery. Anarchism and syndicalism, with their "denial" of the state, revealed their theoretical inadequacy, their bankruptcy, despite their grandiloquent revolutionary pretensions. Revolutionary Marxism, Bolshevism, alone stood up under the test of war and revolution. The Russian Bolsheviks taught us this in word and deed. The American militants learned from them, for the first time, the full meaning of the program, and simultaneously, the significance, the role, of the vanguard party.

The revolutionary workers of the whole world went to the same school. A world-wide realignment of forces began to take place under the impact of the war and the revolution. Lines were sharply drawn. Sentimental unification gave way to ruthless splits, and the splits became definitive, irreconcilable. The revolutionary militants, instructed by the war and the revolution, learned to counterpose the Marxist program to all other programs. Instructed by the precise teachings of Lenin, they learned the necessity of organizing their own party, separate and apart from all others, and to build it, not in fraternal tolerance of other parties, but in ruthless struggle against them.

Once these ABC lessons were assimilated — and, I repeat, we learned them 25 years ago — the revolutionary vanguard broke decisively with the old tradition of mish-mash parties and loose coalitions, with free-lance radicalism and bohemian irresponsibility. In place of all that the organizational principles laid down by Lenin were adopted: unity on the basis of a principled program; all devotion, all loyalty, to one party and only one party; strict responsibility and accountability of every member to the party; professional leadership; democratic centralism. The pioneer American Communists, and we, their heirs and continuators, have worked on these lines consistently and unswervingly since 1919.

If our party stands today on far higher ground than that occupied by the amorphous rebel workers' movement prior to the First World War — and that is indubitably the case — it is not due solely to the superiority of our program, but also to the consistent application in practice of the principles and methods of Bolshevik organization. The experience of a quarter of a century has convinced us over and over again that this is the right way, the only way, to build a revolutionary party.

It is absurd to think that we can unwind the film of this experience and go back to where we started. But if Morrison's criticism and formulas mean anything seriously, that is what they mean. We cannot entertain any such propositions for a moment. In politics, nothing is more stupid, more infantile, than to retrace ground that has already been covered, to go back and start all over again as if nothing had happened and nothing had been learned. Serious revolutionists must learn from every experience and apply what they have learned in new experiences. We insist on that. The new generation must not begin from the beginning. The fruit of the experience of the past, all that has been acquired and learned by others, is their heritage. They begin with that. Translated into terms of the "organizational question", this means that

609

they begin not from the pre-historic confusion of pre-war days — where Morrison's conceptions would take them — but from the most recent experiences in which our organizational principles and methods were tested in life, the great struggle against the petty-bourgeois opposition, in 1939-40.

All the 40-years experience of Bolshevism — in organization, as well as in theory and politics — was recapitulated in that historic struggle. The new party recruits can learn about Bolshevism and Menshevism on the organization question by a study of the documents of this fight. It is not without interest to note that the party leadership, in the dispute over the incident of the New York membership meeting, shows its unqualified hostility to any sign of looseness or irresponsibility — to say nothing of disloyalty — in relations with the Menshevik traitor clique of Shachtman & Co.; while Morrison, in his plea for unsupervised fraternization, manifests a more conciliatory attitude. On both sides, here as always, the organizational method serves the political line.

SWP Internal Bulletin, Volume 6, No. 10, Nov 1944

Gross sentimentality, unbending rigidity, unfair attacks

James T Farrell (1944)

DEAR FRIENDS AND COMRADES: For some time, I have been disturbed by two articles which have appeared in your pages, *How the Trotskyists Went to Jail,* by Joseph Hansen (February 1944) [about the 18 SWP members jailed in 1944 for sedition after the Minneapolis Smith Act trial of 1941] and *A Defamer of Marxism,* by Harry Frankel (May 1944) [Braverman; this volume, p.393]. I have decided to send you this public protest against them.

What is most lamentable in Joseph Hansen's article is the gross emotional reaction to events which it reveals. Such an attitude must be condemned. There are fine models of Marxist writing; there are other fine models of writing, such as the letters of Vanzetti. Instead of learning from these, it seems as if Hansen imitated the very worst of bourgeois journalism, the sob sisters. I cannot escape the conclusion that Hansen used the Marxist conception of history and the Marxist conception of morality as a means of mere sentimental personalization. If such is not the adulation of leadership, I do not know what it is. I admire the fine example which the eighteen showed during the trial: I admire them for the way in which they have preserved their morale while in jail. But this does not mean that I should adulate them, no more than that I should hope for them or anyone else to adulate me for any reason whatsoever. I also wish strongly to object to the assertion that only the Trotskyists are moral. When party leaders and leading party journalists make such assertions in public, the time has come for such a party to turn a sharp lens of criticism on itself. Hansen's attitude can only create distorted images of reality. I consider it dangerous. The other criticism of Hansen's article – his bad taste, his sloppiness, his bathos – which one can make – these are secondary to its dangerous orientation. I deem it absolutely necessary to criticize that – the emotional reaction to events, and with it, the emotional concept of history.

I reject the theory of bureaucratic collectivism. But I consider that Harry Frankel's review of Max Shachtman can well be described as literary apache work. It was not principled in its arguments. It substituted vituperation for argument and analysis. In consequence, it destroyed the effect of the good points which it made. For instance, Frankel indicated that during the Finnish War, Max Shachtman used the low morale of the Red Army as one argument substantiating his position. Thereby, he established morale as a criterion of argument. In consequence, it should be obligatory for him to explain the high morale of the Red Army in repulsing the Nazi invasion. But the fact that I agree with some of the points made by Frankel does not mean that I should defend his unfairness, his uncouth efforts to strip his adversary of all dignity, all honor, all sincerity. I consider it highly objectionable to polemicize with shabby arguments. And that is precisely what Frankel did in this article.

For instance, he wrote that Shachtman had issued a "new edition" of Trotsky's *The New Course*. Here is an innuendo which helps Frankel discredit Shachtman, to call him, in the manner of a fishwife, a black market charlatan. Now, where is the old edition of *The New Course*? Who sells it? When has it been advertised in your press? When I read this book, I immediately regretted that it had not been available sooner; I regretted in particular that it was not available during the period of the struggle against the Moscow Trials. Among other things, this book contains a brilliant description of the methods of Leninism, one which I hope will be widely read. I hope Harry Frankel will read it again. For I am convinced that he has much to learn from it.

Also: Harry Frankel asked an empty question as a means of discrediting his opponent. Issuing a challenge, he asked why Max Shachtman did not republish *The Revolution Betrayed*. First of all, there is easy access to this book for all who want to read it. Second, it is a known fact that the publication rights to this book are owned by Doubleday, Doran & Co. If Max Shachtman published it, he would, undoubtedly, be faced with a lawsuit. And if that happened, I am rather sure that Frankel, or one of his comrades who is equally rigid in attitude, would then write of this lawsuit in order to prove the low morals of Max Shachtman.

When one indulges in such cheap argument, what moral right has one to call anybody a black market merchant in tripe? Why ask empty questions as a means of destroying the character of an adversary? Also, Harry Frankel would have us believe that in the United States, Max Shachtman has abandoned the Marxist conception of a trade union: in other words that he is a scab and a strikebreaker. I wonder who will believe that?

And while he indulges in such miserable means of refutation, Frankel is, at the same time, guilty of one serious omission. Trotsky conceded that it might happen that history will prove Bruno to have been correct, and that if this turns out to be the case, then Marxists will have to reorientate themselves totally. But, Trotsky, added, he was not convinced that events had, as yet, justified Bruno, and that therefore, it was wrong for Marxists to abandon their program. This concession was a very important one. Frankel should have discussed it. It would have been more important to have it discussed than to have wasted space in the cheapest of abuse. The fact that I reject Max Shachtman's acceptance of the theory of bureaucratic collectivism does not, in my eyes, justify me in approving of unfair, unprincipled, utterly unjust attacks upon him and his character. I consider such methods to be unworthy of Marxism.

I am, as is well known, not a member of your party. But I have collaborated with you on defense cases. I have expressed sympathy with you. On more than one occasion, I have made it clear to Max Shachtman and his collaborators that I did not agree with the theory of bureaucratic collectivism. The fact that I have done this causes me to feel all the more imperatively that it is my duty to send you this protest. Also: I admire the organized will which your party has shown. I admire your spirit of optimism and confidence. I admire the many examples of dedication to ideals and sacrifice for superpersonal loyalties which your party has displayed. But none of these virtues can, in any way, excuse the Frankel attack.

I am fearful that if articles such as these two continue to appear, their only effect will be that of working harm, not good. Gross sentimentality, unbending rigidity, unfair attacks on opponents – these are all dangerous. I hold them to be indefensible.

Fraternally yours,

James T. Farrell. July 30, 1944

New International, November 1944

We should make revisionists hateful

Harry Braverman (1944)

I SHOULD LIKE TO bring a few points to the attention of the party in connection with the letter of James T. Farrell objecting to two articles in our
press. (Internal Bulletin, Vol. VI; No. 6). I need deal only with the attacks on
our review of Shachtman's book, *The Struggle for the New Course*, that appeared in the *FI*...

If the charges against the review of Shachtman's book are reduced to their
essence, they constitute an accusation of demagogy. It should be made absolutely clear that we reject such methods of struggle. We reject demagogy
because the demagogue disarms the party, depriving it of the proper principled arguments, which are the weapons of Marxists. The demagogue provides us with treacherous weapons which will explode in our hands at the
first encounter. That is why the demagogue is the enemy of the party.

Our press is written and edited with that injunction in mind. The review
of Shachtman's book is no exception. Not one word of the review need be
altered to make it comply with the requirements of principled polemic. As
for the harshness of the "attack", any improvement that the article requires,
and it could stand many, would be in the direction of increasing the hostility
and irreconcilability of our attack against this most recent and least original
school of revisionism as represented by Shachtman.

I have read and re-read Farrell's letter with care, but I cannot find in it
any support for his attack on the review. Farrell, apparently, read the review
with his political eye closed, and his subjective, emotional eye open. That is
the only way I can interpret his avoidance of the main political points of the
article, and preoccupation with secondary, insignificant points. For example:
The review opens with the point that, in his edition of *The New Course*,
Shachtman makes an unprincipled attempt to use Trotsky's writings as a vehicle for an anti-Trotskyist, anti-Marxist position on the Soviet Union. What
other significance can the linking of Trotsky and Shachtman in one volume
have? But Farrell detours just before coming to this point and attacks us
wildly for referring to a "new" edition of *The New Course*, construing this in
some way as an attack on Shachtman for publishing a pirated edition of the
book! If Farrell will permit me to explain: to publish *The New Course* is no
crime; to publish it together with Shachtman's attack on Trotskyism is charlatanism.

Farrell makes a similar detour on his second point. In our review we develop the point that Shachtman, in writing about the Trotskyist position on
the Soviet Union, chose as his springboard one of the very few of Trotsky's
writings on the Russian question which could not by political and even by
chronological necessity (it was written in 1923) present the Trotskyist analysis of the Soviet Union. We point out that Shachtman should attempt to re-

fute *The Revolution Betrayed,* or The Soviet Union and the Fourth International, or even to review *In Defense of Marxism,* which he has never done. Farrell seizes upon our mention of *The Revolution Betrayed* with the shout that Shachtman could not republish it since the publication rights are owned by a bourgeois firm!

Copyrights are not involved in this matter. How can Farrell replace the main political point with such a technicality? If Shachtman undertakes to revise Trotsky's analysis of the Soviet Union, it is incumbent upon him to answer the main works dealing with that analysis and take them as his point of departure. Farrell might have noticed that we mention two other of Trotsky's writings in addition to *The Revolution Betrayed.* One of them was published by us recently. All Shachtman need do is review it. We are told that Shachtman is prevented from replying to Trotsky's analysis of the Soviet Union as it is presented in his many books, articles and resolutions because... Doubleday Doran holds publication rights to one of them! No, that is false. Shachtman's sidestepping on this matter is part of his renegacy; his desire to hide behind Trotsky's name while betraying Trotsky's ideas as so many renegades before him have attempted to do with Marx and Lenin. Our point here is scrupulously principled, and exposes the Shachtmanite unprincipledness.

I must say that I read with indignation Farrell's misinterpretation of the review in his third point. Let me repeat his words. "Also, Harry Frankel would have us believe that in the United States, Max Shachtman has abandoned the Marxist conception of a trade union, in other words, that he is a scab and a strike breaker. I wonder who will believe that?" How can Farrell give this false twist to our characterization of Shachtman's venture into the field of the trade union analogy? The review says nothing of the sort. It is clearly stated that Shachtman adopts an "ultra-leftist" criterion for the trade union movement to justify his arbitrary normative method in determining the nature of the Soviet Union. If the Shachtmanites are scabs and strikebreakers thus far it is in relation to the Soviet Union.

Piling one final error on all the others, Farrell adds that Trotsky made an "important concession" to Bruno, Shachtman's revisionist predecessor. Trotsky conceded, he says, that history "might prove Bruno to have been correct" in his theory of bureaucratic collectivism, and I should have discussed this But Trotsky discussed it himself, denying categorically that he had made any new "concessions". He explains this fully, pointing out that; "Marxists have formulated an incalculable number of times the alternatives; either socialism or a return to barbarism".

The claim that Trotsky had made concessions to the Bruno type notions, concessions which amounted to a "revision" of Marxism, was one of the innumerable phantasmagoria conjured up by the Shachtmanites during the factional struggle of 1939-40. Answering them, Trotsky wrote: "If we are to speak of a revision of Marx, it is in reality the revision of those comrades who project a new type of state, non-bourgeois-and non-worker. Because the alternative developed by me leads them to draw their own thoughts up to their logical conclusion, some of these critics, frightened by the conclusions of their own theory, accuse me... of revising Marxism. I prefer to think that it is simply a friendly jest."

It is Shachtman who makes all the concessions to the Bruno type notions that Trotsky discussed. We bear no responsibility whatsoever for that. Such are the points upon which Farrell bases his many epithets against the review. Those who can find a basis for all his epithets in his arguments could also succeed in erecting a building on sand piles. Such serious charges demand more serious proof. Among the most amazing aspects of Farrell's letter is his interpretation of our branding Shachtmanism for what it is as an attempt to besmirch Shachtman's "personal character". "Unjust attacks on him and his character", "strip his adversary of all... sincerity" are among his comments. We can assure Farrell that there are very few things that interest me less than Shachtman's "character". There not one argument in the review that is not aimed at the political position and political methodology of the Shachtmanites. Can it be that his too personal view of the polemic caused Farrell to miss the main political points? We fear that is what happened. For non-political, personal denigration, Farrell will have to consult the writings of Shachtman. In answering my review, this poor slandered character makes reference more than once to my youth, an indubitable fault, but one which I hope to correct in time. Will Farrell write a letter protesting such arguments "ad hominem"...?

Farrell advises me to reread Trotsky's *New Course* in order to learn more about the "methods of Leninism". (How can Farrell forgot that Trotsky characterized Shachtmanism just as the review did, only far more harshly?) I as well as all of us have much to learn in this field. But I can assure Farrell that, study as I may, I will not find conciliationism towards revisionists among the methods of Leninism.

During the early days of the Comintern, Trotsky once wrote in July, 1921, the following words of advice to a young French party that had the problem of dealing with a revisionist grouping: "A split is a very, very serious matter, and once we have recognized the inevitability of split, it is necessary that the masses should understand its full significance. It is necessary mercilessly to expose the policies of the Dissidents (the minority followers of Longuet who split in 1919 — H.F.) It is necessary to make their leaders and their press ludicrous and hateful in the eyes of the masses".

Not a "comradely discussion" but a ruthless struggle; not a polite polemic but a head-on attack to make the opponents "ludicrous and hateful" — such was Trotsky's advice. Are these not authentic words of advice as to the methods of Leninism? There is no more Leninist way to deal with splitters and revisionists.

"Comments on the letter from James T. Farrell". Under the pen-name Harry Frankel. SWP Internal Bulletin vol.6 no.8, October 1944

An arbitrary, factional, self-serving attitude

Albert Goldman (1944)

SEPTEMBER 3, 1944: The following information has reached me [Goldman was in jail at the time]. Jim Farrell wrote a letter to the *FI* criticizing the Hansen article and Frankel's review of *The New Course*. For about a month Jim received no word as to whether or not his letter would be published. Then someone told him that the questions raised in his letter would be discussed in the pre-convention period. It was not made clear whether Jim's letter would be published in toto even in the [internal, SWP-members-only] bulletin. I gather that Jim is disturbed at the refusal of the *FI* to publish his letter and would like my advice.

I must, in the first place, state that from the excerpts I have read, I consider the letter as one from a loyal friend of the party, whose main interest in writing it is to call attention to a type of article which he disapproves and considers harmful to the party.

As a friend of the party there is nothing for him to do except to bring the matter to the attention of the party membership. In this way he will act, as he should, an a party member whose right and duty it is to bring to the membership any decision of a higher body, which he considers to be a serious error and hope that the error will be corrected. You can tell him that I shall try my best to get the whole question before the membership.

September 4, 1944: The membership should carefully consider the significance of the Political Committee's refusal to publish James T. Farrell's letter to the *FI*, in which he criticizes the Hansen article and Frankel's review of *The New Course*. A valuable lesson can be learned from the refusal to publish Farrell's letter. Once a mistake is made and obstinately adhered to, other mistakes are almost certain to follow; a problem not solved correctly is almost certain to lead to further problems. A mistake was made when Hansen's article was published. That mistake could have been easily rectified if Morrison's letter answering Macdonald had been published. The refusal to publish Morrison's [i.e. Goldman's own] letter, which, in all probability, would have ended the discussion on the Hansen article, has now placed us in an absurd position of refusing to publish a letter of criticism from a friend of the party.

The mere fact that a problem has arisen by virtue of Farrell' s sending the *FI* a friendly letter criticizing two articles shows that there is something wrong in the attitude of the people who make the decisions as to what to publish and what not to publish. A party would never be confronted with a problem because of the receipt of a letter of criticism from a friend if the people in charge of the publications would make correct decisions as to the material that should or should not be published. Such a letter would be published as a matter of course. If the author is wrong an answer would be forthcoming showing wherein he is wrong; if he is correct an admission of his correctness would end the matter.

Are we dealing here with a situation where an opponent of the party disagreeing with its basic principles writes a letter or an article against party policy? Are we, in other words, dealing with a situation where an opponent wants to utilize our press for the presentation of his views, which are antagonistic to ours? The answer must of course be an unhesitating and emphatic "No!"

We are confronted by an altogether different situation — where a friend of the party writes a letter of criticism with reference to articles that do not involve party policy. There can be no doubt whatever amongst those who know Farrell and his attitude to our party that he is friendly to the party. It is clear from the letter itself that it is written by a friend who does not approve the contents and tone of two articles, who thinks that those articles are harmful to the party and wants to call attention to that fact. To designate such a letter as unfriendly to the party is completely arbitrary and can convince no reasoning person.

For the party it is not primarily a question of what Farrell and others will think of our refusal to publish a critical letter from a friend. It is a question of correct procedure to follow in such cases. It is a question of creating confidence in our own ranks that we fear no criticism because we can answer any adverse criticism or admit its correctness. The membership should demand the publication of Farrell's letter.

SWP Internal Bulletin Volume 6, No. 6, October 1944.

Criticisms by intellectual amateurs is an insult to the party

James P Cannon

THE LEADERS OF THE opposition showed a great deal of disregard for the opinions and sentiment of the party membership. Perhaps the worst manifestation was the demand that James T. Farrell's letter be published; the attempt to impose his pompous strictures on the party as some kind of authority which the party was bound to recognize. That was a coarse and brutal insult to the party. The party would not be a party if it had not learned to rely on itself and to reject out of hand every suggestion of guidance from outside sources.

We learn and correct our mistakes through mutual discussion and criticism among ourselves. We Leninists have studied the art of revolutionary politics and organization and our decisions receive the constant corrective of the workers' mass movement. We work at it every day. Such individuals as James T. Farrell, whose main interest and occupation lie in other fields, haven't yet started even to think about it seriously. His banal letter alone is sufficient proof of that. Before he, or anyone like him, can presume to teach us he must himself first go to school. We take our ideas and our work far too seriously to welcome instruction from people who haven't the slightest idea of what they are talking about; who mistake vague impressions and philistine prejudices for professional competence.

It is remarkable how politics lures the amateur. Every other art and science, every profession and occupation, has its own recognized body of knowledge and its own rules and standards which amateurs and laymen respect from a distance and take for granted. People who don't know the business do not presume to lay down the law to those who do. Neither James T. Farrell, nor anyone else who didn't wish to make himself ridiculous, would ever dream of intruding – with a ponderous air of authority, at that – on a discussion among practitioners of another art or profession outside the field of his own special study and experience.

But in the art of revolutionary politics and organization – which is not the least difficult nor the least important of the arts, since its aim is to change the world – any dabbler feels free to pontificate without the slightest sign of serious preparation. Dwight Macdonald is the arch-type of these political Alices in Wonderland. But Farrell, as the most cursory reading of his childish letter shows, is not much closer to the real world. There is nothing we can do about it. We can't prevent such people from committing their half-baked notions to paper as soon as they pop into their heads and then waiting for the earth to quake.

But we have people in our ranks – worse yet in our leadership – who excitedly demand that we set aside our rules and suspend our business to listen to these preposterous oracles and even to heed their revelations. We should in all conscience object to that. That is downright offensive. We now learn that James T. Farrell's letter has finally found its place in Shachtman's magazine. That is where it belonged in the first place.

January 16, 1945

SWP Internal Bulletin vol.7 no.2, April 1945

Zinoviev: a great hero

James P Cannon (1955)

I WAS GREATLY INFLUENCED by Zinoviev in the early days of the Comintern, as were all communists throughout the world. I have never forgotten that he was Lenin's closest collaborator in the years of reaction and during the First World War; that he was the foremost orator of the revolution, according to the testimony of Trotsky; and that he was the Chairman of the Comintern in the Lenin-Trotsky time.

It was Zinoviev's bloc with Trotsky and his expulsion, along with Trotsky, that first really shook me up and started the doubts and discontents which eventually led me to Trotskyism. I have always been outraged by the impudent pretensions of so many little people to deprecate Zinoviev, and I feel that he deserves justification before history...

In the exigencies of the political struggle it has not been convenient for the Trotskyist movement to make a full and objective evaluation of this man's life; and others have shown no interest in it. But historical justice cries out for it and it will be done sometime by somebody. In spite of all, Zinoviev deserves restoration as one of the great hero-martyrs of the revolution.

Letter to Theodore Draper, 26 July 1955, from *The First Ten Years of American Communism*

Zinovievist? I learned from Trotsky

James P Cannon (1945)

NOW THE SECOND POINT is about Zinoviev. You know I have had a practice for twenty years in the movement of making very few answers to personal attacks because I always have the good luck to have so many personal attacks made against me that if I took time to answer them all I would never have time to get down to the issues in dispute, never get to the meat of the situation...

But this question about Zinoviev I want to answer briefly because I think it has some historic importance. Zinoviev was not one man. There were four Zinovievs at least — I would say there were six Zinovievs. There was the Zinoviev who was the most intimate collaborator of Lenin in exile during the war, who did great historic work. Then there was the Zinoviev who... together with Kamenev, lost his nerve on the eve of the [October 1917] insurrection... Then there was the] Zinoviev who corrected himself after that, who became the chairman of the Comintern and Lenin's agent, really, in leading the Comintern.

All the great worldwide propaganda against Zinovievism and Zinoviev was set in motion by the group of centrists who were attracted to the Comintern in its first years and recoiled from it in its first years under Lenin: Balabanov and others of that sort who gave to the whole organization and method of Lenin, the organization of the Comintern, the twenty-one points, they gave the name of Zinoviev, making it synonymous with Leninism. When anybody waves the flag of Zinovievism you can do very well to trace it back to which Zinoviev they mean...

Then there was a fourth Zinoviev, the Zinoviev of the troika with Stalin and Kamenev after the death of Lenin. This is the Zinoviev who began to backslide, and it is correct, as Goldman said, that the organizational methods that began to be introduced into the Comintern, in contradistinction to the earlier years, were sort of a bridge toward Stalinism. Not Stalinism by a long way, but a bridge toward a beginning of the bureaucratism.

In that period Zinoviev was chairman of the Comintern. All the most influential pronouncements and articles coming from Moscow came in the name of Zinoviev. He was the leader of the Fifth Congress. The writings of the Left Opposition under Trotsky were suppressed. We got only faint snatches of them here and there and I, like every other leader of the American party in those days, could be said to be a Zinovievist. We were taken in by that campaign of the troika.

In that time, the campaign twenty-one years ago, when my sin is cited, I would say it would be very safe to say at that time I was a Zinovievist in the sense that every other leader of the party was, in the sense that they were taking for good coin the whole line from Moscow and not examining it too critically. But then there is another Zinoviev, the fifth Zinoviev, who in 1926-27 broke away from the bloc with Stalin and concluded a bloc with Trotsky, and made as one of the issues of his campaign... the demand for party democracy.

Now I was not a Trotsky-Zinovievist in that period, but I began, as I recounted in my history, to be very disturbed about that question. But I didn't become a Trotskyist until 1928 and that was when the bloc of Trotsky and Zinoviev had been broken and the sixth Zinoviev, the capitulator, appeared and went back to the camp of Stalinism, and I, on the other hand, supported Trotsky. I didn't support Zinoviev number six.

My re-education on all the principles of Marxism, including party organization, took place under the tutelage of Trotsky from 1928 on. And if you blame me for having been a sort of Zinovievist for the period of 1924-25, you have to find me, I think some one of my accusers who was wiser. I don't know what the organizational and political views of Goldman were at that time as I am not familiar with his writings at that period. (As far as I know, he was a) supporter of the official line and swallowed it whole; but I became a Trotskyist. And it might be said in exculpation of the sin that is alleged against me, I was the first leader of American Trotskyism to become a Trotskyist and I think that should counterbalance. And I remained a Trotskyist, since 1928 up to the present.

From "A Reply to Goldman in Three Points", 7 October 1945, in *The Struggle for Socialism in the 'American Century'* pp.186-8

Don't strangle the party

James P Cannon (1966)

AS FAR AS I CAN SEE all the new moves and proposals to monkey with the Constitution which has served the party so well in the past, with the aim of "tightening" centralization, represent a trend in the wrong direction at the present time. The party (and the YSA [the SWP's youth group]) is too "tight" already, and if we go much further along this line we can run the risk of strangling the party to death...

I am particularly concerned about any possible proposal to weaken the constitutional provision about the absolute right of suspended or expelled members to appeal to the convention. That is clearly and plainly a provision to protect every party member against possible abuse of authority by the National Committee. It should not be abrogated or diluted just to show that we are so damn revolutionary that we make no concessions to "bourgeois concepts of checks and balances." The well-known Bill of Rights is a check and balance which I hope will be incorporated, in large part at least, in the Constitution of the Workers' Republic in this country. Our constitutional provision for the right of appeal is also a "check and balance." It can help to recommend our party to revolutionary workers as a genuinely democratic organization which guarantees rights as well as imposing responsibilities, and thus make it more appealing to them.

I believe that these considerations have more weight now than ever before in the thirty-eight-year history of our party. In the present political climate and with the present changing composition of the party, democratic centralism must be applied flexibly. At least ninety percent of the emphasis should be placed on the democratic side and not on any crackpot schemes to "streamline" the party to the point where questions are unwelcome and criticism and discussion stifled. That is a prescription to kill the party before it gets a chance to show how it can handle and assimilate an expanding membership of new young people, who don't know it all to start with, but have to learn and grow in the course of explication and discussion in a free, democratic atmosphere.

Trotsky once remarked in a polemic against Stalinism that even in the period of the Civil War discussion in the party was "boiling like a spring." Those words and others like it written by Trotsky, in his first attack against Stalinism in *The New Course*, ought to be explained now once again to the new young recruits in our party. And the best way to explain such decisive things is to practice what we preach.

> Letter to Reba Hansen (partner of Joseph Hansen), with copy to Ed Shaw (organisation secretary of the SWP at the time), 12 November 1966. From a pamphlet entitled *Don't Strangle the Party!* published in 1986 by the Fourth Internationalist Tendency (Trotskyists expelled from the SWP, which was by then Castroite).

The Bolshevisation of the Party

James P Cannon (1924)

THE FOUNDING OF THE WORKERS PARTY school in New York City has a great significance for the party and must be regarded as a real achievement [This is the Workers Party which was the legal name of the early Communist Party USA, not the post-1940 WP.] It is one of many signs that the American Communist movement, which already has five years of struggle behind it, is hammering itself into shape, overcoming its weaknesses, striving in real earnestness to throw off the encumbrances which it inherited from the past and to transform itself into a genuine party of Leninism.

We are well aware that our party is not yet a Bolshevik party in the complete sense of the term. But we can say that after five years we have succeeded in crystallizing at least a strong nucleus within the party which endeavors to adopt a real Leninist standpoint on every question which confronts the party. It is characteristic of such comrades that they regard the adherence of our party to the Communist International not as a formal affair, bur as an inseparable part of its being, which shapes and colors all of its activities, something that penetrates into the very marrow of its bones. For them, the word of the Communist International is decisive in all party questions. It is as one of such comrades that I wish to speak here tonight.

The Fifth Congress of the Communist International [June 17-July 8, 1924] has completed its work. It has examined and appraised the world situation. It has gone deeply into the experiences of all of the most important parties during the period since the Fourth Congress [Nov. 5-Dec. 5, 1922], as well as into the work of the International as a whole. The judgment finally arrived at has been compressed into a series of resolutions and theses which are now available for the Communist parties of the entire world. They constitute a clear guide for our future activities.

The congress found that all of the parties of the International, with the exception of the Russian party, are still far short of the requirements of a Bolshevik party. The traditions, customs, and habits of the past are like leaden weights on their feet. They lack the Bolshevik discipline, the iron hardness, the capacity for decisive action, the mobile form of organization, and the strong theoretical foundation which a party of Leninism must have.

The congress demanded an energetic struggle against all these weaknesses and defects, and the slogan of this struggle is "The Bolshevization of the party!"

Our educational work, as well as all other phases of our party life, must be carefully scrutinized and examined in the light of this slogan. When we come to speak of theory and theoretical work, we put our finger at once on one of the weakest spots in the American movement. This has always been the case. The American labor movement, in common with the labor movements of practically all the Anglo-Saxon countries, has a traditional indifference to theory. There is a widespread tendency to draw a line between theory and practice. The typical labor leader boasts of being a practical man who "has no time for theory." We encounter the same point of view quite often even in the ranks of our party.

Such a tendency is bound to lead the party into a blind alley. We must fight against it in a determined and organized manner. The party educational work must be organized in a systematic way and pushed forward with tenfold energy. Our educational work up now has been practically negligible and that is all the more reason for making haste now.

In connection with this work it is necessary continually to stress the fundamental importance of revolutionary theory. Comrade Lenin said, "Without a revolutionary theory, a revolutionary movement is impossible." These words must become a part of the consciousness of every member of the party. It must become obvious to all that the working class will be able to come into open collision with the capitalist order, to dismantle it and to set up in its place the Communist form of society — to accomplish the task which history has set for it — only if at every turn of the road, in every phase of the struggle, it is guided by a correct revolutionary theory.

The spectacle is familiar to all of us, of militant workers starting out with a great hatred of capitalist oppression and a will to fight against it, but drifting along, because of lack of knowledge of the capitalist system and of the means by which it may be overthrown, into a policy which leads them to actual support of the capitalist system. The participation of many thousands of discontented workers in the La Follette movement is an instance of this [US Senator Robert La Follette, a maverick Republican of the type of Theodore Roosevelt and the "Progressives", set up his own "Progressive Party" and ran for president in 1924]. We know that the typical labor leaders of America, who say they have no theory, carry out in actual practice the theory of the bourgeoisie and constitute strong pillars of support for the bourgeois system. There is no such thing as "no theory" in the labor movement. Two social systems are in conflict with each other, the capitalist system and the Communist. One must be guided either by the theory of revolution which leads to the Communist order of society or he will follow a line of action which leads to support of the present order. That is to say that, in effect, he adapts himself to the theory of the present order. "No theory " in the labor movement is the theory of the bourgeoisie.

Without revolutionary theory, the workers, even with the best will in the world, cannot fight the capitalist system successfully. This statement holds good, not merely in the question of the final revolutionary struggle for power, it applies equally in every aspect of the daily struggle. Workers who have no understanding of the theory of revolution cannot follow a consistent line of action that leads toward it. Behind every action aimed at the bourgeoisie, there must be the theory of the revolutionary overthrow of the bourgeoisie. False policies in the ranks of the workers, whereby even their own good will and energy is transformed into a force operating against their own interests, spring in the first place from false theory. Only by an understanding of the revolutionary nature of their struggle, and of the necessity of shaping their actions in the light of this theory and adapting them to the execution of it, can the workers follow a systematic policy of opposition to the bourgeoisie and of defense of their own interests. Revolutionary theory is not something separate from action, but is the guiding principle of all revolutionary action.

The Fifth Congress of the Communist International dealt with the mistakes made by various sections during the period between the Fourth and Fifth Congresses which, in the case of the German party, led to most disastrous results, and laid these mistakes at the door of incorrect theory, of deviation from the line of Marxism and Leninism. It declared that both the opportunistic errors of the right and the sectarian errors of the left represent deviations from the line of the Communist International, which is the embodiment of the theory of Marx and Lenin.

The crisis in the German Communist Party, which became evident at the time of the October 1923 retreat, was declared by the Fifth Congress to be the result of the influence of the remnants of the old social-democratic ideology which still existed within the Communist Party of Germany. This also applies to our party and the remedy for this state of affairs, in the language of the propaganda thesis of the Fifth Congress, is to "Bolshevize the party!"

The propaganda thesis says: The Bolshevization of the party in this sense means the final ideological victory of Marxism and Leninism, or in other words, of Marxism in the period of imperialism and the epoch of the proletarian revolution, and to reject the Marxism of the Second International and the remnants of the elements of syndicalism.

The Bolshevization of the party, therefore, like all slogans of the Communist International, means not a mechanical formula, but a struggle. In this case it is a struggle against false ideology in the party. The Bolshevization of the party, for us, means the struggle for the conquest of the party for the ideology of Marxism and Leninism.

To quote again from the thesis: "The complete and rapid Bolshevizing of the Communist parties can be obtained in the process of the deliberate revolutionary activity of the sections of the Communist International, by more deeply hammering Marxism and Leninism into the consciousness of the Communist parties and the party members."

The Bolshevization of the party is a process and the means towards the end is an ideological struggle. The Workers School, in common with all educational institutions set up by the party, must be a weapon for this struggle. Under no circumstances can we conceive of it as a neutral academy standing between the various tendencies and currents of the party, but as a fighting instrument against all deviations both to the right and to the left, and for the overcoming of the confusion of the party members and for the "hammering into the consciousness of the party and the party members, of Marxism and Leninism." This conception imposes giant tasks upon the Workers School. There is much confusion in our ranks. This we must all admit frankly. Such a state of affairs is to be expected in a party which up to now has devoted little attention to theoretical work and which has had little revolutionary experience, but we must begin now in a determined fashion to cope with this condition and to overcome it.

A particularly dangerous form of confusion and irresponsibility, which we must conquer by frontal attack without delay, is the formal and even frivolous attitude which is sometimes manifested in regard to the relations of our party and our party members to the Communist International. We hear the Bolshevization of the party spoken of here and there as though it were a joke, not to be taken seriously. The very utterance of such a sentiment is in itself an evidence of theoretical weakness. Communists cannot take such a lighthearted altitude towards the Communist International. Let us say at the very beginning, and let everybody understand once and for all: The international organization of the revolutionary proletariat and the leadership of the World Congress is, in itself, an inseparable part of our theory. The very fact that any party members are able to regard the slogan of the Fifth Congress as a joke is a great proof of the need for this slogan in our party.

If we examine closely the state of affairs within our party now, and for the five years that it has been in existence, we are bound to come to the conclusion, as did the Fifth Congress in regard to the International as a whole, that the internal conflicts and crises, as well as the mistakes made by the party in the field of its external activities, can be traced directly to ideological weakness, to the incomplete assimilation by the party of Marxism and Leninism. In other words it still carries with it the dead weight of the past and has not yet become a Bolshevik party.

The thesis on tactics of the Fifth Congress lays down five separate specifications which are the special features of a really Bolshevik party. One of them is the following:

"It (a Bolshevik party) must be a centralized party prohibiting factions, tendencies and groups. It must be a monolithic party hewn of one piece."'

What shall we say of our party if we measure by this standard? From the very beginning, and even to the present day, our party has been plagued with factions, tendencies and groups. At least one-half of the energy of the party has been expended in factional struggles, one after another. We have even grown into the habit of accepting this state of affairs as a normal condition. We have gone to the extent of putting a premium upon factionalism by giving factional representation in the important committees of the party.

Of course, this condition cannot be eliminated by formal decree. We cannot eliminate factions and factional struggles by declaring them undesirable. No, we shall make the first step toward eliminating factions, tendencies and groups, toward creating a monolithic party in the sense of the Fifth Congress declaration, only if at the beginning we recognize the basic cause of the condition, if we recognize that the existence in our party of factions, tendencies and groups runs directly counter to Leninism, to the Leninist conception of what a revolutionary proletarian party should be.

Then we will proceed, in true Leninist fashion, to overcome the difficulty. Not mechanically, not by organizational measures alone, but by an ideological and political struggle which has for its object the creation of a uniform and consistent proletarian class ideology in the party ranks. The problem of factions, tendencies and groups is not an organizational problem merely, it is a political problem and for political problems there are no mechanical solutions.

We must conceive of the Workers School as one of the best weapons in our hands for the fight to develop a uniform proletarian ideology in the party ranks and to overcome all deviations from it.

The American revolutionary movement has had in the past, and still has in many sections, even in a section of the party, queer and false conceptions of the nature of revolutionary education. We are all acquainted with that class of "educators" who reduce education to the study of books and separate the study of books from the conduct of the daily struggle. We know of that old school of "educators" whom we used to call the "surplus value" school, who imagined that if a worker learned something of the nature of the capitalist system of society, the process by which it exploits him and by which it expropriates the major product of his labor, then his education is complete.

We have no place for such a static and one-sided conception of revolutionary education. In all our work, the analysis of capitalist society and the study of the mechanics of capitalist exploitation must be directly and originally connected with the Marxian theory of the state and the process by which the proletariat will overthrow it and set up their own order of society. We must give short shrift to those pseudo-Marxists who convert Marxism into a "theory" separate from struggle. According to our conceptions, Marxism and Leninism constitute both the theory and practice of the proletarian revolution, and it is in this sense that the Workers School must teach Marxism, and must impart it to the students of the school.

Genuine Leninist education cannot by any means be separated from the daily activities and the daily struggles of the party. It must be organically connected with these struggles. No one can become a real Leninist if he studies in a glass case. We must discourage, and the Workers School must fight with all its means against, any such conception.

Correct revolutionary education is partisan education. It must bear the stamp of Marx and Lenin, and no other stamp. Only the theory and teachings of Marxism and Leninism are revolutionary. They cannot be harmonized with any other theory, for no other theory is revolutionary. The Workers School cannot be natural or tolerant. It must scrutinize, ten times over, every item in its curriculum, and every utterance of its instructors from the standpoint of their adherence to the teachings of Marx and lenin.

There is a phrase entitled "labor education" which is current in the labor movement. There is no such thing as "labor education". "Education" is given from the revolutionary standpoint of Marx and Lenin or it is "education" which leads to a conformity and an adaptation to the bourgeois order. This fact must never be lost sight of in any of our educational work. We must be intransigent in this conception of education and so must the Workers School. We must be "narrow-minded" and intolerant on this score, imparting knowledge or culture not from any "general" standpoint, which in the last analysis becomes the standpoint of the bourgeoisie, but from the standpoint only of Marxism and Leninism. There is a conception of this so-called labor education, in my opinion utterly false, which has become widespread. Scott Nearing recently expressed the opinion that the "United Front" tactic should be applied in workers' schools. Our answer to this point of view is that if there is one place where the united front should not be applied it is the field of education. According to our point of view, the only theory which correctly analyzes capitalist society and correctly maps out the road of the struggle for its overthrow is the theory of Marxism and Leninism. We cannot find a common meeting ground with any other theory or any other brand of education. The Workers School does not represent a united front in the field of education. The Workers School must be a partisan school, a weapon in the hands of the party for implanting the party ideology in the minds of the students who attend its classes.

I should like to deal now with the question of education in connection with our trade union activities. I speak with particular reference to the trade union activities because at the present time it is our main field of work, although the points made apply to all fields of activity in the daily struggle. Our party members in the trade unions are obliged to carry out widespread and many-sided activities, the sum total of which comprises a very large percentage of our party work. This is rightly so, because the trade unions are the basic and elementary organizations of the proletariat, and the success of our party, in its efforts to become a party of the masses, depends to a very large extent upon its ability to work in the trade unions and to follow out a correct policy in all of its work there.

To arrive at the correct policy in dealing with the complex problems which constantly come up in the trade unions, a firm grasp on theory is absolutely indispensable. However, theory is badly lacking in this field amongst the comrades in the ranks, who have to carry out the work.

The reason for this is obvious. The members who join our party directly from the trade unions come to it as a rule because they are drawn to the party in the daily struggle over immediate questions. They become convinced, by seeing our party in action and working with it, that it is a real party of the workers which fights for the immediate interests of the workers, and on that basis the workers come to the party. As a rule they do not go through a course of study before admission and do not inquire very deeply into the fundamental theory upon which the party's whole life and activity is founded.

Consequently, for our comrades in the trade unions to attempt to work out a line of tactics in relation to the employers, in relation to the reactionary labor leaders, progressive labor leaders and various other currents and tendencies in the trade union movement, and to coordinate everything with our general political aims, their own empiric experience is not a sufficient foundation. They are bound to become overpractical if they have no other guide, and to drift into tactics which lead them inevitably away from the revolutionary struggle. The Communists in the trade unions can be successful only if they approach all of their tasks from the standpoint of correct revolutionary theory and have all of their activities imbued with this theory.

Two serious errors manifest themselves in the party in connection with theory and practical work in the trade unions. On the one hand we are confronted, every now and then, with a prejudice on the part of the rank and file workers in the trade unions against theory and theoreticians and a resentment against any interference of this kind in their work. All the party leaders, especially the comrades leading our trade union work, have encountered this prejudice. On the other hand we frequently see comrades who have gained all their knowledge from books and who have had no experience in the actual struggle of the workers, especially comrades who can be classified under the general heading of "'intellectuals," adopting a condescending and superior attitude towards the comrades who do the practical work of the party in the daily struggles in the unions. They take a pedagogical and supervisory attitude towards the trade union comrades and thus antagonize them and lose the possibility of influencing them and learning from them.

Both these attitudes are false, and in my opinion the Workers School must help the party to overcome them by systematic, persistent, and determined opposition to both. We must oppose the prejudice of some of the practical trade union comrades, who are new in the party and who have not yet assimilated its main theories, against theory and party workers theoretically trained. We must oppose and resist in the most determined fashion any tendency on their part to separate their work from the political and theoretical work of the party and to resent the introduction of theoretical and political questions into their discussion of the daily work in the unions. And likewise, to the comrades who have book knowledge only, we must make it clear that the theory of the party gets its life only when it is related to the practical daily struggle and becomes a part of the equipment of the comrades who carry on the struggle. They must learn how to approach the practical workers and collaborate with them in the most fraternal and comradely manner, and they must not under any circumstance adopt a superior and pedagogical attitude towards them. This very attitude in itself manifests an ideological defect. A Communist intellectual who cannot identity himself with the trade unionists in the party and make himself one with them is not worth his salt.

The separation of theory and practice, the arbitrary line between theoretical work and practical work, the arbitrary division of activity into theoretical activity and practical activity, must be combatted and overcome. We must set up against it the conception of the organic connection between theoretical and practical work, and of fraternal collaboration between theoretically trained comrades and comrades carrying out the practical work in the daily struggle, especially in the trade union movement.

Our party, in common with the other parties of the International, is confronted by two dangers which militate against its effectiveness in the class struggle. One of the dangers is left sectarianism, which is a deviation from the line of Marxism and Leninism in the direction of syndicalism, and the other is right opportunism, which is defined in the Fifth Congress resolution as a deviation from Leninism in the direction of the emasculated Marxism of the Second International.

These dangers can be overcome and the party remain on the right road only if it succeeds in carrying on a successful struggle against these deviations. Educational work is an important means to this end.

Educational work therefore is not a mere academic activity. In a certain sense it is a fight. It is a fight to overcome these dangers by building in the party ranks a true and firm and uniform proletarian ideology. It must help the party in the fight against right deviations without falling back into the error of deviations to the left. The Workers School must be for the party one of the most important means by which we impress in the minds of the party members a knowledge of Marxian and Leninist theory, of developing a respect for theory and an understanding of its fundamental importance, without falling into the error of teaching theory in an abstract manner and separating it from the daily activities of the party.

Our party must be at the same time a party of theory and a party of struggle, with theory and struggle closely interlocked and inseparable. Without allowing the party members to develop into mere faultfinders, the school must help them to acquire the faculty of criticism, of subjecting every action and every utterance of the party to criticism from the standpoint of its conformity to the basic theory of the movement. We do not want a party consisting half of critics and half of practical workers, but every party member must be at the same time a critic and a constructive worker.

The party must be a party of study and struggle. All the party members must be trained to become thinkers and doers. These conceptions carried out in actual practice will be the means whereby we can rapidly transform our party into a Communist Party in the true sense of the word.

We have every reason to be proud of the response the Workers School has met in the ranks of the party membership of New York. The enthusiastic support it has already gained gives us the hope that our educational work, which we have so long neglected, can now be developed extensively and that all who are most active and alive in the party will join in the task of making it move forward.

The party members in New York should look upon the Workers School as their own institution, as their own party educational center which, by fraternal collaboration of all the comrades, can be built and maintained as a real leader in the fight for Leninist ideology in the party, in the light to shake off the paralyzing inheritance of the past and to merge in the shortest possible time, through the process of careful study and vigorous struggle, into a party complying with the specifications of a Bolshevik party which were laid down by the fifth Congress.

That is: "A central monolithic party hewn of one piece."

That is: "Essentially a revolutionary and Marxist party, undeviating, in spite of all circumstances proceeding towards the goal and making every effort to bring nearer the hour of the victory of the proletariat over the bourgeoisie."

Speech of 5 October 1924, published in *The Workers Monthly*, Nov. 1924.
Reprinted in *James P. Cannon and the Early Years of American Communism:
Selected Writings and Speeches*, 1920-1928

Keep the necessary equilibrium between democracy and centralism

Leon Trotsky (1937, 1938, 1939)

TO THE EDITORS OF SOCIALIST APPEAL (USA): During the past months I have received letters in regard to the inner regime of a revolutionary party from several apparently young comrades, unknown to me. Some of these letters complain about the "lack of democracy" in your organisation, about the domineering of the "leaders" and the like.

Individual comrades ask me to give a "clear and exact formula on democratic centralism" which would preclude false interpretations. It is not easy to answer these letters. Not one of my correspondents even attempts to demonstrate clearly and concretely with actual examples exactly wherein lies the violation of democracy.

On the other hand, insofar as I, a bystander, can judge on the basis of your newspaper and your bulletins, the discussion in your organisation is being conducted with full freedom. The bulletins are filled chiefly by representatives of a tiny minority. I have been told the same holds true of your discussion meetings. The decisions are not yet carried out. Evidently they will be carried through at a freely elected conference. In what then could the violations of democracy have been manifested? This is hard to understand.

Sometimes, to judge by the tones of the letters, i.e., in the main instance by the formlessness of the grievances, it seems to be that the complainers are simply dissatisfied with the fact that in spite of the existing democracy, they prove to be in a tiny minority. Through my own experience I know that this is unpleasant. But wherein is there any violation of democracy?

Neither do I think that I can give such a formula on democratic centralism that "once and for all" would eliminate misunderstandings and false interpretations. A party is an active organism. It develops in the struggle with outside obstacles and inner contradictions.

The malignant decomposition of the Second and Third Internationals, under severe conditions of the imperialist epoch, creates for the Fourth International difficulties unprecedented in history. One cannot overcome them with some sort of magic formula. The regime of a party does not fall ready made from the sky but is formed gradually in struggle. A political line predominates over the regime. First

631

of all, it is necessary to define strategic problems and tactical methods correctly in order to solve them. The organisational forms should correspond to the strategy and the tactic.

Only a correct policy can guarantee a healthy party regime. This, it is understood, does not mean that the development of the party does not realise organisational problems as such. But it means that the formula for democratic centralism must inevitably find a different expression in the parties of different countries and in different stages of development of one and the same party.

Democracy and centralism do not at all find themselves in an invariable ratio to one another. Everything depends on the concrete circumstances, on the political situation in the country, on the strength of the party and its experience, on the general level of its members, on the authority the leadership has succeeded in winning. Before a conference, when the problem is one of formulating a political line for the next period, democracy triumphs over centralism.

When the problem is political action, centralism subordinates democracy to itself. Democracy again asserts its rights when the party feels the need to examine critically its own actions. The equilibrium between democracy and centralism establishes itself in the actual struggle, at moments it is violated and then again re-established. The maturity of each member of the party expresses itself particularly in the fact that he does not demand from the party regime more than it can give. The person who defines his attitude to the party by the individual fillips that he gets on the nose is a poor revolutionist.

It is necessary, of course, to fight against every individual mistake of the leadership, every injustice, and the like. But it is necessary to assess these "injustices" and "mistakes" not in themselves but in connection with the general development of the party both on a national and international scale.

A correct judgement and a feeling for proportion in politics is an extremely important thing. The person who has propensities for making a mountain out of a mole hill can do much harm to himself and to the party. The misfortune of such people as Oehler, Field, Weisbord, and others [people who had splintered from the Trotskyist movement in the early and mid 1930s] consists in their lack of feeling for proportion.

At the moment there are not a few half-revolutionists, tired out by defeats, fearing difficulties, aged young men who have more doubts and pretensions than will to struggle. Instead of seriously analysing political questions in essence, such individuals seek panaceas, on every occasion complain about the "regime", demand wonders from the leadership, or try to muffle their inner scepticism by ultra-left prattling.

I fear that revolutionists will not be made out of such elements, unless they take themselves in hand. I do not doubt, on the other hand, that the young generation of workers will be capable of evaluating the programmatic and strategical content of the Fourth International according to merit and will rally to its banner in ever greater numbers.

Each real revolutionist who notes down the blunders of the party regime should first of all say to himself: "We must bring into the party a dozen new workers!" The young workers will call the gentlemen-sceptics, grievance-mongers, and pessimists to order. Only along such a road will a strong healthy party regime be established in the sections of the Fourth International.

From "On democratic centralism", December 1937

Genuine, honest democracy

By Leon Trotsky

I BELIEVE DEMOCRACY is very important in the organization. Why? Because democracy is perishing everywhere in the States, in, the trade unions, in the old revolutionary parties. Only we can permit genuine honest democracy so that a young worker, a young student can feel he has the possibility of expressing his opinion openly without being immediately subjected to persecution. Ironical statements from someone in authority is also persecution. We can attract new members to the youth [organisation] as to the party only by genuine intelligent democracy. Everybody is tired of the lack of democracy....

We cannot establish with one blow or with one resolution the authority of the party. We cannot create the authority for the party with one resolution. If the young comrades have two, three, five, or ten experiences proving to them that the party is more wise, more experienced, then they will become more cautious in their opposition to the party and more moderate in the forms of this opposition. Anyone who speaks in a tone of contempt to the party will immediately feel around himself a vacuum of irony and contempt and it will educate the people. But if we approach the young comrades with a general conception such as this: "Boys and girls, you acted very well against the Socialist Party because it was a bad party; but we are a good party. Don't forget it. You must not oppose us." How can you convince them with such a general conception? It is very dangerous. "You believe it is a good party, but we don't believe it!"... "You are bureaucrats, no more, no less."

It is very dangerous. Theoretically it is correct like the question of discipline. Iron discipline, steel discipline, is absolutely necessary, but if the apparatus of the young party begins by demanding such iron discipline on the first day it can lose the party. It is necessary to educate confidence in the leadership of the party and the party in general because the leadership is only an expression of the party.

We can fail now in two directions. One in the direction of centralization; the other in the direction of democracy. I believe now we should exaggerate the democracy and be very, very patient with centralism in this transitional time. We must educate these people to understand the necessity of centralism.

From "Towards a Revolutionary Youth Organisation", 18 November 1938

No reason to hinder discussion

By Leon Trotsky

DEAR COMRADE ROSE: I send simultaneously the Russian text of the USSR article [*The USSR in War*] to Vanzler for translation. I don't see, I must confess, any reason to hinder discussion on this matter. Better to take the initiative and to show that the events did not take us unaware. It would be good if you communicate to me the reactions of comrades of both camps to the last article on the USSR.

With warmest comradely greeting, L. Trotsky

Letter to Rose Karsner (James P Cannon's partner), 28 September 1939. Published for the first time in Trotsky's *Writings, Supplementary Volume 1934-40*, p.843; and not included in *In Defence of Marxism*.

A serious educational discussion

By Leon Trotsky

DEAR JIM: TWO THINGS are clear to me from your letter of October 24: (1) that a very serious ideological fight has become inevitable and politically necessary; (2) that it would be extremely prejudicial if not fatal to connect the ideological fight with the perspective of a split, of a purge, or expulsions, and so on and so forth.

I heard for example that Comrade Gould proclaimed in a membership meeting: "You wish to expel us." But I don't know what reaction came from the other side to this. I for my part would immediately protest with the greatest vehemence such suspicions. I would propose the creation of a special control commission in order to check such affirmations and rumours. If it happens that someone of the majority launches such threats I for my part would vote for a censure or severe warning.

You may have many new members or uneducated youth. They need a serious educational discussion in the light of the great events. If their thoughts at the beginning are obsessed by the perspective of personal degradation, i.e., demotions, loss of prestige, disqualifications, eliminations from Central Committee, etc., and so on, the whole discussion would become envenomed and the authority of the leadership would be compromised.

If the leadership on the contrary opens a ruthless fight against petty-bourgeois idealistic conceptions and organizational prejudices but at the same time guarantees for the discussion itself and for the minority, the result would be not only be an ideological victory but an important growth in the authority of the leadership.

"A conciliation and a compromise at the top" on the questions which form the matter of the divergences would of course be a crime. But I for my part would propose to the minority at the top an agreement, if you wish, a compromise on the methods of discussion and parallelly on the political collaboration. For example (a) both sides eliminate from the discussion any threats, personal denigration and so on; (b) both sides take the obligation of loyal collaboration during the discussion; (c) every false move (threats, or rumours of threats, or a rumour of alleged threats, resignations, and so on) should be investigated by the National Committee or a special commission as a particular fact and not thrown into the discussion and so on.

If the majority accepts such an agreement you will have the possibility of disciplining the discussion and also the advantage of having taken a good initiative. If they reject it you can at every party membership meeting present your written proposition to the minority as the best refutation of their complaints and as an example of "our regime".

It seems to me that the last convention failed at a very bad moment (the time was not ripe) and became a kind of abortion. The genuine discussion comes some time after the convention. This signifies that you can't avoid a convention at Christmas or so. The idea of a referendum is absurd. It could only facilitate a split on local lines. I believe that the majority in the above-mentioned agreement can propose to the minority a new convention on the basis of two platforms with all the organizational guarantees for the minority.

The convention is expensive but I don't see any other means of concluding the present discussion and the party crisis it produces.

J. HANSEN [Leon Trotsky]. October 28,1939

P.S. – Every serious and sharp discussion can of course lead to some desertions, departures, or even expulsions, but the whole party should be convinced from the logic of the facts that they are inevitable results occurred in spite of the best will of the leadership, and not an objective or aim of the leadership, and not the point of departure of the whole discussion. This is in my mind the decisive point of the whole matter.

Letter to James P Cannon, October 1939, printed for the first time in James P. Cannon's *The Struggle for a Proletarian Party*, with the explanation that it had been omitted in error from the collection *In Defence of Marxism*.

13. The working class is central

A letter to the workers of the USSR

Leon Trotsky (1940)

GREETINGS TO THE SOVIET WORKERS, collective farmers, soldiers of the Red Army and sailors of the Red Navy! Greetings from distant Mexico where I found refuge after the Stalinist clique had exiled me to Turkey and after the bourgeoisie had hounded me from country to country!

Dear Comrades! The lying Stalinist press has been maliciously deceiving you for a long time on all questions, including those which relate to myself and my political co-thinkers. You possess no workers' press; you read only the press of the bureaucracy, which lies systematically so as to keep you in darkness and thus render secure the rule of a privileged parasitic caste.

Those who dare raise their voices against the universally hated bureaucracy are called "Trotskyists," agents of a foreign power; branded as spies — yesterday it was spies of Germany, today it is spies of England and France — and then sent to face the firing squad. Tens of thousands of revolutionary fighters have fallen before the muzzles of GPU Mausers in the USSR and in countries abroad, especially in Spain. All of them were depicted as agents of Fascism. Do not believe this abominable slander! Their crime consisted of defending workers and peasants against the brutality and rapacity of the bureaucracy. The entire Old Guard of Bolshevism, all the collaborators and assistants of Lenin, all the fighters of the October revolution, all the heroes of the Civil War, have been murdered by Stalin. In the annals of history Stalin's name will forever be recorded with the infamous brand of Cain!

The October revolution was accomplished for the sake of the toilers and not for the sake of new parasites. But due to the lag of the world revolution, due to the fatigue and, to a large measure, the backwardness of the Russian workers and especially the Russian peasants, there raised itself over the Soviet Republic and against its peoples a

637

new oppressive and parasitic caste, whose leader is Stalin. The former Bolshevik party was turned into an apparatus of the caste. The world organization which the Communist International once was is today a pliant tool of the Moscow oligarchy. Soviets of Workers and Peasants have long perished. They have been replaced by degenerate Commissars, Secretaries and GPU agents.

But, fortunately, among the surviving conquests of the October revolution are the nationalized industry and the collectivized Soviet economy. Upon this foundation Workers' Soviets can build a new and happier society. This foundation cannot be surrendered by us to the world bourgeoisie under any conditions. It is the duty of revolutionists to defend tooth and nail every position gained by the working class, whether it involves democratic rights, wage scales, or so colossal a conquest of mankind as the nationalization of the means of production and planned economy. Those who are incapable of defending conquests already gained can never fight for new ones. Against the imperialist foe we will defend the USSR with all our might. However, the conquests of the October revolution will serve the people only if they prove themselves capable of dealing with the Stalinist bureaucracy, as in their day they dealt with the Tsarist bureaucracy and the bourgeoisie.

If Soviet economic life had been conducted in the interests of the people; if the bureaucracy had not devoured and vainly wasted the major portion of the national income; if the bureaucracy had not trampled underfoot the vital interests of the population, then the USSR would have been a great magnetic pole of attraction for the toilers of the world and the inviolability of the Soviet Union would have been assured. But the infamous oppressive regime of Stalin has deprived the USSR of its attractive power. During the war with Finland, not only the majority of the Finnish peasants but also the majority of the Finnish workers proved to be on the side of their bourgeoisie. This is hardly surprising since they know of the unprecedented oppression to which the Stalinist bureaucracy subjects the workers of nearby Leningrad and the whole of the USSR. The Stalinist bureaucracy, so bloodthirsty and ruthless at home and so cowardly before the imperialist enemies, has thus become the main source of war danger to the Soviet Union.

The old Bolshevik party and the Third International have disintegrated and decomposed. The honest and advanced revolutionists have organized abroad the Fourth International which has sections already established in most of the countries of the world. I am a member of this new International. In participating in this work I remain under the very same banner that I served together with you or your fathers and your older brothers in 1917 and throughout the years of the Civil War, the very same banner under which together with Lenin we built the Soviet state and the Red Army.

The goal of the Fourth International is to extend the October revolution to the whole world and at the same time to regenerate the USSR by purging it of the parasitic bureaucracy. This can be achieved only in one way: By the workers, peasants, Red Army soldiers and Red Navy sailors, rising against the new caste of oppressors and parasites. To prepare this uprising, a new party is needed a bold and honest revolutionary organization of the advanced workers. The Fourth International sets as its task the building of such a party in the USSR.

Advanced workers! Be the first to rally to the banner of Marx and Lenin which is now the banner of the Fourth International! Learn how to create, in the conditions of Stalinist illegality, tightly fused, reliable revolutionary circles! Establish contacts between these circles! Learn how to establish contacts through loyal and reliable people, especially the sailors, with your revolutionary co-thinkers in bourgeois lands! It is difficult, but it can be done.

The present war will spread more and more, piling ruins on ruins, breeding more and more sorrow, despair and protest, driving the whole world toward new revolutionary explosions. The world revolution shall reinvigorate the Soviet working masses with new courage and resoluteness and shall undermine the bureaucratic props of Stalin's caste. It is necessary to prepare for this hour by stubborn systematic revolutionary work. The fate of our country, the future of our people, the destiny of our children and grandchildren are at stake.

Down With Cain Stalin and his Camarilla! Down With the Rapacious Bureaucracy! Long Live the Soviet Union, the Fortress of the Toilers! Long Live the World Socialist Revolution!

Fraternally, Leon Trotsky. May, 1940

WARNING! Stalin's press will of course declare that this letter is transmitted to the USSR by "agents of imperialism." Be forewarned that this, too, is a lie. This letter will reach the USSR through reliable revolutionists who are prepared to risk their lives for the cause of socialism. Make copies of this letter and give it the widest possible circulation. L.T.

Fourth International, October 1940

Trotsky's partner, Natalia Sedova, broadcasts to the Russian workers

Natalia Sedova (1956)

THIS IS NATALIA IVANOVNA SEDOVA, widow of Leon Davidovich Trotsky, speaking from Mexico City. I am addressing myself to the workers and peasants and, in the first place, to the young people in Soviet Russia. The present rulers, Khrushchev, Bulganin, Mikoyan and others, having inherited the Stalinist dictatorship, are conducting an intensive propaganda campaign so as to distract from themselves the powerful wave of dissatisfaction and hatred for the thieves of the victories of the proletarian revolution, a wave which grew in your hearts.

They are the same men who supported Stalin in all his bloody massacres, the aim of which was to frighten you with terror and thus to retain power in the hands of the Stalinist bureaucracy. The very method of the campaign through which these men hope to absolve themselves of responsibility for their heinous crimes bears witness to the fact that the ruling clique is Stalin's faithful successor.

Stalin always followed the "scapegoat" method for failures of plans and orders arbitrarily enforced from above. Local bureaucrats tagged the blame on helpless workers and peasants and the GPU (secret police) did the rest.

Stalin himself did not spare even his most devoted servants, especially if they betrayed any trace of indecision or doubts. Stalin forced them to confess uncommitted crimes and heaped on them the blame for the decay and corruption of the regime. This method was already devised during the period of the old struggle against the Left Opposition headed by Leon Trotsky, and this method subsequently became the chief characteristic of the Stalinist system.

What then is the present campaign if not a continuation of the same method, but with one serious difference — today's scapegoats are really guilty of crimes of which they are accused. Beria was first. Then three years passed — three long years — before the present bosses dared to expose the criminal in the corpse of their leader. Now they declare to the entire world that in the process of building up the "cult of personality" Stalin lost his mental balance. His ailment, it appears, consisted in lacking complete confidence in the Molotovs, Khrushchevs, Kaganoviches and their like who were nonetheless completely devoted to him.

Just try and think: Who are these direct heirs of the unbalanced Stalin who declared themselves collective leaders of Soviet Russia? They admit, they admit to the entire world, that for many decades not one among them, among the collective leaders, dared — for fear for his own life — to come out with a proposal for steps which would have saved the lives of millions of workers and peasants who were banished to concentration camps.

These are the nonentities who dare to demand from Russian workers and peasants unimaginable sacrifices in the struggle for a great cause. How long will they hold on under the pressure of great events? All their lives they showed no interest in improving the lot of the toilers; they were interested only in holding on to power and to all the privileges that go with power. Besides, the training they received from Stalin makes the realization of a collective leadership unlikely even in the imperfect form they have in mind. How can they trust each other knowing full well that while Stalin was alive each one among them would have been happy to sacrifice all and everything just to hold on to his own power and position? Events unfold slowly but it is unlikely that this leadership will last long. I realize with bitterness that many of my listeners were brought up completely in a Stalinist spirit. Young people were taught history which was thoroughly permeated with lies. Even those grains of truth which the rulers were forced to admit now make impossible the use of old history textbooks. Yet the new textbooks which are now being prepared, will they be more truthful than the old ones? The rulers of Russia are in a dilemma: which lies to admit and which lies to retain intact?

How can Khrushchev admit that the campaign of annihilation of the Stalinist leadership in the Ukraine, including Kossior, Antonov-Ovseyenko and others — a campaign which Khrushchev himself conducted while Stalin was alive — was based on lies? How can Voroshilov, this venerable chairman of the Supreme Soviet of the USSR, dare to admit openly that while signing the death sentences of the Red Army commanders Tukhachevsky, Yegorov, Gamarnik and others, he knew full well that all this was nothing but lies and frame-up? And the statesman Molotov — will he tell of the beautiful friendship with Hitler and Ribbentrop which culminated in Stalin's signing of the Hitler pact and which gave a green light to a world war? The murder of Kirov in 1934 gave impetus to an unequaled campaign of executions and slander directed against entire strata of the Russian population. Will the leaders of the present regime tell us who is guilty of this crime? Will they admit that behind this bloody affair and all its consequences stood the sinister figure of the "father of the peoples" who organized Kirov's murder? Should they admit this fact, then the entire campaign of slander which was directed at that time against Trotsky, Zinoviev, Kamenev and hundreds of others will fall to pieces and the entire affair will reappear as it was in reality, as a nightmare and a frame up.

The government leaders are in a dilemma. Where should they stop? They have already begun to put the brakes on further unmasking of lies.

The reason for this is clear: their own power is based on this truly monstrous tissues of lies — of lies of the bureaucracy against Trotsky, Zinoviev, Kamenev and hundreds of other members of the Opposition. They dare not continue repeating the lies nor denounce them.

Here they try to divide the Stalinist period into two periods: the first period during which they enthusiastically elevated Stalin to the dictator's throne, and the second period when Stalin elevated himself to the status of a deity and thrust on his followers the "cult of personality." The world press is full of quotations from the old speeches of Khrushchev, Mikoyan and others. It is impossible to repeat these speeches without revulsion. Besides, I am sure that you in Soviet Russia are familiar with these quotations even better than the world press. No, the crimes began not from the moment the leader became mentally unbalanced. The so-called "cult of personality" was a natural consequence of the entire period after the death of Lenin and the banishment of Trotsky.

Everything you were taught about Trotsky since that time is vile slander.

Those who participated in the revolution and went through its first heroic stages could not believe those lies. But serious changes in the balance of social power will be required before you, young people, will be able to uncover historical truth.

In his testament Lenin warned the party as follows: "I propose to the comrades that they find a way to remove Stalin from that position and appoint to it another man... more patient, more loyal, more polite and more attentive to comrades, less capricious, etc." These lines were written on the 25th of December 1922. Further, on the 4th of January 1923 Lenin condemned Stalin's position on the Georgian problem and entrusted Trotsky with launching a fight against it. And in a third document Lenin declared that he breaks off all personal and comradely relations with Stalin. While Lenin was still alive Stalin concentrated in his hands tremendous power by placing his men in important posts. Lenin's testament was not carried out and its publication was forbidden.

Lenin and Trotsky not only recognized collective leadership within the party but also acted in complete accordance with this principle. To them collective leadership meant not only discussion in upper party echelons where decisions were made by a majority of votes after a broad exchange of views. They could not envisage collective leadership without an active, democratic party organization, from top to bottom.

And not just in peacetime, either. Animated discussions sharply expressing different views existed even in the most critical periods. It was the suppression of party democracy, and the subjugation of the weakened party to the Stalinist sham of a monolithic party organization which tolerated no disagreements, which resulted in the destruction of the party as a Bolshevik party and in the establishment of a dictatorship on the summit, that is, in the "cult of personality."

Leon Davidovich [Trotsky] understood that by continuing the exposure of the counterrevolutionary regime he was undoubtedly risking his own life. Yet this consideration did not prevent him from merciless criticism [of the regime]. Day after day, until the last hour of his life, he continued to appeal to revolutionary workers of the world to rise against these oppressors. The plan for the industrialization of the country was worked out by Trotsky. However, at that time Stalin and his clique put their stakes on the peasants and fought this plan. Only after Trotsky was exiled to Alma-Ata and after the opposition was suppressed was Stalin forced to begin the industrialization of the country. He did it in his own manner, with unheard-of cruelty and at the cost of tremendous sacrifices on the part of the population.

Trotsky sharply condemned this method, as well as the forced collectivization of the peasants which was accompanied by savage repressions, mass deportations and arrests, and which resulted in the general famine in the Ukraine during which millions of peasants died. Trotsky also fought against the system of slave labor in the concentration camps.

His unmasking and condemnation of all these evil-doings of Stalin, and finally his eloquent response to the sham Moscow Trials, enraged the Stalinist clique, which decided to get rid of Trotsky. This was done by the dictator's henchmen on the 20th of August 1940. It is unlikely that the news of the famous commission which investigated the Moscow Trials, the chairman of which was the noted American philosopher John Dewey, has reached you. This commission, which heard the testimony of Trotsky and others, which carefully examined all the accusations, arrived at the conclusion that Trotsky and his son, Leon Lvovich Sedov, who were accused during these trials, were innocent. The press throughout the world closely followed the work and the verdict of the commission.

From my distant exile where I have already spent so many years I find it difficult to estimate the number of people in Russia who would believe the accusations against Trotsky and others. Abroad no one believes any longer in the vile slander that Trotsky allegedly was linked with fascists, foreign powers, espionage and the like.

Russia's present rulers look into the future with some confidence. They know that during the reign of the Leader all the heroic figures of the proletarian revolution were done away with. They believe that nowhere in the world are there any forces that, might threaten them. Among themselves they have signed a temporary truce under the guise of collective leadership, since the only danger they see is discord among themselves. But they are wrong. Even a weak blow to the myth which they themselves created, even a partial unmasking of the falsehood of the regime on which their rule is based, cannot but sow doubts and discord among the new, growing generation. Idealism was always the characteristic and the strength of youth. I am convinced that the doubts will crush the hard convictions and that youth will not abandon its search for truth until it will find all the truth. Woe then unto the false leaders!

Lately the press throughout the world has been busy with the so-called anti-Stalinist speech of Khrushchev, which he made at a closed meeting before the end of the 20th Congress. Foreign delegates were not permitted to attend and the speech itself was not published in Soviet Russia and hence you are not familiar with it.

In his speech, which lasted for a few hours, Khrushchev continued the downgrading of Stalin. It was a terrible and at the same time a pitiful speech. The enumeration of crimes could not fail to shaken the listeners, and later also readers.

How could this happen? How could one reach such a monstrous downfall? "Cult of personality" they say... Yet an individual is linked to the environment which supports him. And the environment, devoid of lofty ideological motivations, was unable to say no to the master in the Kremlin, to criticize the totalitarian regime of decay and falsehood in front of the Leader. Stalinist bureaucrats are now forced to rid themselves at least of part of the load by passive admissions, and out of fear of the masses, by the slogan "back to Lenin." Stalin also claimed verbally Lenin's mantle, but in his actions he contradicted Lenin.

In the end no admissions and promises can save the decayed Stalinist oligarchy.

The task of overthrowing Stalinism is the task of the Russian workers and peasants.

I send you my greetings and fiery confidence in your victory.

Labor Action, 30 July 1956. Text of a broadcast to Russia via Radio Liberation.

The Fourth International's French-language magazine from October 1936, March/April 1937, February 1937, March/April 1938 and September/October 1938.

Why the working class is central

Max Shachtman (1953)

WE CONSIDER OURSELVES as heirs of the Trotskyist movement when it was a living movement in the full sense of the word, when it represented the imperishable tradition of revolutionary Marxism. And today, 25 years after the founding of that movement [i.e. of the US Trotskyist movement, in 1928], looking backward with a minimum of maudlin sentimentality and a maximum of calm, objective and reasoned analysis – what do we celebrate on this 25th anniversary?

What do we seek to represent in the working class movement as a whole, of which we are an inseparable part? What fundamentally justifies our independent and separate existence, our stiff-necked obduracy in maintaining that existence, in refusing to give up in insisting, not only that we will hold on to what we have, but get more and more, until our ideas infuse the bloodstream of the whole working class movement?

It is the essence of revolutionary Marxism – that respect in which it always differed, as it differs today, from every other social and political tendency, from every other movement, from every other mode of thought in society. And that essence can be summed up in these four words: Marxism is proletarian socialism. They say – by "they" I mean professors, former professors, aspirant professors – that there are as many schools of socialism as there are socialists. Every Princeton student bursts his seams when he hears this: "There are other socialisms, and which of the 57 varieties are you referring to?"

I, who like a joke as well as the next man, would be the last man in the world to dream of depraving these poor, intellectually poverty-stricken apologists for a decaying capitalist social order of their little joke. And you will admit it is little.

So I will say: Yes, historically and actually – if it will make you happy, and after all we socialists are for the extension of happiness – there are 57 and even a greater number of socialisms. When Marx came on the intellectual scene, in Germany, in France, in Belgium and in England, there were any number of socialisms; and there were socialisms before Marx was born; and there were socialisms promulgated after he died. Marx mentioned a few in his deathless Communist Manifesto. There were the "True Socialists", the Christian socialists, the reformer socialists, cooperative socialists, bourgeois socialists, feudal socialists, agrarian socialists, royal and imperial Prussian socialists. They existed and continue to exist. In our time we had "National-Socialists"; we have had if I may say so "Stalinist socialism". Stalinist socialism – I don't like to say that, but we do have all sorts of "socialists".

But even if it gives the professors and the Vassar students another burst seam, I say there is one socialism that we adhere to. Even if we will not say that this is the "true" socialism, that it is the "right" socialism, that it is the "genuine" socialism – we will say that it is our socialism. If you don't find it "true" you can become a royal and imperial Prussian socialist, you can become a Stalinist "socialist", you can become (every man is entitled to his joke) a "Sidney Hook socialist". For we believe in everybody having the right to be any kind of socialist, or anti-socialist, he wants. We claim no more for our socialism, than the fact that it is ours.

Marxian socialism is distinguished from all the others, not in the fact that it holds to the so-called labour theory of value, and not even in the fact that it developed the ideas of dialectical materialism, and not even in the fact that it participates in and prosecutes the class struggle. Its fundamental and irreconcilable difference with all the others is this: Marxism is proletarian socialism.

The great discovery of Marxism – what distinguished it as a new socialism in its day, what distinguished the great discovery of Karl Marx in his search for a "bearer of philosophy" as he used to say in his early days, in his search for a "carrier" out of the contradictions of capitalism – the great discovery of Marxism was the revolutionary character of the modern proletariat. That is the essence, that is the durable characteristic, of Marxian socialism. Proletarian socialism, scientific socialism as distinct from all other socialist schools, from utopian socialism, dates from that great discovery – the social revolutionary character of the modern proletariat.

When speaking of socialism and socialist revolution we seek "no condescending saviours" as our great battle hymn, the International, so ably says. We do not believe that well-wishing reforms – and there are well-wishing reformers – will solve the problems of society, let alone bring socialism.

We are distinguished from them all in this one respect above all others – we believe that task belongs to the proletariat, only the proletariat itself. That is a world-shattering idea. It overshadows all social thought. The most profound, important and lasting thought in Marxism, the most pregnant thought in Marxism is contained in Marx's phrase that the emancipation of the proletariat is the task of the proletariat itself. It is clearly the most revolutionary idea very conceived, if you understand it in all of its great implications.

That is why we are in the tradition of the Paris Commune, for example, the first great attempt of the proletariat to emancipate itself. That is why we are in the tradition of the great revolution in Russia – the Bolshevik revolution – the second great attempt of the proletariat to emancipate itself. That's why we defend it from its detractors. That's why we are so passionate about it. That's why we are, if you will, so "dogmatic". We know what we are defending even if they do not always know what they are attacking.

And that is what we learn all over again from Trotskyists what we have begun to forget, what we have begun to ignore, what we have begun to take for granted. If I may speak for myself, I can tell you I will never forget the explosion in my Communist smugness when for the first time I read Trotsky's criticism of the draft programme of the Comintern, written when he had already been banished to Alma-Ata in 1928, written for the Sixth World Congress of the Communist International. What a commentary it is on the Communist movement in 1928 that, so far back, that precious Marxian document, which is so fresh to this hour, had to be written in exile in Russian in 1928 – in exile! It had to be transmitted by theft; Cannon had to steal his copy in Moscow from the Comintern secretariat and smuggle it into the US. It had to be disseminated here in the Communist Party illicitly, to three or four people who would read it behind locked doors – because if the leaders of the CP found out that we had it (let alone that we were reading it, let alone that we were favourably influenced by it) they would put us on trial and expel us, and they did.

To read that work and to know what was really going on in that fight of Trotskyism, that it was always a question of international socialism versus national socialism, the coordinative efforts to bring about socialism of the entire working class of the world as against the messianic, nationalistic utopian idea that it could be established in one country alone by the efforts of a benevolent bureaucracy of the working class – that had a shattering effect upon our thinking.

We learned then from Trotskyism what we hold so firmly to now: There can be no socialism without the working class of the world, no socialism without the working class of Russia. Twenty-five years later we see the results of building socialism without the international working class – without the Russian working class and against the Russian working class. No matter how many books you leaf through, no matter how old they are, where will you find the story of such an unendurable tyranny as has been established in the Stalinist countries, where "socialism" has been built without the working class and against the working class?

We are the living carriers and embodiment of the ideas to be learned from these events. We are its living teachers, for those whom we can get to listen in these days of darkness, confusion and cowardice.

In this country we have learned far more about the meaning of the idea of an American labour party, a labour party based on the trade unions, than we ever dreamed was represented by that idea when we first put it forward in 1922 in the American Communist movement, than when we put it forward again and again later in the Trotskyist movement. To us it represents a declaration of independence of the working class, its first great step in the country toward self-emancipation, and also to us it represents the remedy for that series of tragedies, calamities, misunderstandings and frustrations represented by New Dealism – that is, collaboration of the working class with a benevolent liberal bourgeoisie.

And what it represents runs through everything we say and everything we do and everything we want others to do in the United States and elsewhere: Not with them – not under them – you yourselves are the masters not only of your own fate but the masters of the fate of all society if you but take control of society into your own hands! That is your destiny! That is the hope of us all.

We are optimistic because that will remain our hope in the greatest hours of adversity, while everywhere else lies pessimism. Our role is to teach Marxism, that Marxism which is proletarian socialism, Marxist politics, socialist politics. Our idea of politics boil down to this revolutionary idea – to teach the working class to rely upon itself, upon its own organization, upon its own programme, upon its own leadership. Upon its own ideas and need for democracy, and to subordinate itself at any time to the interest, the needs, the leadership, the programme, the movement, the organization, or the ideas of any other class.

We regret that in other branches of the socialist movement or what is called the socialist movement, that idea does not dominate every thought. We are proud that in our section of the socialist movement it does dominate every thought. We are proud that in our section of the socialist movement it does dominate every thought and every deed. That's why we are Marxists; that's what we learned all over again in many intellectual and political battles under that peerless teacher and peerless revolutionary Trotsky. And we start by teaching socialists to rely upon themselves.

When we read for the first time *The New Course* by Trotsky, his work directed against the first big and dangerous manifestations of bureaucratism in the Russian Soviet state, another explosion took place in our smugness. I venture to call it – it's an awkward phrase and I hope it's not too badly misunderstood – a bible of working class democracy. This was Trotsky's brilliant simple overwhelming pamphlet on how a socialist movement should act inside and outside, how a socialist state should act, how socialist leaders and socialist ranks, the socialist elders and the socialist youth, should act toward themselves and one another ...

What we have learned more sturdily than every before, what is more completely a part of our Marxian idea of proletarian socialism, is that there is no socialism and no progress to socialism without the working class, without the working class revolution, without the working class in power, without the working class having been lifted to "political supremacy" (as Marx called it) to their "victory of democracy" (as Marx also calls it). No socialism and no advance to socialism without it! That is our rock. That is what we build the fight for the socialist future on. That is what we're unshakably committed to.

Look at what has happened – I hold them up as horrible examples – to all who have renounced this struggle after having known its meaning. They have no confidence in the social-revolutionary power of the proletariat – that is the alpha and omega of them all. One will embroider it with colour thread and another with another, but at bottom that is it.

I claim to know whereof I speak because I know so many of them and know them so intimately – excuse me, knew them so intimately and know also what caused their renunciation of the struggle. They have been corrupted by that most ancient of corrupt ideas: that as for the lower class, there must always be one; that the lower class must always be exploited and oppressed; that there is no other way. That's their real feeling and that's what caused their renunciation of the struggle.

They are the Stalinists in reverse. They have lost their faith in the socialist faith for that reason and for that reason primarily and fundamentally.

They have lost their respect for the working class because for so long a period of time it can, and it has, and it does, lie dormant and stagnant and seems to be absolutely passive, immobilized in permanence. In other words, they have doomed it – this working class which has shown itself so capable of so many miracles in the past hundred and two hundred years of its struggle against the bourgeoisie and against oppression in general – doomed it to eternal servitude. That's why they are not Trotskyists; that's why they're not socialists; that's why they're not democrats; that's why they're not people with human integrity any longer.

Ask any of them point-blank (if you're on sufficiently good terms with them): do you believe that the working class can every rule society and usher in a classless socialist regime? Do you believe that the working class has that capacity innate within it? Not one of them, if he is honest, will admit agreeing with it. You will notice everyone of them beginning to hedge and to hem and to haw and to talk about 25 other subjects – because in all of them the corrupt idea has taken sound and firm roots that the working class will always be oppressed and exploited by someone or another.

Look at Burnham and his "Machiavellians" – the whole theory is there, the whole snobbish bourgeois theory that goes back to feudalism and goes back to slavery before that: there have to be exploited workers and the best they can hope for is that the rulers fight among themselves and that in the interstices of this fight they may be able to promote their own interests just a little bit without ever changing their exploited status.

What is this at bottom but a variety of that notorious philosophy which the Stalinoid intellectuals and apologists used to whisper to us in justification of their support of the Kremlin: "You don't mean to say that you really believe that the working class can emancipate themselves, can themselves take power? ... They need a strong hand over them ..."

These people can't absorb the idea that the workers can free themselves. Take that diluted variety of these sceptics, the pro-war socialists (if you can call them socialists):

We would be for a Third Camp, you see, if it existed. Show us a Third Camp and we would be the first ones to be for it – if it were big and powerful and had lots of dues-paying members. But there is no Third Camp now, so why be for it? But the minute it comes into being – we don't believe that it will ever happen, of course, but if despite our scepticism it should come into being against capitalism (which were are not really for) and against Stalinism (which we detest), we will support it with all the power of speech and pen at our command. But until then allow us to be the snobs and careerists that we are.

Those who swoon with delight at being accepted nowadays in respectable society (of which, alas, we are not a part) have lost all respect for themselves – that's what it is with the cynics, with the somewhat milder version, the sceptics, the climbers, the turncoats and the veterans who never saw combat in the class struggle and who nevertheless have the effrontery to live off pensions from the bourgeoisie today in various institutions reserved for them exclusively.

For us who have nothing in common with such people and want nothing in common with such people, in all their 57 schools, the 25th anniversary comes after a quarter century of defeats and setbacks, yes, but defeats and setbacks accumulated only because men and movements left the working class in the lurch.

But although it is silent so often, and silent for so long, and although it is disoriented, this proletariat – today's proletariat, or tomorrow's like yesterday's – will outlast this trial as it will outlast its old leaders and resume its iron march to socialist freedom. Our confidence in it, maintained these 25 years, is undiminished 25 years after we took up the banner of renewed faith in it and renewed willingness to learn from it, as well as to teach it what we know.

For the man who lives for himself, alone like a clod of mud in a ditch, like a solitary animal in a savage forest, 25 years of dedication to socialism is an incomprehensible as it is unendurable. But we are, thank god, not like the clods of mud, the careerists and the opportunists, the philistines of all sorts and varieties who have specially strong fountains of strength in this last trench of world capitalism, the United States. We are people who have been intellectually and spiritually emancipated by the great philosophical and cultural revolution in thought that Marx began and Trotsky so richly expanded. We are the fortunate ones who are not resigned and know that they need not resign ourselves, to the inevitability of advancing barbarism, to the decay and disintegration of society.

We know with scientific sureness that no reaction – not matter how strong at the moment, no matter how prolonged – can destroy that social force whose very conditions of existence force it into a revolutionary struggle against the conditions of its existence, the proletariat.

We know with scientific sureness that no matter how dark and powerful reaction may be at any given time, it not only generates but regenerates its gravedigger – that same proletariat, the only social force which class society has endowed with infinite capacity for recuperation from temporary defeat.

And we know with scientific sureness that the achievement of the fullest development of democracy, which is socialism, is in safe hands when entrusted to the proletariat and in safe hands only when it is in its charge, for it alone must have democracy for its existence and it alone can realize it in full by its irrepressible aspiration for socialism and its unceasing fight for it.

For the man to whom the debasement and oppression of others is a mortal offence to himself, who cannot live as a free man while others are unfree, who understands that without resisting the decay of society there is no life worth living – for him the informed struggle against exploitation and social iniquity is the blood-stream of life. It is indispensable to the self-realization of humanity and therefore to the attainment of his own dignity. It is the mark of his respect for his fellow man, of his yearning to gain the respect of others, and therewith to assure his respect for himself.

For such men, and we count ourselves as such, these turbulent 25 years are a long episode that has given richer and stouter meaning to the moral life of all who passed through it with their loyalties unimpaired, and it is in this life, the life of freedom, that the founder of our contemporary movement Leon Trotsky was a startling example. It is to the grand vindication of this life that lies ahead that we renew our bond tonight – the oldest and noblest bond in history, the bond that will be redeemed only on the day when the last chain has been struck from the body and mind of man, so that he may walk for the first time among his equals erect.

From a speech delivered on 18 November 1953. *Labor Action*, 30 November 1953

The "New Democracy" at Work

Top: *The Militant*, 13
July 1953, after the
workers' rising of that
month against
Stalinism in East
Germany. Adenauer
was Chancellor of
West Germany;
Malenkov was then
on top in the USSR
after the death of
Stalin. Right: *Labor
Action*, 14 June 1948,
commenting on fake
election results in
Czechoslovakia after
the Stalinists took full
power in February
1948.

Essays

Isaac Deutscher and the end of socialism

Max Shachtman (1954)

A BIOGRAPHY OF LEON Trotsky written by an author [Isaac Deutscher, in his youth active in the Polish Trotskyist movement, later a well-known writer in Britain] who understands that his life was nothing more than his political ideas and political activities, is of necessity a political document. The fact that this biography is written by Isaac Deutscher gives it more than ordinary importance.

He brings to his work the extensive knowledge of his subject acquired through active participation in the revolutionary movements with which Trotsky was so prominently associated and through earnest research into materials not easily available to others. He knows he is writing about a man of heroic gifts and attainments, of such stature that it seems society must rest up for generations before being able to produce his like again.

Deutscher has performed a precious service, in general to all those who are interested in historical truth and accuracy and in particular to those who are interested in the revolutionary movement. Although this book is actually only the first part of the biography he planned to write it covers the period from Trotsky's birth in 1879 to about the mid-period of his life, in 1921, leaving the remainder of his life to be dealt with in a second volume called *The Prophet Unarmed*, it already supersedes, in respect to documentation on the life of Trotsky, everything else that has been published, not so much in particular as on the whole.

A political writer does not have to speak in the first person to reveal his views; they appear even when he speaks in the second and third. Deutscher does not announce his conceptions in his own name, as it were, but they are announced nevertheless. It would appear from his writings, then, that he still regards himself as an opponent of capitalism, a supporter of socialism and not of the more conservative school but of the more radical, and, on the whole, a Marxist. But it is precisely in this last respect that the results are nothing less than a disaster.

After you rub your eyes with your knuckles to make sure you have read what you have read, you ask the question: what was this man doing all those years in the communist and Trotskyist movements (above all in the Polish movement which always had so high and serious a regard for Marxism), that allows him to end up with theories that are at once superficial, preposterous and downright reactionary, even though they are put forward in the name of socialism? To try to answer would lead us too close to aspects of life which are not our field. It will have to do if we say that by the side of exceptional talent in the exhaustive work of bringing together the facts and documents, of honourable contempt for the small-minded carper and the forger, the picayune adversary and the "tomb-robber," of writing skill which is most unusual in a second language, Deutscher discloses a paucity and shallowness in the theoretical domain which is startling by comparison. And it has invariably been a grave weakness in this domain that has proved to be the obstacle to reaching an understanding of Stalinism and worse than an obstacle.

Take, as one example, the disagreement between Lenin and Trotsky during the First World War on the question of "revolutionary defeatism." Deutscher disposes of the matter in a paragraph. It is not a matter of terseness that is involved, although the writer devotes far more space to matters of far smaller importance and greater transparency. It is, however, a matter of the very great theoretical importance of Lenin's position during the war and of its political implications and consequences, at the very least from the standpoint of the historian, not to say the enlightener of readers. To Deutscher, "actually, the difference [between Lenin and Trotsky] was one of propagandist emphasis, not of policy.... Each attitude had, from the viewpoint of those who held it, its advantages and disadvantages." This is pious enough, especially from one who proclaims himself "free from loyalties to any cult," but it does not even scratch the surface below which lie rich ores for the theoretical or historical assayer.

What makes matters worse, is that he does not anywhere pursue the subject to its obvious conclusion, namely: what relation did Lenin's conception or slogan of "revolutionary defeatism" and Trotsky's conception that "the revolution is not interested in any further accumulation of defeats," have to the actual defeats at the end of the war, if not in general then at least in Russia? What relation did they have to the actual revolutions at the end of the war, at least to the Russian revolutions in March and November?

Worthwhile if limited generalisations can be drawn from such an examination. To conclude the subject, as Deutscher does, by saying that: "In 1917 these two shades of opposition to war merged without controversy or friction in the policy of the Bolshevik party," is simply to state a truth that has no great relevance to the controversy in question. After all, Deutscher might have used the same phrase with regard to the pre-1917 dispute over the "permanent revolution," but nobody has yet argued that the dispute on this question between Lenin and Trotsky represented "two shades" of opinion.

The other example is precisely the dispute over Trotsky's theory of the "permanent revolution" and Lenin's formula of the "revolutionary democratic dictatorship of the proletariat and the peasantry." The theory which is Trotsky's distinctive contribution to Marxism and to the course of the Bolshevik revolution itself, which is, so to speak, the head and heart of his entire political life, is given surprisingly cursory treatment here. The reader gets a fifth-carbon copy of Trotsky himself, uninspiringly presented, which is a matter of taste, but also uncritically presented, which is something else again.

Why did Lenin combat Trotsky's theory so persistently, not to say violently? Why did he cling so long and so doggedly to his own formula? Were the differences serious, or primarily the product of a misunderstanding on Lenin's part, or of his failure to read Trotsky's elaborated version of the theory — a possibility suggested by Trotsky at one time and repeated by Deutscher? Deutscher gives his view of Lenin's position and summarizes the dispute in these words: "Lenin's formula of a 'democratic dictatorship of the proletariat and the peasantry' seemed broader and more cautious than Trotsky's 'proletarian dictatorship,' and better suited for an association of socialists and agrarian revolutionists. In 1917 events in Russia were to confirm Trotsky's prognostication."

To reduce the dispute to these terms is an all but incredible feat. We are here altogether uninterested in the monstrous inventions and falsifications concocted by the Stalinists. Nevertheless, the fact remains that the dispute hinged on two radically and irreconcilably different views about the character of the Russian revolution and the nature and prospects of socialism in Russia, least of all on whether Trotsky would "prejudge [the] potentialities" of the peasantry and Lenin "would not", and not at all on whether one view was "broader and more cautious" and the other narrower and more reckless. It is hard to believe that an ex-socialist like Bertram Wolfe (in his *Three Men Who Made a Revolution*) presents a far more comprehensive and well-documented picture of the conflict as seen by the two protagonists (regardless of Wolfe's own arbitrary conclusions from the conflict) and even grasps it better than Deutscher does.

As for the second statement — about the confirmation of Trotsky's views in 1917 — that is good enough for an article or a popular pamphlet, or it is good enough "on the whole." As an unqualified assertion in a critical biography of Trotsky it is inadequate. A critical evaluation or re-evaluation of Trotsky's conception of the permanent revolution, without detracting an inch from its remarkable theoretical power and insight into the actuality of future developments, would nevertheless add some observations as to exactly where the "1917 events in Russia" did not confirm Trotsky's prognostications. It would become clear exactly how important, indeed, vitally important from the standpoint of the concrete political struggle during a decisive period in the development of the revolution, this error in the theory would have turned out to be, if Trotsky had not been so free from dogmatism. Trotsky himself has provided the clue to the error and it would not require too great an effort to make it plain, specific and instructive for the political problems of today.

Here again, Deutscher is either indifferent to theoretical questions or incapable of finding his way among them, even when the political consequences that clearly follow from them are of immense and active importance. It may as well be added that, on the basis of the theories he propounds about Stalinism, the latter is more likely the case. It is a pity. Where he should have his greatest strength, there lies his most glaring weakness. The weakness, we shall see, is not less than fatal. At the least, it is fatal to the entire conception of socialism as a revolutionary movement and as a social objective that was set down in the name of science by Marx and Engels, and supported for a hundred years thereafter by all those who professed their views to any substantial degree.

Deutscher does not set forth his own conception about the development of the Russian revolution and its relationship to the socialist goal in any forthright way or as any sort of systematic theory. One might say that he is under no obligation to the reader to do so, that he is satisfied to let the reader draw his own conclusions from objectively presented facts of history. Whatever may be said about such an assertion — and we regard it as absurd — the fact nevertheless remains that in one way or another, Deutscher does draw conclusions of his own along the lines of his own theoretical and political views. If one is to express an opinion about these conclusions and views, it is necessary first of all to do what Deutscher fails to do, that is, to bring them together from the various parts of his work in which they are loosely scattered and give them the maximum cohesiveness that they allow for, to make them succinct and explicit to the greatest extent that this is made possible by the diffuse, ambiguous innuendo-ism and the even irresponsible way in which they are often stated.

To Deutscher, the Russia of Lenin and Trotsky, the Russia of the Bolshevik revolution, is organically continued in the Russia of Stalin (and his recent successors). Although generally sympathetic to Trotsky's point of view and full of praise for his theory of the permanent revolution in particular, he points out that there was indeed one aspect of the theory that was a "miscalculation."

Not for a moment did Trotsky imagine, however, that the Russian Revolution could survive in isolation for decades. It may therefore be said, as Stalin was to say twenty years later, that he "underrated" the internal resources and vitality of revolutionary Russia. This miscalculation, obvious in retrospect, is less surprising when one considers that the view expressed by Trotsky in 1906 was to become the common property of all Bolshevik leaders, including Stalin, in the years between 1917 and 1924. Hindsight, naturally, dwells on this particular error so much that the error overshadows the forecast as a whole. True enough, Trotsky did not foresee that Soviet Russia would survive in isolation for decades. But who, apart from him, foresaw, in 1906, the existence of Soviet Russia?

The important thing in this passage is not that the author is more severe toward the critics of Trotsky's "miscalculation" than toward Trotsky himself, but that he holds that "Soviet" Russia is still in existence despite its long isolation and the triumph of the Stalinist regime in the country. What there is about the regime that warrants calling it a "Soviet" regime today, when there is not a microscopic trace left of Soviet power or even of a Soviet institution, is nowhere discussed or even so much as mentioned by Deutscher. That is evidently the least of his preoccupations.

That Stalinism represents the organic continuation and maintenance of the Bolshevik revolution as it inherited it, or took it over, from the regime of Lenin and Trotsky, is indicated by Deutscher in a dozen different ways as a fact which he considers established. That is not because he is oblivious to the differences or denies them.

The Bolshevik Revolution was the great revolution of democracy and socialism in Russia, and so also was the regime it established in 1917. Since that time, great changes have taken place. The world revolution did not come, yet "Soviet" Russia survived in isolation for decades. "A man like Trotsky could not imagine that the revolution would seek to escape from its isolation and weakness into totalitarianism." It is this totalitarianism that Stalinism represents. The masses of the people are held in cruel and ruthless subjection by tyrannical rule. That is true, and Deutscher will not blink at the fact. But it is nevertheless also true, in his eyes, that this rule represents the continuation and even the extension of the same revolution.

The whole theme of his book, as was the whole theme of his earlier biography of Stalin, is, first, that the change from the Lenin/Trotsky regime to the Stalin regime was an inescapable necessity for this revolution in particular. Second, that the change was inevitable not only for this revolution but so it always has been and presumably always will be for every popular revolution in general. And third, that the outstanding and apparently distinctive characteristics of the regime established by the change are not only to be found in the regime that preceded it, and are not only the products of an organic outgrowth from it, but were originally directly but inconsistently prompted by Lenin and Trotsky. Their program is being simply if brutally carried out by their successors.

This theme is more blatantly asserted in the present friendly biography of Trotsky than in the previous unfriendly biography of Stalin. It is not a new one. Up to now, it has been almost exclusively the property of all the opponents of Stalinism who are opponents of the Bolshevik revolution as well, on the one hand; and on the other hand of all the upholders of Stalinism who profess their support of the Bolshevik revolution. It is worthy of special attention again because it is now presented by a supporter of the Bolshevik revolution, in fact by a not entirely reformed former Trotskyist, who is not a Stalinist, and worthier yet because of the arguments Deutscher musters.

Why was the evolution of Stalinist totalitarianism necessary for the revolution?

Because, in the first place, the working class itself could not be relied upon to maintain and develop the socialist revolution. Proletarian democracy may be established in the early days of a socialist revolution, when the fumes of naive illusions befuddle the thoughts of the idealistic utopians who lead it. But if the revolution is to survive, proletarian democracy must be dispensed with, and the Utopians who believe in it, and their place taken by the realistic despot who will rule against the will of the proletarians but for their own good. Deutscher refuses to entertain any vulgar socialist illusions about the working class, the Russian working class in particular, and most particularly in the period of 1917 onward. He calls attention extensively and with a special sort of relish to the fact that the "grotesque sequel to the October insurrection, a sequel to which historians rarely give attention, was a prodigious, truly elemental orgy of mass drunkenness with which the freed underdog celebrated his victory." The reader is left to "draw his own conclusions," as it were, from the highly detailed picture of the saturnalia drawn by Deutscher.

The reader who, out of obtuseness or out of a knowledge of what the "freed underdog" of the Russian revolution was in his all-sided reality, does not draw the right conclusions, is given them directly by Deutscher in his picture of the same underdog three years later. The country, in 1920, was in a severe crisis; and so was the Bolshevik party that led it. In describing its inner debates on the crisis, Deutscher describes the then Workers' Opposition, whose views on workers' democracy he says, and rightly, were later taken up substantially by the Trotskyist Opposition, as follows:

They were the first Bolshevik dissenters to protest against the method of government designed "to make the people believe by force" [the quoted words are from a passage in Machiavelli which is the motto of Deutscher's book — S.] *They implored the party to "trust its fate" to the working class which had raised it to power. They spoke the language which the whole party had spoken in 1917. They were the real Levellers of this revolution, its high-minded, Utopian dreamers. The party could not listen to them if it was not prepared to commit noble yet unpardonable suicide. It could not trust its own and the republic's fate to a working class whittled down, exhausted, and demoralised by civil war, famine, and the black market.* (*The Prophet Armed*, p.508)

Because, in the second place, there was only one working-class party that could be relied upon to maintain the revolution, and only one, the Bolsheviks. The working class had to be deprived of its right to political existence because it could not be trusted to defend socialism. All other parties, past or future, therefore also had to be deprived of their right to political existence because they could not be trusted to take power in the interests of socialism.

If the Bolsheviks had now [in 1920] *permitted free elections to the Soviets, they would almost certainly have been swept from power. The Bolsheviks were firmly resolved not to let things come to that pass. It would be wrong to maintain that they clung to power for its sake. The party as a whole was still animated by that revolutionary idealism of which it had given such abundant proof in its underground struggle and in the civil war. It clung to power because it identified the fate of the republic with its own fate and saw in itself the only force capable of safeguarding the revolution. It was lucky for the revolution — and it was also its misfortune — that in this belief the Bolsheviks were profoundly justified. The revolution would hardly have sur-*

vived without a party as fanatically devoted to it as the Bolsheviks were.
(*The Prophet Armed,* p.504)

Rather than grant the right to legal existence only to parties that promise solemnly not to try to win a majority — or if despite their best efforts they win such a majority, promise even more solemnly not to exercise it — it was better to make it a principle of the socialist revolution in Russia that only the Bolshevik party had the right to exist. As a matter of fact, it is in the nature of revolutions to wipe out all parties but one — the one that wipes out all the others in the name and interests of the revolution.

The revolution cannot deal a blow at the party most hostile and danger-ous to it without forcing not only that party but its immediate neighbour to answer with a counterblow. The revolution therefore treats its enemy's im-mediate neighbour as its enemy. When it hits this secondary enemy, the lat-ter's neighbour, too, is aroused and drawn into the struggle. The process goes on like a chain reaction until the party of the revolution arouses against itself and suppresses all the parties which until recently crowded the political scene. (*The Prophet Armed,* p.339)

Which is why the advance to socialism required the suppression not only of the working class but also of all parties, including all past and future working-class parties, except one. And even this one had to be, in the nature of things, also suppressed in the end.

And because, in the third place, inside of that one and only party that could be relied upon to save socialism, there was only one point of view that could really be relied upon. For once you have two views, you have a contest; and once you have a contest, you may have a split and there are your two or more parties again. And Deutscher knows where that would lead:

Almost at once it became necessary to suppress opposition in Bolshevik ranks as well [as outside these ranks]. *The Workers' Opposition (and up to a point the Democratic Centralists too) expressed much of the frustration and discontent which had led to the Kronstadt rising. The cleavages tended to become fixed; and the contending groups were inclined to behave like so many parties within the party. It would have been preposterous to establish the rule of a single party and then to allow that party to split into fragments. If Bolshevism were to break up into two or more hostile movements, as the old Social Democratic party had done, would not one of them — it was asked — become the vehicle of counterrevolution?... Barely two years were to elapse before Trotsky was to take up and give a powerful resonance to many of the criticisms and demands made by the less articulate leaders of the Workers' Opposition and of the Democratic Centralists, whom he now helped to defeat, and before he, too, was to cry out for a return to proletarian democracy.* (*The*

Prophet Armed, p.520)

The one that could really be relied upon was, then, certainly not the point of view or the group represented by Trotsky. For, with all his high-minded idealism and selflessness, what else could he represent when he took up the struggle against the bureaucracy in 1923 except the criticisms and demands of the old Workers' Opposition and the D.C.ists to which he gave a powerful resonance?

And what else could they represent except "the Levellers of this revolution," its "Utopian dreamers"? What else could the party do, speaking through Stalin this time, but refuse to "listen to them if it was not prepared to commit noble yet unpardonable suicide"? Being Utopians, the Workers' Opposition and the Democratic Centralists, like the Trotskyists after them, wanted the party to "trust its own and the republic's fate to a working class whittled down, exhausted and demoralised by civil war, famine, and the black market."

Under the circumstances, then, it follows with brass-stitched logic that the attempt of these inner-party oppositions to restore proletarian democracy in the country, accompanied inevitably by the risk of creating another party, could only promote the ends of counterrevolution and kill (by suicide if not homicide) the prospects of socialism in Russia. Correspondingly, the work of the Stalinists to establish and consolidate a regime which ruled "regardless of the will of the working class," of the will of all other political parties and the will of all other factions of their own party — in fact by crushing and suppressing all of them — was necessary to prevent the counter-revolution and to produce socialism in Russia and elsewhere.

That is how it happened that the revolution which began with the naively Utopian idea of Bolshevism that the road to socialism lies through the fullest achievement of democracy found it necessary to learn the hard lesson that the road to practical and successful socialism lies through the fullest achievement of totalitarian tyranny.

Thus Deutscher. And he is not at the finish line, he has only just started.

Anyone who imagines that Deutscher is concerned here only with explaining the transformation necessary for a revolution that occurred in a backward country under exceptional circumstances from which a socialist revolution in more favoured countries would be exempted, is luring himself to disappointment. To Deutscher, the evolution to Stalinist totalitarianism was the inevitable outcome of the Bolshevik revolution, in the same way that an equivalent tyranny has always been and must presumably always be the inevitable outcome of any popular revolution. The idea that the masses of the people can ever directly manage and control their destiny is as erroneous as the assumption that such control is essential for human progress in general or socialism especially. How does he reach this not entirely novel conclusion?

Readers of Deutscher's biography of Stalin will recall the theory — "the broad scheme" — by which he explains not only "the metamorphosis of triumphant Bolshevism" into Stalinism but, much more generally, the basic processes which have "been common to all great revolutions so far." In the first phase of all these revolutions, "the party that gives the fullest expression to the popular moods outdoes its rivals, gains the confidence of the masses, and rises to power." Civil war follows.

The revolutionary party is still marching in step with the majority of the nation. It is acutely conscious of its unity with the people and of a profound harmony between its own objectives and the people's wishes and desires. It can call upon the mass of the nation for ever-growing efforts and sacrifices; and it is sure of the response. In this, the heroic phase, the revolutionary party is in a very real sense democratic....

This phase lasts little longer than the civil war. By then the revolutionary party, though victorious, faces a country and a people that are exhausted. A reaction sets in among the people.

The anti-climax of the revolution is there. The leaders are unable to keep their early promises. They have destroyed the old order; but they are unable to satisfy the daily needs of the people. To be sure, the revolution has created the basis for a higher organisation of society and for progress in a not very remote future. This will justify it in the eyes of posterity. But the fruits of revolution ripen slowly; and of immediate moment are the miseries of the first post-revolutionary year. It is in their shadow that the new state takes on its shape, a shape that reveals the chasm between the revolutionary party and the people. This is the real tragedy which overtakes the party of the revolution.

If it obeys the mass of the petulant and unreasoning people, it must relinquish power. But, "abdication would be suicide." In order to safeguard the achievements of the revolution, it must disregard the voice of the people in whose interests the revolution is made.

The party of the revolution knows no retreat. It has been driven to its present pass largely through obeying the will of that same people by which it is now deserted. It will go on doing what it considers to be its duty, without paying much heed to the voice of the people. In the end it will muzzle and stifle that voice. (Deutscher, *Stalin*, pp.174ff.)

That was in his Stalin book, and that it was not a momentary aberration is shown in his Trotsky biography, where this theory is not only expanded upon and underscored, but becomes the heart and soul of his work. *The Prophet Armed* — the title of the book — comes from a famous passage in Machiavelli's *The Prince*, where he is discussing the difficulties facing "the innovators" who seek to replace an old order with a new. Can they rely on themselves or trust to others, asks Machiavelli?

... that is to say, whether, to consummate their enterprise, have they to use prayers or can they use force? In the first instance they always succeed badly, and never compass anything; but when they can rely on themselves and use force, then they are rarely endangered. Hence it is that all armed prophets have conquered, and the unarmed ones have been destroyed. Besides the reasons mentioned, the nature of the people is variable, and whilst it is easy to persuade them, it is difficult to fix them in that persuasion. And thus it is necessary to take such measures that, when they believe no longer, it may be possible to make them believe by force.

By 1920, says Deutscher, the Bolsheviks were faced with the choice which every revolutionary party in power faces, in its essence, at one time or another: Let the masses speak, and they will remove you from power and destroy the revolution; stifle the masses, and "it would deprive itself of historic legitimacy, even in its own eyes."

The revolution had now reached that cross-roads, well known to Machiavelli, at which it found it difficult or impossible to fix the people in their revolutionary persuasion and was driven "to take such measures that, when they believed no longer, it might be possible to make them believe by force." (*The Prophet Armed*, p.506.)

To vouchsafe democracy to the masses may have meant the removal of the Bolsheviks from power, and as we have seen above, Deutscher does not believe they had the right to give up power. That would have encouraged the White Guards to resort to arms; and the Bolsheviks "could not accept it as a requirement of democracy that they should, by retreating, plunge the country into a new series of civil wars just after one series had been concluded". But there is a deeper reason, in Deutscher's mind, why the crushing of the proletariat was inevitable — and by that, it should now be clear, Deutscher means desirable from the standpoint of preserving the revolution. That reason, too, lies in the very nature of the revolution — not the Russian alone, but all revolutions. Every "great revolution" has its Utopian extremists who do not understand that the revolution cannot really satisfy the unreasonable demands of the masses it inspired, of the masses who assured its triumph, of the very masses who were told that the revolution will satisfy their demands. With the best intentions in the world, these Utopians — Levellers in Cromwell's England, Hebertists in Robespierre's France, and in Bolshevik Russia the Workers' Opposition, the Democratic Centralists and then the Trotskyist Opposition — can only imperil the revolution, its conquests and its future. They are among those who:

... cry in alarm that the revolution has been betrayed, for in their eyes government by the people is the very essence of the revolution. Without it there can be no government for the people. The rulers find justification for themselves in the conviction that whatever they do will ultimately serve the interests of the broad mass of the nation; and indeed they do, on the whole, use their power to consolidate most of the economic and social conquests of the revolution. Amid charges and countercharges, the heads of the revolutionary leaders begin to roll and the power of the post-revolutionary state towers over the society it governs. (Stalin, p.175)

It is not necessary for us to emphasise that Deutscher applies this conception — the new tyranny against the people nevertheless does, "on the whole," use its power to strengthen the conquests of the revolution — to the revolution that established capitalism and to the revolution that is to establish (and according to him, has already established in Russia) socialism. The analogies between the industrial revolutions that consolidated the social revolutions in both cases, he finds "are as numerous as they are striking." He summarises the "primitive accumulation of capital" that marked the bourgeois revolution in England as "the first violent process by which one social class accumulated in its hands the means of production, while other classes were being deprived of their land and means of livelihood and reduced to the status of wage earners." A similar process took place under Stalin in the Thirties.

Marx sums up his picture of the English industrial revolution by saying that "capital comes [into the world] dripping from head to foot, from every pore, with blood and dirt." Thus also comes into the world — socialism in one country. In spite of its "blood and dirt," the English industrial revolution Marx did not dispute this marked a tremendous progress in the history of mankind. It opened a new and not unhopeful epoch of civilization. Stalin's industrial revolution can claim the same merit. (Stalin, pp.342ff)

That a new despotism is the inevitable product of every revolution, after its first stage, should not generate unperforated gloom. For if the masses cannot be trusted to continue the revolution they began or, in any case, made possible, they may console themselves with the thought that the despots are tyrannising over them for their own good. Even if against their will, and by cruelties which drip blood and dirt from every pore, the achievements of their revolution are being protected in the only way that is practical — by suppressing them. A new and not unhopeful epoch lies ahead. It is a relief to know it.

The final proof of this not wholly discouraging theory lies, in Deutscher's revelation, in the concrete circumstances from which it is contemporaneously deduced. They show the organic link between Lenin and Trotsky and their regime, and Stalin and his regime. There is no rupture between the two but a relentless continuity. Deutscher claims to have

... *traced the thread of unconscious historic continuity which led from Lenin's hesitant and shamefaced essays in revolution by conquest to the revolutions contrived by Stalin the conqueror. A similar subtle thread connects Trotsky's domestic policy of these years with the later practices of his antagonist. Both Trotsky and Lenin appear, each in a different field, as Stalin's unwitting inspirers and prompters. Both were driven by circumstances beyond their control and by their own illusions to assume certain attitudes in which circumstances and their own scruples did not allow them to persevere — attitudes which were ahead of their time, out of tune with the current Bolshevik mentality, and discordant with the main theme of their own lives.* (*The Prophet Armed*, p.515).*

The world revolution, the extension of the revolution westward which was to save Russia from the disintegration to which its isolated position, according to the Bolsheviks, surely doomed it — was it one of their illusions?

Precisely, says the now disintoxicated Trotskyist. If Lenin and Trotsky "had taken a soberer view of the international revolution" they might have "foreseen that in the course of decades their example would not be imitated in any other country... History produced [sic] the great illusion and planted and cultivated it in the brains of the most soberly realistic leaders..." (Ibid., p. 293.) "What was wrong in their expectations was not merely the calendar of revolutionary events but the fundamental assumption that European capitalism was at the end of its tether. They grossly underrated its staying power, its adaptability, and the hold it had on the loyalty of the working class." (*The Prophet Armed*, p.449) As for the organisation of the Communist International, which was to organize, stimulate and lead the world revolution, it was an illusion and a mistake — "fathered by wish, mothered by confusion, and assisted by accident."

Yet, a veritable horror of isolation reigned among the Bolsheviks, Trotsky more than any of them. Since world revolution proved to be an illusion, year after year, the Bolsheviks were driven — "true ... in the heat of war, under abundant provocation, without grasping all the implications of its own decision" — to break out of isolation by embarking for the first time, in violation of their hallowed principles, upon the course of revolution by conquest. The first time was in the 1920 war with Poland. "If the Red Army had seized Warsaw, it would have proceeded to act as the chief agent of social upheaval, as a substitute, as it were, for the Polish working class." It is true that Trotsky and Stalin were against making the attempt to pursue the defeated forces of Pilsudski that were retreating back to Poland. But Lenin was for it. The attempt failed.

Lenin [then] *grew aware of the incongruity of his role. He admitted his error. He spoke out against carrying the revolution abroad on the point of bayonets. He joined hands with Trotsky in striving for peace. The great revolutionary prevailed in him over the revolutionary gambler. However, the "error" was neither fortuitous nor inconsequential.* (*The Prophet Armed*, p.471)

Because it was not fortuitous, it reasserted itself. If Lenin did not persevere in the course of revolution by conquest (the "revolution from above" in contrast to the revolution of the masses which was an illusion), it was, among other reasons, because of his "scruples," that is, his revolutionary socialist principles, ideals and traditions. The difference in Stalin's case is simply that he was not burdened with such scruples and inhibitions. With the failure of this first attempt, Lenin's, at revolution by conquest, the revolutionary cycle, which the First World War had set in motion was coming to a close. At the beginning of that cycle Bolshevism had risen on the crest of a genuine revolution; toward its end Bolshevism began to spread revolution by conquest. A long interval, lasting nearly a quarter of a century, separates this cycle of revolution from the next, which the Second World War set in motion. During the interval Bolshevism did not expand. When the next cycle opened, it started where the first had ended, with revolution by conquest.... In 1945-6 and partly even in 1939-40 Stalin began where he, and in a sense he and Lenin had left off in 1920-1.

The victory of socialism in Poland as the product of the proletarian revolution — "a genuine revolution" — was an illusion. The victory of socialism in Poland as the product of invasion, occupation and subjugation by the armed forces of a totalitarian despotism, that is not an illusion. It is simply Stalin's uninhibited continuation of Lenin's course. It is a comfort to hear this.

As in foreign policy, so in domestic policy. In 1920, with the revolution at that crossroads, so familiar to Machiavelli and now even better understood by Deutscher, "Trotsky ... stumbled ... he initiated courses of action which he and the Bolshevik party could carry through only against the resistance of the social classes which had made or supported the revolution." His proposals for loosening the bonds of War Communism, an anticipation of the New Economic Policy soon to be advocated by Lenin, having been rejected by the party leadership, Trotsky proposed in its stead to carry the policies of War Communism to the bitter end, as it were. He "advanced the idea of complete state control over the working class."

The reference is to Trotsky's proposals during the so-called trade-union dispute in 1920 for the "militarisation of labour" and the "incorporation" of the unions into the state machine. The divorce between dictatorship and proletarian democracy, which Stalin carried to its inevitable conclusion, was clearly obvious. But Lenin refused to proclaim the divorce. For although he, too, "was aware that government and party were in conflict with the people… he was afraid that Trotsky's policy would perpetuate the conflict." And even Trotsky was his own antidote to the program he proposed.

Accustomed to sway people by force of argument and appeal to reason he went on appealing to reason in a most unreasonable cause. He publicly advocated government by coercion…. He hoped to persuade people that they needed no government by persuasion. He told them that the workers' state had the right to use forced labour. . . . He submitted his policies to public control. He himself did everything in his power to provoke the resistance that frustrated him. To keep politically alive he needed broad daylight. (The Prophet Armed, pp.516ff)

Trotsky did not direct the transformation of the revolution into a despotism not only because circumstances then prevented it but because it was not in his character to do it. But a different one was available, luckily for socialism. "It took Stalin's bat-like character to carry his [Trotsky's] ideas into execution." Neither Trotsky nor Stalin, each for his own reasons, would admit this. But it was true.

There was hardly a single plank in Trotsky's program of 1920-1 which Stalin did not use during the industrial revolution of the Thirties. He introduced conscription and direction of labour, he insisted that the trade unions should adopt a "productionist" policy instead of defending the consumer interests of the workers; he deprived the trade unions of their last vestige of autonomy and transformed them into tools of the state. He set himself up as the protector of the managerial groups, on whom he bestowed privileges of which Trotsky had not even dreamed. He ordered "socialist emulation" in the factories and mines; and he did so in words unceremoniously and literally taken from Trotsky. He put into effect his own ruthless version of that "Soviet Taylorism" which Trotsky had advocated. And finally, he passed from Trotsky's intellectual and historical arguments ambiguously justifying forced labour to its mass application. (*The Prophet Armed*, p.515)

Therein lay and still lies Trotsky's victory in spite of all, the victory of which he himself was one of the outstanding victims. That is what Deutscher means by titling the last chapter in the present work "Defeat in Victory". "All armed prophets have conquered, and the unarmed ones have been destroyed." Trotsky could not, in the crucial hour, arm himself against the people so as to make them believe by force after persuasion had failed to sustain their beliefs. Stalin could. He became the true prophet armed.

The revolution itself had made that necessary, for such is its nature; it made it inevitable; it prepared for it willy-nilly. Fortunately, the new prophet armed proved, again, to be one of those rulers who, "on the whole, use their power to consolidate most of the economic and social conquests of the revolution." The result has been the victory of socialism in Russia, and not only in Russia but wherever else — and that reaches far across two continents by now — the armed prophet has extended the revolution by conquest. In the crude environment in which the revolution was obliged to entrench itself for so long, it could only produce a "brand of socialism," as Deutscher puts it.

The brand of socialism which it then produced could not but show the mark of its historic heritage. That socialism, too, was to rise rough and crude, without the vaulting arches and spires and lacework of which socialists had dreamed. Hemmed in by superior hostile forces it soon delivered itself up to the new Leviathan state — rising as if from the ashes of the old. (*The Prophet Armed*, p.521.)

As every good American knows, you can't get something for nothing. For the blessings of Stalin's "brand of socialism," which lacks such gewgaws as arches, spires and lacework, hundreds of millions are paying with the Leviathan-state. If, to realize these blessings, the totalitarian regime was indispensable, it is not entirely to Stalin's discredit that he knew or felt which was the right way and took it absolutely. And Trotsky, the gifted revolutionary Utopian? "It was another of history's ironies that Trotsky, the hater of the Leviathan, should become the first harbinger of its resurrection."

This is as good as an epitaph, even if it is written before the second volume of the biography has appeared. But only in a manner of speaking. It is not merely a matter of Deutscher having written a libel of Trotsky, and not of Trotsky alone. In his biography of Stalin he already showed how far he has travelled from Marxism. His biography of Trotsky shows he has not retraced a step but gone farther away and to ever stranger fields. Deutscher has put a cross over himself. It is his own epitaph as a revolutionist and a socialist that he has written.

If justice were half as prevalent as prejudice, Deutscher's book would be acclaimed far more widely than it is likely to be. Even those who did not find cheer in its main theories would find quiet solace in it, from one standpoint or the other. The revolutionary socialists — the Utopians — are presently in such a small minority that they do not count; besides he abandoned them to their own devices years ago. But the others, those who make up the big majorities and the big minorities, for them the book should be a box of bonbons.

The Stalinists — if not the official Stalinists then the sophisticated Stalinist, the openly cynical Stalinist, the Stalinoid by design and the Stalinoid by gullibility — might ask for better, but not expect it. What else has he been saying in justification of his whole regime, his whole course, his whole political philosophy — not of course on the platform before the vulgar mob but in the less exposed intimacy of the enlightened? There it is safer to explain the simple truth that the donkey is a donkey, and should be grateful that the driver is determined to lash him toward the new and not unhopeful pasture where he may some day roam unsaddled, unleashed and with an abundance to nibble on.

The professional Mensheviks of both schools have equal delights in store for them, equal parts of confirmation for each bias. The one school, all the way down to and including Shub, who feed their detestation of the Bolshevik revolution on its Stalinist outcome, can feel vindicated by this avowal from a hostile camp that there could be no other outcome — they never said otherwise. The other school, represented by the late Th. Dan, who justified their late-in-life capitulation to Stalinism, can feel, at least secretly vindicated by the thought that the Bolshevik revolution which they opposed was indeed led by irresponsible utopians. Leftist Labourite demagogues and ignoramuses, to whom Marxian theory was always a redundant nuisance we can well do without in Britain, and social-democratic or radical "neutralists" in France, should feel easier about their conciliatory inclinations toward the slave state when it is brought home to them so clearly that, unlike the capitalist states where the workers are oppressed and exploited in the name of capitalism, they are oppressed and exploited in Russia in the name of a brand of socialism which has opened a not unhopeful epoch of civilization.

The classical bourgeois opponents of socialism, ranging all the way from the academicians of the von Mises and Hayek type to plain blatherskites like Kerensky, owe lavish thanks to Deutscher for such a rich replenishment of their thinning arsenal of arguments, dating back to Spencer, that all efforts at freedom based on collectivism cannot but lead to the Servile State, the new tyranny, and that the high minded socialist idealist is at best a Utopian — moreover one who, it turns out, is more dangerous to socialism than to capitalism itself.

The new snobocracy, the neo-pseudo-proto-Machiavellians, has a rich morsel here over which to quiver with delight ever so fastidiously, for ever since they had the theory explained to them third hand by second rate dabblers in Machiavelli, and Mosca, Michels and Pareto, they have understood how preposterous is the Marxian myth that the working class and it alone has the historic mission of emancipating itself and therewith all of humanity.

The tired and retired radical of yesterday, and his name is indeed legion, can find here some justification for the clod-of-earth existence to which he has degraded himself, as can his blood-kin, the ex-radical cynic and sceptic now turned pusher and climber up the ladder of bourgeois respectability — financial, social, literary, academic or all together. For what else have they been saying for some time now except that the struggle for socialism can lead only to totalitarianism and that the working class, as the socialist self emancipator, has failed atrociously to live up to the confidence which they vested in it for so many months and in some cases even years?

Whether this motley public does justice to Deutscher's book or not, we have our own responsibility to discharge. It obliges us to say:

If Deutscher's theory is valid, it is not as an explanation for the "brand of socialism," as he calls it. It is the end of socialism. And so, in one sense, it is. It is the end of socialism for an entire generation. That generation is finished and done for so far as the fight for human dignity is concerned. It started well, even magnificently. It has ended, except for a handful of individuals, in a state of utter demoralization, helpless and hopeless victim of Stalinism and all other forms of reaction associated with it in one way or the other.

Deutscher is an example of that generation, and one of the sorrier ones. His conscious, rational life he devoted to the fight for proletarian socialism, the only socialism there is or ever will be. In the accursed years of worldwide reaction and despair we are living through, he has abandoned that fight to become the vehicle of a theory which is a mockery of Marxism, a grotesque libel against socialism, unscientific through and through and reactionary from top to bottom. It is an unabashed apology for Stalinism in the name of socialism. It could take shape only in a mind that has come apart under the steady blows of reaction instead of understanding and resisting it. If I did not know from my disheartening discussions with Deutscher, here and in England, that he has lost all belief in the socialist capacities of the working class, and that he refuses to follow the logic of his view by becoming an out-and out Stalinist only because he considers himself a "civilized" person, his writings would anyhow make it plain enough. His writings are a capitulation to the Stalinist reaction; at best, if the best is insisted on, they represent his resignation to Stalinism, and in the round the difference is not worth quibbling over.

If the generation of yesterday is finished, we are as confident that a new generation is entering the scene to pick up the socialist banner again as one did after the dark and critical years opened up by the first world war. Its mind must be as clear as can be of all the accumulated rubbish in which the old generation has been choked and blinded and worn to death. Deutscher's theory is part of that rubbish. If for no other reason than that, we shall try to clear it away.

At the basis of Deutscher's apology for Stalinism — an apology which we have stigmatized as the end of socialism — lies an utterly fantastic miscomprehension of the difference between the bourgeois revolution which assured the triumph of capitalism and the proletarian revolution which is to assure the triumph of socialism.

Deutscher only gives open and crass expression and besprinkles with Marxian jargon those ideas which have poisoned the thinking of tens and hundreds of thousands, and even more, and disposed them to passionate partisanship for Stalinist reaction, at the worst, or to cynical capitulation to it, or to terrified resignation to it, or at best, to piteous hopes for its self-reformation.

One of the most important keys to the understanding of capitalist society is this: *in order to rule socially, the bourgeoisie does not have to rule politically*. To this should be added: *in order to maintain its rule socially, the bourgeoisie is often unwilling and most often unable to rule politically*. And to go back, as it were, to the beginning, this should be added too: *the bourgeois revolution which has the aim of establishing the social power of the bourgeoisie does not at all have to aim at establishing the political power of the bourgeoisie; indeed, it establishes the bourgeoisie as the social power in the land even when it is carried out without the bourgeoisie or against the bourgeoisie or by depriving the bourgeoisie of political power in the land*. And covering all these conceptions is this: no matter who the leaders and spokesmen of the bourgeois revolutions were, or what they thought, or what they aimed for, the *only possible* result of their victory was the establishment of a new, if more advanced, form of class rule, class exploitation and class oppression by a minority over the majority.

These insights, thoroughly acquired, automatically give the Marxist an understanding of bourgeois society, from its inception to its close, that is far superior to anything that any bourgeois scholar or statesman, no matter how liberal, can possibly attain. While the bourgeois flutters and fumbles, the Marxist already has the key to such apparently disparate phenomena, as for example, the New Deal and Fascism.

Deutscher nowhere shows that he possesses this key. If he ever had it, everything he has written on the subject of Stalinism shows that he has thrown it away. There is no doubt about it, for it is precisely in the five above quintessential respects in which the bourgeois revolution differs from the proletarian revolution, that Deutscher makes the two analogous. The disastrous result could have been anticipated and so it was, for the differences between the two are not only fundamental but irreconcilable.

At its inception, as it was emerging from the economic era and developing the economy, the interests and the class character that distinguish it, the young bourgeoisie needed only one thing to guarantee its rule over society: to remove the fetters with which feudalism restricted the expansion — no matter how or by whom or for what immediate reason — the dominance of self-expanding capital was assured and with it the class dominance of its owners. The political power, the state, under whose sway these barriers were eliminated, might be constituted out of bourgeois, non-bourgeois, anti-bourgeois. But, once the traditional barriers of feudalism were thrust aside, capital rapidly and spontaneously took command of the economy as a whole, incessantly revolutionizing and transforming it, inexorably sweeping aside and subordinating other forms of economy — and doing all this *with or without* the conscious efforts or support of the state power.

To be sure, where the state power was exercised in close harmony with the new, developing economic power, there the capitalization of the economy proceeded more rapidly and smoothly. But what is important here is the fact that even where the state power sought in one way or another to impede the capitalization, that process continued nevertheless, more slowly, either by bending the state power to its needs or by replacing it by one better adapted to them.

The modern world went through an epoch of change from feudal to bourgeois society because under the conditions of the time there was no way of releasing the productive forces with which society was pregnant, of expanding them to an undreamed of extent, than the capitalist way. For this reason, both feudalism and communism were doomed in that epoch, even where their representatives held or had the chance to hold political power. The one was doomed because it was obsolete and the other because it was premature; the one was doomed because the productive forces were already so far developed that they could develop no further under feudalism and the other because the productive forces were not yet sufficiently developed to permit the establishment of communism.

There lies the basic reason why, no matter who held the political power during this long epoch, the capitalist economy, the capitalist mode of production and exchange, was strengthened, expanded and consolidated. This made the capitalist class the "economically dominant" class in society, that is, established its social rule regardless of the form assumed by the state. In turn, again regardless of the form assumed by the state, the fact that it maintained the dominance of capitalist property and therewith the capitalist mode of production, made it willy-nilly a capitalist state.

Or, to put it in other words: the social power, the class power, the state power of the capitalist class is determined and assured by its economic power, that is, its ownership of capital, of the capitalist means of production and exchange. Without this economic power, the bourgeoisie is nothing, no matter what else it has on its side, even if it is the direct aid of God's vicar on earth is nothing and less than nothing. With it, the bourgeoisie is the ruler of society, no matter what else is against it.

That is still a very general way of indicating the relationship between the political and economic power in the bourgeois state. As soon, however, as the relationship is examined as it developed concretely, a much more revealing light is thrown upon it and we can move much more surely to the heart of the present-day problem. The sum of the concrete experiences from which our generalizations are derived shows that the earlier the bourgeois revolution was carried through — the more thoroughgoing it was, the more revolutionary was the bourgeoisie, the more directly did it lead the revolution against the old order, the more freely did it arouse the revolutionary and democratic spirit of the people as a whole.

By the same token, the later the bourgeois revolution was carried through the more stultified and distorted were its results, the more conservative and even reactionary was the bourgeoisie, the more prudently did it shun the role of leader of the revolution, the more eagerly did it seek guidance and protection from despotism and dynasties, and the more antagonistic was its attitude toward the mobilization and activity of the populace as a whole. This can be set down as a law of the development of the bourgeois revolution. It flows from the nature of bourgeois society, not as an abstraction, but as it naturally unfolds.

Call the bourgeois revolution progressive or not, necessary or not (Marxists of course regard it as progressive and necessary), its objective aim is incontestable: the establishment of a new social order in which a new class is brought to power in order to rule over, exploit and oppress the majority of the people. The new social order, no matter what else is said about it, cannot be conceived of without the class rule, class exploitation and class oppression which are the very conditions of its existence.

At the beginning of the revolution and the constitution of the new order, its prophets, its idealists, its inspired supporters among the toilers, may well have been moved by other considerations. But even if no one sought to deceive them, they could only deceive themselves. If they looked for that revolution to bring equality and freedom for all, they were mistaken in advance and for certain. Freedom and equality in the bourgeois revolution mean, fundamentally, the free market and equal right of all commodities to exchange at their value; and at best, all political and human freedoms that do not destroy the freedom needed by the owners of capital to exploit the proletariat. More than that could not be granted by the leaders of the bourgeois revolution and the upholders of the new order regardless of who they were, what they thought, what they wanted, or what they did.

But this is a situation which only reflects one of the basic contradictions not only of the bourgeois revolution but of bourgeois society as a whole. It is a contradiction rooted not in the conflict between easily tired masses and untiring revolutionists, utopians and realists, but in the conflict between irreconcilable classes. The early bourgeois revolutions did indeed bring forth Utopian leaders and movements. Deutscher, with a faint trace of affectionate condescension, speaks of them as the "high-minded, Utopian dreamers" of the revolution. Among them he includes the Levellers of the English Revolution, the extreme communistic left in the time of the French Revolution, and the Democratic Centralists and Trotskyists in the Bolshevik Revolution. To some of them, not to quibble about words and decorum among "Marxists," the term Utopian does apply. But it applies solely and exclusively for reasons inseparably connected with the class character of the bourgeois revolution.

To the primitive proletariat (or pre-proletariat) of that revolution, there corresponded a primitive communist or pre-communist movement. Such movements appeared in Cromwell's day, in Robespierre's day, in the days of the German peasant wars, to mention only a few. The struggle against absolutism and feudalism was to be crowned, in their conception, by a more or less communistic equality for all. What was it that fatally doomed these movements and the struggles they conducted, noble and idealistic in purpose though they were, as Utopian? Nothing, absolutely nothing, but the fact that while the development of the productive forces, among the most important of which is the proletariat itself, had reached the level which made possible and necessary the class rule of the bourgeoisie (and the subjugation of the proletariat implied by it), that level was not yet high enough to make possible the rule of the proletariat and the inauguration of a free and equalitarian society of abundance.

It is exceedingly interesting to note what Engels says about this social phenomenon, trebly interesting in connection with Deutscher because firstly, he quotes from Engels in a deplorably chopped-down version; secondly, it does not seem to occur to him that the application of Engels' thought to the subject he is treating would destroy his whole construction, root and branch; and, thirdly, because everything which Engels wrote to lead up to the section quoted might, so far as Deutscher is concerned, have been written in untranslated Aramaic. The whole of his *Peasant War in Germany* is devoted by Engels to this problem as it manifested itself in 16th-century Germany, and his forewords are as if written to illuminate the present debate. In writing about the plebeian revolutionary government over which the peasant leader, Thomas Münzer, presided in Thuringia in 1525, Engels deals with a dilemma facing a revolutionary leader who comes before his time, as it were.

The worst thing that can befall a leader of an extreme party is to be compelled to take over a government in an epoch when the movement is not yet ripe for the domination of the class which he represents and for the realisation of the measures which that domination would imply ... he necessarily finds himself in a dilemma. All he can do is in contrast to all his previous actions, to all his principles and to the present interests of his party; what he ought to do cannot be achieved.... Whoever puts himself in this awkward position is irrevocably lost.

That is how far Deutscher quotes Engels. Toward what end? To emphasize the suggestion that even Lenin may have been thinking (in 1918) that the Bolshevik Revolution was premature, "a false spring," thus reminding Marxist ears that "Marx and Engels had repeatedly written about the tragic fate which overtakes revolutionaries who "come before their time" as exemplified by Engels' commentary on Münzer. And toward what "broader" end? To support "Marxistically" his view that Stalin only carried on in a despotic way the proletarian revolution which Lenin (and Trotsky), because of their dilemma, could not carry out in that way or in a democratic way which would correspond to "all his principles and to the present interests of his party." But that is not at all the sense of Engels' view, and as soon as we supply the words which Deutscher supplanted with three periods between the last two sentences he quotes, the reader will be able to judge what Engels was talking about:

In a word, he [the leader of the extreme party who takes power prematurely] *is compelled to represent not his party or his class, but the class for whom conditions are ripe for domination. In the interests of the movement itself, he is compelled to defend the interests of an alien class, and to feed his own class with phrases and promises, with the assertion that the interests of that alien class are their own interests. Whoever puts himself in this awkward position is irrevocably lost.*

And further:

Münzer's position at the head of the "eternal council" of Mühlhausen was indeed much more precarious than that of any modern revolutionary regent. Not only the movement of his time, but the whole century, was not ripe for the realization of the ideas for which he himself had only begun to grope. The class which he represented not only was not developed enough and incapable of subduing and transforming the whole of society, but it was just beginning to come into existence. The social transformation that he pictured in his fantasy was so little grounded in the then existing economic conditions that the latter were a preparation for a social system diametrically opposed to that of which he dreamt. (The Peasant War in Germany)

We cite Engels at some length not because a quotation from Engels automatically settles all problems, and not even because the best way to know what Engels said is to read what he said. We cite the quotation because it underscores the contrast and the gulf between the supra-historical mystique with which Deutscher invests all revolutions without exception, and the concrete manner in which a Marxist analysed the class conflicts in every revolution and the specific economic conditions underlying them. From the way in which Engels deals with the problem, we get an entirely different conception of what exactly is the "tragic fate" of the Levellers, Babouvists and other Utopian revolutionary movements.

The Utopians of the early days were Utopians only because objective conditions were not ripe for the victory of their class or for the social order that they dreamed of, but only for the victory of a new exploiting class. They were Utopians only because even if they somehow gained political power for a while all they could do with it was "to defend the interests of an alien class, and to feed his own class with phrases and promises, with the assertion that the interests of that alien class are their own interests." They could only help establish the social rule of a new exploiting class.

Engels' commentary on Münzer is no more isolated or accidental in the works of the two great Marxists, than is the use of that commentary by Deutscher. The same thought voiced by Engels is supplemented and rounded out in the familiar comment made by Marx in 1848 about the social problem faced by the Jacobins in the Great French Revolution more than two centuries after Münzer.

In both revolutions [the English revolution of 1648 and the French of 1789] *the bourgeoisie was the class that really stood at the head of the movement. The proletariat and the fractions of the citizenry that did not belong to the bourgeoisie either had no interests separate from those of the bourgeoisie or else they did not yet constitute independently-developed classes or class segments. Hence, when they clashed with the bourgeoisie, as for example from 1793 to 1794 in France, they fought only for the carrying out of the interests of the bourgeoisie, even if not in the interests of the bourgeoisie. The whole of French terrorism was nothing but a plebeian way of finishing off the foes of the bourgeoisie, absolutism, feudalism and philistinism.* (*Aus dem literarischen Nachlass von K. Marx and F. Engels,* Vol. III.)

With the true significance of the Utopians, be they primitive communistic or jacobinistic movements, now indicated by Marx and Engels, the true significance — historical, social, class significance — of the brilliant Florentine's "prophet armed" becomes evident. The fact that the Levellers of all kinds and the Jacobins of all kinds came "before their time," does not suffice to have them leave the political scene with an apologetic bow. The social reality that follows the revolution only strengthens their determination to carry through the revolution to the ends they dreamed of originally, and in the interests of the broadest masses of the toiling people. The trouble is that the social reality of the bourgeois revolution is and cannot but be the class rule of the bourgeoisie. The more apparent that becomes, the more pronounced is the tendency of the masses to "believe no longer."

What is this tendency, after all? Nothing but the first important manifestation of the irreconcilability of class antagonisms between bourgeoisie and proletariat, which proves to be a permanent characteristic of bourgeois society till its last gasp, which is indeed the motive force determining the course of this society to the end. And inasmuch as the bourgeoisie must strive for the maximum degree of stability and order in which to carry out and maintain its social functions, this disorganizing tendency which appears with its ascension to power (and even before) must be kept in restraint.

It is then, and only for that reason, that the "prophet" must be at hand. He is absolutely indispensable to the class rule of the bourgeoisie because "it is necessary to take such measures that, when they [the exploited classes] believe no longer, it may be possible to make them believe by force." No wonder Marx thought so highly of Machiavelli, that unmoralising, realistic, arch-intelligent thinker of the new order and the modern state.

The "armed prophet" turned out to be the only thing he could be, what he had to be: the armed power, the police and prisons, required to preserve the oppression and exploitation of the proletariat by the bourgeoisie. The "armed prophet" is nothing but the armed bourgeois state. Everything is as it should be, for the bourgeois order cannot exist without class exploitation, and that cannot be maintained without the armed prophet who makes them believe by force.

But is that how it should be, or how it has to be, or how it may be, in a socialist society, or in a social order which can be legitimately regarded as a "brand of socialism"? That has become the life-or-death question for the socialist movement. Deutscher's answer is equal to pronouncing the death sentence upon it.

Deutscher is overwhelmingly fascinated — you might also say obsessed — by undiscriminating, uncritical and unthought out analogies between the bourgeois revolutions (the French in particular; but never the American, it is interesting to note) and the Bolshevik revolution. He explains the outcome of the latter only in terms of the evolution of the former. But if his comparisons are to make any sense, they must be tied together into some sort of systematic thought (if this is not too outrageous a demand to make in our times, when the intellectual disorder and frivolity are the peevish but popular form of rebellion against any kind of disciplined and systematized thinking). In which case we will for sure get the following seven tightly-linked points:

1. The Trotskyist Opposition, in fighting for workers' democracy, that is, for the rule of the workers, disclosed its Utopian character.

2. What the Opposition wanted was not only the program of the Democratic Centralists before them, but basically the program for which and with which the Bolsheviks in general won the Revolution of 1917.

3. The Bolshevik revolution itself, then, was Utopian.

4. That was so not only and not even because the socialist proletariat and the socialist revolutionaries came to power "before their

time," but precisely because for the necessarily short time that they are in power, they are, like Thomas Münzer, "compelled to represent not his party or his class, but the class for whom conditions are ripe for domination... compelled to defend the interests of an alien class."

5. The Lenins and Trotskys, under relentless objective pressures, could only prepare the ground for the direct and despotic rule of the alien class represented by the "prophet armed" who is needed to make the people believe by force — Stalin.

6. Under the aegis of the new but this time energetic and forward-driving revolutionary despot, the alien class in power nevertheless establishes a "brand of socialism," without the working class and against the working class inasmuch as "the revolution" cannot be entrusted to a class that "had proved itself incapable of exercising its own dictatorship."

7. The totalitarian dictatorship against the working class is nevertheless "promising," as capitalism once was, presumably because while the present "brand of socialism" in Russia (and China? and Poland? and East Germany?) established by a class alien to the proletariat (that is, exploiting and oppressing it), will be (or may be?) succeeded by another (less totalitarian?) "brand of socialism" carried out by a class which is not alien (or not so alien?) to the working class, which exploits and oppresses the working class not at all (or not so much?), or which is (perhaps?) carried out by the working class itself which can at last (for what reason?) be "entrusted" with the task of a socialist reconstruction of society (superior to the present "brand"?).

There is one difficulty, among many others, with this chain of monstrous and downright reactionary ideas which rattle around in Deutscher's mind. It is the difficulty facing every capitulator to Stalinism who is himself not an authentic Stalinist but who has lost all belief in the self-emancipating capacity of the proletariat: Not a single one of them dares to present these ideas directly, candidly and simply to the proletarians themselves! How we should like to attend a working-class meeting at which any of the multitude of Deutschers of all varieties would say in plain language:

"The socialist revolution, which you will make in the name of democracy and freedom, cannot be allowed to submit to your fickle will ('the nature of the people is variable,' says Machiavelli). It is you who will first have to submit to the totalitarian rule of revolutionary despots. For theirs is the inescapable task of wiping out all the Utopians who were your idealistic but quixotic leaders and of making you believe by force that they are establishing a brand of socialism."

Yet — the question is put by people, especially those who have

been influenced by analogies once drawn between bourgeois Bonapartism and what Trotsky so questionably called "Soviet Bonapartism" (and Deutscher is one of those who have been very badly
influenced by the very bad analogy) — yet, is it not an historical fact
that the ruling class can be brought to power by another, in the manner in which Bismarck of the German Junkers consolidated the power
of the German capitalist class? And is it not a fact that the bourgeoisie
has more than once been deprived of its political power and yet maintained its economic, its social power? By analogy, is that not substantially the same thing that has happened to the Russian proletariat
under Stalinism?

The alloy in Trotsky's argument was already a base one; in
Deutscher it is far worse because he mixes into it what was so alien
to Trotsky — a wholesale capitulation to Stalinism, that is, a capitulation to Stalinism historically, theoretically and politically.

We have already indicated how and why the early plebeian and
even communistic enemies of feudalism, who did indeed come before their time, could not, with the best will or leadership in the
world, do anything but establish and consolidate the class rule of the
bourgeoisie, even when for a brief period they took political power
without or against the bourgeois elements. The very primitiveness,
the very prematurity, the very Utopianism of these plebeian movements made it possible for a long time for the bourgeoisie to arouse
them against feudalism and to be allied with them in the common
struggle. What risk there was, was tiny. But the bourgeois social order
is a revolutionary one. It constantly revolutionizes the economy; it
creates and expands the modern classes; it expands immensely the
productive forces, above all the modern proletariat. And before the
struggle with the old order is completely behind it, the bourgeoisie
finds itself representing a new "old order" which is already threatened by an infant-turning-giant before its very eyes, the modern socialist proletariat.

Now comes a "new" phenomenon, the one already implicit in the
futile struggle of yesterday's Utopians against yesterday's bourgeoisie. What is new is that the bourgeoisie dares less and less — to
the point finally where it dares not at all — stir up the masses against
the old privileged classes of feudalism. What is new is that the bourgeoisie fears to take power at the head of a mass movement which
may acquire such impetus as will at an early next stage bring to
power the new revolutionary force, the proletariat, as successor to
the bourgeoisie. The bourgeoisie tends now to turn to the reactionaries of the old order as its ally against the young but menacing prole-

tariat. Engels marks the dividing line between two epochs of the development of bourgeois society with the year 1848 — the year of a number of revolutionary proletarian uprisings throughout Europe:

And this proletariat, which had fought for the victory of the bourgeoisie everywhere, was now already raising demands, especially in France, that were incompatible with the existence of the whole bourgeois order; in Paris the point was reached of the first fierce struggle between the two classes on June 23, 1848; after a fortnight's battle the proletariat lay beaten. From that moment on, the mass of the bourgeoisie throughout Europe stepped over to the side of reaction, and allied itself with the very same absolutist bureaucrats, feudalists and priests whom it had just overturned with the help of the workers, in opposition to the enemies of society, precisely these workers. (Reichsgründung und Kommune)

It is out of this relationship between the classes that the phenomenon of Bismarckism (or Bonapartism) arose. The bourgeoisie, faced with a revolutionary opposition, needed a "prophet armed" to protect itself from this opposition and it found one:

There are only two decisive powers in politics [continues Engels]: the organized state power, the army, and the unorganized, elemental power of the popular masses. The bourgeoisie had learned not to appeal to the masses back in 1848; it feared them even more than absolutism. The army, however, was in no wise at its disposal. But it was at the disposal of Bismarck. (Ibid.)

In a letter to Marx (April 13, 1866), dealing with Bismarck's proposal for a "universal suffrage" law which was a part of the war preparations against Austria, Engels extends his analysis of Bismarckism beyond the field of German class relations and to the bourgeoisie in a more general way: . . . *after all Bonapartism is the true religion of the modern bourgeoisie. It is always becoming clearer to me that the bourgeoisie has not the stuff in it for ruling directly itself, and that therefore where there is no oligarchy, as there is here in England, to take over, in exchange for good pay, the management of state and society in the interests of the bourgeoisie, a Bonapartist semi-dictatorship is the normal form. It carries through the big material interests of the bourgeoisie, even if against the bourgeoisie, but it leaves it no share of the domination itself. On the other hand, this dictatorship is in turn compelled against its will to promote these material interests of the bourgeoisie.* (Marx-Engels Gesamtausgabe, III, 3.)

And again, some ten years later, looking backward on the significance of the rise of Bismarck-Bonapartism, Engels pithily analyses its essential characteristics:

Even the liberal German philistine of 1848 found himself in 1849 suddenly, unexpectedly and against his own will faced by the question: Return to the old reaction in a more acute form or advance of the revolution to a republic, perhaps even to the one and indivisible republic with a socialistic background. He did not stop long to think and helped to create the Manteuffel reaction as the fruit of German liberalism. In just the same way the French bourgeois of 1851 found himself faced by a dilemma which he had certainly never expected — namely: caricature of Empire, Praetorian rule, and France exploited by a gang of blackguards — or a social-democratic republic. And he prostrated himself before the gang of blackguards so that he might continue his exploitation of the workers under their protection. (Selected Correspondence.)

The whole of Bonapartism implies the existence of a revolutionary danger from below ("they believe no longer") with which the ruling class of exploiters cannot cope in normal ways, against which they must summon the more-or-less open dictatorship of a reliable armed force (again the "prophet armed"), to which they have to yield political power in order to preserve their social power. And whatever form it has taken, regardless of where and when, from the time of the first Bonaparte to the last Hitler, it was always a matter of the bourgeois being so terrified by the revolutionary spectre that he "prostrated himself before the gang of blackguards so that he might continue his exploitation of the workers under their protection."

Whether consciously or only half-consciously, in cold blood or in panic, the bourgeois was right from his class standpoint, and he showed that he grasped the problem a thousand times more firmly and clearly than Deutscher has with all his superficial and helplessly muddled analogies. The bourgeois knows that his social power — the dominant power that his class exercises over society and the relative power that he as an individual exercises in his class and through it upon all other classes — rests fundamentally upon his ownership of capital, of the means of production and exchange, and upon nothing else. It is not titles or privileges conferred upon him by monarchs or priests, and not armed retainers within his castle walls, but ownership of capital that is the source of his social might. Deprive the bourgeoisie of this ownership, and it becomes a nothing, no matter who or what the political power may be. But if the political regime is republican or monarchistic, democratic or autocratic, fascist or social-democratic, clerical or anti-clerical, so long as it maintains and protects the ownership of capital by the bourgeoisie and therewith the capitalist mode of production, then, regardless of what restraints it may place on one or another derivative power of the capitalist class, it is the political regime of capitalism and the state is a capitalist state.

Basically, it is the private ownership of capital that enables the bourgeoisie, in Marx's oft-repeated words, "to determine the conditions of production." From that point of view, Marxists have never had any difficulty in explaining the political difference between the monarcho-capitalist state and the republican-capitalist state, the autocratic or fascist-capitalist state and the democratic capitalist state, and at the same time the fundamental class or social identity of all of them.

Or, to put it otherwise: the "norm" of capitalist society is not democracy or even the direct political rule of the bourgeoisie. The norm of capitalism is the private ownership of capital. If that norm is abolished, you can call the resulting social order anything you want and you can call the ruling class anything you want — but not capitalist.

How is it with the working class, however? Its unique characteristic, which distinguishes it from all preceding classes, may be a "disadvantage" from the standpoint of the shopkeeper, but from the Marxian standpoint it is precisely what makes it the consistently revolutionary class and the historic bearer of the socialist future, is this: it is not and it cannot be a property-owning class. That is, its unalterable characteristic excludes it from any possibility of monopolizing the means of production, and thereby exploiting and "alienating" other classes.

In the period between the class rule of capital and the classless rule of socialism stands the class rule of the workers. And it is precisely in this period that the unique characteristic of the proletariat is either corroborated in a new way, or else we may be dead certain that its class rule has not yet been achieved or has already been destroyed. For once the power of the bourgeoisie has been overturned, and the private ownership of the means of production and exchange has been abolished (more or less), it is on the face of it impossible to determine who is now the ruling class by asking: "Who owns the means of production?"

The question itself is unanswerable. The revolution has just abolished ownership of the means of production. The bourgeoisie has been expropriated (i.e., deprived of its property). But the proletariat does not now own it; by its very nature it cannot and it never will. Until it is communistically owned, really socially owned (which means, not owned at all, inasmuch as there are no classes and no state machine), it can exist only as nationalized property. More exactly: as state property. What is more, there is no longer a capitalist market to serve as the regulator of production. Production is now (increasingly) planned production; distribution is planned distribution. Anarchy of production and the automatism of the market must give way more and more to consciously planned production (and of course distribution). This is the task of the state which now owns the means of production and distribution.

As yet, it should be obvious, we know and can know nothing about the class nature of the state in question or the social relations which it maintains. And we cannot know that from the mere fact that property is now statified. The answer to our question can come only from a knowledge of who is master of the state, who has political power.

There is the point, precisely there! The bourgeoisie is such a class that if it retains ownership of the economy, the political regime protecting that ownership maintains, willy-nilly, the rule of capital over society. The proletariat, on the contrary, is such a class that if it retains mastery of the state which is now the repository of the economy, then and only then, in that way and only in that way, is it assured of its rule over society, and of its ability to transform it socialistically.

The bourgeoisie can turn over the political power, or allow the political power to be taken over completely, by a locum tenens, to use Deutscher's favourite term for "deputy," so long as the dictatorial deputy preserves the ownership of capital which is the fundamental basis for the power of the bourgeoisie over society in general and over the threatening proletariat in particular. But once the proletariat is deprived — and what's more, deprived completely — of all political power, down to the last trace of what it once had or has in most capitalist countries, what power is left in its hands? Economic power, perhaps? But the only way of exercising economic power in Russia (or China, Poland and Albania) is through the political power from which it has been so utterly excluded by the totalitarian bureaucracy.

We know how the bourgeoisie, be it under a democracy or an autocracy, is able to "determine the conditions of production" which in turn enable us to determine who is the ruling class in society. But under Stalinism, the workers have no political power (or even political rights) of any kind, and therefore no economic power of any kind, and therefore they do not "determine the conditions of production," and therefore are no more the ruling class than were the slaves of Greek antiquity.

The "true religion" of the bourgeoisie is Bonapartism because, as Engels wrote about Bismarck, he carries out the will of the bourgeoisie against its will. That, in two respects; in that it protects private property from the revolutionary class that imperils it; and in that it, maintains private property as the basis of society. To maintain it is all that is essential (not ideally desirable in the abstract, but absolutely essential) to carrying out the will of the bourgeoisie, for the "coercive power" of competition and the "blindly operating" market to keep everything else running more or less automatically for bourgeois economy — running into the ground and out of it again, into the ground and out of it again, and so on.

But what sense is there to this proletarian, or Soviet or socialist Bonapartism? None and absolutely none. Against what revolutionary class that threatened its social power did the Russian proletariat have to yield political power to a Bonapartist gang? We know, not just from quotations out of Marx and Engels, but from rich and barbaric experiences in our own time, why and how the bourgeoisie has yielded political power in order to save its social power (which is, let us always bear in mind, its right to continue the exploitation of the proletariat). What "social power" was saved by (for) the Russian proletariat when it yielded political power to Stalinist "Bonapartism"?

"Social power" means the power of a class over society. Under Stalinism, the working class has no such power, not a jot or tittle of it, and in any case far less than it has in almost every capitalist country of the world. And it cannot have any social power until it has in its hands the political power.

Or is it perhaps the case that the Stalinist bureaucracy carries out the will of the proletariat against the will of the proletariat, that is, in the language of Deutscher, the Marxist-by-your-leave, tries "to establish socialism regardless of the will of the working class"? It turns you sad and sick to think that such a point, in the year 1954, has to be discussed with a "Marxist," and such an urbane and ever-so-bloodlessly-objective Marxist at that. But we know our times, and know therefore that what Deutscher has the shamelessness to say with such above-the-common-herd candour is what has so long, poisoned the minds of we-don't-know-how-many cynics, parasites, exploiters, slaveholders and lawyers for slaveholders in and around the working-class movement. So it must after all be dealt with, but briefly.

Bourgeois Bonapartism (the only Bonapartism that ever existed or ever can exist) can carry out the will of the ruling bourgeoisie against its will, and do it without consultation of any kind. The political ambitions, even the personal ambitions, the imperialist ambitions of the Bonapartist regime coincide completely with the self-expansion of capital, as Marx liked to call it. Each sustains the other. In the course of it the will of the bourgeoisie, which is nothing more than the expansion of capital — the lifeblood of its existence and growth — is done.

Even where the Bonaparte represents, originally, another class, as Bismarck represented the Prussian Junkers, the economic interests of that class, as it is by that time developing in the conditions of expanding capitalist production, are increasingly reconciled with the capitalist mode of production and exchange. (The same fundamental process takes place as noted by Marx in the English revolution, when the bourgeoisie unites with the landowners who no longer represented feudal land but bourgeois landed property.) But where the state owns the property, the "socialist" Bonaparte who has established a political regime of totalitarian terror has completely deprived the so-called ruling class, the proletariat, of any means whereby its will can even be expressed, let alone asserted. Indeed, the totalitarian regime was established to suppress the will of the proletariat and to deprive it of all social power, political or economic.

If Deutscher is trying to say — as Trotsky so often and so wrongly said — that by "preserving state property" the Stalinist Bonapartes are, in their own way, preserving the class rule or defending the class interests of the proletariat, as the bourgeois Bonapartes did for the bourgeoisie in preserving private property, this comparison is not better but worse than the others. By defending private property, the Bonaparte-Bismarck-Hitlers made it possible for the bourgeoisie to exploit the working class more freely, a favour for which the bourgeoisie paid off the regime as richly as it deserved. But by defending and indeed vastly expanding state property in Russia, the Stalinist bureaucracy acquires a political and economic power to subject the working class to a far more intensive exploitation and oppression than it ever before suffered. If it protects the country from the "foreign bourgeoisie" (as every qualified exploiting class does), it is solely because it does not intend to yield all or even part of its exclusive right to the exploitation of the Russian people.

And finally, if Deutscher is trying to say that socialism has to be imposed upon the working class against its will, if need be, or even that socialism (a "brand of socialism") can be imposed upon the working class against its will, he is only emphasizing that he has drawn a cross over himself and over socialism too. You might as well try to make sense out of the statement that there are two brands of freedom, one in which you are free and the other in which you are imprisoned.

The proof of the pudding is before us. If a vast accumulation of factories were not merely a prerequisite for socialism (and that it is,

688

certainly) but a "brand of socialism," then we had it under Hitler and we have it in the United States today. If the expansion of the productive forces were not merely a prerequisite for socialism (and that it is, without a doubt) but a "brand of socialism," then we have had socialism under Hirohito, Hitler, Roosevelt and Adenauer.

Under capitalism, the working class has been economically expropriated (it does not own the means with which it produces), but, generally, it is left some political rights and in some instances some political power. Under feudalism, the landed working classes were deprived of all political power and all political rights, but some of them at least retained the economic power that comes with the ownership or semi-ownership of little bits of land. It is only under conditions of ancient slavery and in more recent times of plantation slavery, that the slaves — the labouring class — were deprived of all economic power and all political power. Those who most closely resemble that ancient class are the working class under Stalinism. They are the modern slaves, deprived of any political power whatever and therefore of all economic power.

If this is the product of a "brand of socialism," necessitated because the working class did not will socialism (why should it?), then the whole of Marxism, which stands or falls with the conception of the revolutionary self-emancipation of the proletariat, has been an illusion, at best, and a criminal lie at worst. But even that would not be as great an illusion and a lie as the claim that Stalinism will yield its totalitarian power as the bureaucracy gradually comes to see that its benevolent despotism is no longer needed in the interests of social progress.

What Engels wrote to the German party leaders in September, 1879, in Marx's name and in his own, is worth recalling:

For almost forty years we have stressed the class struggle as the immediate driving force of history, and in particular the class struggle between the bourgeoisie and the proletariat as the great lever of the modern social revolution; it is therefore impossible for us to cooperate with people who wish to expunge this class struggle from the movement. When the International was formed we expressly formulated the battle-cry: the emancipation of the working class must be achieved by the working class itself. We cannot therefore cooperate with people who say that the workers are too uneducated to emancipate themselves and must first be freed from above by philanthropic bourgeois and petty bourgeois.

That remains our view, except that to "philanthropic bourgeois and petty bourgeois," we must now add: or by totalitarian despots who promise freedom as the indefinite culmination of the worst exploitation and human degradation known, with the possible exception of Hitler's horrors, in modern times. That view Deutscher has discarded. On what ground he continues to proclaim himself a Marxist passes understanding.

There remains Deutscher's justification of Stalinist "socialism" in the name of Russia's backwardness, and the responsibilities for Stalinism which he has ascribed to Lenin and Trotsky. It is one of the favourite themes of the apologists, but it has the right to be dealt with.

Drive the apologists for Stalinism out of all their other trenches and they will take tenacious refuge in the last one. It is their deepest one and affords them the most obdurate hold on their defences. It is buttressed with solid learning direct from Marx, has historical breadth, roots in economics, and the sociological sweep that lifts it above the transient trivia of journalistic polemics. It is the trench, one might almost say, of the Old Crap, "die ganze alte Scheisse," as it is written in the original Marx.

In brief: socialism (or the most eminently desirable brand of socialism) presupposes a most advanced stage of the development of the productive forces which alone can assure abundance for all and therewith freedom; but for forcibly-isolated and exceedingly poor Russia to be brought to such a stage required the crude, violent, at times unnecessarily expensive but basically unavoidable excesses (alte Scheisse) of the practical realists. The proof of the pudding lies in the statistics and who is so quixotic as to argue with statistics?

Under socialism

a) Production — enormous increase

b) Capitalists — enormous liquidation

c) Bureaucratism — enormous, but:

1. inevitable, or

2. necessary, or

3. exaggerated, or

4. declining, or

5. self-reforming.

Net, after all deductions: an understandably inferior brand of socialism, but socialism just the same.

On this score, as on so many others, Deutscher feels, like scores of contemporaries, that his demoralisation invests him with a special right or obligation to cruise freely, with accelerator lashed to the floor and steering gear disconnected, from imprecision to imprecision and muddle to muddle.

The conception was first elaborated by Trotsky, who while not himself an apologist for Stalinism but a most implacable critic, nevertheless provided the apologists with far more weapons than they deserved. In Trotsky, the idea was developed much more persuasively and roundedly than in Deutscher. Above all, the former was free of those unpleasant observations which the latter weaves into all his writings in deference to the low-grade antisocialist prejudices of the intellectual philistine. In its thought-out form, it is to be found in the most probing and most instructive of Trotsky's studies on Stalinist Russia (and therefore the one which, re-read, most plainly shows the basic mistake in his analysis), *The Revolution Betrayed*, which he wrote in 1936. Early in the book he says:

Two years before the Communist Manifesto, young Marx wrote: "A development of the productive forces is the absolutely necessary practical premise [of Communism], because without it want is generalized, and with want the struggle for necessities begins again, and that means that all the old crap must revive".... the citation, merely an abstract construction with Marx, an inference from the opposite, provides an indispensable theoretical key to the wholly concrete difficulties and sickness of the Soviet regime.

Employing this key, he comes to the conclusion that the "old crap" is represented by the transformation of the Soviet state into "a 'bourgeois' state, even though without a bourgeoisie" in so far as the Stalinist totalitarian regime "is compelled to defend inequality — that is, the material privileges of a minority — by methods of compulsion." That the bureaucracy should have established such a regime, he continues later, has its basis in

... the poverty of society in objects of consumption, with the resulting struggle of each against all. When there is enough goods in a store, the purchasers can come whenever they want to. When there is little goods, the purchasers are compelled to stand in line. When the lines are very long, it is necessary to appoint a policeman to keep order.

But hasn't the totalitarian state become even harsher with the rise in production? Yes.

Soviet economy had to lift itself from its poverty to a somewhat higher level before fat deposits of privilege became possible. The present state of production is still far from guaranteeing all necessities to everybody. But it is already adequate to give significant privileges to a minority, and convert inequality into a whip for the spurring on of the majority.

In different terms, Deutscher draws, or seems to draw, similar conclusions:

... after its victory in the civil war, the revolution was beginning to escape from its weakness into totalitarianism.... Rich in world-embracing ideas and aspirations, the new republic was "poor with the accumulated poverty of over a thousand years." It mortally hated that poverty. But that poverty was

its own flesh and blood and breath.... For decades Bolshevism had to entrench itself in its native environments in order to transform it. The brand of socialism which it then produced could not but show the marks of its historic heritage. That socialism, too, was to rise rough and crude, without the vaulting arches and spires and lacework of which Socialists had dreamed. (The Prophet Armed, pp.519ff)

Let us try to convert these loose literary flutterings into more precise thoughts related to more precise realities in order to judge whether the "poverty of society in objects of consumption" (Trotsky) or the "accumulated poverty of over a thousand years" (Deutscher) produced Trotsky's "degenerated workers' state" or what is Deutscher's more extravagant synonym for the same thing, the "rough and crude ... brand of socialism" — or it produced something as different from a workers' state and socialism as a prison is from a presentable home.

The part played by poverty in the transformation of the Bolshevik revolution is too well known to require elaboration here. Poverty which is induced by a low level of industrial development never has been and never will be the foundation on which to build the new social order. That was known in Russia in 1917, as well as before and after. Without exception or hesitation, every Bolshevik repeated the idea publicly a thousand times: "For the establishment of socialism, we ourselves are too backward, poor and weak, and we can achieve it only in class collaboration with the coming proletarian powers of the more advanced western countries. Our strategical objective, therefore, requires laying primary stress upon the advance of the world revolution and, until its victory, working for the maximum socialist accumulation which is possible in a backward, isolated workers' state." In these thoughts the science of Marxism was combined with the virtues of political honesty and forthrightness, sagacity and practicality.

The big difficulties manifested themselves, it is worth noting, in this: the more the victory of the world revolution was delayed (and contrary to Deutscher's hindsight, it was delayed primarily by the course and power of the newly-rising leadership of the revolutionary state), the more restricted became the possibilities of any socialist accumulation. It is not a matter of accumulation "in general," which is always possible, but socialist accumulation. That signifies a harmonious social expansion resulting from such cooperation in the productive process as requires less and less strain on the body, nerves and time of the labourer and less and less public coercion, on the one hand, and on the other, affords more abundance and the possibility for unhampered intellectual development to everybody, increasingly free from inherited class divisions and antagonisms of all kinds.

From 1918, when Lenin first outlined the masterful and brilliant conception that later got the name of NEP (New Economic Policy), through the NEP itself, through the struggle of the Trotskyist Opposition, through the rise of the Stalinist bureaucracy, and down to the days of the "self-reforming" bureaucracy that has followed Stalin, all important questions, conflicts and developments that have appeared in Russia were related to or depended upon the problem of accumulation.

The fight of the Russian Opposition coincided with the end of the possibilities of a socialist accumulation in Russia given the continued repression (or undermining, or retardation) of the revolution in the West. It was therefore as significant as it was fitting that the Opposition intertwined its program for a socialist accumulation inside Russia with that stiff-necked fight against the theory of "socialism in one country" which was the obverse of its fight for the world revolution.

In this sense, the defeat of the Opposition put an end to the socialist accumulation in Russia as decisively as it put an end to the socialist power in the country. But it did not put an end to accumulation of any kind, any more than it eliminated political power of any kind. The defeat merely changed the form and content of both. It had to. No society with class divisions, and therefore class conflict, can hold together for a day without a political power, that is, a state power. And no society, least of all in modern times, can live without accumulation. There was accumulation in Russia under the Tsar, and accumulation of another kind under Lenin, and accumulation of still another kind under Stalin. The whole question revolves around the "kind." Trotsky noted that:

In its first period, the Soviet regime was undoubtedly far more equalitarian and less bureaucratic than now [that is, in 1936]. But that was an equality of general poverty. The resources of the country were so scant that there was no opportunity to separate out from the masses of the population any broad privileged strata. At the same time the "equalizing" character of wages, destroying personal interestedness, became a brake upon the development of the productive forces. Soviet economy had to lift itself from its poverty to a somewhat higher level before fat deposits of privilege became possible. (Op. cit.)

There isn't a line in all of Deutscher's analysis that even approaches this in the clarity with which it points to the answer of the "riddle" of Stalinism. Yet for all its compact clarity, it requires modification and some close study.

Let us start with the provocative statement that the "equalizing" character of wages "became a brake upon the development of the productive forces." The idea is absolutely correct, in our opinion. It remains correct if it is expressed in a broader and more general way, always remembering that we are speaking of an isolated, backward Russia: The political power of the workers, represented and symbolized, among other things, by the equalizing character of wages, became a brake upon the development of the productive forces. Does that mean that with a proletarian power the productive forces could no longer develop? The term "brake" must not be understood in so absolute a sense. It merely (and "merely" here is enough) meant that such a political power did not allow the productive forces to develop as fast and as strongly as required by the concrete social needs of the time. This formulation brings us a bit closer to the reality.

The fact is that with the introduction and expansion of the NEP, which, with Lenin, presupposed the unwavering maintenance and strengthening of the state power of the proletariat, there was a steady development of the productive forces all over the land, a rise in the socialist accumulation in particular, and a gradual rise out of the depths of the "accumulated poverty." But (still remembering the fatal absence of the world revolution) the general development of the productive forces soon disclosed its dual nature: the rise of the socialist forces of production and the rise of the private-capitalist sector of production, not only in agriculture but also in industry and commerce.

The character of the economic development as a whole was called into question with challenging sharpness. The whole literature of the time (1923-1930), as well as the whole of the factional conflict, hinged on the question: Russia — toward capitalism or toward socialism? To overcome the trend toward capitalisation of the economy, a trend with powerful roots in the retarded and petty-bourgeois character of Russian agriculture, required not only a vast but above all a rapid industrialisation of the country. When Lenin used to say, "Germany plus Russia equals socialism," he meant nothing less than that advanced Germany, controlled by a socialist proletariat, would make it possible for backward Russia so to industrialize itself as to assure a socialist development for both countries. But what could Russia do if forced to rely upon her own resources?

The proletariat in power could not produce an industrialisation of the country rapid enough to overcome the bourgeois tendencies surging up with such unexpected speed and strength from its primitive agriculture and it was not strong enough to assure a socialist development in both spheres of economic activity. To do that, it would have had to subject itself to such an intensity of exploitation as produced the surpluses that made the capitalist classes, in their heyday, the beneficiaries of all pelf and privilege and at the same time the superintendents of the miraculous economic achievements that have at last made it possible for man to rise from his knees.

The trouble, as it were, was this: others can exploit the working class, but it cannot exploit itself. So long as it has the political power, it will not exploit itself nor will it allow others to do so. That is why the workers' state, the workers' power, the workers' democracy established by the revolution turned out, in its enforced isolation, to be a brake on the development of the productive forces at a pace required by the relation of class forces in Russia in the Twenties. And that is why, again in its enforced isolation, the workers' power had to be destroyed to allow free play to the development of productive forces in Russia.

By whom? What force would take over the power in order to carry out this exploitation that was demanded for Russia's industrialisation under the extraordinary concrete conditions of the time?

Trotsky says that "the resources of the country were so scant that there was no opportunity to separate out from the masses of the population any broad privileged strata." But this is patently wrong. On the basis of the same or even less easily available or more poorly managed resources, Tsarist society had "separated out" and maintained such privileged strata in the form of the capitalist and feudal classes. It is not to the scant resources or to them alone that we need look for the answer. There simply was no bourgeoisie on hand to take over the organization and management of Russian society and the exploitation of its resources (the proletariat included) implied by its rule: there was none on hand and, as it turned out, none in sight capable of such a task.

The native bourgeoisie? In agriculture, it did not exist at all, except in the form of an incohesive rural petty bourgeoisie which needed an urban bourgeoisie to organize, lead and dominate it. In industry, it was confined to the periphery of production and the field of trade. If the comparatively potent bourgeoisie of pre-Bolshevik Russia never really raised itself to the position of ruling class, either before or after the Tsar was overturned, the ludicrous remnants of it, even if supplemented by the neo-bourgeois elements of the NEP period, could hardly hope to achieve the same position "except as tools or vassals of the world bourgeois".

The foreign bourgeoisie? Abstractly, yes. Concretely, no. Such was the unusual and unforeseen concatenation of social and political forces, that the world bourgeoisie completely failed to unite in a resolute assault upon the Bolshevik regime of 1917-1920, thus making its survival possible. It could only dream of another attack in the following years. And when it seemed on the brink of finding a practical, effective rallying centre for a renewed assault with the rise to power of Hitler (the "super-Wrangel" that never materialized), the conflicts and contradictions in its own midst were so acute, or else so easily exploited by the now Stalinized Russia, that more than half the world's bourgeoisie found itself in the deadly combat with Hitler that assured the survival, not the crushing, of the Stalinist state.

Society, like nature, abhors a vacuum. The more complex and modern the society the greater is its abhorrence — and more ingenious and variegated are its improvisations. Scant though Russia's resources were, they had enough magnetic power to attract from the nethermost regions of society a new coagulation that was to perform — one way or another — the social task awaiting it. In so doing it was to consolidate itself as a new, reactionary ruling class, which established and continues to maintain its domination over society by means of the most ruthless, most unashamed, most intensely organized, centralized, and consciously directed terror against the people it exploited that has ever been known in history — without exception.

It is true that it performed its task. It industrialised the country to a tremendous extent, unforeseen by itself, its friends or its foes. It accomplished, in its own unique way, the absolutely inevitable revolution in agriculture, subordinating it to industry, integrating it into industry, in a word, industrializing it (the work is not complete, but the trend is utterly irrepressible). But to achieve this goal in the only way that this social force can achieve it, it destroyed (as it was destined to do) the power of the working class, destroyed every achievement of the Bolshevik revolution, established the power of the most absolutist ruling class in the world, and reduced the entire population to the grade of slaves, modern slaves, not plantation slaves, but slaves, who are deprived of any and all public recourse against the most exploitive and oppressive regime known to our time, with the possible — and we stress the word — exception of Hitlerism.

That is how the "old crap" revived and that is what its revival has meant. To Trotsky, the "old crap," meant as an indictment of the bureaucracy and a rebuff to its apologists (it is no accident that his *Revolution Betrayed* has as its last chapter an attack on such "friends of the Soviet Union" as the Webbs and Durantys, of whom Deutscher is only a present version), nevertheless left the proletariat the ruling class of Russia. To Deutscher, the "old crap," meant as an apology for the bureaucracy, is a brand of socialism which lacks only vaulting arches, spires and lacework which were the dream stuff of socialism. Not, however, to Marx, let us note, if we go back to the original text in which Trotsky found his now familiar quotation [2].

Marx, in his violent attack upon the German "critical critics," is presenting his ideas on communism in systematic polemical form even though they are still taking shape for their climactic presentation two years later in the Manifesto. He is seeking to free communism from all trace of utopianism, of wishful-thinking, you might say, of abstract idealism. He wants to show the scientific foundation under its inevitable unfoldment as the last historic achievement of the self-emancipating proletariat, which "must first conquer political power in order to represent its interest in turn as the general interest." But if this political power is to lead to effective communism, he points out again and again to "the premise-less Germans," it must be preceded or based upon material conditions prepared by the past, that is, by capital. Without such things as the development of machinery, extensive utilization of natural power, gas lighting, steam heating, water supply, and the like, "the communal society would not in turn be a new force of production — devoid of a material basis, reposing upon a merely theoretical foundation, it would be a freak and end up only as a monastic economy."

He goes further to emphasize his point. The "alienation" which is as characteristic of capitalism as of all class societies, can be abolished only if two practical premises obtain: It must become a power so intolerable that the mass makes a revolution against it inasmuch as it faces them with the contradiction between their own propertyless-ness and the "existing world of wealth and culture, both of which presuppose a great increase in productive power — a high degree of its development." Such a development "is an absolutely necessary practical premise also because without it only want is generalized, and with want the fight over necessities would likewise have to begin again and all the old crap would revive."

It is a thought scattered and repeated through hundreds of pages of Marxian writings, especially against the Utopians and "pure-and-simple" anti-capitalists. The thought is as clear as day: the "old crap" is not a deformed workers' state or a crude brand of socialism. It is the revival of the old, even original and not very far advanced rule of capital, that is, of class domination, of class exploitation and oppression, of the struggle of each against all.

Is that precisely what happened in Russia? The abstract generalization as thought out by Marx was manifested in and applied concretely to a country with unique class relations at a given stage in its development as a unique part of a world capitalism at a specific stage in its development. The "old crap" of class rule revitalised not in its old capitalist form but in a new, anti-capitalist but nonetheless anti-socialist form.

From a reading of Deutscher's books and articles, there is not to be found so much as a hint that the question of the exploitive class character of the bureaucracy has been submitted to his critical scrutiny. Only by implication can the reader permit himself the inference that, if the question has been considered at all, the indicated conclusion has been dismissed without appeal. To Deutscher, the bureaucracy is the "locum tenens" of the socialist proletariat which is incapable of self-rule, just as Napoleon, Cromwell and Bismarck were the deputies of the capitalist bourgeoisie, each despot opening up progressive vistas for the class he (or it) represented, consolidating the revolutionary gains and prospects of his (or its) class, and more of the same wisdom which is now familiar to us.

In the first place, the theory of the "old crap," in Deutscher's version, completely and shatteringly destroys his entire theory of the Russian revolution, which is as much as to say that it makes tabula rasa of four-fifths of what he has written on the subject. His "basic" explanation, i.e., apology, for Stalinism consist of a general theory of all revolutions. According to it, the Stalinist bureaucracy rose to take command of the Russian revolution for exactly the same reasons that the Cromwells, Napoleons and Bismarcks rose to take command of the bourgeois revolutions in England, France and Germany. It lies in the nature of all revolutions, it is a law of all revolutions.

But all that becomes patent rubbish the minute he advances the theory that negates it utterly, that is, that Stalinism rose in Russia because, unlike the West with its wealth, culture, traditions of respect for the human personality, etc., etc., she was "poor with the accumulated poverty of over a thousand years," so that the "brand of socialism" which "Bolshevism" then produced "could not but show the marks of its historic heritage."

One or the other! Both it cannot be.

Either Stalinism (or "revolutionary despotism") is the invariable result of all revolutions, at least for a long stage in their development, in which case the reference to Russia's poverty is irrelevant.

Or, Stalinism is the inevitable result of a particular revolution, of an attempt to establish socialism in a backward country which was materially unprepared for it. From this it follows that Stalinism would not result from a revolution in a country or countries which have the material and cultural prerequisites for socialism. In this case the whole theory of "the prophet armed" in all revolutions is pretentious nonsense, and worse than that reactionary nonsense (and even hilarious nonsense since its author cannot rightly say if the "prophet armed" is represented by the tragic hero of his work or by the man who murdered him).

That's in the first place. And normally that would be enough for one man and more than enough. But there is also a second place.

Out of the clear blue, we learn that Deutscher has, in fact, been asking himself whether the bureaucracy is a new exploiting class or not. In his books up to now? No, for as we said, there is no trace of such an announcement in them. But in one of his recent articles, as translated from the French review, *Esprit*, in *Dissent* (Summer 1954) we note his awareness that there is a point of view that holds the Stalinist bureaucracy to be a new ruling class.

The managerial and bureaucratic class, it is said, has a vested interest in maintaining the economic and social inequality of the Stalin era. It must therefore preserve the whole apparatus of coercion and terror which enforces that inequality.

This argument assumes that there exists:

a. a high degree of something like class solidarity in the Soviet bureaucratic and managerial groups; and

b. that the ruling group is guided in its policies by a strong awareness of, and concern for, the distinct class interest of the privileged groups. These assumptions may or may not be correct — in my view the evidence is still inconclusive. A weighty argument against them is that we have repeatedly seen the privileged and ruling minority of Soviet society deeply divided against itself and engaged in a ferocious struggle ending with the extermination of large sections of the bureaucracy. The victims of the mass purges of 1936-1938 came mainly from the party cadres, the managerial groups, and the military officers corps, and only in the last instance from the nonprivileged masses. Whether these purges accelerated the social integration of the new privileged minority, or whether, on the contrary, they prevented that minority from forming itself into a solid social stratum is, I admit, still an open question to me.

The argument Deutscher invokes against the theory that the bureaucracy represents a class is downright trivial. If applied to any number of the ruling classes that have existed throughout history, it would rule them out of that category instantly. But for a moment that is beside the point. What is positively incredible is to read that Deutscher has been writing all this time about the rise of the Stalinist bureaucracy in Russia (and elsewhere) and about how it has established socialism in Russia, or some brand thereof, without having determined in his own mind if this bureaucracy is a new exploiting class or not.

In our time, we have made our fair share of mistakes about the famous "Russian question" and according to some not wholly friendly critics, we have even oversubscribed our quota in this field. But yet we can say, with tightly reined pride, that we do not have and do not want anything like this to our dubious credit.

To speak of Russia as a socialist society (and with such casualness) while the exploitive class character of those who established this "brand of socialism" is still "an open question to me" that requires a brand of Marxism that it has not been our misfortune to have encountered anywhere else to date.

Yet we realise that there is one hurdle that many Marxists find it impossible, or at least exceedingly difficult, to take: the class character of the Stalinist bureaucracy, and the class character of the society they have established and defended with such murderous ardour. It is by no means superficial, this reluctance, and by no means trivial, as are so many of the views that are expressed with amazing lightmindedness in Deutscher's works. It is in harmony, this reluctance, with virtually a century of Marxian and historical tradition. Who else, in most of the past hundred years, but an abstractionist, a pedant, a constructionist, would have sought a field for contemporary political speculation outside the perspective of capitalism or socialism? Support of one automatically implied (except for a few incorrigible or romantic feudalists) opposition to the other and vice versa. "Down with capitalism!" was as plainly the battle cry of socialism as "Down with socialism!" was the battle cry of capitalism.

But with the advent of Stalinism, which is so unique that it continues to baffle and disorient tens of millions, and tens of thousands of the intellectual and political vanguard in particular, it becomes increasingly absurd, not to say criminal, to be imprisoned, in our analysis of it, by two dimensions, as it were: since it is so obviously not socialism, it must perforce be some sort of capitalism — or, since it is obviously not capitalism, it must of necessity be some brand of workers' or socialist regime. History allows only one or the other.

History is not an obsequious engine whose wheels are so set that it can only move forward along a route firmly prescribed by Marxism, without pauses, without ever running backward and without ever leaving the main rails to go off on a blind spur. Neither is it a precisely organized Cook's tour which meticulously sets a timetable for all nations and peoples to travel through primitive communism, then through chattel slavery, then through feudalism, then through capitalism, then through the dictatorship of the proletariat, then through the dictatorship of the secretariat, to be allowed entry finally into the best brand of socialism, with vaulting arches, spires and lacework included — but with wandering off on side trips of any kind strictly forbidden. To attribute to Marxism such a conception of the historical route of march is, in Plekhanov's words, "an interesting psychological aberration."

Society has wandered off on side excursions and even blind alleys before, just as it is doing in some countries today, though we are strongly convinced that the wandering is not for long, not as long as the historical era of capitalism and certainly not as long as the historical era of feudal stagnancy.

The origin of the new historical phenomenon lay in the poverty on which socialism could not be built. But because under the concrete conditions capitalism could not be built either, a new social order was inaugurated which overcame the poverty in a reactionary way – reactionary first of all, last of all and above all because it set back and delayed the victory of the only revolutionary and liberating class in present society, the socialist proletariat.

Those among the avowed Marxists who have been seduced by the vague arguments about the "old crap" into rejecting the notion that the Stalinist bureaucracy represents a ruling class might bear in mind that Trotsky, stoutest adversary of the idea that the bureaucracy represents a new class, and proponent of the idea that it represents "only" a caste, not only never proved his contention and not only never tried to prove it but ended up by acknowledging in so many words that it was not a caste. The same Marxists may be interested in this reminder from Engels which does not "solve the problem" but which is nevertheless not inappropriate:

Since the emergence in history of the capitalist mode of production, the taking over of all the means of production by society has often been dreamed of by individuals as well as by whole sects, more or less vaguely and as an ideal of the future. But it could only become possible, it could only become an historical necessity, when the material conditions for its realisation had come into existence. Like every other social progress, it becomes realisable not through the perception that the existence of classes is in contradiction with justice, equality, etc., not through the mere will to abolish these classes, but through certain new economic conditions. The division of society into an exploiting and an exploited class, a ruling and an oppressed class, was the necessary outcome of the low development of production hitherto. So

*long as the sum of social labour yielded a product which only slightly ex-
ceeded what was necessary for the bare existence of all; so long, therefore, as
all or almost all the time of the great majority of the members of society was
absorbed in labour, so long was society necessarily divided into classes.
Alongside of this great majority exclusively absorbed in labour there developed a class, freed from direct productive labour, which managed the general
business of society; the direction of labour, affairs of state, justice, science,
art, and so forth. It is therefore the law of the division of labour which lies at
the root of the division into classes. But this does not mean that this division
into classes was not established by violence and robbery, by deception and
fraud, or that the ruling class, once in the saddle, has ever failed to strengthen
its domination at the cost of the working class and to convert its social management into the exploitation of the masses. But if, on these grounds, the division into classes has a certain historical justification, it has this only for a
given period of time, for given social conditions. It was based on the insuf-
ficiency of production; it will be swept away by the full development of the
modern productive forces. And in fact the abolition of social classes has as
its presupposition a stage of historical development at which the existence
not merely of some particular ruling class or other but of any ruling class at
all, that is to say, of class differences themselves, has become an anachronism,
is out of date. (Anti-Dühring – my emphasis – MS)*

Is this not an excellent description, especially to those who recall
the rational and appropriate kernel of the theory of the "old crap",
of the fundamental basis upon which Stalinism rose in Russia? And
is it not also an adequate refutation, at the same time, of all theories
as to the "progressive" or "relatively progressive" character of the
Stalinist bureaucracy – theories which cannot but be based upon na-
tional-isolationism as distinguished from the international premises
of socialism and Marxism?

Of all the Marxists who, in our own day, allowed themselves to
think out theoretically the possibilities of a new exploitive society,
Bukharin stands out as the most searching mind, and that over a long
span of time. It may further help those avowed Marxists who are immobilized between the two rigidly-conceived social dimensions to
read what Bukharin wrote almost on the eve of the Bolshevik revolution.

In discussing the growth of state capitalism, he insists, and quite
rightly, that the "capitalist mode of production is based on a monopoly of the means of production in the hands of the class of capitalists
within the general framework of commodity exchange." Thereupon
he adds this most remarkable theoretical extrapolation:

Were the commodity character of production to disappear (for instance), through the organization of all world economy as one gigantic trust, the impossibility of which we tried to prove in our chapter on ultra-imperialism, we would have an entirely new economic form. This would be capitalism no more, for the production of commodities would have disappeared; still less would it be socialism, for the power of one class over the other would have remained (and even grown stronger). Such an economic structure would most of all resemble a slave-owning economy where the slave market is absent. (N Bukharin, *Imperialism and World Economy.*)

The Stalinist state did not, of course, arise out of capitalism and the development of a state capitalist economy, but out of an economy that was socialist in type. But is not the terse definition of a new exploitive class society, where commodity production has disappeared (more or less) and the ruling class has concentrated all ownership and control into one hand, the state's, perfectly applicable to the slave-state of Stalinism?

In 1928, after eleven years of the Bolshevik Revolution and with God-knows-what unspoken thoughts roaming about in the back of his mind, the same Bukharin had occasion to return to the same subject from a somewhat different angle, in the course of a speech delivered to the Program Commission of the Sixth Congress of the Communist International. In discussing, from the purely theoretical standpoint, the possibility of classical capitalist economic crisis in a society in which all the means of production are owned by the state (naturally, not by a proletarian state), he points out that in such a society "only in world-economic relations do we have trade with other countries, etc." Thereupon he continues with these equally remarkable insights:

Now, we raise the question whether in such a form of capitalism which actually represents a certain negation of capitalism, because of the fact that the internal market, the circulation of money, has disappeared, a crisis can occur. Would we have crises there? I believe not! Can there exist in this society a contradiction between the restricted consumption of the masses (consumption in the physiological sense) and the growing productive forces? Yes, that may be. The consumption of the ruling class grows continuously, the accumulation of the means of production, calculated in labour units, can grow to enormous dimensions, but the consumption of the masses is retarded. Perhaps still sharper here is the discrepancy between the growth of the consumption of the masses. But just the same we will not find any crises. A planned economy exists, an organized distribution, not only with regard to the connections and reciprocal relations between different branches of industry but also with regard to consumption. The slave in this society receives his share of fodder, of the objects that are the product of the total labour. He may receive very little, but just the same crises will not take place. (*Kommunistische Internationale*, 1928, No. 33/34.)

Is this not an astoundingly apt description of the most basic relations in Stalinist society? Bukharin did not hesitate to call such a society slavery, even if of a modern kind, but it would never occur to him to speak of such an abomination as socialism of any brand whatever. Or if, at a tragical stage of his life, he did speak of the Stalinist inferno as socialism, the pistol of the GPU was already jammed against the base of his skull. Deutscher has no such excuse.

Let us say that we close our mind to Deutscher's utterly wretched apology for the Stalinist dictatorship, his pseudo-historical justification for the massacre of the "Utopians" by the regime of the new Russian slave owners, his sophomoric theories about revolutions in general, his logical preposterousness which would be derided by anyone accustomed to think with his mind instead of with his pyloric valve. To forget all these things is next to impossible but let us say it is done. Then we would have to reduce Deutscher's violence against the basic tenet of socialism — the self-emancipatory role which is exclusively assigned to the revolutionary proletariat — to a case of the opinion that capitalism can give way only to socialism. The opinion is as erroneous as it is common. Understandable fifty years ago, and for adequate reasons rightly so, it is inexcusable today, in the light of the Stalinist experience. The common notion has to be revised for accuracy, and the revision, far from upsetting the provisions of Marxism, amplifies and above all concretizes them:

Capitalism, nearing the end of its historical rope, is decreasingly able to solve the problems of society on a capitalist basis. The problems will nevertheless be solved anyhow and are already being solved. Where the proletariat takes command of the nation, the social problems will be solved progressively, and mankind will move toward the freedom of a socialist world. Where the proletariat fails for the time to discharge its task, the social problems will be solved nevertheless, but they will be solved in a reactionary way, solved at the cost of creating a dozen new social problems, solved by degrading and enslaving the bulk of mankind. That is the meaning today of the conflict between capitalism and socialism, socialism and Stalinism, Stalinism and capitalism.

That is the meaning that can and must now be read into the historical warnings of the great founders of scientific socialist theory and the proletarian socialist movements. They did not and could not hold that the decay of capitalism, which is a spontaneous and automatic process, would just as spontaneously and automatically assure the victory of socialism — of any brand.

In the most mature and instructive of his works, *Anti-Dühring*, Engels clarifies the standpoint of Marxism on this score, not once but repeatedly:

By more and more transforming the great majority of the population into proletarians, the capitalist mode of production brings into being the force which, under penalty of its own destruction, is compelled to carry out this revolution.

... modern large-scale industry has called into being on the one hand a proletariat, a class which for the first time in history can demand the abolition, not of one particular class organization or another, or of one particular class privilege or another, but of classes themselves, and which is in such a position that it must carry through this demand or sink to the level of the Chinese coolie.... if the whole of modern society is not to perish, the revolution of the mode of production and distribution must take place, a revolution which will put an end to all class divisions.... [the bourgeoisie's] *own productive powers have grown beyond its control and, as with the force of a law of Nature, are driving the whole of bourgeois society forward to ruin or revolution.* (My emphasis — MS.)

These do not have their value in determining if Engels was gifted with apocalyptic vision — that has no importance. But they reveal how Engels judged the relationship between the disintegration of capitalist society and the part of the proletariat in the process — victim of the outcome or master of a regeneration. The failure up to now of the proletariat to play the latter part successfully is not our subject here. Except to say that ninety-five per cent of those "socialists" who have in effect capitulated either to the American bourgeoisie or the Stalinist bureaucracy are possessed in common by a thoroughgoing disbelief in the capacity of the proletariat to play that role, we leave the subject for another occasion. But it is incontestable that up to now it has not played the role triumphantly.

And the result of this failure? Is it perhaps the victory of a "rough and crude... brand of socialism" established without the proletariat and against it, not only in Russia but also in China (where the even vaster poverty should produce an even rougher and cruder and more monstrous form of "socialist" totalitarianism, should it not?), and throughout Eastern Europe (with some modest but unmistakeable aid from Deutscher), and even in far from backward Czechoslovakia and Germany? Not at all. The essence of Engels' insights, amazing for their content even though they could not be marked off with clear lines, has been confirmed by the events.

For its failure, the proletariat has already paid the penalty, in the

Stalinist countries, of its own destruction, that is, its reduction to modern slavery; in more than one sense it has been driven to the level of the Chinese coolie; where bourgeois society is not transformed by revolution it is transformed into the ruin of Stalinism; the alienation ("to use a term comprehensible to philosophers") which the development of capitalism brings man to the verge of abolishing, is enhanced by Stalinism to a degree which does not have its equal in our memory.

We have no greater confidence in the longevity of Stalinism than of capitalism, less if anything. It is not reasonable to believe that at the time when the greatest of all class societies is approaching its death, the meanest of class societies is entering a new and long life. But shortlived or longlived, it will not quietly pass away. It will have to be pushed into its delayed oblivion. The essential precondition for the social emancipation from Stalinism is intellectual emancipation from its mythology, be it in the crass form in which it is presented officially or in the form of urbane and cynical apologetics in which it is presented by Deutscher. In either form it implies the end of socialism, for it would indeed be an unrealizable Utopia if conceived as anything but the direct achievement of a self-conscious, self-mobilized socialist proletariat. The rebirth of the proletarian socialist movement requires not the revival of the mythology in a revised form but its entire demolition.

1. One of the outstanding, curiosa of political terminology today is the persisting but anachronistic reference to "Soviet Russia" in journals of every political line. Where the press speaks of "socialist Russia" that too is wrong, but it is understandable. But there is plainly less Sovietism in Stalinist Russia than in Germany, France, England or the United States.
2. It is from the chapter on Feuerbach in the Marx-Engels Deutsche Ideologie. The quotation as given in *The Revolution Betrayed* is inexact, and evidently suffers from double translation (from German into Russian and then from Russian into English. For all of its roughness, the translation in Trotsky does no violence to the thought of the original. Cf. the original German in the first version.

Shachtman's review of Deutscher's first volume was published in the *New International*, March-April, May-June, and July-August 1954

Did Stalinism grow organically out of Bolshevism?

Max Shachtman (1950)

IT IS HARD TO SAY who has written more absurdities about Lenin's "organisational principles": the Stalinists who seek to prove that their totalitarian party regime conforms identically with the views set forth by Lenin or the modern anti-Bolsheviks who argue that if the two are not quite identical it is nevertheless Lenin's views and practises that led directly to the present Stalinist regime. They represent complementary and mutually parasitic parts of a division of labour which has successfully devastated the thinking of millions of people, with one saying that the totalitarian tyranny leads to (or is!) socialism and the other that socialism can lead to nothing but this totalitarian tyranny.

Either as perpetrators or victims of falsification, both are so thoroughly and extensively wrong that it would require volumes just to exhume and properly correlate the facts. It is not merely a matter of setting the historical record right — that is of secondary importance. It is above all a matter of resuming the lagging fight for socialism, which a Stalin abandoned so completely to pursue one reactionary course and a Wolfe has abandoned just as completely to pursue a different reactionary course.

In Lenin's conception of the "party machine," of its role in relationship to the working class, Wolfe finds (as what popular writer nowadays does not?) "the germ of a party dictatorship over the proletariat itself, exercised in its name," that is, the germ of Stalinism. It is out of this feature of Bolshevism that Wolfe erects the third pillar of his analysis. He reminds us that at the beginning Trotsky warned against the inevitable outcome of Lenin's conception:

The organisation of the party will take the place of the party; the Central Committee will take the place of the organisation; and finally the dictator will take the place of the Central Committee.

"Was ever prophecy more fatefully fulfilled by history?" exclaims Wolfe. The truth is that if prophets had no better example than this of how they are confirmed by history, the profession would be in sorry shape. With due respect to Trotsky, it can be said that to find in Stalinism a fulfilment of Trotsky's "Cassandra-like prevision"

707

(Wolfe's phrase) of Lenin's conception requires a well-trained capacity for superficiality assisted by an elaborate ignoring — we will not say manipulation — of the historical facts. The "prevision" was not fulfilled at all; and Trotsky himself was not the last to understand this.

But before this is established, let us see what it is that makes Lenin's views so reprehensible in Wolfe's eyes. Rather, let us try to see, for on this score Wolfe is either ambiguous or obscure, or just plain silent. He makes the task of the reviewer almost baffling. Attentive reading of page after page of Wolfe fails to disclose exactly what it was in Lenin's ideas about the "party machine" that led to Stalinism.

Was it Lenin's conception of who is entitled to party membership? Wolfe describes the dispute at the party congress in 1903 on the famous Article I of the party constitution. Lenin's draft defined a party member as one "who recognizes the party's program and supports it by material means *and by personal participation in one of the party organisations.*" Martov, leader of the Mensheviks-to-be, proposed that the phrase in italics be replaced entirely by the following: "and by regular personal assistance under the direction of one of the party organisations." Martov's formula was supported by the majority of the delegates.

Wolfe describes Lenin's view unsympathetically, which is his God-given right. But what was wrong with it? Wolfe's answer is a significant wink and a knowing nod of the head, as if to say, "Now you can see where Lenin was heading from the very start, can't you? Now you know what Bolshevism was at its very origin. If you really want to trace Stalinism to its historical roots, there indeed is one of the sturdiest and most malignant of them."

But wink and nod notwithstanding, all that Lenin proposed was a provision that had been and was then and has ever since been a commonplace in every socialist party we ever heard of, namely, that to be considered a party member, with the right of determining the policy and leadership that the membership as a whole is to follow, you have to belong to one of the units of the party. That would seem to be, would it not, an eminently democratic procedure, to say nothing of other merits.

By Martov's formulation, the policy and leadership of the party to one of whose branches you belong are determined for you by persons who are given the title of party members in exchange for "assisting" it without the obligation of belonging to any of its established branches. It is the thoroughly bureaucratized bourgeois political machines that are characterized by the kind of party "membership", that Martov's draft proposed, and it is one of the ways in which leadership and party policy are divorced from control by the ranks. But what socialist party, regardless of political tendency, does Wolfe know that has ever adopted a party statute such as Martov defended? The Social Democratic Federation of August Claessens and Algernon Lee is not entirely corroded by Bolshevism, it is said. But suppose someone were to advocate that membership in the SDF be extended to persons who assist the Federation under the direction of one of its branches without actually joining a branch. These nonagenarians would immediately summon every remnant of their remaining muscularity to crush the hardy advocate as a madman who threatens the integrity of the SDF and the "Leninist organisational principle" which they take even more for granted than they do the atrocity stories about the history of Bolshevism.

Or suppose the roles had been reversed, and it was Lenin who had advocated the Martov formulation in 1903. Just imagine the speed with which heads would bob knowingly and eyes blink significantly, and how profound would be the conclusions drawn about the sinister character of Bolshevism as far back as the date of its birth! And the whole joke is that there was a reversal, at least on the part of Martov! Wolfe is oblivious to it; but in his history of the Russian Social Democracy Martov reminds us that under the influence of the 1905 revolution, the Mensheviks, at their Petersburg conference in December of that year, "abandoned Paragraph I of the old party statutes [that is, the Martov formula of 1903] which weakened the strict party-character of the organisation in so far as it did not obligate all the members of the party to join definite party organisations." So, about two years after the London debate, the Mensheviks themselves adopted Lenin's definition of party membership and there is no evidence that they ever altered it subsequently. From then on, at least, Lenin's view was never really in dispute. It is only in our time that it is splattered across the pages of anti-Bolshevik literature, with all sorts of dark but always undefined references to its ominous overtones, undertones and implications.

Was it Lenin's intolerance toward difference of opinion within the party, his conception of a party monolithism that allowed only for obedience to a highly-centralized, self-appointed and self-perpetuating leadership, his autocratic determination to have his own way regardless of the consequences, with a penchant for splitting the movement when he did not get his way? These are familiar charges against Bolshevism, and against Lenin in particular. Wolfe might have made an original contribution to these charges by providing some facts to sustain them. Instead he preferred to repeat them, and more than once.

We feel neither the desire nor the need to canonise Lenin as a saint, or to regard his works as sacred texts. He was the greatest revolutionary leader in history, and that is more than enough to assure his place against both detractors and iconographers. If we knew nothing at all about him, it would be safe to assume that he had his faults, personal and political; learning about him only confirms this innocent and not very instructive assumption. He was devoted to the cause of socialist freedom and his devotion was durable and passionate. As an adversary, Paul Axelrod, said, "there is not another man who for twenty-four hours of the day is taken up with the revolution, who has no other thoughts but thoughts of the revolution, and who, even in his sleep, dreams of nothing but revolution." This made him, in the eyes of dilettantes and philistines, let alone defenders of the old order, a fanatic. It was his strength. He was, in consequence, a passionate partisan of the instrument he regarded as indispensable for the revolution, the party, of the sharpness and clarity of its thought. This necessarily brought him into conflict with others, and not only with dabblers but with revolutionists no less devoted to socialism than he. In polemic and in factional struggle generally (neither of which was really invented by Lenin, and which can be avoided only by eschewing politics altogether), he was resolute, self-confident and uncompromising. It is easy to think of worse qualities. But they were qualities that made him incomprehensible or insufferable in the eyes of tergiversaters and cobwebheads. If, as was often the case, he exaggerated or overreached himself, it was generally because nobody helped him by inventing a method of carrying on polemical and factional struggle without risk of exaggeration. (Reading Wolfe, for example, shows that such a method has still to be invented. Only, for his exaggerations there is not even that excuse.) But all this about Lenin, and a good deal more, does not begin to prove the "standard" charges against him.

Take splits. Wolfe says that "in the matter of splitting, Lenin was invariably the aggressor". It is a categorical statement — one of the few made by Wolfe who generally prefers indirection. To illustrate how much dehydrated bunk there is in the statement, we can take the famous 1903 party congress which split the Russian Social Democratic Party. There was a furious fight over the above-mentioned Paragraph 1 of the party statutes. Lenin was defeated after a two-day debate. But he did not bolt the congress or the party. Earlier in the sessions, however, the delegates led by Lenin and Martov, Axelrod, Trotsky and Plekhanov, overwhelmingly defeated the position of the Jewish Bund on the question of autonomy. The Bund, refusing to bow to the majority, split from the congress. No sermon from Wolfe on the virtue of unity and the vice of splitting.

Then the congress, Lenin and Martov included, voted against the separate organisation around the "Economist" journal, *Rabocheye Dyelo*. Whereupon, two Economist delegates split from the congress. Still no sermon from Wolfe. Then the congress, by a slender majority but nonetheless a majority, adopted Lenin's motion for an *Iskra* editorial board of Plekhanov, Lenin and Martov, as against the outgoing board which had included old-timers like Axelrod and Zasulich. Whereupon Martov announced his refusal to abide by the decision — to serve on the board — and the split between the now-named Mensheviks (Minority) and Bolsheviks (Majority) became a fact. Conclusion? "In the matter of splitting, Lenin was invariably the aggressor."

Of course Lenin was responsible for a split here and a split there! To deny it would be absurd; to feel apologetic about it, likewise. But it is interesting to see how Wolfe applies different standards in different cases — so sternly moralistic toward the Bolsheviks and so maternally tender toward their opponents. He quotes Lenin as writing that he could not understand why the Bund split from the congress since "it showed itself master of the situation and could have put through many things"; and then observes with haughty severity:

Since, all his life, Lenin attached a feeling of moral baseness to "opportunism," he found it hard to understand that these men of the Bund and Rabocheye Dyelo *could have firm convictions, principles of their own, and, defeated on them, would not content themselves with "putting through" what he regarded as opportunistic measures.*

Happy Bundists to have so sympathetic an advocate! Lenin found it hard to understand, but he, Wolfe, he understands. After all, if people have firm convictions and principles, they will not, if defeated in their own organisation, consent to forego them just for the sake of unity. They will not and they should not. Better a split than that! All this applies to Bundists, Economists, Mensheviks and other opponents of the Bolsheviks. But not to the Bolsheviks themselves. Even though their principles and convictions were no less firm, they deserve no such affectionate consideration. Why not? Because... because... well, because in the matter of splitting Lenin was invariably the aggressor.

The tale of Lenin's "intolerance" toward opponents inside the party has been told in a dozen languages. In the best of cases (they are rare enough), the record is seen through the completely distorting glasses of the present-day Stalinist regime; in the worst of cases (that is, as a rule), the record is falsified in whole or in part. At least nine times out of ten, Lenin's "intolerance" consisted, for the opponents, in the fact that he refused to accept their point of view on a question.

The phenomenon is familiar to anyone who has been active for any length of time in politics, especially in those working-class movements where politics is not an intellectual pastime but is taken most seriously. A man who puts forward a point of view on some question, but adds that his opponent's view is probably just as good if not better — there is a tolerant man for you. If he says that it really doesn't matter much whether the organisation adopts his view or not — there's a tolerant man. If he is not so impolite as to try vigorously to win supporters for his view and to plan, with his initial supporters, on how to win a majority for it — he is tolerant too. Or if his point of view miraculously wins the support of, let us say, the organisation's convention, and he then announces that he is ready to concede the leadership to his opponents who are against his position and who, with the best will in the world, could not carry out the adopted policy with enthusiasm or understanding — there is a most tolerant man. He is not at all like Lenin, granted. He differs from him in that he does not take his views or his organisation — or himself — very seriously. He is in politics for a week-end, warmed by the sunny thought that after he has returned to his normal pursuits he will have left behind a memory unmarred by the tiniest Leninist stain.

The references generally made to Lenin's "intolerance" are actually calculated to convey the impression that he imposed upon the Bolsheviks a uniquely dictatorial regime in which his word, or at best, the word of his Central Committee was law that could be questioned only under penalty of the severest punishment. The unforearmed reader tends to think of Lenin's organisation in terms of Stalin's — not quite the same, to be sure, but as an only slightly modified version.

The comparison is utterly monstrous. Up to 1917, the Russian revolutionary movement was an illegal, underground movement, working under the onerous conditions of czarist autocracy. In spite of that, the Bolshevik movement had, on the whole, more genuine democracy in its organisation, more freedom of opinion and expression, a freer and healthier internal life, than at least nine-tenths of the other socialist or trade-union organisations of Europe, most of which enjoyed legality and other facilities beyond the dreams of the Russians.

This was true not only of the relations between the Bolsheviks and Mensheviks when they represented only contending factions within a more-or-less united party, but likewise true among the Bolsheviks themselves, first as a faction and, after 1912, as an independent party. The hideous monolithism of Stalin's regime was entirely unknown — it was not even dreamed of — among the Bolsheviks. Political tendencies were formed without let or hindrance, and if they dissolved it was not under compulsion of any kind. The official leading committee always had its central organ — the spokesman of the faction or the party — but time and again periodicals would be issued on their own responsibility by political groupings or tendencies inside the party and even (or rather particularly!) inside the Bolshevik faction (later inside the Bolshevik Party) itself. Even after the Bolsheviks took power, this tradition was so strong and normal and deeply rooted that, in the most perilous period for the new Soviet regime, it was possible for groups of dissident Bolsheviks not only to publish newspapers and reviews of their own independently of the Central Committee but to attack that committee (and of course Lenin!) with the utmost freedom and... impunity.

These separate organs of tendencies or groups or factions discussed all questions of party theory, party policy, party organisation, and party leadership with a fullness, a freedom and an openness that was known to no other working-class organisation of the time and has certainly had no equal since the rise of Stalinism. The idea of "secret" or "internal" discussion of political or theoretical questions of the movement, introduced by Zinoviev and Stalin in the period of the revolution's decline and now considered perfectly good "Bolshevik" practise, alas, even by self-styled Marxist organisations, was simply not known among the Bolsheviks — mind you, among the Bolsheviks even while they were an illegal, police-hounded and police-infiltrated movement! Lenin's collected works, which are composed largely of open "inner-party" polemics and the files of a dozen different factional papers and pamphlets, provide inundating evidence of this rich, free and open party life. In this respect, no other socialist organisation of those days could even equal the Bolsheviks.

Even in its best days, the German Social Democracy did not have anything like so free and democratic an organisational-political life, while it was an outlawed party or afterward in the period of legality. Why, even Marx and Engels sometimes had to fight to get their views published in the German party press and their fight was not uniformly successful. Among the Bolsheviks, such a thing was unheard of, and not just with respect to a Marx or Engels or Lenin, but also to the spokesman of some unpopular grouping in the party or faction.

Read, or re-read, all the anti-Bolshevik histories or commentaries with the closest care, and see what facts are related about how Lenin's "organisational principles" worked out in party practice. You will find all sorts of hints, suggestions, innuendo, clouded allusions, grunts, grimaces, pursed lips, winks and nods; you will find gossip, chit-chat about factional excesses which are "normal" in heated factional fights, titillating tales about the "dubious" sources of Bolshevik funds calculated to shock the sensibilities of our pious business and trade-union circles and of course a lot of plain kiln-dried falsification without filler, shellac or varnish. But it would be astounding if you found even one fact about the regime in the Bolshevik party or fraction that contradicts the record cited here about what the regime actually was. And it is this regime, as it really existed, that is supposed to have led to Stalinism! This is the tradition that is said to have helped Stalinism appear and triumph! Stalinism rests upon it exactly the same way a stiletto rests on the heart it has stabbed.

Or just suppose that, in the search for facts about Lenin and the old Bolshevik movement, Wolfe or any other anti-Bolshevik writer had discovered about them the things that are known about other leaders and other political groupings. For example, in the early *Iskra* days, Plekhanov, in order to assure his domination of the editorial board that was evenly divided between the "old" and the "young," was given two votes as against one for all the other members! If that had happened with Lenin — then or at any other time in his life — can you imagine the pages — no, the chapters — filled with outrage in every line, that would be written to argue that this was the very essence of Bolshevism, the core itself of Leninism, the proof positive and irrefutable of how it was pregnant with Stalinism from the day it was born?

Or take the party of Rosa Luxemburg, who was, writes Wolfe generously and rightly, "the outstanding advocate of revolutionary policy and the outstanding defender of democracy within the labour movement." Yet, she shared the theory of the permanent revolution which, says Wolfe, led to Stalinism; her party was opposed, and not on very democratic grounds, to the Soviets of Workers' Deputies in the revolution of 1905; she and her party were opposed to the democratic slogan of the right of self-determination and on grounds that were, objectively, reactionary; her party (we refer to the Social Democratic Party of Poland and Lithuania) was opposed to the idea of mass, formally non-party trade unions and insisted that the unions must declare their allegiance to the revolutionary party; and in spite of her criticisms of Lenin's "organisational principles," the regime in her own party in Poland was exceptionally factional, narrow, super-centralistically disciplined and far more "bureaucratic" than anything the Bolsheviks were ever guilty of.

The anti-Bolsheviks, who have exactly nothing in common with Luxemburg, ghoulishly drag her into court against Lenin, but if that record were to be found in the history of the Bolsheviks, can you imagine the uproar in twelve languages?

Or take the Narodniks (Populists) for whom Wolfe has such an extravagant reverence. In their early days, these spiritual (and political) ancestors or the Social Revolutionists, convinced but primitive revolutionists, exploited — with the best intentions in the world — the anti-Semitic pogrom feelings of the Russian peasants and even issued leaflets spurring them on. Can you imagine what the anti-Bolshevik professionals would make of such a thing if it could be found in the record of the Bolsheviks or their forebears? Or what they would say if some Bolshevik argued that Kerensky's role in 1917 "flowed from" the anti-Semitic aberrations of the Narodniks four decades earlier?

Such examples could be cited almost indefinitely — but not with reference to Lenin and the Bolsheviks. If they and they alone are the targets today, it is not as a result of objective historical re-examination but because of the frenetic campaign against socialism by a desperate and dying bourgeoisie and by disoriented and disillusioned ex-revolutionists. And by the same token, if we defend the Bolsheviks today it is in the interest of historical objectivity but also because we remain loyal to the emancipating fight for socialism.

Wolfe does deal with two aspects of Lenin's "conception of the party machine" that are indeed of decisive importance. He separates them when they should be connected. Properly connected and focussed, they would throw a most revealing light on Bolshevism, the Russian Revolution, its decline and on the rise and meaning of Stalinism. Right here, perhaps, is Wolfe's most glaring failure. He fumbles the problem helplessly and hopelessly, where he is not utterly oblivious to its significance. You cannot help asking yourself what in heaven's name this man learned about Marxism during his long years in the communist movement — or since.

First, Wolfe finds in Lenin's views on the interrelations between the revolutionary movement, socialist consciousness and the spontaneous struggles of the workers, as he expressed them early in the century, the

... dogma, obscure as yet in its implications, [that] was at the very core

of "Leninism." From it flowed an attitude toward the working class, toward its ability to think for itself, to learn from experience, toward its capacities and potentialities for self-rule, toward its "spontaneous" movements such as might take place without orders and control from the party of socialist theoreticians and professional revolutionaries. From it would spring a special attitude toward trade unions, toward the impromptu strikers' councils or Soviets, even toward two revolutions — in 1905 and the spring of 1917 — that would come not on order but by surprise. Elsewhere, Wolfe finds something else that makes up "the real core of 'Leninism,' separating him by an abyss from the Mensheviks, and blurring to the vanishing point the dogmatic line which divided him from Trotsky." The "core" is this:

In short, Lenin's real answer to the question: what happens after we get power? is: Let's take power and then we'll see.

This "core" separated Lenin not only from the Mensheviks but from Marx as well, and Wolfe argues the point with a brevity, if not erudition, which merits full quotation:

To Marx it might have seemed that "the forms of the state are rooted in the material conditions of life," that "the economic structure of society. .. independent of men's will... determines the general character of the social, political and spiritual processes," and that "no social order ever disappears before all the productive forces for which there are room in it have been developed." But to Lenin's political-power-centred mind, for all his Marxist orthodoxy, such formulae were intolerable fetters unless subject to the proper exegesis. And the exegesis literally turned Marx on his head until the Marxist view that "in the last analysis economics determines politics" became the Leninist view that, with enough determination, power itself, naked political power, might succeed wholly in determining economics.

Wolfe has more to say about these two points, but very little more.

Lenin's ideas about socialist consciousness and the struggle of the working class were not invented by him nor were they uniquely his own. They are nothing less than the intellectual underpinnings of any genuinely socialist party, and it is inconceivable without them. In an even deeper sense they underlie the very conception of a rationally-ordered socialist society. No one developed these ideas more sharply and profoundly, even if with polemical vehemence, than Lenin, and that was his special contribution. But the ideas themselves go back to the beginnings of the scientific socialist movement, back to Marx and Engels. A serious examination of Lenin could not have failed to establish this fact and draw conclusions that it indicates Wolfe cannot help but know that Lenin's views were an almost literal copy of those expressed earlier, just as the century turned, by Karl Kautsky. And his present-day venerators would be horrified to hear that, by virtue of what he wrote at that time, he was the fountainhead of what was inevitably to become Stalinism! Kautsky, before Lenin, wrote:

Many of our revisionist critics believe that Marx asserted that economic development and the class struggle create, not only the conditions for socialist production, but also, and directly, the consciousness *of its necessity ... In this connection socialist consciousness is presented as a necessary and direct result of the proletarian class struggle. But this is absolutely untrue. Of course, socialism, as a theory, has its roots in a modern economic relationship in the same way as the class struggle of the proletariat has, and in the same way as the latter emerges from the struggle against the capitalist-created poverty and misery of the masses. But socialism and the class struggle arise side by side and not one out of the other; each arises out of different premises. Modern socialist consciousness can arise only on the basis of profound scientific knowledge. Indeed, modern economic science is as much a condition for socialist production as, say, modern technology, and the proletariat can create neither the one nor the other, no matter how much it may desire to do so; both arise out of the modern social process. The vehicles of science are not the proletariat, but the bourgeois intelligentsia: It was out of the heads of members of this stratum that modern socialism originated, and it was they who communicated it to the more intellectually-developed proletarians who, in their turn, introduce it into the proletarian class struggle where conditions allow that to be done. Thus, socialist consciousness is something introduced into the proletarian class struggle from without, and not something that arose within it spontaneously. Accordingly, the old [Austrian] Hainfeld program quite rightly stated that the task of Social Democracy is to imbue the proletariat with the* consciousness *of its position and the* consciousness *of its tasks. There would be* no *need for this if consciousness emerged from the class struggle.* (Kautsky's emphasis.)

To this should be added: neither would there then be any need for a distinct, separate political movement of socialism — a socialist party — except, perhaps, to fulfil the not very useful function of passive reflector of the welter of ideological and political confusion that, to one extent or another, will always exist in the working class, at least so long as it is a class deprived of social power and therewith of the means of wiping out its own inferior position in society. It is kept in this inferior position under capitalism by force but only in the last analysis, only at times of crisis. As a rule, be it under democratic or even under fascist capitalism, the ruling class maintains or seeks to maintain itself by ideological means.

The whole of capitalism's "headfixing industry", as one Marxist wittily called it, is directed toward keeping the working class in ignorance or confusion about its social position, or rather about the purely capitalist reasons for its position, toward concealing from the working class the emancipating historical mission it has and the road it must travel to perform it.

So long as the workers do not acquire an understanding of their social position and their social task, their battles against the ruling class, be they ever so militant or massive, can only modify the conditions of their economic subjugation but not abolish them. Indispensable to their abolition is the socialist consciousness (an exact mathematical formulation of which is neither possible nor necessary) of the working class, which means nothing more and nothing less than its realisation of its position in society today, of its power, and of its obligation and its ability to reconstruct society socialistically.

Now the dispute over the ideas of Kautsky-Lenin on the subject boils down to this: either the working class, organised in its elementary trade union organisations or not, acquires this consciousness by spontaneous generation in the course of repeated struggles for the improvement of its conditions — or in its decisive section, it acquires it, in the course of these struggles, to be sure, with the aid of those who already possess this socialist consciousness and who are banded together (in a group, a league, a movement, a party — call it what you will) in order more effectively to transmit it, by word of mouth and by the printed page, to those whose minds are still cluttered up with bourgeois rubbish, that is, the products of the "head-fixing industry."

Between these two, there is not a single person today who calls himself a socialist of any kind who would venture to defend, flatly and frontally, the former conception. All you get from the anti-Bolsheviks is, as in Wolfe's case, murky reference to the "special attitude" that flowed from Lenin's formulation of the position, in which the only thing definite is a sneer at the very conception of a socialist party — the "socialist theoreticians and professional revolutionists." The reformists who distinguish themselves from Lenin by saying that while they too are for a socialist party, they look upon it as a "servant" of the working class and not as its "master" or "dictator"; as a means of the "socialist education" of the working class in whose "ability to think for itself" they devoutly believe and not for the purpose of "ordering and controlling" it from above — are either hypocritical or inane. Their daily practice, inside the labour movement and in politics generally, would indicate that it is less the latter than the former.

The question of socialist consciousness which Lenin developed has wider implications. Wolfe sees in it only the source for establishing a new slavery for the working class, the Stalinist tyranny in the name of the "dictatorship of the proletariat". The truth is not merely different, but in this case it is the exact opposite!

Workers' democracy and, indeed, that complete realisation of democracy which inaugurates the socialist society, are not only inseparable from Lenin's ideas on socialist consciousness but, without them, become empty words, unattainable hopes, illusions at worst.

What was the obvious meaning of Lenin's insistence that the specific role of the socialist movement was to "introduce" a socialist consciousness into the working class? What, for example, was the clear implication of Lenin's "Aside from the influence of the Social Democracy, there is no conscious activity of the workers," which Wolfe quotes as a sample of the "dogma [which] was at the very core of 'Leninism'"... and from which "flowed an attitude toward the working class"? It should be obvious.

The "party of socialist theoreticians and professional revolutionaries" was not assigned thereby to trick the incurably blind and incurably stupid workers into lifting it to power so that it might establish a new kind of dictatorship over them. That makes no sense whatsoever. It was assigned the job of making the workers aware of the fundamental reasons for their exploited and subjected position under capitalism; of making the workers aware of their own class strength and having them rely only upon their class strength and independence; of assembling them in a revolutionary party of their own; of making them aware of their ability to free themselves from all class rule by setting up their own government as the bridge to socialist freedom.

Without a socialist consciousness, there would be working-class activity but the workers would continue to remain the ruled and never become the free. For the workers to rule themselves required conscious activity toward socialism.

What is Wolfe trying to convey with his suggestive prose? That Lenin dwelled so emphatically upon the need for the party to instil socialist consciousness or stimulate it in the working class because he did not believe in "its ability to think for itself, to learn from experience"? Or because he was sceptical about "its capacities and potentialities for self-rule"'? Did Lenin expect to imbue the unable-to-think-and-lead proletariat with socialist conceptions by intravenous hypodermic injections? Or is Wolfe just a little... careless with his innuendoes?

Let us go further. Lenin knew — he referred to it often enough and nowadays it is especially necessary to emphasise and elaborate it — one of the most basic and decisive differences between the bourgeois revolution and the socialist revolution. One of the outstanding characteristics of the former was that it could be carried through without a clear ideology, without an unequivocally-formulated consciousness on the part of the bourgeoisie whose social system it was to establish. In fact, not only could it be carried out in this way, but generally speaking that is how it was carried out.

The greatest bourgeois revolution the French, was carried out by plebeians, without the bourgeoisie and in part against it; and it was consolidated by Napoleon, in part without the bourgeoisie and in part against it. In Germany it was carried out, that is, the supremacy of capitalism over feudalism was assured, in the Bismarckian or Junker-landlord way — again, in part without the bourgeoisie and in very large part against it. The passage from feudalism to capitalism in Japan is only another example of the same phenomenon. Yet, in all these and other cases, including those where the bourgeoisie was not raised to political power, the bourgeois revolution was nevertheless effected, consolidated, guaranteed. Why? As Lenin once wrote, in 1918:

One of the main differences between the bourgeois and the socialist revolution consists in this, that for the bourgeois revolution which grows up out of feudalism the new economic organisations, which continually transform feudal society on all sides, gradually take form within the womb of the old society. The bourgeois revolution faced only one task: to throw off and destroy all the fetters of the former society. Every bourgeois revolution that fulfils this task, fulfils everything that is demanded of it: it strengthens the growth of capitalism.

But if the bourgeois fetters upon production are thrown off and destroyed, that alone does not and cannot assure the growth of socialist production. Under capitalism, production is assured by the irrepressible tendency toward accumulation of capital which is dictated primarily, not by the will of the capitalist, but by the blindly-operating market as the automatic regulator of capitalist production. Socialist production is incompatible with market relations.

It is production for use and therefore planned production, not automatically regulated by a blind force. Given a certain level of development of the productive force available, everything then depends upon planning, that is, upon the conscious organisation of production and distribution by human beings.

Now, under capitalism, what and how much is produced is determined by the market, and the distribution of what is produced is determined basically by the relations between the class that owns the means of production and exchange and the class that is divorced from them. Overturn capitalism, and it is found that there is no market to determine what is produced and in what quantities, and there is no class that owns private property.

Until the distant day when all classes are completely abolished and socialism fully established, the conditions of production and distribution must necessarily be determined by politically-associated human beings — no longer by the blind market but by the state.

In other words, where the state becomes the repository of all the means of production and is in complete control of them, economy is for the first time subject to planned and conscious control by those who have the state in their hands. In this sense, politics determines economics! This may sound startling to Wolfe, as well as to all sorts of half-baked half Marxists But if this simple and irrefutable fact is not understood, then the whole idea of the working class taking power in order to organise a socialist society becomes absurd and even meaningless. In revolution, but above all and most decisively in the socialist revolution, the relationship between economics and politics is not only reversed, turned upside-down, but it must be reversed!

But if politics now determines economics (again, within the limits of the given productive forces), or to put it differently, if the conditions of production and distribution are now determined by politically conscious individuals or groups, the question of the nature of the determining politics is immediately thrown open. What assurance is there that the politics will be socialist in nature, so that production relations are socialist or socialistic (by which is meant socialist in tendency or direction) and that distribution corresponds to them, so that what is produced is for the use of the people and not of a small privileged group?

To rely for that on the good will, the honourable intentions or the socialist past or professions of faith of a group of planners who hold the state power to the exclusion of the rest of the people, is naive, where it is not reactionary. In any case, it is not a socialist idea and certainly not Lenin's. A socialist development of the economy can be assured only by those who are to be its principal beneficiaries, the working class, and only if it has the power to make the decisions on production and distribution and to carry them out, hence only if it holds the power of the state. For politics now determines economics! And it cannot acquire this power or wield it unless it is permeated by a socialist consciousness, which means, among other things, an understanding of the decisive role it has to play in the new state, and therefore and only by that means, the role it has to play in assuring a socialist direction to the operation of the economy.

That is why Lenin, in distinguishing between bourgeois and socialist revolutions, underlined the fact that the Bolshevik revolution "found at hand" not socialist economic relations that had developed under capitalism as capitalist economic relations had developed under feudalism, but rather a democratic political factor: "victory depended solely upon whether already finished organisational forms of the movement were at hand that embraced millions. This finished form was the Soviets."

The same thought was in his mind when he urged that every cook should become an administrator, so that with everyone exercising the power of "bureaucrat" no one would be a bureaucrat. And the thought was even more pregnantly expressed in his famous saying that "Soviets plus electrification equal socialism." (It is impossible even to imagine Lenin saying that a totalitarian prison for the workers plus nationalized property equals a degenerated workers' state!)

The Soviets, before the Bolsheviks took power, were acclaimed by every Menshevik and Social Revolutionist as the "revolutionary democracy." That was right. What is more, the Soviets were a magnificent example of a spontaneous movement of the workers and peasants themselves, not set up by order of any party or according to its plan.

Wolfe finds that from Lenin's "dogma" about socialist consciousness "flowed" an attitude toward the working class which was uncommendable because, it would seem, it was most undemocratic and even contemptuous toward the working class, including "its 'spontaneous' movements such as might take place without orders and control from the party..." Like the Soviets of 1917, for example? Then how explain that every party in Russia, except the Bolsheviks, fought to keep the Soviets (the "revolutionary democracy") from taking over all power, and worked to keep them as a more or less decorative appendage to the never-elected but self-constituted Kerensky regime?

True to Lenin's "dogma", the Bolsheviks alone strove to imbue the Soviets with a genuinely socialist consciousness, which meant concretely that the workers (and even the peasants), more democratically and representatively organised in the Soviets than ever before or ever since in any other movement in any country of the world, should take command of the nation and therewith of their own destiny.

This example of what really was the "attitude" of Lenin and his party toward the "spontaneous" movements of the workers, their ability to think and learn for themselves, and their capacities and potentialities for self rule — not in some thesis or polemical article or speech, but in one of the most crucial periods of history — is so outstanding, so overshadowing, so illuminating about Lenin's "conceptions" that Wolfe passes it by. We will not ask what this historian would have said about Lenin's "dogma" if the Bolshevik attitude toward the "revolutionary democracy" in 1917 had been the same as, let us say, that of Kerensky. But we wonder what he will say in succeeding volumes about the Menshevik and SR "attitude" toward the Soviets and the "dogma" from which it "flowed".

The revolution of 1917 was the decisive test for all political parties and groups. In spite of conservative trends in the ranks (all parties tend toward conservatism about some of their "dogmas"), Lenin showed that he had been able to build and hold together a party which proved, in this most critical hour, to be the only consistent champion of revolutionary democracy and revolutionary socialism, and the only "political machine" ready and able to lead both to victory. This is what brought Trotsky to the side of the Bolsheviks and caused him to "forget" his "Cassandra-like prevision" about how "the dictator will take the place of the Central Committee" and the party itself.

If Wolfe finds that Trotsky's prediction was "fatefully fulfilled by history", it is primarily because of his method of separating the history of the conflict of social forces from specific political events, or worse, of simply ignoring the former. The fact is that whatever grounds there may have been or seemed to have been in 1903-04 for Trotsky to utter his warning, the main tendency of the development of Lenin's group or party, particularly from 1905 onwards, was in an entirely opposite one from that feared by Trotsky.

The apparatus did not replace the party, nor the Central Committee the apparatus, nor the dictator (Lenin!) the Central Committee. The inner-party democracy and freedom of opinion and discussion of the Bolsheviks as an illegal movement, it is worth repeating, can be matched, without apology, against the regime of virtually every other working-class organisation, legal or illegal, that ever existed.

Here, too, the decisive test was 1917 itself. At least, you would think so, on the basis of almost universal experience in such matters. A working-class movement which is suffering from a fatal disease — opportunism, let us say, or bureaucratism — does not usually reveal it, not clearly, at any rate, in normal periods, in periods of social calm or political decay. It shows it, and most disastrously for itself and its followers, in the most critical and troubled periods of society, above all in the crisis of war and the crisis of revolution. But precisely in the critical period of 1917, the Bolshevik party passed the test, and so well that Trotsky found it possible to abandon his early apprehensions about it.

Now, why didn't Lenin's conception of organisation, which was one of the "roots of Stalinism", manifest itself in 1917 in a way that would cause the Bolshevik party to play a conservative or reactionary role in the revolution, to be a brake upon the workers and peasants? The question is of first-rate interest. Therefore, Wolfe passes it by.

Did the Bolshevik party measure up to its task early in 1917? Of course not! But that was not because Trotsky's prophecy about Lenin's conception of organisation had been fulfilled, fatefully or otherwise. It was an entirely different prophecy of Trotsky's that was fulfilled or almost. Years earlier, Trotsky had written that the Bolshevik formula of "democratic dictatorship of the proletariat and peasantry" had its revolutionary side, as opposed to the Menshevik conception of a revolution in which it would he the role of the proletariat to bring the bourgeoisie to power. But, he added, if the Bolsheviks persisted in this formula, the coming revolution would reveal its reactionary side, that is, that which inhibited the proletariat from carrying the democratic revolution through to proletarian power and the inauguration of socialist measures.

Steeped in Lenin's old formula, most of the party leaders in 1917 adopted a position which paralysed the revolutionary possibilities of the party. It took a further fight by Lenin, after his arrival in Russia in April, to effect that "rearmament" of the party which finally assured the victory in October. But, this "prophecy" of Trotsky's — or rather, Lenin's rearming of the party in the direction of Trotsky's theory — is regarded by Wolfe as one of the sources of Stalinism!

Important is the fact that Lenin did not replace the Central Committee by a dictator in any sense indicated by Trotsky. He enjoyed, justly, immense authority among the Bolsheviks, but he had won it and kept it to the end of his life by his intellectual ability and character as a leader and not by any dirty manipulation or usurpation.

In 1917, most of the party leadership opposed his famous "April Theses." He was not only unable to dictate to the others, but did not dream of it. He won them over, one by one, partly by the pressure of the party ranks whom he convinced and partly by convincing the leaders as well. In 1917, or before, when his point of view won, it was not because the dictator had replaced the Central Committee; and when his point of view lost, as was more than once the case, it was not because the apparatus had replaced the party.

Yet, the Bolshevik party did degenerate; Soviet democracy was replaced by a unique Bonapartist dictatorship. But the process did not conform with Trotsky's prediction, which Wolfe transforms into an abstraction raised to the nth power. Reading Wolfe, you would think that the Bolshevik party was a sort of supra-mundane evolving out of some purely internal mechanism, unaffected by the strains and influences exerted by terrestrial forces.

It is only necessary to read what the Bolsheviks said and wrote in the period of the revolutionary upsurge to see what their real attitude was toward Soviet and socialist democracy, what ideas of working-class self rule they sought with all their strength to instil into the Russian people. The bureaucracy rose not because of these ideas, but in spite of them.

The revolution was soon plunged into a fierce civil war, and if it had not been for the Bolsheviks, including their "machine", the Soviet power would not have lasted 48 hours, to be replaced, in all likelihood, not by bourgeois democrats but by the czarist reaction which Anglo-French imperialism was sponsoring.

Civil war, unfortunately, is not the ideal culture for the growth of the democratic bacillus. The days of War Communism were harsh and stringent. At the front and at home, command inevitably took the place of free discussion and voting. The tendency to bureaucratic command gripped and held not only Bolshevik leaders, but rank-and-file militants, Bolshevik and non-party, as well.

Even so, Soviet democracy could have been restored after the civil war if the accursed backwardness of Russia had been overcome rapidly by the aid which a successful revolution in the advanced West could have contributed on a grand scale. It could have been maintained if, to start with, the Menshevik and SR parties had allied themselves with the "revolutionary democracy" in the civil war and not with the monarchist reaction. Russian Populists of the old days once exclaimed: "Never will history forgive the autocracy for making terrorists out of us." With far more justice the Bolsheviks might have declared: "Never will history forgive the Mensheviks and Social Revolutionists for joining the war against the Soviets and forcing us to substitute our party for the Soviets."

Soviet democracy might have been restored by another road, the re-democratisation of the Bolshevik Party itself. And here it is interesting to note that the big fight for party democracy was launched by an outstanding section of the Old Bolsheviks who rallied to Trotsky's position; in fact, by the time Zinoviev broke with Stalin and joined the Trotskyists, it can be said that the bulk of the militants who had been most thoroughly trained in the old school of Bolshevism and in Lenin's "conception of organisation", lined up against the Stalinist bureaucracy, which was represented primarily by comparatively recent members or by obscure personages who had never played an important part in the life of the party. Well or badly, consistently or not, the old Bolshevik cadres resisted the rise of the new Stalinist bureaucracy. If they failed, it was not due to the overpowering force of Lenin's organisational principles, but to an overpowering force of a radically different kind.

In passing, Wolfe writes:

Nineteen five and nineteen seventeen, the heroic years when the machine was unable to contain the flood of overflowing life, would bring Trotsky to the fore as the flaming tribune of the people, would show Lenin's ability to rise above the confining structure of his dogmas, and would relegate Stalin, the machine-man, to the background. But no people can live forever at fever heat and when that day was over and Lenin was dead the devoted machine-man's day would come. [** see note at end of article]

Just in passing! But these two sentences contain more insight than can be found in any two chapters of Wolfe's book. Revolutions are periods of turbulence precisely because the people are so free to choose their course and their leaders for themselves and so hard to control by a machine. Wolfe merely sets down the two deeply significant sentences and then goes on as though they were no more than a chance collection of words.

He seems to shy away from matters and statements of social importance spontaneously, without special effort, as if by instinct. But the sentences are important regardless of Wolfe. When the masses were free to choose democratically in the revolutions of 1905 and 1917, Trotsky and Lenin were lifted to power. (Their names can be used here as symbolic of Bolshevism as it really was.) And it is only when the masses were exhausted or apathetic or prostrate, that is, when revolution was succeeded by reaction, that the Stalinist counter-revolution could triumph over the masses and over the Bolshevik party.

There is the "core of Stalinism" indeed! The Stalinist bureaucracy did not grow out of an organic evolution of the Bolshevik party, as was implied by Trotsky's "prophecy". Its growth paralleled and required the destruction of that party. And its destruction, root and trunk and leaves and branch, until absolutely nothing is left of it today except the plagiarized name. This fact, too, is of such capital importance that the anti Bolshevik writers pass it by. Destroyed: the principles of Bolshevism, its program, its tradition, its history, its personnel down almost to the last man, including (how significant this is!) even those Bolsheviks who tried to capitulate to Stalinism, and yes, including even the big bulk of the original Stalinist faction of the old party! Preserved: the name of the party and a few renegades from the second and tenth ranks of the old Bolshevik party — that and nothing more.

The destruction of the Bolshevik party meant the destruction of socialist consciousness. The measure of the growth of the Bolshevik party was the growth of this consciousness among the workers it influenced; and in turn it grew among the workers to the extent that the party remained attached to the ideas which Lenin most conspicuously advocated. It is of tremendous interest that for the Stalinist faction to extend its initial victory inside the party apparatus (that's where its first victory occurred) to a victory inside the party generally, it had to flood the party.

The first big public step, so to speak, taken by the Stalinist bureaucracy was the notorious Lenin Levy organised right after Lenin's death. Hundreds of thousands of workers were almost literally poured into the party. Who were they? Generally speaking, the more conservative workers and employees, people who had not shown any interest in joining the party in the tough days of the revolution and civil war but who could, in 1924-25, be persuaded to join it now that its power seemed consolidated, now that membership seemed to guarantee employment, privileges, a career.

Almost to a man they could be counted on by the bureaucracy in the fight against the Opposition, against the Bolsheviks, their principles, their revolutionary and socialist and democratic traditions. It was Stalin's first and least important step in literally dissolving Lenin's "machine" in order to substitute a despotic police regime that was utterly alien to it. This first step was typical of those that followed.

There is as much justification, then, for the theory that Stalinism was rooted in the Bolshevism which it extirpated, as there is, for example, in the kindred theory that the socialist movement, its methods and its theories in general form the roots of the fascist movement and its methods and theories.

The anti-Bolshevik democrat would feel outraged at seeing the latter argument put forward. He would declare indignantly that to explode such nonsense, nothing more is needed than the fact that Hitlerism crushed the socialist organisations, imprisoned or killed their leaders, outlawed their ideas, and so on and so forth. Yet the argument that Hitlerism had its authentic roots in the German Social Democratic Party is advanced in all coolness by so eminent an anti-socialist as Frederick von Hayek, and with the same reasoning, with the same analogies, with the same cavalier attitude toward decisive facts as is displayed by those who argue that Stalinism is rooted in Bolshevism. Hayek is a defender of the capitalist status-quo-ante-state intervention and a sworn foe of socialism, and he has his means of discrediting its good name. The aim of the democratic or reformist anti-Bolsheviks is somewhat loftier, as it were, but the means they employ to discredit Bolshevism are in no essential different from Hayek's.

On the flyleaf of his book, Wolfe quotes, for his motto, the noble words of Albert Mathiez:

The historian has a duty both to himself and to his readers. He has to a certain extent the cure of souls. He is accountable for the reputation of the mighty dead whom he conjures up and portrays. If he makes a mistakes, if he repeats slanders on those who are blameless or holds up profligates or schemers to admiration, he not only commits an evil action; he poisons and misleads the public mind.

Mathiez devoted much of his great work to defending the great French Revolution and its Jacobins from detractors. The socialist today has the duty to defend the great Russian Revolution and its Jacobins in much the same spirit. As to how faithfully Wolfe has heeded the injunction of Mathiez, the reader of his book will judge for himself.

[**] Then why the title "Three Who Made a Revolution"? Up to now, only Stalinist forgers have presented Stalin as one those who outstandingly led the revolution. The facts presented by Wolfe show this to be a falsification and the above quotation confirms it. The title he gives his book is therefore utterly misleading. It would of course be very awkward to load a book with a title like "Two Who Made a Revolution and One Who Made a Counter-Revolution", but one merit it would have: it would be accurate.

From Shachtman's review of *Three Who Made a Revolution*, by Bertram Wolfe, in *New International*, Jan-Feb, Mar-Apr, and Jul-Aug 1950: this is the third (July-August) part of the review.

Trotsky and Cannon

Max Shachtman (1953)

IT IS NOW TWENTY-FIVE YEARS since the Trotskyist movement was launched in the United States under circumstances which had already ceased to be unusual for that movement. The date was 27 October 1928.

On that day, an enlarged session of the Political Committee of the Communist Party, upon hearing a statement by three members of the party's Central Committee in which they aligned themselves with the then Russian (or Trotskyist) Opposition, voted to expel the three from the party: James P. Cannon, Martin Abern, and Max Shachtman (an alternate member).

This action, as the expelled knew before they made their avowal, was a foregone conclusion. The Sixth Congress of the Communist International held only a few months earlier had made the espousal of "Trotskyism" incompatible with membership in the International or any of its affiliates. But if the three clearly expected expulsion the minute after they read their statement to the rest of the Central Committee members, it might almost be said that everything else related to the founding of the Trotskyist movement in this country was unexpected. Indeed. looking backward, it offers an excellent example of how the inevitable often asserts itself in politics through the accidental and in spite of it.

Unexpected, in the first place, was the extraordinary stupidity and criminality of the Communist Party leadership in its proceedings against the expelled. The party leadership was then in the hands of the Lovestone faction. To embarrass their rivals of the Foster faction, out of whose leading group the expelled Trotskyists had come, and to show Stalin how reliable they were in hunting Trotskyism, the Lovestoneites promptly launched a reign of terror in the party ranks.

Every branch and every member of the party and the youth organization was compelled on the spot to declare his loyalty to the Central Committee in the fight against the Trotskyists, to condemn the three Trotskyists themselves as well as everything they stood for or were said to stand for, and to disavow any "conciliatory" attitude toward them.

Conciliationists were designated as those who asked to withhold

729

their vote on the resolution of condemnation until they could see and read the statements of the three expelled members. In this way, dozens of communists were expelled overnight throughout the country without having anything but a vague idea of the opposition's views. Most of them were recruited to the side of the expelled who now called themselves, after their Russian comrades, the Left Opposition, and afterward took the name of Communist League of America.

To this service the Lovestoneites added another, most often with the active aid of the Fosterites as well, who did not want to be outbidded in the Kremlin. For the first time in the history of any radical or socialist movement, we saw not only an expulsion which resulted in the formation of another movement but also an attempt made by the older organization to smash the new group in the egg by the open, direct, conscious and organized use of force and violence.

This was not a spontaneous outburst of indignant or exasperated individuals, but the result of deliberate planning by the leadership and mobilization of the organs at its disposal. The three of us were physically assaulted by party toughs armed with clubs and knives when we first appeared round the party centre to distribute our paper, *The Militant*, and for a long time afterward. Our very first meeting in New York – probably the first Trotskyist public meeting in the Western hemisphere! – was never really held. The police had to intervene to prevent even greater bloodshed than had already been caused, when literally scores of party hoodlums, mobilized that very evening at party headquarters and equipped with blackjacks, knives, lead pipes, brass knuckles and other subtle political arguments, broke into the hall to terrorize the audience and the speakers

At our next meeting in the same New York Labor Temple, we were better prepared for the same mob that came to visit us, as is evidenced by the emergency treatment records of neighbouring hospitals and by the fact that after some initial incidents the meeting – a magnificent one – went on peaceably to its end. But for two or three years thereafter, literally from one end of the country to the other, our comrades and our public meetings were subjected to the same kind of organized Stalinist gangsterism, which subsided only when groups of sturdy, valiant and resolute militants – female as well as male! – drummed some wholesome homilies in workers' democracy into the skulls of the hooligans and, in general, helped bring a sense of shame into the hearts of the better elements in the CP ranks.

The Trotskyist movement was certainly not weaned on meek milk. The campaign of violence against it helped it win more supporters from outraged members and sympathizers of the official party. But it must be admitted that, as with all the madness of Stalinism, there was method in it – cunning, base, sinister method. It not only aimed at intimidating actual and prospective Trotskyists; but it also aimed, probably primarily, to draw between the followers of the official party and the then "unofficial opposition" of Trotskyism the most difficult of all lines to cross in politics: the line of blood.

Probably because it was so unexpected, despite what was being done to the oppositionists inside Russia, this virulent violence of the Stalinists made a deep impression upon us. Eight years after the Trotskyists were expelled from the Communist Party in this country, they were expelled on grounds just as flimsy and by means just as brusque and bureaucratic – from the Socialist Party which they had joined earlier. Yet the bloody violence that followed our expulsion from the Stalinist party was totally unknown after the split in the Socialist party.

The impression which the violence made upon us caused some supercilious souls and empty bonnets to chide the Trotskyists in the following years for their "Stalinophobia." It was as if they regarded us, with condescending comprehension, as obsessed victims of traumatic personal experiences. To us, however, it never was a psychological problem; it became with increasing clarity a social and political phenomenon of specific significance.

The assaults upon us were, it should certainly be obvious now, not a passing incident produced by factional excitations, but manifestations of an essential and distinguishing characteristic of Stalinism. Stalinism is by its social nature a totalitarian movement. It can triumph, it can maintain itself only by the physical extirpation of its adversaries in the popular movements, and therewith extirpation of any and all forms democracy that impede its rule. The Trotskyists were the adversary with the most perspicacious insight into Stalinism. The violence against us was all the more ruthless and cynical. It was not an "excess" but authentic and durable, and in its most brutal flaring in this country it was nothing but an anticipation and preparation of what Stalinism aspires to achieve.

The early hooliganism against us was a disgrace and discredit to the revolutionary movement as a whole. But it not only helped win us additional recruits; it sealed in us a conviction that any group in the labour movement that resorts to violence against any other group in it – except in self defence – has no place or right in the organized working-class movement and must be driven out of it without mercy. And it also helped our minds reach into the heart of darkness of Stalinism itself. Unexpected, in the second place, was the development

731

of the Stalinist movement and, with it, of our own perspectives. We assumed that the CP was going to remain ever more firmly under the Lovestone leadership, that the Comintern endorsement which it seemed to get at the Sixth Congress would be reiterated and strengthened, that it would be given an ever freer hand in demolishing the Foster faction or driving it into unhappy but silent subservience. This triumph of the Lovestoneite right wing would, as we saw it, speedily bring a large section of unrepentant Fosterites to our side. So we concentrated our fire on the Lovestoneite leadership as the authentic representatives of the Moscow revisionism and on the Fosterite leadership as centrists and capitulators without a future in the/our party.

The deep antagonism that the best militants in the Foster faction felt toward the Lovestoneites as petty-bourgeois intellectuals, snobs, cynics, low grade manipulators and manoeuverists, encouraged us to expect decisive support in the very near future from these militants with whom, after all, we had been so closely tied factionally and even personally up to yesterday.

In this entire analysis we were only following the essentials of Trotsky's views on the unrolling of the Russian Thermidor. He looked upon all the victories of the Russian Stalinists over the Russian Bukharinists – inside the Russian party or in the Comintern – as only apparent, trivial and momentary. The right wing would unquestionably and very soon show its real and overwhelming strength in Russia.

The centre – the Stalinist bureaucracy – would unquestionably and very soon show its real and disastrous weakness. At worst, it would capitulate completely to the right wing; at best, it would try to wage a faltering, apologetic, defensive, ever-eager-for-compromise fight against it. But such a fight it was foredoomed to lose, unless the Left Opposition snatched the banner from its palsied hands and took command of the fight to save the revolution from the capitalist-restorationist classes represented by the right.

As we know, nothing of the kind happened. The Stalinist centre not only took up the fight with the Bukharinists but wiped them out root and branch, wiped out all important traces of the possessing classes, wiped out the last remnants of the Bolshevik party, its leaders, traditions and principles, wiped out every shred of democracy, wiped out all possibility of simply restoring the old Trotskyist Opposition, and forced Trotsky himself to the subsequent conclusion that from the standpoint of the centrist bureaucracy – the Stalinists, that is – the right wing represented a threat from the left. He never explained this

732

enigmatic assertion.

It goes without saying that not a single self-styled "orthodox Trotskyist" today would grasp the meaning of this assertion, let alone try to explain it. In any case, Trotsky's perspective was radically wrong and he never succeeded in ridding himself of the basic ambiguity it contained.

Our perspective in the USA was likewise wrong, although the consequences were far less serious here than in Russia. A bewilderingly few months after our own expulsion by the Lovestoneites, the entire Lovestoneite leadership and the bulk of its national cadre – except for such dregs as Stachel, Minor and their kind – were unceremoniously booted out of the party and the Comintern. A faster case of biters bit is not on recent record.

After a few years of stertorous breathing, the Lovestone group performed the most outstandingly honest act of its existence – it voted to dissolve for want of any contribution it could make to the working class as an organization. Of it too, then, could be said that nothing became it so well in life as its way of taking farewell of it. (It is strange how other futilitarians, so numerous today, spurn the encouragement offered by this example of decent self-interment. It would seem that in politics, at least, some refuse burial services as stubbornly as if they were alive.)

Unexpected, in the last place, was the source from which the American Trotskyist movement sprang. A veritable mythology has been created on this score, modest when compared with the mythology of Stalinism but patterned after it nevertheless. If its sole result were to feed the vanity that requires such a diet, it could be overlooked with the compassion felt by any Marxist to whom nothing human is alien. But it cannot be ignored when it serves questionable political ends and distorts historical events which demand clear understanding in the interests of today's needs.

The Trotskyist group in this country was founded by some of the leaders of the Cannon faction in the Communist Party, most prominently by Cannon himself. But the idea that this faction had been, as he likes to say, "prepared by its past" for this distinguished action and role, that it had been moving inside the Communist Party straight or even more or less in the direction of Trotsky's ideas, that its appearance as a Trotskyist group was only the logical and natural culmination of its preceding fight inside the party, is absurd where it is not pernicious.

It is accepted only by uninformed people whose credulity has been cooly imposed upon in the hope that facts will not rudely intrude upon rhetoric and say-so. The reality is quite different from the tales of the myth makers.

The entire Communist Party was astounded, not to say stupefied and even incredulous, at hearing that Cannon had come forward as a supporter of the Russian Opposition. The announcement came as a bombshell, not only to the opponents of his party faction but also to its supporters. There was nothing in the past position or conduct of the faction that offered the slightest advance indication of the announcement that its leader and two of his associates were to make on October 27, 1928. Indeed the indications were of a distinctly different kind. The very way in which the group was born is an example.

The Cannon faction came into existence in the CP as an independent group as a result of a split which it organized in 1925 in the Foster-Cannon group, which was by far the more healthy and proletarian of the two contending party factions. When Zinoviev, by an unprecedented cablegram from Moscow, robbed the Foster-Cannon faction of its legally-won majority at the party convention in order to turn the leadership over to the Lovestoneite minority, the rightly embittered Fosterites threatened a passive strike against Zinoviev's outrage. Cannon thereupon split from the Fosterites, condemned them for "disloyalty to the Comintern" and even charged them with planning a "right-wing split" from the party. Those days and the three years of the party struggle that followed, including the part played in it by the Cannon faction, are like an unbelievable nightmare which a participant cannot recall with pride.

From its birth, the Cannon faction never had a distinguishing programme of its own, never played an independent role, never had a meaningful solution for the factionalism that incessantly corroded the party but whose roots it did not even begin to understand. If, as a small minority, it nevertheless had the support of a number of excellent militants, it won them not because of any of its virtues in principle or programme – in general it had none that anyone, its spokesmen included, could ever define – but because of the out-and-out vices that marked the leadership and program of the Foster and Lovestone factions. Its sole attractive power lay in the repulsive power of the others.

Having nothing or virtually nothing to offer the party in its own name, it was doomed to recommend itself to the party in the name of the others. Soon after its birth, it was completely federated with the Lovestoneites, and jointly with then sought to smash the Foster group on the grounds that it represented a low grade of "trade-union communists" distinctly inferior to the "party communists" or "political communists" of the Lovestone faction. But before very long it created a new group out of a sordid alliance with disgruntled Lovestoneites like Weinstone, Ballam and for a moment Stachel – respectively a careerist, a cynic and plain scum.

The alliance began to place distance between itself and its confederates of yesterday, the Lovestone faction, when rumours came from Moscow that new winds were blowing, that Lovestone's patron, Zinoviev, was finished, that a new star was looming who favoured decency, native leadership, worker-communists and simplicity in the Comintern parties and against "intellectuals" and "cablegram leaderships" (this star was Stalin!)

The more emphatically this grotesque rumour was repeated, the more energetic became the Cannon and Foster faction in "developing differences" with the Lovestoneites of a kind that they felt would place them in the most favourable position before the new star rising in Moscow. On the eve of the Sixth World Congress, the two factions were reunited against the Lovestoneites on a trumped-up "programme" of which around nine-tenths was political and economic rubbish. But this re-unification meant far less than appeared. Emissaries of the American factions in Moscow and emissaries of the Moscow factions in the United States made it clear that whether Lovestone or Foster was recognized as the official Governor-General for the American party, the Cannon faction would carry no weight and would receive no recognition. No wonder Cannon refused to go to the Sixth Congress and consented to attend only when driven to it by his own faction.

It was obvious or it should have been that the Cannon faction had reached the end of its road in the party. It goes without saying that the prospect of supporting Trotsky was never so much as mentioned at formal or informal gatherings of the faction. Indeed it is not too much to say that of the three American factions, the Cannonites were generally marked out as those least interested or concerned with what was going on in the Russian party.

The best that can be said for us in those days is that while we automatically voted to "endorse the Old Guard" and "condemn Trotskyism" the dubious honours for the outstanding work of denouncing Trotskyism throughout the party ranks and in the party press went to Lovestoneites like Wolfe, Stachel and Olgin and Fosterites like Bittelman and Browder.

Far, then, from being "prepared by our past" for Trotskyism, we were no less startled by Cannon's first (and of course exceedingly confidential) announcement of his support of the Russian Opposition than was the party as a whole when the three of us proclaimed that support to the Political Committee meeting at which we were expelled. I will never want, or be able, to forget the absolutely shattering effect upon my inexcusable indifference to the fight in the Russian party, upon my smug ignorance about the issues involved, upon my sense of shame, that was produced by the first reading of Trotsky's classic *Critique of the Draft Program of the Comintern*. But to Cannon's eternal credit he smuggled out of Moscow and illicitly circulated here among two or three of his personal and political friends the numbered copy, wretchedly translated and brutally excised, of the Critique which the Congress Secretariat had loaned to selected delegates with "read-and-return" instructions imperiously stamped on the top page. (What a regime, where Trotsky's writings had to be smuggled out of the country the way revolutionists used to have to smuggle writings into the Russia of the Tsars! What a party, where Trotsky's writing had to be shown, furtively and only in the assured secrecy of a private dwelling, by one Central Committee member to another!)

But neither can I forget the equally explosive effect the Critique had in lighting new horizons, in clarifying the problems of the revolutionary movement and pointing out new roads to tread in resolving them – horizons and roads, thoughts and perspectives, which the endless, pointless, unprincipled jungle-fighting of the American party factions had so completely obscured that one first-rate militant after another was poisoned by the lack of clean light and air of Marxist principles and Marxist thought, and rotted away to a Stalinist leprosy.

So long as there are classes, the class struggle is irrepressible. The formation of a scientific socialist movement – a complex process – is an inevitable product of the modern class struggle and so is its re-formation. The fight begun by Trotsky against the undermining of the Russian Revolution was unquestionably the most important step in the re-formation of the socialist movement since a handful of Marxists set about reconstituting the international socialist movement after its collapse in 1914.

The rise of the new, authentically socialist international was inevitable. When it began to take on flesh and blood in the form of the Communist International and the Communist Parties throughout the world, the inevitable very often asserted itself, then too, through the accidental. Many were the unexpected situations and the unexpected individuals who made the new movements growth possible. So it was a quarter of a century ago with us.

That Cannon should have decided in 1928, out of the clear blue, to support the Russian Opposition, was an accident, and the motives that prompted him have been the subject of all sorts of speculation in the past (some interesting; others preposterous), which it would be out of place to consider here. But it was a lucky accident for us. The Cannon faction in the CP was tiny but close-knit. Yet the majority of its leading militants and its supporters in the ranks did not follow Cannon in his adoption of the Trotskyist position, and most of them soon became the most delirious anti-Trotskyists. If a few of us (myself, Marty Abern, Rose Karsner, Tom O'Flaherty and then Arne Swabeck, Abert Gates, V.R. Dunne and Karl Skoglund) did become Trotskyists, it was thanks primarily to the fact that Trotsky's views were sponsored by a party leader who enjoyed the prestige and authority that Cannon had in our eyes.

And if the Trotskyist movement in this country showed greater substance, stability, seriousness and tenacity than in many other lands, that, in turn, was thanks primarily to the fact that Trotsky's views were popularized and defended by a basic cadre of communists experienced and known in many fields of activity and habituated to effective collaboration by years of common practice.

History would be mystical in nature, wrote Marx in 1871 if "accidents played no part in it." That holds true in particular for the history of the revolutionary movement. Anyone in it with eyes in his head has seen Marx corroborated a hundred times over for any given period, "accidents" can play a decisive role in advancing or retarding it, "including the 'accident' of the character of the people who first stand at the head of the movement." This sort of "accident" makes it possible to speak not only of the "Trotskyist movement in the United States" but also of an "American Trotskyism." And without grasping what is signified by that, a good deal of the life of the Trotskyist movement in this country is bound to be incomprehensible and a very great deal that is instructive in it is bound to be lost.

The American Trotskyist movement was born with two distinct advantages. Trotsky's views, at the end of five intensive years of struggle in the party, had had a chance to develop far more fully and clearly than they appeared to be in 1923 or even in 1926. Many who solidarized themselves with Trotsky in the earlier years were really under misapprehension about what he stood for in reality and in the long run; and as his views unfolded more extensively, they took their leave with the adequate excuse that they had not realized where they were going. Those who solidarized themselves with Trotsky in 1928 and afterward, had no such excuse and they never dreamed of invoking it – they knew where Trotsky stood and where they themselves stood and they joined him without political reservations. That was one advantage we had over every other Trotskyist group in the world, with the exception of the French. With them we shared another advantage, one that was derived from the acknowledged leader of the organization (at least for the time when Alfred Rosmer was its spokesman in France), in our case from Cannon. We have listened to many attempts to ignore or deny this fact but we never heard one of any merit.

Cannon gave the American Trotskyist movement a personal link with the preceding revolutionary movements and therewith helped to preserve the continuity of the movement, a factor disdained by the dilettante and inordinately worshipped by the bureaucrat but nevertheless regarded as highly important and precious by any responsible militant. Cannon was among the first in this country to become a firm champion of the Bolshevik Revolution; as one of the leaders of the left wing in the old Socialist Party he became a leading founder of the Communist Labor Party in 1919; he helped defeat the faction of professional illegalists who insisted on keeping the communist movement of this country in a sub-cellar; and became first national chairman of the party when it re-emerged as an open, legal organization in 1923. Even before the First World War, Cannon had already attained prominence among the younger militants of the International Workers of the World (IWW), being one of the adherents of Vincent St. John, whom he almost succeeded in later years in winning to the communist ranks.

From the beginning of the movement, he was outstanding and steady in his insistence that the organization would never amount to much unless it oriented itself primarily and mainly toward the proletariat, unless it rooted itself strong and deep in the organized labour movement, unless it became itself an overwhelmingly proletarian movement. These ideas may be regarded as the most obvious commonplaces of the Marxist movement, and of little importance. But it must be remembered that as late as the 30s in this country, the communist movement never had more than scanty, isolated or haphazard contact with the broad labour movement and was to a large extent alien to it; and that the Trotskyist movement, except for estimable but incidental connections with parts of the labour movement, was completely isolated from it for many years. It should be borne in mind, further, that because we were so intensely concerned with profound theoretical problems and so preoccupied with "Russian" or "international" questions to the exclusion (whether real or apparent, is beside the point here) of "American" questions, we tended in the early days to attract mainly the younger people, students, intellectuals good and bad, very few workers, even fewer active trade unionists, still fewer trade unionists active in the basic and most important unions, but more than a few dilettantes, well-meaning blunderers, biological chatterboxes, ultra-radical oat-sowers, unattachable wanderers, and many other kinds of sociological curiosa.

Most of them made bivouac with us for a while, but not for too long. Of the movement, the best were those who completely assimilated the meaning of the proletarian character that the living and genuine socialist movement must have. If he sometimes injected an unjustified polemical or factional warp into his emphasis, it was nonetheless Cannon who was most persistent throughout the early, difficult years of isolation in imbuing all the serious people with an alertness to the need of a proletarian movement; and on the whole he was likewise the most effective of us all.

These two advantages that the American Trotskyist movement drew out of its own midst, particularly from the leadership which founded it, were much more considerable than might appear to the passing observer. Yet, if it were not for the ideas and leadership of Trotsky himself, which were obviously the really decisive factors in maintaining the integrity and cohesiveness of the American movement, these advantages would long before now have been cancelled out by the disadvantages that stemmed from the same source.

Cannon received his first training in the revolutionary movement as an IWWer and in the better half of it, at that. But, as the final development of the IWW underscored with such tragic finality, its great and even glorious contributions to the advancement of the revolution in this country were undermined and finally destroyed by its negative aspects. Of these, no matter how understandable they are in the light of conditions of the times, there were not few. The most disastrous in the long run was its attitude toward revolutionary theory, ranging from indifference to derision to contemptuous hostility.

French syndicalist theory was skinny enough in its best day, but it was positively robust compared to what came out of the IWW. On the battlefields of the class war, the IWW was an exemplar of brotherhood, combativity, incorruptibility and uncompromising hatred of exploitation and injustice. But theoretically and politically, the IWW was simply a desert with only occasional and seldom-used oases which were not enough to sustain its life in the ripping crises of the World War and the Bolshevik Revolution. Like many European syndicalists and anarchists, some notable Wobblies found the basic dilemma of their movement resolved by the ideas that triumphed in the Bolshevik Revolution and the Comintern and many of them remained better revolutionists than scores of incorrigible social-democratic parliamentarians who hastily jumped on the new bandwagon.

Among the Wobblies who came over to the communist movement, men like Bill Haywood and George Andreychine were better known, but Cannon was nevertheless outstanding as a party man. So were the contributions he made to a movement which, above all in this country, was cursed at the outset by a predominance of elements alien to a proletarian movement, to a socialist movement, to an internationalist movement and even to an American movement. But while he left far behind him the prejudices which most Wobblies carried as their distinguishing badge, he did not (or could not) free himself in reality from the worst of them — that corroding contempt for theory.

The communist movement was not the IWW, and no leader could live long in it who expressed the same attitude toward scientific thinking and generalization which was so popular among Wobblies (including Wobbly demagogues, of whom there was a countable number). Everyone learned to repeat Lenin's phrase "Without revolutionary theory, no revolutionary practice," and Cannon learned it and repeated it as often and as devoutly as the next man. Unfortunately, that changed very little and most of the change was on the surface.

The American communist movement did not live in an atmosphere which encouraged Marxian thought beyond the assimilation of some of the basic ideas put forward by Lenin or popularized by Zinoviev. It encouraged instead the kind of fraudulent, unprincipled factional polemics that helped to destroy it eventually.

The Trotsky movement which succeeded it was radically different in this respect. It was compelled to start and for a long time to remain almost exclusively a movement passionately and earnestly devoted to a theoretical reconsideration of many basic suppositions, theoretical re-evaluations, theoretical criticism, clarity and preciseness, as the prerequisites of revolutionary political practice.

In this field Cannon was, to put it bluntly, helpless, much more so than had been so notoriously the case with him in the Communist Party. As his equipment in this field, he had a considerable quantity of commonplaces and truisms which he accumulated from his extensive experience and sparse studies in the revolutionary movement. They were not merely valuable, but indispensable, especially in a movement whose recruits included people with little or no experience or well-assimilated knowledge of many of its basic principles.

To the untutored mind, a truism is a revelation indeed and one, more-over, that he needs more than he thinks.

But as the critical thinker – including the man of action, who has learned how greatly preliminary thought adds to the effectiveness and lasting value of his action – passes beyond the ABCs and the simple formulae for simple situations, and confronts more complex political problems, more intricate social relations and conflicts, he feels more acutely the importance and power of Marxian theory.

These are situations and problems for which "common sense" (as Marx used to call it derisively) and "sound intuition" are inadequate at best and unreliable as a rule. In the Trotskyist movement in particular, very few people could be impressed by a solemniferous repetition of Lenin's famous phrase. From their leaders they expected more than the sonorous phrase, and even more than an ability to repeat the theoretical propositions so brilliantly put forward by Trotsky. They expected their leaders to show a respect for Marxian theory that would be manifested in a knowledge of its historical development and an ability to employ that knowledge in dealing with problems of the day. Cannon had neither the knowledge nor the ability, as was known to all his old friends and critics, but above all to himself; and it did not take a new recruit many years in the movement to become painfully aware of this grave, if not fatal, defect in the leader of a Marxian revolutionary movement.

As the movement grew, so grew also the number of comrades who realized that the most prominent leader of their organization could go from year to year (to date, the record covers twenty-five unbroken years) without writing a single article on any question of Marxism, on any vital theoretical problem of the movement, historical or contemporary, on any question of international politics or even, for that matter, on any vital question of American politics.

There are some articles in which some of these questions are dealt with and disposed of by quoting or paraphrasing what Trotsky wrote; there are some agitational articles against capitalism, Stalinism, or reformism; there are many, many articles or speeches on factional fighting – and that is all. If some of it rises above the trivial, none of it bursts out of the commonplace by design.

The ideas that Cannon accumulated in the movement were not only enough but more than enough to enable him to explode the position of any defender of capitalist exploitation or politics, any apologist for Stalinism, any spokesman for class collaboration. But in any debate in the party over questions that directly involved Marxian theory and politics, his performance, where it was not banal, could only

741

create the embarrassment that it did, not only among older comrades, but, alas, among many younger ones as well.

Extremely conscious of this shortcoming, and just as sensitive to the awareness of it in others, Cannon choked off the potential for political development in literally dozens of comrades who came under his influence by instilling in them a disdainful attitude toward "theory" and "theorizers" and "intellectuals" in general. His insistence on a proletarian orientation for the movement – so incontestably right in and of itself, now as much as at the beginning – was subverted to the denigration of "theorizers" and people "abnormally" concerned with analysing political and theoretical problems.

As a result he raised up, by and large, factional adherents to a cult of pseudo-proletarian ignorance, instead of earnest revolutionists anxious to suck as much scientific knowledge and understanding as they can out of the riches available in the movement in order to make themselves increasingly free from enforced reliance upon authority. The kind of leadership that he produced in this image and the kind of education it gave to the organization is practically without precedent in the Marxian movement and, in one harsh word, is a disgrace to its traditions.

While Trotsky was alive, the vast esteem in which he was held by the movement made it possible for him to exert a counteracting influence so great that it heavily mitigated the baleful effects of Cannon's leadership. It was thanks to Trotsky's efforts that a small but precious generation of militants was trained in an understanding and respect for the achievements of socialist thought, a knowledge of its history and traditions, a realization of the innate shortcomings of that unique American brand of vulgar practicalism which, however it is explained in the light of the historical development of the country, is nevertheless the curse of the radical and labour movements.

With very few exceptions, the intimate followers of Cannon never played more than a passive role in sustaining Trotsky's efforts in this respect. Cannon himself played as good as no role at all. It is hard to believe that of the leader of the American Trotskyist movement – now the officially crowned leader of something called "orthodox Trotskyism" – but it is true.

Cannon liked to repeat again and again to his cronies and to young comrades who came under his fleeting influence that "In politics I am a Trotskyist; but in organizational questions I am a Leninist." It was his way of saying that he left all the big political and theoretical questions to Trotsky, provided he remained in control of the organization (Lenin's "organizational principles" he understood solely in the form in which they were transcribed and taught to him in the Communist Party by Zinoviev, who had infinitely more in common in this field with Stalin than with the real Lenin; and to this day Cannon does not clearly know the difference between Zinoviev and Lenin).

So it was, on the whole. Cannon never showed more than the most nominal interest in the tremendous work done in this country, by myself in particular, to select, translate, edit and publish the theoretical, polemical and political works of Trotsky.

The *New International* was founded against Cannon's opposition and maintained year in year out against his indifference. He never showed any interest in its work and development and of course practically never wrote for it. If questions of theoretical or historical importance or of wider political importance and value interest him, he has not allowed himself to be carried off by them. His concern has always been: questions of trade union tactics and manoeuvre, inner-party and factional manipulations, questions of leadership, above all the prestige and control of the leadership.

Trotsky always refused to support the complaints against Cannon that were made repeatedly by comrades who enumerated not only his theoretical and political shortcomings but his bureaucratic regime inside the organization. There is ample reason to believe that Trotsky had few illusions about Cannon on either score.

With regard to the first complaint, he used to repeat to the critical and often embittered comrades that he would not support any struggle against Cannon's leadership on such grounds. To some of them he would add, as discreetly as possible, that Cannon was not to be attacked but, within certain limits, supported. As he indicated to some of the critics, it was necessary to understand that Cannon was a product of the American labour and revolutionary movements as they have developed in their own social and historical environment; that if he had some of the shortcomings of these movements he also had their virtue; and that he would be superseded by a superior leadership not as a result of a factional fight in which opponents would win a numerical majority, but only when the advancement of the class struggle in the United States would lift the proletariat to a higher level and lift out of itself leaders who in turn stood on a higher level. These views, carefully reflected in some of his writings on the factional struggles in the American movement, were rather objective but somewhat philosophical.

With regard to the other complaint, he was less philosophical, because he had fewer illusions. He understood that Cannon was not only a product of the American working class (and in an even wider sense, of the American type of politics – that is, American bourgeois politics), but also a product of the Comintern of Zinoviev's days. This eminent and tragic figure was not only a highly successful popularizer of Lenin's ideas but also a highly successful distorter of them. He taught a whole generation of communists some of the fundamental ideas of modern Marxism whose validity remains essentially intact today. But he also mistaught and ruined most of that generation, some only in part and others completely. More than any other individual, he poisoned the Comintern's life with methods, procedures, and party conceptions that contributed heavily to the eventual triumph of Stalinism.

What Cannon learned about Lenin's conceptions of the role of the party, of the party cadre, of the party leadership, of party democracy, he learned not from Lenin but, like virtually all the Communist Party leaders of his time, from Zinoviev, that is, from the ridiculous caricature of Lenin's ideas and traditions that flowered in the disastrous days of Zinoviev's "Bolshevization" campaign.

In the American Communist Party, Cannon was one of the first and most ardent champions of that ill-begotten, ill-fated, anti-Bolshevik "Bolshevization." To this day, he acts no better; worst of all is the fact that he does not even know that better exists and that Zinoviev's campaign was a forgery and a calamity from start to finish, from purpose to consequence. Trotsky did know it, however.

In the course of the very first factional struggle which Cannon precipitated in the Trotskyist organization here, Trotsky found himself impelled to write to us that he could not fail to see in it the methods and traditions of Zinovievism. It was a gentle and restrained rebuke to Cannon, but its meaning was unequivocal.

It is doubtful if Cannon has grasped its real import to this day. In any case, his conduct in a whole series of factional struggles does not betray any awareness of it on his part. He suffers, as he always did, from that Zinovievist evil which endeavors to solve significant political differences and conflicts primarily by organizational means and preferably by ruthless splits – to say nothing of half a dozen other evils which helped to make up the name of Zinovievism in the history of the movement. In some of Cannon's own speeches can be found instance after instance of how Trotsky, aware of the Comintern school that had produced Cannon, tried as diplomatically and pedagogically as possible to induce Cannon to follow a democratic and reasonable course in a factional situation or in the organization of the internal life of the party, rather than the bureaucratic and surgical methods toward which Cannon turned almost spontaneously.

Fortunately, Trotsky was often successful, even if he was not right in every instance. However that may be, Cannon has not had to suffer from this sort of intervention for many years. The utterly bureaucratic regime that he has succeeded in establishing in his organization – up to and including the idolatrous burning of incense to The Leader in the Party press, to say nothing of party-sponsored public birthday banquets to various leaders (the mere thought of which is like a cathartic to a self-respecting socialist) – is of a piece with the utter theoretical, political and, in general, intellectual aridity which reigns there.

While Trotsky was alive, it was, after all, his ideas which prevailed and they were the ones that fertilized and fructified the movement. But even in the last political conflict inside the movement, he involuntarily gave us an adequate glimpse of his real appraisal of the Cannonite leadership. That was the conflict produced in 1939 by the war crisis. Even though our own position (that of the minority combination) was not clearly thought out or, at any rate, fully developed, we were not only on the right path but were already politically sound enough to shatter the traditional position of the Trotskyist movement which the Cannonite leadership tried to defend (namely, Russia is a degenerated workers' state and must be unconditionally defended in the war). The word "shatter" is used deliberately and without a trace of boastfulness or exaggeration.

In the debate that opened up on the "Russian question," the position of the Cannonites was so hopeless that their leader, after one or two incredible speeches, withdrew completely from participation in the discussion on that question and settled down instead to the factional task of organizing the mass expulsion of the minority and therewith the split. Trotsky's intervention in the conflict was, so far as I can recall, absolutely without parallel in the history of the international leadership of the Marxist movement.

World leaders like Marx, Engels, Lenin and Trotsky himself had intervened more than once in the disputes of this or that national section of the movement, for it was their right and duty to express their opinions and to seek to influence the outcome. But never before in such a way and on such a scale as did Trotsky in the SWP in 1939-1940.

Virtually from the first day of the fight to the day of the final break, he took over completely the conduct and direction of the fight against the minority in every respect and in every particular, from the decisive political question itself down to the most trivial detail. He brought to bear every ounce of his knowledge, his experience, his polemical talent, his esteemed authority, to gain support for his views. The official party leadership, the majority, the Cannonites, were simply relieved of all initiative, all enterprise and at bottom all responsibility in the discussion – just as if they simply did not exist. That they were not overcome with a sense of humiliation was itself a sad sign.

Every document we put out was immediately subjected to a counter-document by Trotsky, who rushed in immediately as if he feared what the party leadership would say in reply to us if left to its own resources. This went so far that Trotsky found it necessary to mail one of his documents against us directly to all the party branches throughout the country, without waiting to have it sent out in the normal way, that is, through the national office of the organization. Down to the sorriest organizational minutiae, Trotsky substituted himself completely for the leadership he supported. The Cannonites became a mimeographing machine for Trotsky's articles and letters. They had nothing whatever of their own to say in the debate except to parrot mechanically what was written in Trotsky's latest polemic, whether they understood it or not.

In no internal dispute in the Trotskyist movement had Trotsky ever before found himself impelled to go to such incredible extremes in his intervention. He always had enough confidence in the group he supported to allow it independent initiative and responsibility in a fight. In 1939, the detailed and, one might say, the desperately anxious way he intervened could only show he had no confidence at all in the ability of the Cannonites to conduct the political or even the organizational fight.

The role he took upon himself in that struggle (regardless for the moment of who was right or wrong in the issues at stake) constituted an absolutely annihilating judgment against the qualities of the Cannonites as party leaders in a serious crisis. Even worse, if that were possible, were the gratitude and glee that the Cannonite leaders displayed in having thus been released by Trotsky from the responsibilities (to say nothing of the dignity) of leadership. Cannon left the discussion to the Old Man and ourselves, and concentrated his talents upon getting rid of annoying critics by organizing the split, that is, the outcome that Trotsky was at the same time trying his best, by means of exerting pressure on both sides, to avert ("in politics I am a Trotskyist; but in organizational questions I am a Leninist").

The outcome of that conflict marks the broad dividing line in the development of the Trotskyist movement all over the world. It only emphasized the damning judgement which Trotsky's very support of the Cannonites pronounced against them. Despite the comparative weakness of our own undeveloped position; despite the power with which long tradition invested the official position; despite the long-standing prestige which Cannon enjoyed, generally speaking, in the party and above and beyond all other considerations, despite the unprecedented authority which Trotsky rightfully had throughout the movement and which he used to the full in the debate – the Cannonites skinned through at the concluding convention with a bare formal majority, that is, a slight majority of the voting party membership, but a minority if the votes of both the party and the youth organizations were counted. (Among the youth, it is significant to note, Cannon had practically no support at all, either then, before or since.) The victory was truly Pyrrhic. Actually it was a resounding repudiation of Cannon. Everyone was aware of this: if Trotsky had not intervened the way he did, or if he had not been in a position to intervene at all, the Cannonites, on their own, would have been routed and overwhelmed beyond recovery. If that was not the case, it is Trotsky and only Trotsky they have to thank. By the same token, it is Trotsky who must bear his share of the responsibility for the subsequent evolution of the movement he inspired and led.

His share, however, should not be exaggerated. Despite some external appearances to the contrary, there was a basic difference between the current in the socialist movement most brilliantly and consistently represented by Trotsky during his lifetime, and the current represented more or less consistently by the present "orthodox Trotskyists."

Of the latter, Trotsky might well say now, paraphrasing the sardonically bitter words Marx used to describe some French "orthodox Marxists" of his time, "I sowed dragon's teeth and reaped Cannonites." For the latter represent a current which, while allied with Trotskyism for some time, was essentially inimical to it and distorted its development.

In this country it can be characterized as a variety of Zinovievism, infused with scattered elements of Trotskyism and with heavy doses of the specifically American contempt for theory and equally American admiration for the concept and practice of the "party boss" or its equivalent in the labour movement, the "trade-union boss."

If this current – contrary to Trotsky's wishes and urgings – found it impossible to tolerate us Marxists in the same organization but instead expelled us en masse in a way that would evoke the admiration of any Stalinist; and if it found it impossible years later to consummate re-unification with us – that cannot be explained away as accidental. We represent indeed two different currents.

"Twenty Five Years of American Trotskyism", *New International*, January-February 1954.

Labor Action, 15 October 1945, calls for reparations to be extracted from the capitalist class, not from conquered countries

James P. Cannon as Historian

Albert Glotzer

This work will not rely in any degree upon personal recollection. The circumstance that the author was a participant in the events does not free him from the obligation to base his exposition upon strictly verified documents. The author speaks of himself, in so far as that is demanded by the course of events, in the third person. And that is not mere literary form; the subjective tone, inevitable in autobiographies or memoirs, is not permissible in a work of history. — Leon Trotsky, History of the Russian Revolution.

IN THE LIGHT OF the above what is one to say about James P. Cannon's, The *History of American Trotskyism*? It violates Trotsky's whole method of historical writing, i.e., the Marxist method. The book would be bad enough if it were presented as memoirs or autobiography. But as history it is almost worthless. Had the head of the Socialist Workers Party written his memoirs, a review of his book would have to take that into account in surveying critically a series of anecdotes which are highly personalized and subjective. One could show where they were factually or interpretatively wrong and dismiss the rest as opinions of the author and the book as the product of particular views which the author held.

Since the book is presented as a history such a conclusion is out of place. The author has a totally different responsibility for his work. As a history, Cannon's book is shallow, totally devoid of ideas, of theory and the politics which flow from it. The only politics which concern Cannon are inner-party, factional politics.

There is hardly a page in the book which does not contain a false reference, a partial fact, an incomplete tale, a conspicuous omission or direct misrepresentation. Coupled with these is a complete lack of objectivity and historical grasp.

The most important objections to the book relate to its omissions. These are of such magnitude as to condemn the author for the butchery he committed to a theme which is so rich and instructive. Cannon replaces ideas and theory with platitudes, clichés and homilies which make wearisome reading. He replaces analysis and history with disconnected but selected events in which the author plays the role of hero against opponents who are all villains.

A reading of the book will make it immediately obvious why it is impossible to review it in the ordinary sense of a book review. A whole book is required to reply to this misrepresentation of the history of Trotskyism in America. But it is necessary to indicate more precisely what is wrong with Cannon's work. And we shall do this in several ways. It is important first, however, to understand something about the author in order to understand why he wrote this kind of history.

Cannon entered the workers' movement when he was quite young. He was a member of the pre-war Socialist Party; the IWW, a founder of the Communist Party and one of its early leaders. He immediately revealed a distinctly revolutionary temper and desire. His interest and understanding of theory aside, Cannon was one of the pioneers of the revolutionary Communist movement in this country. Cannon exhibited an easy talent for leadership and a deftness at inner-party politics. This he joined with good native instinct and experience. In the infant days of the Communist movement, these qualities enabled him to rise to the top leadership of a growing party.

Cannon's knowledge of revolutionary theory and history is primitive and cursory. Of and by itself, this is fatal in one so anxious to be acknowledged as the leader of the Fourth International, the inheritor of the role of Trotsky. When it appears in combination with a deep-rooted antipathy to theoretical study, a "know-nothing" attitude toward history and politics, it is extremely dangerous. Inside the movement, it takes the form of open and covert attacks on people who are interested in theory and who realize that without proper theoretical training and understanding, it is impossible to build a revolutionary party.

Cannon covers up his attacks on theory and study with slashing indictments of "intellectualism," that paralyzing form of dilettantism which very often makes its appearance in the movement. The movement sometimes attracts intellectuals who have no solid interests in the program of the Party but who find membership in the revolutionary party a form of intellectual exercise. When Cannon attacks such elements it is, of course, impossible to disagree with him. But behind these attacks against intellectualism, he always wages a campaign against serious intellectuals capable of giving inestimable service to the movement.

Even more important than this, his attacks on "intellectualism" often cover up his attacks on ideas and theory and those who champion them inside the party. In so doing, Cannon, by his role and place in the movement, raises ignorance to a high plane and feeds the most backward prejudices against theory and theoretical pursuits. No wonder that at the 1939 convention of the Socialist Workers Party, one of Cannon's most trusted aides made a speech in which he demanded that the theoretical organ of the party, The *New International*, he abandoned because it was of no interest or value to the workers in the party and the working class in general. That this speech went unrebuked by the leader of the party is not accidental. It was widely known by many party members that Cannon had little or no interest in the theoretical press.

These characteristics of the author are not recently acquired. They were present from the days when he was a leader in the Communist movement. There too, Cannon became known as an "expert" in factional conflict, inner-party politics. The "organization question" always held a fascination for him. It was so much like politics in America in general and it offered him a field of activity to compensate for his disqualification from more important fields of revolutionary thought. In the long run, Cannon's adeptness at organization politics has always proved his undoing. He was trained in the wrong school, the Zinovievist-Stalinist school of organization.

Time alone has served to smother the fact that Cannon was one of the exponents of "Bolshevization" in the American movement — that corroding and degenerating influence on the Communist International. The "Bolshevization" of the Comintern was the means by which the whole International was bureaucratized. The parties lost their independence of thought and action; they became dominated by the ruling group in the Russian party. It was the product of Zinoviev's fertile imagination, cunningly assisted by Stalin. It later served to hasten the downfall of Zinoviev as party after party was drawn into the net of an organizational system which bureaucratically subordinated them to the Stalin regime in Russia.

Cannon became known as the "captain of Bolshevization" in this country, just as in other countries the reporters and advocates of this theory and practice were to become known. The "Bolshevization" theory merely paid lip-service to Lenin's concept of democratic centralism. The essential idea of the "Bolshevization" program was the creation of "monolithic parties," without factions and disputes — that is, without life. Bolshevism as a great theory and practice was reduced to a simple system. The young Communist parties came to learn now that Bolshevism did not mean essentially correct theory and practice, but "toughness," rigidity, inflexibility — in a word, bureaucratism.

In October, 1924, Cannon made a report to the New York Workers' School on "The Bolshevization of the Party". He was then heralding the decisions of the 5th Congress of the Comintern, sometimes called "Zinoviev's congress." Referring to the question of Bolshevization, Cannon said:

"A particularly dangerous form of confusion and irresponsibility, which we must conquer by frontal attack without delay, is the formal and even frivolous attitude which is sometimes manifested in regard to the relations of our party and our party members to the Communist International. We hear the Bolshevization of the party spoken of here and there as though it were a joke, not to be taken seriously. The very utterance of such a sentiment is in itself an evidence of theoretical weakness ... The very fact that any party members are able to regard the slogan of the Fifth Congress as a joke is a great proof of the need for this slogan in our party".

And what is this most important decision of the Fifth Congress? It relates to the Bolshevization of the party in this respect, which Cannon quotes approvingly:

"It [a Bolshevik party] must be a centralized party, prohibiting factions, tendencies and groups. It must be a monolithic party hewn of one piece".

It would, of course, be unfair to say that Cannon subscribes openly to this theory and practice today. But it remains true that he was educated in this school, became saturated with its ideas and its practices and has never fully thrown off their detrimental influence. In one form or another, the Trotskyist movement, from its founding days, has had to struggle against Cannon's bureaucratic organizational practices which resemble so strongly those of the Zinovievist-Stalinist school. It is, for example, one of the strongest factors in the present struggle now taking place in the Socialist Workers Party.

With these preliminary observations, it is easier to understand how Cannon came to write this kind of history. But one other element is missing: it is Cannon's concept of his own role in the movement and his evolution toward Trotskyism and in the Trotskyist movement. We refer to the not-so-celebrated "gestation" theory Cannon propounded during the early factional struggles in the Communist League in which he developed the theme that, since "there are no accidents in history," his emergence as a Trotskyist and as founder of the Trotskyist movement was logically necessary and inevitable. Needless to say, this theory was rejected by the Communist League in 1930, '31 and '32, but Cannon has never given it up nor his determination to dominate bureaucratically the affairs of his party.

We have no doubt that in the SWP of today, the "gestation" theory is accepted in fact as one of the great contributions to Marxism, when as a matter of fact, it is merely the theoretical justification for Cannon's leadership under any and all or circumstances.

Cannon's chapter devoted to the great historical period after the First World War, when Communist parties emerged all over the world, is shallow. Here his lack of accumulated knowledge and an inability to carry out indispensable research has resulted in a completely jammed-up picture of those days, just as every other important stage of development in the history of American Marxism is jammed-up. What is now "telescoped" in the book, and which takes many pages, is the anecdotes, the platitudes and the clichés.

Certain events in the early history are accurately portrayed and the general problem of the young Communist Party are, correctly stated. They give an inkling of deadening effect of the protracted factional struggles which paralyzed the party. But an objective analysis of the great issues of the time is missing. As in all other chapters, the theoretical and political questions are not even referred to. Obviously, Cannon never made a full estimate of the period which so heavily influenced his own thinking and practices.

He speaks of the early struggles against the right wing group of Ruthenberg and Lovestone. It was, without doubt, a progressive struggle on the whole. Until the end of 1923 this struggle was decided on the basis of the respective strengths of the Foster-Cannon faction and that Ruthenberg-Lovestone. Relations with the Communist International were then still primarily political. The struggle against Trotskyism had only begun and the transformation of the Comintern into an instrument of the Zinovievist-Stalinist bloc was still incomplete.

In 1924, however, a great change had taken place. From then on the lives of the parties in the Comintern were completely controlled by the Kremlin bureaucracy. Leaderships and policies were determined in Moscow and very often by the mere transmission of a cablegram. The American party was no exception, and one of the leaders of party expressed it accurately when he said that the party was "suspended by cables from Moscow." The Foster-Cannon leadership was itself removed by a cable at a convention where it had the support of the overwhelming majority of the delegates and the party membership. This did not end the factional struggles in the American party. They continued to be fought more sharply. But henceforth, no matter what the relationship of strength was between the factions, the leadership of the party was determined by the Kremlin. Except that where there had been two groups contending for the leadership of the party, after the transference of this leadership to Ruthenberg, there were now three.

Cannon makes note of this change in the factional line-up but he deliberately avoids the explanation of how it came to pass that the Foster-Cannon group split immediately after the Comintern decision which handed over the leadership of the CP to the right wing. He must evade this question because it conflicts with other things he writes about his role in the CP, and his theory of gestation.

How does Cannon explain his split with Foster? Well, the Foster group was made up primarily of trade unionists, people unschooled in Marxism and Bolshevik politics. The Cannon group was more a pioneer Communist group with a stronger Communist tradition. In a way, this is true. But during those stormy days Cannon justified the faction because in the party it represented the fusion of the Communist elements with native American revolutionary trade unionists. The fusion of these two basic elements which made up the Communist movement was necessary to the future development of the party.

By purely objective reasons, Cannon's explanation of the split is a mystery. He cites the difference in character between the two elements of the faction and then abruptly says that this "implicit division became a formal one." And that is all. Cannon passes on to other matters.

But the split in the Foster-Cannon group occurred over the attitude to be taken to the bureaucratic action of the Comintern (Zinoviev-Stalin bloc) in turning the leadership of the party over to the right wing and doing so in defiance of the will of the party membership and a convention of the party. For all its primitiveness and backwardness, the Foster group's reaction was healthy. It said: We will not accept the decision, but fight it.

Cannon thereupon split, not the party, but the faction. Cannon personally played the leading role in the fight to have the decision accepted. "You cannot fight the Comintern," he thundered at the Foster group. His fight was so determined that he finally broke down the resistance of the Fosterites who, in turn, gave in to the persistent pounding of one of their ex-leaders.

Is Cannon to be condemned for having played a role which, when reviewed in the light of history, was wrong, but which at that time he could not have fully understood for a number of good reasons? No. But then he owes it to the movement to tell the truth about that period now when all the facts are known not only to him but an entire new generation of revolutionaries who did not live through the old days. This marked the beginning of the great degeneration of the Comintern and the American movement. Yet Cannon, in the role of myth-creator, cannot tell the whole truth about it lest it reflect upon past, present or future glory.

The story of the CP from that point until the expulsion of the Left Opposition is hastily sketched. Some of it is accurate, other parts are suspect. The factional struggle continued unabated. The split in the Foster-Cannon group was repaired by the final establishment of a new bloc against Lovestone who had taken over the leadership of the party following Ruthenberg's death. Prior to the reestablishment of the bloc, the Cannon group had made a short-lived but intimate bloc with Lovestone, and then another with dissident elements of the Lovestone group. The great problem in the party always remained: how to get rid of the deadening leadership of the right wing. It could never be effected even with a majority because the "Comintern would not permit it."

It became clear to all the factions that the way to change the leadership and policies of the party was by courting the "proper people" in Moscow. That meant continued rivalry and mad dashes to Moscow by the leaders of contending factions. There was obviously something wrong in Moscow. All the groups felt that way. What it was, namely, the struggle against Trotskyism and the rise to power of Stalinism, none of them knew fully and some not all, neither Lovestone, Foster, nor Cannon.

By implication, Cannon would now have us believe that in those years of 1925, 1926 and 1927, he was gradually moving toward an acceptance of Trotskyism. In describing some attack of the Comintern upon him for reasons which he could not understand, Cannon writes: "They must have suspected something." What? Perhaps Cannon was reading Trotsky's writings and talking about them in the Party? Perhaps he was developing views approximating those of Trotsky? No, he cannot say these things because too many people know otherwise, knew that he was ignorant about the fight in the Russian party and cared even less. And when he adds that the Comintern: "... went far out of their way to take cracks at me ...", he is merely "suggesting" a legend.

On another page he describes how he came across the 1926 Left Opposition document on the Anglo-Russian Trade Union Unity Committee and favored its position. How? Was it publicly manifested? Did he present his views to his faction? Or, is this an afterthought which occurred in the writing of this book? No one in the party knew of this "opinion"; more important, none of his intimates in the faction was aware that Cannon had any thoughts whatever on Trotsky, the Left Opposition, or the International. As far back as in the CP Cannon's "international" interest was the subject of humor.

By 1928, however, Cannon was completely fed up in the CP. He wanted to get away, he said, to get "a bath in the mass movement." So he went on a speaking tour for the International Labor Defense. He went, he added, because he wanted to "think out ... the Russian question which troubled me more than anything else." So far as was known then, the only thing that troubled Cannon and which had anything to do with the Russian question was how to get the Russians to stop supporting Lovestone. If he had any ideas about Trotsky and the Left Opposition, they were kept completely secret from the party, from his faction and from his most intimate collaborators. But, if Cannon did go on the tour to think out the Russian question, nobody was ever informed what it was he had thought out.

As a matter of fact, the leaders of the American party and the party as a whole were completely divorced from the politics of the Kremlin. They were really political neophytes. The struggle against Trotsky was to them quite remote and never to be taken too seriously. Certainly no one then believed that Trotsky would be expelled from the Russian CP and subsequently deported from the country where he had helped to make the revolution. Nor did the American leaders understand the international ramifications of that struggle. They were completely absorbed in their own factional conflict and what troubled them was the solution to this fight rather than the struggle against Trotsky.

The struggle against Trotskyism in this country took the form of "enlightenment campaigns" initiated in Moscow and carried out by the factions in an effort to show the Comintern bosses which was the more loyal faction and worthy of Moscow's support. The individuals in the Cannon group did less than those of the other factions in these "educational" campaigns, as they were also called, but they participated too.

The real truth about Cannon's role in those days was that he had lost all heart for the struggle. He had no wish to continue it further. He even refused to go to the Sixth Congress and it was only after the most persistent urging by the faction leaders that Cannon agreed to go to Moscow. His position was that the whole business was hopeless and a waste of time. But if he had any thoughts about Trotsky before his departure to the Sixth Congress in 1928, this too was unknown to anyone in the faction.

There has been a great deal of speculation on how or why Cannon became a Trotskyist. To us, this of no fundamental importance. Whether he discovered Trotskyism in Moscow for the first time, or whether he had secret views on it before he left in no way invalidates the fact that he was the first in this country to accept the views of Trotsky and was the individual responsible for the establishment of a Trotskyist movement in America. This much is history already and for that alone, if not for his role in the CP, Cannon has earned his place in the history of the Marxist movement of America. What is objectionable, as objectionable as the speculations of those who wonder why and how he did it, is the attempt to create a legend about something which is really not mysterious, in order to strengthen a theory which is utterly false and contains dangerous implications.

We come now to the actual formation of a Trotskyist organization in America. It was necessary to deal at some length on the antecedent period in the Communist Party because those events led directly to the subsequent emergence of a Trotskyist group in this country and because they shed light on Cannon's background, his activities and his outlook. These had an important influence on the events of the future.

The most important period in the history of American Trotskyism is the worst part of Cannon's book. The period between the wave of expulsions in the CP and the formation of the Communist League of America at its May 1929 conference in Chicago is dealt with adequately for a book of this type. But the actual formation of the Communist League, which was indeed a historic day, since it marked the organization of the Trotskyists in this country, is dealt with in less than two and half pages! The conference was of enormous significance. It gathered the scattered elements throughout the country, welded them into an organization, adopted a program which was based on a Marxist estimate of the world situation, elected a National Committee, made a decision to issue a weekly *Militant* and to initiate a campaign for it. Most important of all about this gathering is that it presented the platform of Trotskyism to the American labor movement.

And of this conference, Cannon has little or nothing to say. The great ideas which inspired our small movement are hardly even referred to, or where reference is made, there is no intelligent discussion of these ideas. Those questions which Cannon does discuss briefly relate to the trade union issue, or the question of whether or not the Left Opposition should have become a party or remained a faction of the Communist Party.

The period between the conference in May 1929 and the issuance of the weekly *Militant* in November of 1929 is omitted in Cannon's book. These were "dog days" too. But it was a period when Cannon's interests and activities had flagged. It transpired that shortly after the founding conference, he had little faith in the future of the organization. At that time he wanted to retire and leave the job to the "younger elements." Only the strongest pressure of his collaborators prevented "America's No.1 Socialist" from leaving the organization in the hands of these "younger elements," and retiring to the Middle West. Thereafter, he opposed the establishment of the weekly *Militant* and expressed his opposition by taking leave completely for a period of time. He was not even present at the affair which greeted the weekly in those dog days.

Yet with the same suddenness that he departed, he reappeared. He returned to carry on a fight against the "youthful leadership" which had not heeded his counsel that the organization ought to "retrench." He organized his group of "older and maturer comrades" to fight against every bold step made by the Communist League. He won over to his side Dunne of Minneapolis and Webster {Swabeck], who were ready at one time to go ahead without Cannon, the latter even proposing that organizational measures be taken against Cannon.

Cannon was against the issuance of a youth paper; he opposed the publication of Jewish and Greek papers. All three of these were issued. He fought against Shachtman's trip to Europe to establish our first contact with Trotsky and to seek aid of the European movement for the weekly *Militant*, which he insisted should become a bi-monthly or monthly. Every step of progress made in the CLA had to be fought out against Cannon. Is it any wonder that all of these important stages in the development of the CLA find no place in Cannon's book?

Every successive period in the development of the Trotskyist movement is similarly treated. The great ideas of the movement, the great struggles of international Trotskyism are replaced by anecdotes and platitudes and by patronizing references to his "boys." For example, Cannon has no place in the book to mention the editor of the *Militant* or the real secretary of the League. But he wastes space to tell an old tale about the linotype operator! He makes no reference to the first contact made with Trotsky by Shachtman and his first tour in this country which had such a profound effect on our movement and an important influence on its followers. He says nothing about Glotzer's visit to Trotsky and his national tour in 1932 which covered Canada and the United States as far as Kansas City. But he does mention Webster's tour in 1934! Why? A slight omission? No, Webster is one of his "loyal" supporters. Webster is one of the comrades who, together with the men of Minneapolis, "always supported me, they never failed me, they held up my hands." There is the finished bureaucratic outlook!

Now you can understand more fully the absence of objectivity and history in the Cannon book. His observation of events is subjective, based solely on his participation in them, and whether his participation looks good in print. Everything else goes out. His treatment of individuals follows the same pattern. Those who are his supporters are fine comrades. Everyone else is a scoundrel.

Throughout the book there is a running attack on the successive New York organizations of the CLA, WP and SWP. The impression created is that the New York organizations were a haven for Greenwich Villagers, intellectual snobs, careerists, etc. It goes without saying that this was untrue. It is true that the Trotskyist movement attracted a number of alien elements who either had to leave the movement when they found it to be a serious revolutionary organization and not merely a stamping ground for "anti-Stalinists", or were expelled from it. But the New York movement was always the political, organizational and financial backbone of the Trotskyist movement in America.

It is true that in later years the Minneapolis organization rivaled it in numbers and financially, but by no stretch of the imagination could Minneapolis be said to be the political and organizational center of the movement. On the contrary, under Cannon's direction and his policy of sheltering it from "Eastern intellectuals and ideas," Minneapolis was always one of the most backward sections, theoretically and politically, in the party. The main reason for this was Cannon's leadership in that city.

The policy Cannon pursued there was consciously predicated on keeping Minneapolis uninformed about the great ideas and inner struggles in the movement; the aim was to prevent the "workers' branch" from becoming infested with ideas, to keep it politically backward. Instead of raising the Minneapolis movement on par with the most advanced sections of the party, Cannon actually sought to reduce the party to the political level of Minneapolis.

Cannon's repeated sneers at the New York movement are based on one fact and one fact only: The New York movement usually opposed Cannon. Cannon could not cope with the most politically advanced section of the Party and that is why he spends so much time and effort in the book in tearing it down.

It is true that the years between 1929 and 1932 were dog days, but no small reason for it was the sharp internal struggle waged by Cannon against the aggressive policy pursued by the CLA in opposition to his conservative program of "retrenchment." His only explanation of how our small band issued the weekly *Militant* is that "somehow the paper came out." But there was more than "somehow" to it. The paper came out because of the great sacrifices of all the members of the organization and those who directed the work of the League in those days.

One could write at great length on every chapter of the book to show how Cannon has not represented the history of the Trotskyist movement. Page after page can be read without finding out, for example, where the Trotskyist movement stood on a series of world-shaking problems. There is not even a single statement of what Trotskyism stands for, what its main ideas are. All we get from Cannon is that "Trotskyism means business." This is, of course, hardly an enlightening description of the theory and politics of Trotsky; it is "revolutionary" rotarianism.

Just as the early history of the CLA is represented as a great struggle between Cannon and men who wear corduroy trousers, who talk a great deal, and argue even more, the later history of Trotskyism in this country, represented by the turn in policy with the coming of Hitler to power, the fusion with the AWP, the entry into the SP is also personalized. Always it is Cannon versus villains.

The struggle over entry in the Socialist Party was an extremely important struggle. For my own part, it is difficult to determine who was right or wrong. It is obvious too, that one cannot argue at this day: would we have gained more by entry or by the independent road. Entry for this writer was not then, nor is it today, a principled question, but rather a tactical one. But we find in Cannon's book a new reason to justify the entry, a reason obviously developed as an afterthought. Following a gratuitous admission that perhaps a number of errors (opportunist) were committed in the Socialist Party, Cannon makes the utterly monstrous statement that:

It was required of us historically, at that crucial moment, to be members of the Socialist Party and by that to have closer access to elements — liberals, intellectuals and half-practical people — who were necessary for the great political task of the Trotsky Defense Committee.

This is, of course, a political libel against Trotsky who opposed many of the policies pursued inside the SP which he thought might be developed on the grounds of expediency relating to his case. So far as was known in the Party, the Trotsky case had nothing whatever to do with the entry!

We have said that the book lacks theory, politics and ideas in general. This criticism is validated by Cannon himself. Let in take a few examples, from the many which fill his history.

On page 81, the great man writes: "It is just as impossible to bluff in the political movement as in war." Why Cannon's own book is a refutation of this platitude. And politics and war are filled with bluffs, a countless number of them. But it sounds good to Cannon to write this. Makes a great impression on young people who are in the process of being miseducated by the kind of training given them by Cannon.

In reference to the hotel strike in New York and the role of the CLA Cannon writes: "That is one of the characteristics of Trotskyism. Trotskyism has never done anything half-way. Trotskyism acts according to the old motto: Whatever is worth doing at all is worth doing well." Never does anything half-way! Whatever is worth doing at all is worth doing well!

On page 146 we learn again: "These Trotskyists mean business. When they undertake anything, they go through with it."

Again on page 179: "Trotskyists mean business."

And on page 198: "They always do things right in Minneapolis." Always!

This is Trotskyism, according to the history written by Cannon, whom George Collins in the *Fourth International* described "as the historian of a movement that has swept the field of revolutionary politics of all rivals [!], it is a tribute the viability of his teachings and their adoption and application in life by the group itself."

One member of the Cannon party said of the history "There was never a history like this!" We heartily concur. We cannot recall another like it.

New International, October 1945

1939: Trotsky and his critics

Max Shachtman (1962)

WHAT DISTINGUISHED TROTSKY from all other opponents of the Stalinist regime was his theory that it represented a bureaucratically-degenerated workers' state.

Why was it still a workers' state, even after the Opposition, representing the revolutionary proletariat, had in the late 1920s been driven out of the ruling party and into prison and exile, even after the consolidation of an exclusive bureaucratic monopoly in the party and state? Because, first, there was still the possibility of defeating the bureaucracy by means of a vigorous but peaceful reform of the party. And, second, the principal means of production were still nationalised, in the hands of the state, and not yet converted into private capitalist property. While the bureaucracy had betrayed the principles of the revolution, it had not yet surrendered this vital material achievement – nationalised property – to bourgeois counter-revolution. The latter was moving rapidly forward under the regime of the bureaucracy, but it had not yet triumphed. In no circumstances should it be allowed to triumph. Therefore, whenever and wherever there was an attack by bourgeois forces on the Stalinist regime, which for all its degeneration remained a workers' state, it was the duty of the Trotskyists and workers throughout the world to stand up for the unconditional defence of the Soviet Union.

In sum: the Stalinist bureaucracy was paving the way for a counter-revolution in Russia. A timely victory of the Opposition would restore the state to Soviet democracy and internationalism. The vacillating, parasitic bureaucracy was not a serious alternative. The alternative was the victory of the counter-revolution. Its social content was bound to be the restoration of private property following the destruction of nationalised property. Proletariat and bourgeoisie were the only two basic and decisive classes. The issue would be joined and determined in open conflict between them; and that conflict was imminent. Up to that moment, even the degenerated Stalinist state must be defended against bourgeois attack...

Banished from the territory of the Soviet Union by police decree at the end of 1928, Trotsky only intensified his war upon the Stalinists upon the basis of this doctrine, analysis and programme. He was now able for the first time to assemble and lead an international communist Opposition based entirely on his theory. But he soon found that he had to defend his theory almost as often and as vehemently from his partisans as from his enemies. From the time of his banishment until his tragic death, there was hardly a year in the existence of the Trotskyist movement abroad or of its counterpart inside Russia (so long as it retained any sort of coherent and articulate form) that did not see a crisis that rent its ranks in disputes over Trotsky's views of the "Russian question". There was hardly a year of his last exile when Trotsky did not find himself obliged, by new developments or by reconsideration, to modify his theory, sometimes drastically, while trying to preserve its essentials. The last year of his life saw another crisis, occurring at the outbreak of the world war. His position on Russia was again challenged by his followers. In this last controversy he allowed for an amendment to his conceptions so far-reaching in its implications as to shatter the very basis of his theory, in particular the theory of his opposition to Stalinism.

Even before Trotsky was banished to Turkey, the process of disintegration of the Russian Opposition had begun and it continued at an accelerated pace. The Democratic Centralists – residue of a faction in the controversies of the early 1920s which had joined with Trotsky and Zinoviev in the United Opposition Bloc of 1926 – were the first to part with their allies. Led by old Bolshevik militants like Sapronov and Vladimir Smirnov, they took the view that the Thermidorian reaction – the counter-revolution – had already triumphed in Russia and that the workers' state was at an end. Relatively, this was a minor loss; graver ones soon followed.

In the middle of 1928, with all the Oppositionists already expelled, it became evident that a new struggle was developing among the anti-Trotskyist leaders, precipitated by a crisis in grain collections. Now the fight was between Stalin's followers and those led by Bukharin, Rykov and Tomsky. It was the prelude to what was to be called the "Great Change" or "Russia's Second Revolution" – the programme of massive industrialisation and forced collectivisation which was to be the decisive feature of Russia's development for the next three decades.

Trotsky, then in Asian exile, treated Stalin's turn with the greatest scepticism and reserve. Indeed, he sounded the alarm against the impending counter-revolution more vigorously than ever. Stalin, he wrote repeatedly in those days and for a long time afterwards, had not adopted and could not adopt a Left course but only a "Left zig-zag". He represented only the bureaucratic apparatus vacillating under the pressure of real and effective classes. Tomorrow, the "Right tail" would come crashing down on his head, because it represented the powerful restorationist and proprietor classes; and to them Stalin would capitulate. In a famous 1928 article, which was one of the pretexts for his expulsion from Russia, Trotsky insisted that the country was facing a "dual power" situation, as it did in 1917 just before the Bolshevik victory, when Kerensky represented the state power of the bourgeoisie and the Soviets were the incipient socialist power. Only, this time, the "film of October is unwinding in reverse" – that is, it was not the bourgeois element of the dual power that was about to be overturned by the socialist element, but exactly the other way around. Voroshilov was even mentioned as the possible "man on horseback" – a counter-revolutionary Bonaparte.

As late as April 1931, even though the Right wing had already been crushed by Stalin, Trotsky still spoke of the "dual power" in Russia and declared that the further degeneration of the party machine – Stalin's faction – "undoubtedly increases the chances of the Bonapartist form" of the overturn of the Soviet state, that is, "the form of the naked sabre which is raised in the name of bourgeois property". (To my knowledge, he never again referred to the "dual power" in Stalinist Russia, or to the outcome of the contest between the two classes it was said to represent.)

This analysis was entirely in keeping with Trotsky's idea of expected developments, but it was almost equally out of keeping with the political and social reality. It could not and did not serve to retard the decline of the Opposition, upon which the Stalinist apparatus was in any case exerting an almost unbearable pressure. As it became clear that Stalin's course was not a "zig-zag" but a sustained and resolute line, that the Bukharin faction was irretrievably defeated; that the propertied, semi-propertied and potentially-propertied people in the country were being economically (and even physically) annihilated, that a restorationist bourgeoisie was not within miles of a struggle for power (then or later) – the Zinovievist and then the Trotskyist Opposition collapsed. First, Zinoviev, Kamenev and their friends capitulated to the regime. Then, of the Trotskyists, came the capitulation of Radek, Preobrazhensky and Smilga. Then (this was an especially hard personal blow to Trotsky) Rakovsky; then, dozens upon dozens and finally hundreds of others. A tiny, dwindling minority remained steadfast, and none of these survived the blood purges of the Moscow Trials period – nor indeed did the capitulators.

In virtually every case – if we set aside exhaustion, apparatus pressure and the like – the political reason given was at bottom the same: the perspective of a rising bourgeois counter-revolution had proved to be false. If anything, Stalin was smashing the economic and political foundations of the bourgeois elements more ruthlessly than the

Opposition had ever proposed to do. And his economic policy was not a momentary tactic but a durable line by which he was expanding and consolidating the basis of socialism. In this they had to work along with him.

This reasoning was not without its defects. It is true that even the soundest theoretical and political arguments would have been of little avail in holding together the Opposition in the extraordinary circumstances. It is true, too, that Trotsky's analysis, criticism and predictions about the Stalinist course in a dozen vital fields of domestic and foreign policy were matchless and were confirmed by events.

But in the basic theory that the bourgeois counter-revolution and the restoration of capitalism were on the order of the day in Russia, that the destruction of the economic and political power of the workers under Stalin was bound to bring about this counter-revolution and this one alone, that the Stalinist bureaucracy could not effectively resist it but would only manure the soil from which it would surely arise – this theory found no confirmation at all.

Yet Trotsky reiterated the analysis and forecast in a dozen different ways in all his writings during the critical decade of the 1930s, emphatically and without reservation. From a mind so luminous and penetrating, it is almost incomprehensible, unless we remember that it was a fixed point in Trotsky's doctrine: a workers' state can be destroyed and replaced only by a bourgeois state based on private property.

Outside Russia, the Trotskyist movement enjoyed far greater continuity and coherence, if only because it was free of the ruthless police pressures of the Kremlin. Trotsky never had to cope among his foreign supporters with the problem of capitulation to Stalinism or conciliation. Except for a few trivial individual cases, no such tendencies manifested themselves. But he was not free from the necessity of defending his views continually from doubts and challenges in his own ranks. It may be said that even those who accepted his theory, including the changes he introduced into it from time to time, did not always agree with the passionate enthusiasm and conviction they shared for his trenchant attacks upon the Stalinist regime and its policies. But Trotsky's prestige and authority in his movement were probably unequalled by the leader of any other branch of the radical movement. For most of his followers this sufficed to turn the balance against doubt, but not for all.

Barely settled in his Turkish exile, Trotsky was forced into a sharp struggle with a large part, if not the majority, of his adherents in Europe. In the Russo-Chinese conflict of 1929 over the Chinese Eastern

Railway, in which Moscow held important rights inherited from Tsarist times, a military clash appeared possible. This raised the question, among the Trotskyists, of the validity of the policy of "unconditional defence of the Soviet Union in wartime". Many of them held that Moscow was displaying an imperialist attitude towards China and that revolutionists should not support it. Trotsky attacked them furiously. Russia was to be defended in spite of Stalin because it was still a workers' state. The ensuing debate ended in the first big split in the Trotskyist movement. Most of the Germans followed their chief, Hugo Urbahns, in separating from Trotsky. In France, most of the communist-syndicalists, around Fernand Loriot and Pierre Monatte, founders of the French Communist Party and partisans of Trotsky as early as 1924, broke with him in the dispute. So did many who were in the Trotskyist group led by Maurice and Madeleine Paz. The split extended to Belgium, where Trotsky lost the allegiance of the group around Van Overstraeten, the former head of the Communist Party and then of the Trotskyist opposition.

This split was a stiff blow. But under Trotsky's tireless hammering, the oppositional groups in Europe and the Americas, though they never became a political force, were reunited around his views. The union did not endure. It was breached, at first in a minor way, during the period of the Moscow Trials and the Spanish Civil War. Up to that time, Trotsky had defended his theory that Russia was still a workers' state on the grounds that the workers retained the possibility of turning the political helm in Russia and bringing the bureaucracy under their control, without resorting to a revolution, by means of an internal reform of the ruling party. By 1936 he could no longer maintain this view, and abandoned it.

The bureaucracy had now, he argued, attained total political power. Indeed, in its political rule, it did not differ from the fascist bureaucracy in Germany. In fundamental distinction from the latter, however, it rested upon different social foundations, defined as nationalised property, which the Stalinist bureaucracy preserved "in its own way", just as the Nazi bureaucracy preserved private property in its way. The Russian workers had been completely expropriated of all political rights and power. Because the "way" in which the bureaucracy defended nationalised property was such as to bring closer the return of capitalism, the bureaucracy had to be removed from political dominance, which had reached such a totalitarian level that it could not be corrected by peaceful reforms. The bureaucracy could be overturned only by a revolution; but this revolution would not be a social revolution as it would not alter the prevailing property forms.

It would be a "political revolution".

It is hardly necessary to dwell on the dimensions of the hole this thesis created in the wall of Trotsky's basic theory. Here it must suffice to refer to two reactions in the ranks of the Trotskyists. The vast majority in Europe and America accepted it out of hand, so to speak, with little reflection on its significance. Few recalled that only a little earlier Trotsky, both in exposition and in polemic, had insisted that Stalinist Russia was a workers' state precisely because, while the bourgeoisie needed a revolution against the regime in its interests, the working class could realise its interests by means of peaceful reform.

The other reaction was shown by those Trotskyists, a very small and ineffectual minority, who rejected Trotsky's thesis. One of them was the young Frenchman Yvan Craipeau. In Russia, he wrote, the loss of all political power by the working class meant that it no longer ruled in any social sense, that Russia was no longer a workers' state, and that the bureaucracy had become a new exploiting and ruling class. Furthermore, this new class, by its military alliance with French imperialism (in the form of the Stalin–Laval Pact), and by its role in the Spanish Civil War (where the Stalinists opposed all steps towards a socialist revolution and proclaimed themselves defenders of private property), ruled out, for revolutionists, the policy of defence of Stalinist Russia in a war.

The other was an American Trotskyist leader, James Burnham, a somewhat unorthodox Marxist who was later to become more widely known in a different capacity. Leaning heavily on Trotsky's contention that the Russian working class had lost all trace of political power, Burnham argued that, though Russia was no longer a workers' state, it was not yet a bourgeois state. The bureaucracy was playing a reactionary role because it had "definitely entered the road of the destruction of the planned and nationalised economy". It expressed only the interests of those social groups that were "now in the process of transformation of a new bourgeois ruling class". However, since nationalised property still existed, the defence of Russia in war was the "imperative and inescapable duty" of the proletariat. This was in 1937. It did not even foreshadow the altogether different position Burnham was to take later. Trotsky's response was moderate, for clearly Burnham did not differ too widely from his own view.

One element in Trotsky's reply is worth recalling, however, for the special light it throws on a later development. Although in a certain sense Hitler and Stalin both served the bourgeoisie, "between the functions of Stalin and Hitler there is a difference. Hitler defends the bourgeois forms of property. Stalin adapts the interests of the bureau-cracy to the proletarian forms of property. The same Stalin in Spain, that is, on the soil of a bourgeois regime, executes the function of Hitler." It was thus shown again, concluded Trotsky, that the bureau-cracy was not an independent class "but the tool of classes" – a tool (a bad one) of the workers in Russia where state property prevailed, and a tool of the bourgeoisie outside Russia where private property existed.

The 1937 dispute was allowed to lapse. Neither Craipeau nor Burnham pressed his views further, and Trotsky seemed content to let it go at that. The new doctrine of the political revolution became official, and in 1938 Trotsky added an amendment that the revolution which was to restore the democracy of the Soviets would exclude the bureaucracy from participating in them.

Two years later the war broke out, and the conflict over the "Russ-ian question" flared up more intensely than ever before. It proved to be the most bitter and most wracking of the internecine struggles of the Trotskyist movement, and the last one in which Trotsky was able to participate.

The theory of "unconditional defence" of the "workers' state" was given its crucial – indeed, its only concrete – political test with the fir-ing of the first gun. The armies of Hitler and Stalin joined forces to conquer and subject Eastern Europe and to divide the spoils of vic-tory. The annexation of the Baltic lands and parts of Poland and Fin-land was undoubtedly required for the defence of Stalinist Russia in much the same way as the subjugation of Korea and Manchuria were required by Imperial Japan. But what had such a course in common with socialist politics, asked a minority of the American Trotskyist leadership. Their answer to this question was: Nothing! Russia was now an integral part of an imperialist war, allied with a reactionary imperialist power, and pursuing with its ally an imperialist policy of conquest and oppression. Russia's invasion of Poland and Finland must be condemned, and the slogan of defence of Russia discarded. They did not advocate support of the Western coalition, which they characterised similarly as imperialist. The break with Trotsky's tra-ditional policy was unmistakable and portentous.

The minority leaders included Martin Abern and Max Shachtman, two of the founders of American communism, and two of the three communist leaders who launched the Trotskyist movement in the United States in 1928. Shachtman founded the theoretical journal of the American Trotskyists and edited Trotsky's works in English. The third, James Burnham, although a later adherent to Trotskyism, was widely respected in its ranks. The three could not easily be dismissed as casual figures. The American organisation was by far the most stable, steadfast and important branch of the international Trotskyist movement, and Trotsky could not let it depart from his position by default or negligible interventions. From Mexico, he plunged into the debate.

Although differing on the sociological question, the "class character of the Russian state" (Abern believed that it was still a degenerated workers' state, Burnham had abandoned that view in 1937, and Shachtman was uncertain), which they agreed not to debate, the three were at one about the political question ("unconditional defence"). It was perfectly obvious that analysis of the theoretical question was in itself far from being decisive in determining policy towards the war.

Trotsky ignored the fact that it had only recently been just as obvious to him, and after starting out with a relatively mild article against the view of the minority, he launched a large-scale attack upon it. Drawing on his exceptional intellectual resources, which the minority could not match, and using his unrivalled gift for irony, he blanketed his opponents under a mounting drumfire of polemic. They stood firmly by their position even though Trotsky exploited its every weakness and gap, reassured by their conviction that he had not answered what was sound and rational in their rejection of "defencism".

A few weeks later, Trotsky expanded the range of his assault. He confronted the minority with questions ranging from the class nature of Russia to the logic of Aristotle and Hegel; from dialectical materialism down to the most trivial of internal organisational matters. He called into question the revolutionary probity of the minority leaders, their personal characteristics, and their records in the movement. They were denounced as a "petty-bourgeois opposition" suffering from "gangrene". The political question, the only one posed by the minority, was all but lost in this universalised turbulence.

With this kind of intervention from Trotsky, his supporters retained control of the American organisation at the end of the dispute, but only by a narrow margin; the minority won the decisive majority of the young Trotskyists and almost half of the party membership as well. After the 1940 convention, the minority were expelled en bloc without trial, and the split was irrevocable. Abern, Shachtman and their friends continued in a new organisation; Burnham, deeply shaken and repelled by the fight Trotsky had conducted, quit the movement entirely with a disavowal of Marxism in general, and soon moved to the position presented a year later in his *The Managerial Revolution*.

Trotsky's victory was as complete as it was dubious. From the vigour and intensity of his participation in the dispute, nobody could have imagined that he was at the same time in such despair about his personal condition that he was seriously contemplating taking his own life. Of this melancholy prospect there was not the slightest sign in his polemical writings.

Yet, oddly enough, it was neither the direct targets of these writings – his party opposition – nor the arguments levelled against them that were the most important aspect of the development of Trotsky's theory in this last period of his life. From this standpoint, the fight against his own opposition was of decidedly secondary, at most of auxiliary significance. Primary importance belongs instead to Trotsky's critical observations on a theory put forward by a non-participant in the dispute. This was a former Italian communist and ex-Trotskyist who, on the eve of the war, published a book in French, *La Bureaucratisation du Monde*, under the name of Bruno R – Bruno Rizzi.

Rizzi rejected Trotsky's theory of the "degenerated workers' state and held that a new revolution was taking place throughout the world. It had brought, or was bringing, to power a new ruling class in a new social order, "bureaucratic collectivism". It was neither capitalist nor socialist in any significant sense. The working class is reduced to totalitarian slavery, exploited collectively by the new bureaucracy. The Stalinist bureaucracy in Russia and the fascist bureaucracy are equally representative of the supremacy of this new class and new social order. So too is the New Deal of Roosevelt, even if in a not yet equally advanced form. Thus, Rizzi. Thus also a little later *The Managerial Revolution*, in which Burnham adopted Rizzi's thesis virtually in toto and with the addition of some extravagant predictions.

Up to the appearance of Rizzi's work, Trotsky defended his theory from those critics in or around his movement (except in the case of Craipeau) who held that the Russian state stood above the contending classes, or that it had become a bourgeois state, usually called "state capitalism". Hugo Urbahns, for example, put this label upon Stalinist Russia as well as upon fascist Italy and Germany. In Marxian terms and in terms of social realities this label was an absurdity. Trotsky had little difficulty in ridiculing and riddling this point of view, and more generally, in rejecting the identification of the Stalinist and Hitlerian social regimes despite the similarities of their political rule.

Rudolph Hilferding, the eminent Austro-German socialist theoretician and economist, who in 1940 linked fascism and Stalinism in the same social category of "totalitarian state economies", likewise gave short shrift to the theory of "state capitalism".

A social order in which there is no capitalist class, no capitalist private property, no capitalist profit, no production of commodities for the market, no working class more or less free to sell its labour power on the open market – can be described as capitalist, no matter how modified by adjectives, only by arbitrary and meaningless definition. In any case, there was no capitalist anywhere in the world who would accept such a definition.

In Rizzi's case Trotsky had a different problem. He did not hesitate to acknowledge the merits of Rizzi's work, or to criticise what he called its mistakes. But in acknowledgment and criticism he managed to subvert the foundations of his own theory:

Bruno R in any case has the merit of seeking to transfer the question from the charmed circle of terminological copybook exercises to the plane of major historical generalisations. This makes it all the easier to disclose his mistake [he wrote on 25 September 1939]. *Bruno R has caught on to the fact that the tendencies of collectivisation* [operating in all modern economy, in Russia, Germany or the United States] *assume, as a result of the political prostration of the working class, the form of "bureaucratic collectivism". The phenomenon in itself is incontestable. But where are the limits, and what is its historical weight?*

The answers given by Trotsky to these questions were little less than startling in view of the tenacity with which he had till then clung to his own theory of Stalinism and the arguments he had mustered in support of it. Three weeks later (18 October 1939), he wrote:

Some comrades evidently were surprised that I spoke in my article (The USSR in the War) of the system of "bureaucratic collectivism" as a theoretical possibility. They discovered in this even a complete revision of Marxism. This is an apparent misunderstanding. The Marxist comprehension of historical necessity has nothing in common with fatalism. Socialism is not realisable "by itself", but as a result of the struggle of living forces, classes and their parties. The proletariat's decisive advantage in this struggle resides in the fact that it represents historical progress, while the bourgeoisie incarnates reaction and decline. Precisely in this is the source of our conviction in victory. But we have full right to ask ourselves: what character will society take if the forces of reaction conquer?

Marxists have formulated an incalculable number of times the alternative: either socialism or return to barbarism. After the Italian "experience" we repeated thousands of times: either communism or fascism. The real pas-

sage to socialism cannot fail to appear incomparably more complicated, more heterogeneous, more contradictory than was foreseen in the general historical scheme. Marx spoke about the dictatorship of the proletariat and its future withering away but said nothing about bureaucratic degeneration of the dictatorship. We have observed and analysed for the first time in experience such a degeneration. Is this revision of Marxism? The march of events has succeeded in demonstrating that the delay of the socialist revolution engenders the indubitable phenomena of barbarism – chronic unemployment, pauperisation of the petty bourgeoisie, fascism, finally wars of extermination which do not open up any new road. What social and political forms can the new "barbarism" take, if we admit theoretically that mankind should not be able to elevate itself to socialism? We have the possibility of expressing ourselves on this subject more concretely than Marx. Fascism on one hand, degeneration of the Soviet state on the other, outline the social and political forms of neo-barbarism. An alternative of this kind – socialism or totalitarian servitude – has not only theoretical interest, but also enormous importance in agitation, because in its light the necessity for socialist revolution appears most graphically.

What "some comrades evidently were surprised" at, and not without cause, was the view Trotsky had set down in his article of 25 September 1939. It is worth citing:

Might we not place ourselves in a ludicrous position if we affixed to the Bonapartist oligarchy [the Stalinist regime] *the nomenclature of a new ruling class just a few years or even a few months prior to its inglorious downfall?...*

The second imperialist war poses the unsolved task on a higher historical stage. It tests anew not only the stability of the existing regimes but also the ability of the proletariat to replace them. The results of this test will automatically have a decisive significance for our appraisal of the modern epoch as the epoch of proletarian revolution. If contrary to all probabilities the October Revolution fails during the course of the present war, or immediately thereafter, to find its continuation in any of the advanced countries; and if, on the contrary, the proletariat is thrown back everywhere and on all fronts – then we shall have to pose the question of revising our conception of the present epoch and its driving forces. In that case it would be a question not of slapping a copybook label on the USSR or the Stalinist gang but of re-evaluating the world historical perspective for the next decades if not centuries: have we entered the epoch of social revolution and socialist society, or on the contrary the epoch of the declining society of totalitarian bureaucracy?

The twofold error of schematicists like Hugo Urbahns and Bruno R consists, first, in that they proclaim this latter regime as having been already finally installed; second, in that they declare it a prolonged transitional state of society between capitalism and socialism. Yet it is absolutely self-evident that if the international proletariat, as a result of the experience of our entire epoch and the current war, proves incapable of becoming the master of society, this would signify the foundering of all hope for a socialist revolution, for it is impossible to expect any more favourable conditions for it; in any case no one foresees them now, or is able to characterise them.

With these pronouncements, Trotsky turned a corner in his thinking so abruptly as to bring him into violent collision with the main pillars of the theory of Stalinism he had long and stoutly upheld.

The doctrine that Russia was still a workers' state because the bourgeoisie had not yet become the ruling class, was essentially exploded. It is possible for Russia (or other countries) to be ruled by a new exploiting class which is neither proletarian nor bourgeois. The doctrine that the maintenance of nationalised property proved that the Stalinist regime was a workers' state, however degenerated, was similarly exploded. It is possible for nationalised property to be the economic foundation for the rule of a new class. The conception of a new ruling class commanding a society which is neither capitalist nor socialist (a conception not long before derided by Trotsky) was not a revision of Marxism at all. "Marxists have formulated an incalculable number of times the alternative: either socialism or return to barbarism." And this conception does not of itself mean the end of socialism or the fight for it. "An alternative of this kind... has... enormous importance in agitation, because in its light the necessity for socialist revolution appears most graphically." It is true, to be sure, that Trotsky endeavoured at the same time to reaffirm his old theory. It was no longer so easy. Having insisted that Russia remained a workers' state because the rule of the bourgeoisie had not been restored and nationalised property still prevailed, he now conceded that the workers' state could be utterly destroyed even if the bourgeoisie did not come to power and even if property remained nationalised.

The Russian state, he argued, remained proletarian because the Stalinist bureaucracy had no prospect of retaining control of it ("its inglorious downfall" might be a matter of "a few years or even a few months", he said in 1939, almost a quarter of a century ago), whereas Trotskyists had the perspective that in all probability the October Revolution would "find its continuation" in advanced countries "during the course of the present war, or immediately thereafter".

To determine the nature of a social order by appraising the prospects for political success of its upholders and its opponents, is extraordinary procedure for a Marxist. The two are closely related, but in exactly reverse order. The nature of cancer is not established by the success of medical science in finding the cure for it or the speed with which it is found. The nature of the atomic bomb is not determined by the use to which it is put, by the appalling consequences of its use, or by society's success in controlling or destroying it. Marx determined the class nature of capitalism by an analysis of its social anatomy, starting with the commodity. The validity (or invalidity) of this analysis is not to be determined by the conclusions he drew from it about the prospects for a socialist revolution in the Europe of 1848 or later.

By reducing the question of the nature of the Stalinist state to a matter of the prospects for success of the bureaucracy and of the socialist revolution in the period he indicated, Trotsky effectively abandoned the essential elements of the theory of the "degenerated workers' state".

The course of the war undermined another of Trotsky's doctrines and drove him to another radical revision. Before the war, he had unremittingly attacked Stalinism for its theory of "socialism in one country". This theory was, to him, the central axis of the bureaucracy's thought, from which it derived, or with which were inseparably connected, all its errors, crimes and betrayals of the revolution. If, on Russian soil, it might still play a positive role in so far as it maintained or defended state property, abroad it played an unequivocally reactionary role in that it defended capitalist private property. In Spain, as has already been noted, "that is, on the soil of a bourgeois regime", Stalin "executes the function of Hitler", wrote Trotsky only two years before the war.

In the first months of the war, it should have been clear, this analysis of Stalinism proved completely indefensible. And it was clear enough to Trotsky to end any attempt to defend it. "On the soil of a bourgeois regime" – that is, the part of Poland which was occupied by the Russian army at the start of the war – Stalin did not "execute the function of Hitler" within the meaning of Trotsky's phrase. Instead, he destroyed the power of bourgeois and landowner, abolished private property, and set up the same economic-political-social regime as the Russian. It was an inconvenient turn of events. Given the theory he would not disavow, Trotsky had no choice but to acknowledge that Stalin's course in Poland (as later in the Baltic lands) was "revolutionary in character... 'the expropriation of the expropriators'"... that "the statification of property in the occupied territories is in itself a progressive measure". This acknowledgment placed Trotsky squarely in the centre of a dilemma from which he was not allowed the time to extricate himself. A few weeks after acknowledging the basic social changes introduced in Poland by Stalin, Trotsky introduced a new modification of his theory. "Some voices cry out: If we continue to recognise the USSR as a workers' state, we will have to establish a new category: the counter-revolutionary workers' state." Well, why not?, he continued in an article on 18 October. The trade unions of France and Britain and the United States were counter-revolutionary since "they support completely the counter-revolutionary politics of their bourgeoisie... Why is it impossible to employ the same method with the counter-revolutionary workers' state?"

The "new category" did not alleviate his position. The term "counter-revolutionary" had been applied to the reformist unions in the West precisely because they "defended private property" and refused to "expropriate the expropriators". The "counter-revolutionary workers' state", however, was now acting in Poland in an exactly and fundamentally opposite sense by carrying out measures that were "revolutionary in character – 'the expropriation of the expropriators'." The dimensions of this "revolutionary expropriation" could not be known to Trotsky. Only after his death were they extended far beyond Poland, nowhere under the auspices of the proletariat, everywhere under the aegis, direction and control of the "counter-revolutionary workers' state".

Yet he saw enough in 1939, and wrote enough, to indicate that his central indictment of Stalinism for its theory of "socialism in one country" was no longer relevant. The bureaucracy was showing that while it remained "counter-revolutionary", it could and would carry out a fundamental revolution against the bourgeoisie abroad, but without the working class and against the workers; indeed, in Trotsky's own words, in order to convert them into its own semi-slaves.

The counter-revolutionary proletarian revolution against the bourgeoisie and the working class was a concept which not even the much-burdened dialectic could sustain. It was too much for the back of a theory which held that a regime under which workers and peasants enjoyed not a shred of economic or political power but were pitilessly exploited, was nevertheless a workers' state because it was not a bourgeois state.

The unique nature of Stalinist society, of its ruling class and of its social relations, and its true international significance both for capitalist society and for socialism – on these crucial problems of our time Trotsky found and offered promising clues to an understanding in the last polemical fight of his life. The assassin's axe soon ended all chance of his pursuing the clues to their end.

Survey, no. 41, April 1962

The Buchenwald Manifesto

The proletariat can fulfill its historic task only under the leadership of a new world revolutionary party. The creation of this party is the most pressing task of the most advanced sections of the working class. International revolutionary cadres have already come together to construct this world party in the struggle against capitalism and its reformist and Stalinist agents. In order to carry out this difficult task there must be no avoiding the issue through the more conciliatory slogan of a new 2-1/2 International. Such an intermediary formation would prevent the necessary ideological clarification and would sap revolutionary will. In the imminent pre-revolutionary period what is necessary is to mobilize the working masses in the struggle against the bourgeoisie and to prepare the construction of a new revolutionary International that will forge the unity of the working class in revolutionary action.

All theories and illusions about a "people's state" or a "people's democracy" have led the working class to the bloodiest defeats in the course of class struggle in capitalist society. Only irreconcilable struggle against the capitalist state—up to and including its destruction and the construction of the state of workers and peasants councils—can prevent similar new defeats. The bourgeoisie and the uprooted petty bourgeoisie brought fascism to power. Fascism is the creation of capitalism. Only the successful, independent action of the working class against capitalism is capable of eradicating the evil of fascism, along with its root causes. In this struggle the hesitant petty bourgeoisie will join forces with the revolutionary proletariat on the offensive, as the history of the great revolutions demonstrates.

In order to emerge victorious from the class battles to come the German working class must struggle for the implementation of the following demands:

—Freedom of organization, assembly and the press! Freedom of collective action and the immediate restoration of all the pre-1933 social gains!

—Total elimination of all the fascist organizations!

—Confiscation of their property for the benefit of the victims of fascism!

—Conviction of all representatives of the fascist state by freely elected peoples courts!

—Dissolution of the Wehrmacht and its replacement by workers militias!

—Immediate free election of workers' and peasants' councils throughout all of Germany and a convocation of a general congress of these councils!

—Preservation and extension of these councils, while utilizing all the parliamentary institutions of the bourgeoisie for revolutionary propaganda!

—Expropriation of the banks, heavy industry and the large estates!

—Control of production by the unions and the workers councils!

—Not one man, not one penny for the war debts and the war reparations of the bourgeoisie! The bourgeoisie must pay!

—For pan-German socialist revolution! Against a dismemberment of Germany!

—Revolutionary fraternization with the proletarians of the occupying armies!

—For a Germany of workers' councils in a Europe of workers' councils!

—For world proletarian revolution!

The Internationalist Communists of Buchenwald (IV International)—20 April 1945. Written by Ernst Federn, Karl Fischer, Florent Galloy, and Marcel Beaufrère, inmates at Buchenwald concentration camp. (Abridged here).

The ABC of Materialist Dialectics

Leon Trotsky (1940)

Some people question what if anything Trotsky's idea of dialectics had to do with that of Hegel, or with different parts of mathematics. However all that may be, what follows is what Trotsky thought dialectical thinking was — "closer approximations, corrections, concretisations, richness of content and flexibility" — the method he applied in his work. He did not bring dialectics into the 1939-40 discussion as a diversionary tactic, as has been frequently alleged. He was explaining the method of thinking that led him to his conclusions on the USSR, its current reality, and its possible developments.

GANGRENOUS SKEPTICS like Souvarine believe that "nobody knows" what the dialectic is. And there are "Marxists" who kowtow reverently before Souvarine and hope to learn something from him. And these Marxists hide not only in the *Modern Monthly*. Unfortunately a current of Souvarinism exists in the present opposition of the SWP. And here it is necessary to warn young comrades: Beware of this malignant infection!

The dialectic is neither fiction nor mysticism, but a science of the forms of our thinking insofar as it is not limited to the daily problems of life but attempts to arrive at an understanding of more complicated and drawn-out processes. The dialectic and formal logic bear a relationship similar to that between higher and lower mathematics.

I will here attempt to sketch the substance of the problem in a very concise form. The Aristotelian logic of the simple syllogism starts from the proposition that "A" is equal to "A." This postulate is accepted as an axiom for a multitude of practical human actions and elementary generalizations. But in reality "A" is not equal to "A." This is easy to prove if we observe these two letters under a lens – they are quite different from each other. But, one can object, the question is not of the size or the form of the letters, since they are only symbols for equal quantities, for instance, a pound of sugar. The objection is beside the point; in reality a pound of sugar is never equal to a pound of sugar – a more delicate scale always discloses a difference. Again one can object: but a pound of sugar is equal to itself. Neither is this true – all bodies change uninterruptedly in size, weight, color, etc. They are never equal to themselves. A sophist will respond that a pound of sugar is equal to itself "at any given moment." Aside from the extremely dubious practical value of this "axiom," it does not withstand theoretical criticism either. How should we really conceive the word "moment"? If it is an infinitesimal interval of time, then a pound of sugar is subjected during the course of that "moment" to inevitable changes. Or is the "moment" a purely mathematical abstraction, that is, a zero of time? But everything exists in time; and existence itself is an uninterrupted process of transformation; time is consequently a fundamental element of existence. Thus the axiom "A" is equal to "A" signifies that a thing is equal to itself if it does not change, that is, if it does not exist.

At first glance it could seem that these "subtleties" are useless. In reality they are of decisive significance. The axiom "A" is equal to "A" appears on one hand to be the point of departure for all our knowledge, on the other hand the point of departure for all the errors in our knowledge. To make use of the axiom "A" is equal to "A" with impunity is possible only within certain limits. When quantitative changes in "A" are negligible for the task at hand then we can presume that "A" is equal to "A." This is, for example, the manner in which a buyer and a seller consider a pound of sugar. We consider the temperature of the sun likewise. Until recently we considered the buying power of the dollar in the same way. But quantitative changes beyond certain limits become converted into qualitative. A pound of sugar subjected to the action of water or kerosene ceases to be a pound of sugar. A dollar in the embrace of a president ceases to be a dollar. To determine at the right moment the critical point where quantity changes into quality is one of the most important and difficult tasks in all the spheres of knowledge including sociology.

Every worker knows that it is impossible to make two completely equal objects. In the elaboration of bearing-brass into cone bearings, a certain deviation is allowed for the cones which should not, however, go beyond certain limits (this is called tolerance). By observing the norms of tolerance, the cones are considered as being equal. ("A" is equal to "A.") When the tolerance is exceeded the quantity goes over into quality; in other words, the cone bearings become inferior or completely worthless.

Our scientific thinking is only a part of our general practice including techniques. For concepts there also exists "tolerance" which is established not by formal logic issuing from the axiom "A" is equal to "A," but by dialectical logic issuing from the axiom that everything is always changing. "Common sense" is characterized by the fact that it systematically exceeds dialectical "tolerance."

Vulgar thought operates with such concepts as capitalism, morals, freedom, workers' state, etc. as fixed abstractions, presuming that capitalism is equal to capitalism, morals are equal to morals, etc. Dialectical thinking analyzes all things and phenomena in their continuous change, while determining in the material conditions of those changes that critical limit beyond which "A" ceases to be "A", a workers' state ceases to be a workers' state.

The fundamental flaw of vulgar thought lies in the fact that it wishes to content itself with motionless imprints of a reality which consists of eternal motion. Dialectical thinking gives to concepts, by means of closer approximations, corrections, concretizations, a richness of content and flexibility; I would even say a succulence which to a certain extent brings them close to living phenomena. Not capitalism in general, but a given capitalism at a given stage of development. Not a workers' state in general, but a given workers' state in a backward country in an imperialist encirclement, etc.

Dialectical thinking is related to vulgar thinking in the same way that a motion picture is related to a still photograph. The motion picture does not outlaw the still photograph but combines a series of them according to the laws of motion. Dialectics does not deny the syllogism, but teaches us to combine syllogisms in such a way as to bring our understanding closer to the eternally changing reality. Hegel in his *Logic* established a series of laws: change of quantity into quality, development through contradictions, conflict of content and form, interruption of continuity, change of possibility into inevitability, etc., which are just as important for theoretical thought as is the simple syllogism for more elementary tasks.

Hegel wrote before Darwin and before Marx. Thanks to the powerful impulse given to thought by the French Revolution, Hegel anticipated the general movement of science. But because it was only an anticipation, although by a genius, it received from Hegel an idealistic character. Hegel operated with ideological shadows as the ultimate reality. Marx demonstrated that the movement of these ideological shadows reflected nothing but the movement of material bodies.

We call our dialectic, materialist, since its roots are neither in heaven nor in the depths of our "free will," but in objective reality, in nature. Consciousness grew out of the unconscious, psychology out of physiology, the organic world out of the inorganic, the solar system out of nebulae. On all the rungs of this ladder of development, the quantitative changes were transformed into qualitative. Our thought, including dialectical thought, is only one of the forms of the expression of changing matter. There is place within this system for neither God, nor Devil, nor immortal soul, nor eternal norms of laws and morals. The dialectic of thinking, having grown out of the dialectic of nature, possesses consequently a thoroughly materialist character.

Darwinism, which explained the evolution of species through quantitative transformations passing into qualitative, was the highest triumph of the dialectic in the whole field of organic matter. Another great triumph was the discovery of the table of atomic weights of chemical elements and further the transformation of one element into another.

With these transformations (species, elements, etc.) is closely linked the question of classification, equally important in the natural as in the social sciences. Linnaeus' system (18th century), utilizing as its starting point the immutability of species, was limited to the description and classification of plants according to their external characteristics. The infantile period of botany is analogous to the infantile period of logic, since the forms of our thought develop like everything that lives. Only decisive repudiation of the idea of fixed species, only the study of the history of the evolution of plants and their anatomy prepared the basis for a really scientific classification.

Marx, who in distinction from Darwin was a conscious dialectician, discovered a basis for the scientific classification of human societies in the development of their productive forces and the structure of the relations of ownership which constitute the anatomy of society. Marxism substituted for the vulgar descriptive classification of societies and states, which even up to now still flourishes in the universities, a materialistic dialectical classification. Only through using the method of Marx is it possible correctly to determine both the concept of a workers' state and the moment of its downfall.

All this, as we see, contains nothing "metaphysical" or "scholastic," as conceited ignorance affirms. Dialectic logic expresses the laws of motion in contemporary scientific thought. The struggle against materialist dialectics on the contrary expresses a distant past, conservatism of the petty bourgeoisie, the self-conceit of university routinists and ... a spark of hope for an after-life.

Abridged from "A Petty-Bourgeois Opposition in the Socialist Workers Party",
dated 15 December 1939 and published in SWP Internal Bulletin vol.2 no.7,
January 1940.

Now More Than Ever!

Labor Action, 26 April 1943

The Fate of the Russian Revolution, volume 1: contents

Index

G indicates a glossary entry, p.121-5